PERSONALITY
THEORIES
A Comparative Analysis

PERSONALITY THEORIES
A Comparative Analysis

SALVATORE R. MADDI
Professor of Psychology and Social Sciences
University of Chicago

1976

Third Edition

THE DORSEY PRESS Homewood, Illinois 60430

Irwin-Dorsey International Arundel, Sussex BN18 9AB
Irwin-Dorsey Limited Georgetown, Ontario L7G 4B3

Third Edition

First Printing, April 1976

ISBN 0-256-01800-6
Library of Congress Catalog Card No. 75–39366
Printed in the United States of America

PREFACE

The first edition of this textbook appeared in 1968 as my attempt to write the treatise that, as a teacher of personality, I had wished for but not found. The book was built around a comparative analytic approach which identified seminal issues emerging from the similarities and differences among theories, and then marshalled research relevant to resolving the issues. Through the second and now third edition, this major commitment to the comparative analytic approach has persisted, and achieved acceptance in the field. Since 1968, there has been a steady stream of reaction from psychologists, teachers, and students. At first, there was an avalanche of letters of appreciation, critiques, copies of term papers, telephone calls, and visits. Even now, barely a week goes by without some sort of communication. I have been amazed and gratified, and I thank you all. Writing is a lonely job, for it is rare to get the feedback by which you know whether what you have done has had the intended effect, or any effect at all. I have been quite fortunate, especially so as your reactions have been overwhelmingly positive. Another sign of this is that the book has enjoyed a consistently large number of adoptions each year. We seem to agree on the value of a comparative analytic approach in personology.

But it is hardly true that there have been no criticisms. Almost all the communications, negative as well as positive, have been strongly felt and argued. I am happy to think that my book does not provoke indifference. I have listened carefully to the criticisms, trying to react as openmindedly as I can. These criticisms, along with my own retrospective analyses of the book, have guided the revisions of the second and third editions. With the help of my readers, the book has evolved into something better than it was.

To the original extensive list of theories, the second edition added Jung, existential psychology, and both moderate and radical behaviorism.

Now the third edition adds a new chapter on the social learning approach, for a grand total of 20 theories. And I have updated, elaborated, or changed many of the original theoretical discussions. Extensive coverage of theories is important in a comparative analytic work, lest the conclusions reached be too slanted by overly narrow sampling. I do not know of a personality textbook that includes such extensive coverage of both older and more recent theories of personality as this one. It is still true that some of the theories included here are almost invariably omitted from other textbooks, regardless of their growing importance or unusual features.

As to personality research, the original commitment to extensive coverage of those groups of studies that are most relevant to the issues emerging from the comparative analysis of theories is adhered to in this third edition. The updating done involves the addition of many new studies. Certainly, I have not been able to include every last study in the literature, but neither have I restricted my purview to a mere example here and there. The coverage of research is systematic and representative so that the conclusions reached can not be easily disconfirmed by some overlooked body of findings. In general, I have avoided reliance upon single studies, preferring to reach conclusions on the basis of weight of evidence.

The organization of the book follows from the emphasis upon comparative analysis. The parts of the theories concerning inherent human nature that is common to us all are discussed in the chapters on the core of personality. Theoretical statements about individuality in life style, or the periphery of personality, are discussed afterward. Statements about development, or that which links inherent nature with individual expression, occur in both the chapters on core and on periphery. This organization has the great utility of classing together the statements in the various theories that have similar logical and explanatory function. Surely, the organization also encourages redundancy, but the material covered is complex enough so that some repetition, especially from such different vantage points as inhere in the chapters on core and periphery, is not a waste.

I have tried to find an organization that does not distort so much as illuminate the various theoretical statements. But for some purposes, it may seem distracting not to find the whole of a theory described in one place. Let me point out that the reader can obtain the experience of theoretical wholeness by simply reading, at one time, all the subsections on the theory in question. Within the chapters on core and periphery, the subsections on each theory are clearly marked, precisely in order to maximize the flexibility with which the book may be read. The table on the inside of both covers will help in finding the desired pages. In obtaining an overview of the theories, the Appendix, which lists and roughly defines the major concepts, will also be useful. To facilitate further flexible use of the book, I have also been careful to separate research discussions from theoretical ones. Finally, I have saved discussion of what the good theory of personality would look like for the end, both because it is meant to point toward the future even more than the present, and because it seemed a matter most meaningfully considered after some knowledge of current practice has been gained.

Inevitably, the general tone of a comparative-analytic approach is evaluative. It is a stance given to the identification of similarities and differences among viewpoints, and the posing of issues to be resolved. There is no way of doing this without being evaluative, without reaching conclusions as to what is promising and what is not. I have tried to reach my conclusions straightforwardly and clearly, writing in the first person to emphasize that they are my conclusions and need not be accepted passively by another, if he can find good counterarguments. Personally, I do not consider the conclusions I have reached so ironclad as to brook no disagreement. Nor do I offer the three models for classifying personality theories as absolute, though they do seem useful to me. If the reader is provoked to think of other models that seem to work better, or just mounts serious and effective arguments against mine, I shall be more than satisfied as to the value of my book. Actually, I regard the book as carrying within it the seeds of its own demise. It defines the field in terms of several issues, which could be resolved in short order if their posing encourages relevant research interest. The book also indicates something of the weaknesses as well as strengths of various ways of theorizing about personality, and this information could well serve as a guide to better efforts in the future. I should like nothing more than to find that my book has been rendered obsolete by changes wrought of a fuller commitment to comparative analysis.

Comparative analysis demands objectivity, and I have tried to be equal to the task. But I have not been willing, for fear of being subjective, to functionally decorticate myself. The result would have been such conservatism, detachment, and unwillingness to make decisions and reach conclusions that any vigorous comparative analysis would have been jeopardized. The situation is further complicated because I have some substantive beliefs (activation theory and existential psychology) within personology. I have talked of these beliefs in the third person to indicate that as a comparative analyst I am not entitled to favor my own substantive beliefs merely because they are mine. My intent has been to operate upon my own theorizing with the same tools of comparative analysis I use on the theorizing of others. It is especially hard to be objective about your own viewpoints. If I have been biased in spite of myself, I shall have to rely on my readers to point this out. As whatever bias may be found is unintended, you can be sure that I will be open to careful criticism that aims at increasing our mutual objectivity.

From all this talk about the difficulty of comparative analysis, you may be forming the conclusion that this is not a book for beginners in the personality field. Actually, it seems to me that comparative analysis is the best kind of approach for introducing a field. This book provides a frame of reference for what personality theory is, and a classification system for ordering particular theoretical efforts. This classification also structures issues pointing out a direction for research efforts. It would take years for a beginner, plowing through the voluminous writings of personologists, to arrive at any comparable point of understanding through his own efforts. And I am not sure that it would be possible at all through reading textbooks less committed to comparative analysis and therefore more limited in scope or biased by a particular substantive belief.

Over the years from 1968 to now, I have accumulated a great debt to many persons who have read this book in its various manuscript forms and commented upon it to me. Unfortunately, I cannot refer to them all here. Noteworthy suggestions and criticisms on the first and second editions were made by my colleagues Susan L. Andrews, David Bakan, A. Stephen Frankel, Marvin Frankel, Gordon A. Haaland, Jerry Higgins, Howard F. Hunt, David C. McClelland, M. Brewster Smith, Mary E. Vermillion, Robert W. White, and David Winter. Also of great value were the reactions of my students Paul F. Costa, Jr., Elizabeth Bates, Bruce Brodie, Patricia Crosson, Tobey Klass, Richard Kopp, and David Wexler, who have since gone on to careers in personology.

Especially helpful in development of the third edition were my colleagues Charles Dicken, Charles T. Sullivan, and Howard F. Hunt, and my students David Clark, Stephen Gessner, Marlin Hoover, Jane McCormack, Leo Maülen, and Linda Lewis. I have a special debt of gratitude to Suzanne C. Kobasa, intellectually more my peer than my student, who has been both supportive and critical in true comparative analytic fashion concerning virtually every aspect of the third edition. Also, Dorothy Ford and Sammye Parsons worked long and well in typing the manuscript.

Finally, I count myself fortunate that, in my development, I have had as teachers a number of the personologists considered herein, namely, Gordon W. Allport, David Bakan, David C. McClelland, Walter Mischel, Henry A. Murray, and Robert W. White. From them I learned to view personality in a broad context.

Chicago, Illinois   SALVATORE R. MADDI
March 1976

CONTENTS

duction? Sixth issue: Does personality show radical change after the childhood years have been passed? Concluding remarks.

nation of behavior. Personality implications of social learning theory: *Core considerations. Development. Peripheral considerations.* Concluding remarks.

Chapter 1 PERSONALITY AND PERSONOLOGY

There are a great many personality books around. Considerations of vanity aside, why write another one? Only because you feel you have something to say that has not been said before. I am no exception. The way I read the many available books on personality, they fall into only two main categories or themes. When it is good, a personality book is likely to be a bit of a variation on one of these two themes: an especially competent expression, or a fulfillment of some aspect of the theme not previously elaborated. When it is bad, a personality book is simply more of the same old thing, with the same biases, errors, and even strengths. Two great books, one expressive of each of the categories, would have sufficed. But as you will see, I believe that these two themes are certainly not the only ones possible, and indeed, are not even the most useful ones at this stage of the development of the personality field. I see my book as standing with a surprisingly few others in a third, and very important category of endeavor.

I will call the two well-explored themes *benevolent eclecticism* and *partisan zealotry*. A book written from the standpoint of benevolent eclecticism tends to include many theories of personality, each given relatively equal time and space. When the book is good, you are made to understand why the theorist felt compelled to make just the assumptions he did. Theory follows theory neatly in the discussion, with little concern for the possible incompatibilities organized within the same two covers. The writer does not consider himself worthy of resolving the differences of opinion and assumption existing among the theorists. An air of humility permeates the whole endeavor. In such books, one often reads two justifications: that it is valuable just to bring the various theories before the reader so he will appreciate the richness of the field, and that the existing differences of opinion are currently beyond our poor power to resolve either by reason or experiment. Sometimes, there is even the pious assurance that someday, in a glorious future of comprehensive knowledge, it will be apparent which of the theories is best. Other times it is considered unlikely that any particular theory will emerge victorious, for theorizing is no more than a game, engaged in primarily for its value as a stimulant.

It is assumed that all theorists are entitled to be heard and appreciated, apparently for no necessarily greater reason than that they felt it important to theorize. Sometimes in such books, there is even a place— usually a short, final chapter—where a bit of attention is given to the similarities and differences among the various theories. But the aim of this is to ensure that the reader will grasp the essential meaning of each theory. There is little or no intent to use catalogs of similarities and differences as springboards to further analysis. When empirical research is included in such books, it does not bear on the differences between theories in any crucial way. Rather, it is included as an example of the kind of research stimulated by each theory. I hope you can see why I consider such books to express benevolent eclecticism. A good example of the type is *Theories of Personality,* by Hall and Lindzey (1970).

The book written with partisan zeal contrasts sharply with what I have just described. Such books intend to express one, and only one, theory of personality. The topics considered, research presented, and conclusions reached are all predictable in advance from the assumptions of the theory. The writer frequently adopts a polemical style, aimed at persuading the reader that his viewpoint is best. Other viewpoints are either slighted badly, or included only for purposes of criticism. When such books are done well, they provide the reader with a vivid account of a theory. When they are done poorly, they are ludicrously one-sided, misinterpreting other theories, or willfully insulating the reader against any possibility of recognizing another point of view. Examples of books written out of partisan zeal are *Personality: Dynamics and Development,* by Sarnoff (1962), *Pattern and Growth in Personality,* by Allport (1961), and *Personality: A Behavioral Analysis,* by Lundin (1974).

It is surprising to me that such an overwhelming number of the available books on personality should fall into one or the other of these categories, because there is another clear possibility having obvious value. This third type of book transcends the limitations of benevolent eclecticism and partisan zeal, though showing some similarity to each. From benevolent eclecticism it borrows the breadth and balance involved in considering many theories of personality, and from partisan zealotry it borrows the conviction that one or a few theories are better than others. The overall aim of this third kind of book is to discover the similarities and differences among many existing theories of personality as a starting point for determining which type of theorizing is the most fruitful. The investigation of similarities and differences forms the basis for posing the issues separating the various types of theorizing. Once these issues are posed, rational and empirical analyses can be conducted in order to determine which types of theorizing are best. In such a book, the reason for including research is that it bears in a specifiable and important way on one or more issues separating types of theorizing. The approach I am describing should be called *comparative analysis* to indicate its concern with being comprehensive, orderly, and evaluative in searching for improved understanding. Whether or not it is excellent, my book is an example of this approach.

Benevolent eclecticism and partisan zealotry are useful orientations in the initial stage of the development of a field. People having partisan zeal ensure that the hard work of formulating, refining, selling, and defending particular viewpoints gets done. It is probably only through the loyalty and commitment of those believing in a theory that it eventually becomes familiar to enough people to ensure it a proper hearing. At the same time that it is useful for there to be partisan zealots, it is equally useful for there to be benevolent eclectics. The latter function to ensure a sufficiently open mind in at least some people constituting a field so that there is freedom to accept or reject the arguments of the zealots. In addition, benevolent eclecticism gives an opportunity for the difficult, heavily intuitive work of theory formulation to go forward without premature hampering by hard-headed, cynical evaluation.

But once a number of coherent theories are available, neither benevolent eclecticism nor partisan zealotry will spur much further development of the field. The zealots will merely continue trusting in, advocating, and seeking rational and empirical demonstration of their particular theories. The benevolent eclectics will stand aside casting a blessing on all the bustling, partisan activity that is going on. No one will make it his primary concern to attempt determination of the relative value of the various existing theories. Succeeding generations of workers will duplicate their predecessors, with slight increments in sophistication, to be sure. But there will be no sweeping changes, no dramatic advances, unless an attitude of comparative analysis develops. If there is enough interest in systematic inquiry into the relative merits of different forms of theorizing, the field can proceed to the intermediate stage of development. This stage is characterized by the conjoining of the efforts of people in the field rather than the dissipation of energy in competitive, partisan disputes. This conjoining of efforts toward the end of determining which are the really worthwhile theories in the area spurs the development of sophistication as to the essential nature of the field, and the best way to express this essence in future theory and practice. The field emerges into a fully mature stage of development, when, armed with really trustworthy and effective theories, it applies its knowledge in some way that significantly changes (hopefully improves) the process of living.

It seems to me that the personality field is in an unnecessarily prolonged infancy. We have had a set of reasonably coherent theories for some time now. To be sure, an occasional theory is added to the store already available. But on further analysis, the theory added invariably seems more a rephrasing or elaboration of an earlier one than a new departure. More and more personality research gets done each year, and yet, we do not progress at all rapidly toward a time when we will be able to abandon some theories as empirically unviable. Mainly, this lack of progress can be traced to the research being partisan in nature, rather than directed squarely at the issues separating various types of theorizing. I fear that the retarded development of an attitude of comparative analysis is beginning to produce stagnation in the personality field. It is in the interest of contributing to the eradication of this problem that I write this book. It is a sense of the importance of the endeavor that has provided the self-discipline necessary for what is admittedly a difficult task. I can only hope that if more books are written on personality they too will reflect a commitment to comparative analysis.

What personologists do

It would be sensible at the outset if we could get an overall picture of what personality is and is not. Having such a frame of reference would make it easier to understand the various assumptions and statements made by particular personality theorists. Unfortunately, personality is so ubiquitous and nebulous as to be very difficult to pinpoint. Nobody in his private life seriously doubts that personality exists. Indeed, we take the personalities of ourselves and others into account a good deal in day-to-day decisions and activities. But once we try to specify the nature of personality in some precise, objective way, it seems to evaporate before our eyes, leaving us frustrated and uncertain. This has even happened to some psychologists, with the result that they have seriously contended that personality does not exist (e.g., Mischel, 1968). Such a contention, it seems to me, is as mad as personality is elusive. We must expect the elucidation of personality to be difficult, for after all, it is the most ubiquitous and human thing about us. We cannot gain much understanding of it by studying subhuman organisms, and we are limited in the accuracy of our observations of other humans by the fact that such observations must be filtered through our own personalities. But personality is here to stay, so I suggest we simply accept the difficulty of our task and plunge into it.

We could start on understanding what personality is by reviewing definitions of it that are available. Indeed, Allport (1937) did just this. But I do not think we will gain much by proceeding in this fashion, for there are many, many definitions, each of which is quite detailed and complex. We would be lost in a maze of words that could not really have much impact. I suggest instead that we look in a general way at the implications of the activities of people in the personality field. From the implications, we can generate a viewpoint on the nature of personality that will be at the same time general and vivid. The generality will come from the fact that we will be looking for the common features in the efforts of a large number of serious people having claim to expertness in the area. There will be vividness because our sense of the nature of personality will come directly out of the everyday actions of people devoted to understanding it. You must realize, however, that the statements I am about to make may not all be accurate to the functioning of every person in the personality field. Unless you grant me the leeway of searching for commonalities that may apply to reasonably large proportions of the workers in the field, but not necessarily to all, we will get nowhere. After all, there are no statistics, or explicit data to be used. Indeed, it is even difficult to be sure just who is in the field and who is not. So, we must approach our task in a rather general way.

Let us start by adopting a name for the kind of person we will be describing. Following Murray (1938), let us call him a *personologist,* or someone who is expert in the study and understanding of personality. There are a good many psychologists and psychiatrists who can be indisputably called personologists. Their work involves any or all of four activities: *theorizing, research, diagnosis,* and *psychotherapy.* Psychotherapy involves sensitively listening to, and interacting with, people toward the amelioration of any of a wide range of difficulties that may be problems to them and to their associates. In diagnosis, broadly speaking, the personologist will use any of a number of techniques, such as tests of personality or skills, in order to pinpoint a person's problems or capabilities, either for the person's own information, or for someone else, such as a prospective employer. In psychotherapy and diagnosis, the personologist will be mainly interested in the specific needs of his patients and clients. In his research, there will typically be more concern with general knowledge. The research may involve many or few tasks to be performed by people, with the aim of determining the similarities and differences in observed behavior both within each person and across all the people. Personality theorizing tends to come out of the personologist's experiences in any or all of these activities, and to formalize the bearing of these experiences on the perceived nature of people in general. With this brief introduction, let us focus more concretely of the implications of the habitual ways of functioning of the personologist.

First, we can observe that *the personologist tends to study groups of people, or if he studies only a few individuals, to be concerned with how representative they are of people in general.* Typically, the personologist will not study only one person for his own sake, as will the biographer. If the personologist focuses temporarily upon one person, as in psychotherapy and diagnosis, it will only be with the idea in mind that he will subsequently compare and contrast him with the next person, and so forth. The personologist is *interested in the commonalities among persons* and will not be happy about running the risk of generalizing erroneously from one person who is not really representative of human beings. Indeed, in research, a technical requirement is that the group observed be representative of people in general. The personologist approaches the task of understanding people with the systematic, orderly thoroughness of the scientist, rather than the impressionistic anecdotalism of the writer of fiction. Hopefully, the personologist need not lose the imaginativeness of his humanist neighbor, merely because of an insistence on systematic sampling.

This deeply ingrained interest in commonalities should not lead us to overlook the fact that the personologist also expends great effort in *the attempt to identify and classify differences among people*. There is no basic incompatibility between the search for commonalities and differences, though individual personologists will frequently show preference for one kind of search or the other. Whereas the search for commonalities goes on at an abstract, interpretive level, that for differences involves a concrete, straightforward analysis of observable behavior. Personologists engaged in diagnosis are especially sensitive to individual differences. Such differences are tapped by the personality tests so often taken on entrance to college, or for purposes of job evaluation. Once again, the personologist is not interested in the uniqueness of a person, in the way that might characterize a biographer. Rather, the personologist would like to know the various ways it is possible for people to be, the various characteristics it is possible for them to have. His aim is a classification of styles of being, with the similarities and differences among the categories in the classification clearly specified. The personologist's interest is much like that of the chemist in the periodic table of elements.

Many social and biological scientists are interested in identifying and classifying the similarities and differences that exist among people. In this alone, there is little individuality for the personologist. But if we look further, we find that social and biological scientists tend to be interested in similarities and differences among people that are produced by pressures in the external environment or biological factors of the internal environment. Thus, a sociologist will concern himself with such things as the similarities in voting behavior produced by membership in the same socioeconomic class, and the differences in such behavior traceable to differences in socioeconomic class. Further, he may study the similarities in behavior of all men playing the social role of father, and the differences between their behavior and that of men not playing this role. In contrast, a neurophysiologist might concern himself with the similarities among people under the effects of LSD, and the differences between them and people under the effects of alcohol. Of all the biological and social scientists interested in similarities and differences in people's behavior, *the personologist is rather unusual in not restricting himself to behavior easily traceable to the social and biological pressures of the moment.* This is not to say that he will necessarily turn up his nose at behavior obviously expressive of social or biological pressures. But while recognizing the importance of much of such behavior, he is also prone to a special peaking of interest when it becomes apparent that not everyone in the same socioeconomic class votes the same way, that not all fathers act similarly in that role, and that there is a wide range of mentation in people under the effects of LSD. In other words, one thing the personologist looks for is *evidence of differences among people when the biological and social pressures seem the same.* The personologist is also intrigued *when the same behavior is observed even though the biological and social pressures are different.* He wants to understand voting behavior that is the same, even though it emanates from people of different socioeconomic class, and so forth.

A philosopher or theologian might share the personologist's special interest in behavior not easily explained in social or biological terms but would tend to consider such behavior as spiritual, inspired by God, or expressive of free will. In contrast, the personologist attributes such behavior to the psychological characteristics and tendencies the person has brought to the immediate situation he faces. It is these characteristics and tendencies that constitute personality. Personality may well have developed out of prior experience involving situational pressures in the family setting, but this does not change the fact for the personologist that whenever you observe a person, his behavior is influenced not only by the momentary social and biological pressures, but by his personality as well. The personologist is not against admitting the contribution to behavior made by social and biological pressures, but he does think that exclusive emphasis on these factors necessarily oversimplifies the understanding of living. He would include personality into the mix, without recourse to any mysterious notions of the supernatural or free will. Of the social and biological scientists, then, *the personologist believes most deeply in the complexity and individuality of life.*

But it is not just transitory similarities and differences among people that intrigue the personologist. Implied in his reliance upon the idea that personality is a structured entity influencing behavior is *his emphasis upon characteristics of behavior that show continuity in time.* If personality changes at all, it changes slowly. Therefore, if personality influences behavior, the direction and intensity of the influence ought to persist, producing behavior that is continuous and regular. If the sexual instinct is part of personality, for example, then sexually relevant behavior, say flirtatiousness or dating, ought to be a stable aspect of the person's living. The personologist is interested not only in the actual repetition of aspects of behavior, but also in sequences of functionally related behaviors occurring over time. This emphasis on behavior of a recurrent nature is clearly one reason why personologists like to study people through prolonged contacts, such as psychotherapy. By repeated observation, the personologist feels that he sees personality more completely and accurately. Even when there is only one observation possible, it is typical to use some test of personality that has been specially developed to be sensitive to just those aspects of the person's behavior most likely to persist. An important gauge of the adequacy of a test is its stability, or likelihood that it will yield the same information on a person at two different points in time.

Actually, it is possible to pinpoint the kind of behavior studied by the personologist even further. He is not interested in every aspect of the commonalities and differences in people's functioning that show continuity in time. Within this extensive category of functioning, *the personologist tends to restrict his attention to behaviors that seem to have psychological importance.* He focuses on thoughts, feelings, and actions, leaving to the biological scientist such continuous aspects of functioning as acetylcholine cycles and blood pressure. The personologist is not even interested in such discrete phenomena as a muscle contraction, or the time necessary to adjust to an increase of light in the eye, unless they are part of some larger unit of functioning seeming to have psychological significance. Roughly speaking, psychological significance inheres in functioning that seems to have some ready relationship to the major goals and directions of the person's life. Thus, the personologist will be much more at home discussing such behavior as studying for an examination, or writing a love letter, than with such behaviors as discriminating accurately between two tones, or even an increase in heart rate. The personologist is generally quite willing to grant that the psychological functioning he studies has a physiological substrate, but he typically does not consider this fact to imply the primary importance of physiological study and explanation. One definite implication of the personologist's emphasis upon understanding thoughts, feelings, and actions *is that subhuman organisms will not be very useful to study.* It is simply too indirect and risky to try to understand jealousy, for example, by seeking to specify its precise, unique physiological substrate in such fashion that it can be studied in a subhuman organism that cannot give you the verbal statements that normally indicate the emotion. In large measure, the study of thoughts and feelings requires complex communication through a rich language. In this sense, the proper study of mankind is man.

Other social scientists besides the personologist concern themselves with thoughts, feelings, and actions, rather than more microscopic or fragmentary aspects of functioning. But the personologist tends to study thoughts, feelings, and actions more comprehensively. The economist will be interested in economic behavior, the sociologist in behavior that affects or articulates with the social system, and the political scientist with political behavior. In contrast, *the personologist is interested in all rather than only some of the psychological behavior of the person that shows continuity in time.* It is often said that the personologist concerns himself with the whole person, and this is reasonably accurate if considered along with the other restrictions already discussed. The characteristics and tendencies called personality have comprehensive effects upon thoughts, feelings, and actions. Hence, behavior must be studied widely. More than any other social scientist and psychologist, the personologist serves an integrative function with regard to knowledge of the human being. He is interested in the economic, social, and political behaviors emphasized by other social scientists. He is also interested in the processes of learning, perception, memory, development, and so forth, focused upon by other kinds of psychologists. He aims to integrate all these bits of knowledge into an overall account of the functioning of persons.

Finally, a perusal of the theorizing and research of personologists makes quite clear that *they are primarily interested in the adult human being.* Probably, there is the implicit belief that personality does not jell until some time after childhood, and hence, its effects are clearly and consistently apparent only after maturity. To be sure, it is common for personologists to explain present personality on the basis of learning experiences in early life. And sometimes, this historical orientation is quite elaborated. Clearly, the process of development is important for the personologist. But the aim of investigation into early life experiences is invariably in order to understand adult functioning. Indeed, some personologists do not even elaborate upon developmental process, finding it sufficient to simply assume that they have taken place. By and large, the personologist is interested primarily in the fruit of development —a congealed personality that exerts a pervasive influence on present and future behavior. The subjects of his observation, research, and psychotherapy tend to be adults.

What personality is

Regardless of the ambiguities and loose ends in the preceding paragraphs, we have come to the point where we can make a statement about the overall nature of personality that will be meaningful in terms of the kinds of things done by personologists. *Personality is a stable set of characteristics and tendencies that determine those commonalities and differences in the psychological behavior (thoughts, feelings, and actions) of people that have continuity in time and that may not be easily understood as the sole result of the social and biological pressures of the moment.* Not only does this statement come clearly out of what was said in the previous section of this chapter, it is broad enough, as you will see, to encompass all of the specific theories of personality we will be considering later. The only part of the statement that may need a bit of elaboration is the reference to *tendencies and characteristics*. Tendencies are the processes that determine directionality in thoughts, feelings, and actions. They are in the service of goals or functions. Characteristics are static or structural entities, usually implied by tendencies, that are used to explain not the movement toward goals or the achievement of functions, but rather the fact and content of goals or requirements. They are also used to explain thoughts, feelings, and actions that do not seem directional so much as repetitive in nature. An example of a tendency might be the attempt to achieve perfection in living, whereas related characteristics would be the ideals, such as beauty or generosity, that define perfection. Later on, I will have much more to say about characteristics and tendencies, but for the moment it is enough that you have a general sense of what is meant.

The personologist's three kinds of knowledge

Psychology claims to be a science, and this may have led you to believe that the personologist's theoretical statements will all follow from research. Initial research procedures involve objective observation of behavior in a reasonably large group of persons chosen so as to be representative of people in general, with the aim of stating hypotheses as to the nature and purpose of the behavior. Then these hypotheses are subjected to test as to their empirical truth or falsity in experiments that are carefully designed to be relevant. Confirmed hypotheses represent *empirical knowledge,* which can be characterized as public, precise, and systematic.

You might as well know right now that personality theories are not based solely—or in some cases, even primarily—on empirical knowledge, whatever claims to being scientific the field may mount. To my mind, this state of affairs is neither surprising nor disadvantageous. It is not surprising because the personality field is still in its initial stage of development. When set alongside the richness and complexity of people and their lives, the empirical knowledge available to the personologist is scanty and sometimes so partisan as to be severely limited in generality. Under these conditions, how can it possibly be surprising that personality theories would not be based completely on empirical knowledge? Far from being disadvantageous, the inclusion in personality theories of statements not firmly based in empiricism is a potentially fruitful procedure at this early stage in the development of the field. The leeway granted by this procedure permits the theorist to address himself to the human being in all its complexity. It is true that the theorist risks being wrong, but he will find out if he is soon enough when the empirical development of the field catches up with him. And there is also the possibility that he will have been right. In the meanwhile, the theorist can feel justified in the certainty that the statements he makes in the absence of a sound empirical base will spur his colleagues to make observations and plan experiments that they might not have envisioned otherwise.

To some, what I have said may sound heretical, but to me, it hardly seems unusual. After all, theory in any field is virtually never restricted to statements based on empirical knowledge alone. In addition, the non-empirical statements do represent two other definite kinds of knowledge that can be accorded some degree of respect, especially if their use is seen as provisional until there is more empirical knowledge. These two other kinds of knowledge are based on the process of intuition and reason. To appreciate intuition, recall the times when you have been seized by an inarticulate, private, emotional, though vivid, immediate, and compelling sense of the meaning of what is happening. The substance of these hunches constitutes *intuitive knowledge*. In contrast, there are times when you have carefully and calmly thought through the meaning, parts, and implications of things, with the resulting conclusions arrived at by deduction from a set of assumptions. In this case you are dealing with *rational knowledge,* which is reflective, explicit, logical, analytical, precise, and intellective. Intuitive and rational knowledge are not arbitrary and mysterious things. They emanate from your own experience, and the exercise of your own mind and senses, and may, therefore, be useful clues to what is true.

Intuitive knowledge, operated upon by reason, may become rational knowledge. Further, both intuitive and rational knowledge may merge with empirical knowledge when the appropriate research is done. But none of this changes the fact that at any point in time you may be a conglomerate of intuitive, rational, and empirical knowledge. So too may a theory of personality—which is, after all, the product of a person—be such a conglomerate. And if further justification for the inclusion of intuitive and rational knowledge in a theory of personality were needed, I would point to endeavors where these kinds of knowledge are paramount, with empiricism considered relatively unimportant. The artist, in his emphasis upon creation, and the theologian, in his emphasis on faith, are dealing primarily with intuitive knowledge. And reason is clearly the hallmark of mathematics and philosophy.

Accepting the three modes of knowing may not only facilitate richness of understanding at this preliminary stage of our study of personality, it may also be advantageous in terms of enabling each to serve as a check upon the others. Something that seems sensible on the basis of reasoning may rankle so much from an intuitive standpoint as to provide a clue to the possible limitations in generality of the rational assumptions being made. Something seemingly clear empirically may loom contradictory when viewed rationally, and this may alert us to an unrecognized and erroneous interpretation of data that has occurred. Something terribly insistent intuitively may seem less convincing when it proves to be illogical on detailed analysis. In the early stages of a field, there is no royal road to truth. Rather, there are three intertwining roads, all of which should be traversed, the better to assail the secrets of the terrain.

Whether or not you find my attempt to justify the use of all three modes of knowing convincing, you should recognize that they are indeed used by personality theorists. Inevitably, the initial stages of theory formulation are, as in any creative act, intuitive in nature. The theorist makes decisions as to where to start and what assumptions to emphasize on grounds that are by no means exclusively rational or empirical. He has a hunch, and he follows it up. He feels comfortable with a particular view of life, and so he celebrates it in theory. Sometimes he realizes the intuitive bases of his theorizing, and sometimes he does not. To be sure, the intuitive early stage of theory construction gives way to a stage in which rationality is uppermost. But this does not change the fact that it is largely intuitive knowledge with which the theorist begins. Because of this, his theory bears the stamp of his intuition in its content even when it has been developed sufficiently to achieve a respectable degree of rationality.

But however intuitive the initial bases of his theorizing may have been, the personologist accepts the task of formulating his views as explicitly as possible in terms of a series of assumptions. Generally speaking, he will try to justify these assumptions to you by indicating the manner in which they articulate with common experience. From these assumptions, he will then deduce the major theoretical propositions of his theory. Sometimes you will be asked to accept these propositions as necessary, inexorable conclusions from the assumptions. Although it is somewhat uncommon to find personologists actually arguing the unequivocal truth of their propositions in a manner indicating sole reliance upon the rational mode of knowing, their obvious investment in those propositions and frequent disdain for the collection of empirical evidence bearing upon their possible truth, suggests a strong commitment to reason.

Sometimes the personologist is more of an empiricist than this. Certainly, he subscribes to the standard that nothing which cannot be supported by empirical evidence in some way at some time deserves inclusion in a theory of personality. In addition, many theorists actively formulate empirically testable hypotheses stemming from their assumptions. Some even conduct the empirical tests of the hypotheses, rather than leave that task for other personologists. But, among psychologists, the personologist is hardly insistent on giving no place to intuition and harboring nothing, even temporarily, that is supported only by reason. To the contrary, he will tolerate intuitive and rational knowledge in his theorizing, though accepting the necessity of relying on empiricism whenever in doubt. This catholicity and lack of skepticism has not made the personologist popular and respected among psychologists. But it has granted him vigor of conceptualization, and willingness to tackle complex problems.

In reading the chapters that follow, it will be educational for you to remain alert to these three kinds of knowledge. Try to see their impact on each theorist. There are various ways in which I shall help you in this. In addition, you should try to analyze the aspects of a theory in terms of your own processes of intuition, reason, and empiricism. In this way, you will not be merely a passive bystander, but someone who is developing his own view on what is valuable in the personality field. It is admittedly difficult to analyze a theory intuitively, for intuition is not really an evaluative process. The two best things you can do are to have a global intuitive reaction to a theory, and also to try to recognize when the theorist's formulations are primarily intuitive. Usually, I will help you by suggesting, at the outset of discussion of a theory, some basis in your own experience for understanding its essence in an intuitive fashion. In addition, I will comment whenever a particular stance taken by a theorist is clearly and deeply intuitive or temperamental in character. Of course, much more detailed analysis of theory can be done rationally and empirically. As you can see from the chapter titles, the major analyses I will attempt involve reason and empiricism. In rational analysis, I will try to alert you to the logical consistencies or inconsistencies among the parts of theories, the explicit or implicit status of their assumptions and propositions, and the conclusions that are presumed to require no empirical test. In empirical analysis, I will attempt to evaluate theories on the basis of whatever research is relevant enough to permit some testing of predictions.

The core and periphery of personality

Before you go on to the other chapters of this book, I should tell you something of their organization and what prompted it. The major organizational principle apparent in Chapters 2 through 10 is the basic distinction between the core and periphery of personality. It is common for personality theories to make two kinds of statements. One kind delineates the things that are common to all people and discloses the inherent attributes of human beings. These common features do not change much in the course of living, and exert an extensive, pervasive influence on behavior. This first kind of statement refers to what I call the *core of personality*. But theorists also tend to make statements about attributes of personality that are much more concrete and close to behavior that can be readily observed. These attributes are generally learned, rather than inherent, and each of them has a relatively circumscribed influence on behavior. They are mainly used by the theorist to explain differences among people. Because of their learned status and circumscribed effect, I consider such attributes to delineate the *periphery of personality*.

Theories of personality typically have both core and peripheral statements, and this seems sensible to me insofar as the personologist is interested in the commonalities and differences among people. Let me be just a little more descriptive concerning the makeup of core and peripheral levels of a personality theory, so that you can have the distinction vividly in mind as you read this book. It is in his core theorizing that the personologist makes his major statement about the overall directionality, purpose, and function of life. This statement takes the form of postulating one or perhaps two *core tendencies.* An example of a core tendency is the assumption that all behavior constitutes an attempt to actualize one's inherent potentialities. No matter how different two concrete behaviors are, they are assumed traceable in some way to the attempt to render potentialities a palpable reality. Core theorizing also includes *core characteristics,* or the structural entities implied in the core tendency. The core characteristics relevant to the actualizing tendency used as an example above would be a specification of the content of the inherent potentialities (e.g., sexuality, aggressiveness). These inherent potentialities would be core characteristics insofar as they are assumed present in all persons.

It is at the peripheral level that the theorist makes his major statement concerning the concrete styles of life that differ from person to person. One way in which he does this is to postulate a number of *concrete peripheral characteristics* which are entities relevant by definition to only some proportion of behavior. The need for achievement or the trait of obstinacy are examples of concrete peripheral characteristics. The need for achievement refers only to competitive behavior in a context permitting success and failure. It does not refer to love, or cooperation, or anything else, and therefore, can be used in the understanding of only some of the behavior observable in people. The function of concrete peripheral characteristics is to permit the understanding of differences between people. One can say that Mr. Oliver has a need for achievement, whereas Mr. Sterling has the trait of obstinacy. One can also say that Mr. Oliver has a higher need for achievement that does Mr. Sterling. Theorists differ as to how many concrete peripheral characteristics they postulate; the greater the number the more concern shown for individual differences. Concrete peripheral characteristics are the smallest, most homogeneous explanatory elements the theorist believes are possible. Many persons will be familiar with the term *trait* for the kind of entity I am describing. I have not wanted to use that term, however, because some theories of personality consider traits to be only one of a number of different kinds of concrete peripheral characteristics.

There is a larger, more heterogeneous concept that is also commonly employed in peripheral theorizing. It is the *type.* Each type postulated is constituted of a number of concrete peripheral characteristics. Thus, the type concept serves the function of organizing the basic elements of peripheral personality into larger units that are more immediately reminiscent of the ways of life commonly encountered. A *typology*, or comprehensive classification of types, is sometimes offered. In doing this, the personologist makes an exhaustive statement of the different styles of life that are possible. Typically, one or more types are designed as ideal ways of life, whereas the others are considered nonideal. The nonideal types are either believed to be predispositions to psychopathology, or actual kinds of psychopathology.

The link between the core and periphery of personality is usually assumed to be *development*. In the beginning, the core tendency and characteristics are expressed in interaction with other persons (e.g., family, strangers) and social institutions (e.g., laws, schools). The resulting experience—reward, punishment, knowledge—congeals into concrete peripheral characteristics and types. Which type of personality is developed by a person is generally considered to be a function of the particular kind of family setting in which he matured. Those developmental conditions recognized to be best are regarded as leading to the personality type or types specified as ideal. The other, less adequate developmental conditions supposedly culminate in the nonideal personality types. The type considered ideal is that which most fully expresses the core tendency and characteristics.

These assumptions are depicted in Figure 1–1. As the circles get big-

FIGURE 1–1

Schematic representation of the parts of a personality theory

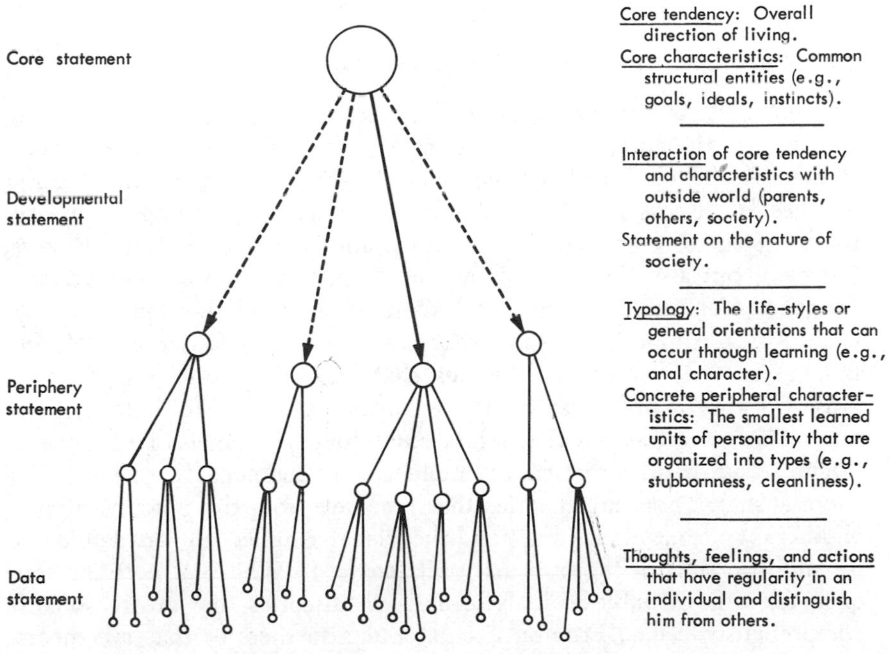

Core statement

Core tendency: Overall direction of living.
Core characteristics: Common structural entities (e.g., goals, ideals, instincts).

Developmental statement

Interaction of core tendency and characteristics with outside world (parents, others, society).
Statement on the nature of society.

Periphery statement

Typology: The life-styles or general orientations that can occur through learning (e.g., anal character).
Concrete peripheral characteristics: The smallest learned units of personality that are organized into types (e.g., stubbornness, cleanliness).

Data statement

Thoughts, feelings, and actions that have regularity in an individual and distinguish him from others.

ger, you are dealing with more general, less homogeneous units. The dotted arrows are intended to show that several lines of development can take place. The one actually occurring depends upon the kinds of experience the person encounters in the process of expressing his core tendency. I have filled in one arrow depicting development to show that it is typical for personality theories to specify an ideal course of development leading to an ideal peripheral personality (e.g., if the core tendency is to actualize inherent potentialities, then ideal development takes place when parents foster and encourage the child, and all this culminates in a self-actualized peripheral personality).

Personality theories arise, I have said earlier, from the activities of personologists doing research, assessing persons, and helping them in psychotherapy. But the theory also influences these activities. When you assess a person's personality, you are working with a particular explicit or implicit sense of typology and its component concrete peripheral characteristics. This is so because it is here that a personality theory permits pinpointing of differences among persons, of the especially "Johnian" quality of John. When you attempt to do psychotherapy, you must decide, on the basis of your view of man's nature (core of personality), and the particular peripheral personality confronting you (is it ideal or not?), what is to be done. Looked at this way, psychotherapy is a special case of development, so the therapist's view of development is also involved. And, as I shall contend throughout the book, research in the personality area should also address itself in precise fashion to the theories available to us.

Selection of theorists for inclusion in this book

A book attempting comparative analysis in the personality area is only as strong as the comprehensiveness and representativeness of the group of theories included in it. I have tried to keep this in mind in selecting theories for discussion. I have included not only theories popular in psychiatry (e.g., Freud, Ego Psychology) and psychology (e.g., Rogers, Murray), but also theories that are not especially popular (e.g., Rank, Angyal). Not only will you find theories postulated some time ago (e.g., Adler, Allport), but some that are recent (e.g., Fiske and Maddi, Bakan) as well. There are theories that stress the core (e.g., Rogers, Maslow) and theories that stress the periphery (e.g., McClelland, Erikson). There are theories that stress emotional phenomena (e.g., Freud, Rogers) and theories that stress intellective phenomena (e.g., Kelly, Existentialism). There are theories that emanate from the practice of psychotherapy (e.g., Adler, Jung) and theories that reflect the academic and research pursuits of the university setting (e.g., White, Allport). I have even taken the trouble to include not only theories that are reasonably comprehensive (e.g., Fromm, Freud) but also theories that are incomplete (e.g., White, Angyal). There is even one position (Behaviorism) that has ambiguous status as personality theory, though it is quite important in contemporary psychology.

If personologists will have any quarrel with my choice of theories, it is likely to involve the absence of Lewin, Sheldon, Sullivan, and Horney. I have omitted them because their thinking no longer seems to have great direct impact on the personality field. Not many personologists would consider themselves followers of these theorists. Such a state of affairs would be understandable in the case of a theory of recent origin, but in an older theory it signifies a decline in importance. But Lewin, and to some extent the others, have been influences upon personologists whose own theories are currently more viable. It seemed sufficient to include these theories in the book. And while Horney has been excluded, many variants on the psychoanalytic theme have been included.

Although I cannot claim to have included all theories of personality. I have included quite a few, and have taken pains to ensure that my sampling is accurately reflective of the field. It seems unlikely to me that the conclusions reached throughout this book would be dramatically or importantly changed if some excluded theory were included instead. Interestingly enough, I found all these thories to express only three basic models for personality theorizing. To be sure, each model has two versions and some variants. Nonetheless, the ways of theorizing about personality are apparently few.

Coverage of theory, research, assessment, and therapy

Among the four functions of the personologist, *theorizing* and doing *research* mainly produce new knowledge, whereas *assessment* and *psychotherapy* mainly apply knowledge that is already available. As such, theorizing and research are intellective or speculative activities, while assessment and therapy are practical activities. By mentioning this difference, I do not mean to imply that one kind of activity is more or less important or grand than another.

Actually, the four activities form a meaningful whole. Theorizing has an integrative function, because whether it is explicit or implicit, it determines what and how research, assessment, and therapy get done. But research is important because it is especially suited, through the collection of systematic and relevant empirical observations, to testing the validity of existing theory and contributing new information that can shape further theorizing. Assessment and psychotherapy are primarily important because they serve those needs of persons which derive from disabled personalities. But assessment and psychotherapy can also help in the process of evaluating theory and contributing new observations that can influence future theorizing. The four functions are organically related to each other. Indeed, some personologists engage in all four types of activity. The most common orientation is for a personologist to engage in at least two functions, and it is rare to find someone isolating himself to only one function.

Although this book will emphasize personological theory and research, it will by no means exclude assessment and therapy from consideration. The choice to emphasize theory stems from its integrative function, as mentioned above. If you understand a personologist's theory, you have a ready basis for appreciating why and how he does his research, assessment, and therapy. Therefore, an emphasis on theory is a sound introduction to personology. The corollary emphasis on research is important, because the comparative analytical approach taken here requires considerable attention to the evaluation and test of existing theory, preparatory to determining whether new theorizing is needed. Because of the importance of theorizing and research to the aims of this book, I will attempt to cover both areas of personology comprehensively and in depth. I have made some theoretical and research exclusions for reasons mentioned where it is appropriate to indicate them, but these exclusions do not seriously limit the emphasis on comprehensiveness and depth. Neither theories nor research are treated as mere examples. I have tried to cover all the essential aspects of the theories and all the relevant research themes.

I cannot claim the same comprehensiveness and depth in coverage of assessment and therapy. These are complex, specialized activities requiring more emphasis than would be possible in this book and in one personality course. There is a craft and many component skills involved in assessment and therapy that take considerable time and effort to explicate, teach, and acquire. But I have discussed in the chapters that follow the theorizing behind the assessment and therapy practices deriving from the various theories of personality. I have done this in part because all four functions of the personologist are an integral whole, partly in order to give a vivid sense of the similarities and differences among the various theories, and partly to provide a bridge to other books and courses on the practice of assessement and therapy.

By and large, discussions of assessment and therapy occur along side of explications of theory in the pages that follow. In this fashion, you can get an organic sense of how the practical activities of the personologist issue from the intellective activities. The research sections are separated off, mainly because what is going on there is the evaluation of theories. To have research discussions follow theoretical ones makes logical sense, but also permits you to use this book in a flexible way that would not be possible if the two were run together.

Chapter 2 THE CORE OF PERSONALITY: CONFLICT MODEL

By now, all the groundwork for our consideration of actual theories of personality has been laid. We know that the personologist's theorizing is expressive of his interest in identifying and understanding the way in which particular people lead their lives. In order to be comprehensive, he must concern himself with the ways in which people are similar to and different from each other. The identification of differences between people forms the basis of theorizing about the periphery of personality, with its emphasis on personality types. The identification of similarities among people is the basis of theorizing about the core of personality, with its emphasis upon the characteristics and tendencies that define human nature and are constantly expressed in living.

In this and the next three chapters, I will present the views on the core of personality of a large number of personologists. I do not offer my list of theorists as complete, but rather as representative of the various kinds of theory existing in the field. In considering the core of personality, one asks the question "What are the basic attributes and long-time directions of the human being?" Core tendencies and characteristics are by their nature at a very high level of generality, so one would not expect to see their influence in any particular small segment of behavior, but rather in the overall pattern of functioning.

When I first began thinking about personality viewpoints, I tended to classify them in some conventional fashion such as trait, dynamic, and cognitive theories, much as in Mischel's (1976) recent book. But no such classifications seemed to capture the essential message of the theories concerning the nature of human life. After many false starts and reconsiderations, I have hit upon three broad categories of theorizing that are convincing to me. The essential meaning of the categories is captured by calling them the *conflict model*, the *fulfillment model*, and the *consistency model*.

19

In the conflict model, it is assumed that the person is continuously and inevitably in the grips of the clash between two great, opposing, unchangeable forces. Life, according to this model, is necessarily a compromise, which at best involves a dynamic balance of the two forces, and at worst involves a foredoomed attempt to deny the existence of one of them. There are two versions of the conflict model. In the *psychosocial version,* the source of one great force is in the person as an individual, and the source of the other great force is in groups or societies. In the *intrapsychic version,* both great forces arise from within the person, regardless of whether he or she is regarded as an individual or as a social entity.

In contrast, the fulfillment model assumes only one great force, and localizes it in the person. This model construes life as the progressively greater expression of this force. Although conflict is a possible occurrence in the fulfillment model, it is neither necessary nor continuous. Indeed, when it occurs, it represents an unfortunate failure in living, rather than something unavoidable. As in the conflict model, there are two versions of the fulfillment model. In the *actualization version,* the great force is in the form of a genetic blueprint determining the person's special capabilities. Living richly, then, is the process of making actual that which is potential at birth. But the *perfection version* does not emphasize genetically determined capabilities so much as ideals of what is fine, excellent, and meaningful in life. The great force constitutes striving toward these ideals of perfection, regardless of whether that entails expressing one's own genetic capabilities or inferiorities. In both forms of the fulfillment model, the content of the great force is explicitly or implicitly considered to be set and specifiable.

In the consistency model, there is little emphasis upon great forces, be they single or dual, in conflict or not. Rather, there is emphasis upon the formative influence of feedback from the external world. If the feedback is consistent with what was expected, or what has been customary, there is quiescence. But, if there is inconsistency between the feedback and the expectation or custom, there is pressure to decrease this uncomfortable state of affairs. Life is to be understood as the extended attempt to maintain consistency. Whereas the conflict of the conflict model is continuous, unavoidable, set in content, and can be held to some minimum, but not eliminated, the inconsistency of the consistency model is avoidable, and can have any of a wide range of contents. In contrast to the fulfillment model, the consistency model assumes no predetermined capabilities or ideals as the guides to living. The consistency model has two versions. In the *cognitive dissonance version,* the relevant aspects of the person in which there may or may not be consistency are cognitive in nature. There may be inconsistency between two thoughts, or between an expectation and a perception of occurrences. In contrast, the *activation version* emphasizes consistency or inconsistency between the degree of bodily tension or activation that is customary for the person and that which actually exists at the time.

I have tried to be clear and succinct in presenting these three models and their versions to you. It has not been my intent to convince you of their meaningfulness and utility for ordering the existing theories of personality. I merely wanted to introduce them, so that you could have them in mind while reading through this chapter and the following eight. If the models leave you a little cold at this point, recognize that it may be simply because we have not yet confronted actual theories, and compared their similarities and differences. When we do, I believe you will find most of the theories clear, pure examples of one and only one version of a model. Further, I do not believe you will find the theories distorted so much as illuminated by the process of ordering them under the models and versions. But I could be wrong. Certainly you will find a few theories that are not pure expressions of a model, but variants instead. To be sure, there are only a few of these variants, but how many does one tolerate before beginning to question the classification scheme? Obviously, I found them few enough to tolerate. But you may not. At the very least, I feel sure that using the classificatory system I have introduced as a heuristic device in reading the pages that follow will serve as a stimulus to your own thinking about the nature of existing personality theories. The personality field is so chaotic at present that all of our classificatory, organizational attempts are to be welcomed.

CONFLICT MODEL: PSYCHOSOCIAL VERSION

In discussing the conflict model, we shall first consider the version that assumes two great and opposing forces, one of which is inherent in a person as an individual, and the other of which is inherent in a person as a social being. The major example of this kind of theory is that of Freud, and I shall discuss it first. Following that, I will consider the theories of Murray and ego psychology, which are rather similar to that of Freud. But Murray and the ego psychologists back away somewhat from the notion that conflict is continual. For them, there is a part of life that is free of conflict. They are theorists who are drifting away from the pure psychosocial conflict model. But they are still so close to it that I have considered them to express a variant of that model.

Freud's position

Sigmund Freud (born in Moravia, 1856; died in London, England, 1939) looms as such a giant, to both his advocates and opponents, that it will certainly be difficult to see him objectively in our time. Nonetheless, we must try. As a man, he was deeply serious about and committed to his work, his wife and family, his friends and colleagues, and his principles. From youth onward, he showed the brilliant intelligence, tenacity, and independence that marked him for greatness, and the social rejection that is a frequent concomitant of this. A physician who strayed far from the orthodox medical emphasis upon physical causes of disease, Freud promulgated views that seemed the work of the devil to most of his colleagues. For most of his life, Freud was considered a fanatic obsessed by sex, and denied recognition by the medical community. In bitterness, Freud drew his circle of admirers even closer around him, insisting on their loyalty to his theoretical principles. It is not surprising that Freud's views would have been so rejected, even though they came directly out of his observation of patients, for they constituted a kind of intellectual indictment of his age, with its stuffy Victorian sterility.

From the beginning, Freud and his inner circle emphasized the mental causation of certain maladies, and set about developing a therapy for the mind rather than the soma. On his own, and through this group, Freud has had an immense influence on personology. So intense was the interaction among the members of the inner circle, mainly young, energetic, ambitious physicians, and their visionary though somewhat paternalistic leader, that sparks flew occasionally. Here and there, a member of this extraordinary group would leave or be rejected. It is a tribute to Freud's intellectual impact on them that these outcasts typically went on to develop influential theories of their own that nonetheless reflect a psychoanalytic parentage.

Freud wrote a great deal, changed his mind often, and left many loose ends where he could not decide which of a number of theoretical alternatives was the most advantageous. Further, he has been interpreted by a great many people, some allies, some enemies, and some revisionists primarily interested in finding a respectable base line from which to develop their own thoughts. In such a complex situation, one must be selective if there is to be any hope of pinpointing the overall thrust of a theorist's position. Accordingly, in what I say here, I will focus on Freud, rather than on his allies, enemies, and revisionists, and in addition, will rely on the things he tended to stress most consistently, rather than on side statements and exploratory forays, however intriguing they may be.

Once you adopt a selective strategy, Freud's view of the basic tendency of living falls readily to hand: *It is the tendency to maximize instinctual gratification, while minimizing punishment and guilt.* It would be well to reflect for a moment on the obvious, commonsense meaning of this statement. Try to think of the last time you wanted to do something selfish, and felt worried about whether someone would hurt you if you acted on the wish, or immoral for having the wish in the first place. If your wish was strong enough, you were clearly in a state of conflict that probably could not be so easily resolved by simply saying to yourself that you would not carry out the wish in action. And if you resolved the conflict by acting on the part or form of your wish that would not be so objectionable to others or to yourself as to engender punishment or guilt, then you are lucky enough to have an intuitive, if homey, basis in personal experience for understanding what Freud meant.

But Freud did, of course, have a more precise, formal meaning in mind than can be completely comprehended from simple experiences of the type I have encouraged you to remember. To uncover this more formal meaning, we will have to use our powers of reasoning because, as I will show later, some of what Freud meant is not strictly speaking available to immediate introspective analysis. In any event, looked at from a formal theoretical point of view, Freud's basic tendency of living includes a position on (1) the instincts, (2) the sources of punishment and guilt, and (3) the mechanism of defense whereby instincts are satisfied while punishment and guilt are avoided.

The instincts. Freud postulates a number of instincts that are common to all human beings as an inherent, unchanging aspect of their nature. In our terminology, Freud's instincts are core characteristics of personality. Although he discusses three types of instinct, all of them have the same general form, differing only in content. All instincts have a *source,* a type of *energy* or driving force, an *aim,* and an *object.* The source of an instinct is invariably rooted in the biological character of the organism—in the very process of metabolism itself. Freud says (1925b, p. 66):

> By the source . . . of an instinct is meant the somatic process which occurs in an organ or part of the body and whose stimulus is represented in mental life by an instinct. We do not know whether this process is regularly of a chemical nature or whether it may also correspond to the release of other, e.g., mechanical forces. The study of the sources of instincts lies outside the scope of psychology.

So the instinct is not the somatic process itself, but rather the mental representation of the somatic process. In this, Freud makes perfectly clear that psychic manifestations, such as thoughts, wishes, and even emotions, are expressive of and dependent upon somatic activities and processes. This is why many personologists have dubbed Freud's theory biological rather than psychological. But while his emphasis is biological, he certainly means to consider the instincts to be influential through their grip on mental life.

You can get a concrete sense of this by considering Freud's attempt to specify the type of energy or driving force entailed in instincts. We approach considerations of type of energy when, having accepted that the source of an instinct is the somatic and metabolic processes of the organism, we ask about the precise nature of the somatic message translated into mental terms. Invariably, we find that Freud considers the message to be about a state of biological deprivation. The energy of an instinct is rooted in such somatic deprivation states as "dryness of the mucous membrane of the pharynx or an irritation of the mucous membrane of the stomach . . ." (Freud, 1925b, p. 61). By statements such as this, Freud means to communicate two general things. One is that the source and energy of instincts is from within the organism itself. So he can say "when a strong light falls on the eye, it is not an instinctual stimulus . . ." (Freud, 1925b, p. 61), because such stimulation is not achieved through processes internal and intrinsic to the organism as a functioning biological system. The other thing Freud means to communicate by referring to such processes as dryness of mucous membranes is that the somatic messages registering in mental life are expressive of the biological requirements of the organism. An instinct is a sign that the organism does not have something it needs, that it is in a state of deprivation. Such deprivation states are experienced as *tension* or pressure. Freud (1925b, p. 65) writes that "By the pressure . . . of an instinct we understand its motor factor, the amount of force or the measure of the demand for work which it represents. The characteristic of exercising pressure is common to all instincts; it is in fact their very essence."

Freud uses the distinction between stimulation entering the nervous system from the outside world and the internal stimulation of instincts to make another important point. In contrast to external stimulation, instinctual stimulation is constant. There is always an amount of instinctual tension, pressure, or energy that is above zero because such tension is an expression of the biological requirements of a functioning organism. An organism metabolizing normally will have such frequent needs for food, water, and the like, that parching or irritation of mucous membranes will almost always be taking place in one part of the body or another. Thus Freud (1925b, p. 62) writes:

> An instinct . . . never operates as a force giving a *momentary* impact but always as a constant one. Moreover, since it impinges not from without but from within the organism, no flight can avail against it. A better term for an instinctual stimulus is a "need." What does away with a need is a "satisfaction." This can be attained only by an appropriate . . . alteration of the internal source of stimulation.

The tension of deprivation states will always be with the person, and what that means is that the instincts will always exert an influence on his living.

Thus far, we have established that instincts have their source in somatic processes and are characterized by the tension and pressure toward action of biological deprivation states. From this information, one can literally guess what Freud considers the overall *aim* of instincts to be. He (Freud, 1925b, p. 65) says that "The aim . . . of an instinct is in every instance satisfaction, which can only be obtained by removing the state of stimulation at the source of the instinct." In other words, the aim of all instincts is to reduce the tension of biological deprivation. The ideal state, never reached because of the constant nature of instinctual demands, is the bliss of quiescence, probably most closely approximated in deep sleep.

The final general attribute of the instinct is its *object,* by which Freud means the thing or things, usually in the external world but possibly within, that serves to satisfy or ease the tension of deprivation. In his own words (Freud, 1925b, p. 65):

> The object . . . of an instinct is the thing in regard to which or through which the instinct is able to achieve its aim. It is what is most variable about an instinct and is not originally connected with it, but becomes assigned to it only in consequence of being peculiarly fitted to make satisfaction possible.

There is typically more than one thing or event that can ease the tension of an instinct, and one or another of these things or events may become especially important to a particular person on the basis of the particular learning experiences he has had. But the range of possible satisfiers of a given instinct can be specified, because they are inherent to the nature of the instinct. For example, only edible things qualify as objects for the hunger need. The process whereby an object becomes recognized as important as an instinctual satisfier for a person is called *cathexis,* rather poetically defined as the investment of an object with libido, or sexual energy.

Some of you may be wondering what all this has to do with mental life. I have said over and over again that the instincts, though basically biological, have important psychic implications. And yet, the terminology employed in discussing the various attributes of instincts does not seem vividly mental. More mental terms can and should be used, as long as you keep in mind that Freud intends the soma and the mind to be closely interconnected. The psychic or mental expression of the source and object of the instinct is a *wish.* A wish for food, for example, expresses the metabolic requirements for nutrients in molar psychological terms. The psychic or mental expression of the tension and aim of the instinct is *uncomfortable emotions.* According to Freud, wishes and associated emotions are accurately expressive of biological requirements by virtue of the close interconnection between the brain (the presumed physiological locus of wishes and emotions) and the soma and viscera (the presumed source of biological requirements) mediated by the autonomic or involuntary nervous system and the endocrine system. Recognize that Freud is saying that a major and unchanging portion of mental life, entailing wishes and associated uncomfortable emotions, is expressive of the biological requirements of the organism. And recognize further that the means to give this portion of mentation a huge role in determining the person's life.

Now that we have a sense of the general form of the instinct concept as developed in psychoanalytic theory, we can profitably consider the content of the instincts postulated by Freud. There are three kinds of instinct present in everyone, and all are subsumed under the concept of the *id*. Whenever you encounter a reference to the id, all you need do is remember that it is a summary term for all the instincts postulated by Freud. The term "id" could easily have been translated "it," which would have been more accurate to Freud's belief that instincts are experienced by persons as foreign rather than part of them. In the terminology of this book, the id is a core characteristic of personality, as are each of the instincts arrayed within the id. The latter is true because although Freud specified three kinds of instincts, he assumed that all three are common to mankind.

Throughout his career as a personologist, Freud argued for the existence of a group of instincts that function to preserve biological life. From the discussion above, it is obvious that he would have assumed the importance of these *self-preservation instincts* (Freud, 1925b), such as those for *food, water,* and *air*. The ultimate source of this class of instincts is an anabolism, or the aspect of metabolism that entails growth. The energy of these instincts is the discomfort and tension associated with irritated mucous membranes in the gastrointestinal and respiratory tracts. The aim is reduction of tension and discomfort through obtaining objects, such as food or water, that have the capability of easing the membrane irritation.

Although the life instincts are obviously basic, Freud gave them much less attention than the *sexual instinct*, which was also an integral part of his theorizing from the very beginning. The source of this instinct is in the metabolic process as it takes place in the parts of the soma differentiated for sexual reproduction in the broadest sense. This includes not only the genitalia per se, but also the secondary sexual areas, such as the breasts, and the orifices, such as mouth and anus, that can participate in the process of sexual arousal. The energy of the sexual instinct, called *libido* by Freud, comes from the sensitivity, irritation, or tension in these various organs of the body when sexual expression has not taken place recently. Obviously, the overall aim of the instinct is release of this tense sensitivity through intercourse, orgasm, and ejaculation. And the most comprehensive object or goal appropriate in this regard are the genitalia of an attractive person of the opposite sex. Any other possible aims and objects, such as kissing, fondling of breasts, genitalia and anus, stimulation of the mouth and anus through activities related to eating and eliminating, masturbation with orgasm, intercourse with an unattractive person, and homosexual relations, are considered only partial by Freud, and therefore capable of producing only partial gratification of the instinct.

When such partial aims and objects are more important to the person than the comprehensive ones, there is a tale to be told. If the person is still below the age of puberty, the tale is simply that of developmental immaturity, for the sexual instinct is considered to be much slower to mature than the other instincts. For a youngster, primary gratification of the sexual instinct through stimulation of the mouth or through masturbation and the like may be quite appropriate to his developmental stage. But if the person favors partial aims and objects in adulthood, the tale to be told is that of faulty development and psychopathology.

Freud's notions of comprehensive and partial objects has led some critics to think his theory very middle class, in the sense that it seems to say that the human's sexual processes are for child-rearing and are not really to be enjoyed. This is not a valid criticism, for Freud well understood the pleasure and satisfaction to be gained from sexual activities not obviously and immediately a part of orgasm and ejaculation during intercourse. But he did see the function of these delightful partial activities as setting the stage for vigorous orgasm and intercourse, the entire sexual expression being deep and truly satisfying. It is only when one or another of the partial goals becomes primary for an adult that Freud would worry. One thing I hope you have recognized is that Freud meant the sexual instinct to cover far more areas of the body and types of activities and pleasures than would be so in a more conventional meaning of sex.

An apparent implication of Freud's having distinguished the sexual instinct from the previously mentioned life instincts is that the former does not have a survival function. But this is not entirely true. Although the sexual instinct does not ensure survival of the individual by providing the impetus for obtaining needed nutrients and raw materials for metabolism (as do the life instincts), it does ensure survival of the species by providing the impetus for procreation. And Freud certainly recognized that survival of the species was ultimately important to survival of individuals. Nonetheless, it must be said that although the sexual instinct is, like all instincts, rooted in biological requirements, these requirements are not immediately relevant to the survival of the individual having the instinct. That the sexual instinct expresses a biological requirement can be shown by the painfully high levels of tension and discomfort that ensue from enforced sexual continence. But that these requirements do not have an obvious, strong effect on individual survival can also be shown by recognizing that some people, such as priests and nuns, live in fairly complete sexual abstinence without taking many years off their lives, as far as anyone knows. Now it is true that once you define sexuality as broadly as does Freud, you can imagine that even celibates can achieve some partial gratification of the sexual instinct, and that maybe it is just this that permits them to survive in an apparently easy manner. And it is also true that Freud would expect the conditions of celibacy to lead to certain symptoms of psychological malady, though they might be so subtle that one would have to observe with discernment. But these things can be well understood by simply postulating that the sexual instinct is rooted in biological requirements, without those requirements having very much to do with the immediate survival of the individual. After all, if you abstained from food or water for very long, there would be no necessity to look with discernment for subtle symptoms. You would die!

The disproportionate attention given by Freud to the sexual instinct certainly cannot be understood as a function of its greater survival importance than needs for food, water, and the like. It received so much attention because it seemed a much greater contributant to conflict than were the life instincts. And in a theory such as that of Freud, conflict forms and shapes the person's life. One reason why the sexual instinct was seen as the major source of conflict is that it matures so slowly and has so many parts that can be satisfied in so many ways. In contrast, the life instincts are simple, needing little maturation, and being capable of satisfaction in just a few ways. One way of summarizing what I have said is that the sexual instinct can be more affected by what one learns in early life than can the life instincts. As we shall see in the following section, Freud's views on the reactions of society to expressions of the sexual instinct make perfectly clear why the end result of this influence-ability should be conflict.

In the latter part of his career, Freud began to be convinced that there is yet a third kind of instinct, and that it functions antagonistically to the life instincts in that its aim is the biological death of the person. It is so extraordinary to assume that a basic tendency of the organism is to push toward death, that consideration of Freud's reasons for doing are clearly in order. He began theorizing in terms of the *death instinct* when he himself was well along in his life. Not only could he note the physiological and psychological changes going on in him as he aged, but he had reached the stage in life where it is increasingly common to find those around you dying. It is not so surprising that Freud would be thinking about death and its causation more in this period of his life than he had earlier. Then there was his own jaw cancer, which though contained by treatment, must have brought the possibility of his own death clearly into the center of attention for the last 16 years of his life. It is clear that Freud had a strong dread of death during his latter years (Bakan, 1966).

It has become fashionable these days to consider death as that which renders much of life meaningless in rational terms, because death, though the only absolute thing in existence, is itself unpredictable. Ours is also a time in which even hard sciences, such as physics, are abandoning the attempt to give causes to each event that can be observed. But in Freud's time, all scientists believed a strong form of the deterministic hypothesis. In other words, they expected to be able to discover a cause for every event. Freud gave evidence very early in his career of the strength of this belief in him when he took phenomena such as dreams and slips of the tongue as important events that were truly caused, a point of view that was not yet so common in medical circles. Such a strong believer in determinism would naturally take death to be a phenomenon with a rational, specifiable cause, especially when his own life circumstances conspired to render death personally salient.

In searching for a rational cause of death, one could take a simply physiological point of view and theorize in terms of the breakdown or fatigue or rigidification of body systems, and let it go at that. But Freud had been so long steeped and committed to a form of theorizing that assumes a psychological component to biological processes, that it is not surprising that the physiological view mentioned above would not have seemed sufficient. Freud had to assume a psychological—indeed, motivational—cause of death that also reflected a profound biological truth, in order to remain consistent with his previous theorizing.

Consistency and personal concern were not, of course, the only reasons for Freud's assumption of the death instinct. The psychological aspects of this assumption provided a rational way of understanding not only death as a natural concomitant of aging, but also death occuring as a result of decision making, such as murder and suicide. War could be understood as mass expression of the death instinct, and in this regard it is not surprising that Freud's major interest in the death instinct followed World War I. And even acts of aggression toward oneself and others could be explained as partial or disguised expressions of the tendency toward death. Like the life instincts, the death instinct could also be considered to have its source in the biological process of metabolism. Even in the individual cell, not only are there anabolic processes, which determine birth and growth, but also catabolic processes, which determine decay and eventual death.

Freud never developed the idea of the death instinct as completely as he had done with the life instincts. To be sure, the death instinct has a reasonably specifiable somatic source, and an aim that is presumably the reduction of tension arising from the biological necessity of catabolism. It is not clear, however, that the latter part of this statement makes much sense. And nowhere do we find detailed discussions of energy associated with the death instinct that would parallel libido theory. Further, while a few objects for the death instinct can be specified, there is an absence in Freud's writings of comprehensive discussions of such matters. A final difficulty with the notion of the death instinct is that it is not embedded in a developmental theory as are the life and sexual instincts.

As if these were not difficulties enough, there is an additional logistical problem created by the assumption that the life instincts are actively opposed by a death instinct. It becomes necessary to specify the precise nature of the relationship between the two antagonistic forces, if there is to be consistency in usage of the theory. Freud's rudimentary statements concerning the relationship are not theoretically satisfactory. He felt that in the normal course of events, the life instincts were stronger than the death instinct until rather late in life, when the trend culminating in just the opposite relationship begins. Also, in some disordered personalities, the death instinct has become more powerful than the life instinct. It is also possible for the death instinct to be stronger at certain times in any person's life, such as periods of sleep and self-condemnation. In statements such as these, Freud is doing no more than taking observations and describing them in terms of the two notions of death and life instincts. As soon as another observation came along, he would, if necessary, have described another kind of relationship between these two forces. There is no basis in such *post hoc* theorizing for consistency in usage from personalogist to personologist. Difficulties such as those mentioned in this and the preceding paragraph have led many psychologists to be particularly skeptical of the concept of death instinct. According to them, everything that Freud can account for with the concept can also be explained by the postulation of aggression resulting from frustration in the attempt to satisfy the life and sexual instincts. In truth, Freud himself believed this until he reached the latter part of his life. But to other educated men (e.g., Brown, 1959), the concept of death instinct has been very intriguing.

In concluding this section on instincts, I would like to remind you of a crucial point, which you must grasp fully if you are to understand Freud's position. The wishes and emotions of the id are deeply self-centered, indeed selfish, in nature. These are the wishes and emotions expressive of the person's basic, unadulterated, biological nature. There are no social refinements in them. The person wants what he needs when he needs it and without regard to what other people may need, prefer, or insist upon. Looked at as an individual, man is basically selfish and uncivilized, according to Freud. As you will see in the next section, it is this inherent selfishness that makes conflict inevitable.

You should also recognize that the instincts, as they exist in the id, are hopelessly ineffective in the external world. What good does it do to have wishes and emotions expressing your biological necessities, unless you have the knowledge of how to reach what you wish, and the capability to carry out the knowledge? Very little or no good, is Freud's answer. Just on the basis of his id alone, a person would only be able to satisfy instincts through wish-fulfilling fantasy (called *primary process* thought). And fantasy will not help much when what you need is real bread. Luckily enough, the infant is ordinarily tended by his parents until he has learned to fend for himself. But learn to fend he must. He must learn which of the appropriate objects of his instincts are available to him in his environment. He must learn where they are likely to be, and what instrumental behaviors on his part are likely to bring him to them. In all this learning, he must express selectivity, accuracy, memory, and self-correction when he fails. In a word, he must act intelligently. In Freud's terms, the person must develop an *ego* (this is the latin word for self).

At birth, the infant's entire mind is comprised of id wishes and emotions. But, as experience accumulates, part of the mind differentiates from the id and becomes ego. In large measure, the ego is the part of the mind comprising the thought and perceptual processes involved in recognition, remembrance, and action relevant to satisfying instincts (called *secondary process* thought). It is important to recognize that one of the two great functions of the ego is to aid in satisfying instincts in the external world. In bringing satisfaction about, the ego has the advantage of control over the voluntary nervous system and musculature. The ego and its component processes, being common to all persons, should be considered core characteristics of personality, along with the id and its components.

Freud has done a very interesting thing in his theorizing. He has made the mind a bridge from the somatic and metabolic requirements of living to the intelligent actions and interactions that constitute psychological living. The somatic and visceral processes produce the wishes and discomforts of the id, and the ego comes into being in order to guide the intelligence and muscles of the body in serving the somatic and visceral processes well. With the advent of the ego, the attempt to achieve biological necessities becomes not only selfish but effective as well. Freud calls this *pleasure principle functioning* to indicate at the same time its selfish and biologically satisfying quality. In the natural state, the human being is an individual, and engages solely in pleasure principle functioning. As you may have surmised, the part of my core tendency statement for Freud concerning maximization of instinctual gratification refers to pleasure principle functioning. But then society rears it head. . . .

The sources of punishment and guilt. The key to understanding Freud's view of the sources of punishment and guilt is in the fact that he believed the instincts to be so selfish in nature. They are not simply self-centered; they are necessarily antagonistic to the principles of orderly, civilized living. The instincts aim only for the reduction of tension due to metabolic requirements. Such requirements are, after all, characteristic of individual organisms alone. According to Freud, if everyone were to act out his natural, uninhibited instinctual demands, i.e., function at the level of the pleasure principle alone, the world would be an unimaginably horrendous place. In the process of grabbing what you want when you want it, you would inevitably encounter someone else who wanted the same thing at the same time, or would be disadvantaged by your gain. You would have to compete with him, or vanquish his defense, and none of this in the stylized and ordered fashion of civilized persons. You would literally fight him for instinctual gratification. The conclusion would be that to the victor belongs the spoils. But, you see, if any person were to accept this conclusion, it would be tantamount to accepting the likelihood that at some time in some place in some way, he would be unable to obtain instinctual gratification. This follows because no one can predict accurately whether he will be victor or vanquished. But accepting that you may not be able to satisfy your instincts is anathema to pleasure principle functioning, which is so selfish. Thus, we find that if people must live together pleasure principle functioning leads to the risk of failure in obtaining the very good that define it! And it is, of course, implausible to imagine a world in which persons would keep to themselves, living as hermits. Actually, Freud's position makes such isolation impossible, as it would lead to frustration of at least one instinct, that for sex, which requires the social interaction of intercourse.

The best that aggregates of persons, or societies, can do is aim for cooperation and order, so as to maximize gratification for all. Societies aim at the common good, which in Freud's terms means equalizing the possibilities of instinct gratification for their members. Of necessity, social living requires the development of civilization in the form of rules and regulations for conduct. These rules and regulations do indeed cut into pleasure principle functioning in the sense of uninhibited, unfettered pursuit of instinctual delights. But since people must live together, rules and regulations are the most effective measures for ensuring a maximum of instinctual gratification for all. Once you grant Freud's assumption that the aims of the individual are selfish whereas the aims of society are for the common good, then if people must function in groups, the seemingly paradoxical development of civilization on the part of persons who have no naturally generous, altruistic interest toward each other actually becomes an enevitability. In that individuals and society are seen to have antagonistic aims, the one selfish and the other communal, we have the essential basis upon which Freud's theory is classified here as an example of the psychosocial conflict model.

I have attempted to trace for you the manner in which Freud derives the importance of civilization from a position that takes selfish natural characteristics of humans as a starting point for understanding life, through simply accepting the fact that persons must live in close interaction with each other. Freud (1952) expressed this view in vivid, parable form in his book called *Totem and Taboo*. It is the story of the beginning of civilization. At the start, there are a father and mother and their many sons. True to the sexual instincts as manifested in the phallic stage of psychosexual development (to be discussed later), the sons wish to murder the father in order to possess the mother sexually. Being pleasure principle creatures, they actually carry out this instinctual wish. But once the father is out of the way, they find themselves thwarted in their selfish desires by the ensuing competition among them, and come thereby to realize the futility of having murdered. So the most direct route to instinctual gratification—pleasure principle functioning—turns out to be ineffective in the long run because all the sons unfortunately want the same commodity. Finally, the sons band together and accept a set of rules designed to avoid future difficulties by restricting the expression of instincts to those forms that are not too damaging to the group as a whole. This, in the parable, is the beginning of civilization, with its emphasis upon obedience toward the father and the taboo on incest, coupled with the institutionalization of marriage. Together, these taboos and sanctions assure as much satisfaction of the sexual instinct for each member of society as is possible without inordinate risk of battle over and deprival of sexual objects.

We are now in a position to consider the matter of punishment and guilt. Punishment and guilt have their source in the communal requirements of society. When people transgress the rules and regulations of civilization then they are punished by other people acting as representatives of the society. Young people are common transgressors, because they function at the level of the pleasure principle, not yet having learned the rules and regulations governing adult life. And parents are common punishers, acting in the role of societal representatives, because they are most often around the youngsters. Such punishments as physical damage, psychological humiliation, and withdrawal of love, are all effective, according to Freudians, by increasing tension in the organism. Even though the increase in tension is caused by an external event, punishment, its discomforting organismic effects are considered similar to those caused by instinctual deprivation. Tension is tension, and whenever it is present, the person must try to decrease it in some way. As society is greater and more powerful than the individual, his method of avoiding punishment, especially when he is a youngster and therefore weaker than he will become, is to curb instinctual expression so as not to brook retaliation.

Punishment comes from outside the person and expresses the societal requirements of communal living. Although expressive of the same requirements, guilt comes from within the person. In order to understand this, you must keep in mind that the child grows up in the context of his parents, who are in large part representatives of society with the assigned task of helping him to accept the rules and regulations that will render him a civilized adult. Certainly, the parents punish the child for unbridled instinctual expression. As the punishments accumulate, their emerging pattern can teach the child something of the nature of the rules. In addition, the parents supplement this dawning knowledge with verbal instruction. The combination of the two techniques leads the child, over a period of time, to internalize the rules. Once they exist in his memory, he can feel guilt. From then on, he can realize for himself when some wish of his transgresses the common good, and can feel morally culpable even if he does not actually express the wish in action. A portion of the mind hitherto devoted to ego processes becomes differentiated for the purpose of abstract representation of the rules and regulations of society in terms of ideas of good and bad, right and wrong. Freud's name for this set of ideas is the *superego*. Because its presence and, to some extent, its contents are common to all persons in the same society, it constitutes a core characteristic of personality in our terminology. As the internal counterpart of earlier punishments, guilt is assumed to have the same effect of raising organismic tension, which must then be reduced. As society was powerful enough to lead the person to inhibit his instincts in attempting to avoid punishment, so is guilt considered powerful enough to force the same sort of inhibition. Only the form and intensity of instincts can be expressed that will keep guilt at a minimum.

Now we have all the elements for understanding just what Freud meant in his core tendency of personality. The person attempts to maximize instinctual gratification while minimizing punishment and guilt because that is the best he can do in decreasing tension given the basically antagonistic nature of the individual and society. With the accumulation of punishment and the development of the superego, the ego takes on its second major function. You will recall that the first function was to provide the cognitive and actional wherewithal for effective satisfaction of instincts in the external world. The second ego function is to translate instinctual demands into expressions that are not inconsistent with superego demands. The ego, therefore, is the architect of the core tendency, which tendency Freud calls *reality principle functioning*. Reality principle functioning takes into account not only instinctual demands but the equally inexorable, and unfortunately opposed demands of society. In reality principle functioning, only socially acceptable forms and routines of instinctual functioning occur. The young man will not sleep with his mother. Instead, he will find another girl, not sexually attracted to anyone, and marry her. The hungry person will not steal bread. Instead, he will get a job and earn the money to pay the baker for the time he has had to spend away from his own instinctual gratification.

Perhaps because of his early biological training in medicine, Freud always considered it important to determine where the energy or fuel came from for particular organismic functions. According to him, the instincts get their energy from their somatic sources, but what about the ego and superego? Strange though it may seem, he thought that these two core characteristics shared the energy of the instincts. When you stop to think about it, this is not really so strange, as it is through the existence of an ego and superego that the maximum instinct gratification possible in a society is achieved. In the healthy personality, id, ego, and superego are deeply consistent in the process of living. All of living has the aim of maximizing instinct gratification while minimizing punishment and guilt, and this is precisely what Freud meant when he said that all behavior is motivated.

We are now in a position to reflect knowledgeably on why Freud emphasized the sexual instinct so much more than the life and death instincts. Actually, the death instinct was a concept of his later life, and he was so uncertain about it that its relative lack of emphasis seems understandable. But the differential in emphasis between the sexual and life instincts requires further comment, as both kinds of instinct were basic parts of his theorizing virtually from the beginning. Clearly, the sexual instinct received the lion's share of attention because Freud believed it to be surrounded with much more psychosocial conflict than the life instincts. The life instincts have an immediately obvious role in maintaining biological survival, a role we can readily be reminded of by the intense levels to which they can rise in just a short time of deprivation. Although unbridled expression of the life instincts comes in conflict with the requirements of society, these instincts are nonetheless so obviously important that all viable civilizations provide institutionalized bases for the regular and rapid satisfaction of them, lest they become too strong. So, three meals a day, with one or two snacks thrown in, are common in our society, and water and other liquids are rather continually available. The life instincts are so readily satisfied, at least in Western societies, that they are not a chronic source of intense conflict. Not so with the sexual instinct. To be sure, we have the institution of marriage, which can provide the socially sanctioned basis for frequent sexual gratification. But what of the person who is not married, and the child with his rudimentary forms of the sexual instinct? Such people's sexual needs are not planned for in any concrete way by society. Sexual gratification can be found, to be sure, but generally not in a socially sanctioned and respectable way. When an unmarried person visits a house of prostitution, he is frowned upon. When a child masturbates, it is imagined that he will damage himself through such monstrous activity. Even if such attitudes are diminishing these days, it must still be said that Western society has provided less extensive and effective institutions for the satisfaction of the sexual instinct than for the life instincts. It is this situation, according to Freud, that surrounds the sexual instinct with so much conflict. Freud emphasized the sexual instinct so much that he defined personality development in terms of it. His well-known oral, anal, phallic, latency, and genital stages are called psychosexual stages of development. And with the biological maturing of the sexual instinct at puberty, the personality jells and changes little thenceforward. It is interesting to speculate that society does not plan well for the satisfaction of the sexual instinct because, though based in biological requirements, it is not immediately relevant to survival, and does not increase in intensity precipitously with brief deprivation.

Defense. Freud's core theorizing not only involves a position on the nature of the instincts and the sources of punishment and guilt, but also includes a position on the mechanism whereby instinct gratification is maximized while punishment and guilt are held to a minimum. This mechanism is contained in the concept of defense. If the person expresses his instincts fully in action he will be punished by other people. If he fully recognizes his instincts even without acting on them he will experience guilt. And yet the instincts are inexorable forces pushing for expression. This state of affairs is the major conflict of life, and is eased somewhat through the process of defense.

The way in which defenses are aroused is simple enough. Whenever an instinct becomes strong enough to make a difference, an alarm reaction occurs in the form of anxiety. Anxiety is a diffuse, and rather contentless feeling of discomfort and impending disaster. This anxiety reaction represents the anticipation of punishment and guilt based on remembrance of past punishment and guilt, and triggers the defensive process. Defense eases the conflict between the demands of instincts and society by striking a compromise between them. The defense limits expression in action, and in personal awareness or consciousness, to only that part or form of the instinct that is acceptable to other people and to one's internalized standards. The ensuing acceptability of actions obviates punishment, and the acceptability of conscious wishes and feelings has the same advantage with regard to guilt. For example, if a son's real instinctual wish is to possess his mother sexually, the defensive form of this may be the awareness of and willingness to act upon the wish to stay close to and nurture her so that no harm will befall her. The defensive wish and actions are not only acceptable to others and one's own superego, but they also permit partial instinctual gratification through closeness to mother and through keeping her for oneself.

From my discussion of the way in which defensive processes are aroused, it may seem as if they are occasional phenomena. In point of fact, this is not true. It is much more accurate to Freud's thinking to realize that defense is a ubiquitous thing, because instincts are never at zero intensity, and hence, conflict between instinctual and societal aims—which is the basis for defense—is never absent. Although one can observe a particular instance of a certain defensive reaction, this does not mean that there was no other kind of defensive reaction already in operation concerning other instincts and other specific forms of the basic conflict. As all behavior is motivated, or infused with instincts, for a Freudian, so too is all behavior defensive!

Be clear about it, this conclusion has extraordinary implications. If all behavior is defensive, then the person is not aware of his true wishes, feelings, and aims. Although these true instinctual elements are represented in the mind, they are represented as mental content unavailable to awareness. The paradoxical ring of this position has been the source of many attacks upon Freudian thinking, and we shall consider it further in Chapter 5 of this book. If all behavior is defensive, then whatever mental content we are aware of is no more than epiphenomenal, or in other words, a pale shadow of the truth. Thus, wishing to remain close to and nurture mother might very well be part of what one would feel if one really wanted to possess mother sexually, but one would never imagine the latter wish from the former.

It should be clearly realized that the defenses function to keep whatever has been repressed out of consciousness more or less indefinitely. Thus, the truth about oneself is rather permanently unavailable. Now mind you, the position that all behavior is defensive has much more alarming implications than would be the case if only some behavior were considered defensive. If, as Freud believed, the truth about oneself is rather permanently unavailable, then how can learning, or any real change in personality take place? Leaving aside for a moment the possibility of change in psychoanalysis—the form of psychotherapy associated with the Freudian position—we should discard as useless some of our most cherished ideas about rationality as the basis for living and educating. If logical thinking and debate cannot even have the real truth to work on, then how can such processes possibly produce any meaningful result? An eminent and anti-Freudian personologist, Gordon W. Allport (1955, p. 100), puts the problem this way:

> Up to now the "behavioral sciences," including psychology, have not provided us with a picture of man capable of creating or living in a democracy. These sciences in large part have imitated the billiard ball model of physics, now of course outmoded. They have delivered into our hands a psychology of an organism pushed by drives and molded by environmental circumstance. . . . But the theory of democracy requires also that man possess a measure of rationality, a portion of freedom, a generic conscience, propriate ideals, and unique value. We cannot defnd the ballot box or liberal education, nor advocate free discussion and democratic institutions, unless man has the potential capacity to profit therefrom.

Because all behavior, according to Freud, is not only motivated but also defensive, we are forced in his frame of reference to accept a view of man as controlled by forces from within and pressure from without, and as so unwise as to not even realize that damning fact!

You may think that especially in this last phrase, I am being unfair to Freud. After all, does he not really mean that since there are conflicts that we ease through defensive processes, we need to be especially careful to recognize that what we consciously believe about ourselves is not necessarily the whole truth? If this is so, then there is no incompatibility, really, between the Socratic injunction to know myself and the Freudian view. Freud is merely making clear how important it is to plumb the full depths of your mind, because what you can easily know is not all there is of importance. You can point to Freud's use of free association as proof that he believed the inhibition of consciousness produced by defense could be circumvented. Although modern-day psychoanalytic thinkers have added to Freud's position in such manner as to make this interpretation plausible, it does nonetheless distort what Freud himself meant.

Most people find the argument presented in the last paragraph compelling because it presents a view of humans as fallible but also perfect-able, a position deeply rooted in Western thought and religion. But be clear about the fact that even if you think you know yourself rather well by now through introspection and experience, even if you think you have seen your own foibles and defensive operations and bedrock instincts, Freud would not have agreed, unless perhaps you had been in psychoanalysis for many years. Freud would have seen your beliefs concerning the nature of your defensive operations and real wishes as themselves defensive! You cannot know the real truth about yourself simply because you have the pious goal of being honest and working hard at it.

The key to understanding why you cannot get behind your own defenses is the notion that the defensive process is itself outside of awareness. If your defenses operated consciously, they would not be effective at all. You would know that you were merely lying to yourself and to the world. A consciously operating process of defense would not insulate you from guilt, though it could be successful in avoiding punishment. Indeed, we all employ techniques for keeping from others what is our conscious intent when we think they will not be accepting of us. Because we do this so much, it was possible for me to suggest to you the intuitive basis for understanding what Freud meant with which I began discussion of his view of the basic tendency of life. But while these techniques for fooling others are somewhat analogous to what Freud meant by defenses, they fall short of the important meaning of that concept. The defense is a way of lying to yourself as well as to other people.

When you lie to yourself, it is only effective if you do not realize you are doing so. Hence, the notion that defense operates unconsciously, and the attendant implication that you cannot penetrate defensive processes to obtain real truth simply by an earnest attempt to do so. Unless you have had the very unusual experience of the momentary breakdown of a defense, you have no basis in personal experience—intuition—for full understanding of the theory or defense. You will have to be satisfied with an understanding on the basis of reasoning, the elements of which I have tried to present here. If you launch forth with what is presumably a very personal account of your own defensive operations and underlying instinctual desires, you must recognize that Freud might well have reacted with chagrin.

As suggested in the last paragraph, there are times when defenses break down, and a glimpse of the real truth ensues. These times occur when the person is in psychoanalysis, or is severely debilitated, through psychological or physical stress. The accompaniment of breakdown in defense is acute guilt and anxiety—the feeling that life is about to end terribly and, indeed, should end for such a worthless person. The person cannot stay in such a state for very long and still maintain much integrity and organization. If defenses are not reinstituted, regardless of whether the source of breakdown was debilitation or psychotherapy, madness or catastrophe will result. I chose strong words because Freud meant them, even though his meaning is often watered down in order to make it consistent with civilized personal experience. Freud felt he was talking about matters of life and death, though it is a tribute to the success of defensive processes that these matters are rarely experienced fully.

If defenses, once breached, must be reinstated in order to avoid catastrophic disintegration of personality, then this must mean that not even in psychoanalysis is the goal of therapy the removal of defenses. Precisely so! But then what did Freud mean when he typified the goal of psychotherapy by the dramatic axiom "where id was there shall ego be" (Freud, 1933, p. 112). In approaching an understanding of this statement, we should be sure that we are clear about the nature of id and ego. The id is the mental representation, in the form of wishes and feelings, of selfish instincts having their source in somatic and metabolic processes. By themselves, instincts are relatively ineffective in the world; instincts do not include knowledge of the instrumentalities governing actions such that gratification is ensured; nor do instincts include knowledge of the necessity of avoiding open conflict with other people simply to ensure a continuing availability of the objects of gratification. Knowledge of instrumentalities effective in instinct gratification, and in conforming to the inescapable requirements of society, are in large part what constitutes the ego. The ego ensures a maximum of instinct gratification and a minimum of trouble through the processes of perception, memory, and judgment, and their relation to the voluntary nervous system, guided throughout by the knowledge mentioned above. And the most important part of the ego is the defenses. It is largely defensive processes that permit successful operation of the basic tendency of life.

Freud's statement about psychoanalysis is often interpreted to mean that unconscious mentation shall be made conscious, and defenses shall be removed in favor of a more open basis for experiencing. This does not appear to be an accurate interpretation. While the id is largely unconscious, it is not true that the ego is largely conscious. Remember that the defenses, which are themselves unconscious, represent the lion's share of the ego according to Freud. So the notion of replacing id with ego is not very likely to mean making unconscious things conscious. Further evidence for this interpretation involves recognition that a large part of the id is unconscious only because of the action of the ego's defensive processes. How can replacing id with ego mean making the unconscious conscious? Indeed, Freud cannot even mean that the id must go, even though it sounds that way, because in this system of thought the id is the natural endowment of man. What did he mean then, by what now emerges as a very figurative, and therefore imprecise, statement? As you may have guessed from my description of id and ego a few paragraphs ago, I think Freud meant that pleasure principle functioning, so characteristic of the id in isolation and so ineffective in the world, must give way to reality principle functioning, if psychotherapy is to be judged successful. Reality principle functioning, you will remember, is what we have been calling Freud's overall core tendency of living.

Lacan (Mehlman, 1972), a contemporary French philosopher, is in essential agreement with my interpretation of Freud's famous statement. Reconsidering the original German "Wo es war, soll ich werden," Lacan asserts that the translation could well have been "Where id (or it) was, there must ego (or I) arrive at." The definite implication of this, is that the goal of psychotherapy is not so much an increase in consciousness as it is an increase in instinctual gratification brought about by rendering the ego an instrument of the id.

So far, I have focused on defensiveness as a general mechanism for striking a compromise between the demands of instincts and of society. Actually, Freud's theory of personality details more different kinds of defense than any other theory using the general concept of defensiveness. His daughter, Anna Freud (1946), lists such examples of defense as *repression, regression, reaction formation, denial, projection, identification, intellectualization, compensation, isolation, undoing,* and *sublimation.* While I will not discuss these different kinds of defense until Chapter 6, on the peripheral characteristics of personality, it is important to recognize here that one crucial distinction between defenses is the degree to which they distort the underlying instincts. The more successful psychosexual development has been, the more the person's functioning is characterized by defenses that minimally distort instinctual reality, such as sublimation. Developmental failings, produced by fixations (or haltings of growth), are partially defined by the existence of grossly distortional defenses, such as projection. But even the highest form of functioning, bespeaking exemplary development, is characterized by defensiveness. The most accurate description of the goal by psychoanalysis, if the position is to have logical consistency, is the substitution, for defenses that heavily distort truth, of defenses that constitute less of a distortion. But as there is no alternative to defensive behavior, there is no alternative to at least some distortion of what is really true, and hence, no alternative to unconsciousness of some of the most basic things about you. Freud's theory of personality is probably the most pessimistic in existence.

A word more about development will aid in fuller understanding of the dimensions of this pessimism. Freud discusses development almost exclusively in terms of the sexual instinct, and delineates the five well-known stages called *oral, anal, phallic, latency,* and *genital.* Fixations at any of the stages preceding the last are considered to result in adult personalities or *character types* including the defenses and traits characteristic of the stage involved. There will be much more discussion of these matters later. For the moment, it is enough to realize that the first three, and most crucial, stages of psychosexual development cover roughly the first five years of life. The latency period, unelaborated by Freud and considered essentially a time of dormancy, extends until the advent of puberty. Puberty opens the genital stage, which extends until death. The extraordinary discrepancy between the attention given the earliest childhood years and the rest of life indicates that for Freud nothing of real developmental importance happens after age five. The outlines of personality are essentially fixed by then, with the rest of life being a repetition of the early patterns. To be sure, the person becomes more complex as he ages, but nothing basic really changes.

Persons familiar with Freud may contend that his pessimism is more characteristic of earlier than later works. But there is continued evidence of pessimism in the later works, where the death instinct is formulated for the first time (Freud, 1922a), and where the inevitability of defensiveness is reasserted (e.g., Freud, 1922b). In the latter work, Freud suggests that the effect of World War I was to strip away the comforting repression of the death instinct humans were all engaging in. If Freud were leaning toward a new found optimism, he could at this point have argued that such a new level of consciousness would spur psychological development. Instead, he predicts that consciousness of our own viciousness will prove too much to bear, leading to a renewal of defensiveness. Some persons may revert to a primitive defense, projection, and imagine that there are really enemies out there, from whom we must protect ourselves (through aggressive self-defense, of course). Others may take a more sophisticated route, by seeming to accept death as the outcome of aggression, but not really accepting it at all. Through such rationalizations as belief in an afterlife or the contention that we achieve immortality in our works and our children, the stark reality of the death instinct is blunted. One way or another, we defend against the instinctual truth because we cannot bear it. If he changed as he aged, Freud probably became more rather than less pessimistic.

Murray's position

Like Freud, Henry A. Murray (born in New York City, 1893) has lived a complex, cosmopolitan life, and began his career as a physician. Throughout his early professional years as a physiologist and surgeon, Murray indicated a searching interest in psychic considerations by conducting serious psychological studies of his colleagues and patients. Eventually, his psychological interests, fired by the psychoanalyst Jung, the study of philosophy, and his own intense life, got the better of him. Having decided on a serious commitment to personology—a word which he coined—Murray was appointed director of the Harvard Psychological Clinic by Morton Prince. The 15 years he gave to this role, which ended with the advent of World War II, comprised an extremely active, exciting, and productive period in the life of the clinic. Much as Freud had done before him, Murray gathered together an extraordinary group of young and capable psychologists, who worked in close collaboration on the development of a theory of personality. But the source of evidence for this theory was not psychotherapy with disturbed people so much as systematic research on the lives of the articulate, gifted undergraduates at Harvard University. Interestingly enough, the aspects of Murray's theory stemming from this source constitute a position on the periphery of personality, and will be discussed in Chapter 6. This peripheral theorizing has had a tremendous impact on personology both directly through Murray and his colleagues, many of whom are extraordinary figures in the field, and indirectly through its effect on the testing movement.

But the core considerations in Murray's theory, which will be discussed here, are distinctly psychoanalytic. At the same time that Murray was heading the Harvard Psychological Clinic, he was becoming trained as a psychoanalyst (by members of Freud's inner circle), and finally became a charter member of the Boston Psychoanalytic Society. His functioning as a psychotherapist for disturbed people expressed the side of him that has been a committed Freudian.

As you may have surmised, Murray's position is frustratingly heterogeneous. Though rich and fertile, his thinking is also disturbingly eclectic. So eclectic is his view, that it is difficult to know whether or not to class it a conflict position. But it is statements about the core of personality that are most relevant to such classing, and in such statements, Murray is quite similar to Freud. But there is a great deal to Murray, as I hope you will realize by the time you have read Chapter 6 as well as this one. His heterogeneous theorizing reflects the nature of his life. In addition to what has been already mentioned, Murray established and directed, in the early days of World War II, the first extensive and systematic assessment service the Office of Strategic Services has had. For his work he was awarded the Legion of Merit in 1946. Over the years, Murray has made a strong commitment to the study of literature, ranking as an expert on the work of Herman Melville. And far from restricting himself to the biological emphasis of Freudianism, Murray has branched out into the study of anthropology and sociology for their relevance to the understanding of humans. For additional information on his life as it relates to his theorizing, see Maddi and Costa (1972).

For Murray (1938), Freud's conceptualization of the core tendency of life will do quite well; *the person tries to maximize instinctual gratification, while minimizing punishment and guilt.* For core characteristics, Murray, like Freud, talks in terms of an id, an ego, and a superego. Murray too considers the id to be the part of personality that contributes energy and direction for behavior. In short, the id summarizes the motivation of the person. In discussing motivation more precisely, Murray uses the language of life and sexual instincts, and gives an important place to considerations of psychosexual development. The superego is for him, as for Freud, a cultural implant, learned through the punishment and approval of parents, which functions to inhibit the socially destructive expression of instincts. So, on the one hand, we see the emphasis upon instincts as self-interested and self-aggrandizing in nature. On the other hand, we see social living depicted as requiring some relinquishment of complete instinctual gratification. Society protects itself by providing for the punishment of antisocial actions, and since punishment is painful, the person avoids antisocial actions. The person attempts to avoid punishment, in the case of social pressures, and guilt, in the case of the superego pressures, all the while he attempts to gain as much instinctual gratification as possible. In the carrying out of this core tendency, the ego has the role of mediating between the poles of the conflict, this role to be accomplished through the use of voluntary nervous system and striated muscle in planning, ordering, and defensive processes. In all this, Murray and Freud are in good agreement. The import of Murray's agreement with Freud is that conflict is inevitable, and life must therefore be, at best, a compromise that minimizes the conflict, or at least makes it bearable. For this reason, I have called Murray a conflict theorist.

But there are differences in emphasis between Freud and Murray in conceptualization of the core of personality. And these differences all go in the direction of decreasing the inevitability of conflict in Murray's approach. Thus, we find that the id, while it certainly contains the familiar selfish instincts, also includes other motivational tendencies less clearly inconsistent with social living. Such things as the needs for love and for achievement are localized in the id by Murray. This means that they are basic motivational tendencies, inherent to the organism, rather than secondary motivations (as they would be for Freud) derived from the selfish instincts through learning and the operation of defenses. Clearly, needs for love and for achievement are not inconsistent with society, indeed they promote it, and if they are inherent, then man, in his most natural state, is not temperamentally incapable of communal living. Hence, Murray's view of the id is, by comparison with Freud's, less in keeping with a conflict position (Murray, 1938).

Turning to the superego, we find that Murray has here too elaborated and eclecticized Freud's view. For Murray, the superego is not only the taboos and sanctions instilled by the parents when the child is at a tender, cognitively uncritical age, but also a sophisticated set of principles and ideals for living based on considerable personal experience with many people and life contexts. Even great literature is a contributant to superego development, according to Murray. The superego grows in individuality and sophistication throughout life, rather than remaining, as it is in Freud, the unshakeable vestige of early trials and tribulations. It is a trivialization of Murray's view of superego to say that it stands in necessary opposition to the id, for, as the id is not completely selfish, so is the superego not completely in the service of the needs of others. So in the treatment of superego, we also see that Murray's modifications of Freud decrease the inevitability of conflict in living.

The upshot of all this is that while conflict and its minimization still remain essential to understanding the core of personality in Murray's theory, it does become possible to consider some functioning of the person that is not conflict defined. Keeping this in mind, it will not be surprising to you to find that Murray has also elaborated the idea of ego much beyond what Freud had in mind. In classical Freud, the role of the ego is essentially only that of carrying out the core tendency of maximizing instinctual gratification while minimizing punishment and guilt. Going beyond this, Murray (Murray & Kluckhohn, 1956, p. 26) elaborates ego functions that relate to the expression in the world of socially acceptable id tendencies. Whereas Freud stressed defensive operations as the substance of the ego, for defenses are the prime basis for resolving conflicts, Murray stresses cognitive and actional procedures for planning and executing behaviors in the absence of conflict. These procedures are such things as *rational thought* and *accurate perception* (Maddi, 1963; Maddi & Costa, 1972). As Maddi (1963, p. 194) points out, Murray even goes so far as to assume, somewhat implicitly, that the ego has an inborn basis separate from that of the id. Murray assumes this when he attributes ego functioning in part to the natural requirement of the nervous system for information.

These modifications of Freud's thinking have a number of general effects well worthy of note. For one, consciousness—true, accurate representation of experience in awareness—is not only logically possible, but actually very important in Murray's position. Each person is some conglomerate of consciousness and unconsciousness, the former expressing conflict-free aspects of personality, and the latter expressing defensive resolutions of conflict. Another difference from Freud is that for Murray, tension reduction is not the most accurate way to state the aim of motivational tendencies. Murray (Murray & Kluckhohn, 1956, pp. 36–37) contends that the absence of tension is not so rewarding as is the process of getting from higher to lower states of tension. This modification leads to the interesting possibility that people may actually increase their tension in order to heighten the experience of pleasure when tension is subsequently decreased. Once again we find Murray unwilling to accept the most extreme form of classical Freudian thinking.

Actually, when we focus on the modifications Murray has made on Freud, Murray looks not unlike some of the theorists I have listed in the chapters on the fulfillment model. But we should not lose sight of the face that Murray is still basically a conflict theorist. Indeed, one can find considerable grounds for being convinced of this in his treatment of development, which follows Freud's lead rather closely. There are modifications here too, but they do not remove the emphasis on conflict. Murray (1938) identifies what he calls *complexes,* which are essentially groups of traits and styles that result from fixations at one or another of the stages of development delineated by Freud. To be sure, Murray does add to the Freudian developmental formulation. At the younger end, for example, Murray describes the *claustral complex,* a group of traits characteristic of the intrauterine stage of life. He also identifies a *urethral stage,* between the oral and anal stages. Nonetheless, Murray's view of complexes as the result of fixations in psychosexual development places him in the conflict camp. This is so because psychosexual development refers to the sexual instinct, which is a basically selfish thing for psychoanalytic thinkers, and because development seems to be essentially limited to early childhood.

All things considered, it may be best to consider Murray's position to be a variant on the pure conflict theory. It is a variant because, though conflict and its minimization still remain the most basic considerations, there is an aspect of personality and functioning which is inherent, and therefore at the core level, that is free of conflict.

Ego psychology

Murray is certainly one of the first theorists of general psychoanalytic persuasion who embraced the possiblity that some proportion of functioning, however small, might be in service of conflict minimization. This possibility has found its most characteristic expression in the writings of Hartmann, Kris, and Loewenstein (1947), who develop the notion of a *conflict-free ego sphere.* They argued that some of the ego's functions were carried forth with energy not derived from the id. In other words, the ego has some functions that are not in service of instinct gratification and the avoidance of pain. They actually go so far as to assume that the ego does not emerge out of the inborn id at all, but that both ego and id have their origin in inherited predispositions and have their own independent courses of development. At least the part of the ego that does not deal with conflict has its own inborn source of energy with which to carry out its functions. The conflict-free portion of the ego has objectives different from the id, and includes functions much like those Murray has stressed; such functions as rational thought processes, accurate perceptual processes, and muscular coordination are used by the person to accomplish intellectual and social objectives that are not psychosexual in nature. Some writers, such as Hendrick (1943), have even assumed that there are ego instincts, such as that *to master.* The source of the mastery instinct is in the environmental challenge to function effectively, and its aim is to reduce the tension resulting from this challenge. Though somewhat different from Murray's need for information, the mastery instinct has a similar logical function in providing a theoretical justification for assuming an inborn ego.

The innate bases of ego autonomy are called *primary,* to distinguish them from *secondary* bases which are rooted in experience. In an authoritative statement, Rapaport (1958) says:

> We no longer assume that the ego arises from the id, but rather that the ego and the id both arise by differentiation from a common undifferentiated matrix, in which the apparatuses that differentiate into the ego's means of orientation, of reality-testing, and of action, are already present. These, termed *apparatuses of primary autonomy,* serve drive gratification and enter conflict as independent ego-factors. They are the memory apparatus, the motor apparatus, the perceptual apparatuses, and the threshold apparatuses (including the drive- and affect-discharge thresholds). They are evolutionary givens which, by virtue of their long history of selection and modification, have become the primary guarantees of the organism's "fitting in" with (adaptedness to) its environment. In other words, the primary guarantees of the ego's autonomy from the id seem to be the very apparatuses which guarantee the organism's adaptedness to the environment.
>
> The *apparatuses of secondary autonomy* arise either from instinctual modes and vicissitudes, as these become "estranged" from their instinctual sources, or from defensive structures formed in the process of conflict-solution, as these undergo a "change of function" and become apparatuses serving adaptation. In other words, the apparatuses of secondary autonomy are not "innate" but arise from "experience." Thus this second guarantee of ego autonomy also involves reality relations. While it is obvious that without relationships to a real external environment we would be solipsistic beings, a long detour was necessary before we could see clearly that the autonomy of the ego from the id—our safeguard against solipsism—is guaranteed by these innate and acquired apparatuses which keep us attuned to our environment.

The "change of function" by which initially instinctual and defensive considerations become autonomous remains a mystery. Rapaport links the process up, somehow, with adaptation, presumably to the demands of external reality. From these ambiguities, and the emphasis upon the necessity of guarantees, it would seem that ego autonomy is precarious at best.

This newer brand of psychoanalytic thinking is called *ego psychology,* and is professed by contemporary psychoanalytic thinkers, many of whom trace their intellectual lineage directly to Freud or members of his inner circle. Ego psychology is currently very popular, because it seems to many personologists to represent an improvement over Freud's cramping view of life that nonetheless preserves his basic insights. Ego psychologists are fond of pointing out that Freud must have held a rudimentary form of their position, because he spoke of the life instincts as ego-preservative (Freud, 1925b). Be this as it may, there is overwhelming emphasis in Freud on the ego as derived from the id and as functioning to strike the conflict-induced compromise of reality principle functioning. Anyone who finds ego psychology a worthwhile elaboration of Freud's thinking must face the implications of assuming an inborn ego and a conflict-free ego sphere. Ego psychology is no mere extension of Freud, rather, it represents a break with psychoanalytic tradition more radical than has often seemed apparent.

It is surely a radical change in psychoanalytic theory to decide that not all, but only some behavior is defensive, and that not all, but only some behavior is expressive of selfish instincts. Immediately, one has modified the theory such that fixations and psychosexual stages are no longer adequately descriptive of development. One can then decrease the overwhelming importance of the early years in understanding life-styles, and this is just what is done by the ego psychologist, Erikson (1950). I will detail his view of development for you in Chapter 6 on the periphery of personality, but for now I would like to have you know that he considers eight developmental stages rendering personality as something that changes throughout the life-span. As you know, Freud considered fewer developmental stages, and saw personality as being rather well set by the time puberty is reached. Ego psychology also permits one to take seriously man's attempts to be rational and logical in reaching decisions and solving problems. As you will be able to see from reading the next chapter, modifications of psychoanalytic theory in the direction of decreasing the pervasiveness and significance of conflict and defense render the resultant body of thought more like what I have come to call the fulfillment model. Ego psychology presents a view of man that is considerably more optimistic than that offered by Freud.

Certainly Murray and the ego psychologists have radically changed psychoanalytic thought. And even though the changes may render that body of thinking more satisfying to contemporary personologists, it must be said that some of the most appealing aspects of the classical Freudian approach are lost. When the ego comprised only the mechanisms of defense whereby conflict could be resolved, the id was still the only inherent aspect of personality. And the id, of course, could be justified on biological grounds. The sexual instinct in particular was tied to physiological processes, and the psychosexual stages of development were considered to follow the biological development of the organism. But are there clear biological bases of the instincts or drives attributed to the conflict-free portion of the ego? And if one also considers the modifications of the id suggested by Murray, whereby motivations other than the survival, sex, and death instincts are considered inherent to the person, then the id loses virtually all of its original meaning. It is only the wish to preserve the name id that underlies Murray's usage, for in his way of thinking id and motivation in its most general sense are one and the same. I do not mean to say that the modifications of the ego psychologists and Murray should not be taken seriously, rather, I simply wish to underscore the shift in thinking that they constitute. One cannot say in any intellectually convincing fashion that the modifications are no more than logical extensions of Freud's thinking.

As you can imagine, I am reticent to abstract from the ego psychology literature, which is heterogeneous enough to border on amorphousness, any one statement of a core tendency to be considered definitive. Nonetheless, if some statement were necessary, the best I could do would be to take seriously the fact that ego psychologists still see themselves as basically in the Freudian camp, and list the same core tendency as for Freud. But it would be important to keep in mind that, like Murray, ego psychologists postulate some instincts that are not opposed to society in any irrevocable fashion.

CONFLICT MODEL: INTRAPSYCHIC VERSION

Thus far, I have discussed theories that are examples of the psychosocial type of conflict model. This type includes a core tendency expressing the necessity for compromise between the requirements of individuals and the requirements of groups. To be sure, psychosocial conflict theories assume the implantation of social aims in the person at some point in his development, following which both great opposing forces are represented within him. But this does not change the basic fact that in such theories the sources of the inevitable conflict are in the individual and the group. In contrast, the intrapsychic version of the conflict model starts with the assumption that the opposing forces rendering conflict inevitable are all inherent, inborn parts of the person. The conflict starts out and remains within the psyche and is not dependent upon the difference between living for yourself alone and living in the company of others. Although the theories I will consider in this section are clearly examples of the conflict model, they are discriminably different in some of their implications from those considered in the previous section. As you will see in more detail later, one important difference between the two types of conflict positions is that the intrapsychic type relies much less heavily upon the concept of defensiveness than does the psychosocial type.

Rank's position

Otto Rank (born in Vienna, Austria, 1884; died in New York in 1939) started out as a member of Freud's inner circle, and was for many years respected by that group as a brilliant and nonmedical contributor to the psychoanalytic movement. Although he did practice psychotherapy, Rank spent much of his intellectual energy applying his view to the understanding of other phenomena than psychopathology. In addition to his own writing, Rank founded or edited three influential European journals on psychoanalysis. The fact that he was not a physician, and that his training was in philosophy, psychology, history, and art, was a welcomed stimulus to Freud and the other psychoanalysts. But as Rank become more and more invested in certain heretical ideas, the relations between himself and the psychoanalytic circle became strained to the point where they finally broke. Today, the version of Rank's thinking available to us seems very different from Freud's position, though there are unquestionable similarities in form. It is perhaps unfortunate for the psychoanalytic movement that Rank left the inner circle, for his stimulating influence must have been largely lost to that group. As we go over his theory now, it becomes clear that he had in mind a good many thoughts that have since flowered in personology.

The core tendency in Rank's (1929, 1945) theory is easily stated, and clearly establishes the position as a pure expression of the intrapsychic type of pure conflict model. According to him, all functioning is expressive of *the tendency to minimize the fear of life while at the same time minimizing the fear of death.* The terms "life" and "death" have special meaning to a Rankian, and that should be discussed before you attempt relating this statement of a core tendency to your own personal experience. Life is equivalent to the process of separation, and individualization, whereas death is the opposite, namely, union, fusion, and dependency. So, the core tendency concerns the opposing fears that you will be a separate individual, and fused with the world and other people. Many of you have a convenient basis for experiencing what Rank meant in having decided whether or not to leave home to go to college. When you thought you should leave home, you experienced, in the prospect of separation from people familiar and dear to you, the fear of life. Conversely, when you thought you might stay at home, you experienced, in the prospect of failing to grow and develop further, the fear of death. To have decided to go, without any plan for continuing your relationship to those left behind would have minimized the fear of death, but greatly intensified the fear of life. Conversely, to have decided to stay, without any plan for extending and broadening your personal development, would have minimized the fear of life but greatly intensified the fear of death. A minimization of both fears might have been struck by deciding to go to a college close by, so that you could continue to live at home, or by leaving to go to school firm in the conviction that you would write and visit home frequently.

According to Rank, life is essentially a series of situations in which you are called upon to either achieve greater separation and individuality, or renouncing that possibility, regress to the old and familiar. And, from his statement of core tendency, it is clear that even the best solution in such situations will constitute a compromise, the two fears involved being unavoidably opposed. As with the other theorists, there is much more than simply this to Rank's position, and we should therefore turn to more detailed consideration of it.

The nature and bases of the two fears. First, it should be pointed out that the two fears are experienced as uncomfortable tension states, much as in the anxiety concept stressed by other conflict theorists. Rank prefers the term fear because it implies a definite object, whereas anxiety is a more diffuse state. Fear is similar in bodily effects to anxiety, but provides, in its more precise cognitive aspects, a format for appropriate action. That the two fears are tension states indicates, according to the wording of the core tendency, that the overall aim of the person can be characterized as tension reduction. In this, Rank is similar to the other conflict theorists. But as soon as one focuses on the origins of the two fears, the differences between him and the others begin to emerge.

Although he might even agree with Freud that each person possesses certain biological instincts, such as those for food, water, and sex, Rank would not consider them of special importance for understanding personality. Whatever biological instincts exist, they do not provide the intrinsic basis for conflict, according to Rank. Much more important is the inexorable tendency for living things to separate and individuate. The very act of launching forth upon life, the act of birth, is a profound separation of the neonate from its mother's body. Rank (1929) believes that being born is a deeply traumatic experience because one must relinquish the warm, relatively constant environment of the womb, in which one's needs are automatically met, for the more variable, potentially harsher world outside, in which for the first time one experiences the discomfort of needs insufficiently and tardily served.

Early in his career, Rank considered the birth trauma the most significant event in life. Later on, though he still gave it a prime position, he came to consider it only the first in a long series of separation experiences that are as inevitable as life itself. The separations are caused by biological, psychological, and social developments that are indistinguishable from life. Typically, the second major separation occurs when weaning takes place, and the child must face the tragedy of relinquishing mother's fecund breast, and the warm, protected place at her side. This separation is rapidly followed by the even greater decrease in contact with mother precipitated by the maturation of locomotor processes. Other common separation experiences are going to school, becoming individuated enough to render meaningless and anachronistic the friendships and attachments of an earlier age, and leaving home to strike out on your own life. To be alive for Rank is to be faced with the continual series of separations through which one becomes a particular psychological, social, and biological person and no one else. Living is a fearful process because it inevitably entails separations, which simultaneously precipitate uncertainty as to what will happen, require the person to assume greater and greater responsibility for himself, and render him ever more alone and lonely.

If separation and individuation arouse so much fear, then why not avoid them completely? According to Rank, to avoid them completely would be to repudiate life, and could only be accomplished by killing oneself. But this is no solution at all, for the human is a living thing, and individuation is an integral, normal part of living. The fact that life is inevitably a process of separation is also the basis of the fear of death. To avoid separation and indviduation in any way, such as refusing to develop or merging mindlessly with other people and things, is so much a violation of the nature of life, according to Rank, that it engenders the fear of obliteration. So the person is caught between two poles of a conflict that is as basic as being alive. Anything done to reduce the fear of living will increase the fear of dying, and vice versa. The only way to achieve a workable existence, therefore, is to strike a compromise which balances, or holds at a minimum, both opposing forces. In this emphasis on compromise, one sees that Rank's is a true conflict theory, even though it is of the intrapsychic rather than psychosocial type.

The existentialists, as you will see in Chapter 3, have a position which appears similar to that of Rank. In the existential view, life is also a continual experience of choice as to whether you will climb the ladder of individuation, which involves separation, or refuse to do so. But, in contrast to Rank, the existentialists advocate achieving individuation, regardless of the toll. They do not endorse the compromise considered ideal by Rank, though this does not amount, as you shall see, to damning the person to social isolation.

Clearly, however, both existentialists and Rank would agree that the attempt to decrease only the fear of life is an unworkable situation in that it negates the very fiber of existence. This a particularly interesting position in light of the recent surge of attention in our society to Zen Buddhism (e.g., Watts, 1957) as a possibly more meaningful way of life than that available in the Western tradition. Zen Buddhism advocates a merging of the person with his social and physical environment, with associated loss of consciousness of self as a force in the world. The teaching of Zen is that man is one with each other man and with the world. Such a belief, and the attempt to implement it in action, constitutes a negation of the nature of life for Rank and May. While neither May nor Rank provides a cogent explanation of how such a negation could even be attempted by people, they clearly would see it as an abberation. Interestingly enough, support for the position of May and Rank is to be found in the research of at least one scholarly Westerner (Koestler, 1960), who interprets Zen Buddhism in both the Western and Eastern worlds as the concerted attempt to die.

The will as a force in life. The other important core characteristic along with fear of life and fear of death is the *will*. The will, in Rank's theory, is somewhat analogous logically to Freud's ego and Sullivan's self. The similarity among all three concepts is in the notion that there is some aspect of personality that has an overall organization function, that integrates all separate experiences into a composite sense of total being. In addition, all three concepts refer to a process of development considered necessary and unavoidable. If the child lives, he will develop an ego, according to Freud, a self-dynamism, according to Sullivan, and a will, according to Rank. Finally, all three concepts are deeply involved in the theorist's explanations of how the core tendency gets carried out. For Freud, the ego is a set of mainly unconscious defensive strategies for ensuring maximum instinctual gratification with minimum punishment and guilt. For Sullivan, the self is a set of beliefs about who and what you are, which beliefs are implanted through the approval and disapproval of others and serve the defensive end of insulating the person against perception of aspects of himself that are incompatible with the beliefs. In contrast, Rank's concept of will refers to an organized sense of who and what you are that in its most vigorously developed form is not defensive at all, and which functions to aid in the establishment of a basis for minimizing both the life and death fears. The outstanding difference among the three concepts is that Rank's will, in contrast to the other two, operates rather consciously in implementing the compromise solution to conflict.

The will begins to develop sometime following birth, when experience has accumulated in such manner that the child realizes that there is a difference between himself and other people or things (this realization is also the beginning of the self-dynamism, according to Sullivan). With this recognition, the will begins to be an active force whereby the child comes to experience his own self as a totality. The will first emerges as *counterwill*. In other words, the child learns that he can say no to adults and to his own impulses. This is already a signal achievement. It is the beginning of a conscious integration of the person as a unit distinct from anything else. According to Rank, counterwill is wholesomely rooted in the basic tendency of life toward separation and individuation. But, as you can imagine, it has the effect of shattering union between the child and his parents, and union is necessary in order to minimize the fear of life. Rank theorizes that the expression of counterwill leads to *guilt,* because of the incompatibility of such an expression of will and the equally necessary pursuit of union. Although the concept of guilt seems somewhat superfluous, there being the concept of fear of life already, it nonetheless makes perfectly clear the disagreement between Rank and May mentioned above. For Rank, it is attempts at separation that can bring guilt, whereas May believes that avoidance of separation brings that emotion. In any event, Rank believes that the highest form of living involves a more mature expression of will than that seen in counterwill with its attendant guilt over forced separation.

The isolation and separation forced by expression of counterwill can be overcome by love of the child by his parents. Ideally, the parent accepts the counterwill of the child as a lovable part of its effort to establish its own self as an independent being but is equally aware of the child's need for support and belonging. If this happens, the child will be able to achieve definition of himself as an independent person, at which point counterwill begins to give way to a more mature expression of will. This mature will incorporates within it both a sense of the separateness and uniqueness of the person, and the ways in which he is tied to other people and things. He recognizes his parts as differentiated from each other, and he recognizes himself as different from other people, but there is also considerable integration of his parts, and of himself with other people. In the words of Munroe (1955, p. 584):

> Ideally the beloved and loving sexual partner supplies the full mutuality of relationship whereby the own will is accepted in and through the "other" and becomes a positive, constructive force. The own will does not arouse guilt because it is loved by the other. The mature person loves himself in the other, and the other in himself. Awareness of difference, of partialization, enriches the new sense of union. This union is not the effortless bliss of the womb, but a constantly renewed creation.

Clearly, it is the mature will that provides the basis for successful expression of the core tendency of minimizing both fear of life and fear of death. In providing recognition of the separate parts of the person and of his difference from others, the will permits an easing of the fear of death. By providing recognition of the organization of the parts of the person into a dynamic totality, and by encouraging a sense of common cause with mutual respect for other people, the will permits an easing of the fear of life. Actually, it is only the simultaneity of both aspects of the will that leads to the minimization of both fears.

The will is not always this vigorously and completely developed, and when it is not, certain limitations in the parent-child relationship can be blamed. There is no need to go into these matters here, however, as they are covered in the section of this theory discussed in Chapter 6 on peripheral characteristics of personality. But I should note one interesting feature of Rank's theory at this time. He does not explicitly rely on the concept of defense in his theorizing, even though his is a conflict theory making even the most successful life a compromise. Clearly, the most ideal, vigorous development of will has little defensiveness about it. There is nothing indicative of distortion of the truth of one's real nature due to its incompatibility with society. This is a great difference from the pure psychosocial conflict theorists, Freud and Sullivan, who make even the highest form of life defensive in character. When he is discussing the nonideal development of the will referred to above, Rank seems to have implicit recourse to a concept of defense. But of all the conflict theorists thus far considered, Rank puts least emphasis on defensiveness. As you will see, the intrapsychic version of the conflict model generally puts less emphasis on this concept than does the psychosocial version.

Angyal and Bakan. Andras Angyal (1941, 1951, 1965) and David Bakan (1966, 1968, 1971) have independently developed positions that are very similar to each other and to that of Rank. Although Angyal's and Bakan's theorizing does not cover all aspects of personality, some discussion of similarities and differences in comparison with Rank will aid in understanding the particular intrapsychic conflict approach they all share.

Angyal's and Bakan's theorizing is similar in form and content to that of Rank. For Angyal, the core tendency is *the attempt to maximize both the expression of autonomy and the expression of homonomy (or surrender)*. Similarly, Bakan's core tendency is *the attempt to maximize both the expression of agency and the expression of communion*.

The core characteristics of personality for Angyal are *autonomy* and *homonomy (or surrender)* whereas for Bakan they are *agency* and *communion*. All four concepts refer simultaneously to pressure on the person to function in a certain way or direction, and to the results in stable aspects of personality of such functioning. Autonomy and agency are similar in signifying functioning that leads the person to be separate from other people and the physical environment, and that leads to the separation of parts of himself from each other. Autonomy and agency also refer to the stable fruits of such functioning, namely, differentiatedness of personality, and independence of other people and things. Whereas the concept of autonomy tends to emphasize aloofness, and the concept of agency tends to emphaize manipulativeness, the differences between them are less important than the similarities. You will have recognized by now the kinship between these two concepts and the assumption by Rank that a basic characteristic of life is the inexorable tendency toward separation and individuation.

In discussing their respective concepts, both Bakan and Angyal make quite clear that they consider them as basic to living as does Rank. According to Angyal (1951, pp. 131–132), when the person is considered from the point of view of autonomy, he seems "to be striving basically to assert and to expand his self-determination. He is an autonomous being, a self-governing entity that asserts itself actively instead of reacting passively like a physical body to the impacts of the surrounding world. . . . This tendency . . . expresses itself in spontaneity, self-assertiveness, striving for freedom and for mastery." Bakan sees agency as a pressure toward individuation that permeates all living matter, not only human, and not only at the level of total organisms. Even cells forming tissues undergo separation.

Surrender and communion also have a lot in common. Both refer to functioning that leads the person to merge or join with other people and with the inanimate environment, and that leads to the integration of the various parts of himself. Surrender and communion also refer to the stable fruits of such functioning, namely, organization of personality, and interdependent relationships with other people and things. As with autonomy and agency, we find that surrender and communion also have slight differences in emphasis. Surrender stresses dependence, whereas communion stresses unity. But again, the similarities among the concepts are more important than the differences. Bakan and Angyal also seem to agree with Rank in making a tendency toward union, however conceptualized, a basic directionality of life. In discussing surrender, Angyal (1951, p. 132) says that the person:

> appears to seek a place for himself in a larger unit of which he strives to become a part . . . he seems . . . to strive to surrender himself willingly, to seek a home for himself in and *to become an organic part of something that he conceives as greater than himself.* . . . The superordinate whole may be represented for a person by a social unit— family, clan, nation, by a cause, by an ideology, or by a meaningfully ordered universe. In the realm of aesthetic, social, and moral attitudes this basic human tendency has a central significance. Its clearest manifestation, however, is in the religious attitude and religious experience.

Bakan describes communion very similarly, stressing the loss of self and self-consciousness through blending with others and with the world.

On the face of it, the two basic forces are irrevocably opposed, agency or autonomy on the one hand pushing toward individuation, and communion or surrender on the other hand pushing toward union. Bakan and Angyal seem to agree that the major task of life is to strike a compromise between these two antagonistic forces. The most successful kind of compromise is that in which both forces are represented as much as possible in living. In discussing such an orientation toward living, Angyal (1951, pp. 135–136) says:

> As in the tendency toward increased autonomy one strives to master and govern the environment, one discovers that one cannot do this effectively by direct application of force, by sheer violence, but can do it by obedience, understanding, and respect for the laws of the environment—attitudes that in some way are similar to those of loving relationships. Similarly: bringing one's best to a loving relationship requires not only capacity for self-surrender but also a degree of proficient mastery of one's world, resourcefulness and self-reliance, without which the relationship is in danger of deteriorating into helpless dependency, exploitation, possessiveness, etc.

Elaborating on love as the prime interpersonal expression of the compromise, or core tendency, Angyal (1951, p. 133) says that it

> consists in a recognition of the *value* and acceptance of the *otherness* of the loved "object" while at the same time one experiences an essential *sameness* that exists between one-self and what one loves.

The highest form of resolution of the basic conflict of life typically involves the simultaneous experience of difference from others and the world, and the sameness and commonality with them and it. In his last statement, Angyal (1965, p. 15) seems of the same mind as before:

> Human behavior cannot be understood solely as a manifestation of the trend toward increased autonomy. Seen from another angle, human life reveals a basic pattern very different from self-assertiveness, from striving for freedom and mastery. The person behaves as if he were seeking a place for himself in a larger unit of which he strives to become a part. In the first orientation [autonomy] he is struggling for centrality in his world, trying to mold and organize objects and events, to bring them under his own control. In the second orientation [homonomy] he seems rather to strive to surrender himself and to become an organic part of something that he conceives as greater than himself.

Bakan is in virtually complete agreement with Angyal's statements, and contributes an emphasis upon simultaneous differentiation and integration as the most constructive expression of the core tendency. In the social realm, differentiation involves a sense of your own individuality, and integration involves the at least partial sense of common cause that might lead to such things as joining a civil rights group or a peace movement or establishing a family. In the personal realm, differentiation involves an appreciation of the different aspects of yourself and your changeability, whereas integration involves the sense of how all the parts are organized together and how there is a thread of continuity that persists through the change.

Oddly enough, along with all their statements of inevitable conflict salved through compromise, Angyal and Bakan include an occasional disclaimer of conflict. For example, Angyal (1965, p. 29) asserts:

> The directions of the autonomous and homonomous trends are different, and they appear to be opposites, but in a well-integrated person the two orientations are complementary rather than conflicting. In fact they logically presuppose each other. As one strives to master and govern the environment, one discovers that one cannot do this effectively by direct application of force, by sheer violence. One must understand and respect the laws of the environment, go along with them, so to say, which means assuming a homonomous attitude. On the other hand, bringing one's best to a loving relationship requires a proficient mastery of one's world, or resourcefulness and self-reliance. Without these qualities one does not have much to offer the other, and the relationship may deteriorate into dependency and exploitation.

I am mystified by this disclaimer of conflict, for it seems to me that the sense of opposition indicated in the first sentence of the quote is only amplified, not nullified, by the statement that follows. That statement is very similar to those quoted earlier, and indicates that one cannot express either autonomy or homonomy in unmitigated form. Ideally, one compromises by trying to be only that kind of individual who can still be open and admirable enough to enter into loving relationships and take on other frames of reference than his own.

Perhaps the intent of such disclaimers is to show that the ideal life, as envisioned by Angyal and Bakan, is not a horror, but a very livable, even satisfying thing. But this can be accepted without any necessity of changing the theory from a conflict model to something else. After all, Freud, too, believed that a person developing an ideal personality would be able to love and to work successfully. Nonetheless, the underlying form of all these theories is conflict, in that there are limits put upon the degree to which each of two opposing personality forces can be expressed without jeopardizing the other. For the intrapsychic conflict theorists, this means that a person cannot be just as individualistic as his tendency toward autonomy or agency would permit, because he must also take into account an equally inherent tendency that leads in the opposite direction. If this position seems very cogent and believable, that is no reason at all to deny it the status of a conflict statement.

The simultaneous process of differentiation and integration, considered by Angyal and Bakan to be the most constructive solution to the problem of the two opposing forces, is also emphasized by Rank. This process, called psychological growth by fulfillment theorists (for whom it is a common emphasis) seems terribly optimistic for the conflict model. Clearly, intrapsychic conflict theorists see the highest form of living to be more a process of development, and less set and defensive than do psychosocial conflict theorists of the pure type. The process of simultaneous differentiation and integration does not smack of distortion of reality, and screening of some things out of consciousness. Indeed, so optimistic do Rank, Angyal, and Bakan seem concerning the most constructive living that you may well question whether it represents a compromise at all. But lest you become confused, I should reiterate that even simultaneous differentiation and integration represents a compromise, because that is the best that can be arranged given the underlying emphasis upon constant, intense conflict as the background upon which personality must develop. The bedrock assumption of all conflict theories, be they intrapsychic or psychosocial in type, is that the person is a house forever divided!

To convince yourself that simultaneous differentiation and integration represents a compromise solution to two opposing forces, consider Rank's position for a moment. According to that theory, the person, though oriented toward reducing the tension of fears of life and death, can never fully achive this aim. At any given point in time, there is some tension from the fear of life, and some tension from the fear of death, for neither complete differentiation nor complete integration can be accomplished. There must be a balance of differentiation and integration. Therefore, the person must live in some degree of fear, even when he has achieved the most constructive solution to the problem of his divided organism. Angyal and Bakan do not celebrate the role of fears in their formal theorizing, though it can be said that they recognize it implicitly. While they never actually postulate fears of separation and union, their more informal discussions and examples seem consistent with assuming that they do not really intend a position very different from that of Rank. In summary, intrapsychic conflict theories seem more optimistic than pure psychosocial conflict theories in stressing growth and de-emphasizing defensiveness. Nonetheless, intrapsychic conflict theories still conceptualize the highest form of living as a compromise, one sign of which is the continual existence of fear. As you will see in the next chapter, the emphasis upon differentiation and integration found in fulfillment theories does not involve such fear.

If more evidence were needed of the necessity of compromise in these theories, there is Bakan's (1968, 1971) recent statements on the psychology of religion and on child abuse, which assert that part of the tendency toward agency in the parent is the impulse to kill his children. The children, of course, are unwanted insofar as they interfere with the individuation process of the parent. But the parent also has communion needs, which can be satisfied by children and a family. In earliest times, according to Bakan, the infanticidal impulse was displaced in defensive manner such that the sacrifice of animals became institutionalized as an expression of religiosity. Religion itself, says Bakan, can be understood as an elaborate defensive attempt to shackle the infanticidal impulse (mitigate the expression of agency) at the same time as the tendency toward communion finds expression not only in merging with the family but with religious ideas bigger than oneself.

Thus far, I have only discussed the highest form of living according to Bakan, Angyal, and Rank. They all postulate less constuctive ways of functioning. These are not compromises which balance the two opposing forces so much as failures to establish a compromise. The failures always amount to expressing in life a disproportionate or overwhelming amount of one of the two forces. In describing the ways in which the person falls short of achieving a workable compromise between the two opposing forces, Rank focuses upon the dangers of renouncing either the tendency toward union or the tendency toward separation. These dangers are the banality of adjustment and the suffering of neurosis, respectively. Angyal and Bakan emphasize only the danger of denying union. Indeed, the entire range of psychological and physical maladies, from alienation to cancer, are traced by Bakan (1966, 1968) to the expression of agency unmitigated by the mellowing effects of communion. Perhaps these differing theoretical emphases can be understood in terms of differences in sociocultural influences acting upon the various theorists. Be that as it may, it does seem that putting together the emphases of all three theorists would result in a more well-rounded position on the relatively destructive ways of life.

Jung's position

Carl Gustav Jung (born at Kessewil, on Lake Constance in Switzerland, in 1875; died in Küsnacht, Switzerland, in 1961) has provided a theory of such complexity and unusualness as to be unlike anything else in the personality field. This does not imply its unequivocal goodness, however, for it is checkered with ambiguities and inconsistencies. Nonetheless, by any calculation, Jung is a major figure in personology, and an influential thinker of our century. Perhaps because of the influence of his father, who was a clergyman, Jung first thought to study philology and archaeology. But a dream of his is supposed to have convinced him to study medicine and science. His early interest in psychiatry was spurred by Eugen Bleuler and Pierre Janet. Jung was very impressed with Freud's first great book, *The Interpretation of Dreams* (1900), and by 1906 a regular correspondence had sprung up between them. Jung became a member of Freud's inner circle. Their mutual admiration was great, and Freud regarded Jung as his successor. Indeed, Jung became the first president of the International Psychoanalytic Association in 1910. But soon after, the relationship between Freud and Jung became fraught with theoretical and personal disagreements, and in 1914, Jung resigned his presidency of and membership in that organization. Freud and Jung never saw each other again, even though both have written interpreting their relationship and differences (e.g., Freud, 1925, 1957; Jung, 1961). After the break, Jung went on to develop his own approach, which he called *analytic psychology.* Once again we have evidence of the kind of excellence in Freud that could attract other strong and creative persons. And once again we have evidence that such persons do not get along easily.

As you can surmise from the name of Jung's approach, it retains much of its Freudian parentage. This is most apparent in the form of the approach, which emphasizes the importance, in understanding and changing a person, of his dreams as expressions of the unconscious, and of the attempt to integrate biological and mental phenomena. But the differences between Freudian and Jungian theory are much more important than their similarities. Generally stated, the main differences entail, on Jung's part, a de-emphasis of sexuality coupled with a greater emphasis on spirituality (in both its mystical and religious senses), and an emphasis on cultural universals in man's experience rather than individual idiosyncrasies. It is these differences more than anything else that won Jung a small but devoted following in the past, and underlie what seems a groundswell of interest in his theorizing on the part of contemporary youth. Jung seems to speak to our spiritual bankruptcy by enabling us to feel grounded in the past and future of mankind, rather than limited to our own puny life circumstance.

It is no simple matter to state Jung's core tendency in a few words. His is probably the most complex personality theory that exists, and as if this were not enough, he tends to take concepts having a common meaning in the personological literature and use them in a different way. And then there is the inevitable indefiniteness associated with his mysticism! But one thing that is clear is that life, behavior, the psyche reek with conflict. At great risk of oversimplification, I would venture that the overall directionality in the theory is *the tendency toward attainment of selfhood.* It is not as simple as you might think to arrive at some intuitive understanding of what Jung means here. For him, the self is definitely not a phenomenologically defined sense of what you are or could be, as is common in personology. Instead, it is a conglomerate of all the conflicting characteristics of personality that exist. Perhaps the best way to gain quick understanding of his meaning is to visualize the self as the hub of a wheel, with the spokes describing the force or tension of opposed, conflicting characteristics of personality. To attain selfhood is to have balanced off all the conflicting polarities. Sometimes selfhood is described as a conflict-free state, but more often it seems a balance between opposing forces instead (Jung 1953b). In any event, complete selfhood is considered an ideal not really possible of attainment.

Core characteristics. There are several core characteristics, and as you shall see, they tend to oppose one another. Of particular importance is the *ego*, which is the conscious mind according to Jung. It is comprised of conscious perceptions, thoughts, memories, and feelings. The ego directs the business of everyday living. Complex combinations of conscious thoughts, feelings, and actions lead to a sense of one's identity and continuity. In defining the ego as completely conscious, Jung deviates from Freud, for whom the ego is at least partly unconscious. The unconscious part, you will recall, is the defenses. Although Jung does assume defensiveness, he emphasizes it less than Freud, and does not localize its processes in the ego.

For Jung, unconscious processes are always in opposition to conscious ones. The sense in which this opposition is inevitable, and even helpful, will become apparent in what follows. For now, it is important to draw the distinction Jung makes between the personal unconscious and the collective unconscious. The *personal unconscious* is very similar to what Freud meant by unconscious and preconscious material, and consists of experiences that were once conscious and have either been forced defensively out of awareness because of their threatening nature (Freud's unconscious), or merely no longer are within the focus of attention (Freud's preconscious). For Jung, the preconscious material can become conscious by a shift in focus of attention, and the unconscious material can become conscious by a relaxation of defenses. Here it is important to recognize that Jung believed it possible for there to be a true alternative to defensiveness, for material defended against to gain accurate, complete consciousness once more. In contrast, Freud emphasized rationalization rather than reason, with what becomes conscious being very partial, no more than a pale shadow of the truth.

The *collective unconscious,* which does not reflect individual experience but rather the accumulated experience of the human species, is Jung's most striking, unique, and controversial concept. According to Jung, all of the events having happened to people for the eons of human history make their contribution to the life of each contemporary person in the form of a sort of species memory. Humans have been in dilemmas, fought to the death, loved successfully and unsuccessfully, reared their young or abandoned them, sought nutriments and found them or not, experienced the power of nature, and so forth, since the beginning of time. The fears, joys, triumphs, tragedies, beliefs, problem solutions, in short, the knowledge they gained has not been lost, according to Jung. Each new child is not a blank slate, who cannot know anything of importance unless he learns it himself. Rather, the accumulated culture of mankind is lodged in his psyche at birth, in the form of a collective unconscious. Actually, Jung even implies that he intends prehuman and subhuman history to have made some contribution to the collective unconscious as well!

To be sure, this collective knowledge is unconscious. Indeed, it cannot, in contrast to the experience constituting the personal unconscious, become conscious through redirection of attention or relaxation of defenses. The collective unconscious was never conscious in the history of an individual, and hence it can never become so, no matter how hard he or his therapist may try. But the collective unconscious does have an enormous influence on behavior, and does affect consciousness indirectly. This indirect effect on consciousness is most clearly seen in such events as the *déjà vu* experience, and the sense of the uncanny.

Probably, Jung came to his view of the collective unconscious out of a fascination with primitive mentality, art, and religion, to say nothing yet of dreams. Jung came to believe that the difference between primitive and modern mentality is not in degree of rationality but rather in the assumptions made about the nature of the world. Modern man assumes that all events ". . . have a natural and perceptible cause" (Jung, 1933a, p. 130), this being one of our principal dogmas. Jung contends that this assumption is only borne out *actually* about one-half the time, but that we shrug this disturbing fact off by references to "chance." But "Primitive man expects more of an explanation. What we call chance is to him arbitrary power," says Jung (1933a, p. 132), who does not find such thinking especially strange. He encourages us to see this primitive belief in the context out of which it emerged, at the same time indicating its hold on him, by engaging accounts of personal experience in the jungle (Jung, 1933a, pp. 138–140):

In the Kitoshi region south of Mount Elgo, I went for an excursion into the Kabras forest. There, in the thick grass, I nearly stepped on a puff-adder, and only managed to jump away just in time. In the afternoon my companion returned from a hunt, deathly pale and trembling in every limb. He had almost been bitten by a seven-foot mamba which darted at his back from a termite hill. Without a doubt he would have been killed had he not been able at the last moment to wound the animal with a shot. At nine o'clock that night our camp was attacked by a pack of ravenous hyenas which had surprised and mauled a man in his sleep the day before. In spite of the fire they swarmed into the hut of our cook who fled screaming over the stockade. Thenceforth there were no accidents throughout the whole of our journey. Such a day gave our Negroes food for thought. For us it was a simple multiplication of accidents, but for them the inevitable fulfillment of an omen that had occurred upon the first day of our journey into the wilds. It so happened that we had fallen, car, bridge and all, into a stream we were trying to cross. Our boys had exchanged glances on that occasion as if to say: "Well, that's a fine start." To cap the climax a tropical thunderstorm blew up and soaked us so thoroughly that I was prostrated with fever for several days. On the evening of the day when my friend had had such a narrow escape out hunting, I could not help saying to him as we white men sat looking at one another: "It seems to me as if trouble had begun still further back. Do you remember the dream you told me in Zurich just before we left?" At that time he had had a very impressive nightmare. He dreamed that he was hunting in Africa, and was suddenly attacked by a huge mamba, so that he woke up with a cry of terror. The dream had greatly disturbed him, and he now confessed to the thought that it had portended the death of one of us. He had of course assumed that I was to die, because we always hope it is the "other fellow." But it was he who later fell ill of a severe malarial fever that brought him to the edge of the grave.

To read of such a conversation in a corner of the world where there are no snakes and no malaria-bearing mosquitoes means very little. One must imagine the velvety blue of a tropical night, the overhanging black masses of gigantic trees standing in a virgin forest, the mysterious voices of the nocturnal spaces, a lonely fire with loaded rifles stacked beside it, mosquito-nets, boiled swamp-water to drink, and above all the conviction expressed by an old Afrikander who knew what he was saying: "This isn't man's country—it's God's country." There man is not king; it is rather nature—the animals, plants, and microbes. Given the mood that goes with the place, one understands how it is that we found a dawning significance in things that anywhere else would provoke a smile. That is the world of unrestrained, capricious powers with which primitive man has to deal day by day. The extraordinary event is no joke to him. He draws his own conclusions. "It is not a good place"—

"The day is unfavorable"—and who knows what dangers he avoids by following such warnings?

"Magic is the science of the jungle."

Jung is saying that in contexts not under human control, thoughts of evil omens, spirits, and bewitchment are universal psychic expressions, not just the illogical bent of primitive mentality. Modern persons also become superstitious when confronting the real capriciousness of nature, from which they are usually protected.

Then Jung asks (1933a, pp. 146–147) himself whether this suspiciousness to which persons are prone might be an accurate response to external, supernatural forces, be they gods or devils:

> Shall we, for the moment at least, venture the hypothesis that the primitive belief in arbitrary powers is justified by the facts and not merely from a psychological point of view? . . . The question is nothing less than this: does the psychic in general—that is, the spirit, or the unconscious—arise in us; or is the psyche, in the early stages of consciousness, actually outside us in the form of arbitrary powers with intentions of their own, and does it gradually come to take its place within us in the course of psychic development?

It is to Jung's credit that he had the courage to actually pose this question for himself, to consider the real possibility of a supernatural order, however antithetical that would be to science. After considerable struggle, he seems to have rejected a supernatural order in favor of the collective unconscious, which though panindividual need not imply anything different in kind from human mentality.

A step on the way to assuming a collective unconscious rather than a supernatural order is taken by Jung when he decides that phenomena such as superstitiousness and sense of the uncanny are essentially elaborate projections. These phenomena occur in primitives somewhat more frequently than in moderns "because of the undifferentiated state of [the primitive's] mind and his consequent inability to criticize himself." (Jung, 1933a, pp. 142–143). Whatever proneness to superstitious belief we moderns retain is due to accumulated memory of the past superstitious beliefs of the human species. While such beliefs are usually activated by some unpredictability or strangeness in the environment, their cause is the collective unconscious nonetheless.

In some sense, then, Jung contends that we are our ancestors. In us live the battles they fought, the fears they experienced, the loves they nurtured. The doctrine of inheritance of acquired characteristics seems to be what Jung had in mind, even though it is in ill repute these days. According to him (Jung, 1933a, p. 148):

> Not only the religious teacher, but the pedagogue as well, assumes that it is possible to implant in the human psyche something that was not

previously there. The power of suggestion and influence is a fact; even the most modern behaviorism expects far-reaching results from this quarter. The idea of a complicated building-up of the psyche is expressed in primitive form in many widespread beliefs—for instance, possession, the incarnation of ancestral spirits, the immigraton of souls, and so forth. When someone sneezes, we still say: "God bless you," and mean by it: "I hope your new soul will do you no harm." When in the course of our own development we grow out of many-sided contradictions and achieve a unified personality, we experience something like a complicated growing-together of the psyche. Since the human body is built up by inheritance out of a number of Mendelian units, it does not seem altogether out of the question that the human psyche is similarly put together.

But it is unclear whether Jung means the collective unconscious to be, literally, the accumulated specific experiences that our ancestors happen to have had, or something less concrete than this. He does refer to recurring themes, problems, preoccupations in the collective unconscious, suggesting that there is something universal about it that reflects the human condition more comprehensively than the mere specifics of actual experience. This quality of universality in the collective unconscious is seen most clearly in Jung's explanation of art and the artist. He is critical of Freud here, on the basis of overspecificity (Jung, 1933a, pp. 167–168):

> Freud thought that he had found a key in his procedure of deriving the work of art from the personal experiences of the artist. It is true that certain possibilities lay in this direction, for it is conceivable that a work of art, no less than a neurosis, might be traced back to those knots in psychic life that we call the complexes. . . . Freud takes the neurosis as a substitute for a direct means of gratification. He therefore regrets it as something inappropriate—a mistake, a dodge, an excuse, a voluntary blindness. . . . And a work of art is brought into questionable proximity with the neurosis when it is taken as something which can be analysed in terms of the poet's repressions. . . . No objection can be raised if it is admitted that this approach amounts to nothing more than the elucidation of those personal determinants without which a work of art is unthinkable. But should the claim be made that such an analysis accounts for the work of art itself, then a categorical denial is called for.

This statement makes two things clear. First, a work of art is not to be understood simply as expressive of what Jung calls the personal unconscious—those once-conscious experiences that have been defended against. Secondly, the collective unconscious, which figures also in the work of art, is probably not just the history of our ancestors' personal unconsciousness. The tone of universality Jung intends (1933a, p. 168) is clearly expressed in statements such as:

> What is essential in a work of art is that it should rise far above the realm of personal life and speak from the spirit and heart of the poet as man to the spirit and heart of mankind. The personal aspect is a limitation— and even a sin—in the realm of art. . . . The artist is not a person endowed with free will who seeks his own ends, but one who allows art to realize its purposes through him. As a human being he may have moods and a will and personal aims, but as an artist he is "man" in a higher sense—he is "collective man"—one who carries and shapes the unconscious, psychic life of mankind.

What Jung means is that the work of art does not issue from the particular experiences and even talents of the artist, but rather from the collective unconscious, to which he has given over. In this sense, the collective unconscious must refer to the age-old considerations that form life, not merely the chronology of each individual ancestor's experiences.

As an aside, let me mention that Jung is taking a position on a battle that still rages as to the proper stance in art criticism. These days, many art critics adopt an approach which analyses the work in order to clarify the particular facets of the artist's personality that have found expression. This is a rather Freudian school of criticism, and it has gained considerable force. There are, however, both traditionalists and a new wave in art criticism that favor an approach which searches for the universality in each creation, regardless of the artist's own personal life. These critics are, according to Jung, on the right track. I should also mention that most artists would favor Jung's view, having long resented what they experience as an overconcretization and devaluation of their art by the Freudian emphasis on creativity as expressive of personal neurosis, or at least idiosyncracy. To generalize beyond art, it seems clear that Jung gives more importance to the collective unconscious than to the personal unconscious. For him, though the personal unconscious is the stuff of neurosis, the collective unconscious permits a valuable identification with what is universal and eternal in man.

Thus far I have mentioned only general conceptions about the nature of the collective unconscious, and some of the observations underlying Jung's having assumed it. It is time now to indicate the content of this highly complicated but intriguing concept. The content is in the form of *archetypes,* which are less frequently called *dominants, imagoes, primordial images,* and *mythological images* (Jung, 1953a). An archetype is a universal form, or predisposition to characteristic thoughts and feelings. Although the archetype is by its nature unconscious and cannot ever become conscious, it tends to create images or visions that correspond to aspects of conscious experience. So, the mother archetype in all of us produces a vague, intuitive image of a nurturant, loving, accepting mother which we then project onto our actual mothers. An archetype is an inherited, generic form of something which determines in part how we perceive our experience. From time immemorial, persons have experienced mothers, and their experiences were homogeneous enough to have permanently emblazoned upon the psyche the essence of mother. Our experience of actual mother is, then, a conglomerate of the generic idea of mother and the particular characteristics our actual mother happens to have. These two sources of experience may or may not match well. Indeed, it is unlikely that they will match completely, even in the best of circumstances, and hence conflict between archetypes and conscious experience (ego) is to be expected. There may well also be conflict between archetypes and the personal unconscious, since the latter is formed out of concrete and troublesome personal experience, while the latter expresses essences.

But the matter is even more complicated than I have indicated. For Jung (1959b, p. 79), the archetypes do not have content in any concrete sense, only form:

> Again and again I encounter the mistaken notion that an archetype is determined in regard to its content, in other words, that it is a kind of unconscious idea (if such an expression be permissible). It is necessary to point out once more that archetypes are not determined as regards their content, but only as regards their form and then only to a limited degree. A primordial image is determined as to its content only when it has become conscious and is therefore filled out with the material of conscious experience. Its form, however, as I have explained elsewhere, might perhaps be compared to the axial system of a crystal, which, as it were, preforms the crystalline structure in the mother liquid, although it has no material existence of its own.

Once you have grasped this emphasis upon archetypes as forms or essences, you can understand why they can never become conscious; it is not that they are defended against, but rather that they are only prototypes or possibilities. In addition, this definition in terms of forms renders more clear why an archetype can, according to Jung, express itself in such a wide range of content. So, the mother archetype can express itself in ". . . the Church, university, city or country, heaven, earth, the woods, the sea or any still waters, matter even, the underworld and the moon" (Jung, 1959b, p. 81). In addition, of course, any actual human being can function as a symbol of an archetype. As you can imagine, it must be very difficult to determine when one is dealing with archetypal experience and when individual experience, and in the case of the former, which archetypes are involved. Jung offers no help beyond recognizing the difficulty and indicating the need for comprehensive, deeply intuitive observation done by persons who are not only sensitive to what they hear and see, but also steeped in the world's cultures and history.

Agreeing with Freud, Jung proposes that the most fertile ground for information about the unconscious in general is imaginative productions, such as works of art and dreams. Indeed, Jung seems to have invented the free-association test, in which the person is presented with various words to which he must respond with the first thought that comes into his head. But by now you can anticipate Jung's disagreement with Freud, which is consistent across all imaginative productions. According to Jung, Freud overlooks the collective unconscious, focusing exclusively upon the personal unconscious. The end result of this is overly concrete explanations. To illustrate this, Jung (1959b) criticizes Freud's interpretation of Leonardo da Vinci's famous painting of St. Anne and the Virgin with the Christ child. Freud concluded that the painting expressed Leonardo's wish to recapture the two mothers he actually had (apparently, he was born to one mother and adopted by another). For Freud, the painting is an expression of repressed personal experiences only. Jung insists, however, that the theme of two mothers is very common in art, myth, and fantasy. Think, says Jung, of the myth of Heracles, born of a human mother and unwittingly adopted by the goddess Hera. Also, it is common for children to fantasize that their parents are not really the true ones. Relevant too is the widespread practice of providing godparents to supplement the blood parents. Not all this could have been promulgated by persons who had actually experienced two mothers in childhood. Rather, the theme of dual parentage is based, according to Jung, on something so universal as to alert us to the presence of an archetype. Leonardo was in the grips of this archetype, rather than playing out some strictly personal drama.

Another aspect of Freud's excessive concreteness, according to Jung, is the use of biological, rather than spiritual, explanations for fantasies. Dreams provide Freud the occasion to trace the vicissitudes of sex and death instincts, structured as biological imperatives. But, says Jung (1933a, pp. 21–22), it is nonsensical to assume that something concretely biological can be symbolically represented in fantasy:

> It is well known that the Freudian school operates with hard and fast sexual "symbols"; but these are just what I would call signs, for they are made to stand for sexuality, and this is supposed to be something definitive. As a matter of fact, Freud's concept of sexuality is thoroughly elastic, and so vague that it can be made to include almost anything. . . . Instead of taking the dogmatic stand that rests upon the illusion that we know something because we have a familiar word for it, I prefer to regard the symbol as the announcement of something unknown, hard to recognize and not to be fully determined. Take, for instance, the so-called phallic symbols, which are supposed to stand for the *membrum virile* and nothing more. . . . As was customary throughout antiquity, primitive people today make a free use of phallic symbols, yet it never occurs to them to confuse the phallus, as a ritualistic symbol, with the [actual] penis. They always take the phallus to mean the creative *mana*, the power of healing and fertility, "that which is unusually potent."

. . . Its equivalents in mythology and in dreams are the bull, the ass, the pomegranate, the *yoni*, the he-goat, the lightning, the horse's hoof, the dance, the magical cohabitation in the furrow, and the menstrual fluid, to mention only a few of many. That which underlies all of these images—and sexuality itself—is an archetypal content that is hard to grasp, and that finds its best psychological expression in the primitive *mana* symbol.

In sharp contradiction to Freud, Jung is actually suggesting that it is essences or archetypes that are at the heart of the unconscious, and that even sexuality derives its importance from the archetype expressed in it. Jung simply does not believe that man's biology (instincts, drives, metabolism) has much to do with psychic life and its hold upon behavior.

This is not to say that sexuality and animal urges are unimportant for Jung, but rather that he does not see them as deriving from biological imperatives. Instead, they derive from an archetype, the *shadow*, which has evolved through time so far as to warrant being treated as a basic core characteristic of personality. The shadow consists of essentialistic forms of the animal instincts man inherited from lower forms of life (Jung, 1959c). As such, it typifies the animal possibility of man's nature. It expresses itself often in thoughts and behaviors of a socially unacceptable sort. These may either be hidden from public view, remaining in the ego, or actually defended against, becoming part of the personal unconscious. The shadow is also responsible for man's conception of original sin, and when it is projected outward becomes the devil or even some concrete enemy. But the shadow is not all bad. It lends vitality and passion to life. Strange though it may seem, Jung believes that it is actually the shadow, which is an essence and not a biological necessity, that underlies the sexual and death wishes figuring so centrally in the Freudian view. This suggests that by endorsing the Freudian view we may actually be defining our lives along lines that are excessively animalistic.

There are several other archetypes which, like the shadow, have evolved far enough to be considered basic characteristics forming life. Especially intriguing are the *anima* and the *animus* (Jung, 1953b, 1959a). These are the archetypes providing a basis for bisexuality. Certainly, it is known that at the biological level, the male and female secrete both male and female sex hormones, not just the one appropriate to their dominant sex. But even if this were not true, Jung would want to postulate an archetypal basis for bisexuality, because he considers it so apparent, once one adopts the purview of anthropology, history, and art, rather than some narrower, culture-bound approach. The feminine archetype in man is called the *anima*, and the masculine archetype in woman the *animus*. These archetypes, though they may correspond to chromosomal realities, are really based on the accumulated experience of man with woman and vice versa. Jung feels that the whole nature of

each sex presupposes the other. This archetype underlies the manifestation in each sex of characteristics of the other (e.g., sensitivity in a man,
aggressiveness in a woman), and determines the attractiveness of the
opposite sex. Through this archetype, each sex can appreciate and
understand the role of the opposite sex. But, if in any concrete instance,
anima or animus are projected onto someone of the opposite sex without
sufficient regard for their real character, misunderstandings and conflict
will result. Perhaps a man will try to find his idealized image of woman
in an actual woman he knows. If he does not realize the inevitable
discrepancies between ideals and actualities, he may suffer bitter disappointment and never know why. Once again we perceive here the ready
potential for conflict between the collective unconscious and the actualities of experience.

Another important archetype is the *persona* (Jung, 1953b), which is
the mask adopted by a person in response to the demands of social convention and tradition, and his own archetypal needs as well. The purpose
of the persona is to make a good impression, both on others and on oneself. Presumably, this archetype has developed out of the accumulated
experience of human beings with having to assume social roles in order
to facilitate that part of life which is lived with others. In fulfilling the
persona archetype by developing a "public" personality, one can defend
against unacceptable thoughts and feelings (thereby swelling the personal unconscious), or one can remain conscious of putting one's best
foot forward (which involves the ego). The latter root leads to a sense
of alienation from others, because one is conscious of tricking them; the
former involves the alienation from self inherent in the personal unconscious.

There are several other archetypes, though no definitive list is available. Jung and his associates have described the archetypes of the *old
wise man, God*, the *child*, the *hero, magic, power, birth, rebirth,* and
death, in addition to those already covered. One more, that of *unity*
(which underlies the *self*) is of great importance, but discussion of it will
be delayed until a more appropriate point.

Intrapsychic conflict and selfhood. There is little question but that
Jung's position exemplifies the conflict model. Polarization, the opposition
of elements, is basic to an understanding of how his theory conceptualizes life. All that is human, indeed everything in the universe, exists,
changes, and thrives due to conflict and opposition, according to Jung.
It is more difficult to determine whether his view is essentially of the
psychosocial or intrapsychic conflict type. Let us examine his concepts
further with a view toward settling this matter.

The existence of a personal unconscious certainly indicates that what
appears to be psychosocial conflict exists. Some conscious thoughts and
impulses are threatening, and hence pushed out of awareness by defenses. As in Freud, the threat is of punishment or guilt, those twin pains

deriving originally from the opposition of the individual to society. It is certainly true that the unacceptable thoughts and impulses do not always have to be sexual or aggressive for Jung, but this does not really shift the form of conflict that is involved.

There are two considerations, however, that do cast doubt on the possibility that Jung's is a psychosocial form of conflict theory. First, it is not clear that the conflict between individual and social pressures is inevitable. After all, Jung makes very little of the personal unconscious, relying for most of his explanations on the collective unconscious instead. In addition, the ego entails true, accurate consciousness, not the half-truth of rationalization. A full-bodied psychosocial conflict theory cannot postulate a true, accurate consciousness, because the conflict between individual and society is inevitable, and the individual—always the weaker—must engage in the distortion of defensiveness. Jung is very clear that the personal unconscious can become conscious, that defenses can be relaxed. Because the personal unconscious could, in his view, shrink to zero, his is probably not best considered a psychosocial conflict theory.

The second reason against a psychosocial-conflict classification is even more compelling. You will recall that in Freud the individual's contribution to the psychosocial conflict is considered to be a biological selfishness that is as somatic and real as metabolism itself. In contrast, biology is incidental to Jung's view of conflict. It is vital to recognize that the shadow, or locus of animalistic thoughts and impulses, is an archetype, not a biological imperative. This essence of animalism is part of the collective unconscious, which is a mental phenomenon expressing essential forms of functioning based on the experiential past of mankind. Thoughts and impulses that are sufficiently selfish to clash with the common good are, therefore, more recapitulations of past human and subhuman experience than biological imperatives. Even if it be said that in the beginning—the first time in history an individual clashed with those around him—a biological imperative was operating (and it is not clear that Jung would even agree), this would not change the fact that every modern person inherits a mental (not biological) predisposition to think and act selfishly because his ancestors have done so.

These may seem like excessively subtle distinctions, but bear with me. I am trying to show that, for Jung, there is basically no causation of any human importance that is other than mental. Mental life is referred to sometimes as spirit by Jung (1933a, pp. 171–195), in contrast to matter, which is everything else of a physical nature, animal, vegetable, or mineral. In extolling the nonbiological nature of mentality, Jung (1933a, p. 176) says:

> But people who are not above the general level of consciousness have not yet discovered that it is . . . presumptuous and fantastic for us to

assume that matter produces spirit; that apes give rise to human beings; that from the harmonious interplay of the drives of hunger, love, and power Kant's *Critique of Pure Reason* should have arisen; that the brain-cells manufacture thoughts, and that all this could not possibly be other than it is.

What a far cry this is from Freud! And notice how the final phrase suggests that once you make mentality your primary explanatory principle, nothing is impossible anymore. The limits on change are only the limits of imagination.

Inevitably, with such a psyche-centered view, one must come to question whether apparently causal considerations like societal pressures (taboos and sanctions) are anything more than figments of the imagination. It seems quite clear that Jung (1933a, pp. 189–190) intends us to believe that since societal pressures must be perceived, they have the status of psychic rather than social realities:

> Without a doubt psychic happenings constitute our only, immediate experience. . . . My sense impressions—for all that they force upon me a world of impenetrable objects occupying space—are psychic images, and these alone are my immediate experience, for they alone are the immediate objects of my consciousness. . . . All our knowledge is conditioned by the psyche which, because it alone is immediate, is superlatively real. Here there is a reality to which the psychologist can appeal—namely, psychic reality. . . . If I change my concept of reality in such a way as to admit that all psychic happenings are real— and no other use of the concept is valid—thus puts an end to the conflict of matter and mind as contradictory explanatory principles.

In the final sentence, Jung makes perfectly clear that what may have appeared as a psychosocial conflict—the contradiction of mind by the "matter" of presumed social imperatives—is really no more than an intrapsychic conflict. If society seems opposed to the individual, it is because he perceives it that way, not because that is its unchangeable real nature. If more documentation were needed, there is the dramatic statement in which Jung (1959b, p. 95) indicates the prepotency of the psyche: "In that one moment in which I came to know, the world sprang into being; without that moment it would never have been."

The basically intrapsychic nature of Jung's conflict theory is apparent in the way he uses it to understand persons and phenomena. There is conflict between a person's conscious perception of his sex and his anima or animus; between his persona, other archetypes, and consciousness; indeed, between any and all of the core characteristics postulated. Intrapsychic conflict is the basic fact of life. But conflict, though inevitable, is not merely painful, something to be defended against. On the contrary, the opposition of elements in the psyche provides energy, as we shall see in the next section, and stimulates growth. It is not surprising, therefore, to find Jung (1933a, pp. 16–17) extolling the unconscious:

> It is well known that the Freudian school presents the unconscious in a thoroughly depreciatory light, just as also it looks on primitive man as little better than a wild beast. . . . Have the horrors of the World War really not opened our eyes? Are we still unable to see that man's conscious mind is even more devilish and perverse than the unconscious? . . . The unconscious is not a demonic monster, but a thing of nature that is perfectly neutral as far as moral sense, aesthetic sense and intellectual judgement go. It is dangerous only when our conscious attitude becomes hopelessly false. And this danger grows in the measure that we practice repressions. . . . That which my critic feared—I mean the overwhelming of consciousness by the unconscious—is most likely to occur when the unconscious is excluded from life by repressions, or is misunderstood and depreciated.

To remain open to emanations from the collective unconscious is to stand on the shoulders of all who have gone before. And to permit the personal unconscious to become conscious again is to recapture the richness of one's own particular past. In contrast to psychosocial conflict positions, intrapsychic ones see conflict as valuable and not to be defended against just because it is inevitable.

Indeed, the ideal, according to Jung, is for the person to actively concern himself with unconscious as well as conscious experiences, and to try to fit the two into a dynamic balance. The tension, pain, and difficulty involved is not to be avoided, for it is the stuff of life itself. Actually, Jung (1953b, p. 219) postulated an archetype called the *self* in formalizing this ideal:

> If we picture the conscious mind with the ego as its centre, as being opposed to the conscious, and if we now add to our mental picture the process of assimilating the unconscious, we can think of this assimilation as a kind of approximation of conscious and unconscious, where the centre of the total personality no longer coincides with the ego, but with a point midway between the conscious and unconscious. This would be the point of a new equilibrium, a new centering of the total personality, a virtual centre which, on account of its focal position between conscious and unconscious, ensures for the personality a new and more solid foundation.

Clearly, in pursuing selfhood, one does not eliminate conflict (the conscious and unconscious remain opposed) so much as set the two conflicting poles of personality into juxtaposition and communication. In contrast to common personological usage, Jung defines the self as a conglomerate of conscious and unconscious experience.

Energy concepts. We have now covered the basic core characteristics involved in the attempt to attain selfhood. But Jung also postulates several energy principles that are intrinsic to this core tendency. The energy involved in the psychological activities of thinking, feeling, and acting is called psychic energy (Jung, 1960a). There is ambiguity as to its sources. Sometimes Jung states that it derives from the very conflict of core characteristics already mentioned; sometimes, in more Freudian fashion, he considers it based on such biological processes as metabolism. In any event, the amount of psychic energy invested in thoughts, feelings, actions, and broader elements of personality is called the *value* of that element. Value is essentially a measure of element intensity, and is related to Freud's notion of cathexis.

We are now in a position to appreciate Jung's two main energy principles, which are psychological versions of the first and second laws of thermodynamics. The *principle of equivalence* (Jung, 1960a) states that if the value of any element of personality increases or decreases, this shift will be compensatorily expressed by an opposite shift in another element. For example, if a person loses interest in someone or an activity, someone else or another activity will increase in interest. Applied to broader elements of personality, this principle indicates that if energy is removed from the ego, for example, it will be reinvested elsewhere, perhaps in the personal unconscious or the persona. The person who becomes concerned with internal experience does so at the expense of attention to external experience, and vice versa.

The *principle of entropy* (Jung, 1960a) states, in its psychological form, that the distribution of energy in the psyche seeks an equilibrium or balance. Thus, if two beliefs are of unequal value, or strength, the general tendency will be for the stronger belief to become weaker and the weaker stronger. As to broad elements of personality, if the ego is, for example, stronger (more relied upon in everyday life) than the shadow, the tendency over time will be for them to come closer together in value.

These two energy principles constitute the main dynamics of the core tendency of seeking selfhood. Indeed, according to Jung, the ideal state in which the total energy is evenly distributed (the ultimate outcome of the two energy principles) throughout the various elements of personality is selfhood. In that state, consciousness and unconsciousness have equal energy, as does any particular thought, feeling, or action, and any other. Do not misunderstand this state of balance for a conflict-free situation. That conflict would still underlie psychic functioning even if selfhood were to be attained is shown by the emphasis on equilibrium. Each element has the same value as the others. The elements have not, however, lost their identity, and the balance is a dynamic one based on the tension of opposition.

In postulating the principles of equivalance and entropy, Jung is emphasizing the psyche as a closed system. It is only in such a system that decreases in the energy of one element would produce compensatory increases in the energy of another, and that there would be a general tendency toward a balance of energies. But Jung (1960a) does not believe that the psyche is a completely closed system. There are inputs of energy from somatic processes such as metabolism, and from the outside world in such forms as punishment or encouragement. These external inputs are regular and inevitable enough to render it impossible, in his view, for complete selfhood ever to be attained. Complete selfhood is in this sense an ideal to be striven for but never completed. Perhaps its unattainability is fortunate, because when perfect entropy is reached in a system, that system runs down and stops, there being no further possibility of the energy differentials that lead to movement. Perhaps we have discovered a basis for rapport between Jung and the later Freud, who came to believe paradoxically that the goal of all life is death.

In this discussion, we have considered three bases for interaction among elements of personality, namely, opposition, compensation, and dynamic balance. These are all consistent with the intrapsychic conflict model. But Jung (1960a) intimates a fourth, namely, unity. On the face of it, this suggests that there is an alternative in his system to conflict. Along these lines, Jung (1960d) proposes a *transcendent function,* the aim of which is to integrate personality elements into an overall whole. This transcendent function, which does not seem to be another energy principle so much as a dynamic rather than static picture of the self, inclines the person toward a unification of the opposing trends within the personality. Other forces, such as the defensiveness associated with the personal unconscious, may oppose the transcendent function, but it tends to work toward unification anyway. If nothing else, it will be expressed at the unconscious level in the desire for wholeness Jung claims is seen in many dreams and myths.

But what sense of unity can a theory so steeped in intrapsychic conflict as a fact of life possibly have? The answer is a paradoixcal or mystical sense. In order to appreciate Jung's ideas on unity, you must recognize his belief that opposites attract, and that the opposite of every truth is also true. The metaphor he adopts for this paradoxical unity is the mandala, or circle, which appears in Sanskrit writings and in many religions. If opposing polarities, such as consciousness versus unconsciousness, can be represented as a straight line, the ends of which race off in opposite directions, then the mandala image transforms the straight line into a perfect circle. In this case, the ends at the same time race apart, but also toward each other. The mandala symbol is closely allied in Jung's thinking to the self and to the entropy principle.

The problem with the mandala metaphor is that it really is not an apt one for the description of polarities and oppositions. One really does not resolve the conflict inherent in a *defined* opposition by suddenly deciding to bend a straight line into a circle, because this only contradicts the defined opposition. Jung is working with a paradoxical sense of unity. Perhaps he even recognized this, for he believed that the transcendent function could not completely triumph, as selfhood could not really be attained.

Selfhood is not possible in the final analysis because the principle of entropy requires a closed system in order to culminate in equilibrium, and Jung is very clear that the psyche is not really a closed system. That Jung talks about unity at all, rather than just compensation, opposition, and dynamic balance, is a reflection of the extraordinary complexity of his theorizing, and his lack of concern about mere inconsistencies in his thinking. He may also have been holding out the possibility that man might evolve, at some time in the future, into a being described better in fulfillment than in conflict terms. This evolutionary possibility is not inconsistent with his emphasis on the collective unconscious as the content of man's past experiences. For the moment, however, we would do well to conclude on balance that Jung's views are of the intrapsychic conflict type.

Developmental considerations.   Once we turn to development, the optimism of this position, in contrast to its Freudian ancestry, is apparent. Jung believes that individual persons are constantly trying to grow, and occasionally meeting with some success in their efforts. The story of personality development is hardly over with childhood, as far as he is concerned. Indeed, as intimated above, the human species, mankind, is also constantly evolving more differentiated and conscious forms of existence. In this regard, the collective unconscious provides a basis whereby each modern person stands on the shoulders of his predecessors, and is therefore able to see a little further than they could.

To be more specific, Jung (1960c) believed that in the earliest years, psychic energy is invested primarily in activities necessary for physical survival. Somewhere around the age of five (the time of Freud's Oedipal conflict), Jung considers sexuality per se to start becoming important. Adolescence is basically an amplification of these early beginnings. Early adulthood involves employing these activities in more broad and complex commitments, such as to a vocation, a family, and a community. Although Jung does not postulate hard and fast developmental stages, his position is thus far similar to that of Freud.

The big contrast with Freud, however, occurs in conceptualization of the last half of life. Jung's position here is an important contribution, taken up by various subsequent personologists. He believed that a radical change takes place in the person when he reaches the late thirties and early forties. Biological and social interests and activities, and orientations to the external, material world recede, to be replaced by an inward-turning spirituality. Wisdom and patience take the place of physical and mental assertiveness. The person becomes more religious, cultural, philosophical, and intuitive. In the ideal case, the strident emphasis on consciousness of the early years is tempered by an acceptance of unconscious experience (e.g., intuitions, mysteries) and an assimilation of it into everyday life. But if the transition is not well navigated, the end result is spiritual bankruptcy, and a hellish end of life. Jung (1933a) felt that especially modern man has difficulty making this transition, because traditional and religious values have deteriorated in the face of industrialization, without their being replaced by any other ideological justification for spirituality. In this, he presaged existential psychology.

Jung used many different concepts to articulate his views on development. He contrasted *causality* with *teleology*, in order to give philosophical sophistication to his optimism. According to the teleological viewpoint, man's personality can be comprehended in terms of future goals. Causality, in contrast, explains the present in terms of the past. Jung felt both were necessary for complete understanding, and criticized Freud for considering only causality. Similar in form is his distinction between *progression* and *regression*. These are not meant as defenses in any strict sense. Rather, he wanted to emphasize the forward thrust of development as progression, and the shrinking to a safe past as regression. Although both occur in any person's life, progression is more a sign of growth than regression. In special instances, however, regression may involve a beneficial tapping of the well of the unconscious. Another similar distinction concerned *sublimation* and *repression,* processes that, once again, are reminiscent of defenses but somehow not as concrete and specific as in Freud. In sublimation, psychic energy is transferred from primitive, instinctual, undifferentiated processes to more cultural, spiritual, complex processes. For example, when energy is withdrawn from sexual activity and given to religious activity, sublimation is said to have occurred. But when discharge of energy is blocked by some internal or external obstacle, repression takes place. The energy is then transferred to the personal unconscious, blocking development. As you may have surmised, underlying the processes of sublimation and repression, and progression and regression are the energy principles of equivalence and entropy.

Another way Jung had of talking about development is as psychological growth, or the progressively increasing tendency toward differentiation and integration. The basis for differentiation is inherent in the opposing, conflictful nature of core characteristics. Integration is expressive of the self archetype, and the transcendent function. The shift in adulthood from material to spiritual concerns is part and parcel of the tendency to attain selfhood and integration. Apparently, Jung (1960b) was willing to carry his notions of spirituality to extremes not very common in a scientist. Late in life, he postulated the *principle of synchronicity,* which is intended to be an explanation of the contiguous or simultaneous occurrence of events that though not causes of one another indicate some commonality in the collective unconscious. Jung intended with this principle to take seriously such disputed phenomena as telepathy and clairvoyance. For him, simultaneous events, such as thinking of a long-lost friend and having him arrive unexpectedly, or awakening with the fear that someone has been hurt only to find out later that this has indeed occurred, express the principle of synchronicity. This principle does not cause the simultaneous events, indicating instead the multiple expressions of archetypes. An archetype can express itself in someone's thoughts and in the occurrence of an external event. With the addition of the principle of synchronicity, Jung has evolved the notion of collective unconscious into something very close to a universal force not even dependent upon the existence of individual psyches for expression. In this principle, he is at his most mystical.

It is extremely difficult to approach evaluation of Jung's position. If the usual procedures of scientific, analytical thought were to be applied, the position could be easily faulted. For example, the principle of synchronicity is actually not an explanation at all, but rather a mere restatement of an observation. All Jung is saying is that two events occurring together do so because sometimes seemingly disparate events occur together. If he were to contend more, namely, that archetypes actively precipitate seemingly disparate though simultaneous events, then archetypes would essentially constitute the very supernatural order Jung has also decried. Similarly, the assumption of a transcendent function seems to contradict the principles of equivalence and entropy, and the other assumptions concerning the inevitability of conflict.

But I have the nagging feeling that in going to work on Jung's theory with the tools of logic, we are missing what there is of value in it. Let us conclude that the theory is full of logical inconsistencies and ambiguities, and try nonetheless to capture its intent. In doing this, we emerge with an emphasis on mind or spirit as the architect of life. Jung is much more humanistic than Freud and others who have given important roles to biological and social forces in the determination of behavior. In this regard, the collective unconscious and its archetypes can be considered the inherent structure of mind. It is this inherent structure that sets limits on man's freedom of imagination and action, not his body or his society. No doubt it is this extreme spirituality that underlies Jung's appeal these days.

Chapter 3 THE CORE OF PERSONALITY: FULFILLMENT MODEL

We have just considered some personality theories that conceptualize the core of personality as reflecting the ongoing conflict between two irrevocably opposed forces. In the conflict model, life is always seen as a compromise, the purpose of which is to minimize the conflict. But the conflict is always potentially large and debilitating, and hence, the compromise has an uneasy quality. The theories I will consider in this chapter conceptualize the core of personality quite differently. Typically, they assume only one basic force in man. Therefore, life is not considered to be a compromise, but rather the process of unfolding of the one force. I have called the position exemplified by these theories the fulfillment model. There are two versions of the fulfillment model, with the difference between them being the nature of the postulated force. If the force is the tendency to express to an ever greater degree the capabilities, potentialities, or talents based in one's genetic constitution, then we are confronted with the actualization version. In the perfection version, the force is instead the tendency to strive for that which will make life ideal or complete, perhaps even by compensating for functional or genetic weak spots. The actualization version is humanistic whereas the perfection version is idealistic.

FULFILLMENT MODEL: ACTUALIZATION VERSION

In considering the actualization version, first I will discuss the theory of Rogers, and indicate how it was based on the work of Goldstein. The other actualization theorist presented here is Maslow. Although his position is similar in many important ways to that of Rogers, you will find that Maslow postulates not one but two forces within the person. The two forces, however, are not conceived in such fashion that they would necessarily be in opposition to each other, and, even if this were not so, one force is considered greatly inferior in importance to the other. Maslow's theory is clearly an actualization version of the fulfillment model, but his postulation of two different forces within the person prompts me to consider him a variant on that model.

Rogers' position

Born in a suburb of Chicago, Illinois in 1902, Carl R. Rogers differs from many psychotherapists in holding the Ph.D. rather than the medical degree and in being Protestant in background. He seems to have considered the strict religious background of his early life to be a heavily restricting, burdensome thing. Early in life, Rogers was primarily interested in the biological and physical sciences, though after graduation from college his concerns shifted sufficiently so that he entered Union Theological Seminary in New York City. Perhaps this shift indicated an attempt to work through his feelings concerning his earlier background. Certainly, the seminary he entered is well known for its liberality. Before very long, he transferred to Columbia University, where he was influenced by the humanistic philosophy of John Dewey, and first encountered clinical psychology. In his initial clinical work, he was exposed to a strongly Freudian view, which even then did not seem convincing to him because it did not consider as important the person's own point of view about himself. Rogers came to rest for some years at the Rochester Guidance Center, of which he became director. In the context of colleagues of heterogeneous personological convictions, and stimulated by the daily practice of psychotherapy, Rogers began to formulate his own position. The person whose work touched him most at this time was Otto Rank, who had by then broken with Freud due to espousal of the position we encountered in the previous chapter.

On leaving his clinical post, Rogers entered university life, taking on the role of teacher and researcher. During the time when he was associated with the University of Chicago, he was elected president of the American Psychological Association (1946–47). With his increasing attention to developing a theory of personality and psychotherapy, an inevitable effect of entering university life, Rogers became more influenced by theorists who stress the importance of one's self-view as a determinant of behavior. Among these theorists were Goldstein, Maslow, Angyal, and Sullivan. Currently, Rogers is continuing his theorizing as a staff member of the Western Behavioral Sciences Institute, an organization, dedicated to the investigation of interpersonal relations, both direct and indirect.

Although there are a number of theorists who are similar to Rogers, his position is at the same time the most comprehensive, developed, and psychological. It is, therefore, a good way of introducing you to that kind of thinking. Rogers (1959) is very clear about the core of personality. For him, *the core tendency of man is to actualize his po-tentialities.* What this means is that there is a pressure in people that leads in the direction of their becoming whatever it is in their inherited nature to be. It is difficult for people to gain appreciation of this actualizing tendency on the intuitive grounds of their own experience. Certainly, we have all had the experience of wanting to achieve something, or feeling impelled to accomplish something. But these experiences are usually at too concrete a level to be directly relevant to the actualizing tendency as slated. We usually experience ourselves as wanting to get good grades, or wanting to learn to dance well, or wanting to be imaginative, rather than in the more abstract sense of acting in concert with our inherent nature. The rather concrete experiences I have mentioned may not be irrelevant, of course, as what the actualizing tendency will lead to in actual functioning depends upon Rogers' view of the content of inherent potentialities. For example, if being imaginative is an inherent potentiality in his theory, then wanting to be imaginative would certainly qualify as one expression of the actualizing tendency. And in our search for some intuitive basis for understanding Rogers' position, we should not overlook the strong possibility that at least some people seem to sometimes have personal experience of an urging to express themselves—somehow, in something—that is difficult to talk about because it is so formless and abstract. Perhaps such occasional experiences are direct representations of the actualizing tendency.

Keeping in mind the questions raised by our attempt to understand what Rogers is saying on the grounds of personal experience, let us turn now to a more formal approach to his theory. Once you assume an actualizing tendency as the basic directionality of the person, you raise consideration of the (1) content of the inherent potentialities, (2) the nature of the actualizing tendency itself, and (3) the manner whereby the inherent potentialities and the actualizing tendency interact in the process of living.

The inherent potentialities of human beings. About the only statement Rogers makes concerning the nature of the inherent potentialities is aimed at differentiating his position from that of Freud. According to Rogers, all the potentialities of the human are in the service of the maintenance and enhancement of life. Hence, one would not find anything such as a death instinct in Rogers. For Rogers, death occurs accidentally, as the end result of biological breakdown with no primarily psychological significance, or through a decision on the part of the person, which decision is necessarily a sign of psychological maladjustment rather than the human's true nature. Actually, I am being much more explicit concerning the view of death in this theory than Rogers ever is, though I believe what I have said is quite in the spirit of his thinking.

But discounting the concept of death instinct, it may seem that Freud and Rogers are not so far apart. Freud would find very congenial the notion that inherent potentialities (he would call them instincts) function to maintain and enhance life. Actually, there is a world of difference between the two theorists, and it has to do with their views on the relationship of the person to society. You will recall that for Freud, the person emerges as selfish and competitive in his pursuit of life. Society is viewed as necessarily in conflict with individuals, as the requirements of corporate living are antithetical to the most direct, straightforward expression of human nature. In contrast, Rogers assumes that what is consistent with the maintenance and enhancement of the individual's life is also consistent with the maintenance and enhancement of the lives of the people around him. For Rogers, there is nothing in human nature that if truly and straightforwardly expressed would obviate the possibility of community by being seriously destructive to other people. While Rogers does not assume, as do the intrapsychic conflict theorists, that it is part of human nature to be communal, he does indicate that the human, in his least corrupted form, will be so appreciative of himself and vigorous in his living as to be capable of deep appreciation of others as well. Although the human does not need community in some imperative way, his nature is such that if he is not maladjusted he can delight in other people.

You may wonder at this point what Rogers would say to the seemingly plausible reasons why Freud assumed human nature to be antithetical to social living. What about all the ways in which person hurts person? And would not mutual destructiveness increase if the rules and regulations of society were relaxed? Is it not merely a pie in the sky to think that the human is so pure deep down? Rogers would answer out of irrepressible optimism. He would point out that more countries are at peace than at war, that world wars are still more unusual than world peace, that societies with many complex laws and taboos do not have less crime than laxer societies, that the overwhelming majority of people abhor death as something foreign to them, and that the infant shows very little behavior indicative of evil and socially destructive tendencies, however limited he may be in his ability to control his processes. In other words, Rogers would not find Freud's reasons for believing the human to be selfish and potentially destructive very compelling. To be sure, one can observe selfishness and destructiveness, but the question becomes that of deciding what such observations really mean about human nature. At one level, Rogers is saying that such observations are occasional enough so that they are best considered expressions of distortions of true human nature, rather than, as in Freud, direct expressions of that nature.

At another level, Rogers has more positive reasons for his view on the constructive nature of the human. These reasons come from observations of people in social contexts, all the way from psychotherapy to international diplomacy. One observation is that misunderstandings and suspiciousness lead to antagonism and even competition between people. When the misunderstandings are spoken to directly, suspiciousness decreases, and antagonistic, competitive behaviors give way to cooperative and appreciative ways of being. This is not to say that people will always agree among themselves, but rather that if there is no misunderstanding, the remaining disagreements will be honest, and mutually respected. Another observation is that when a person feels hopeless and unworthy, he will disregard others, and in many ways treat them poorly. But when he begins to accept himself, he also gains in appreciation and acceptance of others. He can appreciate and accept not only the ways in which others are like him, but also, and probably more importantly, the ways in which they differ from him. These kinds of observations incline Rogers to the belief that the person's true nature—his inherent potentialities—are not only consistent with the maintenance and enhancement of his own living, but of social living as well. It is only when the inherent potentialities achieve distorted expression due to maladjustment that behavior destructive to oneself and others is found.

The most important thing about the observations included above for the theoretical difference between Freud and Rogers, is that it is contended by Rogers that behavior destructive to others always occurs along with behavior destructive to oneself. Rogers believes that if Freud were right, then one would characteristically see behavior constructive to oneself taking place as the other side of the coin of behavior destructive to others, at least when society was least vigilant. Rogers finds little evidence of this.

Of course, the weakness in Rogers' observations is that they do not occur outside of the regulatory function of society, and hence, while they are reasonably compelling, they are not definitive. In attempting to find observations uncontaminated by social pressure, one could go to the infant or the subhuman organism. The infant is unfortunately not a good source of information because it is so undeveloped that one might erroneously decide that it was basically selfish, confusing maturational primitivity with disinterest in the welfare of others. Even at that, Rogers contends that there is little in the child's behavior to show that it is self-seeking at the expense of other people. But anyone awakened to the wail of a youngster in the middle of the night is justified, it seems to me, in not finding Rogers' contention completely convincing. While Rogers would surely agree that the child was preoccupied with his own needs at that point, he would ask whether the observation was really sufficient for the extreme conclusion that man's nature is basically incompatible with community. And, in truth, the observation is not sufficient.

This state of nondefinitive information prompts turning to the lower animals. Rogers has indeed done this, and, as you will see later, this is thoroughly appropriate logically, for the actualizing tendency is not restricted to humans, or even subhumans, referring rather to all living things, be they vegetable or animal. At one point, Rogers (1961, pp. 177–178) asks that we consider the lion, certainly a worthy, and reasonably representative, member of the animal world. Presumably the lion is unencumbered by societal restrictions, in any sense such as that meant by Freud. While this can certainly be disputed, I suppose it is more or less true. The lion, it turns out, is rather benign, having intercourse mainly with its mate and only occasionally with other lions, caring for its children in a rather loving way until they are old enough to go out into the world, and killing only when hungry or in defense of self and family. Here there is no gratuitous evil, nor any evidence of self-interest that is really incompatible with the interests of others. The similarity between the life of the lion and the life of the human is not accidental, according to Rogers. If the human expressed his natural potentialities, he would live a reasonably ordered, constructive, moral life without needing to be held in check by society.

At this point, I will have to call a halt to this controversy, for it cannot be easily settled. Certainly, someone holding Freud's view could find in the animal world organisms that murder fairly typically, such as the wolverine or weasel, or focus on the severe limitation of self-actualization caused by the lion to its prey. And so the argument goes. It will suffice for the present to recognize that the fulfillment model exemplified by Rogers is a serious and worthy alternative to the psychosocial conflict model.

Having appreciated the view that the inherent potentialities function to maintain and enhance life, we are in a position to inquire further as to their precise content. Extraordinary though it is, Rogers is almost mute on this matter! About the most insight one can gain through careful reading of Rogers is that he is thinking in terms of some sort of genetic blueprint, to which form and substance is added as life progresses. But the precise outlines of the blueprint are a mystery. Does it have to do with such biological considerations as the size and tonus of muscles, the excellence of brain structures and organization, and the rapidity of metabolic functioning? Does it have to do with more psychological considerations such as needs to master or be imaginative or gregarious? Rogers gives virtually no guidance. Another kind of question that goes unanswered is whether—and if so, how—there are differences among people in inherent potentialities. As we will see, when one considers the peripheral level of personality, it is very useful in a theory of this type to be able to postulate such individual differences. In truth, one has the sense that Rogers agrees, but nowhere is he explicit enough to inspire certainty.

Surely it would be very difficult to make a list of the things constituting a genetic blueprint from a personologist's point of view. This is undoubtedly part of the reason why Rogers is mute. But there is a reason beyond difficulty, for Rogers is an intelligent, perceptive man who has shown no reticence to tackle and solve difficult problems before. I think that the basic reason for the muteness is that to make a list of inherent attributes would do violence to Rogers' intuitive sense of human freedom. For him, life is seen so much as a changing, shifting, unfolding, unpredictable, vibrant thing, that to theorize about some set list of characteristics would amount to shackling something wild and free.

A word about the history of this theory will make what I have just said more convincing. Rogers' first and abiding interest has been in psychotherapy, in helping people who are beset by problems of living, to find the bases for a more adequate, meaningful existence. He quickly broke away from orthodox theories and techniques of psychotherapy, such as the psychoanalytic approach, and for a period of time was known in psychology as an antitheoretical practitioner. He did not rush to develop a theory of psychotherapy because he was so deeply enmeshed in helping people that he could not have cared less whether he had formal clarity on what was happening as long as it was beneficial. And it seemed to be. After a time, when his therapeutic experience had accumulated, he began to develop a theory about how successful therapeutic outcome could be understood.

His theory of personality was an even later outgrowth of his theory of psychotherapy. And here is the crux of my point. In psychotherapy, it is very helpful to believe in a view of the organism as unlimited in what it can become—helpful for patient and therapist alike. It is helpful because you are already dealing with a patient who is terribly limited by self-destructive symptom patterns, and who has lost conviction that he can be anything other than the sorry person that he is. In such a situation, it is necessary to hold out a view of life that is extreme enough in its opposition to the patient's view to be able to serve as the needed corrective. Once he begins to believe it, the patient can draw tremendous strength from the Rogerian emphasis upon freedom, a strength that helps him find the persistence and energy to change entrenched and destructive life patterns. Rogers' emphasis upon unlimited possibilities in life has been so valuable in psychotherapy that it is not surprising that he would have retained it in his theory of personality.

But a theory of personality is not a theory of psychotherapy. In a theory of personality, you are not starting with an already disordered person. Rather, when you make statements about core tendencies and characteristics, you are talking about the true nature of humans. While we may admire Rogers' temperamental unwillingness to set limits to life's possibilities, we should also recognize that the model of personality theory he has adopted sets up the logical requirement of precision concerning the genetic blueprint if his position is to be complete enough to be usable. Without doubt, in being mute on the substantive characteristics of the genetic blueprint, once having assumed its existence, Rogers is doing what in Freud's position would amount to considering instincts to be important determinants of action without saying what they are. All of the richness of understanding contributed by Freud's view that there are life, sexual, and death instincts would, of course, be lost.

It might seem that in view of the obvious difficulty of deciding in an a priori way upon the content of inherent potentialities, one is justified in looking at the actual behavior of particular people and inferring from that what must be their potentialities. Certainly this is one important way in which theories get built. But it must be recognized that while such a strategy is useful in theory construction, it is thoroughly unacceptable except on this temporary basis. It behooves the theorist employing such a strategy to make clear that in his view it is simply an expedient, and that he realizes the limitations on the adequacy of his theory denoted by the necessity of using the strategy. Unless he adopts such a cautionary stance, he will seem to be falling into the logically unacceptable dilemma of circular reasoning. In Rogers' case, the dilemma would go as follows. He would propose that inherent potentialities determine behavior all the while he advocates using observed behavior as the measuring operation which will tell you what are the inherent potentialities. The circularity in this involves defining that which is to do the explaining in terms of that which is to be explained. With such an approach, you as a theorist can never be shown to be wrong, and because it is logically impossible to show you are wrong, it can never be determined that you are right either. Acceptance of such a circular position can only occur on the basis of faith, or intuition. It is necessary to be able to say what a person's inherent potentialities are by some logical or empirical means that are independent of the behavior to be explained by these potentialities. Only then will it be possible to determine the soundless of Rogers' position. Until then, the lack of specificity as to content of inherent potentialities remains a dangerously seductive elastic clause.

The actualizing tendency. I have already pointed out that the actualizing tendency is the organism's push to become what its inherent potentialities suit it to be, these potentialities though imprecisely specified aiming nonetheless toward the maintenance and enhancement of life. It is time now for a closer look at the nature of the actualizing tendency.

The first thing to note is that the actualizing tendency is indeed an organismic—really biological—rather than psychological tendency. It is rooted in the physiological processes of the entire body. It is a way of talking about the tendency of organic matter to develop and multiply. In this, the actualizing tendency is more like Freud's life instincts than his sexual and death instincts. But the actualizing tendency is much broader than the life instincts per se. The actualizing tendency certainly includes things such as food and water requirements, but only as a special case of the much more general characteristic of living matter to develop along the lines of its function. So when a fetus develops from a fertilized egg, when muscle and skin tissue differentiate, when secondary sex characteristics appear, when there is hormonal instigation of an inflammatory reaction in the case of injury to the body, we see the working of the actualizing tendency fully as much as in the more obvious case of voluntary utilization of function such as flexing the muscles because they are made to be flexed, and singing because the vocal apparatus permits such a delightful use of it.

Indeed, Rogers must find the expression of the actualizing tendency in involuntary growth even more important than is voluntary expression. I say this because he has made quite clear that the actualizing tendency is characteristic not only of human beings, not only of animals, but of all living things as well. Waxing poetic, he clearly makes this point at the beginning of a paper (Rogers, 1963, pp. 1–2):

> During a vacation weekend some months ago I was standing on a headland overlooking one of the rugged coves which dot the coastline of northern California. Several large rock outcroppings were at the mouth of the cove, and these received the full force of the great Pacific combers which, beating upon them, broke into mountains of spray before surging into the cliff-lined shore. As I watched the waves breaking over these large rocks in the distance, I noticed with surprise what appeared to be tiny palm trees on the rocks, no more than two or three feet high, taking the pounding of the breakers. Through my binoculars I saw that these were some type of seaweed, with a slender "trunk" topped off with a head of leaves. As one examined a specimen in the interval between the waves it seemed clear that this fragile, erect, top-heavy plant would be utterly crushed and broken by the next breaker. When the wave crunched down upon it, the trunk bent almost flat, the leaves were whipped into a straight line by the torrent of the water, yet the moment the wave had passed, here was the plant again, erect, tough, resilient. It seemed incredible that it was able to take this incessant pounding hour after hour, day after night, week after week, perhaps, for all I know, year after year, and all the time nourishing itself, extending its domain, reproducing itself; in short, maintaining and enhancing itself in this process which, in our shorthand, we call growth. Here in this palmlike seaweed was the tenacity of life, the forward thrust of life, the ability to push into an incredibly hostile environment and not only hold its own, but to adapt, develop, become itself.

The actualizing tendency is the biological pressure to fulfill the genetic blueprint, whatever the difficulty created by the environment. This quote also indicates that the actualizing tendency does not aim at tension reduction, as do the core tendencies of conflict theorists. The life and development of the seaweed, as described by Rogers, is simply not to be understood as the pursuit of comfort and quiescence. If the aim of the actualizing tendency is to be characterized in tension terms at all, it must involve tension *increase* rather than reduction. Certainly, the expression of "tenacity of life" and "forward thrust of life" and such extraordinary phenomena as "to push into an incredibly hostile environment" would precipitate increased rather than decreased organismic tension. Satisfaction of the actualizing tendency is to be understood in terms of fulfillment of a grand design rather than in terms of ease and comfort. As you will see, all the fulfillment positions involve tension increase, in sharp contrast to the conflict positions, all of which involved tension decrease in one form or another.

While the actualizing tendency is common to all living matter, it is not particularly surprising that some of the expressions it takes in the human being, according to Rogers, would be unlikely at the subhuman level. As do all living things, the human shows the basic organismic or biological form of the actualizing tendency, the aim of which is to express the inherent potentialities. But the human also shows rather distinctly psychological forms of the actualizing tendency. The most important of these is the *tendency toward self-actualization* (Rogers, 1959, p. 196). This is different from the actualizing tendency in that the *self* is involved. The self (Rogers, 1959, p. 200) is

> . . . the organized, consistent conceptual gestalt composed of perceptions of the characteristics of the "I" or "me" and the perceptions of the relationships of the "I" or "me" to others and to various aspects of life, together with the values attached to these perceptions. It is a gestalt which is available to awareness though not necessarily in awareness.

Thus, the self-actualization tendency is the pressure to behave and develop—experience oneself—consistently with one's conscious view of what one is. As you will see in what follows, Rogers' concept of self is similar to Sullivan's self-dynamism, Rank's will, and Angyal's symbolic self.

The self-concept is presumably a peculiarly human manifestation, and to understand how it comes into being, we must consider two additional offshoots of the actualizing tendency. They are the *need for positive regard* and the *need for positive self-regard* (Rogers, 1959, pp. 108–109). Both are considered secondary or learned needs, commonly developed in early infancy, that represent specialized expressions of the overall actualizing tendency. The need for positive regard refers to the person's satisfaction at receiving the approval of others, and frustration at receiving disapproval. The need for positive self-regard is a more internalized version of this. In other words, the need for positive self-regard refers to the person's satisfaction at approving, and dissatisfaction at disapproving of himself. Because the person has a need for positive regard, he is sensitive to, or can be affected by, the attitudes toward him of the significant people in his life. In the process of gaining approval and disapproval from them, he will develop a conscious sense of who he is, called a self or self-concept. Along with this, he will develop a need for positive self-regard, which assures that the tendency toward self-actualization will take the form of favoring behavior and development that is consistent with the self-concept. The person is unlikely to persist in functioning incompatibly with the self-concept because this would frustrate the need for positive self-regard.

To summarize in the terminology of this book, Rogers considers the core tendencies of personality to be (1) the inherent attempt of the organism to actualize or develop all its capacities in ways which serve to maintain and enhance life, and (2) the attempt to actualize the self-concept, which is a psychological manifestation of (1). The needs for positive regard and positive self-regard are secondary or learned offshoots of these core tendencies explicating the motivational mechanism whereby the actualization of self-concept is attempted. The characteristics at the core of personality are (1) the inherent potentialities, which define the ways in which the actualizing tendency will be expressed, and (2) the self-concept, which defines the ways in which the self-actualizing tendency will be expressed. These tendencies and characteristics are at the core of personality because they are common to all persons, and have a pervasive influence on living.

The way to actualization of potentialities. It is crucial to an understanding of maximal fulfillment to recognize that while the inherent potentialities are genetically determined, the self-concept is socially determined. This makes it possible to imagine discrepancies between these two sets of core characteristics; a person's sense of who and what he is may deviate from what his organismic potentialities actually suit him to be. But in order for this kind of discrepancy to exist, the person must have been failed by society. Although society often fails the person in this way, it does not have to do so. Society is not inevitably antagonistic to the individual, as it is assumed to be by Freud and the psychosocial conflict theorists. Rogers (1961, pp. 31–48) has a good deal to say about the nature of society's failure. He calls it *conditioned positive regard.* What he means is the situation in which only some but not all of the person's actions, thoughts, and feelings are approved of and supported by the significant people in his life. Thus, when the person develops a self-concept, the fact that what other people think of him is important, will lead him to see himself only in terms of those of his actions, thoughts, and feelings that have received approval and support. His self-concept will be based on what Rogers calls *conditions of worth;* i.e., standards for discerning what is valuable and what is not valuable about himself. Conditions of worth as a concept serves much the same logical function as does the superego in Freud's theory. Both concepts represent something implanted by society that serves as an ethical monitor on the person's functioning.

The existence of conditions of worth in the self-concept brings into operation defensiveness that is similar to that postulated by Freud. Once you have conditions of worth, some of the thoughts, feelings, and actions that you could well engage in would make you feel unworthy or guilty, and hence, a process of defense is set in motion. As in Freud, the defense is activated when the person has some small inkling or cue, in the form of *anxiety,* that unworthy behavior is about to occur. Rogers details two general kinds of defenses, *denial* and *distortion.* His approach is similar to Sullivan, and falls short of Freud's elaborate list of defenses. But I will not discuss these matters further until Chapter 7.

Although there is much similarity between Rogers and Freud in the notion of societal implants concerning ethical functioning, and defensive operations to shield the person from the pain of considering himself unworthy and to aid in bending behavior to moral standards, there is a critical difference as well. For Freud, defensive operations lead to the most successful life, whereas for Rogers, defensive operations lead to a crippling restriction on living. This difference follows from other differences in the positions. For Freud, the conflict between individual and society is inevitable because the individual is not by his nature suited for community, even though social living is obviously necessary to the broader matters of survival of the species and development of culture. In contrast, for Rogers, though there is often conflict between individual and society—witness conditional positive regard as a reaction to expressions of inherent potentialities—the conflict is not at all inevitable. There is no necessary incompatibility between individual and society, because there is nothing in the individual's genetic blueprint that obviates community. While for Freud the good life involves maximal expression of your true nature within the necessary limitations of the rights of other people, for Rogers the good life involves nothing less than maximal expression of your true nature. Conditions of worth and defensive processes are considered crippling because they lead to a rejection of thoughts, feelings, or actions that truly express inherent potentialities, a state called *incongruence.* In other words, once conditions of worth and defense exist, it is impossible to fully actualize your potentialities. You cannot become all that you could be. You have lost out on some of your genetic birthright.

How can these dire consequences be avoided? You have to be lucky enough as a youngster to have experienced *unconditional positive regard* (Rogers, 1961, pp. 31–48) from the significant people in your environment. Unconditional positive regard means that these people value and respect you as a person, and therefore, support and accept your behavior, even if it is something with which they disagree. Rogers does not literally mean that every possible action must be approved, regardless of the consequences to yourself and others. Obviously, if a young child tries to run into the path of a moving truck he must be restrained. But if he is to experience a continuance of positive regard even though he is being restrained, it must be clear from the adult's way of restraining that there is no diminution of respect and general approval. If the child is hit, or told he is bad for wanting to run across the street, then he is not being positively regarded. If, in contrast, he is simply held back and told in words that are appropriate to his age level that it is dangerous to run across the street, he still is being respected as a human being. In his emphasis on unconditional positive regard, Rogers means an atmosphere of valuing and loving more than he means an absence of all constraints. There are obviously a whole host of things that the child must learn about the world in order to negotiate its complexities effectively. But he can learn these things either in an atmosphere fostering self-acceptance or self-denial, and this makes all the difference for Rogers.

If you grow up in an atmosphere of unconditional positive regard, then you develop no conditions of worth and no defensiveness. Your self-concept is broader and deeper, including a much larger proportion of the thoughts, feelings, and actions that are expressive of your inherent potentialities. In addition, your self-concept is more flexible and changing. This is because new thoughts, feelings, and actions brought about by the continual unfolding of the actualizing tendency can be consciously appreciated (there being no defense) and incorporated into the self-concept (there being no limiting conditions of worth). The state where the self-concept embraces more or less all of your potentialities is called *congruence,* to signify that the self-concept has not shriveled to only part of what you are and can be. The state of flexibility where new experiences can occur and be consciously appreciated is called *openness to experience,* to signify that no watering down through defenses is taking place.

So, for Rogers, the way of actualizing your potentialities in the fullest manner is to possess a self-concept that does not include conditions of worth, and therefore precipitates no defenses. It follows from this that you will (1) respect and value all manifestations of yourself, (2) be conscious of virtually all there is to know about yourself, and (3) be flexible and open to new experience. In this way, the work of becoming what it is in your nature to be can go forward undisturbed. You will be what Rogers calls a *fully functioning person.* And, as indicated earlier, far from being self-interestedly antisocial, as would be expected in the Freudian view of a person without defenses, you will value, appreciate, enjoy, and support other people because you value, appreciate, enjoy, and approve of yourself.

Rogers and Goldstein. Many of the concepts found in Rogers and other actualization theorists can be traced to the position of Kurt Goldstein (1963). A physiologist interested in how people adjust to brain damage, Goldstein did not really offer a theory of personality so much as a theory of the organism. Nonetheless, it will be helpful in understanding Rogers' views to note their similarity to and difference from those of Goldstein.

As does Rogers, Goldstein assumes that the core characteristics of personality are the inherent potentialities, and the core tendency is the push toward realization in actual living of these inherent potentialities. Furthermore, both theorists agree that the core tendency and characteristics ensure the maintenance and enhancement of life, and are not in any necessary way incompatible with community. Although both theorists assume a basic push in the person toward realizing his potentialities, Rogers calls this the actualizing tendency, whereas Goldstein calls it the *self-actualizing tendency.* Rogers saves this latter term for the push to realize one's subjective sense of who one is, preferring the former term to refer to a more organismic, biological process of development. Goldstein can agree to the organismic, biological nature of the basic push to realize one's potentialities, and still call this a self-actualizing tendency because he does not have a psychological sense of the concept of self. For Goldstein, the self is virtually the same as the organism. Nowhere in Goldstein's theory is there recourse to the importance of a phenomenal self-concept.

This means that no formal theoretical role is given to such matters as conditions of worth, and attempts to become in actual behavior what you think or imagine you should be. There is also no formal theoretical role for conflict due to expressions of the actualizing tendency threatening to, or actually falling outside of, the limits set by conditions of worth. And hence, there is no formal theoretical role for defense, at least as a mechanism for avoiding psychologically determined anxiety and guilt. There is also no role in Goldstein's thinking for offshoots of the basic push to actualize potentialities that could be called the need for positive regard and the need for positive self-regard. As you can see, Goldstein's theory is a much simpler one than that of Rogers. It also cannot explain as much. Strictly speaking, Goldstein cannot consider phenomena such as guilt, unconscious cognitions, and acting in terms of one's aspirations.

Generally speaking Goldstein does stay away from the kinds of phenomena mentioned above. Actually, the only one of the three receiving significant attention is unconscious cognition, and the point of view taken is that there is no such thing in Freud's sense. For the unconscious, in the sense of cognitions in the mind but actively barred from consciousness, Goldstein substitutes the view that cognitions not actually in the center of attention at the moment may remain in the mind in unsalient form. But whenever the situation the person faces warrants it, the unsalient cognitions can be called to the center of attention, according to Goldstein.

As is typical of all fulfillment theorists, Goldstein fails to see society as having requirements that not only must be served if civilization is to survive, but that are also in opposition to man's basic nature. For Goldstein, as for Rogers, the external environment serves two functions for the person. First, it provides him with contexts, even tasks, for him to perform in the enactment of his fulfillment. And second, the environment can interfere with normal, vigorous actualization of potentialities. As would be expected from his minimally psychological viewpoint, Goldstein does not have any very complicated or detailed account of development through interaction with society and the physical world, but what he does have is consistent with the fulfillment position. The self-actualization tendency will lead to the fulfillment of the genetic blueprint, unless normal social support and freedom from physical danger are lacking. If there is danger, or actual damage to the person, then *catastrophic anxiety* results. Catastrophic anxiety is fear of coming to an end, or being overwhelmed, or disintegrating. Catastrophic anxiety in turn leads to a diversion of self-actualization pressure away from the vigorous pursuit of life enhancement to the equally valuable, but more conservative pursuit of life maintenance. In this case, the person does not grow so much as survive. Although the life maintenance reaction to catastrophic anxiety may sound less remarkable than the growth taking place in the absence of such anxiety, it should be clearly recognized that for Goldstein, the one is as much an expression of the self-actualization tendency as is the other. They simply differ in that one is the best that can be done with an injured organism, while the other involves no such limitation.

You should note that Rogers' theory parallels that of Goldstein at a more psychological level. In Rogers, functioning defensively because of conditions of worth amounts to the maintenance of life. Life can only be enhanced rather than merely maintained when there is freedom from defensiveness due to an absence of conditions of worth. Conditions of worth, in Rogers' theory, are psychological entities analogous to physical injury, in Goldstein's theory. Another way of viewing this is that threat to the person from the outside takes a social form for Rogers more than for Goldstein, though neither believes threat to be inevitable. The counterpart in Rogers for Goldstein's emphasis on physical injury to the organism is psychological injury in the form of conditions of worth. As a physically damaged organism orients toward maintenance rather than enhancement of life, so too does the psychologically damaged organism considered by Rogers, through the action of defensive processes.

I wish to make a final point about the inherent potentialities. On this matter, we find both theorists agreeing on something like a genetic blueprint. Although Goldstein, as well as Rogers, does not really specify the content of the blueprint, he does suggest a technique whereby one can diagnose the inherent potentialities from the behavior one observes. It is Goldstein's belief that in a person's preferences, and in what he does well, one can see evidence of the underlying genetic blueprint. You should recognize that this is only a bare beginning toward the goal of content specification, for you can say nothing as a theoretician about that content that is general and prior to concrete observations. You must have a person in front of you to observe, so that you can diagnose his preferences and competencies. Having done so, you can speculate about his inherent potentialities. Such speculation does not necessarily tell you anything valid about the next person's potentialities. Nonetheless, Goldstein's technique of diagnosis is a step forward in precision if it can be used in a manner that avoids complete circularity of reasoning. If we can assume that not all, but only some, of any person's behavior will express his preferences and competencies, then we can say that only these behaviors clarify the nature of his potentialities. Behavior that does not express preferences and competencies is to be understood in some other way. Because Goldstein's position focuses on only some behavior, it avoids the banal circularity inherent in saying that all behavior expresses potentialities and it is potentialities that produce behavior.

Maslow's position

The other actualization position I will discuss is that of Abraham Maslow. Born in New York City in 1908, Maslow received his Ph.D. in 1934, and died in 1970 at LaJolla, California. Throughout his career, he concentrated on research, teaching, and writing. The observations he used in theorizing tend to stem from research on normal and creative people, rather than from psychopathology and psychotherapy. An abiding concern of Maslow's was the betterment of society and the individual life. After serving at a number of universities, Maslow became chairman of the Department of Psychology at Brandeis University in 1961. Recently, this distinguished personologist was elected president of the American Psychological Association. At the time of his death, he had emerged as a popular leader of humanistic trends in our society.

Maslow developed his position slowly over many years, and was responsive to and influenced by the work of other like-minded personologists such as Allport, Rogers, and Goldstein. I have included discussion of his view here, even though he is in strong agreement on many points with Rogers and Goldstein, for three reasons. First, he is more detailed and complete on some very important matters than are the other two theorists. But paradoxically enough, the second reason for inclusion is that his discursive, highly eclectic approach to theorizing and writing renders his position ambiguous, at the very same time that he is willing to tackle problems others leave alone. Thus, there are both good and bad practices to be learned from Maslow by the student of personology. The third reason for including his position is that it is an example of what I have been calling a variant on the fulfillment model. In other words, for Maslow, fulfillment is the most important, but not the only, directionality in the person. In view of the complexity introduced by this fact, the ensuing discussion will have to be broken into three broad topics: (1) the core tendencies of personality, (2) the core characteristics of personality, and (3) the interaction between the two.

The core tendencies of personality. Maslow (1962, 1967, 1969) agrees with Rogers and Goldstein in imputing to the person as a core tendency, the *push toward actualization of inherent potentialities*. Although Maslow seems to recognize the importance of the person's own self-concept in much of his writing, he does not explicitly give it the significance and type of role that we found in Rogers. For Maslow, actualization of inherent potentialities virtually ensures development of a self-concept, and while mental illness is considered associated with faulty actualization, the faultiness is not considered the result of a restricting self-concept. It seems to me that Maslow's position is somewhere between that of Rogers and Goldstein. To wit, Maslow names the push toward realizing one's potentialities the *self-actualizing tendency,* and appears to emphasize the physiological organism sometimes, and the phenomenal self sometimes.

Now to what makes Maslow's theory a variant of the fulfillment model. He (Maslow, 1955, 1962) recognizes another tendency, common to all persons, and therefore part of the core of personality, that does not have the same connotations of fulfillment inherent in the actualizing tendency. Although he never quite puts it this way, this other tendency is *the push to satisfy needs ensuring physical and psychological survival.* The model appropriate to this tendency is that of succorance, rather than fulfillment.

The survival tendency is prior to or prepotent over the actualization tendency in that a certain modicum of satisfaction of the former is necessary before the person can engage in any very vigorous expression of the latter. But this is not to say that the survival tendency is more important than the actualization tendency in any other way. The survival tendency can only maintain life, it cannot enhance it. Only the actualization tendency can ensure expression of the person's special individuality and worth. Only the actualization tendency can lead to a rich and deeply meaningful life. Thus, although both survival and actualization tendencies are clearly part of the core of personality, the special importance given to the latter makes Maslow's position a fulfillment theory, albeit a variant on that theme. His position is not in the conflict tradition, because the survival and actualization tendencies are not conceptualized as antagonistic to each other. It is true that if the survival tendency does not lead to a measure of satisfaction, the actualization tendency will not be vigorously expressed, but this is not the same as saying that one tendency inhibits or counteracts the other.

Maslow makes some statements concerning the concrete nature of the actualizing tendency that are especially lucid while being representative of the actualization position as taken by other theorists as well. He starts by saying that "it is necessary to understand that capacities, organs, and organ systems press to function and express themselves and to be used and exercised, and that such use is satisfying and disuse irritating" (Maslow, 1962). And further, "In the normal development of the normal

child, it is now known that *most* of the time, if he is given a really free
choice, he will choose what is good for his growth. This he does because
it tastes good, feels good, gives pleasure or *delight*" (Maslow, 1962).
These statements make the concept of actualizing tendency more concrete and tangible by pinpointing its physiological sources and their
psychological concomitants. The physiological source is the tendency
of somatic components of the organism to function according to their
design. The psychological concomitant is the tendency of the person to
make choices that satisfy him. When he uses satisfaction as a guide, he
will make choices consistent with the proper functioning of the somatic
components of his organism because it is the use of these components
according to their design that yields up satisfaction. Note the similarity
between this position and that of Freud in which somatic requirements
are represented in mental life in such fashion that decisions and actions
suit those requirements. As you already know, once you consider more
concrete matters of the content of organismic requirements, the similarity
ends. Maslow's position clearly indicates that the person does not actualize his potentialities out of any sense of his destiny or any self-conscious
desire to use himself well. Indeed, the person truly actualizing his potentialities experiences little more than a general sense of well-being,
nothing more teleological than that. Actualization theorists tend to distrust more self-conscious attempts to do well by oneself.

As Maslow includes two basic tendencies in the core of personality,
we should expect him to make some statement concerning the nature of
their relationship, the kind of statement irrelevant for other actualization
theorists who postulate only one basic tendency. Actually, I have already
mentioned his view of the relationship between the survival and actualizing tendencies, though it remains to describe more fully. But once
you try to describe more fully, you encounter ambiguities. The survival
tendency is stronger than—takes precedence over—the actualizing
tendency. The actualizing tendency is strong and vigorous only when
the survival tendency has been satisfied. This relationship is certainly
meant to hold developmentally—the major task of childhood is to satisfy
the survival tendency, though once this is firmly accomplished, the
actualizing tendency increases in saliency—but can also be applied at
any point in life. For example, a person having achieved vigorous expression of the actualizing tendency might, through environmental circumstance, find his survival threatened anew, and revert temporarily or
more chronically to expressions of the survival tendency. Interestingly
enough Machiavelli must have subscribed to this kind of viewpoint, for
he believed that refined, civilized, cultured men were only that way
because they lived in an environment devoid of threat to them, and
that once they were threatened, they would be much meaner in appearance and easier to control. But Machiavelli believed that this showed
the greater importance of the survival tendency, whereas Maslow feels

that the survival tendency is only important because it sets the stage for the actualizing tendency. Both beliefs are logically possible and Maslow's choice exemplifies his irrepressible optimism.

Maslow's decision to cast the survival and actualizing tendencies in motivational terms has been a popular one with actualization theorists in general. According to Maslow (1955), the actualization tendency is *growth motivation,* whereas the survival tendency is *deprivation motivation.* Deprivation motivation refers to urges to strive for goal states, presently unachieved, that are necessary in order to ease the pain and discomfort due to their absence. The aim of deprivation motivation is to decrease the organismic tension built up through deficit states that represent deviations from homeostatic balance. Organismic survival requires nutritional substances, and hence, when food has not been ingested for a while, visceral organ activity produces a rising tension level, experienced psychologically as hunger, which precipitates instrumental actions designed to reach the goal state. The goal state is satiation, which is considered the normal, homeostatic state, characterized as tensionless. This is an old model for motivation, that achieved its definitive modern statement in the writings of the physiologist, Walter B. Cannon. You will note that it is the model subscribed to by Freud and the other conflict theorists.

In contrasting deprivation motivation with growth motivation, Maslow may have been taking another cue from Cannon (1929), who said that once the homeostatic needs were satisfied, the "priceless unessentials of life" could be sought. In any event, growth motivation, which Maslow claims has not been adequately recognized in the past, refers to urgings to enrich living, to enlarge experience, because to do so increases our delight at being alive. Growth motivation does not involve the repairing of deficits so much as the expansion of horizons. Its goal states, if they exist at all, are very general in nature. It does not start with sharp discomfort that must be eased. And its aim is not the reduction of tension so much as its actual increase. Satisfaction has to do with realization of capabilities or ideals, through a process whereby the organism becomes more complex, differentiated, and potent. This enlargement of the organism seems to require, if anything, that satisfaction go hand in hand with tension increase.

Unfortunately, growth motivation as an idea is logically inconsistent. It assumes that there exists a kind of motivation which does not involve striving toward something that is lacking. But the motivation construct is such that in order to define a motive, you must specify a goal state that is to be achieved, and the course of action instrumental to reaching the goal (Peters, 1958; Maddi & Costa, 1972). A motive without a specifiable goal state would not be a motive at all. And once you define a goal, you are of necessity assuming that the person having the motive is in a deprived state until he reaches the goal. In a logical sense, then, there is no way of defining a motive that does not follow the so-called deprivation model. I think Maslow is reaching for a distinction between kinds of motivation that is of value, but the value is poorly stated by the terms deprivation and growth motivation. I shall amplify what I mean in Chapter 9. But for the moment let us return to the actualizing tendency.

I am not by any means suggesting the abandonment of the concept of actualizing tendency. Rather, what is at issue is its status as a motive. In this regard, I have tried to convince you that if Maslow and the others wish to consider the actualizing tendency to be a motive, then it must conform to a deprivation model because that is appropriate to the logic of the motivation construct. The actualization tendency as motive must refer to a goal state that is valued but not yet achieved (and that is where the deprivation comes in), and the instrumental actions relevant to its achievement. But I should also make clear that the actualizing tendency need not be considered a motive at all, simply because it exerts a causal influence on behavior. A theorist could decide to consider it an organismic tendency, much like metabolism or maturation, that does not engage the intelligence and decision-making capabilities of the person. Since such a model does not imply purpose in a psychological sense (Peters, 1958), the language of motivation is irrelevant. Indeed, Maslow could easily give up the motivational model for the actualizing tendency, for he has said "Maturity, or self-actualization, from the (motivational) point of view, means to transcend the deficiency needs. This state can be described then as meta-motivated, or unmotivated" (Maslow, 1962).

Although it would seem that Maslow might recognize the value of casting the actualizing tendency in nonmotivational terms, the disconcerting inconsistency and ambiguity of his writing is well exemplified by the appearance of the quote cited above directly following the point in an article where the idea that self-actualization is growth motivation has been developed! It is as if Maslow, in thinking in terms of the intuitively apparent difference between a tendency to actualize one's capabilities and a tendency to satisfy one's survival needs, and in recognizing the inherently motivational nature of the latter, could not resist the symmetry produced by generalizing the motivational model to the actualizing tendency as well. Although such generalization may have seemed neat to him at first, the very kind of logical difficulty I pointed out must have arisen to plague him on reflection, leading him to make contradictory statements in the same breath. In Chapter 9, I will try to show just how it is plausible to consider core tendencies, such as that to actualize one's potentialities, to be forces producing directionality in living without casting them in motivational terms.

The core characteristics of personality. Now let us consider the core characteristics of personality that correspond to the two core tendencies. The tendency to satisfy physical and psychological survival needs virtually expresses what is the content of those needs. Maslow has provided us with a list of needs organized in terms of the degree to which satis-faction of each is a prerequisite to the search for satisfaction of the next. He lists *physiological needs, safety needs, needs for belongingness and love,* and *esteem needs.* The earlier in the list, the more physiological and less psychological is the need. But even the needs at the end of the list, though heavily psychological, are more relevant to survival, or the re-pairing of deficits, than to the fulfillment of one's potentialities. Notice that the intent is an hierarchical organization. In other words, when the physiological needs are satisfied, the safety needs become salient and can be attended to; when the physiological and safety needs are both satisfied, the needs for belongingness and love become salient and can be attended to; and so forth.

Maslow has also specified the core characteristics relevant to the actu-alizing tendency. We should greet such specification with special interest and anticipation, as we have already noted that most actualization posi-tions suffer from the weakness of being mute concerning the content of inherent potentialities. Maslow is, in this company, a worthy exception, but he misses the laurel wreath through being confusing once again. I will try, however, to piece together the essence of his position concerning the inherent potentialities. One relevant kind of information comes in his discussions of the hierarchy of needs mentioned above. Actually, Maslow lists two additional needs that stand higher than those already discussed. These two are the *need for self-actualization,* which is succeeded by the *need for cognitive understanding.* His manner of identifying these two needs in the hierarchy suggests not only that they are independent of each other, but also that the need for cognitive understanding is an even higher expression of man's nature than is self-actualization. But he can-not really mean this, because his position would then become fraught with contradictions and incompletions. So, taking all he says into ac-count, it seems to me most likely that these two needs are referring to different aspects of the inherent potentialities which unfold due to the action of the actualizing tendency. The need for cognitive understanding could be considered a psychological reflection of the inherent function of the nervous system, namely, the processing of information. A number of other theorists considered in this volume (e.g., Murray, Rogers, White, Allport) would also find such an assumption useful. Actually, this kind of view is creeping into psychology these days, and even finds direct expression among two theorists in the Rogerian tradition. Butler and Rice (1963) develop the notion that self-actualization occurs as a result of the nervous system's hunger for stimulation. But to return to the main theme, if the inherent potentialities referred to as "need for self-actualiza-tion" and "need for cognitive understanding" do indeed represent ex-pressions of the actualizing tendency, then the former is inaccurately labeled, as can be seen by its redundancy. Let us delve further into

Maslow's writing to see whether we can discover the proper label for this content.

Of particular relevance are the statements he makes about human nature. At the outset, he emphasizes that people are both similar to and different from each other (Maslow, 1962). And then, in agreement with Rogers and Goldstein, he says, "This inner nature, as much as we know of it so far, is definitely not 'evil,' but is either what we adults in our culture call 'good,' or else it is neutral. The most accurate way to express this is to say that it is 'prior to good and evil' " (Maslow, 1962). Now we come to statements purporting to provide even more concrete specification of the content of human nature. According to Maslow (1962),

> We have, each one of us, an essential inner nature which is intrinsic, given, "natural" and, usually, very resistent to change. . . . I include in this inner nature instinctoid needs, capacities, talents, anatomical equipment, physiological balances, prenatal and natal injuries, and traumata to the neonatus. Whether defense and coping mechanisms, "style of life," and other characterological traits, all shaped in the first few years of life, should be included, is still a matter for discussion. I would say "yes" and proceed on the assumption that this raw material very quickly starts growing into a self as it meets the world outside and begins to have transactions with it.

You may experience an initial flush of enthusiasm of first reading this statement, but I ask you to reflect on it for a moment. To me, the statement teaches us little because it is too omnibus. As a specification of the inherent potentialities relevant to the actualizing tendency, it is really no advantage over muteness. As a statement of all that is in man's nature, i.e., the inherent potentialities plus the deficiency needs, then it might be somewhat helpful if we were told what things went in which of the two categories. Indeed, it is not clear that this is even the right track to follow, for Maslow includes such things as defenses and coping mechanisms. In his own terms, these things are not even clearly innate, rather than learned, and yet they occur in a statement of man's "inner nature."

There are a few other relevant statements in the same article that could be put down here, but they are equally discursive and confusing. At one point, Maslow (1962) indicates that because the human evolved away from strong instincts, it is hard for him to know and experience his inner nature. The same seems to be true for the theorist regarding the inherent potentialities! The conclusion to reach is that Maslow's attempt to specify the content of these potentialities is, because of its omnibus and loose nature, no more useful than the absence of such statements on the part of other actualization theorists.

The way to fulfillment. The conditions under which fulfillment occurs are very similar for Maslow and for Rogers, although there are some superficial differences in terminology. According to Maslow, satisfaction of the survival tendency is all that is necessary to ensure that self-actualization will occur. While the existence of the survival tendency guarantees that the person will seek the goal states that are prerequisites to self-actualization, whether he will be successful really hinges on the nature of his physical and social environment. This is true when the person is young because he is not developed enough to be independent of the assistance of others, and when he is an adult because if his environment does not include the basis for physical and psychological survival, no amount of effort on his part will result in success. But if the survival needs, both physical and psychological, are assuaged, then the natural unfolding process of fulfillment is ensured by the existence of the actualizing tendency and inherent potentialities. When you recognize that satisfaction of the deficiency needs requires that the person be loved, respected, and accepted, along with being provided with the stuff to assuage physiological want, and being kept out of harm's way, it becomes clear that Maslow is in essential agreement with Rogers. The difference between them is that the actualizing tendency incorporates both the maintenance and the enhancement of life for Rogers, whereas it incorporates only enhancement for Maslow, with maintenance being the function of the survival tendency. As far as I can tell, however, this difference does not lead to much discrepancy in the views of person and society held by the two theorists.

The theorists are also in essential agreement on what the person achieving self-actualization would be like. Rogers speaks of the fully functioning person as characterized by congruence between sense of self and organismic qualities, love of self and others, openness to experience, and fairly continual change in living. Maslow uses slightly different words, such as *creative living, peak experiences, unselfish love, unbiased understanding,* but, in point of fact, means very much the same things.

In closing this discussion of Maslow's position, I would like to call your attention to the general implications of the view that survival needs must be met before vigorous actualization of potentialities can occur. Clearly, this means that the person must be nurtured, loved, respected, in order to amount to much. Charmingly humanistic though this viewpoint is, I think it can be seriously criticized. There are countless examples of people who have been significantly creative in spite of early lives that hardly included much nurturance, love, and respect. From the contemporary scene, James Baldwin is certainly an example. It is hard to imagine a developmental environment more destructive than his. Assailed on all fronts by psychological, social, and economic deprivation to the point of inhumanity, he still emerged as a productive, creative writer and critic. And to carry this criticism further, let me point out that an implication of Maslow's position is that when survival needs are frustrated at any point in time—not simply in childhood—there ought to be a concomitant temporary decrease in vigorous self-actualization. But, as I have pointed out elsewhere (Maddi, 1965), there are many contradictory examples to be found in the lives of great men:

> We should keep in mind that John Bunyan began *Pilgrim's Progress* in the humiliating and rigidly regulated environment of a prison, and that Christ developed and preached his new ideas in a societal context that had become oppressively structured, to say nothing of the dangers he encountered. The blossoming of creativity during the Renaissance used to be attributed to the newly found wonder of leisure time, of time in which to contemplate and imagine. But it is now recognized that the Renaissance was an era of tremendous unheaval, chaos, and strife, in which flourished not only creativity, but also vice and intrigue of wondrous variety. Far from being free and permissive, it was an environment in which the artist and scientist had to scramble to get and keep the indulgence and protection of a patron, and hope that the patron would remain more powerful than his enemies for a while at least. And if further evidence were needed . . . I could turn to the concentration camp. Even in this environment so bent on psychological and physical destruction . . . some people could still think and observe creatively enough to develop the kernels of new philosophies of life, later to be written about in such books as *The Informed Heart* and *From Death Camp to Existentialism*. . . . And picture Galileo as he prayed on his knees by the side of the bed at night that he might gain God's aid in finding the inspiration for a creative idea to be converted into money to placate his creditors. Toulouse-Lautrec and many others were in rather constant physical pain as they expressed their creativity. I hardly need mention that Van Gogh created under the pressure of a fantastic assortment of torments. Finally, in *A Moveable Feast,* Hemingway specifically blames the atrophy of his creativity on his transition from a poor artist, who frequently went hungry and cold, to a pampered associate of the rich, for whom life had become easy and placid.

Is it really clear than when survival needs are unsatisfied, self-actualization will be curtailed?

Maslow might have responded to this criticism by saying that his position is accurate in general, regardless of the fact that one can point to exceptions, as in the examples above. For most people, he might argue, the realization of potentialities requires the prior satisfaction of survival needs. There will always be a few people, presumably, who are so extraordinary that their lives will be creative whether or not they are nurtured. Maslow might want to suggest that these people could have been even greater if their survival needs had achieved more satisfaction. This is a plausible, but by no means devastating retort to my criticism. We shall not solve the disagreement here. It is enough that you be aware of it.

FULFILLMENT MODEL: PERFECTION VERSION

In the actualization version of the fulfillment model, the person is conceptualized as trying to become what his inherent potentialities actually suit him to be. If the person has the genes pertaining to high intelligence, then fulfillment will involve a life in which intellectual endeavor is frequent. Fulfillment follows the course determined by something like a genetic blueprint. The perfection version of the fulfillment model is actually quite different than this. In the perfection version, fulfillment follows the course determined by ideals and values concerning the good life. These ideals and values need not mirror the person's inherent or genetically determined capabilities. Indeed, it is frequent for perfection theorists to stress the person's attempt to overcome real or imagined inferiorities. The perfection version is an expression of idealism, whereas the actualization version is an expression of humanism. The purest example of the perfection version is the word of Alfred Adler, although Robert White's recent writings are clearly in the same genre. Gordon Allport and Erich Fromm emerge as primarily perfection theorists, but with some tendencies toward the actualization position as well. Finally, existential psychology emerges as a surprisingly pure example of the class.

Adler's position

Alfred Adler (born in Vienna, Austria in 1870; died in Scotland in 1937) received the M.D. in 1895, and practiced general medicine in the earliest days of his career. Soon, however, he shifted to psychiatry, and became a charter member of the Vienna Psychoanalytic Society. Ironically, as Adler came to serve as president of that august group, the ideas he was developing seemed so heretical that he was severely criticized and denounced, whereupon he resigned his office and membership. He then formed his own group, known as Individual Psychology, which became quite active. Following World War I, in which he served as an army physician, Adler expressed his commitment to public service by establishing the first child guidance clinics in connection with the Viennese school system. In 1935, Adler came to the United States, where he taught his point of view at the Long Island College of Medicine, and continued to be a prolific and forceful writer.

Although there is a clear thread of continuity running through Adler's writings at various stages in his life, there is also considerable evolution. I shall therefore emphasize his final views, though attempting to give some sense of how he got there as well.

The core tendency of personality can be simply stated for Adler. It is *the striving toward superiority or perfection* (Adler, 1927, 1930; Ansbacher & Ansbacher, 1956). Superficially, this core tendency seems similar to that of the actualization theorists, but it is actually quite different. If you had to refer the actualization tendency to your own intuitive experience, you would do so by remembering when you had a vivid sense of who and what you were, and attempted to function consistently with that. But when you think of striving toward superiority or perfection, you are inevitably led to remember those times when you were dissatisfied with your talents or capabilities as you saw them, and actively tried to transcend them to a higher level of functioning.

Sources of striving toward perfection.   It would be well to start this section with a greater sense of Adler's thinking concerning his postulated core tendency of personality. Although originally part of Freud's inner circle, Adler became convinced early in his professional life that aggressive urges are more important in life than are sexual ones. He elaborated this conviction by identifying as the basic drive in man the now famous *will to power*. At this middle stage in his thinking, Adler clearly emphasized self-interest and Machiavellianism as the wellsprings of life. But, as he became older and attempted to find some greater compatibility between his theoretical view of man and his personal commitment to public service, he shifted the emphasis of the core tendency from power to superiority or perfection. The goal of the striving toward perfection is not social distinction, or a position of power. Rather, it is the full realization of the ideal life. In describing the striving for perfect completion, Adler (1930, p. 398) says:

> I began to see clearly in every psychological phenomenon the striving for superiority. It runs parallel to physical growth and is an intrinsic necessity of life itself. It lies at the root of all solutions of life's problems and is manifested in the way in which we meet these problems. All our functions follow its direction. They strive for conquest, security, increase, either in the right or in the wrong direction. The impetus from minus to plus never ends. The urge from below to above never ceases. Whatever premises all our philosophers and psychologists dream of—self-preservation, pleasure principle, equalization—all these are but vague representations, attempts to express the great upward drive.

It may sound to you as if Adler means something very like the actualization tendency, with its emphasis upon inherent potentialities. This is not the case. Adler draws the analogy to physical growth only to dramatize his belief in the inevitability and ubiquitousness of the tendency toward perfection. Achieving perfection, however, is not a matter of expressing potentialities so much as a matter of achieving completion. Adler's emphasis is clearly seen in his concept of *fictional finalism*, which expresses the goal of the core tendency. The word finalism merely refers to the reaching of an end or goal state, and the tendency to go in that direction. The word fictional is crucial in that it indicates that what the person is striving to reach is an ideal, or fiction. Ideals are not potentialities, rooted in the genetic blueprint. The most abstract and general ideal is that of perfection, which is the core characteristic associated with the core tendency. In Chapter 7 on peripheral personality, I shall discuss the more concrete fictional finalisms that develop as a function of one or another of the developmental courses outlined by Adlerians.

Another important aspect of the core tendency reflected in the quote presented above is that, in tension terms, Adler presumes that all people strive toward the increase, rather than the decrease of tension. The references to attempting to be superior, to physical growth, and to a great upward drive that goes from minus to plus all strongly suggest increases in complexity, effort, and energy. Clearly, Adler does not see the person as striving for peace, quiet, and tension reduction. In this emphasis upon tension increase we see that the perfection version of the fulfillment model is similar to the activation version.

But these two versions are different in an important way. In the actualization version, it is enough not to be encumbered by a destructive society. The core tendency will express itself spontaneously, because it is based on a genetic blueprint. In contrast, the perfection version requires that the person work hard to make a reality of what is only a vague possibility in him at birth. The person's striving for perfection will only occur if he holds it as an ideal and disciplines himself accordingly. Witness Adler's (1964, p. 31) words on the matter:

> The high degree of cooperation and social culture which man needs for his very existence demands spontaneous social effort, and the dominant purpose of education is to evoke it. Social feeling is not inborn; but it is an innate potentiality which has to be consciously developed.

Although he is speaking here mainly of the part of superiority striving that involves trying to perfect your society as well, he has the same emphasis for more individualistic efforts to better oneself.

At this point, we must pursue the question of the content of the core tendency in much the same manner as we did with Rogers and Maslow. You will remember that Rogers assumed inherent potentialities to be the core characteristics of personality, but then neglected to specify their content. Maslow attempted such specification, but was so scattered, amorphous, and confusing that he did not shed much light on the problem. Essentially, neither theorist gives us enough formal theoretical basis for determining what the assumed inherent potentialities are so that we can avoid the circular position of deciding that everything that the person has already done must have stemmed from some potential of his. A position as circular as this cannot be put to empirical test, and hence cannot achieve the status of accepted empirical knowledge. Content specification is no less important for Adler simply because his core characteristics are ideals, or fictional finalisms, rather than potentialities.

What has Adler to say about the content of his core characteristics? First, he indicates that the striving toward superiority is innate, and that

it may manifest itself in a large number of different ways. Going on
from there, Adler offers a number of ideas concerning the precise
sources of "the great upward drive." These ideas are *organ inferiority,
feelings of inferiority,* and *compensation,* which in their most general
forms should be considered core characteristics of personality. Early in
his career, when Adler was still concerned with medicine, he developed
the notion of organ inferiority as an explanation of the localization of
illness in one part of the body rather than another. The notion is simply
that the body breaks down at its weak spots, these weak spots being
caused by peculiarities either of heredity or of development (Adler,
1917). As Adler became more psychological in orientation, he developed
the notion that people attempt to compensate for organ inferiorities, and
that this compensatory effort has important implications for their living.
The compensatory effort can be directed at the organ inferiority itself,
as in the case of Demosthenes who stuttered as a child, and became,
through striving, one of the world's greatest orators, or at the strengthening of related, though different organs, as in the case of the blind person
who develops extraordinary auditory sensitivity. Also consistent with the
concept of compensation is the shift in reliance to other, stronger capabilities. Demosthenes could have, for example, gone into painting or
some other essentially nonverbal activity in his attempt to compensate
for his stutter.

As Adler's psychological sophistication deepened, he broadened the
notion of organ inferiority to include any feelings of inferiority, whether
they arise from actual physical handicaps or from subjectively felt psychological and social disabilities. The final step was settling on the view
that *feelings* of inferiority are of paramount importance, and that such
feelings arise from incompleteness or imperfection in any sphere of life
(Adler, 1931). Indeed, an important and valuable sense of inferiority is
that which comes from the contemplation of complete perfection. Says
Adler (1956, p. 23): "In comparison with unattainable ideal perfection,
the individual is continually filled by an inferiority feeling and motivated
by it." For Adler, feelings of inferiority are the subjectively appreciated
aspect of the striving for superiority. As such, feelings of inferiority are
not only constructive forces in living, they are a ready basis for the
diagnosis of the lines along which the core tendency of personality will
be expressed in any given person. While Adler has not provided us with
a complete catalog of specific ways in which the striving toward superiority can manifest itself in all people, he has provided us with a sign for
the identification of specific manifestations of the striving toward superiority that will always be consistent with his theoretical meaning. The
identification of inferiority feelings does not depend upon achieved
superiority. Indeed, feelings of inferiority will normally precede attempts
to achieve superiority, and so such feelings cannot only be determined
independently of strivings toward superiority but can also be used as

predictors of such strivings. Adler's formulation of the fulfillment position
has avoided the circularity found in the actualization positions of Rogers
and Maslow. Adler is very similar to Goldstein in postulating a technique
for diagnosing the content directions that the core tendency will take. I
submit that Adler's emphasis on feelings of inferiority is true to the
perfection position as Goldstein's emphasis on preference is true to the
actualization position.

The emphasis in Adler on feelings of inferiority and in Goldstein on
preferences dramatizes the basic difference between the perfection and
actualization versions of the fulfillment model. Actualization positions
assume that the core tendency acts along the lines of real, usually innate,
organismic potentialities. If a person has a strong inclination toward
wrestling, for example, actualization theories would assume wrestling to
express some inherent potentialities, perhaps strength, resilience, and
suppleness of skeletal musculature. But Adler would not reach the same
conclusion. For Adler, it is feelings of inferiority that would lead to strong
inclinations toward wrestling. And feelings of inferiority might as easily
stem from characteristics of skeletal musculature opposite to those mentioned above. Feelings of inferiority might also develop from having been
beaten in wrestling or some other physical combat. Thus, for Adler,
though the tendency to strive toward superiority is itself innate, the
directions in which it leads the person are expressive of idealizations of
life. Indeed, the most likely directions are those in which inherent potentialities are meager. The aim of the tendency to strive toward superiority is complete perfection, and this carries the definite connotation of
overcoming any limitations in potentialities that may exist in the person.
To hazard an analogy from the game of bridge, actualization theorists
tend to see fulfillment as the result of playing your long suit, whereas
Adler tends to see fulfillment as the result of playing your short suit
capably enough to make it as effective as your long suit.

So, in determining the lines along which the superiority tendency will
find expression, the content of feelings of inferiority is of diagnostic
importance. The other thing in Adler's position relevant to determining
the content expressive of the superiority tendency is the assumption that
man is both an individual and a social being. In the realm of individual
living, man will strive for perfection of himself, and in the realm of group
living, he will strive for the perfection of society. The individualistic and
social expressions are simply different facets of the same tendency to
strive for superiority. Agreeing with the actualization theorists, Adler
sees man and society as essentially compatible (Adler, 1939).

It is interesting to note that the assumption that fulfillment requires
constructive social as well as individual functioning occurs late in Adler's
thinking. In breaking with Freud, Adler shifted emphasis in the content
of the core tendency from sexuality to aggressiveness. But during this
early and the middle portion of his career, Adler did not explicitly reject

the Freudian model of the individual as inevitably in conflict with society. Adler's "will to power" clearly views social interaction as dog-eat-dog in character. But paradoxically enough, Adler held the private, extratheoretical belief that constructive social living is valuable and rewarding. Perhaps it was this belief that pried him loose over the years from the conflict aspects of the Freudian model. For certainly, in Adler's final position, both individual and social sides of man are inherent, and there is no antagonism between them. It is my speculation that the early association with Freud actually hindered Adler from the rapid and vigorous development of a personality theory natural to his experience of, and convictions about, life.

The results of expressing the superiority tendency.   This concluding section on Adler will be brief, as the relevant concepts are actually more appropriately considered at the periphery of personality. But just to round out the picture of Adler's theory, you should note that the expression of the superiority tendency over time results in the formation of a *style of life*. The style of life is a pattern of characteristics, determined both by the feelings of inferiority and the compensatory attempts engaged in by the person. But the style of life is not the same as these feelings and compensations, rather it is the habits and traits resulting from them. As does the character type concept of psychoanalytic theory, the style of life concept accounts for differences between people and is therefore a peripheral characteristic of personality. One broad distinction between styles of life groups those that are constructive versus those that are destructive. It is the *family atmosphere* during the early years that leads to the development of styles of life that are destructive or constructive. If your parents respect and encourage you, a constructive style will develop. A destructive style results from parental disrespect and abandonment. Constructive styles, which are the highest form of living, are defined in terms of cooperation and generous interaction with people in the process of striving for perfection. Destructive styles are defined in terms of competitiveness and jealousy toward others in the striving for perfection. In neither constructive nor destructive styles of life is there much formal emphasis upon the concept of defense. Clearly, defensiveness is even less important in Adler's theory than it was in the actualization positions of Rogers and Maslow. Another important influence on life-style is *family constellation,* notably involving birth order, but this will not be discussed until Chapter 7.

Adler offers a related concept, the *creative self,* which, though it has been very popular among certain personologists, is nonetheless quite vague. It seems to cover the same ground as style of life, but has more the connotation of free will on the part of the person. Read one way, writings on this concept seem to indicate no more than an emphasis upon the person as an active influence upon his own life. This is a common emphasis among fulfillment theorists. But read another way, writings on the creative self suggest a truly mystical process whereby behavior can occur that bears no historical relationship to prior behavior or development. The semisupernatural implications of this emphasis can be taken to indicate a temperamental disposition to view man as free that links Adler with Rogers. Be assured that we will encounter this disposition again among fulfillment theorists.

White's position

Robert W. White was born in 1904, and received his Ph.D. in 1937 in history and government. At the outset of his career, he taught in these fields, but quickly shifted his interests to personology. White was part of the extraordinary group of psychologists gathered together by Murray at the Harvard Psychological Clinic. During these years, White began to formulate his views concerning psychopathology and personality, drawing his observations from the psychotherapeutic interaction and from research. From 1957 to 1962, he served as chairman of the influential Department of Social Relations at Harvard.

White has a position that is properly classed with that of Adler, the differences between the work of the two men being less important than the similarities. Although White's view constitutes the beginning of what may well become a complete theory of personality, at the moment it is somewhat incomplete. White (1959) talks about the core tendency in two ways: as *the attempt to produce effects through one's actions (effectance motivation), and as the attempt to achieve competence in one's functioning (competence motivation)*. It is not entirely clear what the relationship between these two tendencies is meant to be. But most of White's writings (1959, 1960, 1963) suggest that effectance motivation is to be considered an early form of the later competence motivation. Effectance motivation can be seen in the young child who takes delight in the sound it makes when he accidentally drops his rattle on the floor, and quickly learns to drop it regularly. And what even greater pleasure if the child can produce the additional effect of having an adult retrieve the rattle each time it is dropped! White sees exploratory behavior and play as ways in which the young child can experience himself as a potent influence in the world. In attempting to encourage readers to take effectance motivation seriously, White (1960) cites evidence indicating that by the end of the first year of life, the typical child is playing six or more hours a day. This amount of time actually exceeds the working day of many adults, at a stage in the child's life usually considered expressive of oral forms of sexuality or of dependency!

On the grounds of its generality, White concludes that effectance motivation must be at least as important as any other tendency that may exist in the child. Effectance motivation may even have a biological basis, according to White (1959), in the requirement of the nervous system for stimulation and information. He suggests that the human nervous system must have developed, through a process of natural selection, into a unit functioning to process information or stimulus input. If this is so, then effectance motivation might well serve the basic biological purpose of keeping the nervous system supplied with a continuous stream of stimulus input. One definite accompaniment of such a view is the notion that the core tendency, looked at from the point of view of biological energy, is best considered in the service of tension increase rather than tension decrease. In this, White is in accord with other fulfillment theorists, and in opposition to conflict theorists.

As the child becomes older, the mere attempt to have an effect on the world shades naturally into the attempt to deal with life's tasks in a competent manner. The transition is produced by the fact that the expression of effectance motivation leads the child to become experienced and knowledgeable, and to grow in *actual competence* and the *sense of competence*. The shift in core tendency from effectance to competence motivation is certainly functional because, as the child ages, he is assigned an ever-increasing number of tasks by society. He must walk alone, feed and dress himself, go to school, meet and interact with people outside the family, get good grades, choose a life's work and pursue it, establish his own family, and so forth. In order to achieve fulfillment in life, he must seek competence and have some measure of success in this search.

White is not specific in detailing the core characteristics associated with the tendency to strive toward competence. The fragmentary nature of his theory at this early stage of its development certainly makes unequivocal classification difficult. Nonetheless there is not really much doubt in my mind that it is a perfection version of the fulfillment model. To be sure, the tendencies toward competence and effectance are innate. But this alone does not constitute an actualization position. I would remind you that Adler also assumes that the striving toward perfection is innate. It is also true that White sometimes implies that he would recognize certain inherent potentialities, and that people might be assumed to differ in the nature of their endowment with such potentialities. I grant you that this begins to sound like an actualization position. But we must keep in mind that White chose to name the mature form of his core tendency in terms of competence. The denotations and connotations of the word competence are much more in line with a perfection than an actualization position. If you are driven to be competent, then you will strive hardest when you perceive some evidence or possibility of incompetence, even though that incompetence might be expressive of some meager inherent potentiality. In striving for competence, you are hardly likely to just do what you prefer, because you have in mind some conception of what it means to be competent. White's theory is much more in the idealistic mold of perfection positions than in the humanistic mold of actualization positions.

Although it is perhaps too early to be sure, White seems to be moving in the direction of adopting a form of the fulfillment position that is a variant in much the same manner as that of Maslow. You will recall that Maslow recognized survival needs as part of the core of personality, though secondary in importance to the actualization tendency. Well, though White's primary emphasis is on competence motivation, he does also consider survival needs, such as that for food and water. As does Maslow, White assumes that only when the survival needs have achieved some measure of satisfaction does competence motivation achieve vigorous expression. Competence motivation, though it under-lies so much of the person's living, is not likely, by its nature, to ever become so intense and persistent as can be the biological survival needs.

Left unsatisfied, the survival needs can, according to White, preempt the person's attention and functioning. One clear result of this distinction of White's is to convince us that competence motivation is different in his view from needs ensuring survival in the most immediate sense. While a certain minimum of competence is undoubtedly necessary in order to survive, competence motivation is meant to refer to the pursuits that make life excellent more than those that simply make it possible.

White certainly feels that any time the survival needs become very strong, expression of competence motivation is curtailed. It is not yet clear that he also means to assume that unless one receives the consistent nurturance with which to ensure survival early in life, later life will fail to show vigorous competence motivation. If he did assume this, then his position would be even closer to that of Maslow, and even more clearly subject to the criticism I made of him to the effect that some very great people have become so in spite of depriving, punishing early environments.

Allport's position

Gordon W. Allport (born in Indiana in 1897; died in Cambridge, Massachusetts in 1967) received a Ph.D. in psychology in 1922. In addition to psychology, he studied philosophy, and taught sociology, showing from the start the kinds of ethical and social concerns that were to mark his personality theorizing. He was an extremely literate man, interested in what was going on in many fields neighboring his own. During a long and prolific career, Allport received many honors, including election to the presidency of the American Psychological Association, and several other psychological organizations. In addition, he was editor for 12 years of the influential *Journal of Abnormal and Social Psychology*. Allport never practiced psychotherapy, and did not see the data of that context as relevant to personality theorizing. More relevant for him were observations of excellent, capable, and gifted people.

Over the course of a long career, Allport wrote extensively on personality, social psychology, religion, and ethics. In all these fields, his views showed steady evolution. This evolutionary change, coupled with the diversity of his concerns, makes summary of his views difficult. As with Freud, I will have to stress those of Allport's statements that are most recent, and that were most consistently made. Even adopting such a strategy, it is much more difficult than with Freud to formulate Allport's view of the core tendency of personality. In the earliest expression of his position, Allport emphasized traits and other peripheral characteristics of personality more than core considerations. But since those days, he evolved concepts more naturally relevant to the understanding of basic, lifelong directions. Nonetheless, it is still rather difficult to point to any specific core tendency. At points, Allport seems to assume an actualizing tendency, though he does not actually make such an assumption explicitly. And yet, he also seems to believe that competence motivation and similar notions are important. In thinking all this over for some time, I have come to the firm conclusion that when Allport refers to such concepts as self-actualization and competence motivation, he gives them the status of examples of the kind of view of humans he has in mind. None of them is to be taken as the core tendency itself in any precise fashion. Allport's view of the core tendency is meant to be more general than these examples.

It seems to me that the most accurate rendition of his thinking states that the core tendency *is functioning in a manner expressive of the self.* He has a technical name for the self—*proprium*—and hence the core tendency may be called *propriate functioning* (Allport, 1955). As life is a developmental process the lines of which are largely determined by the self or proprium, his viewpoint is properly considered a fulfillment position. As I will show later, although there are elements of the actualization version represented, his theory is best considered an example of the perfection version. But first I should point out that there is an additional core tendency in Allport's system. As in Maslow, it is the *tendency to satisfy biological survival needs.* This tendency is clearly meant to be different, though not incompatible with, propriate functioning. In addition, satisfying biological needs is definitely seen as less important in determining the value and meaning of life than is the heavily psychological propriate functioning. Hence, Allport's theory is a variant on the fulfillment position in much the same way as is Maslow's actualization viewpoint and as White's position may well become. Like all variants of the fulfillment position, Allport's theory assumes that one core tendency—propriate functioning—is in the service of the highest development of the person, whereas the other core tendency—satisfaction of biological needs—merely ensures the physical survival of the organism. Indeed, Allport (1955) calls the tendency toward biological survival by the disparaging name of *opportunistic functioning.*

Just to start you thinking along the lines of Allport's meaning, let me suggest a basis in common personal experience for intuitive understanding of propriate functioning. Remember the last time you wanted to do something or become some particular way, because you really felt that doing or becoming that would be expressive of the things about yourself that you believe to be most important. Such ideals are an important part of the self, according to Allport. If the wish to reach the ideals was strong enough, you very likely also experienced energy and determination ample to working toward them. Such personally relevant striving is also part of the self for Allport. And finally, some of you may have been aware at the time of the deep way in which the ideals and striving came out of the most personal, not necessarily even expressed, sense of who and what you are. These senses of self are also relevant. I shall certainly have to go over the aspects of self more formally, but for the moment it will be sufficient if you get some intuitive sense of the meaning of propriate functioning. Such functioning impells the person toward the future, according to Allport, whereas opportunistic functioning is experienced as little more than the placation of biological forces within one that are tangential to the important things in life.

The specific propriate and opportunistic functions. As Allport (1955, 1961) says so little about the opportunistic functions, it will be easiest to consider them first. About all there is to point out concerning their content is that he is rather willing to accept whatever biological needs other psychologists and physiologists have uncovered. Needs for food, water, air, the avoidance of pain—all may be considered relevant. If there is any defining attribute of the class of needs indicating opportunistic functioning, it is that they aim toward the reduction of physiological tension. Actually, this is why Allport considers the functioning involved opportunistic in nature. To be motivated by a welling up of tension and discomfort within you such that your actions are aimed at removing the tension, regardless of whatever that must mean you actually do, is opportunistic because it does not involve such psychological considerations as values and principles in the determination of behavior. However useful such functioning may be in ensuring physical survival, it is opportunistic from the psychological point of view because, in Allport's (see Maddi, 1963; Maddi & Costa, 1972) view, it does not reflect psychological considerations.

Allport's (1955, 1961) stance makes abundantly clear that the important thing in life is propriate functioning. It is the *self* that defines the lines along which life is meaningfully led, and the self has little to do with questions of biological survival. One can die physically all the while one is leading a meaningful life, and indeed, many of the martyrs did just this. The meaningfulness of life is a psychological consideration, and one cannot derive the psychological level of understanding from the biological one. In this position, Allport is completely opposed to Freud and other instinct theorists. And, as you will have begun to see, his view of propriate functioning is not even as organismically or biologically based as is the core tendency of actualization theorists. His is basically a perfection position.

As you can imagine from his emphasis as presented above, Allport has a great deal to say about the content, or core characteristics, of propriate functioning. Of all theorists who consider the self important, Allport is distinguished in his detailed elaboration of just what he takes that aspect of personality to include. Allport feels that such detailed specification of the contents of self is important not only because your readers can thereby be more sure of what you mean, but more specifically because the concept of self has been the source of such misunderstanding and bitterness among psychologists in previous years. The concept of self has seemed to many to be nothing more than a slightly dressed-up version of the old notion of soul, with all attendant implications of divine implantation and independence of the mortal laws governing organismic functioning. Allport's heroic attempt to specify precisely what comprises the self is not simply an effort after clarity, but is also an expression of the view that this concept need not be mysterious or supernatural. Rather, it is a collection of executive functions, clearly within the purview of psychology.

The first step for Allport in the specification of the content of self is to assume that it includes only those aspects of experience that seem essential, warm, and of central importance to the person. Thus, his definition of self is phenomenological, or follows what the person himself believes to be of significance. The second definitional step for Allport is to detail a set of functions of the self that are common to all sound adults. In what was perhaps a too extreme attempt to demonstrate the unmysterious nature of the self, Allport (1955, pp. 41–56) first considered the proprium to be a set of ongoing functions without underlying structure. More recently, however, he (Allport, 1961, pp. 110–138) seemed ready to recognize that function necessarily implies structure, even though his emphasis was still on function. In any event, the functions of the proprium are *sense of body, self-identity, self-esteem, self-extension, rational coping, self-image,* and *propriate striving.*

You can easily demonstrate the pervasiveness and importance of your sense of your body, even though it is usually automatic and outside the focus of attention, by performing a little exercise suggested by Allport. Think of spitting saliva into a glass and then drinking it down. You are likely to feel revolted, even though you swallow the saliva in your mouth all the time. The saliva in your mouth is part of your sense of body, whereas the same saliva outside the confines of your body becomes a foreign thing. In less-striking fashion, pain, injuries, and the like, can make you aware of the sense of body that is always operating on the fringe of attention. Allport contends that bodily sense is a factor in the life decisions that you reach, though in truth, it is the most rudimentary of the propriate functions.

Whereas you have a sense of your body primarily through kinesthetic, proprioceptive, and tactual cues, the propriate function of self-identity is the set of ideas you use to define yourself. You may conceive yourself to be a lawyer, or a generous person, or a great lover, but whatever the set of ideas about yourself, the ones that comprise self-identity are those that are most central and important to you. Self-esteem, another propriate function, is closely related to self-identity. Self-esteem defines the bases upon which you feel worthwhile. These bases will be ideas of self, much like those comprising self-identity, with the added feature of giving more precise guidelines for living. If you have a certain self-identity, then you will try to function consistently with that identity. But functioning inconsistently with the identity will not necessarily be a source of pain. Once you begin to have ideas about yourself that are tied to your worthiness, however, you have much fewer degrees of freedom for your behavior.

By including self-extension in the propriate functions, Allport gives recognition to the importance of things, people, and events that are actually different from ourselves, but are nonetheless defined by us as central to our existence. It is as if we extend ourselves, or at least our definition of self, so as to include other aspects of the world. So for a particular person, his car, wife, daughter, and stamp collection may, for all intents and purposes, be parts of his self. This means more than that these things are important in any usual way or sense. They are parts of his self when he sees them as really indistinguishable from, and governed by the same laws as he, and when, therefore, their fate and his fate are the same. So a dent to the fender of the car is in some sense as painful as would be a disfigurement of his own face; his daughter's failing grade in school injures his own self-esteem; and his wife's unfaithfulness is the same as if he had betrayed his own principles.

By including rational coping as a propriate function, Allport means to indicate the centrality for the person of thinking about, and dealing with, problems and tasks in a reasoned, logical way. Allport is contending that people actually define themselves as rational beings, and that this aspect of self-definition is very important in understanding the kinds of lives they lead. If you defined yourself as irrational, you would indeed be a very different, and for Allport, opportunistic person.

For Allport, the propriate functions, or core characteristics of personality, do not operate independently. Rather, they intermingle, producing a life expressive of the core tendency of personality, called propriate functioning. As you can tell from the core characteristics, propriate functioning involves the capacity to work hard for what you want, with what you want defined by a set of values and principles, and by a less-abstract, though pervasive, sense of who you are, all this guided by a deep commitment to rationality. Thus, propriate functioning is *proactive, future-oriented* and *psychological.*

In calling propriate functioning proactive, Allport means to contrast it with reactive functioning, which is opportunistic according to him. In distinguishing proactive behavior, Allport (see Maddi, 1963; Maddi & Costa, 1972) makes the point that psychology has a painfully ready tendency to deal only with behavior that is a response to some external environmental pressure. Even the fact that behavior goes by the technical name of *response* for the psychologist is indicative that the psychologist believes life to be a reaction to influences external to the person. For Allport, reactive behavior is the least important thing to understand about the functioning of sound, adult human beings. For such people, only behavior having the purpose of satisfying the requirement of biological survival is reactive in nature. Such opportunistic functioning is determined by the biological needs of the organism in conjunction with the features of the external environment that either are frustrating or satisfying of these needs. The person exercises little choice or flexibility or individuality in opportunistic functioning. In contrast, functioning in a manner that is expressive of the proprium or self is proactive because it influences the external environment rather than being influenced by it. When you are expressing your own sense of who you are, your behavior shows choice, flexibility, and individuality, for, after all, your sense of self is not tied to inexorable biological considerations that are at the same time simple and not very different from what characterizes lower animals. The proprium is developed out of the rich store of psychological experience coming through imagination, judgment, social interaction, and familiarity with culture and the history of the human. The aspirations and convictions contained in the proprium lead the person to manipulate the world in such fashion that those aspirations and convictions become realities. To call such behavior reactive misses the extraordinary degree to which the human can be a force influencing his own destiny.

In calling propriate functioning future-oriented, Allport means to contrast it with opportunistic functioning in yet another way. Opportunistic functioning is governed by unchanging biological needs, and hence, is characterized by the development of habits. If you are hungry, you learn the most efficient ways to obtain food from the environment around you, and then, each subsequent time you are hungry, you react in the same way that was efficient before. Opportunistic functioning is past-oriented in the sense that it involves the operation of long-standing habits which have proven fruitful in ensuring biological survival. Each time a biological need is aroused, the person is faced with the task of diminishing a state of tension in order to get back to a relatively tensionless state. According to Allport, propriate functioning is wholly different from this.

The goals of propriate functioning involve bringing about states that have no precise precedent in the person. Think of aspirations, and recognize that they attempt to bring the person to an existential state he has never experienced before, at least for himself. The fact that propriate functioning relies so heavily on imagination as a guide to action means that the person will not be functioning habitually and in keeping with what has happened in the past. In addition, propriate functioning will not be an attempt to return to a past state of lack of tension. Indeed, it will very likely bring tension increase, as the proprium is not necessarily complementary to the biological needs. So a person driven by the propriate ambition to express something in a poem may work long into the night, caring little for the mounting tension of lack of food and physical fatigue. The whole point here is that propriate functioning is aimed at future, previously unexperienced states, in contrast to opportunistic functioning which aims to reestablish "the good old days."

There is little more that needs saying concerning why Allport typifies propriate functioning as psychological in nature. Opportunistic functioning is underlain by the biological givens of the organism. In contrast, propriate functioning has much more to do with ideas, feelings, introspections, and other considerations more properly considered at the psychological rather than biological level of experience. This is not to say that there is no physiological substrate for mentation and emotion. Rather, it is to say that propriate functioning is not understood very well until one adopts the point of view that ideas and feelings are genuine and important determiners of behavior, and that the behavior thus determined is very likely to be different than that determined directly by considerations of biological survival. In this emphasis upon the difference between the psychological and biological aspects of life, Allport comes close to being a conflict, rather than fulfillment theorist. But I think he is more appropriately considered a variant on the fulfillment position, because opportunistic functioning can compliment, as well as oppose, propriate functioning, and because opportunistic functioning is considered to play a negligible role in the life of the sound, human adult.

Among fulfillment theorists, Allport is unique in the explicitness with which he specifies the content of core characteristics. You will remember that actualization theorists gave us little with which to know what is contained in people's inherent capabilities, and Adler did only a little better in providing us with a diagnostic aid—feelings of inferiority— with which we could identify the particular directions the push toward superiority was taking in concrete instances. Allport goes still further with his specification of the content of the propriate functions. Having his statements, we may expect, if the theory is correct, to find a sense of body, self-identity, self-esteem, rational coping, self-extension, and propriate striving in all people. To be sure, these core characteristics may take somewhat different shape in different people as a function of differences in previous experience and even genetic constitution, but nonetheless Allport has been much more explicit and precise concerning the directions life will take than have been other fulfillment theorists.

Certainly, it must be said that the kind of life—proactive, future-oriented, psychological—ensuing from expression of the propriate functions is much the same as that envisioned by other actualization and perfection theorists. These theorists are also similar in emphasis on the self and introspection as factors determining life directions. But if we strain to discern the essential spirit of these theories, keeping in mind the possibility of error due to the insufficient precision of most of them, we arrive at certain differences in emphasis. Of the propriate functions, only sense of body seems very rooted in the inherent nature of the organism. The other propriate functions bear little necessary relation to inherent potentialities. Add to this the fact that Allport stresses aspirations (self-image), and working hard to reach them (propriate striving), and it becomes clear that his position is closer to the perfection theorists, Adler and White, than it is to the actualization theorists. Of course, it goes without saying that Allport's position is diametrically opposed to that of Freud. The propriate functions are noninstinctual, conscious, rational processes whereby life is led in an ever-changing way that shows proaction, future-orientation, and choice. In contrast, Freud saw unconscious, inexorable, unchanging, biological instincts as the only real determiners of life.

A final point needs to be made here. Fulfillment theorists generally stress individuality. You will recall I even suggested that the vagueness as to content of core characteristics seen in actualization theorists, and the emphasis on free will in Adler, are partly due to reticence to infringe upon the assumed freedom to be an individual. Now of all fulfillment theorists, Allport has traditionally been the most adamant supporter of the doctrine of individuality. Indeed, he said early in his career (Allport, 1937) that each person is so unique that the concepts used to describe him cannot even be employed on anyone else. While he more recently adopted a less severe version of this position (Allport, 1962), it is still true that he emphasizes individuality to an extraordinary degree. In Chapter 7 on peripheral characteristics of personality, you will see this emphasis more clearly. Actually, Allport has been severely criticized by many other psychologists for having such an extreme notion of individuality that no generalizations from person to person seem possible. But with the publication of his notion of the proprium, Allport clearly took a long step away from his previous position. Whether this was because he was criticized is immaterial. What you should recognize is that the propriate functions appear in all persons, and therefore, they define the commonality among people.

Developmental course of propriate and opportunistic functions. Allport (1955) believes that at the beginning of life, the person is mainly a biological organism, with the psychological dimension of life developing gradually. Initially, then, man's functioning is primarily opportunistic, with all the indications of reactivity and past-orientation. The infant has little personality, his opportunistic behavior being determined by ongoing chemical processes and environmental pressures. At first, the infant can only express discomfort in rather reflexive ways when strong viscerogenic drives exist, and functions according to the principle of tension reduction alone. During this early period, the infant is extremely dependent upon others, particularly his mother, for nurturance and affection.

For Allport (1955), what the child's future life will be like depends in significant measure on whether or not he gets the nurturance and affection. If he does, then the preconditions for the development of a gradually more differentiated and personally integrated life-style or personality are met. With enough security, the kernels of selfhood begin to develop near the end of the first year of life. The first signs of consciousness take the form of recognizable experience of the body (bodily sense). The second and third years see the beginnings of self-identity and then self-image, and from 6 to 12, the rational coping qualities of the proprium become apparent. In adolescence, propriate striving is in increasing evidence. Although the various propriate functions begin their development at different ages, they all act interdependently by the time adulthood is reached.

As the propriate functions are ever more richly and vigorously expressed, they lead to the development of a gradually increasing set of peripheral characteristics of personality. Allport calls these peripheral characteristics *personal dispositions,* and means to refer with the term to concrete, readily expressed and observed consistencies in people such as gregariousness or honesty. But I will not consider personal dispositions until Chapter 7. Just recognize now that as the proprium develops, undifferentiated, reactive, opportunistic behavior concerned with reducing tension caused by survival needs recedes in importance as a determinant of behavior, being replaced by propriate functioning, which involves increases in tension, is proactive, and leads to greater and greater subtlety and awareness.

According to Allport (1961), the infant begins as a relatively undifferentiated organism, reacting more or less as a totality. As the proprium develops, the person becomes more and more differentiated, through the accrual of an increasing number of personal dispositions. With even more experience and development, ever more embracing bases for integrating all the differentiated parts are achieved. In short, Allport sees development as the simultaneous increase in psychological differentiation and integration. He calls this *psychological growth* (see Maddi, 1963; Maddi & Costa, 1972). The differentiation is seen in the set of personal dispositions, a matter to be discussed later. The integration is seen in what Allport calls *psychological maturity*. The aspects of psychological maturity he recognizes suggest that they are the structural or stable resultants of a history of expression of the propriate functions. The aspects of maturity are (1) specific, enduring extensions of the self, (2) dependable techniques for warm relating to others (such as tolerance), (3) stable emotional security or self-acceptance, (4) habits of realistic perception, (5) skills and problem-centeredness, (6) established self-objectification in the form of insight and humor, and (7) a unifying philosophy of life including particular value orientation, differentiated religious sentiment, and a personalized conscience. The more vigorous is the expression of propriate functions, the greater the likelihood of developing all aspects of psychological maturity in adulthood. These aspects can serve an integrative function in the personality because, as you can see, they deal with general questions relating to the meaning and value of life, questions concerning every man. It is these characteristics of maturity that permit organization of the personal dispositions, which are, of course, much more concrete, habitual orientations toward life. Clearly, psychological maturity is a state characterized by tension-increasing, perfection-oriented behavior. Such behavior is not defensive, according to Allport (1955). In these emphases, Allport is very like the other fulfillment theorists.

The preceding paragraphs depict the course of development when the infant's early dependency has been warmly met. But if succorance and affection are not readily available, the child may react with signs of insecurity, initially including aggression and demandingness, and later including jealousy and egotism. Vigorous development of propriate functioning will be jeopardized, the individual remaining relatively undifferentiated and deficient in integrative characteristics of maturity. Tension reduction will remain an important aim. Such an adult would show evidence of defensiveness, with attendant lack of awareness of himself. Allport would consider such a person mentally ill, though he is uninterested enough in the matter to give it no further consideration.

In the specification of the developmental course of propriate and opportunistic functions, Allport is once again more explicit and more complete than other fulfillment theorists. And once again, if I am not mistaken, he is closer in spirit to the perfection than to the actualization theorists. The actualization theorists would probably be uneasy with Allport's strong emphasis on a structure to the self, in the form of values, principles, and conscience, that is rather stable and serves an integrative function by ordering and rendering meaningful more concrete experiences. In contrast, actualization theorists see the self-concept as a flexible entity, as something in process of continual change, and as much less vividly conscious. Allport's view of psychological maturity might seem to actualization theorists to stand in the way of real openness to experience.

Fromm's position

Erich Fromm was born in Frankfurt, Germany in 1900, and studied psychology and sociology in his college years. He received a Ph.D. from the University of Heidelberg in 1922, after which he received training in psychoanalysis in Munich and Berlin. In 1933 he came to the United States as a lecturer at the Chicago Psychoanalytic Institute, and subsequently entered private practice in New York City. Still later in his career, he taught at a number of universities and institutes in this country, finally leaving to head the Mexican Psychoanalytic Institute in Mexico City. In recent years Fromm not only continued to write but also trained many students in his psychotherapeutic techniques and theorizing.

Fromm's intriguing viewpoint unfortunately includes elements of the conflict model, and of both actualization and perfection versions of the fulfillment model. As you can see from where I have placed him in this chapter, I believe the perfection aspects of his position to be paramount. In what follows, I hope the reasons for this decision will become clear to you. By now in your reading of this chapter, nothing in Fromm's theory will seem totally surprising and hence my treatment will be brief.

To begin at the beginning, you should know that Fromm (1947) distinguishes between *animal nature* and *human nature*. Animal nature is roughly defined by biochemical and physiological bases and mechanisms for physical survival. While the human certainly has an animal nature, he is the only organism possessing a human nature as well. This fact has, according to Fromm, rendered the human's animal nature the least important part of him. Even without my discussing the specific content of human nature, you should recognize the similarity between Fromm, Allport, and Maslow. Fromm is especially close to Allport, for both de-emphasize the animal nature or opportunistic functioning in the human, considering his human nature or propriate functioning so much more characteristic. Indeed, the only really accurate rendition of a core tendency for Fromm would be *the attempt to fulfill one's human nature*. Implied in his theory may be another core tendency concerning the satisfaction of one's animal nature, but nowhere does Fromm emphasize this. Even when a person shrinks from vigorous expression of human nature, he is best characterized in Fromm's terms as avoiding humanness rather than embracing creatureness. The human being can never really become a creature, simply because he happens to possess biological survival needs. Obviously, it is because of this emphasis upon pursuing one's human nature that I have classed Fromm a fulfillment theorist.

Probably, he should be considered a variant on this position, as he does assume an animal nature along with the human nature. But it is not without uneasiness that I designated him a fulfillment theorist, for in at least one place in his writings (Fromm, 1947, p. 41), he specifically suggests that it is the antagonism between the person's human and animal natures that provides the impetus to development and living. This is clearly a conflict statement. Happily, it is a rare occurrence in his writings, which generally stress the pursuit of humanness to an intense degree, with the fact of the person's animal nature barely acknowledged, and definitely lost in the shuffle. Taking all of Fromm's writings into account, it is not even clear that one is justified in proposing a core tendency referring to the animal nature. Fromm's position most resembles that of Allport, as I have already indicated.

In order to understand Fromm's position more fully, and determine whether it is properly considered an actualization or perfection version of the fulfillment model, we must scrutinize the proposed content of human nature. Fortunately, Fromm has a good deal to say about what human nature entails, and in this, achieves a degree of theoretical precision like that of Allport and superior to that of the actualization theorists. Fromm (1947) starts by saying that organisms whose nature is primarily animal are one with the world of nature. There is no sharp separation between themselves, other organisms, and the environment around them. They have no experience of separateness.

But human nature is unique under the sun, and it therefore leads to extraordinary potentialities and problems. Perhaps the most basic characteristic of human nature is the ability to know itself and the things that are different from it. Once an organism is endowed with such knowledge, it is inevitably separate from nature and other organisms. This separateness looked at positively is freedom, and looked at negatively is alienation (Fromm, 1941). It is the freedom and independence stemming from the person's human nature that can lead him to great heights of creative accomplishment. It is fear of the loneliness and isolation involved in acting on his human nature that often leads persons to forego their birthright of freedom. The human can never function as if his nature were solely animal, but he can approach this by shrinking from the freedom which could come through acting vigorously on his human nature. But this shrinking is not straight-forward acting on an animal nature, and hence, is never as satisfactory as the simple life of animals, and is clearly inferior to the vigorous expression of humanness. This shrinking from freedom is what amounts to conformity on the social level, and what Allport would call reactive behavior on the individual level. It is a defensive way of life, though Fromm does not discuss defense in any systematic manner. In contrast, acting on one's human nature leads to productiveness, and a way of life that is not defensive. Fromm's emphasis upon freedom, productiveness, individuality, and lack of defense as expressions of the highest form of living are thoroughly consistent with other fulfillment theories. But conflict positions like that of Freud also stress productiveness in the highest form of living, and you may wonder, therefore, whether Fromm is really making a fulfillment statement. He is, because for him productiveness is not cast in the light of adjustment to society, as it is in conflict theories. A productive person would only be adjusted to society, according to Fromm (1955), if the society were constructive or sane. If it were not, the productive person would not be adjusted—only the conformist, shrinking from his human nature, would be.

True to the fulfillment model, Fromm does not assume a basic antagonism between individual and society. What he does stress is that the human's nature will achieve expression in the ways that are effective and possible given the societal, cultural climate in which he exists. As in other fulfillment positions, it is true of Fromm that he believes that when human nature is pervertedly expressed (in the shrinking from freedom leading to conformity and reactivity) the blame is society's. Authoritarian, dictatorial, monolithic, punitive societies increase the likelihood that their members will fall short of vigorous humanness. But society need not be coercive, so when it is, Fromm (1955) is quick to condemn it as pathological. Fromm is often considered a social psychological theorist by personologists of psychoanalytic persuasion. In a way, this is a mistake. Actually, Freud more than Fromm emphasized the importance of society by assuming it to be a force that cannot be avoided, transcended, or changed. Fromm, like all fulfillment theorists, gives primary importance to the full expression of the individual and cares little for adjustment to society. The only sense in which it is reasonable to consider Fromm a social psychological theorist is that he has been consistently a critic of past and contemporary societies, setting himself the task of clarifying how pathological societies pervert human nature. In this, he is similar to, though perhaps more systematic than, other fulfillment theorists.

Fromm has specified the content of human nature even more concretely than what has been discussed above. The core characteristics associated with the core tendency are the *needs for relatedness, transcendence, rootedness, identity,* and *frame of reference.* The need for relatedness stems from the stark fact that the human, in becoming man, has been torn from the animal's primary union with nature. In place of this unthinking, simple merging with nature, the human must use his reason and imagination to create his own relations with nature and other people. The most satisfying relationships are those based on productive love, which always implies mutuality, generosity, and respect. The need for transcendence is the motivational basis for proactive functioning. It is the urge to become a productive individual rather than merely a creature. The need for rootedness is apparently very similar to the need for relatedness. Fromm says that it is part of human nature to seek roots in the world, and that the most satisfying roots are those based on a feeling of brotherliness with others. The person's need for a personal identity is a bit similar to his need for transcendence, since both needs lead in the direction of individuality. In striving for an identity, the most satisfying procedure is to rely on your talents, and productive capabilities. Failing that, identity of a less-satisfying sort can be achieved through identification with other people or ideas. Finally, a person needs to have a frame of reference, a stable and consistent way of perceiving and comprehending the world. Once you get down to this level of concreteness concerning the content of human nature, the tension-increasing nature of its pursuit becomes apparent. Again Fromm emerges as a fulfillment theorist.

The similarities between Fromm's needs and Allport's propriate functions should not have escaped your attention. The need for transcendence is like propriate striving, the need for rootedness is like self-extension, the need for personal identity is like self-identity and self-esteem, and the need for a frame of reference is like the rational coping out of which develops a philosophy of life. The similarities in content between the core characteristics in these two positions is one piece of evidence inclining me to the belief that Fromm's position is best considered a perfection rather than actualization theory. The human, according to Fromm, seems to be striving toward an ideal conceptualization to the perfect life, rather than merely expressing his inherent capabilities in an unselfconscious fashion. To be sure, perfection is defined in terms of what it is in human nature to be. But for any given person this nature is not merely the sum total of his particular strengths and weaknesses; the conceptualization of human nature is more universal than that. Fromm believes that it is within the person's power to perfect himself, but the way to perfection is not simply that of expressing inherited strengths. The person must practice to be human in order to get good at it. This will frequently involve overcoming inherent weaknesses. This emphasis is clearly seen in Fromm's (1956) book, *The Art of Loving*, in which is described a set of exercises whereby one can practice loving, and with persistence, become capable in that regard. In contrast, actualization theorists are likely to believe that adequate loving and such obviously constructive things come quite naturally to the undefensive person. Fromm seems more a perfection theorist than anything else.

Existential psychology

There has been sharply increased interest of late in existentialism. This interest has shown itself over a broad spectrum of society, and not only includes personologists and psychotherapists, but also professionals of every stripe, political activists, clergymen, students, and the man on the street. This has happened even though the body of thought commonly labeled existentialism is extremely amorphous, shifting in emphases from country to country, continent to continent, and even individual theorist to individual theorist. It seems to me that much of existential thought really constitutes a set of attitudes for living, a manifesto more than a systematic theory of personality. On these grounds, existentialism could have been omitted from this book. But there is simply too much interest in it, and its emphases are too unique, for me to have done that with any sense of satisfaction.

What I shall try to do is select the threads in existential thought that seem most rigorous and relevant to personality theory. Because of this, what follows will not concern the theorizing of any one person, but rather a plurality. I shall not refer much to the philosophical founders of existentialism, Kierkegaard and Heidegger, favoring instead those of their followers who have attempted to translate their thinking into statements about personality. Foremost among these are Europeans, Ludwig Binswanger (born in Kreuzlingen, Switzerland in 1881; died in the same place in 1966), Medard Boss (born in St. Gallen, Switzerland in 1903; has resided in Zurich for most of his life), and Victor Frankl (born in Vienna in 1905, where he still lives). Major figures who have worked in the United States are Rollo May (born in New York City in 1909, and lives there still), and Paul Tillich (born in Starzeddel, Kreis Guben, Prussia in 1886; died in Chicago in 1965). But it will also be necessary to refer to work by other existential psychologists.

Binswanger, Boss, and Frankl all knew Freud, and were heavily influenced by his thinking early in their careers. But the major intellectual influences on them have been Kierkegaard and Heidegger. It is not inaccurate to characterize Binswanger, Boss, and Frankl as having attempted to translate Heidegger's philosophical stance into a viable approach to psychotherapy. All physicians, Binswanger served for many years as chief medical director (a post his father held before him) of the Bellevue Sanatorium in Kreuzlingen, Boss was professor in the medical school of the University of Zurich as well as director of the institute of Daseinsanalytic Therapy, and Frankl is professor in the medical school of the University of Vienna and director of the Neurological Polyclinic there. Tillich's career was as a theologian, an interpreter of Christianity in our modern times of spiritual emptiness. He taught at such prominent schools as Harvard University and the University of Chicago, and had an enormous effect upon modern religious theory, to say nothing of psychology. May is a psychologist, and serves as a training therapist at a distinguished center for psychotherapy, the William Alanson White Institute in New York City.

It is no mean feat to state a core tendency for existential psychology in a few words. Not only is there the difficulty of many different voices, all using slightly different words, there is also the complication that the words are often poetic, metaphoric, seeming sometimes to have polemic, emotional intent rather than that of intellectual precision. What is clear, however, is the emphasis on being genuine, honest, true, and on making decisions and shouldering responsibility for them. All in all, an apt phrasing on the core tendency might be *to achieve authentic being*. The word being, or existence, or *Dasein* (to use the German) is pregnant with meaning for the existentialist. It does not refer to some passive creatureness, though it partially includes this. Rather, it signifies the special quality of existing characteristic of humans, a quality that heavily involves mentality, intelligence, and awareness. The adjective authentic is meant to carry some of these connotations, and also to indicate the emphasis of existential psychology on honesty, a stance difficult to manage due to the inherently frightening and demanding nature of life. More often than not, according to existentialists, people shrink from authenticity.

In order to gain an oversimplified but nonetheless relevant intuition concerning what it means to achieve authentic being, search your memory for times when you understood and accepted yourself most, when you were aware of your vanities, sentimentalities, follies, weaknesses, and were somehow able in spite of this to assert the importance of your life and anticipate with vigor the experiences you might have in the future, even though you could not entirely predict or control them and this frightened you. As you will see in what follows, the main emphases of existential psychology are expressed in such experiences.

Core characteristics.   In writing this, I am very much aware that my attempt to render the existential viewpoint as systematic theory will do violence to the sensibilities of existentialists as to what is important. They are steeped in the phenomenological approach, which is the attempt to understand in no other terms than immediate, vividly appreciated, but unanalyzed sensory experience. In a sense, what I have been calling intuitive understanding is considered by many existentialists as the only important psychological knowledge. Once you commit yourself to a phenomenological approach, it follows fairly readily that you will consider one person's reality to differ from that of his neighbor, for each of them is likely to perceive things differently. Thus, the existentialist's aversion to formal, abstract theorizing is two-pronged. Intuition is the antithesis of abstraction, and different persons have different intuitions.

This antitheoretical stance seems strongest among European existentialists. For example, Hall and Lindzey (1970, p. 580) quote a personal communication from Boss to the effect that:

> I can only hope that existential psychology will never develop into a theory in its modern meaning of the natural sciences. All that existential psychology can contribute to psychology is to teach the scientists to remain with the experienced and experienceable facts and phenomena, to let these phenomena tell the scientists their meaning and their references,

and so do the encountered objects justice—in short, becoming more "objective" again.

Let me pose a conundrum which may help here. Is that object I am sitting on a mass of relatively slow-moving atomic particles, a construction of shaped and polished woods having low brittleness and therefore able to carry weight, or a chair? Of course, it is all three, and any existentialist would agree. But in human terms, the existentialist would hasten to add, it is a chair, nothing else, except perhaps colors and textures readily perceived with the senses. To talk of atomic particles, and even of brittleness, is to theorize in the manner of natural sciences.

Presumably, Boss would accept theorizing in some human fashion. But once you have called a chair a chair, and blue blue, about all you can do without becoming abstract and analytical is to recognize that chairs may differ in shape and colors in intensity. Boss and other European existentialists seem to accept this sort of thing as the natural limitation of theorizing if it is to remain true to the human experience of things. But American existentialists are less sure, being somewhat more willing to theorize about antecedents to the phenomenal experience (e.g., what learning experiences condition the perception of something as a chair?). And even the Europeans are not quite consistent, for it they were, it would be rather impossible to define core characteristics of personality. Yet it is the Europeans who have gone furthest in formulating them. As you will see, even though these core characteristics adhere strictly to phenomenological givens, they nonetheless imply capabilities of the human organism. As such, a statement on man's nature can be derived from them; a statement which, like all others, is abstract and essentialistic. Although the vivid appreciation of immediate sensory experience is all the more important because so often excluded from a role in everyday life, Boss does seem to be fighting a losing battle in insisting that existentialism avoid formalization. Formalization does inevitably mean abstracting, but without it the transition from mere attitudes to working theories probably cannot be made.

Being-in-the-world (Binswanger, 1963; Boss, 1963) is a basic core characteristic intended to emphasize the unity of person and environment. The emphasis is not merely one of interaction between the person and his environment, as in Sullivan's thinking. Rather, person and environment are essentially one and the same. This is because both being and world are human creations, so interdependent as to be inseparable. Of course the human body and the things in our environment have physical reality—shape, size, weight. But these physical properties are irrelevant for the existentialist. When he speaks of being, he emphasizes the sum total of intuitive sensory experiences, combined with memories, fantasies, and anticipations. When he speaks of world, he emphasizes the environment a person creates for himself through exercizing the capacities producing being, and the expression of that being in action. Both being and world are intensely personal. Being is mentality considering our individual selves, and world is mentality considering our surroundings.

In order to understand a person's existence, the manner in which being and world merge must be appreciated. In explicating being-in-the-world, May (1958, pp. 59–60) says:

> *World is the structure of meaningful relationships in which a person exists and in the design of which he participates.* Thus world includes the past events which condition my existence and all the vast variety of deterministic influences which operate upon me. But it is these *as I relate to them*, am aware of them, carry them with me, molding, inevitably forming, building them in every minute of relating. For to be aware of one's world means at the same time to be designing it.

It is instructive to contemplate his (May, 1958, pp. 41–42) words concerning being, for they are complementary to those about world, and also imply something about human nature:

> The full meaning of the term "human being" will be clearer if the reader will keep in mind that "being" is a participle, a verb form implying thart someone is in the process of *being something*. It is unfortunate that, when used as a general noun in English, the term "being" connotes a static substance, and when used as a particular noun such as *a* being, it is usually assumed to refer to an entity, say, such as a soldier to be counted as a unit. Rather "being" should be understood, when used as a general noun, to mean *potentia*, the source of potentiality; "being" is the potentiality by which the acorn becomes the oak or each of us becomes what he truly is. And when used in a particular sense, such as *a* human being, it always has the dynamic connotation of someone in process, the person being something. Perhaps, therefore, *becoming* connotes more accurately the meaning of the term in this country. We can understand another human being only as we see what he is moving toward, what he is becoming; and we can know ourselves only as we "project our *potentia* in action." The significant tense for human beings is thus the *future*—that is to say, the critical question is what I am pointing toward, becoming, what I will be in the immediate future.
>
> Thus, being in the human sense is not given once and for all. It does not unfold automatically as the oak tree does from the acorn. For an intrinsic and inseparable element in being human is self-consciousness. Man . . . is the particular being who has to be aware of himself, be responsible for himself, if he is to become himself. He also is that particular being who knows that at some future moment he will not be; he is the being who is always in a dialectical relation with non-being, death. And he not only knows he will sometime not be, but he can, in his own choices, slough off and forfeit his being.

This passage clearly identifies self or being as process rather than as some static, unchanging content, and in that sense is reminiscent of the actualization fulfillment model as epitomized in Rogers. But the crucial difference is that the process of becoming described by May is not a natural one in the sense of being easy or linking humans with lower animals. May could never, as did Rogers, give as an example of becoming a sea-weed growing and flourishing though pounded incessantly by waves. Seaweeds do not have mentality, self-consciousness and therefore never choose. For May and other existentialists, being is so essentially a matter of choice that humans can even choose against it by commiting suicide, by precipitating nonbeing. When May and other existentialists refer to fulfilling one's potentialities they mean something closer to Fromm and other perfection fulfillment theorists than to the actualization fulfillment position. Achieving one's potentialities involves, for May, a painful and continual process of soul-searching and decisions, in the face of doubt and loneliness. This is more a matter of striving to do the best one can than indulging a genetic birthright. Much of what follows will lend additional evidence for this interpretation.

But what are these potentialities that are expressed in the process of authentic being? Like actualization fulfillment theorists, existentialists are far from clear on this matter. Probably, such theorizing would be too abstract and essentialistic for their phenomenologically conditioned tastes. But there are some clues available. One is that these potentialities are expressed in a process, rather than in something fixed once and for all. The biggest clue involves the distinctions made between three broad modes of being-in-the-world. These are the *Umwelt, Mitwelt,* and *Eigenwelt,* to use the original German (Binswanger, 1963; Boss, 1963; Frankl, 1960; May, 1958). Umwelt literally means the world around you, but has the connotation of the biological and physical world. Mitwelt, or with-world, refers to the world of persons, of one's fellowman. Eigenwelt means own-world, and refers to the internal dialogue of relationship to oneself. It is important to recognize that in all three modes, the operation of mind, awareness, is assumed. So the Umwelt is not some objective consideration of the biological and physical characteristics determining a person's relationship to the world around him. Rather, it concerns *his construal* of the biological and physical tie between himself and the world. So too with the Mitwelt, which refers to a person's perceptions of and orientations toward his interactions with others and social institutions. It is hardly necessary to point out this operation of self-consciousness in the case of the Eigenwelt, for it cannot be defined at all unless it includes a consciousness that can consider itself an object.

It is best to interpret these three modes of being as general frames of reference. In any being-in-the-world, there will have to be some general orientation to biological, social, and personal experiences. But the precise nature of these three orientations can shift considerably, and differ from person to person. An example of the difficulties ensuing from a narrower interpretation of the three modes, which ascribes to them some content considered necessary because of their biological, social, and personal nature can be found in Keen's (1970) recent explication of existential thought. He presents the three modes of being as being-in-the-world, being-for-others, and being-for-oneself. For him, being-in-the-world involves natural, rather unreflective experiencing, while being-for-others adopts external, social criteria for functioning, and being-for-oneself involves self-conscious reflection upon one's existence. Although these distinctions seem similar to those presented previously, they are quite different in their emphases. Being-for-others has the negative emphasis of being subjugated to convention that is not the defining characteristic of Mitwelt. One's Mitwelt may involve conventionality, but it might also involve intimacy and even an unconventional social commitment. In Keen's concepts, there is an implied antagonism between being-in-the-world and being-for-oneself, in that the former is easy and natural and the latter incessantly introspective. Small wonder that he seems to favor being-in-the-world as the mode of existence leading to the good life. This, of course, leads to an inconsistency in spirit, for his being-for-oneself carries the major possibility for the considered, rational life so important to existentialists, and is clearly more uniquely human than is his being-in-the-world. And yet, it is the latter that is considered most advantageous.

It is closer to the original meaning of Binswanger and Boss, who are primarily responsible for the three modes of being, to consider Umwelt, Mitwelt, and Eigenwelt to refer to biological, social, and personal experiencing, leaving aside for additional consideration what is good and bad about the person's commitment in each mode. From this position, it is possible to discern a meaning for the human potentialities referred to by May. Following Frankl's (1960) lead, Maddi (1967, 1970) has assumed that human nature is comprised of biological, social, and psychological needs. The biological needs include those for food, water, and air, and refer to functions that must be expressed if the person is to survive physically. The social needs include those for contact and communication, the frustration of which leads to intense loneliness and loss of sense of self. The psychological needs are considered to be for symbolization (or classification), imagination, and judgment. Although the three sets of needs are reminiscent of Maslow's biological, security, and cognitive-understanding (or self-actualization) needs, Maddi does not propose them as organized into a hierarchy.

Of the three sets of needs, it is the psychological ones that are the least usual to assume, and that carry the meat of the existential emphasis. The process of symbolizing or classifying involves abstracting from the specifics of an experience that which is general enough to be considered similar to other experiences. When you symbolize, the end results are categories with which to recognize and order experiences. Because you literally will not recognize some experience for which you have no category, it can be said that the more categories that exist in your cognitive mass, the greater will be the meaningfulness of experience for you. Imagining involves combining and recombining categories, memories, and ideas in a manner that does not require input from the external world. According to Maddi, the aim of imagining is change, in the sense that the imagined state is invariably thought of as more interesting or advantageous than present actualities. With every change that takes place (whether in thought or action), the amount of information available is increased. Thus, meaning, in the sense of amount of information, is greater the more active the imagination. Finally, judgment involves evaluating experience in a manner that leads either to considering it good or bad (moral judgment), or pleasant or unpleasant (preferential judgment). The values and preferences resulting from the judgmental process also increase meaning by giving the person a personal basis for orienting toward experience.

What Maddi is saying is that the human needs to symbolize, imagine, and judge in order to feel satisfied and avoid frustration because that is the nature of his organism. One argument he offers (Maddi, 1970) for assuming psychological needs to be core characteristics is the universality of symbolization, imagination, and judgment. Once you recognize that words are symbols, it becomes apparent that thought and communication, if not perception as well, would be impossible without symbolization. That every society ever studied has a mythology suggests the universality of imagining on a grand scale. And Osgood (1962) indicates that the tendency to make evaluations was universal in all the societies and culture areas he studied. A supplementary argument based on evolutionary theory can be formulated (Maddi, 1970). After all, the human's mind is the ultimate wonder of evolution, winning for him a preeminent place among the creatures even though he is puny and frail physically. The strength of that mind is that it can take in, order, evaluate, and anticipate vast amounts of information, thence acting effectively. Once such a marvelous nervous system evolved, it could hardly lie fallow. Its requirement is that it perform the operations for which it was designed. There is some research (Riesen, 1961) to indicate that the use of neural structures is necessary in infancy if they are to develop normally. The human needs to symbolize, imagine, and judge because that is what his central nervous system is designed to do. And since symbolizing, imagining, and judging all create meaning, it would seem that the search for meaning—note that this is a process, not an end point—is an inherent, unlearned aspect of human nature.

Let us return now to all three sets of core characteristics, namely, the biological, social, and psychological needs. The mere existence of neither biological nor social needs differentiates the human from lower animals. Biological needs reflect metabolic requirements, and in their most straight-forward sense, there is little room for taste and subtlety. Cooked meat tastes better and is more digestible than raw meat, but in the absence of the wherewithal to cook, raw meat will undoubtedly be eaten. Although it may be much nicer and more hygienic to eliminate in a modern toilet, the pants will be fouled sooner than the biological organism damaged. Insofar as our biological needs do not differ from those of lower animals, there is no basis in them for decorum, subtlety, and taste. So too with social needs, which would also seem to exist in lower animals, to judge from the prevalence in even rather primitive species of a rudimentary social structure involving simple social roles. When social needs are most straightforwardly met, it would seem to be by engaging in a wide range of interactions with people. Talking with service personnel, colleagues, acquaintances, friends; dating; going to and having parties, dinners, and lunch meetings are ways to communicate and have contact. Even simply watching people go by or having them around as background will work, as is attested by the ubiquitous sidewalk café in Europe. All these things satisfy the social needs by increasing the number and variety of people interacted with. But another way to meet these needs is to work in depth toward increasing the richness of some few intense relationships. This way involves intimacy and love, in that you come to feel that some other person or persons are very important to you and you to them. You do not wish to keep your mutual experience just on the surface, preferring instead to go progressively deeper, creating new levels of experience all the while. Insofar as our social needs do not differ from those of lower animals, there is no basis in them for intimacy and love.

Working from Maddi's rendition of human nature, let us return to the Umwelt (biological experience), Mitwelt (social experience) and Eigenwelt (personal experience) emphasized by Binswanger and Boss. Maddi would argue that the more vigorous the expression of psychological needs (symbolization, imagination, and judgment) the more will the Umwelt include taste and subtlety and the Mitwelt intimacy and love. And the more vigorous the expression of psychological needs, the more will the Eigenwelt show complexity and individuality. This is because intense symbolization, imagination, and judgment would result in many categories with which to classify experience, many ideas about change, and many values and preferences. Also, the larger the number of these cognitions, the more unusual they would be. This individuality is one criterion of an ideal personality according to existentialists (Binswanger, 1963; Boss, 1963; Frankl, 1960; Maddi, 1970; May, 1958). But you should note that it is uniqueness that is intended in the terminology of individualism, not any stony isolation from people. Indeed, vigorous expression of psychological needs is considered an encouragement toward intimacy and love rather than more superficial forms of socializing.

Once it is assumed that human nature includes biological, social, and psychological needs, it is natural to consider the ideal to be vigorous expression of all three. When this happens, there is a tendency for Umwelt,

Mitwelt, and Eigenwelt to merge, producing a unitary whole. This unitary quality will be apparent not only at any given point in time, but in the manner in which present experience will be tied to the past and the anticipated future. Spatial and temporal unity occurs because the vigorous expression of symbolization, imagination, and judgment tends to order, interpret, and influence biological and social expressions. This unitary quality of being-in-the-world is another criterion of an ideal personality according to existentialists (Binswanger, 1963; Boss, 1963; Frankl, 1960; Keen, 1970; Maddi, 1970; May, 1958).

Thus far, the emphasis has been upon vigorousness of psychological need expression as that which lends humanness to the human being. Actually, it is impossible for a human being to fail entirely to express psychological needs, because they are rooted in the very nature of his central nervous system. But this does not mean that everyone expresses them as vigorously as possible. Maddi (1967, 1970) believes that through developmental failures some persons will learn to make only rudimentary use of symbolization, imagination, and judgment. These persons will have only a few categories for recognition, ideas about change, and values and preferences. In addition, the contents of these cognitions will be common, stereotyped, and conventional. Such conforming persons will resemble lower animals as much as is possible in humans; their Eigenwelt will be simple and conventional, their Umwelt and Mitwelt will show a relative absence of taste, subtlety, intimacy, and love. In addition, Umwelt, Mitwelt, and Eigenwelt will be fragmented rather than unified. Their sense of the present will not be tied to past or future. Though they may feel nagging dissatisfaction with their lives, they will not be able to pull themselves up by their mental bootstraps. Their personalities will be nonideal.

Existential dynamics. The heart of the existential position is its view of directionality in living. Basic to an understanding of what is concretely involved in the core tendency of striving for authentic being is the assumption that everything in life can be profitably depicted as a situation requiring decision or choice. As there is no alternative envisaged to decision making, every moment in life expresses *intentionality* (Boss, 1963; Keen, 1970). Freud too believed that all behavior was motivated, but whereas motivation to him was largely unconscious, to existentialists it is largely conscious. Indeed, it is the human's propensity for consciousness that necessitates formulating his life as a series of decisions or choices. The human is by nature intelligent—a symbolizing, imagining, and judging organism—and he cannot therefore avoid decisions however he might wish for some easier path.

As there is no alternative to decision making for the human, he will lead his life to the fullest if he recognizes and accepts this fact. In order to properly recognize the necessity of continual decision making, it is useful to practice vigorous symbolization, imagination, and judgment, because this will ensure a complex and sophisticated cognitive mass. And rich expression of those psychological processes is certainly an aid in actually making decisions, for such expression underlies the ability to pose problems, consider alternatives and possible outcomes, and then enact plans. Life is a series of decisions whether or not one recognizes it. But life is best led by preparation for and commitment to the decisions that must be faced.

It is in the decision-making process that emotions play an overshadowing role. Whatever the content of a decision, it always takes the form of posing one alternative that pushes the person into the future, the unknown, the unpredictable, and another alternative that pulls the person into the past, the status quo, the familiar. While choosing the future is attractive because of challenge and growth possibilities, it is uncharted and therefore anxiety-provoking. And while choosing the past is attractive because it is comfortable and relaxing, it involves sacrificing the possibility of development and brings with it the guilt of missed opportunity. Existentialists speak of this anxiety and guilt as *ontological* (e.g., May, 1958), or an inevitable part of being. This formulation is reminiscent of Rank who emphasizes the inherent opposition of fear of life and fear of death. But where intrapsychic conflict theorists advocate a compromise which minimizes both fears, existentialists do nothing of the kind. What is ideal for existentialists is to choose the future, and accept ontological anxiety as an unfortunate concomitant of authentic being (Binswanger, 1963; Boss, 1963; Frankl, 1960; May, 1958; Tillich, 1952).

Of course, it is impossible to grow to adulthood without having shrunk from some chances to push forward into one's future, so there will be in any person some accumulated ontological guilt. And this guilt must also be accepted, like the anxiety, for it is a genuine expression of the life one has led. One cannot alleviate this guilt by resolving not to be so hard on oneself, because this would amount to a falsification of the reality of one's life. Such a falsification would corrupt one's being-in-the-world through the denial that by certain choices one has inevitably limited other opportunities. To falsify, to deny ontological guilt, is to forfeit attainment of authentic being.

But merely accepting ontological guilt is not enough. One must also arrange to minimize it by choosing often on the side of realizing future possibilities. One must find some way of persisting in the face of ontological anxiety. Persisting does not mean denying the really frightening nature of moving toward the unknown. To deny ontological anxiety all the while appearing to choose the future is to make a pseudo choice, and to jeopardize attainment of authentic being through lying to oneself (Binswanger, 1963; Boss, 1963; Frankl, 1960; May, 1958; Tillich, 1952). Indeed, much of what existentialists mean by the necessity of taking responsibility for your own life is just this recognition of the hazards of choosing the future, and choosing it nonetheless. You must recognize that through your own commitments you may end in tragedy in order to win the possibility of triumphing. And this is not to say that you will triumph if you do this—you only win the possibility of so doing. In the emphasis on remaining aware of ontological anxiety and guilt, and choosing to optimize the former at the expense of the latter in order to realize one's possibilities, we see vividly why existential psychology is a perfection fulfillment rather than an intrapsychic conflict position. Although existentialism conceives of an inherent conflict between anxiety and guilt, it does not advocate a compromise designed to minimize both. It assumes that only through persisting in the face of anxiety can one win through to a full realization of his potentialities for being.

Before considering the important question of how one can manage to persist in spite of ontological anxiety, it would be well to consider further the precise nature of this emotion. Tillich (1952) has identified three forms of ontological anxiety, namely, fear over human finitude, fear over the necessity of action in the absence of knowledge of outcomes, and fear of meaninglessness. In the first the emphasis is on the sheer terror over the fact, presumably known to the human alone, that he will die, perhaps when he least expects it. The second recognizes that one tries to make decisions in order to bring about goals one cherishes. But there is no guarantee that this outcome will occur, and if one realizes that the decisions are one's own (and could presumably have been made differently, if one had only known), this is very frightening. The final emphasis is upon the ultimate question of what existence is worth, if one not only can but has the responsibility to shape it, but may yet die or end losing all one wanted. This contemplation raises the awful suspicion that life is meaningless, a very disconcerting experience indeed! To these fears, Bugental (1965) adds a fourth, the fear of isolation. This refers to the recognition which is part and parcel of consciousness that you make your own decisions, namely, that you may be rejected by all and end completely alone.

In the face of all this, how comforting it would seem to reject individuality and personal initiative in favor of convention and tradition. If you do not take chances, if you let others be your guide, if you agree at all costs, if you give up these foolish fantasies that life could be better than it is, if you stop trying to reflect on your experience in the vain attempt to understand, if you accept rather than judge, then you will not have to face the anxieties mentioned above. You can have a nice, solid, respectable, happy life, right? Not at all, according to existentialists. If you abnegate the birthright of individuality contained in the psychological needs, you will only gain comfort in the short run, if that. You will become conventional and banal, showing little taste and complexity, and relating to others in only superficial ways. You will have to avoid using your own wits not only in order to remain conventional, but also so that the incredible lie (Keen, 1970) you have perpetrated on yourself can persist. Worse than all that, yours will be an inauthentic being not only in the eyes of serious men, but your own as well. You are, after all, a human being and cannot avoid self-scrutiny entirely, no matter how hard you try. Here and there, a stray thought of beauty, a daydream of love, the observation of someone who seems truly himself, will haunt you. As life goes on, and the lie's inevitable effect of halting development and enthusiasm for life persists, you will wonder at why conventional success and approval do so little to lift your spirits. You will be in the grips of severe ontological guilt. This is what provoked Thoreau to exclaim that "most men lead lives of quiet desperation," and Kierkegaard to warn of "the sickness unto death."

You cannot defend successfully against the necessity of self-reliant decision making, according to existentialists. If you try, all that will happen is that ontological anxiety and guilt, those natural concomitants of living, will get transformed into neurotic, inauthentic forms of themselves. *Neurotic anxiety* heavily involves shame, taking the form of fear that others and yourself will know how frightened you are (Keen, 1970). Because you deny that ontological anxiety is a natural part of living, you try to hide it. But even worse is what happens to ontological guilt, which when accepted, takes the form of dissatisfaction because of specific things you did or did not do, which things stifled opportunities. *Neurotic guilt* is much more devastating, taking the form of condemnation of one's entire being, rather than only particular acts. There is some hope of rectifying particular acts, but little of reclaiming a being comprehensively rejected (Keen, 1970; May, 1958). Suicide is, for existentialists, frequently a response to massive neurotic guilt.

However dreadful is the psychopathology emanating from the avoidance of decision making and growth, this does not change the fact that ontological anxiety, honestly faced, is gravely painful indeed. How can the human hope to face it and have a satisfying life? An early existential answer (Kierkegaard, 1954) was *faith in God*, who made the human mind a godlike thing. Through the exercise of intelligence in decision making, one draws closer to a unity with God after death, this position contends. For modern-day existentialists, faith in God will not be convincing as a basis for persisting in the face of ontological anxiety. A particularly pessimistic contemporary position (Camus, 1955) extolls the strength to go on that is constituted by full appreciation of the *absurdity* of a life in which people search for meaning when there is none to be found. More compelling, it seems to me, is the modern view that what people need is *courage* (Tillich, 1952), or recognition of their true power and dignity among living things. In a sense, the courage to persist is the other side of the coin of ontological anxiety. If you hold on to the sense of power involved in recognizing that it is precisely because the human is so beautifully intelligent as to be able to fashion life rather than be fashioned by it that he can experience anxiety, then the anxiety is bearable. It may seem a bearable burden in exchange for the power to create one's own meaning through symbolizing, imagining, judging, and the actions following therefrom.

This emphasis on ontological anxiety as a sign of freedom and power is why Tillich (1952) considers doubt to be the "god above God." Powerful expression to the idea that ontological anxiety or doubt is actually a sign of ideal functioning is given by Frankl (1960, p. 30) when he says:

> Challenging the meaning of life can . . . never be taken as a manifestation of morbidity or abnormality; it is rather the truest expression of the state of being human, the mark of the most human nature in man. For we can easily imagine highly developed animals or insects—say bees or ants—which in many aspects of their social organization are actually superior to man. But we can never imagine any such creature raising the question of the meaning of its own existence, and thus challenging that existence. It is reserved for man alone to find his very existence questionable, to experience the whole dubiousness of being. More than such faculties as power of speech, conceptual thinking, or walking erect, this factor of doubting the significance of his own existence is what sets man apart from animal.

Nothing so centrally part of human nature as ontological anxiety could ever be defined as psychopathological. And there is considerable dignity in confronting this anxiety, for to do so is to reach a high point of humanity. Only when you have clearly seen the abyss and jumped into it with no assurance of survival can you call yourself a human being. Then, if you survive, shall you be called hero, for you will have created your own life.

Freedom and necessity. A theme running throughout existential theorizing is that through vigorous symbolization, imagination, and judgment, one can achieve freedom. Through his mentality, the person is supposed to create his own world. And yet, there seem to be limits on this freedom, to judge from the frequent referral of existentialists to the necessities or givens of life. These givens are variously called *facticity* (Sartre, 1956), and the *ground* or *thrownness* of existence (Binswanger, 1958). Just what is necessity and what possibility?

Perhaps as much as any personological position, existentialism shows respect for necessities or givens. The major, unassailable given, after all, is that each person will die. Nonbeing is an inherent part of being. But there are other givens as well. If you are born a woman, then menses and the child-bearing function are givens. And there are particular social situations in which necessity abounds. Frankl (1960) is especially eloquent in this regard when he talks of being forceably imprisoned in a concentration camp during World War II. Perhaps it will surprise you a little to find existential psychologists advocating acceptance of givens. For example, Binswanger (1958, p. 340) says "The more stubbornly the human being opposes his being-thrown into his existence . . . the more strongly this thrownness gains in influence." The end result of this is debilitating, in "that a person does not stand autonomously in his world, that he blocks himself off from the ground of his existence, that he does not take his existence upon himself but trusts himself to alien powers, that he makes alien powers 'responsible' for his fate instead of himself" (Binswanger, 1963, p. 290). In other words, accepting the limits set upon the possibilities of your existence by certain imposed biological and social forces enables you to be more authentic because you do not have to lie to yourself. The value of accepting givens is the same as accepting ontological anxiety and guilt as inherent aspects of living. It is only by remaining honest that one has any chance at all of pursuing those possibilities that could be available. Accepting that you cannot influence certain things makes you more aware of what you can influence, paradoxical though that may seem at first blush.

This is not to say that existential psychologists advocate passive acquiescence to social and biological forces. Actually, Frankl (1960) believes that those persons who could not survive the concentration camps succumbed either because they considered themselves completely and unalterably trapped, or because they denied that they were incarcerated at all. But those who survived did so through a frank acceptance that some portion of their existence was not under their control, and a continual exploration through symbolizing, imagining, and judging of what freedom or maneuvering space was left to them. The first value of this approach is that they discovered some portion of freedom and therefore could retain some sense of human dignity. The second value is that, as they set their wits to work constructively on the matter, they carved out more freedom than they would initially have imagined and than was available to others not so fortunate. But recognize that their fortunateness was self-determined, by their own courage to face straightforwardly a horrendous imposition on freedom, in spite of the pain of such honesty. It was their persistence in being authentic regardless of suffering that permitted them to use their wits in gaining greater freedom. Thus, one accepts a necessity in order more clearly to explore what possibilities of freedom are left. In this, one often discovers that the necessity is smaller and less important than initially thought.

But there are very few *actual* necessities, according to existentialists, beyond some biological factors. Most of us never experience forcible incarceration. Much more debilitating than failing to accept an actual necessity is construing things which are actually only possibilities as necessities. A person unhappy in his job or his marriage may complain that he cannot make any changes. Perhaps he feels he could not get another job, or that his responsibilities as husband and father preclude dissolving the marriage. It would not be unusual in such a situation to hear an existential psychotherapist questioning whether there really are no other jobs and no other ways of fulfilling obligations. The person in the example has construed particular life commitments, which were freely made and can be freely changed, as necessities. This confusion of possibilities as necessities is at the heart of psychopathology, according to existentialists (Binswanger, 1963; Boss, 1963; Keen, 1970). Typically, when a person makes this conclusion, he wants to abdicate personal responsibility, blaming his failures on a destructive society that he can do nothing about. He wants to lie down and die and be pitied for it. He lacks the courage that would permit authentic being, choosing to lie to himself and others instead.

Existential psychology is definitely a perfection fulfillment position. There is little sympathy in the existential position for treating possibilities as necessities, for the person is considered to have the wherewithal to do better than that, if he would only try. Some positions exemplifying the conflict model would be much more sympathetic to the failure to attempt some wanted goal, because the conflict model is built on compromise. For the existentialist, the guilt one feels on staying in a marriage against one's will is *true* or ontological guilt. An existential psychotherapist would not try to remove so much as amplify the experience of it, in order that the person be forced to recognize the portion of freedom he has surrendered unnecessarily. In contrast, a classical Freudian psychotherapist might try to help the person decrease guilt, on the grounds that it was only due to an overly harsh superego in the first place. Such a superego would stand in the way of establishing a workable compromise between individual and social pressures, both conceived as necessities. Similarly, an intrapsychic conflict therapist would find the person's guilt due to an overbearing autonomy, and encourage its diminution in paving the way for a compromise expressing more communion. Even an actualization fulfillment therapist might be skeptical that the guilt pointed toward a beneficial direction of movement, on the grounds that it is feelings of well-being that augur personal fulfillment. He too might try to decrease the guilt.

We are now in a position to understand more fully what the existential psychologist means by freedom. It is not some mysterious free will, undetermined in any way by past experience, constituting something virtually supernatural and not to be understood. Rather, as Gendlin (1965–66) makes clear, it is the process of using one's wits—symbolization, imagination, and judgment—to construct possibilities. In discussing freedom, Gendlin (1965–66) says

> An oversimplified existentialism would have it that you can choose yourself to be any way you wish. You simply leap out of your situation and your past. This would be a flat denial of all our sufferings and failing attempts to be a certain way just by wishing we were. That is not what existentialism means at all. But, then, what is choice and freedom? Sartre, discussing the example of a cafe waiter, points out that "cafe waiter" is, of course, only a role. The living man fills the role, rather than

being defined by it. But, says Sartre, that does not mean that he can just simply choose to be a diplomat instead. There is "facticity," the situation and conditions about us which we cannot arbitrarily wave away. We must "surpass" situations in our interpreting them and acting in them; we cannot just choose them to be different. There is no such magic freedom as simply choosing ourselves to be other than what we are. Without difficult, sensitive steps, we do not become free of the constraints we are under.

The same may be said about a man's past, his upbringing, his learnings. The past is surpassed in the present, but this is no arbitrary anything-you-please. The same relationship between a given (facticity) and a movement (freedom, surpassing) holds here . . . the given does not have in it what we later make of it; and yet, what we make of it is related to what was given, must follow from it in certain ways, and just some ways fit. How I can surpass my past is not logically or analytically deducible from it. Surpassing is living action; but not just any arbitrary action brings the felt response of authentic surpassing. It is hard to devise such a mode of action, and we often fail to do so.

What we construct through symbolization, imagination, and judgment is freedom in the sense that it changes us, and is not strictly deducible in advance from a knowledge of our past. It represents a new frame of reference and format for action that we worked at creating, that we rendered consistent with our past, and that we can truly believe. We worked hard, and were not breathed upon mysteriously by God. This achievement of freedom is properly called *transcendence*, and though its specific content in any case would be very difficult to predict in advance, the process of thought which renders it likely is predictably common in some persons and uncommon in others. This is the story of development, and will be taken up in Chapter 7.

Suggested in Gendlin's (1965–66) position on freedom is a more full-blown sense than we had before of what it means to conceptualize life as a series of decisions. As he (Gendlin, 1965–66, pp. 135–136) makes clear, the alternatives in any decisional situation are as much posed by the person as they are given:

> Another error committed when [the person's mental process of] explication is left out is to view choice as between already given alternatives. This is not existentialism but a bad misunderstanding of it. . . . Situations are all in terms of what we may do, not do, suffer, avoid, succeed in, or miss. A situation is never pure facticity. . . . The facticity of. . . . *posed* alternatives is not to be accepted as though the binding facts I now see were ultimate; but neither can we simply wave away the facts. We don't always succeed in explicating new alternatives so well that we combine all we desire in one, while avoiding all that we wish to avoid. But free choice is not the choice between the two, bad, given alternatives. Free choice necessitates the creation of new alternatives which make stepping stones of what were obstacles.

Thus, the involvement of symbolization, imagination, and judgment in the very posing of alternatives to decide among is also a part of the transcendence of what seemed necessary by rendering it only a possibility instead.

This discussion permits pinpointing of the existential position on defensiveness. Although existentialists do assume defensiveness, they mean something quite different from the usual emphasis on dropping out of consciousness that which is socially unacceptable. The occasion for defensiveness, according to existentialists, is cowardice in the face of ontological anxiety (this is virtually the same as the inability to believe in one's own power of intelligence). The end result is the distortion involved in neurotic anxiety and guilt, and the confusion of possibilities for necessities. The whole emphasis is on not having done the real cognitive work involved in achieving transcendence, rather than on hiding one's antisocial tendencies from scrutiny.

Concluding remarks. At this time existential psychology is hardly a unitary body of theory with no ambiguities and disagreements. What I have tried to do is select those parts of various theorists' emphasis that seem to fit together into something approaching a coherent position. It is premature to indulge in any very rigorous analysis of the strengths and weaknesses of the approach, which can barely be called a position yet. At the moment, it seems best to immerse oneself in the main emphasis presented here, and to gain a sense of their similarities to and differences from other personological positions.

Chapter 4 THE CORE OF PERSONALITY: CONSISTENCY MODEL

In stating the core tendency of personality, the consistency model emphasizes the importance of the information or emotional experience the person gets out of interacting with the external world. The model assumes that there is a particular kind of information or emotional experience that is best for the person, and hence, that he will develop a personality which increases the likelihood that he will interact with the world such as to get this kind of information or emotional experience. The personality is determined much more by the feedback from interaction with the world than it is by inherent attributes of the human.

In comparison with consistency theories, both fulfillment and conflict theories put much greater emphasis upon an inherent nature, as a component of personality determining life's course. According to fulfillment theories, life is an unfolding of the human's inherent nature. And even when conflict theories stress society as an important force in living, they assume that personality is in large measure an expression of the human's inherent characteristics. For both fulfillment and conflict theories, the content of personality is much more set by virtue of the attributes the human brings into the world than is true of consistency positions.

To be sure, consistency positions do make some assumptions about what is inherent in humans, but these assumptions involve very little content. Consistency positions concern themselves much more with the compatibility between aspects of content than with what the content actually is. For consistency theorists, the content of personality is largely learned, and represents the history of feedback resulting from interacting with the world. To be sure, the feedback influences the content of personality along the lines of the assumed core tendencies of personality, and these core tendencies are inherent in human nature, but there is no particular content that one would expect to find in people more than any

141

other content. As you will see, the implications of this kind of position are very different from those of fulfillment and conflict positions.

CONSISTENCY MODEL: COGNITIVE DISSONANCE VERSION

There are two basic versions of the consistency model. In one of them, which I have called the cognitive dissonance version, the important elements in the determination of consistency are cognitions. The cognitions may be thoughts, expectations, attitudes, opinions, or even perceptions. Consideration of the discrepancy or consistency between cognitive elements may occur either within or across the categories just mentioned. Agreement or disagreement may be between two thoughts, or a thought and a perception, and so forth. All cognitive dissonance versions of the consistency model assume that discrepancies between cognitive elements produce an emotional state that provides the energy and direction for behavior. In the pure form of this position, exemplified by the theory of Kelly, discrepancies both large and small produce discomfort, anxiety, and tension. These emotional reactions in turn produce behavior the aim of which is to reduce the discrepancy and ensure that it will not occur in the future. After Kelly's position is presented, it's similarity to that of Festinger will be explored. The final theorist discussed in this section will be McClelland. His point of view is properly classed as a variant on the cognitive dissonance version of the consistency model. For McClelland, only large discrepancies result in emotional discomfort and avoidance, whereas small discrepancies are actually considered to result in pleasurable emotion and approach behavior.

Kelly's position

George A. Kelly (born in 1905; died in 1966) received his Ph.D. in psychology from the University of Texas after having studied both in the United States and England. He spent his career in university settings, where he combined teaching with student counseling. For a number of years he was director of the Psychological Clinic at Ohio State University, and held a professorship at Brandeis University at the time of his death. Although Kelly did not publish as much as some other personologists, he influenced many students over the years.

Kelly's theory of personality is not at all like that of the other theorists covered so far. And yet, as you will see, he seems to be able to address himself to a wide range of phenomena in living. Although he was developing his position over a period of many years, it was not presented in the literature until rather recently. This is part of the reason why it is not too well known among psychologists. But a reason that is easily as important is that Kelly's approach has a distinctly intellectual or mentalistic ring, and is therefore somewhat at a disadvantage in having to compete in a field long dominated by views of the human as emotional and instinctual. Actually, it is a position well worth a hearing, precisely because it is so different from prevailing views, and because it is rather complete and carefully wrought.

The core tendency of personality from Kelly's (1955) point of view is easily stated. It is *the human's continual attempt to predict and control the events he experiences.* Kelly advocates taking as a model for the human, not the biological organism, or the frame of reference of happiness and unhappiness, but rather, the scientific pursuit of truth. Truth is not necessarily what pleases or satisfies us in the straightforward terms of our desires and needs, but rather, what convinces us of its inexorable reality. The scientific pursuit of truth is the empirical procedure of formulating hypotheses, and testing them out in the tangible world of actual experience. If a hypothesis is supported by facts or events, the scientist retains it regardless of how popular it is with him, but if it is disconfirmed by facts, he discards or changes it again regardless of how popular it is with him. Kelly deeply believed that it is as scientists that people approach the task of living. The only important difference between actual scientists and people in general is that the actual scientist is more self-conscious and precise about his pursuit of truth, but his methods and procedures are in other ways the same as those of people in general. After all, the scientific method was invented by the human, and can be clearly seen as a formalization of what he tended to do rather normally in the process of deciding what to believe and do.

In arguing for the centrality for living of the scientific model, Kelly (1955, p. 5) says:

> It is customary to say that *the scientist's ultimate aim is to predict and control.* This is a summary statement that psychologists frequently like to quote in characterizing their own aspirations. Yet, curiously enough, psychologists rarely credit the human subjects in their experiments with having similar aspirations. It is as though the psychologist were saying to himself, "I, being a *psychologist,* and therefore a *scientist,* am performing this experiment in order to improve the prediction and control of certain human phenomena; but my subject, being merely a human organism, is obviously propelled by inexorable drives welling up within him, or else he is in gluttonous pursuit of sustenance and shelter.

Kelly is arguing that, from the point of view of reason, if the psychologist and his subject are both normally capable and intelligent humans, and if the psychologist knows he is attempting to predict and control, then the most likely conclusion to reach about the subject is that he is making the same attempt. It is only naïveté that leads to any other conclusion.

Kelly could well bolster this logical argument by an empirical one. Psychologists who do personality research are very sensitive to the possibility that their measurement operations will be contaminated by the subject's wish to appear in a socially desirable and appropriate light.

It seems that virtually whenever you give subjects a set of questions to answer about themselves, they will tend to answer in ways that make them look good, or that seem to give the psychologist what he wants. It is also clear that subjects are terribly interested in what the purpose of the measurement is, and in what will come of their participation in the research. A personologist naïve enough not to recognize that subjects are very interested in predicting what the experiment is about and controlling what is made of their performance will very likely fail in his research efforts. Or if he succeeds, it will only be apparent success produced by his having been unintentionally clever enough to use the subject's attempts to predict and control for his own ends. The most sophisticated approach to this problem of measurement is to construct tests that employ techniques for canceling out the effects of subjects trying to determine the goals of the research and responding in a socially desirable manner. The empirical support lent to Kelly's logical argument is quite extensive (e.g., Edwards, 1957; Jackson & Messick, 1958) though it is neither necessary nor appropriate to review it here.

Actually, if you have even participated in a psychological experiment as a subject, you may well have an intuitive basis for understanding Kelly's insistence on the importance of the attempt to predict and control one's experience. Perhaps you can remember wondering what was going to be done to you, and what was the point of the research. Perhaps you can also remember trying to find out what was going on, by asking questions, or by watching very sensitively. And whether or not you ever felt sure you had figured it all out, perhaps you remember trying to have only a particular impact rather than to leave the matter undefined. You may even recall simply not trusting the psychologist if he gave you some account of why he wanted your participation. All of these possible remembrances express one facet or another of the disrupting effect of uncertainty and the attempt to achieve certainty. Those of you who have not been subjects in psychological experiments can probably remember other instances in which it seemed very important to predict and control what was going to happen.

Now if all Kelly meant was the kind of thing we can understand intuitively on the basis of memories such as those mentioned above, he would not have much of a personality theory. We could even agree with him on the importance of being able to predict and control and still remain unconvinced that he had clarified the human condition in any very comprehensive way. But Kelly actually has a great deal more to say about personality, as we shall see through focusing upon the (1) development, (2) use, and (3) change of constructs and construct systems.

Development of constructs and construct systems. According to Kelly, the person's first step in attempting to predict and control his experience is to engage in the construing of events. Before much construing has taken place, experience is made up of a seemingly random and continuous flow of events. For Kelly, events have an actual existence separate from the person, but do not achieve importance for understanding personality until they are construed by him. The process of construing is one in which certain events are classed together with others that are considered similar, and contrasted with others that are considered different.

In the initial stages of construing, the person begins to focus upon certain general features of the events flowing by in a seemingly random series in such a way that he can recognize what he considers to be repetitions or replications of events. Because he has abstracted what is for him the essence of a particular event that is occurring, he can identify a repetition of that event in the future. He has transcended the literal event, and achieved abstract representation of the essence of the event. It is only through such a process of generalization and abstraction that the events of one's experience can become meaningful and orderly. Without active attempts to construe, it would not be possible to find the world a familiar place and to form expectations about what is likely to happen next. Kelly is very clear in the belief that since construing is an interpretive process, not a mere description of literal reality, it will be done differently by different people. He means that there are many possible ways of ordering events in similarity and difference classes, and these ways are all plausible because there are so many events that are all so literally different from each other. What Kelly fails to give us is an explanation of why people will construe along particular lines. He simply does not deal with this question. In addressing this question, one could say that there are certain core characteristics of personality, e.g., inherent capabilities, that influence the directions of construing, but such a possibility would not be in the spirit of the consistency model with its emphasis upon environmental experience as the contributant of personality content. If Kelly dealt with the question of why different persons construe along different lines, he would probably have to do so in terms of their different histories of environmental experience. This amounts to saying either that you construe along the lines that have been taught to you by significant others, or that you construe along the lines that are a natural outgrowth of the type of events your own particular world of experience has happened to include. That Kelly has been reticent to develop his theory along these lines should be kept in mind, as there are other reticences I will mention that can all be construed by us as having a particular meaning.

In any event, the result or product of the process of construing is the *construct*. A core characteristic of personality, the construct is an idea or abstraction that has a dichotomous nature. Good-bad, for example, is a construct. Chromatic-achromatic is another. Constructs are categories of thought that grow out of the interpretations we place on events, and, as we shall see in the next section, serve the purpose of aiding us to anticipate future events. In considering the construct to be dichotomous in nature, Kelly deeply believes that he is mirroring the nature of common thought. In order to develop a construct at all, he believes, you must have noted, at a minimum, that two events seem similar to each other and different from a third. The process of perceiving similarity is deeply bound up with the process of perceiving difference. Whenever you say that two things, say wood and metal, are similar, perhaps in being hard, you are at least implying that they are also different from soft things, such as water. The recognition that there are hard things requires that there also be soft things to serve as contrasts. If there were not both soft and hard things in the world, none of us would ever have construed hardness and softness as characteristics of things. In a more general sense, anything that we see as a thing, we see because it contrasts with something other than it. On these kinds of bases, Kelly feels that constructs are inherently dichotomous in nature. This is not changed for him by the fact that a person may seem to be using only one pole of a construct. If a person is, for example, talking only in terms of the goodness of people, without reference to badness at all, this merely means that the badness pole of the goodness-badness construct is implicit. It does not mean that it is nonexistent. There are no unipolar constructs.

Thus far, I have been using language very much like that of Kelly. It is in itself an abstract, intellectualized language. As I am not entirely sure that what a construct is and how it is formed is as vivid as it could be to you, let me pause and give an extended example that may come reasonably close to your own experience. Imagine that you have no constructs in the area of heterosexual relationships. You do, however, have a basic tendency to predict and control the events of your experience. In the normal course of events, you will find yourself in the company of people of the opposite sex, and your urge to predict and control your experience will find expression in attempting to understand, interpret these encounters. So, in the encounters, you will be looking for similarities and differences that can serve as the bases for abstractions, generalizations, ideas that will render the encounters meaningful and predictable. Consider three encounters with people of the opposite sex. The first and third may leave you enthusiastic and joyous, while the second may threaten and disturb you. You could develop the idea or construct of *satisfying-dissatisfying* as a relevant dimension of heterosexual relationship. The first and third encounters may also involve people who are excitable, imaginative, inconsistent, and unusual, whereas the second encounter involves someone who is orderly, even tempered, pragmatic, practical, and acquiescent. On the basis of these observations, you could develop the construct of *creative-banal* as something that applies to heterosexual relationships. Thus far, I have discussed similarities between the first and third encounters and differences of both from the second. But other possibilities could arise. For example, the first and second encounters could involve people who get good grades, who have no trouble finishing papers, and who make contributions of a tangible nature to the lives of other people, whereas the third encounter might involve a person who shuns evaluations, does not complete courses, and does nothing for other people. On the basis of these observations, you could formulate the construct of *productive-nonproductive* as yet another relevant dimension of heterosexual relationship.

Perhaps this gives you some intuitively relevant sense of what Kelly means when he talks of the development of constructs. How constructs are used and changed are topics for the following sections. When you have read those sections as well as this one, it should be clear how the development, use, and change of constructs is relevant to the prediction and control of experience. But before proceeding to the next sections, there are a couple of things to be accomplished in this one.

In the course of experiencing events, a person will develop many constructs. You can see how easily three separate constructs could have developed out of encounters with three people of the opposite sex. Actually, I could have cataloged many more potential constructs in that example. In point of fact, many constructs are developed in living, because events are numerous and multifaceted enough to stimulate many separate interpretive conclusions. But rather than remaining separate, the many constructs developed by a person tend to become organized into a *construct system*. The organization of constructs in a system tends to be hierarchical in nature, according to Kelly, although I must say that he is none too clear concerning the lines along which hierarchization will take place. There seem to be two kinds of relationships between constructs rendering one superordinate and the other subordinate. First, "a construct may be superordinate to another because each pole of the subordinate construct forms a part of the context for the two poles of the superordinate" (Sechrest, 1963, p. 214). In our extended example, the construct satisfying-dissatisfying would be superordinate to the construct creative-banal if people who are creative are satisfying and people who are banal are dissatisfying, and it is also true that there are other things besides creativity and banality that contribute to their satisfying and dissatisfying nature. In other words, creativity-banality is parallel but subordinate to satisfying-dissatisfying because of the lesser generality of the former construct.

In order to illustrate the other kind of superordinate-subordinate relationship, I will have to extend our already extended example. But first, recall that the construct productive-nonproductive was formed on the basis of similarity between the first and second encounters, with the third being different. Regardless of whether that construct is more or less general than the other two, it remains independent of them and cannot be organized in the same hierarchy with them. The productivity-nonproductivity of a person has nothing to do with whether or not they will be considered creative or banal, of whether interaction with them will be satisfying or dissatisfying. This is because productivity-nonproductivity is a construct that was formed on the basis of different groupings of event attributes than the other two constructs. Observations such as this led Kelly to theorize that although constructs tend to be organized into systems, some constructs will be so independent of, or incompatible with, each other that they will either exist alone, or as part of separate (possibly competing) construct systems.

Now on to the extension of our example whereby it will be possible to illustrate the second kind of hierarchical organization of constructs. Add a fourth encounter with someone of the opposite sex, and assume that the experience is such that the creative pole of the creative-banal construct is relevant. So, the first, third and fourth encounters were with creative people, whereas the second was with a banal person. Assume further that there are characteristics of the first and fourth encounters that suggest generosity, while the third encounter suggests stinginess, and the second is neutral with regard to these two considerations. The resulting construct *generosity-stinginess* has a hitherto undiscussed type of relationship with creative-banal. Regardless of which is the more general, and hence higher in the hierarchy, the entire construct generosity-stinginess fits in the creative pole of the creative-banal construct. What this means is that while it is relevant to consider the generosity or stinginess of creative people, it is meaningless to do so with banal people. This is the second type of hierarchical relationship mentioned by Kelly. It is important to note that in both types of hierarchical relationship, the constructs to which a given construct is superordinate or subordinate is a matter of relative generality.

In closing this section, let me say a bit more on the matter of the actual content of constructs and construct systems. As I indicated before, Kelly does not theorize about the lines along which construing will take place, even though he could do so within the framework of a consistency position by focusing upon environment determinants of construing. It is not surprising, therefore, to find that nowhere in Kelly's writing is there a list or typology of likely constructs. Kelly could, within the context of a consistency position, provide such specification of the content of personality by describing the kinds of constructs one can expect to find in persons with particular histories of environmental interaction. So we have encountered another point in his theorizing where it falls short of complete understanding of personalities. There is still another example of this shortcoming, and I will delay a general discussion of the problem until we have encountered it.

In fairness to Kelly, it must be said that although he does not provide theoretical apparatus whereby one can know what kinds of constructs to expect in people who have lived in particular kinds of environments, he does indicate an explicit, effective procedure for discovering the content of constructs that exist in any person with whom you may be confronted. In other words, in Kelly's approach you can determine what a person's constructs contain once you are faced with him, even though as a theorist you could not have predicted them in advance of actually examining him. Thus, while Kelly's theory cannot be completely predictive—an interesting fault in a position that takes the scientific model as the measure of the human—it is usable in moderate degree in that you can at least describe people once you encounter them. The procedure for determining a person's constructs is called the Role Repertory Test (Kelly, 1955) and it is thoroughly consistent with the theory. Briefly, it involves providing people with the names of the significant people in their lives (e.g., mother, father, best high school teacher) and then having all possible combinations of three of these people judged in a dichotomous fashion. The judgment requires that two of the three people in each combination be specified as similar in some way, and different from the third. Then, by analyzing and summarizing all the dichotomous judgments made by the person you are testing, you can determine the number and content of the constructs comprising his system. It is quite an ingenious test!

It must also be said of Kelly that although he does not provide precise specification of construct content that is likely in people with particular histories, he does conceptualize certain general attributes of constructs that are helpful in rendering his position concrete and usable. He thinks it important to know whether a costruct is *permeable, preemptive, constellatory,* and *propositional* in nature (Kelly, 1955, pp. 156–157). If a construct is permeable, hitherto unencountered events can be subsumed within it, whereas an impermeable construct can only be used to understand events that went into its original formulation. A preemptive construct is one that renders the events it subsumes unavailable for subsumption within other constructs. It is not necessary in this summary of Kelly's position to describe constellatory and propositional constructs. It is enough to know that, in general, all four characteristics of constructs seem relevant to how flexible and adaptable the person is likely to be.

The use of constructs and construct systems. Thus far in understanding how the person goes about attempting to predict and control the events of his experience, we have seen that he develops constructs organized into one or more hierarchical systems. Constructs are interpretations of events arrived at through what amounts to a process of inductive reasoning. A construct system is essentially a theory of the world or of subportions of the world of experience. All this is quite consistent with the model of the human as scientist, as is the use to which constructs and construct systems are put, according to Kelly. Once the scientist develops, through inductive reasoning, a theory concerning the significance of observed events, he will then use that theory in a deductive fashion to anticipate and influence events that have not yet occurred. His deductive processes will lead him to make hypotheses or predictions and to manipulate or control the environment so as to test those hypotheses. A person's use of his constructs and construct systems follows this model, as far as I can tell from Kelly's writing. I must say, however, that the most ambiguous and fragmentary part of his position is the matter of precise explanation of the translation of constructs and construct systems into anticipation and action. To a certain extent, what I say below involves reading between the lines of Kelly's writings. Hopefully, I have done this in the spirit of his approach.

In understanding the way in which constructs and construct systems are used in anticipation and action, it is first necessary to recognize that events only achieve significance for the person when they are subsumed within constructs. And obviously, the particular significance construed events have is determined by the number and content of the constructs they fall within. Let me say essentially the same thing in words that are more immediately relevant to anticipation, or at least, to future perception. What Kelly is saying is that the constructs and construct systems that you have right now will determine what future events will be important to you, and also, what will be the nature of their importance. The usefulness of constructs in attempts to predict and control is that they give you a tangible basis for expecting what kinds of events are likely to occur, and for interpreting their meaning. Suppose you are on the verge of a heterosexual encounter. If you have the constructs relevant to such encounters that I mentioned earlier in the extended example, you will look forward to this new encounter with the expectation that it will be satisfying or dissatisfying, creative or banal, productive or nonproductive, and involve generosity or stinginess. You will not expect the encounter to involve anything more or less in the way of possibilities. The higher a construct concerning heterosexual encounter is on the hierarchy, the more it will determine expectation. Thus, if satisfying-dissatisfying is the most general of these constructs, you will expect it to apply without a doubt to the imminent encounter, whereas, you may be less certain of the applicability of some less-general construct such as productive-nonproductive.

So the first way in which construct systems are relevant to prediction and control is that they provide you with the set of expectations which you can use in imagining what future experience will be like. You cannot seriously expect that a future heterosexual encounter will be, say, revealing or unrevealing unless you have such a construct in your system already. But the predictions that can be reached solely on the basis of having a set of hierarchically organized constructs that seem relevant to you, are very general in character. All you can say at this level is that the forthcoming heterosexual encounter will be satisfying *or* dissatisfying, creative *or* banal, and so forth. You cannot expect that it will be definitely satisfying, rather than dissatisfying, or definitely creative, rather than banal. The decision as to which pole of each of the relevant constructs to favor in forming expectations is a terribly important matter for Kelly's theory, if it is to provide precise understanding of people's attempts to predict and control.

When people favor one pole of a construct rather than the other in anticipating the future, they are making what Kelly (1955, pp. 64–68) calls the *elaborative choice*. The important theoretical question is the basis upon which the choice is determined. Kelly does not stress such a possible basis as favoring the pole that has turned out to be most accurate in the past, though such an actuarial basis is certainly plausible for his kind of theory. Instead, he says that "A person chooses for himself that alternative in a dichotomized construct through which he anticipates the greater possibility for extension and definition of his system" (Kelly, 1955, p. 64). This statement seems quite consistent with the core tendency of prediction and control. If your aim in life is prediction and control, you must be interested in perfecting the construct system upon which the success of your aim depends. But there is an ambiguity here stemming from the fact that there are really two strategies whereby one can succeed in prediction of events. The most obvious way is to develop a construct system that works well for a given set of events, and then to constrict the world of your experience to just those events or ones so similar that it is unlikely that anticipation of what will happen is either difficult or inaccurate. The least obvious way of succeeding in accurate prediction is to develop a construct system that is so comprehensive and valid that no restriction of experiential possibilities is necessary because virtually any event can be accurately anticipated.

How does Kelly's statement quoted above articulate with these two strategies? Although Kelly is rather ambiguous in this regard, a careful reading discloses that he recognizes both strategies, and means to incorporate them in the notion of elaborative choice. This choice is made adventurously when the pole of the construct favored is considered likely to lead to expansion of the construct system so that it is more comprehensive. The elaborative choice is conservatively made when the pole of the construct favored is considered likely to lead to maintenance or protection of the construct system as it exists at present. The conservative choice leads to constricted certainly whereas the adventurous choice leads to broadened understanding.

Although Kelly has provided descriptive terminology for recognizing conservative and adventurous choices, he gives no theoretical rationale for why or when one kind of choice will take precedence over the other. This is a severe drawback in the position, as it is the elaborative choice that determines the anticipations so directly expressive of the core tendency of the human. In recognizing this drawback, Sechrest (1963, p. 221), a student of Kelly who has written an interpretive analysis of the position, says:

> There is probably in the [elaborative choice] an implicit assumption of some alternating extension and consolidation of the construction system. When the person feels secure and capable of anticipating events correctly, he will make choices that offer possibilities of extending his system, even at the risk of being wrong, but then a period of consolidation will follow in which he will make choices that reduce exposure to error but are confirmative.

Although this is an ingenious hypothesis, there is little direct evidence for it in Kelly's writings. It seems to me that we will have to make do with a theory that, while descriptively complete, falls short of explaining when conservative as opposed to adventurous strategies will be followed in using constructs to arrive at predictions.

It seems to me that this drawback needs to be understood along with the two others mentioned earlier. Kelly fails to be specific about the lines along which construing takes place, the actual content of the ensuing constructs, and finally, the bases upon which constructs are used in adventurous or conservative ways. When theorists in the conflict and fulfillment traditions are confronted with the explanation of such directional behaviors, they tend to assume the determining influence of instincts, inherent potentialities, emotions, emotional conflicts, or motives. It is understandable that Kelly would not have recourse to such possibilities, as his is a consistency position which not only stresses the learned nature of personality, but also is billed as free of hedonic and motivational assumptions. What the human is trying to do, according to Kelly, is predict and control, not to express some inner nature or set of needs or delight in pleasure. But his disavowal of fulfillment and conflict assumptions does not solve his problem as set forth above. He must find a basis for rendering his position more complete and predictive that is also consistent with his kind of approach. But I am not sure Kelly would agree to the need for theoretical additions. He is so insistent on the individual's freedom of choice in life, that he may actually be temperamentally unwilling to infringe upon his idealistic stance with theorizing rendering life a precisely determined thing. Recall that I also suggested this of Rogers, Adler, and Allport. These theorists, though in different theoretical traditions, have been vociferous, uncompromising exponents of freedom of choice in living.

Thus far in the discussion of the use of constructs and construct systems in the prediction and control of experience, I have focused upon anticipations or expectations rather than upon actions. With regard to anticipation processes, we have seen that Kelly provides a partial basis for understanding how they come about and what will be their content.

They come about as a natural concomitant of the constructs that come to mind whenever one is faced with the possibility of certain kinds of events, and they have the content involved in the favored poles of the relevant constructs. Kelly's position is only partial because we are not told why and when particular poles will be favored, and earlier in the whole process than that, because we are not told why certain directions of construing are chosen instead of others.

Turning to the determination of action, we find that Kelly's position is even more sketchy and ambiguous than it was with regard to anticipation. In agreement with this criticism, Sechrest (1963, pp. 219–220) says:

> [The notion of elaborative choice] is the most directly related to the prediction of overt behavior, but, as will be seen, there are serious problems in moving from an individual's construct system to his behavior in any particular situation. . . . If [the elaborative choice] provides the essential link between the construction system and observable behavior, the nature of the link has not been precisely described. One gets the impression that the predictions to be made from [the elaborate choice] are not at all exact.

In general, Kelly does not really discuss action, presumably subsuming it under anticipation broadly conceived. This indicates that insofar as one wanted to focus upon action per se, one would imagine Kelly's position to be that it is complementary to, or an extension of, expectation. So, if your constructs led you to expect that a forthcoming heterosexual encounter would be creative, then you should presumably act in a fashion consistent with that. But what this would mean more concretely remains a mystery in Kelly's position. We can speculate on what action complementary to anticipation might be, and say, for example, that someone expecting an interaction to be creative might act on it in terms of what creativity means to him. Perhaps he would be sensitive, free associational, and unevaluative in the things he said and did in the interaction.

As you can imagine, if a person's actions were complementary to his expectations, and also successful, then he would be heavily influencing his experience in such fashion as to render his construct system valid. If your construct system leads to expecting a creative encounter, and you therefore act effectively in a creative manner, then you are much more likely to conclude that you were right in your expectation than if you had acted in some other way. Now the only reason I bring this up is that it is not at all clear that the scientist model for the human would lead to the view that action should be complementary to expectation. When the scientist has an hypothesis, he sets about testing it. Testing it involves actions designed to show, not only whether the hypothesis is true, but also, and more importantly, whether it is false. The scientist essentially tries to disprove his hypothesis, and only if he is unsuccessful in this, will he accept it as valid. Generalizing from the scientific model, we would expect Kelly to take the view that a person would not act in a fashion complementary to his expectations so much as in a fashion that would provide a rigorous test of them.

To be sure, this strategy of test would require a rather cold-blooded attitude toward life, but such an attitude seems to be an integral part of Kelly's basic assumptions. If your aim in life is to predict and control experience accurately, and experience is made up of events that actually exist independently of you, then you must spend all your time testing your expectations in order that your construct system will conform well to reality. One could argue cogently that it is most natural logically for someone holding Kelly's position to conceptualize actions as primarily hypothesis-testing in nature.

What would hypothesis-testing action look like? Kelly gives no help whatsoever in this. But, working in the spirit of his approach, we could take a stab at answering the question. If the construct you deemed relevant to an imminent heterosexual encounter is *productive-nonproductive*, and you have made the elaborative choice leading to the expectation that the encounter will be productive rather than nonproductive, then hypothesis-testing action would involve stimulating either productiveness and nonproductiveness alike, or neither of these. In any event, hypothesis-testing action would not involve attempts to stimulate just productiveness or just nonproductiveness in the encounter. To encourage experience relevant to only one pole of the construct, would be to jeopardize any possibility of determining whether the expectation based on elaborative choice was really accurate.

In trying to talk specifically about hypothesis-testing action, I am already beyond the formal theoretical apparatus provided by Kelly. It must be concluded that he is rather unconcerned about action as a category of human functioning separate from mentation. From some personological points of view, this is a serious limitation. Some personologists would believe that if Kelly were to elaborate his theory such that action were given a more important status as something to explain, the intriguing purity of the approach with its singular concern with prediction and control as the core tendency would come under attack. Bruner (1956) raises one form of this belief when he asks if it is really true that the attempt to avoid the disruptive surprise associated with inaccurate prediction is the only force directing life. In specific criticism of the maintenance and expansion of the construct system as a whole as the only basis for decisions, Bruner says, "I rather suspect that when some people get angry or inspired or in love, they couldn't care less about their 'system as a whole.'" Later in the same book review, Bruner (1956) makes even more clear that he is criticizing Kelly's unwillingness to assume that emotions have a determining influence on anticipation and actions:

The book fails signally, I think, in dealing convincingly with the human passions. There was a strategy in Freud's choice of Moses or Michelangelo or Little Hans. If it is true that Freud was too often the victim of the dramatic instance, it is also true that with the same coin he paid his way to an understanding of the depths and heights of *la condition humaine*. By comparison, the young men and women of Professor Kelly's clinical examples are worried about their dates, their studies, and their conformity. If Freud's clinical world is a grotesque of *fin de siècle* Vienna, Kelly's in a gloss of the post-adolescent peer group of Columbus, Ohio, who are indeed in the process of constructing their worlds. Which is more "real"? I have no idea. I wish Professor Kelly would treat more "most religious men in the most religious moments," or even just Nijinsky or Gabriel d'Annunzio.

Bruner suggests that even if many young college men and women can be well understood by assuming that they are trying to develop construct systems with which they can successfully predict and control events, this is not necessarily true of everyone. Even if only a few people seem more ruled by their passions than that, and certainly if the emotions have some degree of determining influence in many people, Bruner's criticism needs to be taken seriously. And the possibility that emotions have a causal influence on functioning is most readily apparent in the realm of action, a realm with which Kelly has little concern.

The change of constructs. In concluding discussion of Kelly's position, I wish to focus upon the bases of change in constructs. Some points raised here will help you gain more comprehensive understanding of the position, and may also make some of my interpretations to this point more convincing.

Essentially, constructs change when they lead to anticipations that turn out to be inaccurate. The whole thrust of Kelly's position is that there are real events, and the major task of life is to predict and control them accurately. Constructs are the bases upon which anticipation and action occur. It follows from this that constructs are only useful when they permit accurate prediction of events. When they do not permit accurate prediction, constructs are changed, and then the new predictions are tested. Thus, a person's construct system represents the results up to that time of a process of rational trial and error in the development of what amounts to a theory of the world of experience. It is the emphasis upon congruence between this theory as a predictive system and the real world of events that puts Kelly's position in the consistency mold.

When there is lack of consistency, or, in other words, when expectations are disconfirmed by events, the person experiences *anxiety*. Kelly's (1955, p. 495) definition of anxiety as "the awareness that the events with which one is confronted lie outside the range of convenience of his construct system" is unusual in personology. In this definition, the content of expectations and of events is really irrelevant to the arousal of anxiety. It is the lack of fit between the two kinds of things—inconsistency—that leads to the uncomfortable feelings we know as anxiety.

You should not imagine, as some serious students of Kelly have done (e.g., Sechrest, 1963), that he sees anxiety as the result of only significant or large discrepancies between events and anticipations. Kelly (1955, pp. 498–499) clearly establishes in quotes like the following that any and all inaccuracies of predictions, no matter how small or seemingly unimportant, precipiate anxiety:

> From the standpoint of the psychology of personal constructs, anxiety, per se, is not to be classified as either good or bad. It represents the awareness that one's construction system does not apply to the events at hand. It is, therefore, a precondition for making revisions. . . . Our definition of anxiety also covers the little confusions and puzzles of everyday living. The sum of a column of numbers does not check. Anxiety! We add it up again, it still does not check. More anxiety! We add it up another way. Good adjustment. Ah, there was our error!

It is statements such as this that led Bruner (1956) to characterize Kelly's core tendency as leading toward the avoidance of disruptive surprises. Such statements also make amply clear that we are dealing with a tension-reduction view. Anxiety is a tension state, and it must be minimized. Note that the anxiety of disconfirmation of expectations is the springboard for construct system change. Even if the anticipation expresses the adventurous form of the elaborative choice, as long as the ensuing events are discrepant from anticipation, anxiety is the result.

While Kelly's emphasis on the discomfort of unexpected events makes sense on the surface, consider its implications further. There is little in the theory that would help us gain understanding of boredom, which is clearly also a state of discomfort. How humdrum life would be if the goal involved in Kelly's core tendency of personality were actually achieved! Do not be misled by the notion that choices could be made adventurously rather than conservatively. In point of fact, the theory specifies that every unexpected event is anxiety provoking, and leads to construct system modification so as to ensure against recurrence of the unexpectedness. Kelly cannot even assert that consistency between expectation and occurrence is only necessary in matters of special concern to the person, for he clearly believes, as exemplified by the quote in the previous paragraph, that even seemingly trivial unexpectednesses are anxiety laden. According to Kelly, therefore the avoidance of boredom and monotony cannot be an important urging of the human being.

However simplistic Kelly's emphasis upon the necessarily discomforting effect of disconfirmed expectations may seem, his position is at least straightforward. Disconfirmation or anticipatory error leads to anxiety, which is uncomfortable enough to precipitate construct system change and hence new anticipations to be tested for their accuracy. There are no instincts, with their immutable content, or defenses, or unconscious determinants of functioning, in the person to interfere with the trial and error process whereby one tries to see the world accurately. The only aspects of the theory that could interfere with the straightforwardness of the trial and error process are guilt and hostility, and they stand out like sore thumbs amidst the other aspects of the theory. *Hostility,* according to Kelly (1955, p. 533), is the "continued effort to extort validational evidence in favor of a type of social prediction which has already been recognized as a failure." *Guilt* is defined as "the awareness of dislodgement of the self from one's core role structure" (Kelly, 1955, p. 533). These two concepts are unnatural to the theory not because it is particularly difficult to see the meaning intended, but rather because there is no additional theoretical structure within which to embed them. They are swimming up stream as it were against the current formed by an otherwise consistent theoretical structure in which constructs are readily changed when they do not permit accurate anticipation. Nowhere in the theory aside from the notion of hostility is there any way of expecting that the person will maintain an invalid construct in the face of evidence of its invalidity. And nowhere in the theory aside from the notion of guilt is there any particular emphasis upon ideas like the self, and its existence independent of the construct system. It is as if in these two notions Kelly makes concessions to ways of thinking about man that are more natural to other theories adopting a model of living as an irrational and defensiveness process.

Kelly and Festinger.   Leon Festinger and a number of other social psychologists have recently developed a consistency position closely related to that of Kelly. But as Festinger is mainly concerned with social psychological phenomena, such as attitude change, his views will not be considered in any detail here. The basic principle of Festinger's (1958) position is *that whenever cognitive dissonance exists, the person will employ procedures for reducing it.* The position, like that of Kelly, takes *cognitions* to be the elements relevant to consistency. In Festinger's position, cognitions can be beliefs, attitudes, ideas, or perceptions. A state of inconsistency or dissonance might exist when the idea of yourself as a fair person was confronted with the perception of yourself as acting in a discriminatory fashion. While many dissonances will involve the ethical domain, this need not be so. Indeed, any expectation that is disconfirmed by one's perception of events constitutes dissonance, regardless of whether the expectation and perception involve you, someone else, or the inanimate world. Kelly and Festinger are also in agreement on the consequences of dissonance or disconfirmed expectations. The consequence in both positions is anxiety, or at least some generalized emotional discomfort and tension, which serves as the mainspring for change, the aim of which is to avoid that which caused the tension. But here there is an important difference in emphasis between the positions of Festinger and Kelly.

You will recall that Kelly emphasizes a rational procedure of trial and error in changing constructs such that they eventually provide an accurate basis for predicting events. In contrast, Festinger's emphasis is not so exclusively on rationality and on fitting cognition to the actual dimensions of a real world of events. Instead, Festinger contends that the person will change one or the other of the cognitions involved in the dissonance, or, for that matter, the nature of the relationship between them, without regard for the niceties of the real world. According to Festinger, the person is as likely to distort reality as anything else in his attempt to avoid dissonance. In this irrational emphasis, Festinger is much closer to Freud than to Kelly. For Freud, you will recall, defenses were procedures whereby reality is distorted so that anxiety over conflict will not be felt. If there is a difference between Freud and Festinger in techniques for avoiding anxiety, it is that the content of conflict for Freud is invariably sexual and moral, whereas Festinger casts his net more widely than this. Some other personologists, like Sullivan and Rogers, who also have use for a notion of defense as a distortion of reality, but do not especially restrict the content of underlying conflict, may therefore come even closer than Freud to Festinger.

An example may help to dramatize the irrational flavor of Festinger's versions of the consistency model. Suppose you believe that a man, whom you respect and love very much is actually immortal—a God. This is one cognition. But also suppose that you see him die what is clearly a mortal's death on the cross. This second cognition is dissonant with the first, and precipitates anxiety. The anxiety is not because you lost a loved one, but rather because you are in turmoil as to what to believe. Therefore, in order to remove the anxiety, you have to decrease the dissonance. You may well do this by developing the third cognition which says that he did not really die, but simply left earthly life. Armed with this belief, you even have the basis for rejoicing. And, in order to protect yourself from the possibility of anxiety in the future—for, after all, the perception of the death on the cross is rather vivid—you proselytize. If you can convince others of your new, dissonance-reducing belief, you can believe it more unequivocally yourself. Kelly's position would have been an agreement concerning this example until the point of dissonance reduction. At this point, Kelly would be much more likely to predict change in the original belief of immortality, as the most realistic procedure.

Festinger has developed his theory in a direction permitting the understanding of attitude change rather than personality. It is understandable therefore, that he offers little that could clarify core characteristics and peripheral aspects of personality. For this reason, we need to go no further into his point of view. It will suffice to record the substantial agreement in basic assumptions between Kelly and Festinger. In Festinger's position, as in Kelly's, we find a point of view within which boredom, or the state of complete consistency between cognitions, cannot be considered a significantly unpleasant human experience. Again, as in Kelly, we find a model of man as painfully frail.

McClelland's position

David C. McClelland was born in New York City in 1917, and received a Ph.D. in psychology from Yale University in 1941. The son of a Protestant minister who later became a college president, McClelland has spent his career teaching and doing research on personality in university settings. He showed his leadership capacity and interest in public service by functioning as chairman of the Department of Psychology at Wesleyan University, and as deputy director of the Behavioral Sciences Division of the Ford Foundation. Following these posts, he became head of the Center for Research in Personality, and then chairman of the Department of Social Relations, at Harvard University. Deeply influenced by Murray and by the broad social science emphasis at Harvard, McClelland spent the early part of his career developing and testing his theory of personality, and has recently been investigating its social applications in underdeveloped societies throughout the world.

For McClelland, as for Kelly and Festinger, the consistency or discrepancy between expectations and occurrences is basic to the understanding of behavior. But whereas Kelly and Festinger find all inconsistency to result in unpleasant feelings and avoidance, McClelland considers this outcome to occur only when the degree of inconsistency is large. For him, small discrepancies between expectation and occurrence are more properly considered to result in pleasant feelings and approach behavior. His position is a variant on the consistency model in which the core tendency of personality is *to minimize large discrepancies between expectation and occurrence, while maximizing small discrepancies between expectation and occurrence.*

In finding an intuitive basis in your own experience for understanding McClelland's position, it would be well for you to think of times of uncertainty and times of boredom. In all of our lives, there are times when the sheer inability to determine what will happen next, and the related inability to know clearly what is happening now, is a real source of threat and discomfort. Also in all of our lives, there are times when everything is so predictable and clear that we wish something novel and unpredictable would happen. The introspective fact that people sometimes want to increase predictability and sometimes decrease it was the starting point for McClelland's theorizing. As indicated in the core tendency, he believes that it is small degrees of unpredictability that people crave, and large degrees that they avoid. I can imagine that at least for some of you, the introspective evidence for this position is not readily available. Because of this, it will be useful now to go on to a more rational analysis of the position, returning later to a point of correspondence between reason and intuition.

   The core characteristics associated with the core tendency. For Mc-Clelland (McClelland, Atkinson, Clark, & Lowell, 1953) there are core characteristics that are present at birth, and core characteristics that develop through learning. The innate core characteristics underlie the core tendency, while the learned core characteristics do not. Let me be less abstract. By virtue of being born, the person has the ability to experience pleasant feelings, or *positive affect,* and unpleasant feelings, or *negative affect.* McClelland is not concerned with distinctions between particular emotions, such as love and joy, in the positive class; and anger and fear, in the negative class. The two broad classes suffice for his theoretical purposes, and although he does not say so, one forms the impression that he may even assume that the innate apparatus for the experience of affect is simple and undifferentiated enough to permit of only two affective states, which, though amorphous and imprecise, clearly differ in whether they are pleasant or unpleasant. Another assumption, closely related to that of an innate basis for experiencing positive and negative affect, is that people find the latter affective state obnoxious enough to avoid, and the former attractive enough to seek. There is nothing, however, in the innate tendency to avoid negative affect and seek positive affect that explains the particular techniques for avoiding and seeking that we may observe in a person. Particular techniques are a matter of learning.

   Having assumed an innate basis for feeling positive and negative affect, McClelland needs to tell us what it is that can trigger one reaction as opposed to the other. As you can tell from the core tendency as stated earlier, he gives this role to the match between expectancies and occurrences. An *expectancy* is a cognitive unit, or thought, referring to what you imagine will be the content and timing of events in the future. Clearly, the expectancy is similar to the construct of Kelly, and the cognition of Festinger. As in Kelly and Festinger, McClelland recognizes events as real aspects of the world, though, of course, they must be appreciated by the person in order to have any significance for his living. As in Kelly and Festinger, McClelland assumes that expectancies are formed on the basis of past experience, and that different people may well form different expectancies owing to peculiarities of their background. McClelland suggests that the mechanism whereby expectancies are learned is contiguity. In other words, if the events in a given set occur in the same sequence often enough, you will abstract from your experience the expectation that the same thing will happen in the future. So whenever you encounter the first of this series of events, you have a definite idea of what is coming next. For McClelland, there need not be any reward at the end of the series, such as the proverbial pot at the end of the rainbow, in order that you learn the sequence. You learn it simply because it is there and is repeated in your experience often enough. Such learning without reinforcement is similar in emphasis to Kelly, though you should recognize that for both theorists, whether or not the expectancy that is learned turns out to be accurate is quite important in understanding when it is retained, discarded, or changed.

In this regard, we have seen that, for Kelly, any degree of inaccuracy of expectation leads to anxiety and the discarding or change of the expectation. Not so for McClelland. Only large discrepancies between expectation and occurrence have those consequences. In contrast, small discrepancies lead to positive affect and the retaining of the expectation. It is this emphasis on the pleasant, attractive effects of small inaccuracies of anticipation in the context of a position that otherwise agrees with those of Kelly and Festinger on the importance for living of considering the match between what you expect and what happens, that makes McClelland's approach a variant of the consistency model.

McClelland's emphasis upon quantifying the match or mismatch between expectation and event, though intriguing, raises the question of the manner in which quantification is to be done, for a number of possibilities suggest themselves. For his part, McClelland is apparently undecided, even concerning the demarcation point between large and small discrepancies. Although he is undoubtedly undecided out of a sense of the complexity of the problem, rather than out of lack of full recognition of it, I feel that we must consider it further in order to really understand the position. Perhaps the most obvious way of quantifying the agreement between expectation and occurrence would be to determine the number of elements or parts of the expectation, the number of elements or parts of the corresponding event, and then calculate the proportion of elements that agreed. This technique, for all its ponderousness, would be useful for at least fairly complex expectancies. Expectancies referring to propositional speech would be good examples. The sentence "a rose is a rose is a rose" is striking because it is an occurrence discrepant from expectations concerning sequence of types of words in intelligible speech. In attempting the identification of elements for purposes of quantifying degree of discrepancy, one might use parts of speech as elements.

But here we encounter a vexing problem. Not all parts of speech are equally important. Indeed, in almost all instances of naturally occurring sequences of events, some of the events will be more significant to the person than others. Perhaps, then, another and more meaningful way to quantify the degree of discrepancy between expectation and occurrence is to order elements of expectation and occurrence by their importance. One could then say that the greater the importance of the event inaccurately predicted, the larger the discrepancy between expectation and occurrence.

I am afraid we will not be able to solve the problem of quantification here. All I want you to recognize is that the problem is important, and has not been overcome as yet. A theory that cannot tell you how to distinguish between small and large discrepancies, when these two orders of discrepancy have effects that are reputed to be drastically different, is severely handicapped in providing believable explanations of phenomena. But while handicapped it is not without utility, as I will show in the next chapter. For the moment, I have tried to alert you to the value of attempts to develop the the theory in such fashion that it can, at some future time, provide consistent, workable bases for quantification.

Influence of the core tendency on personality development. McClelland's theory differs in two important ways from the consistency positions already considered. The first way—the emphasis on moderate rather than total anticipational accuracy as the ultimate goal of living—has already been mentioned. The other important differences is the emphasis McClelland puts on action in addition to the more purely cognitive-affective considerations of consistency. These two emphases in McClelland's thinking are usefully considered together in attempting to understand the way in which expression of the core tendency leads to personality development.

Strange though McClelland's position may seem at first, I ask you to reflect on the problem of boredom. I have already indicated that positions such as that of Kelly cannot logically consider boredom to be an important factor in life. McClelland has made moderate anticipational accuracy the ideal because of the belief that complete accuracy, over any significant period of time, would be too monotonous and boring for comfort. If you consider boredom to be an unpleasant state, you have an intuitive basis for understanding McClelland's position, however strange it may sound initially. In sum, McClelland's position grants a hardiness and vivacity to man not really found in other consistency positions. For McClelland, as for other consistency theorists, the greater the discrepancy between expectation and occurrence, the more intense is the organismic tension. But his position is not a simple tension reduction view, as are the others. Rather, McClelland considers the moderate tension associated with moderate anticipational inaccuracy to be ideal. Not only too much, but also too little, tension is avoided. This is the first position we have encountered which explicitly takes this stance.

Of all the consistency positions, McClelland's is most oriented toward the explanation of action. You will recall that Kelly's theory put us in the position of considering actions to be more or less synonymous with anticipations. While this is perhaps understandable in a position that stresses total accuracy of prediction as the ultimate goal of life, there is still a critical problem created by the collapsing of the distinction between anticipation and action, because it is no longer logically possible, then, to consider action strategies that are aimed at providing tests of anticipations rather than merely being extensions of them.

The crux of the difference of opinion hinges on the fact that while Kelly makes the achievement of total accuracy the real aim of life, for McClelland, considerations of accuracy of anticipation are the basis for the development of personality characteristics that are not particularly in the service of anticipating accurately. Let me be more specific. For example, in Kelly's theory, constructs, which are the elements of personality, are formed, used, and changed for the single purpose of ensuring better and better prediction. In McClelland's theory, expectations are only one kind of element of personality. The other major kind of *motives* (McClelland, 1951). But while the nature and content of motives certainly reflect the person's history of anticipational accuracy and inaccuracy, the motive is not primarily in the service of either increasing or decreasing anticipational accuracy. I will make this more clear in a moment. For the present, just keep in mind that motives are influencers of action in the direction of specific goals having little direct relationship to considerations of accuracy.

The point I have been making will become more clear if I trace for you the manner in which expression of the core tendency leads to the development of motives. Remember that the positive affect associated with moderate inaccuracy and the negative affect associated with great inaccuracy lead, respectively, to approach and avoidance actions. When the person has experienced a small discrepancy between expectation and occurrence, he approaches, or in some way brings himself closer to, the area of experience involved. And if the discrepancy is large, he avoids, or in some way forces himself farther away from, the area of experience involved. Let us consider two common areas of experience: that of affiliation with people, and that of achievement in work.

Suppose that the person's most frequent experience in the affiliative domain is that of having his expectations greatly violated by occurrences. This can happen if the particular people with whom he interacts are complex, inconsistent, and inconsiderate enough to be unpredictable. Assume that the person we are talking about is young enough to be impressionable, and unable to choose his associates easily. His predominant affective tone in interpersonal relationships will be unpleasant. If this condition goes on for any length of time, he will learn an enduring orientation (or motive) to avoid people. Every time the possibility of interaction arises, the memory of painful emotional consequences will also arise, leading the person to avoid the interaction as much as possible. But what you must see is that the goal of the motive is avoidance of interaction, not the achievement of total accuracy of predicion!

Now consider the area of work achievement. Suppose our young person's most frequent experience in this area is that of having his expectations violated only a little by occurrences. His expectations are not so greatly discomfirmed that he is discouraged, and not so completely accurate that he becomes bored and indifferent. Instead, he comes to regard working as a source of mild and pleasant surprises. This kind of accumulation of experience can be brought about by parents (McClelland *et al.* 1953, p. 62) who watch the child carefully enough to know when he has mastered some task he is working on, and are sensible enough to then give him another task that is a little beyond his grasp, but not completely outside of his capabilities. Under such conditions, the person will learn an enduring orientation (or motive) to strive for success (or achievement) in work. Every time the possibility of work arises, leading him to accept the work challenge as much as possible. Again, the goal of the motive is to approach or seek work, not to try for total accuracy of prediction!

I should point out that if the parents in the example about the affiliation area were more like the parents in the work area example, then a motive to approach interaction would have been learned. Similarly, if the parents in the work example were more like those in the affiliation example, then a motive to avoid work would result. In every area of experience, there is an approach motive and an avoidance motive possible, according to McClelland. But I will not pursue this further here, as motives are actually peripheral characteristics of personality in his thinking, their usefulness being mainly the understanding of individual differences.

In closing, I should make clear that the absence of reference to the concept of defense is not an oversight on my part. Like Kelly's position, that of McClelland gives no role to this concept. Even avoidance actions and motives are not strictly speaking defensive in the sense of debarring mental content from awareness.

CONSISTENCY MODEL: ACTIVATION VERSION

The cognitive dissonance version of the consistency model considers the match or mismatch among cognitive elements, typically expectations and perceptions of events. In contrast, the version of the consistency model to be discussed here considers the match or mismatch between customary and actual levels of activation or tension. As in all consistency positions, content is relatively unimportant. The theory of Fiske and Maddi is virtually the only activation position that has relevance for personality. As you will see, it is more comprehensive than the cognitive dissonance positions.

Fiske's and Maddi's position

Donald W. Fiske was born in Massachusetts in 1916, and after an early education at Harvard, received his Ph.D. in psychology from the University of Michigan in 1948. In a career of teaching and research in university settings, his major interests have been measurement of personality variables and understanding the conditions under which human behavior shows variability. At Harvard and in the Office of Strategic Services during World War II, Fiske came under the influence of Murray, Allport, and White. Fiske has been president of the Midwestern Psychological Association and is associate chairman of the Department of Psychology, University of Chicago.

Salvatore R. Maddi was born in New York, New York in 1933, and received a Ph.D. in psychology from Harvard in 1960. During his time at Harvard, he was fortunate enough to have as teachers Allport, Bakan, McClelland, Murray, and White. In a career emphasizing teaching and research in the university setting, Maddi's predominant interests have been in the need for variety, personality change, and existential psychology. Maddi's collaboration with Fiske began in 1960 and produced, over the years, the position described below. Maddi has been director of the Clinical Training Program and the Undergraduate Psychology Program in the Department of Psychology, University of Chicago.

Activation theory is a contemporary development in psychology that is having considerable impact on many subfields of the discipline. Understandably enough, given its complexity, the personality field has been among the last and least affected by activation theorizing. But Fiske and Maddi (1961; Maddi & Propst, 1971) have offered a version of activation theory that is not only more systematic and complete than most, but that also is quite relevant to personality. In the cognitive dissonance version of consistency theory, the emphasis is on the discrepancy or match between two cognitive elements, usually an expectation or belief on the one hand, and a perception of some event on the other. In the activation theory offered by Fiske and Maddi, discrepancy is also the major determinant of behavior. The discrepancy is not between two cognitive elements, however, but between the level of activation to which the person is accustomed and the level of activation he actually has at a given moment. Discrepancies between the customary and the actual levels of activation always produce behavior the aim of which is to reduce the discrepancy. Therefore, Fiske's and Maddi's position is exemplary of the pure consistency model.

Let me precipitate us into discussion of the position by stating its core tendency, which is that *the person will attempt to maintain the level of activation to which he is accustomed (that is characteristic of him).* In order to get some basis in personal experience for understanding the meaning of this core tendency, recognize that activation is a word referring to your level of excitement, or alertness, or energy. Try to remember times when what was going on made you more or less excited than usual, or required more or less alertness and energy than usual. If you found the situation too greatly or meagerly exciting and tried to do something about it, or found the alertness and energy demands too great or too slight and tried to do something about them, then you have within yourself a basis for intuitive understanding of the core tendency offered by Fiske and Maddi. Actually, some of you may have difficulty in recognizing the relevance of your own experience without additional, detailed consideration of the position. I think this is because the position is rather new and unfamiliar and because the psychological import of the concept of activation is not immediately apparent. Let us hasten, therefore, to more detailed study of the position.

Customary and actual levels of activation. According to Fiske and Maddi (1961, p. 14) activation is a neuropsychological concept, referring on the psychological side to the common core of meaning in such terms as alertness, attentiveness, tension, and subjective excitement, and on the neural side to the state of excitation in a postulated center of the brain. It is clear that on the psychological side, Fiske and Maddi are concerned with a general quality of organismic excitation similar to what so many other theorists we have considered refer to as tension. Fiske and Maddi attempt to make this view more plausible and convincing by exploring its neural substrate. On the neural side, they suggest that the reticular formation, a large subcortical area of the brain, is the focus of activation. In this, they are following much precedent (e.g., Jasper, 1958; O'Leary & Coben, 1958; Samuels, 1959), and attempting to integrate psychological and physiological levels of theorizing.

Having offered a rough definition of activation, Fiske and Maddi concern themselves with the determinants of this state of excitation. They implicate three dimensions of stimulation and three sources of stimulation, subsuming all these activation-influencing characteristics under the term *impact*. The three dimensions of stimulation are *intensity, meaningfulness*, and *variation*. Intensity, to be defined in terms of physical energy, is an obvious attribute of stimulation. The kind of difference referred to is that between a loud noise and a soft noise. Meaningfulness requires more clarification. In a sense, anything that can be called a stimulus at all has to have meaning. If it had no meaning, you would not even recognize it. Defined this way, meaningfulness would be such a general attribute of stimulation as to underlie all others, including intensity and variation. Fiske and Maddi have a more restricted meaning of meaningfulness. They refer primarily to the significance or importance of a stimulus for the experiencing organism. For example, the word "leave" has less meaningfulness for most people than does the word "fire" or the word "love." In considering variation, Fiske and Maddi make a number of points. First, variation refers to a state in which the current stimulus is different from that which preceded it—different in either intensity, meaningfulness, or both. So one aspect of variation is *change*. Another aspect of variation is *novelty*, or the state in which the current stimulus is unusual, infrequent in the person's total experience, regardless of whether or not it differs from the stimulus immediately preceding it. The final aspect of variation is *unexpectedness,* or the state in which the current stimulus deviates from what the person had come to believe was going to happen, regardless of whether it constitutes a change or is unusual in an overall sense.

Talking about the dimensions of stimulation that can influence activation prompts consideration of the sources of stimulation, for reasons of completeness if nothing else. The three sources stipulated by Fiske and Maddi are *exteroceptive, interoceptive,* and *cortical.* Extroceptive stimulation involves chemical, electrical, or mechanical excitation of the sense organs sensitive to events in the external world. In contrast, interoceptive stimulation refers to such excitation of the sense organs sensitive to events within the body itself. These two sources of stimulation are already well known and require no jutification. But it is unusual to consider cortical stimulation. Most psychologists who consider physiological events in the cortex tend to see them as reflecting stimulation from other places in the body or the outside world. What Fiske and Maddi are suggesting is that the cortex itself be considered one of the actual sources of stimulation. They are on logically sound ground in so doing, as the brain locus of activation is considered to be a subcortical center. That they are possibly on sound anatomical and physiological ground is suggested by the recent discovery that the cortex not only receives, but also sends nerve fibers to the reticular formation, which, as you will recall, is the implicated subcortical center. Hebb (1955) has suggested that the fibers sent to the reticular formation by the cortex may constitute the physiological substrate for understanding "the immediate drive properties of cognitive processes."

Fiske and Maddi make activation level a direct function of impact. Impact is, in turn, some direct function of the moment to moment intensity, meaningfulness, and variation of stimulation from interoceptive, exteroceptive, and cortical sources. Activation, impact, and the dimensions and sources of impact, being common to all men, are core characteristics of personality. Thus far, the theorizing of Fiske and Maddi may seem too complex and removed from phenomena of psychological significance to be very useful to the personologist. But bear with me, for the psychological significance of their position will soon emerge. And as for complexity, you should recognize the possibility that the kind of completeness aimed for by Fiske and Maddi may not only require such complexity but may also be quite useful in fostering understanding. You may have noticed, for example, that the discrepancy between expectation and occurrence stressed by McClelland and Kelly is represented as merely one aspect of variation by Fiske and Maddi. The other theorists make unexpectedness the basic determinant of tension or anxiety, terms which differ little in meaning from activation as used by Fiske and Maddi. But once you are introduced to the broad definition of stimulus characteristics producing impact that Fiske and Maddi prefer, you are likely to begin to wonder whether the other theorists have not indeed oversimplified their thinking concerning the determinants of tension.

Having considered actual level of activation, which is given at any moment in time by the total impact of stimulation, we can turn to the *customary level of activation*. Fiske and Maddi assume that the levels of activation experienced by a person over the course of many days tend to be fairly similar. After all, the regularities and continuities of living should result in day-to-day similarities in the intensity, meaningfulness, and variation of stimulation from the various sources. Over time, the person should come to experience a particular level of activation as normal, or usual for a particular part of the day. These normal, usual, customary levels of activation can be roughly measured by averaging the actual activation curves for a person over a period of some days. Such measurement was accomplished by Kleitman (1939), who found a regularity which he called the "cycle of existence." This cycle of existence has a single major rise and fall during the waking period. After waking, higher organisms typically show an increasing degree of alertness, then a relatively long period with a gradual rise and later a gradual decline, and, finally, a sharper decline toward drowsiness and return to the sleeping state. A number of physiological variables, such as heart rate and body temperature, follow the same course (Kleitman & Ramsaroop, 1948; Sidis, 1908). Fiske and Maddi assume that the curve described as the cycle of existence is the curve of customary level of activation. As everyone has a customary level of activation, whatever differences in shape it may take from person-to-person, it is a core characteristic of personality. So too, of course, is the previously discussed actual level of activation.

Once you have postulated an actual and a customary level of activation, it is almost natural to consider the match or mismatch between them to be of importance. And this is just what Fiske and Maddi do. Their core tendency refers to the attempt on the part of the person to maintain actual activation at the level which is customary for a given time of the day. If actual activation deviates from customary level, *impact-modifying behavior* is instituted. Two kinds of deviation are possible. When actual activation level is above that which is customary, *impact-decreasing behavior* occurs, and when actual activation level is below that which is customary, *impact-increasing behavior* occurs. You should note that impact-decreasing behavior must involve attempts to decrease the intensity, meaningfulness, or variation of stimulation from interoceptive, exteroceptive, or cortical sources, and that impact-increasing behavior must be oppositely defined.

Fiske and Maddi are classed as consistency theorists because they consider the overall directionality of living to be the search for a match between actual and customary levels of activation. In clarifying why people show the core tendency, Fiske and Maddi (1961) assume that the coincidence of actual and customary levels of activation is experienced as a state of well-being, whereas discrepancies between the two lead to greater degrees of negative affect the larger they get. It is to avoid the discomfort of negative affect that people attempt to reduce discrepancies between actual and customary levels of activation, and success in this attempt is experienced as positive affect.

The theory of Fiske and Maddi is a pure consistency position because the ideal state is a complete absence of discrepancy between actual and customary levels of activation. There is no notion, as in McClelland's variant position, that a small degree of discrepancy is a positive thing. But McClelland's insistence that positions like that of Kelly are limited because they cannot give importance to boredom and the attendant interest in unexpected events is incorporated by Fiske and Maddi. The incorporation involves theorizing that the customary level of activation cannot only be overshot by actual activation, but undershot as well. When it is undershot, the person will actively seek out stimulation of greater variation, meaningfulness, and intensity. In part, this means he will seek our unexpected events. This property of the position of Fiske and Maddi is associated with two others important enough to mention. The first is that they are not postulating a position making tension reduction the aim of all functioning, as are the other pure consistency theorists. Although theirs is a pure consistency position, Fiske and Maddi agree with McClelland that some of the person's functioning aims to reduce tension or activation, whereas some aims to increase it. The other property I should mention is that Fiske and Maddi assume that usual, everyday life situations involve some variation (change, novelty, unexpectedness) as well as some intensity and meaningfulness. In other words, some more than minimal degree of variation is assumed to be normal. This assumption is implicit in the notion that the customary level of activation is high enough at all times in the day that it can indeed be undershot by the actual level of activation. To Fiske and Maddi, the assumption of other pure consistency positions that an absence of unexpectedness is the ideal situation is a little ludicrous because it seems so inconsistent with everyday life. Fiske and Maddi agree with McClelland that the human being would be bored in a situation of total certainty and predictability, in that such a situation would be too low in impact to produce activation that came up to customary levels.

The theory of Fiske and Maddi is a good example of what is called a homeostatic position. In other words, whenever there is a deviation from a norm of some sort, in this case customary level of activation, there is an attempt, which gets stronger the greater the deviation, to return to the norm. There is a general tendency in psychology for all tension reduction theories to be considered homeostatic in nature. Thus, the theories of Freud, Sullivan, Angyal, Bakan, Rank, Kelly, and Festinger, if not a few others as well, would be considered homeostatic positions. Actually it strikes me that these theories are really only half of the homeostatic model, because the norm that is assumed is a minimum state. This means that the norm can only be exceeded, but not undershot. The theory of Fiske and Maddi seems, by comparison with the others, a true homeostatic position in that the norm is some quantity greater than minimum and less than maximum. Once having a theory like that of Fiske and Maddi, the partial inapplicability to the other theories of the concept of homeostasis becomes apparent.

Many concepts have been mentioned in the preceding pages, and perhaps it would be well to bring this subsection to a close by summarizing them in the terminology of the core of personality. The tendency of the person to maintain the level of activation which is characteristic or customary for him at each point in time is the core tendency of personality. There are no differences between people in this tendency, which infuses all of living. There are a number of core characteristics of personality associated with this core tendency. They are actual level of activation, customary level of activation, discrepancy between the two, impact-increasing behavior, and impact-decreasing behavior. These concepts bear the same invariant relationships to each other in all people. To be sure, there are many sources of individual differences—customary levels of activation may differ, and there may be many different strategies of increasing or decreasing impact, to name a few—but these are matters for discussion in Chapter 8 on the periphery of personality.

Formation of the characteristic curve of activation. Fiske and Maddi do not consider the customary curve of activation to be present at birth; it is probably formed out of experience. To be sure, they do suggest the possibility that genetic considerations, presently not well understood, may predispose the person to a customary curve of activation having a particular shape and height. But the accumulated experience of particular levels of activation at particular times of the day is considered the major formative influence on the characteristic curve of activation. So, the first importance of the environment for the person is as the major determinant of his characteristic curve of activation. This determination takes palce sometime during childhood, though Fiske and Maddi are quite vague on this. In a way, their vagueness is not very surprising, for we have seen that the consistency model gives little concern to the content of experience and of inherent nature. In Kelly and McClelland, it is the fact of discrepancy between expectation and occurrence, not the content of the discrepancy, that influences behavior. For Fiske and Maddi, it is the impact of early stimulation, not its content, that has a formative influence. Once you de-emphasize the importance of stimulus content and of inherent nature, then you have little logical impetus to develop elaborate theories of stages of development during which the content of your own wishes and the content of reactions from specific important people are important.

But Fiske and Maddi do believe that as experience accumulates, as the stimulation patterns of successive days recur and recur, the characteristic curve of activation begins to solidify. Once set, this curve does not change very much under ordinary circumstances. This is because of the nature of the effects on personality and experience of the impetus to maintain activation at the characteristic level. At this point it is essential to distinguish between *correction* for discrepancies between actual and characteristic levels of activation that really occur, and *anticipatory attempts* to ensure that such discrepancies will not occur (Maddi & Propst, 1971). I will discuss anticipatory functioning now, as it is basic to understanding why the characteristic curve of activation does not change once solidified, and delay consideration of correctional functioning until later. As experience accumulates, the person learns certain habitual ways of functioning that are useful in ensuring that large discrepancies between actual and characteristic levels of activation will not occur. These ways of influencing the impact of present and future intensity, meaningfulness, and variation of stimulation from interoceptive, exteroceptive, and cortical sources form a large part of the peripheral personality. If peripheral personality is a successful expression of the core tendency, then the conditions under which the characteristic curve of activation would change are not encountered. The person's range of experience and activities is selected and maintained in order to yield degrees of impact at various times during the day resulting in actual levels of activation that would match those which are characteristic. If anything, the longer the person lives, the more deeply entrenched will be his characteristic curve of activation. Only if he were forced to be in prolonged circumstances of unusual impact levels—an example might be the battlefield—would there be conditions of stimulation likely to shift the characteristic curve of activation.

Anticipational and correctional attempts to maintain consistency. It may seem to you that Fiske and Maddi, like Freud, consider personality to remain essentially static after childhood, but actually this is not the case. Although the customary curve of activation is considered to remain roughly the same under ordinary circumstances, behavior and personality processes expressing the anticipatory function of the core tendency must actually change in order that this curve remain steady. This may seem paradoxical, but it is really very simple and understandable. One function of the anticipatory processes is to ensure that future levels of activation will not fall below those which are characteristic. But this statement must be understood alongside the fact that any stimulation, regardless of its initial impact, will lose impact as it is prolonged. We adapt to stimulation that has appreciable duration. A sound that seems initially loud becomes overlooked if it continues long enough. Something initially meaningful becomes ordinary as time goes on. Variation is especially short-lived, for any novel or unexpected stimulus loses so much impact after a while that it may become boring. A great deal of research testifies to the conclusion that the initial impact of stimulation decreases as its experience is prolonged (see Fiske & Maddi, 1961).

What this means is that as the person lives longer and longer, he must continually shift his anticipatory strategies for ensuring that future levels of activation will not be too low for comfort. In action, he must continually broaden his range of activities and interests. In thought and feeling, he must become more and more subtle and differentiated, for one can thereby ensure that future stimulation will actually be experienced as more impactful than it would be if experienced now. If you see a Jackson Pollack painting right now, it might have a low level of impact for you because it seems nothing more than a smear of colors, repetitive at best. But, if you increase the subtlety of your cognitive and affective processes, you will be much more sensitive to the same painting on seeing it in the future. Then it may have great impact, for you will perceive the many strands of paint built up layer on layer, and the subtle differences between various parts of the canvas. Whether or not we agree on Jackson Pollack, I think you can see what is meant by ever-increasing cognitive and emotional differentiatedness as a basis for ensuring that activation will not fall too low in the future. Attempting to approach the point where one can see the universe in a grain of sand is expressive of cognitive, affective elaboration of experience in order to offset its natural tendency to lose impact as it is prolonged or reexperienced.

But in order to properly maintain characteristic activation, the person must also develop anticipatory strategies to ensure that future impact not be higher than characteristic level. This is especially necessary to balance off the possible, though unintended side effects of anticipatory attempts to keep activation from falling below the characteristic level. When you try to ensure this by becoming more cognitively, affectively, and actionally differentiated, you cannot very precisely predict where the thing will end. If you are forever increasing your search for new, and more meaningful and intense experiences, you increase the likelihood of precipitating a crisis in which your ability to keep what happens to you within manageable limits is threatened. You might unwittingly precipitate yourself into a state of impact so great that an uncomfortably high level of activation is the result. To be sure, if this were to happen, then the person, according to the theory, would scramble to correct the high level of activation. But it is inefficient of the person to wait until activation is already too high before acting, just as it is inefficient of him to rely on correction of levels of activation that are already too low.

Progressively greater cognitive, affective, and actional differentiation is the anticipatory technique for keeping up activation, but what is the technique for keeping activation low enough? Maddi and Propst (1963) indicate that the strategy for ensuring that future levels of activation will not be too high is the progressive increase in principles and techniques for integrating the elements of cognition, affect, and action differentiated in order to ensure that activation will not be too low. The essence of integration is the organization of the differentiated elements into broad categories of function or significance. Integrative processes permit you to see how some experience is similar in meaning and intensity to other experiences, regardless of how different it may be in terms of the more concrete analysis expressive of differentiation processes. There is no conflict between the processes of differentiation and integration. No matter how sensitive you become to our Jackson Pollack painting on the basis of differentiation processes, you can also place it in the overall scheme of his work, the work of contemporaries, and the history of art through exercise of integrative processes. Integrative processes function to ensure that activation levels experienced in the future will not be wildly high, without blanketing out the possibility of the sensitive experiencing needed in order to avoid dismally low activation levels.

Actually, as you can tell, the picture of personality offered is one in which there is continual change through the life-span, this change being in the service of ensuring a minimum of discrepancy between actual and customary levels of activation. The change involves progressively greater differentiation and integration, or what we have encountered before as psychological growth. With varying emphasis, this notion appears in actualization and perfection versions of the fulfillment model. It is not particularly characteristic of psychosocial conflict theories, but it does play some role in intrapsychic conflict theories. Fiske and Maddi are the only consistency theorists to refer to psychological growth. Indeed, their approach seems more advantageous than those of the actualization and perfection theorists, because it explains psychological growth rather than simply assuming it.

Now it is possible to return to correctional rather than anticipatory processes, in order to understand their special significance. First, it is obvious that a correction for discrepancy between actual and characteristic levels of activation is only necessary when anticipatory processes have failed. Correctional attempts, for the adult, have the quality of emergency maneuvers (Maddi & Propst, 1971). Simply put, Maddi and Propst (1971) believe that impact-decreasing behavior aimed at reducing an actual level of activation that is already higher than charcteristic operates to distort reality in the sense of screening out stimulus impact that is really there. They see impact-increasing behavior aimed at augmenting an actual level of activation that is already lower than characteristic to be equally distorting of reality, but to involve the kind of distortion that adds something to the stimulation that is not really there. These sensitizing and desensitizing aspects of correctional behavior come close to one aspect of the traditional meaning of defense. But we must be careful to recognize that Maddi and Propst do not mean to imply the active debarring from awareness of impulses and wishes forming a real but dangerous part of the person himself. They merely assume a mechanism for exaggerating or underestimating the real impact of stimulation. In this, they come closer than any other consistency theorists to emphasizing a concept of defense.

In summary, the position of Fiske and Maddi is a consistency theory, which focuses upon discrepancy between actual and customary activation, rather than accuracy of prediction. As worded, it is broad enough to subsume other consistency positions having this latter focus. Fiske and Maddi conceptualize behavior and personality as partially oriented toward tension reduction, and partially oriented toward tension increase. In this, their approach resembles that of McClelland, though theirs is a pure rather than variant consistency position. Fiske and Maddi, like other consistency theorists, are eclectic with regard to content, in that their conceptualization of humans and society includes little that is necessary and immutable. They believe that the essential features of the core of personality remain fixed, but that peripheral personality changes continually throughout life, in order to satisfy the requirements of the core tendency. This continual change is in the direction of simultaneous increases in differentiation and integration, or psychological growth.

Chapter 5 RATIONAL AND EMPIRICAL ANALYSES OF CORE CONSIDERATIONS

The previous chapters covered the theorizing of a goodly number of personologists, and yet, only three basic models for personality theorizing have emerged. These models characterize the inmost recesses of psychological man in terms of conflict, fulfillment, or consistency. There are, of course, some variants on these three models, and, in addition, each of the models has two discernible versions. Further, each personologist has his own special emphases and verbal nuances. Nonetheless, it is a very significant thing to learn that there are so few ways of conceptualizing the overall directionality and universal features of life.

Whereas in the previous chapter I was concerned with distinguishing among the various theories exemplifying each of the three models, in this chapter I would like to emphasize some conclusions about the essential nature of the models. Having considered their essential nature, I will then pinpoint some issues regarding the core of personality raised by the similarities and differences among the three models. These matters constitute the rational analysis mentioned in the title of this chapter. Having posed issues, I will also conduct the empirical analysis promised in the chapter title by discussing the results of systematic research that bear on the issue. This will constitute a beginning on the arduous but nonetheless necessary task of determining the strengths and weaknesses inherent in the three models for personality.

ESSENTIAL FEATURES OF THE THREE MODELS

The conflict model

Everything essential to the conflict model can be understood once the idea is grasped that in this view the human is inextricably caught in the opposition of two great forces. In the intrapsychic version of the conflict position, exemplified by the theories of Rank, Angyal, Bakan, and Jung, great forces originate within the person. Although it may not be immediately apparent, Jung's position also stresses two great forces. They are the individualistic, worldly, practical activities of the ego (or conscious mind), and the communal, ancient, racial memories of the collective unconscious. In the psychosocial version of this model, only one of the forces is inherent to the person, with the other being inherent to society. The theories of Freud, Murray, and the ego psychologists, make this kind of conflict assumption. In all conflict theories, conflict is experienced as an uncomfortable state of tension and anxiety. The overall aim of life, therefore, is to reduce tension and anxiety as much as possible by minimizing conflict.

In all versions of the conflict model, life is at best a compromise. This view is inevitable once you assume an inherent and unavoidable conflict at the core of personality. The compromise cannot take the form of erasing one of the two great forces, for both forces are inherent and basic, even if one of them does not originate in the person. Therefore, psychological sickness or maladjustment is usually defined by conflict theorists as the attempt to live as if only one of the two forces existed. Such an attempt must be considered a failure, if the logic of the conflict model is to be served. In Rank's theory, excessive placation of the death fear leads to neurotic isolation, whereas excessive placation of the life fear leads to herd conformity. In the theories of Freud and Murray, unmitigated expression of instincts, the force inherent to the person, is defined as psychopathy and leads in the direction of destruction of self and others, whereas unmitigated expression of the force inherent in society, in the form of superego, leads to the excessive, unrealistic, punitive guilt and defensiveness which is responsible for neurosis. Clearly, then, the attempt to live as if there were only one and not two great forces is unworkable.

What will work is a compromise in which balance is achieved between the opposing forces. Thus, the concrete patterns of living must always express both forces at the same time, in order for the life to be effective. While it is certainly possible, within the limits of the conflict model, to imagine a workable compromise in which one of the forces will occasionally gain ascendancy over the other, these occurrences must be superimpositions upon an underlying dynamic balance between the forces. In Rank's terms one must minimize both the fear of life and the fear of death. Jung dignifies the achieved balance between ego and the unconscious (personal and collective) by the term selfhood. And for Freud, Murray, and the ego psychologists, the highest purpose of life is to gain a maximum degree of instinct gratification with a minimum degree of pain and guilt. Here too we see the notion of a balancing of the two great forces, in the form of id and superego requirements. There is much in Sullivan that agrees with this. With a conflict model, the best that can be achieved in life is the compromise of balance.

But there is more that needs saying about the version of the conflict model that assumes one force to be inherent in the person and the other in society. Since the forces must be opposing for conflict to ensue, this version necessarily defines the human as an individual with selfish aims, because society must, of course, be defined in group terms, in terms of the corporate good. Because society is made up of other intelligent beings, the individual's selfishness can be detected and severely punished. Because, in his selfishness, he is against these other people, the individual can be made to feel ashamed and guilty. What all this means is that one of the two forces, that inherent in society, has the power to detect and thwart the other, individualistic force. But the individualistic force does no have any similar power. Therefore, if a compromise involving balance is to be achieved, the individualistic force must have some protection to offset the detecting and thwarting power of the societal force. If there was no such protection, the person would have to renounce his nature, and this would obviate a compromise.

What I am trying to show is that the logic of the psychosocial version of the conflict model leads easily to the concept of defense as a continuous, necessary process in successful living. It is defensiveness that offsets the special detecting and thwarting power of the societal force. In attempting to avoid the pain and guilt he would suffer due to his selfish instincts, the person institutes defenses that have the dual purpose of shielding him from recognition of his selfishness and of encouraging instinctual expression in ways that are relatively innocuous from the standpoint of society. Freud's theory, of course, is the prime example of this kind of position. Recall that he even dubs unmitigated expression of instincts, *pleasure-principle* functioning, whereas functioning so as to maximize instinctual gratification at the same time that pain and guilt are minimized is called *reality-principle* functioning.

So, whenever you encounter a conflict position in which one force is inherent in the person and the other in society, you can expect, if the position is logically consistent, that the concept of defense will be preeminent in the achievement of a compromise of balance, which is the healthiest state. The distinction in such positions between mental health and illness is not made in terms of whether or not there are defenses, for there are always defenses. The distinction is made in terms of whether the defenses promote the effective compromise of balance, or the ineffective denial of one of the two opposing forces.

Turning for comparison to the version of conflict theory that assumes both opposing forces to be inherent to the person, we do not find the emphasis on defense that can be found in the psychological version discussed above. Because both forces originate in the person, there is no special problem of one force stressing detection and thwarting of the other. Hence, there is no logical necessity for the more vulnerable force to be supplemented by some concept serving a protective function. To my way of thinking, it is not surprising that Rank, Angyal, and Bakan have not emphasized the concept of defense in their theorizing, even though one could say with some truth that their theories are not as completely developed as those of the psychosocial theorists. In this context, Jung's emphasis on eliminating the personal unconscious and accepting the collective unconscious becomes understandable. In point of fact, the intrapsychic theorists do not need a protective concept, and therefore, their view of a compromise of balance does not emphasize defensiveness.

In the psychosocial position, involving as it does such emphasis upon compromise and defense, the highest or healthiest form of living is defined primarily in terms of the adjustment of the person to the socially determined corporate good. Such a position inevitably involves defining the highest form of living in terms of dependability, considerateness, responsibility, generosity, morality, and conformity. Indeed, one finds this emphasis upon what might be called good citizenship in the theories of Freud, and the other psychosocial theorists. A little of this emphasis is also found in the intrapsychic theorists. That the intrapsychic version of the conflict model has less emphasis on adjustment to the pressures of society in its definition of the healthiest state is to be understood in terms of the relatively low reliance of this position on the concept of defense, coupled with the assumption that both opposing forces originate within the person.

Another concomitant of the emphasis in the conflict model upon compromise and defense is the view that the personality is rather completely set in its general outlines by the time childhood is finished. The rest of life can be reasonably well characterized as a filling out and elaboration of the patterns established early in life. Whatever change in personality takes place during adulthood is more a matter of degree than of kind. And indeed, stability of personality is a more salient fact for conflict theorists than is personality change. Once again, what I have just said is more true for the psychosocial than for the intrapsychic versions of the model, because the former emphasizes defense more than the latter.

An additional word of emphasis concerning the content of the two forces in conflict theories is in order. All versions of the conflict model tend to stress one force as individualistic and the other force as communal, regardless of whether or not both forces are seen to arise from the organism itself. Death fear is a tendency toward independence and uniqueness, whereas life fear is a tendency toward dependence and similarity with others. The ego, for Jung, is a mainly individualistic thing, whereas the collective unconscious is that which relates you to mankind. While there is perhaps no strict logical necessity that the two opposing forces of a conflict theory stress individualistic and communal content, they nonetheless do so.

The fulfillment model

In order to understand the fulfillment model, you must realize that it assumes only one great force in living rather than the two of conflict theories. Although fulfillment positions sometimes conceptualize a way in which the person can get into conflict, conflict is not inevitable or basic. Hence, the fulfillment theories do not see life as necessarily a compromise. Rather, they see it as the unfolding of the one great force, with the most successful living involving the most vigorous expression of the force. In the fulfillment model, the more vigorous is the expression of the force, the greater is the experience of tension. Tension is not intimately associated with anxiety, however, as it is in the conflict model. Although fulfillment positions do not strictly speaking assume that the person aims at the increase of tension per se, such increases are integrally a part of expressing the great force, and are not, in any case, particularly uncomfortable.

In one version of the fulfillment model, emphasis is upon realization of one's own inherent capabilities. Here you will recognize the actualization theories of Rogers, and Maslow. Adler, White, Allport, Fromm, and existential psychologists define another version of the fulfillment model that stresses the perfection of life through striving toward ideals. Rather than considering individually unique potentialities, as would actualization theorists, perfection theorists stress the capabilities of the human species. This can be seen in Fromm's emphasis upon human nature, and in Adler's and White's emphasis upon mastery and the compensation for initial inferiorities.

Turning to a more concrete consideration of the content of the great force, we find fulfillment theorists in agreement that it is heavily psychological in nature. It is not so much oriented toward mere survival through use of capabilities as toward the enhancement of living, above and beyond survival, that can come through perfection or the expression of capabilities. Many fulfillment theorists, such as Maslow, Allport, Fromm, and the existentialists actually separate the person's animal nature from his human nature. The pursuit of animal nature, which leads to survival, is really rather unimportant alongside the pursuit of human nature. Although the great force tends to be identified with human nature alone, there are exceptions among fulfillment theorists. Rogers is the only personologist in this group who does not make much distinction between animal and human nature, preferring to consider the great force to be that which underlies both enhancement and survival.

Although the great force of the fulfillment theorists tends to be individualistic in nature, it is not so in the manner of conflict theories. Fulfillment theorists generally see no special difference between successful individual living and successful group living. If the person is vigorously expressing the great force, his life with himself and with others will be rich, varied, and satisfying. Adler's is perhaps the most formal statement of this emphasis, in that he specifies both mastery and social interest as facets of the core tendency of personality. As the requirements of individual and group living are by no means different for fulfillment theorists, they do not conceptualize any inevitability of conflict here.

But as existentialism makes especially clear, it is not conventionality that marks the most constructive social commitment. Probably because of this, conflict can come about between the person and his social context. Those fulfillment theorists who have elaborated this matter, notably Rogers, Maslow, Fromm, and existential psychologists make it clear that when conflict occurs, it is due to the existence of a societal context that has become inhuman and punitive in some way. Only when it is failed by society can expression of the great force lead to conflict. Although fulfillment theorists are generally somewhat vague about how society can become inhuman and punitive, they do tend to stress, with Rogers, significant people in the person's life who are too crabbed to accept him completely and lovingly, and suggest, with Fromm, the unfortunate roots of such difficulties in the economic, political, and cultural milieu.

It is this kind of conflict, according to fulfillment theorists, that jeopardizes vigorous expression of the great force, eventuating in an unnecessarily trivial, conforming, unsatisfying life. Mental illness is defined by fulfillment theorists as the attempt to live as if the great force did not exist, in order to avoid conflict between it and a societal context. As you can see, the way in which mental illness is defined is similar in fulfillment and conflict theory, with the difference, of course, that as there is in fulfillment theory only one great force that can be denied, there is only one class of illness, whereas conflict theory, with its two great forces that can be denied, conceptualizes two ways of becoming ill. Interestingly enough, some fulfillment theorists, in considering the conflict between the person and an inhuman social context, have recourse to the concept of defense. This is true most notably of Rogers, but appears in Maslow, Fromm, Allport, and existential psychology as well. In some ways, the concept of defense used works similarly to that of psychoanalytic theory. In talking of a punitive, inhuman society, fulfillment theorists are postulating an intelligent force which is set upon the detection and thwarting of part or all of the great force. The person can be punished and feel pain and guilt. Therefore, he protects himself by instituting defensive processes such that (1) he does not see the parts of the great force that would frighten him concerning retribution, and (2) he channels expression of the great force in socially innocuous paths.

Although the concept of defense works in the same manner and has purpose similar to what it does in conflict theory, there is a very important difference to be recognized. For fulfillment theorists, conflict is not inevitable, and the highest form of living is not a compromise. So defense only has a logical function in their thinking if, and when, conflict actually develops. Even if conflict is found to develop fairly often, this does not change the fact that fulfillment theorists have no reason to define defensiveness as part of the highest state of being, or mental health. This is the major significance of the difference between fulfillment and conflict positions. It means that the fulfillment model defines the highest form of living in terms of transcendence of society, rather than conformity to it. Emphasis in ideal living is upon imaginativeness, spontaneity, individuality, self-reliance, openness to experience, and an unflinching knowledge of the inmost recesses of oneself. This emphasis contrasts sharply with that on good citizenship found in the conflict model.

When they consider the entire life-span, fulfillment theorists think in terms of a fairly continual developmental process such that personality changes throughout childhood, adolescence, and adulthood. The changes are generally considered to indicate progressively greater differentiation and integration, or psychological growth, at least when conflict and defense do not interfere. This emphasis on personality change in the direction of growth is very understandable considering the fulfillment theorist's assumption that there is only one great force which normally leads the person to attempt to realize his capabilities and perfect himself. Continual personality change is as logically a part of fulfillment theory as is the emphasis of the conflict model on personality stability once the childhood years are past.

The consistency model

In order to appreciate the meaning of the consistency model, you must recognize that it does not stress the importance of the specific content of personality and inherent forces, considering instead the importance of the congruence, compatibility, or fit between various aspects of personality or elements of content. In the cognitive dissonance version of the model, these elements of content are cognitive in nature. For Kelly, one of these cognitive elements is the construct, or conceptualization, and the other element is the perception of actual occurrences. McClelland's emphasis is very similar in that one kind of element is the expectation, and the other is the perception of events. Festinger's theory includes these two elements as well, but is perhaps more broad in that the consistency between two conceptualizations, or for that matter, the consistency between two perceptions, is also of importance. Regardless of the differences among these theories, they all agree that one kind of element has primarily to do with ideas or expectations as to what the world and you are like, whereas the other kind of element has primarily to do with observations or perceptions as to what the world and you seem actually to be doing. In contrast, the version of the consistency model exemplified by Fiske and Maddi concerns itself with the match between the level of excitation or tension that is customary for the person, and that which he is actually experiencing at some particular point in time. The activation version is similar to the cognitive dissonance version, nonetheless, in stressing the goodness of past experience as a basis for coming to grips with what is happening now, and in considering any content of experience as important as any other content.

The cognitive dissonance version of the consistency model, when it appears in pure form, is strictly a tension-reductive viewpoint. Its major message is that inconsistency or incompatibility between a certain idea or expectancy and a certain observation is an intensely uncomfortable state of high tension and anxiety. So uncomfortable that in the attempt to avoid incompatibilities and thereby reduce tension, the story of life is contained. For Kelly, the entire personality is either the result of attempts to avoid and resolve incompatibilities, or the expression of unresolved incompatibilities. Once you get to McClelland's variant on the cognitive dissonance position, however, you find a viewpoint that agrees with the purer theories only for large incompatibilities, but considers small incompatibilities to be actually pleasant and therefore sought after. Incompatibilities are still characterized as tension states, but it is no longer assumed that all degrees of tension are unpleasant. McClelland's position amounts to portraying the person as seeking small increments in tension, but avoiding large increments. Concerning tension, the activation version of the consistency model is more similar to McClelland than to Kelly and the other cognitive dissonance theorists. Activation is characterized as tension, but the person is not portrayed as uniformly avoiding or minimizing tension. When his tension level is higher than customary, he will reduce it, but when it is lower than customary, he will increase it. The person finds tension of a too meager degree as unpleasant as tension of a too intense degree.

According to the consistency model, the only attributes of the person considered both inherent and important for understanding personality are (1) the bases for reacting affectively to incompatibilities, and (2) the broad techniques whereby unpleasant affective experiences can be terminated. But the content of thoughts and perceptions are learned, as is the customary level of activation. Unlike conflict theory and fulfillment theory, there is no definition of great forces in terms of concrete, immutable content. This eclecticism with regard to what the content of personality is likely to be is the major reason why consistency theories stress individual uniqueness and the peripheral rather than core level of personality.

Because they do not stress conflict where one of the two opposing forces has the power to detect and thwart the other, consistency theories should have no logical necessity for the concept of defense. And lo and behold, they do not use it! In Kelly's view, when a construct fails to predict accurately an observed occurrence, the construct is modified so as to be potentially more predictive of the real world of events. This process of modification is properly considered rational trial and error. McClelland believes that the person straightforwardly approaches those domains of experience that have typically yielded small unexpectedness, and avoids those that have typically yielded great unexpectedness. Actually McClelland and Kelly explicitly indicate that the concept of defense is unnecessary. This emphasis is even more extreme than in fulfillment theory, which though it does not make defense constant, recognizes its occasional importance depending on the circumstances of living.

Although Festinger incorporates this emphasis upon rational trial and error in his cognitive dissonance theory, he also tends closer to the use of a concept of defense. He comes closest when he recognizes that the ways of reducing incompatibilities include not only the rational alternatives of modifying one's concepts and avoiding certain domains of experience, but also the more irrational techniques of distorting and denying aspects of the real world. This is, after all, what defenses are supposed to do. Fiske and Maddi also tend toward the conceptualization of defensiveness. They refer to the attempts on the part of the person to correct for situations in which a discrepancy between actual and customary activation has already taken place. Such correction is achieved by manufacturing or denying stimulus impact, depending upon whether activation level needs to be raised or lowered. Such corrections distort the real impact of the stimulation. But as with Festinger, Fiske and Maddi do not explicitly use the concept of defense, and do not refer in their notion of correction to any inhibition of real parts of human nature, to avoid conflict with society. All in all, it seems reasonable to conclude that the concept of defense is not very important in the consistency model.

In considering the entire life-span of the person, the consistency, like the fulfillment model, portrays personality as changing fairly continuously. This emphasis on change seems understandable in a position that does not emphasize conflict, defense, or inherent characteristics of personality with their immutable content. Personality change should occur as a concomitant of the natural process of encountering different events in the world of experience. If there is any difference between the fulfillment and consistency models regarding the nature of personality change, it is that the former emphasizes patterned change in the form of ever-increasing differentiation and integration, or psychological growth, more than does the latter. But this distinction is very close to splitting hairs. After all, psychological growth is a notion implicit in Kelly's thinking, and it achieves explicit importance in the theorizing of Fiske and Maddi, who actually provide an explanation for it, rather than merely assuming it as do most of the fulfillment theorists.

SOME ISSUES RAISED BY THE THREE MODELS

As you have seen, conflict, fulfillment, and consistency models differ in a number of ways. Some of these ways are at a very abstract level, such as the assumption of conflict theories that the person and society basically aim at different things versus the assumption of fulfillment theory that the goals of the person and society are compatible. Such abstract differences raise issues that are difficult to resolve, certainly in terms of empirical evidence and even in terms of rational argumentation. From my point of view, the most fruitful inquiry that can be conducted with such extremely abstract characteristics of theories is to see whether each position has logical consistency. Thus, if a theory makes the assumption that the person and society are antagonistic, then it is only logical to also assume that life is, at best, a compromise. To see life otherwise would be rather inconsistent with the assumption of inevitable conflict.

In the preceding section of this chapter, I have tried to consider the three models as to their internal logic, and to determine, in some rudimentary way, how well particular theories exemplifying the models conform to that logic. This is a very difficult task, partly because the particular theories are sometimes incompletely explicit and metaphorically stated. Nonetheless, it seems reasonably clear to me that most conflict, fulfillment, and consistency theories show decent logical consistency. But even more important, the essential features of conflict, fulfillment, and consistency models, aside from any particular theories that fall within them, are quite consistent. These three models, then, emerge as serious descriptions of the core of personality.

But is there anything more we can do toward deciding which of the models, or which features of the models, are the most fruitful for understanding personality? Certainly, I have just said that further consideration of very abstract issues raised by the differences between them is not likely to be useful. But it seems to me that there are some slightly more concrete issues that can be deduced from differences among the models which may well bear further consideration here. The issues I have in mind can be discussed with regard to more empirical considerations. Hence, there is much to learn from addressing these issues. As you will see, some of them involve differences between two of the models only, whereas others involve the agreement of two of the models, and disagreement with the third.

First issue: Is the concept of defense tenable?

Both conflict and fulfillment positions use the concept of defense, whereas consistency positions are examples of theories of personality that do not ordinarily consider the concept necessary. The concept of defense has also come in for considerable criticism from psychologists who are not personologists and from philosophers, mainly on the grounds that it seems too implausible and illogical. Therefore, this first issue is very important in our attempt to determine the most fruitful directions in theorizing about human personality.

We should approach discussion of this issue by first ensuring that we are in agreement concerning the meaning of the concept of defense. According to all theorists who use the concept, a defense is a technique for avoiding the anxiety that would be aroused by recognition that there existed in you some thought or action that would lead to punishment, guilt, or feelings of unworthiness. The bases of punishment, guilt, and feelings of unworthiness, according to most theorists using the concept of defense, are in conflictful parent-child relationships, the conflict being produced either because the aims of the person and the society are inevitably incompatible, or because these aims have become incompatible through society's failure. The defense is instituted virtually at the same time as the arousal of anxiety, and therefore not much anxiety is actually experienced, if the defense is effective. Once instituted, the defense tends to persist, because the underlying conflict also persists.

The successful defense avoids anxiety by distorting or denying to awareness the underlying conflict. This is accomplished by blocking recognition of the thoughts or actions that would bring the person into difficulty with society or its internalized form in the conscience. This blocking of recognition is an active process, not merely the absence of awareness through inattention or habit. Rather, the person would not be able to become aware of the thoughts or actions even if he tried, or were pushed by others. The underlying conflict would have to be resolved or at least accepted before any awareness could occur.

As you can see, any theory of defense is a complicated thing. It includes a conceptualization of conflict and of unconscious mental content. Additional complication is added by the fact that theorists using the concept of defense generally recognize different kinds of defensive operations. The smallest number of defenses is found in Roger's theory, which considers only out-and-out denial, and then less-extreme distortion. The largest number of defenses is to be found in psychoanalytic thinking, which includes such examples as repression, projection, denial, reaction formation, intellectualization, undoing, and sublimation. In psychoanalytic theory, each of these defenses has different effects upon living, though all have the general purpose of warding off anxiety by rendering conflicts unconscious.

The development and popularity of the concept of defense came about through the observations of personologists primarily interested in psychopathological states. By and large, these observations represent semiempirical evidence in the form of insight-provoking cases. Summarizing them would be a useful way of approaching a precise, sharp appreciation of the issue concerning the tenability of the concept of defense. Many of the most dramatic and compelling of these observations were made by Freud and his early collaborator (Breuer & Freud, 1936) in their study of hysterical women. These women had the most peculiar symptomatology—paralysis or anesthesia of the hands, blindness, incessant aches, inability to speak—for people who seemed free of physical defects. Not only did they seem free of physical defects, but in addition, their symptoms often were nonsensical from a physiological point of view. For example, an inability to feel in the hands—the so-called glove anesthesia —would be almost impossible to come by on the basis of injury to the nervous system (Freud, 1893). The nerve groupings in the hands are such that it would be much more likely to lose feeling in one side or the other of a hand, rather than in the whole hand. And injury to the nerve tracts in the arm or shoulder would produce more widespread defects than in the hand alone. In addition, when both hands are rendered without sensation, then whatever strange injury that took place in one arm or shoulder would also have had to occur in the other one. A most unlikely prospect! One could think that damage to the central nervous system was the cause, but once again, such damage would have more widespread effects than on the hands alone. As a further example of the physiological nonsense of hysterical symptoms, it was observed that paralyses in these people were not associated with progressive deterioration of muscular tonus, even though the muscles were apparently unused. These weird phenomena inclined many physicians at the time to the belief that the apparent absence of physical injury was not simply due to their own limited diagnostic capability, but rather signified the nonphysical basis of the symptoms.

In an urgent attempt to learn more about this disorder, Freud and Breuer began hypnotizing their patients, in hopes of overcoming the symptoms. Picture their amazement when it became apparent that hysterical symptoms are lost in the hypnotized state! Glove anesthesias, paralyses, blindness, all were removed, only to return once more soon after the termination of the hypnotic state. This was the definitive observation of the nonphysical basis of hysterical symptoms. So as to learn more about what these hysterical women were like, Freud and Breuer began asking them questions and also encouraging them to say whatever was in their minds. Two things were clearly established. One was that these people were not particularly disturbed by their symptoms, however bizarre they were. One would think that such extreme symptoms, in the absence of apparent cause, would move anyone to anxiety. Instead, these women showed what Charcot had already dubbed *the beautiful indifference of the hysteric.* The second conclusion reached was that these women knew and understood and remembered less about themselves than was true of people free of such symptoms. Often friends could be more helpful in relating the patient's past than she could be herself. In addition, the patients showed little curiosity and awareness of what was happening to them and to the world around them. They were intellectually uncritical to an inordinate degree. But, when pushed to remember specific events from childhood through the combined effects of saying whatever came into their heads and having their utterances interpreted by the physician, they often became extremely anxious. And lo and behold, as confrontations accumulated, the anxieties diminished and so did the symptoms, all the while that it became progressively easier for them to remember the events of their past.

These observations led Freud and Breuer to an explanation of hysteria stressing the concept of defense. For them, hysteria is clearly caused psychologically, rather than physically. The immediate cause is a mechanism of defense, repression, which has the effect of blocking action and thought. What actions and thoughts? Obviously ones that could be anxiety provoking. What would they be? Obviously ones that would bring retaliation from society or that would make the person feel guilty. So the deeper cause is conflict, which, because of its ability to arouse anxiety, leads to defense. But since the actions and thoughts defended against are important and strong to the person, they cannot be rendered nonexistent through defense. They must find some sort of expression. The symptoms are their distorted expression. From here, it was only a hop, skip, and jump to the identification of other defenses and conflicts as underlying other psychopathological states. The extraordinarily powerful model of defense was launched. Later personologists interested in psychopathology have in some cases elaborated and in others simplified the theory of defense, but have left it essentially unchanged. When that theory is found, it invariably involves conflict, leading to anxiety, leading to defense, which takes the form of denying the conflict to awareness in order to avoid the anxiety.

The issue as to whether the concept of defense is tenable is raised most insistently by psychologists for whom the concept seems preposterous. If there is an active process whereby conflicts are held out of awareness, then there must be some part of the person that can perceive reality, and decide what the rest of the person shall and shall not be permitted to know about. On the face of it, this idea of a man within a man seems nonsensical to critics of the concept of defense. In the following discussion, we shall consider a number of specific criticisms of attempts to demonstrate empirically the action of defenses. You should recognize that every one of these specific criticisms follows from the general stance that theorizing about men within men is foolish. Be clear that the men-within-men criticism does not refer to the fact of different parts of the organism—a fact easy enough to accept—but rather to the attribution of characteristics of the whole organism, such as intelligence and choice, to the separate parts. So the part of the organism that does the defending, as well as the part being affected by the defense, are considered intelligent, perceptive, and capable of choice. This leads the critics of the concept of defense to say that the concept merely amounts to talking about one organism as if it were two. But since it is obviously not two organisms, defense is a nonsensical concept, regardless of how dramatic it may be.

Clearly the organism is only one, and hence, if the concept of defense necessitates the treatment of the organism as two, it would be rather untenable on rational grounds. But the question to be asked at this point is whether it would be possible to translate the terribly figurative language used by defense theorists into terms less implicative of men within men? Surely Freud did far too much talking about superegos *fighting* ids, and egos *siding* with, or *deceiving* one or the other. Words such as fighting, siding, and deceiving properly characterize relations between people, and when used to describe relations between parts of the same person are at best analogical and at worst illogical. It may be possible, however, to describe the relations between parts of personality in terms that capture the essential import of defense while avoiding nonsense. If possible, this will amount to demonstrating the analogical status of current statements concerning defense through translating them into statements describing the techniques whereby consciousness is denied in terms consistent with the known capabilities of single organisms.

But before any attempt at such translation, it must be clear that there is empirical evidence such that a concept of defense seems useful to invoke. Certainly, the semiempirical anecdotal observations I mentioned earlier are partial evidence, but only partial, as they have not been made systematically. What I mean is that the psychotherapists making the observations did so only on people who came to them as patients, and by and large did not require even that observations of defense be made on all or at least a high proportion of the patients. Psychotherapists have been known to make conclusions on the basis of striking observations of as few as one or two patients. However exciting these conclusions may be, they may not apply to people in general, even though it is typical to assume that they do. In addition, the conclusions of psychotherapists are often so highly interpretive that it is not at all clear that disinterested psychological observers would agree. The bases upon which the interpretations have been made are sometimes unstated, raising questions concerning the consistency and objectivity with which these bases have been applied. Such a state of affairs requires that there be a body of more rigorously systematic empirical observations before it is agreed that there is evidence suggesting the action of something like a defense.

Fortunately, over the past 30 years or more, a large number of research studies have been done concerning the existence and operation of defenses. It will not be possible to cover them all here, but I can refer you to a number of able reviews (Allport, 1955; Chabot, 1973; Eriksen, 1963; Eriksen & Pierce, 1968; Holmes, 1974; MacKinnon, 1962; Sears, 1944). What I will do here is discuss some of the more representative and instructive of these studies. Most often the research effort has been devoted to investigations of repression or denial, a type of defense relevant to all theories incorporating this concept. Some attention has also been given to projection and regression, methods of defense more specific to psycho-analytic theory.

The bulk of the studies I will review here concerns a general form of defensiveness that might be called repression. This process is important not only in psychoanalytic theory, but in many other positions as well. The studies concern defensiveness effects on perception and memory. I shall save consideration of research on the specific, highly differentiated defenses associated most exclusively with Freud's position until Chapter 10, where they will be more appropriate. But before turning to repression, I wish to consider two studies on regression, because they will permit me to make an important point about how and on whom studies of defensiveness should be done.

The first study concerning regression is famous, but, though often cited, is not very useful. In this study, Mowrer (1940) used small numbers of rats in an experiment involving electric shock. One group of rats was permitted to learn by trial and error that the shock in the grilled floor on which they stood could be turned off by pressing a foot pedal. Another group was given shocks for an approximately equal amount of time but had no pedal to press. Eventually, these latter rats learned to avoid shock by sitting up on their hind legs. When sitting up had been well learned, a foot pedal was inserted and they were permitted to learn to use it. From this point on, both groups were frustrated by having shock introduced to this foot pedal, so that when they tried to turn off the floor shock they got a shock from what had been the instrument of salvation. The rats that had originally learned to avoid shock by standing on their hind legs almost immediately regressed to that habit, while the other rats persisted in pushing the pedal.

What is wrong with this experiment as a demonstration of regression? The major problem is that it does not take into account that regression is a notion inextricably embedded in a broader theoretical framework. For psychoanalysts, regression involves going from a later stage of psycho-sexual development to an earlier one, in a partial or more complete sense, this movement being a function of fixation and frustration. By fixation, Freud means the overly strong attachment to a particular stage of psy-chosexual development, and by frustration he means the prevention of instinctual gratification in whatever stage the person finds himself. When frustration becomes strong, retreat to a previous, fixated psychosexual stage may take place. This is called regression. Now it is possible, I sup-pose, that rats have psychosexual development in some rudimentary sense. At least, their mating behavior improves with practice. But even if this were considered to qualify the rat as an organism on which the con-cept of regression might be tested, it seems clear that no test has been made by Mowrer because standing up or pushing a pedal to avoid shock really does not bear sensibly on psychosexual development. This experiment has nothing to do with the concept of regression, even though it may be regarded to have demonstrated that a newly learned habit may be relinquished, when no longer effective, for a previously learned one. One thing is clear: if defensiveness is to be studied on subhuman organisms, they must at least have some form of psychosexual development, and the specific behaviors studied must be convincing analogues of the human behaviors focused upon by psychoanalytic theory (cf. Hunt, 1964). As these criteria are essentially unreached in animal studies, they are thus far of little utility for testing psychoanalytic notions of defense.

You might be thinking that if regression were divested of its psychoanalytic parentage, Mowrer's demonstration might be positive evidence. But the concept of defense, even without consideration of psychosexual stages of development, requires some active process of debarring from consciousness in order to reduce anxiety. In regression, this debarring is effected through returning to some earlier state of being. If rats are to be proper organisms for study, then they must have consciousness, for only if they do will debarring from consciousness constitute a useful procedure of defense. Many psychologists might be willing to assume that rats or some even higher organisms have consciousness. But even if consciousness analogous to what can be obtained in humans through self report exists in animals, the fact of its methodological inaccessibility is a formidable barrier. Consciousness may or may not exist in an animal, and if it does, it may or may not provide sensible analogies to the human conflict, guilt, and anxiety considered to be the springboards of defense. Even with an emancipated concept of regression, it becomes clear that the study of subhuman organisms is so imprecise as to be of marginal utility. The same is true for the study of other defenses as well, as all require an organism the consciousness of which can be scrutinized.

Somewhat more convincing is a study of regression by Barker, Dembo, and Lewin (1941), also very well known. They used 30 preschool children as subjects, turning them loose in a free play situation. All were above average in intelligence. Each child was encouraged to play alone with some toys for a half hour. The next day he was brought back, but this time played first with some much more desirable toys. After the first 15 minutes, the investigator returned the child to the other end of the room without explanation, and permitted him to play with the original, less-attractive toys for a half hour. During this half hour, the desirable toys were in full view, though unavailable. Barker et al., reasoned that if regression is a reality, the frustration involved in giving up the desirable toys should lead to more destructive play with the less-desirable toys than the child had shown on the first day of play. The investigators tried to establish age norms for constructiveness of play, so that they could see whether any decrease in constructiveness of play could indeed be considered to represent becoming more childish. Their results show clearly that the expected destructiveness occurs. This study incorporates one important element of the regression notion, namely, that it is a process of primitivization, of becoming more like a child. But the study is not particularly relevant to the psychoanalytic notion of regression, because there was little concern with the specifics of psychosexual development. The results can certainly be used, however, to support a concept of regression emancipated from the rest of psychoanalytic theory. The only fly in the ointment, and it will crop up constantly in the following discussion, is that there is no way of knowing if the primitivization shown really occurred without conscious awareness, as it would have had to in order to be a bona fide expression of defense. This shortcoming might have been avoided, as the subjects were humans and not rats, and could therefore have been questioned.

We are now ready to traverse the terrain of repression research. You should remember that the concept of defense contains within it the notion that something mental of an unpleasant sort is being denied awareness. It is important, therefore, to employ human subjects and to attempt to determine whether the defensive process, though measurable by the experimenter, is really unavailable to the subject's awareness.

The defense mechanism of repression involves debarring from awareness any sensation, perception, thought, or action that would be in conflict with values and principles instilled in you by society, and has the immediate function of avoiding the anxiety that would accompany awareness of the conflict. The meaning of the concept of repression in psychoanalytic theory is much the same as in other theories of defense, except that in psychoanalytic theory the personal contribution to the conflict invariably can be traced to the life, sexual, or death instincts. In considering research studies of repression, we will be working at the heart of the issue of the tenability of the concept of defense, as repression is ubiquitously recognized in theories of defense, and even in psychoanalytic theory, is considered the basic defense. Indeed, Freud first used the concept of repression before hitting upon the concept of defense, and switched to primary emphasis on the latter only when it became clear to him that there were additional, more elaborate techniques than repression for avoiding consciousness.

It is fortunate that consideration of repression comes so close to the heart of the concept of defense, for there has been quite a large number of studies of repression. Indeed, such studies, dubbed the "new look" in perception, abounded and attracted intense interest in the 1950s. The basic issue concerning the tenability of the concept of defense waxed hot in the form of specific research controversies during this exciting time in personology.

Certainly, there were studies of repression before the 1950s, but they tended to involve memory of action more than perception, and were therefore less amazing than the "new look" work. Let us turn to the more perceptual work before considering the memory work.

The notion that people can be especially defensive or especially vigilant in their perception of things, as a function of aspects of personality such as needs and values, was introduced in a series of three articles by Bruner and Postman (1947a, 1947b) and Postman, Bruner, and McGinnies (1948).

All of these experiments used the tachistoscope, a devise for presenting visual stimuli for controllable and very brief lengths of time. Generally speaking, tachistoscopic procedure involves presenting the stimulus at too short a time for recognition, and then, gradually increasing the duration of subsequent presentations. The subject is to say what he thinks the stimulus is after each exposure, with the important data being the length of exposure that accompanies correct perception. Stimuli that have different content, or have been presented under different conditions may have different exposure lengths associated with correct perception. Recognizing this is basic to understanding the notions of perceptual vigilance and defense. Indeed, the existence of a group of stimuli that requires shorter and longer exposure times for correct perception than did the general run of stimuli led these investigators to invoke the ideas of perceptual vigilance and defense.

The study of Bruner and Postman found that those stimuli associated with experimentally produced anxiety had lower recognition times than did stimuli not associated with anxiety. In developing the notion of perceptual vigilance, these investigators suggested that stimuli of special importance to the person are enhanced in perception and recognized sooner. The other studies concerned the concept of perceptual defense. In the first of these (Bruner & Postman, 1947b) a word association task was initially administered. Subjects varied, of course, in the speed with which they could think of an associate to the words the experimenter presented. Then these words were presented to the subjects again, only this time tachistoscopically.

Bruner and Postman found that for some subjects, words associated with long association times—this presumably indicating emotional disturbance—required much longer tachistoscopic exposures for recognition than did words with medium or short association times. They dubbed this lengthened recognition time perceptual defense and likened it to repression, whereby anxiety-provoking stimuli are defended against in perception or prevented from attaining awareness. But Bruner and Postman also found that in certain other subjects long association time words had lower tachistoscopic recognition times, suggesting again the relevance of the notion of perceptual vigilance.

The Postman, Bruner, and McGinnies study supplements the two already discussed, in suggesting that values can affect perception as well as can anxiety and underlying emotional disturbance. They chose words for tachistoscopic presentation that were representative of six broad value areas, e.g., religion, economics, aesthetics, and sought to determine beforehand their subject's commitments to these value areas, through the use of a standard psychological test for that purpose. Sure enough, they found a relationship between the intensity of a subject's commitment to each value area and the speed with which he recognized tachistoscopically presented words relevant to those areas. Subjects who had an intense commitment to theoretical values, for example, had lower recognition times for words from this value area and had higher recognition times for words from value areas to which they had minimal commitment. The concepts of perceptual vigilance and defense were again used to explain the results.

Although these three studies have more or less bearing on the concept of repression, it was not until the subsequent study of McGinnies (1949) that the relevance of this kind of research became precisely clear. McGinnies selected a group of socially taboo words, such as whore, bitch, belly, and Kotex, and a group of neutral, acceptable words for tachistoscopic presentation to college student subjects. All the while that his subjects were trying to tell him what they saw in the tachistoscope, McGinnies was also measuring their galvanic skin response. The galvanic skin response is essentially an index of the electrical conductivity of the skin, which electrical conductivity increases in a very sensitive way when sweating increases. Such increases in sweating have generally been considered indicative of emotional arousal, or anxiety.

McGinnies obtained striking results. Not only did the taboo words require longer tachistoscopic exposures for correct recognition, but also, subjects showed increases in sweating on the tachistoscopic exposures of the taboo words that were too brief to permit visual recognition. No comparable increase in sweating prior to conscious recognition occurred with neutral words. These findings are shown in detail in Table 5-1 with the measures of sweating appearing in the first two columns, and those of recognition time in the last two. The higher recognition time for taboo words was considered a manifestation of perceptual defense and the greater sweating accompanying prerecognition trials with taboo words was considered to be not only an indication of the active nature of defensive processes but also to suggest an unconscious detection or manifestation of anxiety elicited by these words. Extraordinary though the results of this study may seem, they are just what you would expect from the action of the defense mechanisms of repression or denial. If some percepts are to be debarred from consciousness, some part of the organism must be able to detect them and rule them out. The findings concerning increased sweating suggest that there is some kind of organismic response to taboo words, and that this incipient emotional response is part of the process of denial to awareness. McGinnies' choice of taboo words was also appropriate, reflecting as they did psychosexual matters inappropriate for polite discussion and thought.

Lest we conclude prematurely that there is clear empirical evidence

TABLE 5–1

Summary of the raw data and statistical tests for all observers
with respect to both galvanic skin response and thresholds of
recognition for neutral and critical stimulus words

Observer	Mean microammeter readings during pre-recognition exposures		Mean thresholds of recognition	
	Neutral words	*Critical words*	*Neutral words*	*Critical words*
1	37.80	40.46	.055	.184
2	40.96	41.53	.044	.094
3	39.31	42.06	.054	.080
4	38.34	40.80	.103	.126
5	41.48	43.76	.040	.064
6	41.41	47.08	.070	.130
7	40.75	39.94	.057	.104
8	39.98	42.85	.063	.076
9	39.44	42.68	.059	.130
10	40.02	42.71	.049	.223
11	39.88	41.55	.046	.077
12	41.27	44.02	.057	.091
13	40.56	41.37	.033	.037
14	40.19	41.42	.034	.054
15	40.85	40.63	.046	.056
16	40.83	41.84	.036	.046
	Mean diff. = 1.98 $t = 5.10$ P < .01		Mean diff. = .045 $t = 3.96$ P < .01	

Source: E. McGinnies, "Emotionality and perceptual defense," *Psychol. Rev.*, 1949.

favoring the existence of the repressive defense, we should recognize that no sooner had McGinnies' results appeared than they were resoundingly attacked. The specific criticisms made reflect the overall disbelief that the concept of defense is tenable because it seems to require theorizing about a man within a man. Howes and Solomon (1950) voiced the criticisms in strong and capable manner. The first criticism was that subjects might very well have known in a conscious way the content of the taboo words for some trials before they felt certain enough of their knowledge to voice it. After all, if you were in their position, and saw what looked like Kotex, you might not have wanted to risk saying that to an adult and an authority—the experimenter—unless you were absolutely sure you were right. But maybe you started sweating as soon as you first thought the word was Kotex. As you can see, this is a serious criticism. If it is true, then all that is meant by the finding concerning longer tachistoscopic times for taboo words is that people decide which of their thoughts and perceptions to express so as to avoid unnecessary embarrassments. There is nothing here of defense in the sense of an unconsciously operating process actively debarring certain percepts from awareness.

The second criticism made by Howes and Solomon concerned the fact that the taboo and neutral words that were used by McGinnies differed markedly in familiarity or frequency of past occurrence in the subject's experience. By consulting the listing of the frequency with which major words appear in written usage prepared by Thorndike and Lorge (1944), Howes and Solomon determined that McGinnies' taboo words appear with much lower frequency than the neutral words. This led to the criticism that the different tachistoscopic lengths required for the perception of words was a function of the frequency with which those words had been experienced in the past, rather than having anything to do with defensive operations. This criticism is general enough to apply to the three experiments described before as well as this one. Teeth were really put into the criticism when these two psychologists demonstrated in further studies (Howes & Solomon, 1951; Solomon & Howes, 1951) that tachistoscopic exposure lengths for word recognition could be predicted from the Thorndike-Lorge tables of word frequency.

Even though the frequency criticism has obvious cogency and some empirical support, there is the rankling thought that it is not really as devastating as it might seem at first blush. After all, if you are interested in the frequency with which a person has experienced a word in the past, you must take into account not only instances coming his way from some external source, e.g., books, speeches, other people, but also instances that he experiences by virtue of his own imagination and thought processes. Once you recognize this fact, the engaging simplicity of the explanation Solomon and Howes put forth is largely lost. Not only does their frequency explanation become extraordinarily more complex, it is not clear that it is even testable anymore. What, I ask you, is a comprehensively adequate measure of frequency of experience of a word in the past? Certainly, the Thorndike-Lorge listings cannot be used, reflecting as they do rather formal written usage for public consumption—the kind of usage one finds in magazines and newspapers. Especially when one is interested in the frequency of experience of taboo words, one cannot possibly trust to the Thorndike-Lorge word lists. Such lists certainly underestimate frequency of exposure to such words, especially when one takes into account the person's own thoughts and fantasies alongside verbal interactions with others that are informal and private in nature. Looking at the word frequency matter in this way makes me wonder what in the world the relationship between Thorndike-Lorge word frequency and tachistoscopic recognition time found by Solomon and Howes (1951) and Howes and Solomon (1951) could possibly mean?

Fortunately, psychologists like Eriksen (1963) have scrutinized the data of these two studies in a manner that bears on the question I have just posed. It turns out that "practically all of the relationship can be traced to a difference between words having 0 or very low frequencies in the Thorndike-Lorge counts and words having high frequency" (Eriksen, 1963, p. 40). For words in the frequency range from 10 to 3,000 occurrences per million in the count mentioned above, there is virtually no relationship between frequency of occurrence and tachistoscopic recognition time! This useful bit of information means that the frequency criticism of Solomon and Howes is only cogent when one works with words having especially high or low frequencies of ocrurrence in formal, public usage. This more accurate version of the criticism hardly destroys the findings of Bruner and Postman (1947a, 1947b), Postman, Bruner, and McGinnies (1948), and McGinnies (1949). Following his reanalysis of the findings of Solomon and Howes (1951) and Howes and Solomon (1951), Eriksen (1963) concludes that "we may note that the empirical relationship between frequency of past occurrence and recognition threshold has been amply demonstrated, although the magnitude of this relationship has undoubtedly been considerably overestimated."

We can now return to the other criticism made by Solomon and Howes, namely, that the relatively long exposure times associated with taboo words merely reflects a conscious decision on the part of the subject not to risk embarrassment should he have been wrong in thinking the word to be improper. This criticism is completely sound from the point of view of reason when leveled at the McGinnies experiment, but has considerably less relevance to the other experiments because they employed not taboo words, but rather anxiety-provoking or value-related words. It should not have been embarrassing for subjects to report such words, even if they turned out to be wrong. Nonetheless, it is the McGinnies experiment that comes closest to a demonstration of the defense mechanism of repression, as it is normally used in theories of defense.

There is no worthy logical counterargument to the Solomon and Howes criticism, but there is one empirical study that escapes the criticism, while still bearing on repression. In this study, McCleary and Lazarus (1949) used nonsense syllables for stimuli in place of meaningful words. For half of the nonsense syllables, an unpleasant, anxiety-provoking effect was established by accompanying a one-second exposure of the syllable with an electric shock. Through a series of such exposures they produced the effect of increased sweating, measured by the galvanic skin response, every time one of the syllables associated with electric shock appeared. After this conditioning had been established, all of the syllables, including the half that had not been associated with shock, were presented at tachistoscopic speeds that ranged from extremely brief up to approximately the time required for accurate perception by most people. As in the McGinnies experiment, the galvanic skin response was recorded on each tachistoscopic trial, along with the subject's verbal report of what he saw. In the tachistoscopic part of the experiment, no electric shock was used. As you can see, the experiment was the same in design as that of McGinnies, except that in place of taboo words, nonsense syllables were used, with some of the syllables rendered anxiety provoking by the pretachistoscopic pairing with electric shock. Thus, one cannot say with any cogency either that the shocked versus nonshocked nonsense syllables had been more frequent in the past experience of subjects, or were socially unacceptable, and therefore the source of potential embarrassment. The study of Lazarus and McCleary successfully avoids both criticisms made by Solomon and Howes.

We should, therefore, be especially interested in the results, in order that we may consider the empirical tenability of the concept of defense. Now let us first consider the trials on which the subject's verbal report was wrong. On these trials, it was found that sweating was greater for the previously shocked syllables than it was for those that had not been accompanied by shock. McCleary and Lazarus (1949) conclude that "at tachistoscopic exposure speeds too rapid for conscious discrimination . . . the subject is still capable of responding in a discriminatory way." They suggested the term *subception* for this apparently autonomic, perhaps subcortical form of perception. Clearly, these results are supportive of the part of the theory of defense that involves a keen sensitivity on the part of some aspect of the organism to potentially threatening perceptions, such that they may be guarded against. But this erperiment does not show that the previously shocked syllables required longer tachistoscopic exposure times for accurate perception than did the nonshocked syllables. Indeed, the opposite result was obtained, something more consistent with the idea of perceptual vigilance than perceptual defense! Taken as a whole, this study is only partially supportive of the repressive aspect of defense. Perhaps this state of affairs can be traced to what was lost in the process of developing a design that could circumvent the criticism of Solomon and Howes. While the shocked nonsense syllables were undoubtedly unpleasant stimuli, it is not at all clear or likely that they articulated in any deep way with the kinds of intense underlying conflicts that all theorists of defense agree should provoke defenses. The Lazarus and McCleary study presents, as laboratory experiments frequently must, a pale shadow of life, and once this is appreciated, it may even seem surprising that the subception part of defensiveness could be demonstrated.

Another approach to circumventing the criticisms of Solomon and Howes is exemplified in a study by Cowen and Beier (1954). They decided to retain taboo and neutral words as the stimuli, increasing the likelihood thereby of engaging more deep-seated conflicts than could be done with the technique of Lazarus and McCleary. Instead of tachistoscopic presentation, these investigators achieved a similar effect by using blurred type-written copies of the words arranged into booklets. The arrangement was such that successive pages went from very blurred to very clear for each word. The important datum was the number of pages that had to be turned before the word was correctly identified.

In order to avoid the criticism involving word familiarity, Cowen and Beier correlated number of pages turned for correct identification with the frequency of occurrence listed for the word by Thorndike and Lorge. They found the correlation to be zero for the words they used. In order to avoid the criticism involving embarrassment to verbalize taboo words, they varied the sex of the experimenter, such that half the subjects reported to an experimenter of the same sex, and the other half to one of the opposite sex. In addition, all experimenters read the entire list of words that would be used, including the taboo ones, to the subjects before the experiment began. Cowen and Beier reasoned that the combination of these two procedures should decrease the embarrassment factor to the point where it could not be invoked in the explanation of findings. In addition, they also demonstrated that there were no important differences in the results they obtained between experiment-subject pairs of same and opposite sex.

The main result of this study was that the taboo words did indeed require more page turns for correct identification than did the neutral words. These results corroborate those of McGinnies, in the context of a design that at least comes close to avoiding the criticisms of Solomon and Howes. Considering these results along with those of Lazarus and McCleary, whose study also avoids the criticisms, the empirical case for the existence of a repressive defense is reasonably sound. One could still say of the Cowen and Beier study that there was some remaining embarrassment, even though the experimenter had alerted the subject as to the nature of the words he would see, but this comes much closer to hairsplitting than it did in the McGinnies study.

Blum (1955) tried another approach to avoid the criticisms leveled at the initial perceptual defense studies. He used as stimulus materials pictures taken from his Blacky Test (Blum, 1949), which show a young dog in various interactions with two older dogs (its parents). As is described more fully in Chapter 10, the interactions were chosen to exemplify facets of parent-child relationships considered important in psychoanalytic theory. Blum presented a slide with four of these pictures tachistoscopically to subjects who had to say which picture was in each of the four positions. All subjects knew the 11 Blacky pictures well, but did not know that in reality it was the same 4 pictures being presented on every one of the 48 trials (the pictures were rotated so that they appeared in each position the same number of times over the trials). After the experiment, all subjects said that they were unable to recognize any of the pictures, so the experiment was for them a kind of guessing game.

On the basis of other information, it was determined that some subjects actually had conflicts relating to some of the pictures, and no conflicts relating to others. Blum reasoned that there should be fewer identifications of conflict-laden pictures than nonconflictual pictures. But you should recognize that, since subjects thought all 11 Blacky pictures would appear, though only 4 actually did, they might well identify pictures that were not presented. Blum argued that there should be no difference in frequency of calling conflictual and nonconflictual pictures that were not presented. This is because the perceptual defense notion requires that a threatening stimulus actually occur, else there is no special reason for defensiveness. The results were as expected. For actually presented pictures, the means on calling conflictual and nonconflictual pictures were 9.42 and 17.12, respectively. For pictures not presented, the mean calls on conflictual and nonconflictual pictures were 15.20 and 16.69, respectively. It is especially interesting that among highly conflictual pictures, those not actually presented were called by subjects much more than those that were presented.

Bootzin and Natsoulas (1965) performed a similar experiment with some additional refinements and which utilized a combination on each trial of threatening and nonthreatening stimuli. Suffice it to say that their results also justified the interpretation of a defensive process. While it is not entirely clear in their study or in Blum's whether the defense takes place in the perceptual process itself or somewhere between perception and the subject's verbal response (see Natsoulas, 1965), there seems to be defensiveness of some kind.

Having concluded that there is at least some empirical support for the concept of repression, we should now turn to the vexing problem posed by the findings suggesting a process of perceptual vigilance. Thus far, we have observed in passing that some subjects seem to be particularly sensitive, rather than insensitive, to words that refer to dominant values in them, and to words and nonsense syllables that are anxiety provoking. It is important for us to decide what meaning to attribute to perceptual vigilance, as it seems to exist, for better or for worse, alongside of perceptual defense. But before pursuing the matter further, let me introduce you to a related body of research that should be taken into account.

The body of research I mean concerns the effects of repression on memory, rather than on perception. Research interest in the effects of repression on memory actually predates concern with its effects on perception. Rosenzweig and Mason (1934) did the first study clearly in this tradition. As subjects, they used 40 children, and each child was given the task of solving a series of jigsaw puzzles, with a prize to be given to the child who did best. The experimenters had arranged things beforehand so that each child was permitted to finish half of the tasks assigned to him, but was interrupted in working on the other half. The interruptions were carried out in such a manner that the children thought they were failing those tasks. After 45 minutes of puzzle solving, followed by a free interval of 1 minute, each subject was asked to name the picture puzzles he remembered having worked on. Of the 40 children, 16 remembered more completed than "failed" tasks, 13 recalled fewer completed than "failed" tasks, 9 recalled an equal number of both, and 2 recalled no tasks. At best, only 16 of the 40 subjects could be thought of as remembering according to a theory of repression. Thirteen subjects seemed particularly sensitive to their failures, which should have been anxiety provoking. In these two groups, we have an analogous phenomenon to perceptual defense and perceptual vigilance. The subjects who were especially good at recalling their failures should not be considered more accurate than those who could only remember their successes. Rather, it is the nine subjects who remembered an equal number of completed and failed tasks whose mental functioning was most accurate to reality. The same thing holds true for subjects showing perceptual defense and vigilance, though the data are not as clear as in Rosenzweig and Mason. When a person takes more exposures to recognize some of a group of stimuli, he is being selectively insensitive, and therefore inaccurate to reality. When a person takes fewer exposures to recognize some of a group of stimuli, he is being selectively sensitive, and this is also a form of inaccuracy to reality. Only people who are neither vigilant nor defendant have perceptual processes accurate to reality. Although such people undoubtedly exist in the perception studies described earlier, they have not been singled out for analysis, in the way they were by Rosenzweig and Mason.

Thinking that the number of subjects showing repression could be increased over what it was in the study of Rosenzweig and Mason by arousing a sense of pride in accomplishment, Rosenzweig (1933, 1943) designed another experiment. He presented the same kind of puzzles to one group of adult subjects as an "intelligence test," and to another group in an informal manner emphasizing the test itself, rather than their own performance. The first group should have had pride aroused, whereas the second group should not have had their self-esteem threatened. Then, as in his original study, each subject completed half the puzzles and "failed" the other half. Under the pride-arousing condition, 17 subjects remembered more finished tasks, 8 more unfinished, and 5 remembered both equally. In the less-stressful condition, only 7 subjects remembered more finished tasks, while 19 remembered more unfinished tasks, and 4 showed no difference between the two. The findings clearly show that the greater the threat to self-esteem, the stronger are repressive tendencies. But it is still true in this study that some subjects seem especially sensitive to their failures, and some show neither sensitivity nor insensitivity. I should point out that it has been typical to criticize these studies for using the interrupted task technique (e.g., Sears, 1950), because it is well known to lead, when there is no special threat to self-esteem and interruption is not structured by the experimenter as failure, to a preponderant tendency to recall the interrupted rather than the completed tasks (see Zeigarnik, 1927). The criticism states that it is unwise to try to demonstrate repression, requiring as it does the opposite recall, on such a procedure. From my point of view, this is not a sensible criticism. Special sensitivity to incompleted tasks has never been convincingly explained, and is an intriguing phenomenon because it suggests defensiveness in its inaccurate rendition of reality and is analogous to the phenomenon of perceptual vigilance.

In another study, MacKinnon (1933) attempted to arouse guilt in his subjects, reasoning that this procedure would initiate defensive reactions. Each of his 93 subjects was left alone, though they were secretly observed by the experimenter through a one-way vision screen, to work on a series of tasks so difficult as to be impossible of solution for practically all people. The subjects had in their possession the answers to all problems, provided in an answer booklet. They were told they could not look at the answers while they were working the problems. MacKinnon argued that repression could be expected to occur only in subjects who violated the prohibition—43 percent of the group—and then only if they felt guilty about their violations.

When subsequently asked to recall the problems they had worked on, violators (most of whom showed no signs of guilt) remembered most often problems whose solutions had been seen in violation of the prohibition, and least often problems whose solutions had not been seen at all. A small, atypical group of subjects, who violated the prohibition and who gave signs of guilt in behavior and verbal report, tended to recall problems whose solutions they had looked up less well than other problems. These results are particularly interesting, because they suggest that one can expect a defensive reaction only when some conflict has been actually created for the person.

Several other studies have employed a different procedure to investigate the effects of repression on memory. Zeller (1950) first constituted experimental and control groups out of pretested subjects so that there were no group differences in number of trials necessary to learn a set of neutral verbal materials (nonsense syllables). Then the groups were given a psychomotor test rigged so that the control subjects performed well and had an enjoyable experience whereas the experimental subjects performed badly and felt threatened. Following this, all subjects had to relearn the originally neutral materials. It was interpreted as a sign of repression (instituted in the face of threat and generalizing to the associated verbal materials) that experimental subjects required more trials to relearn than did the control subjects. The final procedure involved explaining the rigging of success and failure on the psychomotor task to the experimental subjects, and then to test once again for speed of relearning. The effect of the debriefing should have been to remove the threat and hence the occasion for repression. Consistent with this, the experimental and control groups were no longer different in speed of learning. This last finding suggests what Freud meant in "the return of repressed." If that which has been repressed is still in the mind, it should be recoverable when defensiveness is no longer necessary.

Zeller (1951) has also demonstrated these effects when the behavior scrutinized for signs of repression is free-recall rather than number of trials to relearn. By now, there have been several independent reports of similar findings (e.g., Flavell, 1955; Penn, 1964).

Predictably, criticisms have arisen from researchers convinced that an alternative explanation to that of repression is best. Aborn's (1953) findings suggest that when subjects in the kind of situation used by Zeller are given special instructions to attend to the material to be learned, there is no difference in performance between those who are threatened and those who are not. This simple instruction to remain alert should not have been effective if repression was indeed operating, because defenses are supposed to operate unconsciously. In a similar assault on the repression interpretation, D'Zurilla (1965) showed that in the kind of situation Zeller used the threatened subjects reported thinking about the psychomotor task more than did the nonthreatened subjects. D'Zurilla argued that if the slower learning of the threatened subjects was indeed due to repression, they should have thought about the materials less, not more.

Holmes and Schallow (1969) tried to provide direct evidence that an interference interpretation is at least as cogent as that involving repression. To a procedure similar to that of Zeller, they added a group that experienced interference (the task they were performing was interrupted at 30 second intervals by portions of a movie). As shown in Figure 5–1, both this group and the more usual threatened group recalled the materials previously learned less well than the control group which was

FIGURE 5–1

Mean number of words recalled on Test 1, before experimental manipulation; Test 2, after experimental manipulation; and Test 3, after debriefing

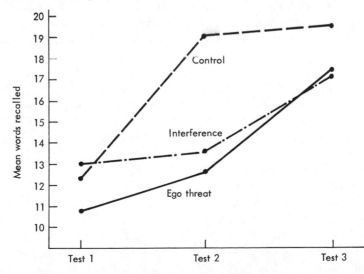

Source: Adapted from Holmes and Schallow, "Reduced recall after ego threat: Repression or response competition?" *J. Pers. Soc. Psychol.*, 1969.

neither threatened nor interrupted. Following debriefing, there were no recall differences among the three groups. Holmes and Schallow believe that not only interruption but also threat is best interpreted as an interference rather than defensiveness phenomenon. It is equally plausible, however, that recall can be worsened in several ways, one of which is interference and another of which is repression. In a way, it is surprising that results should emerge from experiments such as these that are at all supportive of the defensiveness hypothesis, because the conditions of threat are not really as extreme assaults upon the person as those provoking personality theorists to their hypotheses about repression.

A flaw in the preceding studies concerning recall and relearning is that only repression was studied. Although repression is admittedly the basic defense, there are others which might even have the effect of especially sensitizing the person. Truax (1957) has reported an experiment of special importance because it took this problem into account. Using a personality test, he selected subjects high and low in the tendency to repress, and reasoned that only the former would respond to threat by decreased recall and slow relearning. Truax introduced another procedural improvement in this research tradition by associating threat with some of the stimulus materials to be learned but not others, and by exposing all subjects to all stimulus materials. In effect, subjects served as their own controls. His findings are consistent with the defensiveness theory in that subjects prone to repression indeed recalled and relearned the threatening stimuli worse than the nonthreatening stimuli. If anything, subjects not prone to repression did better on threatening than nonthreatening stimuli. Although this study is formidable support for the existence of defensiveness, controversy still abounds. Tudor and Holmes (1973) have reported a similar study using recall for completed and incompleted tasks under stress and nonstress conditions. They did not find that subjects prone to repression recalled fewer incompletions under stress, as one might expect from the standpoint of repression. But their findings are severely complicated by differences in the original learning of completed and incompleted tasks.

As is so often the case, in research, a number of groundbreaking studies have to be done in order for the methodological and substantive problems in the area to become clear. Research on defensiveness is no exception to this process. The maturing of defensiveness research is seen clearly in the work of such personologists as Eriksen, who have joined together emphases on perception and memory in the context of a more sophisticated version of defense theory than was employed by earlier investigators. Eriksen (1963, pp. 42–43) points out

> . . . that the clinical concept of repression is more sophisticated than to assume that all people or even a majority of people automatically repress any sexual or aggressive ideation, or that all anxiety-arousing thoughts or feelings are repressed. Instead, repression is a defense mech-

anism used sometimes by some people to handle anxiety-arousing thoughts or feelings whose anxiety-provoking nature is a function of the individual's own unique past experiences. Thus one would not expect a great deal of communality among people in terms of the kind of stimuli that should lead to repression. Furthermore, theories of personality dynamics also recognize that there are other types of defense mechanisms. Represion is not the only way individuals defend against ego-threatening stimulation.

Intellectualization, reaction formation, and projection are defensive mechanisms that one might expect actually to lead to a sensitization for a stimulus related to the conflict. In the instance of reaction formation, the person manifesting this defense seems to be particularly alert to finding and stamping out the evil that he denies in himself. Similarly, in the case of projection, those manifesting this defense are considered to be hyper-alert to detecting the presence of the defended-against impulse in others. Intellectualization frequently leads to a considerable preoccupation with the subject matter of the unacceptable impulse.

These differences in defensive mechanisms would be expected to have different perceptual concomitants. In the case of repression or denial one might expect a tendency for the subject to manifest avoidance or higher duration thresholds for stimuli related to the sources of conflict. On the other hand, those manifesting defenses of intellectualization, reaction formation or projection might be expected to show a lower duration threshold for anxiety-related stimuli.

There are two things of great importance in this passage. The first is that perceptual vigilance may reflect the sensitizing defenses, such as reaction formation and intellectualization, whereas perceptual defense reflects the desensitizing defenses, such as repression and denial. I would suggest, further, that sensitization and desensitization effects on memory, in the form of recall for failed or completed tasks, also reflect these two kinds of defensive process. The second important point made by Eriksen is that research concerning the effects of defense on perception should include independent information concerning the kinds of defenses the subject generally tends to use, so that you can predict precisely what kinds of perceptual effects you should find. It seems to me that this point is as well taken in the study of defensive effects upon memory and other aspects of cognition.

Eriksen has done a number of studies guided by these criteria. In the first of them, he (Eriksen, 1951a) used hospitalized mental patients who were selected on the basis of having conflicts in particular, specified need areas and in whom desensitizing defensive operations might be expected. The amount of emotional disturbance in the three need areas of aggression, homosexuality, and succorance was assessed through use of a modified word association technique. Disturbance scores on this test were then related to the subject's tachistoscopic recognition time for pictures, some of which related to the three need areas, and some of

which did not. Patients whose word associations showed much disturbance in a need area were found to require longer exposure intervals for
recognition of the corresponding need-related pictures than for neutral
pictures. The correlations describing this effect are those appearing in
the first three rows of the final three columns in Table 5–2. In another
similar study, Eriksen (1951b) found that emotional stimuli did not
necessarily lead to high tachistoscopic recognition times. Subjects who
showed extensive overt aggressive behavior and who expressed aggressive
content in composing stories about pictures were found to have lower
recognition times for tachistoscopically presented pictures having aggressive content.

In their study, Lazarus, Eriksen, and Fonda (1951) pinpointed the
meaning of the opposing trends found in the two studies just summarized. Psychiatric outpatients were used as subjects and were classified
on the basis of their therapeutic interviews and other clinical tests as
either sensitizers or repressers, depending upon whether they characteristically responded to anxiety in terms of intellectualization as a defense, or whether they tended to avoid and deny thoughts and ideas
related to the conflicts. The results, as shown in Table 5–3, indicate that
the sensitizers tended to give freely aggressive and sexual endings to a
sentence completion test whereas the repressers tended to block or distort
into innocuous forms sentence completion stems that would normally
suggest either aggressive or sexual content. Further, when performance
on the sentence completion test was compared with auditory perception
of hostile and sexual sentences heard against a noise background, the
sensitizers were superior to the repressers in recognition of the emotional
content.

Eriksen (1952) has also done a study relating the effects of repression
on perception and on memory. He put a group of college freshmen
through a series of tasks, half of which they were permitted to finish, and
the other half of which involved interruption, in much the manner of

TABLE 5–2

Intercorrelations of the word association and perceptual recognition scores for the
three need areas*

		Word association			Perceptual recognition		
Score		Agg.	Suc.	Homo.	Agg.	Suc.	Homo.
Word association.........	Aggression	.636	.582	.417	.435	.216
	Succorance		.282	.281	.611	.180
	Homosexuality			−.101	.264	.314
Perceptual recognition....	Aggression				.352	.180
	Succorance					.060

* *Eta* is used as the measure of relationship. Evaluated via the *F* test, an *eta* of .415 is significant at
the .95 level.
 Source: C. W. Eriksen, "Perceptual defense as a function of unacceptable needs," *J. abnorm. soc.
Psychol.*, 1952.

TABLE 5–3

Comparison of intellectualizers and repressers on perceptual recognition and sentence completion test

	Repressers (N = 12)		Intellectualizers (N = 13)		
	Mean	S.D.	Mean	S.D.	t
Auditory perceptual recognition					
Sex*......................	− .25	1.18	+1.60	1.48	3.32
Hostility*.................	−1.10	1.32	+ .30	1.25	2.67
Neutral*..................	5.27	1.59	6.17	1.59	1.36
Sentence completion test					
Sex.......................	6.20	1.39	9.10	4.52	2.02
Hostility..................	5.50	1.70	8.00	4.31	1.77

For a one-tailed test, *t* values of 1.71 and 2.50 are significant at the .05 and the .01 levels, respectively.
* Using adjusted sense-perceived scores (that is, subtracting neutral score from score on critical materials—sex and hostility respectively; if less critical material was correctly perceived than neutral, score would be minus).
Source: R. S. Lazarus, C. W. Eriksen, and C. P. Fonda, "Personality dynamics in auditory perceptual recognition," *J. Pers.*, 1951.

Rosenzweig's work. The tasks were structured as measures of intelligence, and the interruptions as failures. As we would expect on the basis of Rosenzweig's work, the subjects showed wide differences in preponderance of recall of completed or interrupted tasks. These two groups of subjects were then administered a word association test and in a subsequent testing session their tachistoscopic exposure times for correct recognition of long, medium, and short association time words were determined. As shown in Table 5–4, the subjects who recalled successfully completed tasks on the memory study showed higher tachistoscopic

TABLE 5–4

Correlations between association times and recognition thresholds for the success-recall and failure-recall groups where recognition thresholds have been corrected for total group performance

Subjects	Success-recall		Subjects	Failure-recall	
	r	z		r	z
A..............	.49	.54	a	.02	.02
B..............	.46	.50	b	.11	.11
C..............	.24	.25	c	.05	.05
D..............	.29	.30	d	.21	.21
E..............	.43	.46	e	.04	.04
F..............	.30	.31	f	.00	.00
G..............	.29	.30	g	−.13	−.13
Mean z score:	.38			.04	
Combined variance estimage:	.012				
	t = 5.73		p < .001		

Source: C. W. Eriksen, "Defense against ego-threat in memory and perception," *J. abnorm. soc. Psychol.*, 1952.

exposure times for correct recognition of long association time words, whereas subjects who recalled their failures on the memory study showed no significant relationship between recognition times and association times. Once you get to a study that is this sophisticated, that concerns itself with the related effects of a defensive process on more than one cognitive function, and that considers more than one kind of defensive process, the sorts of criticisms that seemed so weighty when leveled at the perceptual studies of Postman, Bruner, and McGinnies have virtually no significance. There are by now numerous other studies like this one, but I will not review them all.

I will, however, consider one more study because it is an example of the gradual broadening, deepening, and enrichment that has taken place in research on defensiveness. In this and subsequent studies, Eriksen and his associates (Eriksen, 1954; Eriksen & Brown, 1956; Eriksen & Davids, 1955) have been successful in relating the difference between sensitizing and repressing to the difference between hysterical and psychasthenic tendencies as measured by a respected test of psychopathological tendencies, the Minnesota Multiphasic Personality Inventory. In current psychoanalytic conceptions of neurosis, the mechanism of repression is predominantly associated with hysteria while intellectualization is considered characteristic of the obsessive-compulsive or psychasthenic neurosis. Eriksen found that subjects scoring high on the hysteria test tended to recall successfully completed tasks on the memory test following task performance, whereas subjects scoring high on the psychasthenia test tended to recall failed tasks.

We have come now to the end of the review of defensiveness research that I had intended. It is not that there is no other research, but rather that what remains will add little that is new to what we have already considered. On the basis of our analysis of the studies covered, it can fairly be said that there is empirical support for the existence of defensive reactions within people that extend across learning, perceptual, and memory processes. To be sure, there seem to be at least two broad categories of defensiveness, namely, desensitization and sensitization. And certainly, there are many loose ends, some of which will prove relevant to issues I will pose later. But with regard to the present issue of whether a concept of defense is tenable, we must clearly conclude that there are systematic empirical findings that recommend the concept to us. Happily enough, the systematic studies are in concordance with the semiempirical clinical observations with which discussion of the issue was begun. By way of more precise summary, the operation of defenses has been shown both when certain stimuli were rendered anxiety provoking through experimental manipulation, and when stimuli were chosen so as to be likely to engage common conflicts permeating the lives of the subjects. The effects of sensitizing and desensitizing defenses have been shown on perception of stimuli exposed for brief periods of time, and on memory for activities engaged in previously. In some of the most recent studies, these two kinds of effect have been shown to occur together, and in a manner consistent with the implications of different kinds of defenses for psychopathological tendencies.

Although we can now say with some authority that there is evidence supporting the notion of defense as an explanatory concept, we are still left with the nagging criticism, underlying this whole issue, of the non-sensical nature of theorizing that assumes a man within a man. It is time to grapple with this criticism now that it is clear that there is rigorously scientific evidence recommending the concept of defense to us. As I suggested earlier, if it is possible to suggest a basis whereby the overly figurative language incessantly surrounding the concept of defense can be translated into language descriptive of known capabilities of single organisms, then the man-within-a-man criticism will lose considerable force. I believe that recent physiological experimentation and theorizing make this translation possible, and propose to discuss this matter now. Much of what I will say follows the brilliant start made by Bruner (1957b) in his introduction of the concept of *gating*. To set the orientation from which the idea of gating emerges, Bruner quotes from the physiologist, Adrian (1954, pp. 238–239), who was knighted for his excellence:

> The operations of the brain stem seem to be related to particular fields of sensory information which vary from moment to moment with the shifts of our attention. The signals from the sense organs must be treated differently when we attend to them and when we do not, and if we could decide how and where the divergencies arise, we should be nearer to understanding how the level of consciousness is reached. The question is whether the afferent messages that evoke sensations are allowed at all times to reach the cerebral cortex or are sometimes blocked at a lower level. Clearly we can reduce the inflow from the sense organs as we do by closing the eyes and relaxing the muscles when we wish to sleep and it is quite probable that the sensitivity of some of the sense organs can be directly influenced by the central nervous system. But even in deep sleep or coma there is no reason to believe that sensory messages no longer reach the central nervous system. At some stage therefore on their passage to consciousness the messages meet with barriers that are sometimes open and sometimes closed. Where are these barriers, in the cortex, the brain stem, or elsewhere?

How far this statement is beyond the old notion of the nervous system involving little more than stimulation of a sense organ, conduction of that stimulation to the sensory area of the cortex, translation into an action message in the motor cortex and transmission from there peripherally to the muscles! Adrian is clearly positing central nervous system control of stimulation coming into the organism. Such control, dubbed gating by Bruner, would, if discovered, render the psychological concept of defense much more plausible. In the possibility of central nervous system control of peripheral stimulation is the basis for translating the concept of defense into the kind of sensible terms that will obviate the man-within-a-man criticism.

There is even some empirical evidence to support the notion of gating. Hernandez-Peon, Scherrer, and Jouvet (1956) did a physiological experiment on cats, in which they arranged to obtain a recording of the electrical discharge, called potential, in the nerve cells just past the auditory sense organ, called the cochlear nucleus, on the way toward the brain. They arranged their apparatus in such fashion that whenever they sounded a click in the cat's ear, they could determine the intensity and rate of electrical impulses in those nerves immediately central to the sense organ. After recording enough to determine the normal level of electrical activity as a response to the sounds, Hernandez-Peon et al. introduced three kinds of nonauditory distractors. While being exposed to the click, cats were shown two mice in a bell jar, were given fish odors to smell, or were shocked on the forepaw; i.e., visual, olfactory, and somatic distractors were employed. Strange and marvelous to tell, electrical activity in the nerves just central to the cochler nucleus was markedly reduced under all three conditions over what it had been without the distractors! Presumably, messages being transmitted to the brain over one sensory channel entered into some central nervous system process whereby stimulation reaching another sense organ was not transmitted beyond that organ. Even without knowing more about this mysterious process, we can recognize that it is clearly indicative of the tenability of the concept of defense at the physiological level of analysis. The nervous system can apparently do that which seemed so nonsensical to many psychologists and philosophers.

Hernandez-Peon and his associates have given evidence suggesting a physiological basis for desensitizing defenses in the auditory perceptual system at least. The work of other investigators (e.g., Galambos, Sheatz, & Vernier, 1956; Granit, 1955;) suggests the generality of this phenomenon beyond the auditory modality, and also gives evidence of a similar physiological mechanism for the sensitizing defenses. One of the clearest demonstrations of the latter, again in the auditory modality, occurs in Galambos et al. (1956). They utilized a recording procedure and experimental design similar to that of Hernandez-Peon et al., except that they made the click presented at the cat's ear a signal for subsequent shock. Once the cats had learned this signal value of the click, the presentation of the click without the shock was enough to produce a greater burst of electrical activity from the nerve cells central to the cochlear nucleus than occurred in control animals for whom the click did not function as a signal for shock. It is as if the learning process involved a tuning of the auditory system so as to be especially sensitive to clicks, more sensitive than would be normal.

More complete and precise evidence that the central nervous system tunes or detunes peripheral sensory systems is provided by Galambos (1956) in an ingenious study. Arranging recording apparatus in similar fashion to his previous study and that of Hernandez-Peon et al., Galambos also stimulated the superior olivary nucleus of his cats. The superior olivary nucleus is a major subcortical center of the brain for the auditory system. He found that whenever he stimulated this nucleus, the electrical activity occurring just central to the cochlear nucleus in response to the clicks presented at the ear was markedly reduced. What Galambos has done is produce the same effect found by Hernandez-Peon et al. by stimulating a brain center directly rather than by providing stimulation in a nonauditory sensory modality. These results are an important link in the chain demonstrating central nervous system control of peripheral sensitivity. Although some of the research findings mentioned here have proven difficult to replicate, some additional research and theorizing has suggested the existence of a gating mechanism for pain (Clark & Hunt, 1971; Melzack & Wall, 1968), a sensation that has for so long resisted explanation.

The kind of evidence provided by the studies just described is clearly relevant to the effects of defenses on perception, but not immediately relevant to other effects of defenses. While this is true, I would encourage you to recognize that there are other sensory systems besides the traditional, obvious ones having to do with stimulation reaching the organism from the outside world. There are sensory systems alerting the organism to its internal world, like the kinesthetic and proprioceptive systems. It is certainly possible that such systems are also tuned by the central nervous system, and if this is so, then there is ample basis for more widespread effects of defense than on exteroceptive perception alone. Although evidence for interoceptive tuning is absent at this point, I would submit that the revolutionary step has already been taken in the work of people like Galambos and Hernandez-Peon, and in the theorizing of Adrian, Bruner, and Melzack and Wall.

Perhaps exteroceptive and interoceptive sensory stimulation entering the central pervous system is compared to a template or model of stimulation existing in the memory. This template or model could well be affected by the past history of reward and punishment encountered in dealing with other people. When incoming stimulation and the template match well, no gating occurs. But when they do not match the discrepancy may constitute the physiological concomitant of conflict and anxiety. The mismatch may instigate some control process sensitizing or desensitizing certain or all exteroceptive and interoceptive sensory modalities such that precisely that stimulation which would match the template better is permitted to pass on to the brain. Stimulation not permitted to pass would then be unconscious because it was literally not in the brain, even though in the organism at the level of sense organs. This resolves the paradox of assuming mental content that is not available to awareness, a paradox that has bothered many critics of the concept of defense. And in a more general sense, the criticism of a man within a man recedes in cogency, for we can talk in more descriptive, less-figurative terms. The evidence concerning the phenomenon of gating renders the concept of defense more plausible than its critics would have admitted some years ago. For the moment I am ready to conclude that the concept of defense is tenable.

This conclusion has an obvious bearing on the three models of personality we have been considering. Clearly, it is not a black mark against a model that it includes, or even relies upon the concept of defense. Far from it, the empirical evidence showing the existence of sensitizing and desensitizing behaviors actually favors the models specifically employing the concept of defense. On this basis, the conflict and fulfillment models, in all their versions, seem fruitful. The consistency model seems less fruitful, for the concept of defense is not a logically integral part of it. This is least true as a criticism of the activation version of the consistency model exemplified by the theory of Fiske and Maddi. In their discussion of corrections for discrepancies between customary and actual levels of activation that have literally taken place, Fiske and Maddi stress behavior which has the characteristics of the sensitizing and desensitizing processes encountered in the research we have been considering. In a general sense, then, Fiske and Maddi could possibly account for sensitizing and desensitizing behavior, even though they do not employ the traditional concept of defense, with its emphasis upon conflict between individual and society.

Second issue: Is all behavior defensive?

Having encountered empirical support for the belief that defensive behavior occurs, it becomes important to consider whether all or only some behavior is defensive in character. There is an issue involved here because the psychosocial conflict model in its pure form would assume that all behavior is defensive, whereas most other models assume only some behavior to be defensive. Actually, the cognitive dissonance version of the consistency model gives no explicit role to defense. Most of the semi-empirical and empirical evidence relevant to this issue has already been discussed in this and the previous chapter. Of particular importance is research permitting one to see whether there is behavior that does not distort reality, in a context entailing pressure toward distortion.

Meager though the findings are, I have pointed out that each time a study was designed and analyzed in such fashion that it was possible to note not only desensitization and sensitization, but normal or accurate sensitivity as well, some subjects fell into this last category. This result is most clear in the experiments on memory, and persisted through all experimental attempts to increase the likelihood of defense through pressuring the subjects. Apparently some people do function nondefensively at least some of the time. It will do no good to say that this shows no more than that the experiment was successful only for some people, that only some people had their anxieties aroused and conflicts engaged. This very statement recognizes that some people function without defensiveness at least some of the time!

Although similar evidence from perceptual studies is harder to come by, I did point out that it is very likely to be there. Because the relevant investigators have not been particularly interested in the proportion of their subjects perceiving accurately, i.e., not in an unsensitive or hypersensitive fashion, they have not analyzed their data in such manner as to make this information available. But a perusal of their findings shows two things clearly: there are marked differences in perceptual speed among the subjects in a typical study, and the average differences in time necessary for perception of crucial as opposed to neutral words is typically quite small. These two characteristics of results strongly suggest that the proportion of subjects perceiving accurately might well be sizable.

In my judgment, the evidence, though not extensive, supports the contention that some people do not appear to distort reality appreciably, even when pressured and threatened. Therefore, we have an empirical basis for resolving the issue posed earlier in favor of the position that some but not all behavior is defensive. This conclusion has far-reaching implications. Perhaps the most basic implication is that the pure conflict model of the psychosocial type is limited in usefulness for understanding personality. You will recall that this kind of model employs a concept of defense because it postulates an individual with essentially selfish concerns and a society with antithetical concerns and the capability with which to ferret out and punish selfishness. The concept of defense is used in such theories to account for the whole orientation of a person's life whereby he can avoid punishment and guilt while still protecting some small basis for self-satisfaction. It is the asserted ubiquitousness of defensiveness in this model that is called into question by our empirical analysis. But the usefulness of the intrapsychic version of the conflict model is not called into question, for this version recognizes the existence of defensive behavior without assuming that all behavior is defensive. The same is true of the variant on the psychosocial version of the conflict model, exemplified by Murray and the ego psychologists. In this variant position, an inherent basis for functioning without conflict, and therefore without defense, is assumed. The conflict theory that fares most badly on the basis of our conclusion concerning the second issue is that of Freud.

As you can see, the fulfillment model is completely supported by our conclusion. This is because the model conceptualizes conflict, anxiety, and defense as possible but not inevitable outcomes of living. In all versions and variants of this model, defense occurs but is not ubiquitous. As already suggested in concluding discussion of the first issue, the cognitive dissonance version of the consistency model is called into question by the empirical evidence indicating the existence of defensive behavior. But the activation version of this model, exemplified by the theory of Fiske and Maddi, was considered tenable. The conclusion reached here reinforces the tenability of this position, because the position certainly does not make correctional (quasi-defensive) behaviors ubiquitous. They only occur when anticipational behaviors have failed. Anticipational behaviors might well fail in laboratory situations, where one cannot completely select one's experiences.

Third issue: Is the highest form of living adaptive or transcendent?

You will recall that according to the pure psychosocial version of the conflict model, the highest form of living was that which involved adaptation to the imperatives of society. Clearly, this position is related to the assumption of ubiquitous conflict between individual and society, with defensiveness being the only protection of the individual. According to this position, maturity involves such traits as dependability, generosity, loyalty, respect for others and society, steady productivity, and evenness of mood. Immature behaviors involve impulsivity, rebelliousness, disrespect for others and social institutions, and general unpredictability. In sharp contrast, the fulfillment model considers repetitive, conforming, unimaginative behavior to be defensive and immature. This is consistent with the position's devaluation of social adjustment as a goal of life. Transcendence of social conventions (they are not considered imperatives) is virtually necessary for vigorous, mature living. Understandably enough, maturity is characterized by the fulfillment model as nondefensive and free of psychosocial conflict. Other versions and variants of the conflict model fall somewhere between the two extremes I have drawn. The consistency model is not especially characterizable on this third issue. Insofar as there is some relevance of this model to the issue it is that the pure cognitive dissonance version tends in the direction of celebrating dependable, repetitive behavior, whereas McClelland's variant and the activation version include some emphases upon both repetitive and novel functioning.

Although the third issue can be precisely pinpointed, it is not clear to me that it can really be settled by empirical analysis. Certainly, we can well expect to be able to find evidence in people for both adaptive and transcendent behaviors. Which of them is considered better will inevitably be a matter of opinion. A conflict theorist can assert with cogency that someone showing good citizenship is an excellent person, and a fulfillment theorist can wax just as eloquent concerning someone whose artistic inclination leads him to function outside of social conventions. In order for empirical analysis to resolve this issue in a definitive manner, both conflict and fulfillment theorists would have to agree upon the admirability of one discernible kind of person. Then a consideration of the behavioral traits of this kind of person might clarify whether he seemed primarily adaptational or transcendent. Perhaps the closest we can come to such agreement is the creative person. Creative people are currently celebrated in our culture as having achieved a pinnacle of living. They are lauded, envied, emulated, and supported by government grants. Both conflict and fulfillment theorists would consider them admirable people. We must be just a bit careful, however, for some people still harbor suspicion that the creative person is really unsavory, dangerous, and lazy. In addition, if you asked people to identify the creative members of their group, there might well be considerable disagreement. Nonetheless, studying the behavioral traits of creative people is probably as close as we can come to an empirical basis for resolving the third issue.

Although there are a number of recent studies of creative people, none is so carefully done and comprehensive as that of MacKinnon (1965; Hall & MacKinnon, 1969). Having decided to concentrate on architects, MacKinnon asked eminent administrators and educators in that field to nominate the most creative members of the profession. By pooling the information thus obtained, he was able to select a sample of architects that were generally agreed to be creative. By comparison with a control group of randomly selected architects, the creative group included a great many prize winners and leaders. Although it is not entirely clear what the measure of creativity means in this study, it is not likely to be far from the current emphases of psychologists. It is rather generally agreed now that the creative act produces something both novel and significant, and that the creative person is someone who produces creative acts consistently (Bruner, 1962b; Jackson & Messick, 1965; Maddi, 1965).

MacKinnon's creative architects were compared with the control group on many tests of personality. One of the most overwhelmingly clear findings of this study is that the creative architects are more transcendent than the control group. The creative architects describe themselves as being rather uninterested in socializing, unconcerned with their popularity and acceptance by others, unusual and idiosyncratic in their habits and beliefs, and more concerned with quality than acceptability or output in their work. Although they consider themselves able to be intimate with friends, they care little for social amenities. In addition, they do not seem overly concerned by their self-preoccupation and disdain for the social system. Lest you doubt whether these self-descriptions bear any relationship to the way other people see these creative architects, let me assure you that they do. MacKinnon's staff of psychologists found the creative architects to be, on the basis of personal contact with them over a period of some days, much as they described themselves. The creative architects were less predictable, repetitive, and conforming, though more imaginative, intense, and original, than were the control architects. Corroboration of the transcendent qualities mentioned thus far was also obtained from the life histories of the creative architects. All in all, they were not adapting to social institutions so much as changing them, or else functioning outside of them.

Although on a less comprehensive scale, many other studies of creativity support the findings reviewed above. For example, Cross, Cattell, and Butcher (1967) compared 63 visual artists and 28 craft students with a matched control group on scores derived from the 16 Personality Factor Questionnaire (devised by Cattell and Stice, 1957). Statistically significant differences in average scores were found on 12 of the 16 factors, with the craft students being typically between the artists and the control subjects. Especially salient features of the artist's personalities were assertiveness (or dominance), self-sufficiency, personal integration, casualness, Bohemian tendencies, and low superego strength. In addition to these transcendent qualities, they were also high in suspiciousness, proneness to guilt, tension, and emotional instability. This hint of inconsistency is also found by Barron (1963) who summarizes 10 years of research as indicating the presence in artistically creative persons of spirituality and a belief in self-renewal but also the possibility of personal conflict. Recently, Helson and Crutchfield (1970), and Helson (1973a; 1973b) have reported that creative mathematicians and writers are more unconventional, assertive, and independent than their less creative counterparts.

Perhaps the intimations of difficulty in relating to others is a somewhat natural sequel of the transcendent orientation present in creative persons. In this regard, Schaefer (1969), like so many other investigators, has found creative adolescents (and, for that matter, adults) to show tolerance for ambiguity, impulsivity, craving for novelty, autonomy, and self-assertiveness.

There is little point in chronicling the other studies of creativity (see Razik, 1965; Stein, 1968), for they are all in essential agreement on the transcendent quality of the phenomenon. Even historical researches into the lives of men remembered as having been greatly creative (e.g., Maddi, 1965) testify to the transcendent nature of their lives. There is a streak of what might almost be called selfishness in great men. Most of them have believed deeply in their own greatness. Even Freud, the arch conflict theorist, seems to have had such a belief (Jones, 1955). Studies of living persons identified as creative support this conclusion (e.g., Taylor, 1963). These various sources of evidence incline me to the conclusion that the highest form of functioning is transcendent rather than adaptive.

This conclusion clearly favors the fulfillment model over the conflict model in its psychosocial version. Not especially hurt by the findings are the intrapsychic version of the conflict model and the consistency model. In classical Freudian thinking, which is the prototype of psychosocial conflict theory, there was no very convincing explanation of creativity. Creativity tended to be seen as somewhat akin to madness. In madness, the person is as close to lacking defenses as it is possible to come, according to classical psychoanalytic thinking. In this state, functioning is chaotic, destructive, and riddled with anxiety. Instincts are fairly directly expressed, to the detriment of the person and those around him. Creativity was considered less violent and psychopathological, but somehow on the same continuum. The creative act was accounted for as an instinctual expression, over which the person had little control. Clearly, this attempt to explain creativity is untenable in the light of the findings of studies such as those reviewed here. It was only with the advent of ego psychology that personologists who found themselves temperamentally in the psychoanalytic camp could explain creativity in a manner that made it distinguishable from madness. But this explanation required the addition to the psychosocial conflict model of aspects of a fulfillment model. The result is really a new theory, as I have pointed out in Chapter 2.

The ego psychology explanation of creativity involves *regression in the service of the ego* (Kris, 1952). Now regression is a defense we have encountered before. But in this context, we find that the retreat to an earlier level of development constituting this defense is not an unavoidable, unrecognized attempt to avoid anxiety, but rather, a consciously precipitated return to a more childish state in order to find inspiration through momentarily relinquishing the very socialization that is considered so valuable in everyday living. So, while regression in the service of the ego retains the element of defensiveness comprising distortion of reality, it is not defensive in that it operates consciously and is under the control of the person. The ego psychologist's explanation of creativity comes as close to the fulfillment model as it can while still retaining something of the conflict model; creativity is for him not properly considered defensive, even though it involves some relinquishment of social realities.

There is very little by way of systematic empirical evidence for or against this psychoanalytic view. One relevant study, however, is that of Gray (1969), who aimed at determining the relationship between a measure of regression in the service of the ego and a measure of creativity, in a sample of 100 male undergraduates. Although he initially found a positive correlation between the two, the correlation was essentially removed by his correcting for the effects of sheer productivity of responses. This suggests that the presumed relationship between creativity and regression in the service of the ego is really a reflection of the more general variable of productivity.

Fourth issue: Is cognitive dissonance invariably unpleasant and avoided?

The pure cognitive dissonance version of the consistency model makes any degree and kind of discrepancy between expectancies, thoughts, and perceptions the source of emotional discomfort and attempts at avoidance. In an obvious sense, this position is very sensible. To perceive something different from what one thought or expected is to have been wrong, and who can rest easy with that? To think one way and perceive yourself as acting another way is to be dishonest or cowardly or inept, none of which possibilities would be very acceptable. To harbor two discrepant thoughts or beliefs at the same time is to be confused, and who wants that? The principle is the same whether the inconsistency be small or large, important or unimportant.

The issue as to whether this position is accurate is raised from a number of sectors of psychology. Within the cognitive dissonance model itself, we have the variant position, exemplified by McClelland, which contends that only large discrepancies are unpleasant and avoided, whereas small discrepancies are actually pleasurable and sought after. Moreover, in the activation version of the consistency model, exemplified by the theory of Fiske and Maddi, there is the view that cognitive dissonance, in the degree required for maintenance of customary levels of activation, will be pleasant and pursued. Rather complete disagreement with the pure cognitive dissonance version of the consistency model is shown by those psychologists, increasing in number these days, who believe that variety has significant positive value for the organism.

In addition, the fulfillment model does not agree with the cognitive dissonance model in any proper sense. If cognitive consistency stood in the way of fulfillment, then for fulfillment theorists, consistency would actually be unpleasant. In this fulfillment theorists would agree with Emerson (1940) in his crackling line from the essay on self-reliance, "A foolish consistency is the hobgoblin of little minds." There is the sense in fulfillment theory that cognitive consistency usually means conformity of the person with an external, or societal definition of life. To be consistent is often to give up fulfillment. The disagreement of fulfillment theorists would not depend on how large the cognitive dissonance was, as in the case of McClelland and Fiske and Maddi, but rather on the content of the inconsistency.

Superficially, the conflict model would seem to agree rather closely with the cognitive dissonance version of the consistency model. After all, conflict is the incompatibility between two opposing forces. But you must keep in mind that in conflict theory it is not any discrepancy which is important, but only discrepancies between the two forces considered to be basic to the person. So at the very least, conflict theory is much narrower in being specific to particular content than is cognitive dissonance theory. But the difference does not end here. You should also recognize that it is possible to imagine a discrepancy which, because it did not involve conflict between the two opposing forces, would not necessarily be considered unpleasant and to be avoided by a conflict theorist. It is only when discrepancy is synonymous with conflict that conflict theory would agree with cognitive dissonance theory. So, like fulfillment theory, conflict theory would only be at issue with cognitive dissonance theory in the case of certain matters of content.

We are ready now to turn to empirical evidence bearing on the issue. Surprisingly, Kelly's theory, the most comprehensive example of the pure cognitive dissonance version of the consistency model, has not generated any systematic research relevant to determining whether dissonance is invariably unpleasant and avoided. Happily, however, study upon study has come out of Festinger's position, which, though not a theory of personality, is certainly in agreement with that of Kelly on the issue before us. I will now consider important and representative examples of this body of research, along with criticisms that have been raised. Following this, I will present systematic research representing the opposing point of view, that of variety theory, also along with criticisms. Finally, we will find some basis for resolving the issue.

Research attempting to demonstrate the avoidance of cognitive dissonance has aroused considerable enthusiasm in contemporary psychology. I think the reason for the enthusiasm is clear. Festinger and his various associates presented in a persuasive, impassioned, and committed way a scheme for understanding social and individual change that was at the same time extraordinarily simple and comprehensive. In addition, they have argued their position, not in the arid arena of pure thought, but in the rich and complex content of important life events. And when they have done experiments, they have focused upon results which though predicted by dissonance theory, would not have been predicted from more familiar and obvious frames of reference. So the position is simple, general, oriented toward important events in life, and predicts surprising, dramatic outcomes that can be followed up in the laboratory. The position's mushrooming popularity is quite understandable.

I would like to start my review of the research in this tradition by quoting at length from an article of Festinger which shows not only dramatic forcefulness of exposition, but emphasis upon significant life events as well. The episode described is from a naturalistic or observational piece of research. Festinger (1958, pp. 74–76) writes:

> Another intriguing example of the reduction of dissonance in a startling manner comes from a study I did together with Riecken and Schachter . . . of a group of people who predicted that, on a given date, a catastrophic flood would overwhelm most of the world. This prediction of the catastrophic flood had been given to the people in direct com-

munications from the gods and was an integral part of their religious beliefs. When the predicted date arrived and passed there was considerable dissonance established in these people. They continued to believe in their gods and in the validity of the communications from them, and at the same time they knew that the prediction of the flood had been wrong. We observed the movement as participants for approximately two months preceding and one month after this unequivocal disproof of part of their belief. The point of the study was, of course, to observe how they would react to the dissonance. Let me give you a few of the details of the disproof and how they reacted to it.

For some time it had been clear to the people in the group that those who were chosen were to be picked up by flying saucers before the cataclysm occurred. Some of the believers, these mainly college students, were advised to go home and wait individually for the flying saucer that would arrive for each of them. This was reasonable and plausible, since the date of the cataclysm happened to occur during an academic holiday. Most of the group, including the most central and most heavily committed members, gathered together in the home of the woman who received the message from the gods to wait together for the arrival of the saucer. For these latter, disproof of the prediction, in the form of evidence that the mesages were not valid, began to occur four days before the predicted event was to take place. A message informed them that a saucer would land in the back yard of the house at 4:00 P.M. to pick up the members of the group. With coat in hand they waited, but no saucer came. A later message told them there had been a delay—the saucer would arrive at midnight. Midst absolute secrecy (the neighbors and press must not know), they waited outdoors on a cold and snowy night for over an hour, but still no saucer came. Another message told them to continue waiting, but still no saucer came. At about 3:00 A.M. they gave up, interpreting the events of that night as a test, a drill, and a rehearsal for the real pickup which would still soon take place.

Tensely, they waited for the final orders to come through—for the messages which would tell them the time, place, and procedure for the actual pickup. Finally, on the day before the cataclysm was to strike, the messages came. At midnight a man would come to the door of the house and take them to the place where the flying saucer would be parked. More messages came that day, one after another, instructing them in the passwords that would be necessary in order to board the saucer, in preparatory procedures such as removal of metal from clothing, removal of personal identification, maintaining silence at certain times, and the like. The day was spent by the group in preparation and rehearsal of the necessary procedures and, when midnight came, the group sat waiting in readiness. But no knock came at the door, no one came to lead them to the flying saucer.

From midnight to five o'clock in the morning the group sat there struggling to understand what had happened, struggling to find some explanation that would enable them to recover somewhat from the shattering realization that they would not be picked up by a flying saucer and that consequently the flood itself would not occur as predicted. It is doubtful that anyone alone, without the support of the others, could have with-stood the impact of this disproof of the prediction. Indeed, those members of the group who had gone to their homes to wait alone, alone in the sense that they did not have other believers with them, did not withstand it. Almost all of them became skeptics afterward. In other words, without easily obtainable social support to begin reducing the dissonance, the dissonance was sufficient to cause the belief to be discarded in spite of the commitment to it. But the members of the group who had gathered together in the home of the woman who received the messages could, and did, provide social support for one another. They kept reassuring one another of the validity of the messages and that some explanation would be found.

At fifteen minutes before five o'clock that morning an explanation was found that was at least temporarily satisfactory. A message arrived from God which, in effect, said that He had saved the world and stayed the flood because of this group and the light and strength this group had spread throughout the world that night.

The behavior of these people from that moment onwards presented a revealing contrast to their previous behavior. These people who had been disinterested in publicity and even avoided it, became avid publicity seekers. For four successive days, finding a new reason each day, they invited the press into the house, gave lengthy interviews, and attempted to attract the public to their ideas. The first day they called all the news-papers and news services, informed them of the fact that the world had been saved and invited them to come and get interviews. The second day, a ban on having photographs taken was lifted, and the newspapers were once more called to inform them of the fact and to invite them to come to the house and take pictures. On the third day they once more called the press to inform them that on the next afternoon they would gather on their front lawn singing and that it was possible a space man would visit them at that time. What is more, the general public was specifically in-vited to come and watch. And on the fourth day, newspapermen and about two hundred people came to watch the group singing on their front lawn. There were almost no lengths to which these people would not go to attract publicity and potential believers in the validity of the mes-sages. If, indeed, more and more converts could be found, more and more people who believed in the messages and the things the messages said, then the dissonance between their belief and the knowledge that the messages had not been correct could be reduced.

Dramatic though this episode is, it cannot be considered a completely convincing demonstration of the principle of cognitive dissonance re-duction. There are just too many other possibly important factors. The situation, as most naturally occurring ones, is so complex in involving so many overlapping factors, that it is ambiguous as a demonstration of the sole importance of any one of the factors. Controlled and systematic laboratory research is needed to supplement naturalistic observation. Festinger (1958, p. 76) clearly agrees, for in the very next paragraph, he says:

These examples, while they do illustrate attempts to reduce dissonance in rather surprising directions, still leave much to be desired. One would also like to be able to show that such dissonance-reduction phenomena do occur under controlled laboratory conditions and that the magnitude of the effect does depend upon the magnitude of the dissonance which exists.

Festinger then goes on to describe an experiment (Festinger & Carlsmith, 1959) which aimed at such precise demonstration of the avoidance of inconsistency. Subjects were told they were participating in a study of measures of performance, whereas in reality they were made to do a boring and repetitive task for one hour. At the end of the time, the subjects were given a false explanation of the purpose of the experiment. They were told that the study concerned the effects of expectation on task performance. Some subjects were then asked if they would stay on and take the place of the research assistant for a few minutes, as he was away for the day. They would have to deceive the next incoming subject that the task he would perform—actually the same boring one the deceiving subject had just finished—was quite interesting and enjoyable. For supposedly taking the research assistant's place, one group of subjects was given $1 each, and the other group was given $20 each. Some subjects refused to be hired, but the others went along with the deception. A control group of subjects was not asked to take part in any deception. At the end of the study, all subjects (deceiving and control subjects) were seen by an interviewer, supposedly part of the psychology department's program of evaluating the experiments done by its members. During the interview, subjects were asked to rate the experiment along four dimensions.

These ratings actually constituted the data of the study, and the averages based upon them are shown in Table 5–5. Three dimensions showed no significant differences between the $1, $20, and control groups. But there were significant differences in ratings of enjoyment of

TABLE 5–5

Average ratings on interview questions for each condition

	Experimental condition		
Question on interview	*Control* (N = 20)	*One dollar* (N = 20)	*Twenty dollars* (N = 20)
How enjoyable tasks were (rated from −5 to +5)	−.45	+1.35	−.05
How much they learned (rated from 0 to 10)	3.08	2.80	3.15
Scientific importance (rated from 0 to 10)	5.60	6.45	5.18
Participate in similar exp. (rated from −5 to +5)	−.62	+1.20	−.25

Source: L. Festinger and J. M. Carlsmith, "Cognitive consequences of forced compliance," *J. abnorm. soc. Psychol.*, 1959.

the experiment. These ratings had been done on a scale from −5 (dull), through 0 (neutral); to +5 (enjoyable). The control group rated the experiment as just a little on the dull side, the $1 group thought it was somewhat enjoyable, and the $20 group was neutral. The small difference between the control and $20 groups was not significant. Festinger and Carlsmith find these results quite supportive of the hypothesis that people tend to reduce cognitive dissonance. They reason that, whereas both the $1 and $20 groups have dissonance due to the inconsistency between their perception of the task as boring, and their perception of themselves as publicly extolling its enjoyability, the dissonance is actually much less for the $20 group. This is because they could at least tell themselves that they were being well paid to lie, while the poor $1 subjects did not even have financial recompense enough for their deception. Therefore, it is understandable, according to the experimenters, that the $1 group should actually report most enjoyment of the task in retrospect, since this shift in their opinion of the task would constitute a reduction of dissonance. I wish you would note that this experiment is really terribly ingenious. Common sense and reinforcement theory would predict that the $20 group, not the $1 group would report subsequently the greatest enjoyment, as they got the most out of their participation, and lied no more severely than did the $1 group. The results obtained are not only consistent with the resolution of inconsistency, they are quite surprising.

Many criticisms have been made of this and similar experiments. But before considering them, let us assume that the results do mean what Festinger and Carlsmith conclude. Even if that were so, there is no evidence to indicate that small inconsistencies lead to avoidance behavior. The difference between the control and $20 groups in rated enjoyment of the task is nonexistent from a statistical point of view. There is only evidence that large inconsistencies, as experienced by the $1 group may lead to attempts to reduce them by concluding that the task must have been enjoyable. So, from the point of view of the issue we are discussing, we should probably conclude no more than that there is evidence that large inconsistencies are unpleasant and avoided.

But the criticism leveled at this and similar experiments has been strong and compelling, raising doubt as to whether the results show anything at all about reactions to dissonance. The major critics of dissonance reduction research have been Chapanis and Chapanis (1964), and I shall rely heavily upon their analyses. They wonder, first of all, how much the experiment was successful in arousing dissonance at all. The experience of dissonance hinges in this study on the repetitive task really being experienced as boring when being performed. And yet, the control group, who did this task, but was not asked to deceive subsequent subjects, rated it as only slightly boring, as very little different from neutral (see the entry corresponding to the first row and column of Table 5–5). Either the task was not really as monotonous as the experimenters thought, or the general instructions given subjects initially about studying the effects of expectation on performance were sufficient to interest them in participating to the point where the monotonous nature of the task was not the single, or even most important, factor in their enjoyment. So, Chapanis and Chapanis conclude that the experiment does not permit us to check whether discrepant cognitions of any important magnitude were in fact produced.

An even more serious criticism involves the difference in plausibility of the \$20 and \$1 remuneration for acting as research assistant. Twenty dollars is a lot of money for an undergraduate even when it represents a whole day's pay. When it is offered for something that must have been less than 30 minutes' work, it is difficult to imagine a student accepting the money without becoming wary and alert to possible tricks. In fact, more than 16 percent of the original subjects in the \$20 group had to be discarded because they voiced suspicions, or refused to be hired! Under such circumstances, Chapanis and Chapanis conclude, it seems likely that those who were retained might have hedged or been evasive about their evaluation of the experiment, because they were generally apprehensive about its nature and purpose. And, of course, the average enjoyment rating of neutral, representing as it does the middle point of a dimension running from unenjoyable to enjoyable, is a very ambiguous result in that it could well represent the canceling out of a number of opposing trends within the group. In any event, whereas the \$1 remuneration seems plausible enough, the same cannot be said for the \$20 one. Chapanis and Chapanis conclude correctly that it is therefore impossible to rule out alternative explanations of the results than that offered by Festinger and Carlsmith.

A cogent alternative has actually been offered by Rosenberg (1965) in a study which attempts to correct some of the pitfalls of a study very much like that of Festinger and Carlsmith. This similar study was conducted by Cohen and reported by Brehm and Cohen (1962). Its general design was similar to that of Festinger and Carlsmith, except that it included four degrees of remuneration, rather than only two. The prediction was that the greater the remuneration, the smaller the dissonance reduction, where such reduction could be seen as a change in original attitude. The subjects were Yale undergraduates, and the study was conducted immediately following a campus riot that had been quelled by the police. The experimenter, appearing at randomly chosen dormitory rooms, ascertained through inquiry that the subject disapproved of the actions of the police. Then he was asked to write an essay in support of the actions of the police, with the justification that the experimenter was interested in obtaining examples of arguments that could justify the police action. The subject was also told that he would receive a certain amount of pay for writing the essay against his own position, with one group being offered $0.50, another group, $1, another $5, and another $10. After writing the counterattitudinal essay, the subject was asked to fill out a questionnaire concerning his real reactions to the police action, on the grounds that:

> Now that you have looked at some of the reasons for the actions of the New Haven police, we would like to get some of your reactions to the issue: *you may possibly want to look at the situation in the light of this.* So, would you please fill out this questionnaire.

A control group was given this final attitude questionnaire but was not required to write the essay and did not receive any remuneration.

Cohen found that the $5 and $10 groups did not differ significantly from the control group in expressed attitude toward the New Haven police. But the subjects in the $0.50 group were less negative toward the police than the $1 subjects, who in turn were less negative than the $10 subjects. In addition, both the $0.50 and $1 groups were significantly different from the control group. As you can see, the results seem to bear out the original prediction rather well. But Rosenberg (1965) suggests the importance, in the explanation of the results, of *evaluation apprehension* and general *annoyance toward the experimenter,* in following up the suspiciousness hypothesis of Chapanis and Chapanis. Rosenberg (1965) writes that his point of view

> . . . would suggest that in this study, as in others of similar design, the low-dissonance (high-reward) subjects would be more likely to suspect that the experimenter had some unrevealed purpose. The gross discrepancy between spending a few minutes writing an essay and the large sum offered, the fact that this large sum had not yet been delivered by the time the subject was handed the attitude questionnaire, the fact that he was virtually invited to show that he had become more positive toward the New Haven police: all these could have served to engender suspicion and thus to arouse evaluation apprehension and negative affect toward the experimenter. Either or both of these motivating states could probably be most efficiently reduced by the subject to show anything but fairly strong disapproval of the New Haven police; for the subject who had come to believe that his autonomy in the face of a monetary lure was being assessed, remaining "anti-police" would demonstrate that he *had* autonomy; for the subject who perceived an indirect and disingenious attempt to change his attitude and felt some reactive anger, holding fast to his original attitude could appear to be a relevant way of frustrating the experimenter. Furthermore, with each *step* of increase in reward we could expect an increase in the proportion of subjects who had been brought to a motivating level of evaluation apprehension or affect arousal.

Rosenberg then performed his own experiment in an attempt to correct the problem he found in previous studies. The general way of improving on previous designs would be to make the collection of attitude information, following performance of the task which is supposed to create dissonance, as separate from the rest of the study as possible. Rosenberg accomplished this in two ways. First, he created a believable situation in which the final attitude information was collected by experimenters other than those who conduced the earlier part of the experiment. Secondly, subjects were paid for their performance in the first part of the study before they progressed to the last part. The first point is clearly an improvement over Cohen's procedure, where the same person collected all data of the study. It is true that Festinger and Carlsmith used different experimenters to administer the task and to collect the enjoyment data, but their design was such that a suspicious subject might well perceive a connection between the two. In contrast, Rosenberg developed an elaborate, though believable rationale for the independence of the part of the experiment designed to arouse dissonance, and the subsequent part designed to reflect the effects of dissonance. The two parts were not only conducted by different people, but involved different buildings, and different institutional affiliations. Therefore, it is unlikely that any forthcoming results like those of Cohen, and Festinger and Carlsmith, could be explained by the effects of fear of evaluation and anger toward the experimenter as easily as by dissonance reduction attempts.

But with this improved design, Rosenberg obtained results that are directly opposite to those expected by dissonance theory. As shown by the averages (M) reported in Table 5–6, he found that the greater the reward, the greater the atttitude change in the direction of the essay the subject had been asked to write that differed from his original attitude. In other words, the more money you get for writing an essay discrepant with your views, the more doing that will change your attitudes. This result is more obvious than that predicted by dissonance

TABLE 5–6

Group means and differences between groups on attitude toward the Rose Bowl ban

Group	M	Group differences*			
		$.50	$1	$.50 and $1	$5
Control.........	1.45	$z = 1.97$, $p < .03$	$z = 1.80$, $p < .04$	$z = 2.31$, $p < .015$	$z = 3.93$, $p < .0001$
$.50............	2.24		$z = .11$		$z = 1.77$, $p < .04$
$1..............	2.32				$z = 1.81$, $p < .04$
$.50 and........ $1	2.28				$z = 2.11$, $p < .02$
$5..............	3.24				

Note: Overall difference between groups as assessed by Kruskal-Wallis test: $H = 17.89$, $p. < .001$.
* Tested by Mann-Whitney z, one-tailed.
Source: M. J. Rosenberg, "When dissonance fails: on eliminating evaluation apprehension from attitude measurement," *J. pers. soc. Psychol.*, 1965.

theory, and throws the previous results of Festinger and Carlsmith and of Cohen into serious doubt.

The question concerning the studies just discussed is whether they demonstrate the effects of attempts to reduce dissonance, or of the guardedness and resentment resulting from the incredulity of the subjects. There is another group of studies by the dissonance experimenters that has been criticized by Chapanis and Chapanis in different, though related manner. Let us take one study (Aronson & Mills, 1959) from this group as an example. College women volunteered to participate in a series of group discussions on the psychology of sex. In a pre-participation interview, some of the girls were told they would have to pass an embarrassment test to see if they were tough enough to stand the group discussion. Girls in this severe embarrassment group had to read out loud in the presence of the male experimenter some vivid descriptions of sexual activity and a list of obscene sex words. Another group of girls, called the mild embarrassment group, read some mild sexual material. All girls in the study were told they had successfully passed the embarrassment test. After this, each subject listened to a recording of a group discussion, which they were told was a spontaneous discussion of the type they might be in, but which was in reality carefully planned and staged by the experimenters. It was planned so as to be a dull and banal discussion of the sexual behavior on animals. Finally, the design called for a control group that listened only to the simulated group discussion, but did not have a previous embarrassment test. All groups then made ratings about this tape-recorded discussion, its participants, and their own interest in future discussions. The results show that the ratings made by the severe embarrassment group were, on the average, somewhat more favorable than those made by the other two groups. Aronson and Mills consider these results to show that the more painful the initiation, the more the subjects subsequently like the group. In successfully passing the severe embarrassment test, the girls had undergone a painful experience in order to gain the right to be part of the subsequent group discussions, which, however, turned out to be so dull and uninteresting that they must have realized that the initiation procedure was not worth it. This produced dissonance, which was reduced by reevaluating the group discussion as more interesting than it really was.

In criticizing this experiment and the conclusions reached, Chapanis and Chapanis (1964) say:

> All this may be so, but in order to accept the author's explanation we must be sure the girls really did hold these discrepant cognitions, and no others. We have to be sure, for instance, that they felt no relief when they found the group discussion banal instead of embarrassing, that success in passing a difficult test (the embarrassment test) did not alter their evaluation of the task, that the sexual material did not evoke any

vicarious pleasure or expectation of pleasure in the future, and that the group discussion was so dull that the girls would have regretted participating. There is no way of checking directly on the first three conditions, although other experimental evidence suggests that their effect is not negligible. However, to check on the fourth factor we have the data from the control group showing that the group discussion was, in fact, more interesting than not (it received an average rating of 10 on a 0–15 scale). It is, therefore, difficult to believe that the girls regretted participating. To sum up, since the design of this experiment does not exclude the possibility that pleasurable cognitions were introduced by the sequence of events, and since, in addition, the existence of "painful" cognitions was not demonstrated, we cannot accept the authors' interpretation without serious reservations.

These critics continue by suggesting that if there is anything to the notion that severity of initiation increases liking of the group, it lies in the feeling of successful accomplishment. "The more severe the test, the stronger is the pleasurable feeling of success in overcoming the obstacle. There is no need to postulate a drive due to dissonance if a *pleasure principle* can account for the results quite successfully" (Chapanis & Chapanis, 1964). The critics point out that the problems with this study of Aronson and Mills crop up in other dissonance studies as well.

The technical term for the problem pinpointed above is confounding of variables. In other words, the results could have been produced either by attempts to reduce dissonance, or by the behavioral effects of relief of some sort. The two variables overlap, or are confounded by the experimental design. Obviously, the principal aim of any experiment is to avoid confounding. In natural situations, confounding often occurs, but the whole purpose of the experiment is to improve upon nature in the sense of holding constant or neutralizing all possible factors save one. That one is made artificially stronger or weaker in the experimental group, so that, by comparing the effects in this group with the behavior of a control group, one can assess the causal influences of the one factor alone. What Chapanis and Chapanis are saying, in all of their criticisms, is that the experiments performed by the dissonance investigator fail in one way or another because of the confounding of two or more factors.

The criticism of confounding is leveled at even more studies in the dissonance tradition than I have presented thus far. In one dramatic instance, Chapanis and Chapanis discuss an experiment reported by Aronson (1961), in which an attempt was made to pit dissonance theory against reinforcement theory. Reinforcement theory says that stimuli associated with reward gain in attractiveness, whereas dissonance thory indicates that stimuli not associated with reward may actually gain in attractiveness if one has had to expend effort in an attempt to attain them. What looks like an ingenious design with which to test this proposition is demolished by Chapanis and Chapanis by making crystal clear that there is confounding of effort expended with rate at which reward is obtained. As a result, no unambiguous conclusions can be drawn as to the effect of effort on attractiveness of stimuli worked for. Similar confounding of factors is pointed out in other studies as well.

To make matters worse, once the catalog of criticisms due to faulty experimental design is exhausted, one finds a whole additional catalog of controversial treatments of data. Chapanis and Chapanis point out that it is a regular occurrence in dissonance research to discard subjects from the analysis of results after the way they performed is already known to the experimenter. This is a severe criticism, as such a procedure undermines the whole idea of scientific objectivity. As Chapanis and Chapanis point out, one can always find a rationalization for excluding subjects that leads to finding support for your hypothesis. Hence, exclusion should always take place before the data have been analyzed. Not only have there been frequent instances of violation of this rule, but the grounds given for exclusion of subjects have often been unconvincing to disinterested observers. Brehm and Cohen (1959), for example, indicate that ". . . [subjects] who failed to choose the alternative initially marked as most liked, were excluded because they gave unreliable or invalid ratings." There is no further explanation of what the investigators might have meant! Using the study of Cohen, Brehm, and Fleming (1958) as an example, Chapanis and Chapanis point out how the reasons given for exclusion of subjects are often self-contradictory. In a study by Ehrlich, Guttman, Schonbach, and Mills (1957), one reason and another were given in justification of excluding what amounts to 82 percent of the original sample! When that large a proportion of a sample is discarded, it is virtually impossible to know what the results really mean, and certainly, it is impossible to know to whom any conclusions reached could possibly apply. In other studies where the proportion of subjects excluded has been lower, it has nonetheless often been true that the proportions excluded from different groups (e.g., high dissonance, low dissonance, control groups) has been different. Chapanis and Chapanis are correct in concluding that some undetermined proportion of dissonance studies may be reporting as fact statistically significant differences between groups that are no more than artifacts due to exclusion of subjects!

Even worse than the exclusion of subjects in the manner described above is the kind of reallocation of subjects from one group to another that is found in the study by Raven and Fishbein (1961). These investigators actually took subjects who did not conform to their predictions, and instead of rejecting them, which would have been questionable enough, actually shifted them from the experimental group to the control group. As Chapanis and Chapanis (1964) conclude "rejection of cases is poor procedure, but reallocation of [subjects] from experimental to control group, across the independent variable, violates the whole concept of controlled experimentation."

Continuing in their demolition of dissonance research, Chapanis and Chapanis point out that in some studies, the number of subjects refusing to participate, once they are informed that they would have to deceive others, or write something they did not believe, is large enough that not taking them into account in reaching conclusions leads to misunderstandings. If a person refuses to participate, he is actually showing himself to be unexplainable on the grounds of dissonance theory, and yet the conclusions reached do not involve any proviso as to what sector of the population may be properly understood on the basis of the results of the studies. Following this, Chapanis and Chapanis close their review with a section on inadequate procedures for the statistical analysis of results, implicating once again many of the studies performed in the dissonance tradition.

What can we conclude about this body of research billed as having demonstrated that cognitive dissonance is always unpleasant and avoided? Well, one thing to note is that investigators in this area have been so concerned with showing how their predictions are different from those of other more familiar and competitive theories, and have also been so concerned with applying their dissonance formulation to complex, important social events, that they have been led to experimental designs involving elaborate instructions and intricate relationships between the subject and the experimenter. Such complex designs are almost bound to confound certain variables, and require the discarding of some subjects. But in dissonance research, there is so much confounding and discarding that it is simply impossible to be sure that results clarify the effects of dissonance and dissonance alone.

Now it may be that the problems of confounding and discarding can be corrected. With less enthusiasm and zeal, perhaps simpler, more believable designs could be arranged that would better permit the testing of dissonance theory. Even so, we would have to conclude now that until such research is done, the case for dissonance as always unpleasant and avoided has not been made. But the situation may be even worse than that. Chapanis and Chapanis (1964, pp. 20–21) seem to think that dissonance theory is such a whopping oversimplification that confounding of variables and exclusion of subjects is inevitable! The concluding statement of their review is:

> The magical appeal of Festinger's theory arises from its extreme simplicity both in formulation and in application. But in our review we have seen that this simplicity was generally deceptive; in point of fact it often concealed a large number of confounded variables. Clearly much can be done to untangle this confounding of variables by careful exper-

imental design. Nonetheless, there may still remain another problem more fundamental than this. In general, a cognitive dissonance interpretation of a social situation means that the relevant social factors can be condensed into two simple statements. To be sure, Festinger does not say formally that a dissonance theory interpretation works only for two discrepant statements; but it is precisely because in practice he does so limit it that the theory has had so much acceptance. Which brings us now to the crux of the matter: *is it really possible to reduce the essentials of a complex social situation to just two phrases?* Reluctantly we must say "no." To condense most complex social situations into two, and only two, simple dissonant statements represents so great a level of abstraction that the model no longer bears any reasonable resemblance to reality. Indeed the experimenter is left thereby with such emasculated predictors that he must perforce resort to a multiplicity of ad hoc hypotheses to account for unexpected findings. We see then that the most attractive feature of cognitive dissonance theory, its simplicity, is in actual fact a self-defeating limitation.

All this was not sufficient to end what has apparently been an extraordinary interest in and commitment to dissonance theory. Silverman (1964) rose to its defense by insisting that Chapanis and Chapanis had only shown that their alternative explanations of research findings in the area was possible, not persuasive. In addition, he asserted that the exclusion of subjects was done without knowledge of results and was therefore sound. But Silverman seems to be missing the point, which is made as soon as alternative explanations are even plausible, and when the exclusion of subjects is so rampant that it is difficult to know of what population the results are representative. When this kind of situation occurs, it can fairly be said that the theory in question has not been proved. Although dissonance research has continued to be done, and believed in, as is witnessed by the appearance of no less than a handbook (Abelson, Aronson, McGuire, Newcomb, Rosenberg, & Tannenbaum, 1969) and of several novel studies (e.g., Cooper & Goethals, 1974; Cooper & Scalise, 1974) on the subject matter, it is clear that this tradition is dwindling.

But virtually with each accumulation of studies in one or another topic relevant to dissonance theory, another review of the literature appears asserting the actual lack of support for the theory once one digs below the surface. Elms (1967) argues that although it is quite true that reinforcement (or incentive) theory and dissonance theory often provide opposite predictions of phenomena, it is the former, not the latter, that seems most supported by research. He reinterprets studies initially appearing to support dissonance theory as actually supporting incentive theory, and also reports several studies which are difficult to construe in any other way than as supporting incentive theory. Among these latter are the studies of Janis and Gilmore (1965) and Elms and Janis (1965), concerning role-playing. In both, student subjects were asked to role-play counterattitudinally in return for either a high or a low monetary reward. Some subjects were led to believe that the sponsor of the role-playing was an organization positively regarded, whereas other subjects thought it an organization negatively regarded. Subjects were given varying amounts of money as an incentive for role-playing, and attitude measures were taken immediately following the experiment. Janis and Gilmore (1965) found that subjects believing that the organization was a positive one showed significantly more positive attitudes about counterattitudinal role-playing than did subjects believing the organization was a negative one. Similarly, Elms and Janis (1965) found that in the positive-sponsorship situation, highly rewarded subjects showed greater positive attitude change than those receiving low reward; in the negative-sponsorship situation, low-reward subjects showed an insignificant trend toward more positive attitude change than did highly rewarded subjects. These studies, reminiscent of Rosenberg's (1965), are quite inconsistent with dissonance theory. Brehm (1965), in an attempt to contend that the study of Elms and Janis was an unfair test of dissonance theory, omits reference to the positive-sponsorship situation, which provides, of course, the major refutation of the position.

As if dissonance theory were not beleagured enough, Rhine (1967) has raised serious problems about its ability to account for findings in the area of information selectivity. He asserts that failure to confirm hypotheses about information selectivity would be a serious blow to dissonance theory, for Festinger (1957, p. 3) has said: "When dissonance is present, in addition to trying to reduce it, *the person will actively avoid situations and information* which would likely increase the dissonance" (italics mine). A main difficulty with available research on information selectivity is that it is not really relevant to the test of dissonance hypotheses, according to Rhine. The degree to which information is avoided or sought will be a U-shaped function of amount of dissonance, by a complicated set of assumptions presented by Festinger (1957, p. 130). Any study attempting to test predictions stemming from this U-shaped curve must include at least three levels of dissonance, preferably quite different in intensity. Yet the available studies involve no more than two levels. In addition, it is important for proper empirical test of the predictions, to be able to separate seeking information from its avoidance. Once again, Rhine demonstrates how available research has failed to permit such separation. He even suggests how this design limitation could be overcome with the proper control groups. In any event, Rhine (1967) concludes that the dissonance explanation of information selectivity has not been proven, and even suggests the plausibility of a curiosity explanation:

> Consider, for example, Adams' (1961) study of mothers who favored environment over heredity as an explanation of children's behavior. He

found that mothers hearing a talk supporting heredity were more interested in getting further information about the heredity—environment issue than those hearing a talk supporting their environment bias. This was interpreted by Adams to mean that dissonance leads to information seeking. If hearing the opposite side of the issue arouses more curiosity than hearing support for a view one already accepts, then the finding could be explained by curiosity instead of dissonance. Curiosity motivation is rarely, if ever, ruled out in selectivity research. If there is any problem for which curiosity should be considered a possible explanation, it is one in which information seeking is a critical dependent variable. Controlling curiosity is particularly imperative when instructions for determining seeking behavior often explicitly request ratings or rankings in terms of interest in the information.

And, of course, if curiosity might explain even some forms of information seeking, it becomes very difficult to contend, as our issue states, that cognitive dissonance is invariably unpleasant and avoided.

Actually, when a position like dissonance theory has attracted so many devoted researchers and generated so many studies, but is still open to the charge of not having been proven, it is a reasonable surmise that something is seriously wrong. Either the theory is so ambiguous as to be unprovable, or it is more wrong than right, however much we can stave off this conclusion by ingenious explanations and counterexplanations. It is beginning to seem as if support for dissonance theory requires very delicately staged experimental situations and carefully primed subjects. At least, there are studies done in naturalistic rather than contrived settings that do not support the theory. For example, Petersen and Hergenhahn (1968) hypothesized that their elementary school subjects, when presented with evidence that they had done more poorly on an academic task than their self-images would tolerate, would consequently make some sort of effort to reduce this dissonance. But there was no difference in this regard between this group and a group whose academic performance matched their self-appraisals.

The next step in considering the issue would seem to be consideration of the body of data accumulated by variety theorists in an attempt to demonstrate that change, novelty, and complexity of stimulation are sought after and desired. If these data are convincing, then at least it can be said that cognitive dissonance cannot always be unpleasant and avoided. This is true because variety almost of necessity is also dissonance, since such aspects of variety as novelty and unexpectedness must be defined as some experiential difference between some set of beliefs or expectancies, on the one hand, and some set of event perceptions, on the other hand. Variety research essentially makes three points: that variety (1) is necessary for effective development and adult functioning, (2) is sought after, and (3) is pleasant, at least in moderate degrees. Fiske and Maddi (1961) have brought together research from various corners of psychology and physiology in support of these three points, and therefore, the discussion that follows will lean heavily upon their formulations. But other psychologists (e.g., Berlyne, 1960; Duffy, 1963) have also provided able reviews of what is now an extensive research literature.

The references to data obtained on subhuman organisms in the pages that follow may strike you as inconsistent with my previous unwillingness to consider such data concerning defensiveness. Actually, there is no inconsistency. Animal data were ruled out of contention for the study of defensiveness largely because such study heavily concerns mentation, which is methodologically inaccessible in organisms below man. But two of the three conclusions concerning variety mentioned in the previous paragraph need not rely primarily, or even heavily, upon the scrutiny of mentation. Subhuman organisms can well be studied in determining whether variety is necessary for effective development and adult functioning, and whether it is sought after, because these questions can be convincingly resolved by observed action and performance. Of course, it is much more difficult to determine whether variety is pleasant without having available mentation in the form of verbal report. Hence, you will see that the data which I review with regard to this question is gleaned exclusively from the human level.

I will not spend much time on the conclusion that variety is necessary for effective development and adult functioning, as it is not as directly relevant to the issue confronting us as are the other two points. Suffice it to say that the studies relevant to this conclusion generally proceed by reducing the variation and intensity of stimulation impinging upon the organism, and then observing the effects of so doing at either the physiological or behavioral level. Whether the study concerns development or adult functioning depends upon the age of the subjects. In studies of young monkeys deprived of variation and intensity of stimulation from infancy, Riesen (1961) has shown subsequent deficits both at the physiological level, in cellular abnormalities of the retina and optic nerve, and the behavioral level, in lack of coordination of actions. Paralleling these behavioral findings at the human level, are the studies of Ribble and Spitz (in Thompson & Schaefer, 1961) comparing infants reared in orphanages with infants reared at home or in prison with their mothers. The children reared in the orphanage were retarded in walking, talking, smiling, crawling, and were generally more apathetic, unemotional, and subdued than were the other infants. In addition, the orphanage children were more susceptible to diseases and showed a higher death rate. Although Ribble and Spitz stress the ambiguous concept of "mothering" in attempting to explain their results, other psychologists, such as Yarrow (1961) argue cogently for the importance of a marked reduction in the intensity and variety of stimulation from what it would be in a more usual environment. The studies

of Ribble and Spitz were so imperfectly performed from a methodological point of view that I would not even mention them here except that
they show such a striking parallel with Riesen's work on monkeys.
More recently, Harlow and others (e.g., Griffin & Harlow, 1966; Harlow,
Harlow, Dodsworth, & Arling, 1966;) have reported results of very
carefully planned studies of monkeys that build upon the start made
by Reisen. Harlow has found that rearing infant monkeys in the absence
of intense and varying stimuli leads to adults that are incapable of
copulating, afraid of other monkeys and living things, and appear very
disturbed emotionally. The monkeys do not seem to be able to learn to
overcome these deficits. If more evidence were needed of the generality
of such effects, there are similar studies involving other species (e.g.,
Konrad & Bagshaw, 1970; Lessac & Solomon, 1969). Apparently, beagles
and cats also showed behavioral deficits at adulthood after having been
deprived of stimulation in childhood. There is strong evidence at the
animal level, and suggestive evidence at the human level, that variety
is necessary for normal development.

The research concerning the need for variety in order to function as
a normal adult has been done largely under the well-known label of
"sensory deprivation." To make a long story short, a number of studies
suggest (see Fiske, 1961), that markedly decreasing the variation and
intensity of stimulation available to adult humans leads, as the time
passes, to a number of signs of disordered functioning. There are such
symptoms as the inability to concentrate, intense feelings of emotional
discomfort, and bizarre mentation reminiscent of hallucinations and
delusions. Some of the deficits persist for a little while after the
sensory deprivation has been terminated. This is not to say that such
strong and disturbing results occur in all subjects or even in all studies
that have been done. Fuerst and Zubek (1968), for example, reported
mild, or in some instances, no impairment on cognitive tests administered
following three days of either darkness and silence, or unpatterned light
and white noise, experienced by their male subjects. But the battery of
tests was also administered prior to sensory isolation, and there was a
relationship between pre- and postexperimental scores. This and other
studies suggest that individual differences and the specifics of the experimental situation have an as yet only partially understood role in
the effects of deprivation of stimulation. Nonetheless, these studies of
adults, along with those done on infants that have been already mentioned, suggest that variety is necessary for normal development and
functioning.

The second conclusion I mentioned before is that variety is sought
after, rather than avoided, as cognitive dissonance positions would
predict. Many of the most important studies supporting this point have
been done at the subhuman level. There have been so many of these
studies, that it is not necessary, let alone possible, to review them all

here. It is more important to grasp the import of the body of research, rather than to know each and every study. The research essentially involves two kinds of experiment. On kind concerns habituation to a particular environment, followed by a change in or addition to that familiar place, and observation of the effects of so doing. A straight-forward example is the study of Berlyne (1955) in which each rat was permitted to become familiar with a rectangular cage with a little alcove at one end. After familiarization had taken place, a series of objects was added to the environment by placing them in the alcove. The rat's reaction to the objects was what interested Berlyne. He found that the various objects produced exploratory behavior, such as sniffing, licking, touching. These findings are typical for such studies; whenever you change or add to an already familiar environment, you get an increase in exploratory behavior. This conclusion applies at the human level also (Maddi, 1961a), even though there are fewer studies there than at the animal level. The other kind of study demonstrating that variety is sought after involves putting the subject in an environment that is ar-ranged in such fashion that he must choose what portion of it to experi-ence. He cannot experience it all at any one time. Subsequent to the first choice, he is put into the environment again, and permitted to choose what portion to experience next. Typical of such studies is that of Dennis (1939), who put rats into a maze shaped like the letter T. In running through the maze, the rats had to turn either right or left when they reached the bar of the T. In this study, as in many similar ones (see Dember, 1961), it was found that after making the choice of either the right or the left arm of the T, when returned again to the beginning of the maze, the rat ran to the opposite arm. This phenomenon has been called "spontaneous alternation." It suggests that variety is sought after, for on the second try, the subject chooses to experience that part of the environment that he did not experience on the first try. There is by now ample evidence that spontaneous alternation also occurs at the human level (e.g., Schultz, 1964).

The major criticism that has been leveled at this body of research is whether it really shows that variety is sought after, or whether some other explanation of exploratory behavior and spontaneous alternation is more adequate. This general criticism finds a number of concrete forms. For example, spontaneous alternation has been attributed by some psychologists to such causes as satiation for the particular muscular movements made in turning one way rather than the other (reactive inhibition), and satiation for the stimuli in the part of the maze first seen (stimulus satiation). Both of these explanations are meant to be alternatives to that concerning variety as an attractive stimulus. Dember (1956) has done an experiment that demonstrates conclusively that the variety explanation is better. It is an ingenious experiment, and deserves our attention. This investigator also used a T maze, but modified it in two ways. In one modification, he installed glass doors at the point where the stem met the arms of the T, such that rats could look into both arms, but enter neither. The other modification involved painting one arm of the T black, and the other white. Thus, on the first try in the maze, rats saw both white and black portions that they could not actually enter. For the second try in the maze, the investigator made two changes. He removed the glass doors, making it possible to enter the arms of the T, and he changed one of the arms from black to white, thereby rendering both of them the same color. Proponents of reactive inhibition, as an explanation of spontaneous alternation, would not expect any difference in the frequency with which the two arms were entered on this second try, because, as no arms were entered on the first try, there would have been no opportunity for the muscular movements involved in turning right or left to become satiated and therefore avoided subsequently. Similarly, proponents of stimulus satiation would not expect differential frequency of entrance into the two arms because on the second try both of them are the same color, and since that color was represented on the first try, there should be no difference in the satiating nature of the two arms. But proponents of the position that variety is sought after would clearly predict that on the second try, rats should enter the arm of the T that was changed in color from what it had been on the first try. In a resounding demonstration of the greater utility of one explanation as opposed to others, Dember found that 17 out of 20 rats entered the changed arm on the second try! This experiment was so incisively designed that in one fell swoop reactive inhibition and stimulus satiation as possible explanations of spontaneous alternation have been demolished.

But there is another alternative explanation of spontaneous alternation and exploratory behavior that is not demolished by Dember's experiment. This explanation, offered by Berlyne (1957, 1960), holds that variety is certainly approached, not because it is pleasant, desired, or needed, but rather because it increases conflict and uncertainty and is thereby unpleasant enough to instigate the attempt to gain greater familiarity with the source of the variety in hopes of decreasing uncertainty and conflict. In exploring a new aspect of the environment, or in alternating spontaneously, the organism is trying to obtain the information with which to render old and familiar—and therefore unthreatening—that which is novel. Clearly, this position would also have predicted entrance into the changed arm of the T in the experiment by Dember, and hence, it is a viable competitor to the position that variety is sought after because it is attractive and interesting. While Berlyne's position can explain the research results thus far mentioned, as well as that which claims variety to be attractive, we cannot conclude that there is empirical support for the contention that variety is not always unpleasant and avoided.

Although Berlyne's position is ingenious, it is unlikely to be true, because it collapses the distinction between approaching a stimulus and avoiding it. What I mean is that if novelty is indeed threatening, then one could as easily predict that it would be run from as that it would be contacted. And yet, running from and contacting it are very different things, not convincingly understood as merely alternative ways of achieving the same end. On logical grounds, Berlyne's position seems weak. And once having pinpointed the collapse of the distinction between approach and avoidance, empirical research suggesting the faultiness of so doing comes to mind. Welker (1959) put rats into a large rectangular box that was well lit and included some objects of different kinds. Off to one side of the rectangle was a small, dark, empty alcove. His rats ran and darted frantically until they found the alcove, and then sheltered themselves in it. After a while, they forayed forth from the alcove, with their movements in the larger rectangle now being calmer and more deliberate. There is a clear observational distinction between the behavior in the large rectangle before entering the alcove and after leaving it. The early behavior seems like avoidance, while the latter seems like approach. If this distinction is important, then we must take seriously the inability of a position like that of Berlyne to account for it. He would have to call both the early and the later behavior exploratory, and explain them in the same fashion, namely, as attempts to decrease the conflict produced by novelty. Berlyne (1967) seems recently to have given up his earlier position, in part on the basis of observations of the sort reported by Welker. In taking seriously that interest in novelty may occur because it is pleasing, Berlyne (1967, p. 29) says:

> There has been much talk of the human craving for excitement and stimulation. . . . Experiments on exploratory behavior . . . and play . . . show that higher animals often find access to stimulation gratifying and that properties known to raise arousal—such as novelty, surprisingness, complexity—may enhance the reward value of exteroceptive stimuli.

Then Berlyne actually goes on to marshal evidence against his former view of the aversive effects of variety through its enhancement of conflict!

Of particular relevance to the argument that variety is attractive are two studies by Maddi and Andrews (1966), in which the degree to which variety is sought after was measured by the novelty of stories composed about pictures. As the pictures were rather unstructured, permitting a wide range of stories, it can fairly be said that people who produce novel stories are actually creating their own variety. That story novelty may well be an indication of seeking variety and nothing else is suggested by the absence of relationship between it and such other general characteristics as intelligence, social class, productivity, the needs for achievement, affiliation, and power, and the tendency to respond in socially desirable fashion (Maddi & Andrews, 1966; Maddi, Propst, & Feldinger, 1965). Also included in the studies by Maddi and Andrews were self-descriptions concerning the attractiveness of variety. These self-descriptions took the form of indicating whether one liked or disliked certain statements, such as "I move my furniture around frequently" and "I often vary my activities." These statements were organized into standard scales from a number of personality tests, such as the Need for Change Scale of the Activities Index, by Stern (1958). As you can see in Table 5–7, Maddi and Andrews found evidence in both studies, that the greater the tendency to seek variety, the greater the preference for, and attractiveness of variety. It would clearly be very difficult to maintain the view that the seeking of variety occurs out of its discomforting and threatening nature in the face of results such as those obtained by Maddi and Andrews. These investigators have shown that it is precisely those people who like variety most who expend effort in seeking it. To be sure, their results also indicate that those who do not like variety do not seek it. This suggests that variety is not attractive for all people all the time, but only for some people some of the time.

There is another study by Maddi (1961c) which concerns the nature of the emotional reaction to different degrees of variety. It is a very important study for reaching a conclusion concerning the issue we have been discussing. Subjects were given a booklet and instructed to perform two simultaneous tasks. Whenever they were given a signal, they were to write down a prediction as to whether the next page of the booklet would have on it a number or the beginning of a sentence. After predicting, they turned the page, and were again given the signal to predict, and again turned the page, and so forth. So the first task was predicting

TABLE 5–7

Product-moment correlations between novelty of productions and variables reflecting preferences for variety

	Novelty of Productions
Study I (N = 78)	
16 PF Factor H (Timid-adventurous)*	−.02
16 PF Factor I (Tough-sensitive)	.33†
16 PF Factor Q (Conservative-experimenting)	.28‡
Study II (N = 56)	
AI *n* Change scale	.25§
AI *n* Play scale	.18
AI Impulsivity scale	.27‖

    * The terms listed are recommended by Cattel for identifying the poles of the factors. The list term is for the low end of the factor.
      † Probability is less than .005 by one-tailed test.
      ‡ Probability is less than .01 by one-tailed test.
      § Probability is less than .05 by one-tailed test.
      ‖ Probability is less than .025 by one-tailed test.
    Source: Adapted from S. R. Maddi and Susan Andrews, "The need for variety in fantasy and self-description," *J. pers.*, 1966.

what would take place, and in the course of the experiment they got rather immediate feedback on the accuracy or inaccuracy of their predictions. Whenever the page they turned to showed the beginning of a sentence, they were also supposed to finish the sentence in whatever manner they wished. So the second task was to complete sentences.

Subjects in the experimental group experienced a regular pattern of stimuli as follows: Each group of three successive pages of the booklet, starting from the first, showed the pattern of number, number, sentence beginning. This pattern recurred eight times without interruption. From the subject's predictions, it was possible to obtain the percentage of accurate predictions within each pattern of number, number, sentence beginning. As you might expect, the average percentage of accuracy increased from a low of 26 to a high of 95 during the eight pattern repetitions. Now the sentence completions made by subjects at the end of each pattern were used as a measure of affective tone, or the degree to which the subjects were having pleasant or unpleasant feelings. Each sentence completion was scored on a five-point scale, according to whether it showed strongly positive affect (5), mildly positive affect (4), neutral affect (3), mildly negative affect (2), or strongly negative affect (1), and mean affect scores associated with each pattern repetition were computed. As shown in Figure 5–2, Maddi found that, in the experimental group, affect was initially negative or unpleasant, but

FIGURE 5–2

Mean affect scores as function of number of series experienced

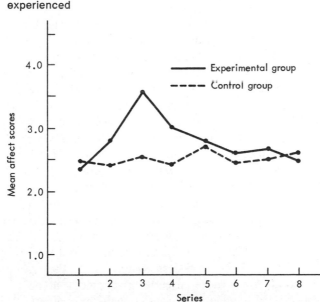

Source: Adapted from S. R. Maddi, "Affective tone during environmental regularity and change," *J. abnorm. soc. Psychol.*, 1961e.

as the pattern was repeated, rose to a peak of positive or pleasant affect, and then became negative once more. Interestingly enough, the greatest intensity of positive affect occurred on the third-pattern repetition, during which the subjects were inaccurate on 33 percent of their predictions. While inaccuracy of prediction decreased from 76 percent to 33 percent during the first three pattern repetitions, affective tone went from negative to positive. And while inaccuracy of prediction decreased from 33 percent to 6 percent during the last five pattern repetitions, affective tone went from positive to negative.

Let us linger over what these results mean. The percentage of inaccuracy provides a precise index of the degree to which there is a discrepancy between what is expected and what actually occurs. Therefore, if theorists stressing the unpleasant nature of unexpectedness and dissonance, such as Kelly and Festinger, were right, Maddi should have obtained results indicating that as percent accuracy increased, negative affect gave way to positive affect. Berlyne should also expect the same thing, as inaccuracy in this case defines what is unexpected, and therefore novel. It becomes terribly important, once you have recognized this, that Maddi's results show the peak of positive affect when prediction is still 33 percent inaccurate, and that further decreases in inaccuracy are associated with progressively more negative affect. These results favor the position that mild variety, call it unexpectedness, dissonance, or discrepancy, is a pleasant experience. Taking all of Maddi's results into account, the most comprehensive conclusion to draw is that small degrees of variety are pleasant, whereas large degrees are unpleasant.

Maddi also reports two other findings from this study that are generally supportive of the interpretation just offered. The first of the findings involves the relationship between prediction and affect when the pattern of numbers and sentence beginnings was changed after the eight repetitions. Some subjects in the experimental group experienced a large change in pattern, whereas others experienced a small change, these effects being confirmed by the amount of increase in predictional inaccuracy. As shown in Figure 5–3, the subjects of the experimental group experiencing the small change showed a striking increase in positive affect, even though they were actually becoming more inaccurate than they had been during the pattern repetitions. In contrast, the experimental group subjects experiencing the large change did not slow a spurt in positive affect, and, of course, they were becoming greatly inaccurate. The final finding of this study concerns a control group, the subjects of which also received numbers and words on the pages of the booklet but found them arranged in a random and therefore unpredictable order. Figures 5–2 and 5–3 show results for this group that are entirely different from those already presented. Affect for the control group was generally negative throughout the experiment.

To tie together the various threads of discussion concerning the third

FIGURE 5–3

Mean difference scores associated with treatments 0, 1, and 2

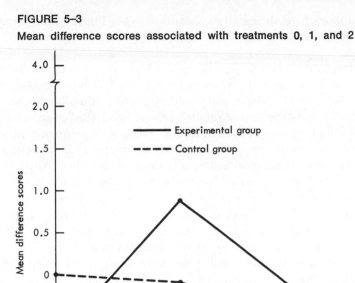

* The treatments represent, respectively, 0, 1, and 2 degrees of change in order of
events for the Prediction and No Prediction groups.
    Source: Adapted from S. R. Maddi, "Affective tone during environmental regularity
and change." *J. abnorm. soc. Psychol.*, 1961c.

issue, we can say that there is empirical support for the conclusion that
cognitive dissonance is not invariably unpleasant and avoided.

The evidence seems to be accumulating that moderate degrees of unexpectedness and novelty are approached and found pleasant, whereas
larger and smaller degrees are unpleasant and avoided (e.g., Berlyne,
1960; Dorfman, 1965; Maddi, 1961b; Munsinger & Kessen, 1964; Vitz,
1966). In addition, some evidence (e.g., Maddi & Andrews, 1966) indicates that persons may differ in the range of variety they consider
pleasant. In light of all this, it is strange to find some psychologists still
holding to the belief that variety is attractive in all degrees (e.g., Nunnally, 1971) or not at all (e.g., Zajonc, 1968). By now, there is enough
known in variety research to suggest that Nunnally's conclusion is based
on his having designed experiments which did not sample subjects'
reactions over a wide enough range of variety to obtain avoidance as

well as approach tendencies (see Maddi, 1971). But Zajonc's argument is more elaborate, and bears very directly upon the issue under discussion here.

In his spirited monograph Zajonc (1968), reviews many linguistic studies, and reports several experiments done by him and his students, to the effect that mere exposure to (familiarity with) stimuli increases their attractiveness. First he collects many correlational studies in which the judged value of words was found to covary with their frequency of usage. Impressive though this array of studies may seem, it must be recognized that correlations do not permit the inference of causality. Although Zajonc construes the studies to show that the more a word is used, the more it takes on positive emotional tone, the very opposite could also have been concluded. Indeed, it makes more common sense to consider the studies to show that it is the positively toned words that get used most. Otherwise, one would be in the odd position of contending that even a word like "friendly" had a negative charge when first entering the language (because it was unfamiliar), and only became positive through use. At that point, the prefixed word "unfriendly" must have been devised in order to offset the positive drift due to increased familiarity. This is not a very plausible position on the creation of language, though it is one to which Zajonc subscribes.

Perhaps the difficulty here is that Zajonc is stretching for a complete explanation of the affective charge of stimuli with only one of the several factors that are important. At some level, familiarity is a factor which can make a contribution to positive affective charge, but so is meaning. After all, words have meaning, not only familiarity. The positive affective charge of a word like "friendly" derives as much if not more from its agreeable meaning (in the form of connotations and remembrances of warm fellowship) as from its frequency of occurrence. Zajonc (1968) does report some experiments, rather than correlational studies, using meaningful stimuli. As I would have expected, he obtains much weaker, even inconsistent, results when trying experimentally to increase the positivity of meaningful stimuli by presenting them often.

Most of Zajonc's reported experiments utilize meaningless stimuli (nonsense syllables, "Chinese" ideographs), which are presented at varying frequencies to subjects, with the expectation that those presented most will be most attractive. In general, he obtains results supporting this expectation. But, the research I reviewed earlier suggests that Zajonc should have obtained a U-shaped curve, in which the stimuli presented with intermediate frequency would be most attractive, whereas those presented less or more frequently would be less attractive. Perhaps the difficulty with Zajonc's procedure is similar to Nunnally's. Zajonc may not have employed a sufficiently large number of repetitions to render the initially meaningless stimuli monotonous and therefore unattractive.

This is possible even though he did use up to 25 exposures of some stimuli. After all, in each experiment, many meaningless stimuli were presented, all with different frequencies of occurrence, and in an essentially unpredictable order. In all this uncertainty, 25 repetitions may have been just enough to render a stimulus moderately familiar and therefore positive in affective charge.

Finally, in an attempt to round out his position, Zajonc (1968) assume that exploratory behavior results from conflict and negative affect over an unfamiliar stimulus, much in the manner of Berlyne (1960) before he changed his mind (Berlyne, 1967). Most of the evidence he marshals for this view shows that unfamiliar stimuli increase reaction time and the Galvanic Skin Response. But these are certainly indirect measures of negative affective charge, the precise meaning of which is hard to determine. The most direct measures are verbal statements, but he reports such data in only one study done by a student of his (Harrison, 1967). In this study, different samples of subjects were used to measure the intensity of exploratory behavior and the preference value evoked by a set of stimuli. A substantial negative correlation was found between exploration and preference, but it is quite possible that this study ran afoul of individual differences. In Harrison's exploratory condition, the subjects who explored intensely might have expressed preference for the novel stimuli had they been asked; whereas in the other condition the subjects who disliked the stimuli might not have explored them if permitted to. Such a state of affairs could have produced the obtained correlation for reasons opposite to those assumed by Zajonc. The study by Maddi and Andrews (1966) mentioned earlier is a better source of information on the relationship between exploration and preference, as both were measured on the same subjects.

Recent research influenced by Zajonc either indicates that the relationship of stimulus exposure to affective reaction is considerably more complicated than he imagined, or takes a developmental direction irrelevant to the issue under discussion here.

The upshot of all this is to render the pure cognitive dissonance version of the consistency model rather untenable, insisting as it does that all degrees of inconsistency are unpleasant and avoided for all people. Our discussion clearly favors the variant position represented by the theory of McClelland and the activation version of the consistency model. As I indicated before, this issue does not have trenchant implications for whether conflict and fulfillment models are more or less tenable than consistency models. Conflict and fulfillment models sometimes agree with consistency models and sometimes do not, indicating that for the former, questions of consistency and inconsistency are not the basic ones. More basic for them are considerations of the content involved in consistencies and inconsistencies.

Fifth issue: Is all behavior in the service of tension reduction?

You will recall that the conflict model and the cognitive dissonance version of the consistency model consider the aim of all functioning to be reduction in tension. So, exponents of these models would answer the question posed above affirmatively. But exponents of all other models would give a flatly negative answer. Fulfillment theorists, if they were at all willing to describe functioning in terms of orientation toward tension, would say that people aim toward tension increase in the major part of their living, and only incidentally at tension decrease. Fiske and Maddi, exemplifying the activation version of the consistency model, actively assume that the person seeks both increases and decreases in tension, depending upon specified circumstances. Let us pursue an empirical answer to this fifth issue, for clearly it is one that has powerful consequences for what we will consider to be the most fruitful manner in which to conceptualize personality.

Most of the research bearing directly on tension dispositions is at the subhuman level. Once again, though I considered empirical study of subhuman organisms virtually useless in clarifying questions concerning the concept of defense, I do not feel similarly regarding the concept of tension. Tension, after all, seems to involve excitation of the nervous system, and is rarely defined as a mental state. Clearly, the concept of tension can be applied to human and subhuman alike, without changing the meaning intended for it by the personologist. Therefore, it should not trouble us that we shall have to rely heavily upon empirical studies of animals in order to reach a conclusion concerning the fifth issue.

Of clear relevance for our purposes is the extensive literature on learning done in the tradition of behaviorism. Many behaviorists have assumed that all behavior has the primary goal of reducing tension, and have provided empirical demonstration after demonstration of this point of view. According to the behaviorist, learning is the establishment of a bond between a particular stimulus and a particular response (S–R bond), such that the response is given by the organism whenever the stimulus is presented to it. This learned link between stimulus and response becomes established when the response brings about a decrease in the level of tension existing in the organism. This decrease in tension is called a reward or reinforcement. For example, if the stimulus is a T maze, seen by the rat from the vantage point of the starting box in the stem of the T, and if the rat has a high tension state produced by having been deprived of food for many hours, then running down the stem of the maze and turning into the right-hand arm—which contains food that the rat is permitted to eat and thereby reduce the tension of hunger—constitutes learning. The next time the rat is put into the maze in a hungry state, he will turn right because the reward of having eaten, or reduced tension there, leads him to try the same behavior again. This type of result has actually been shown in hundreds of experiments (see Hilgard, 1956). A wide range of deprivation states has been used (e.g., food, water, and sexual deprivation), all with the same overall result: If the organism experiencing a high tension state can reduce that state by giving a particular response when faced with a particular stimulus, he will learn to do that, whereas an organism lacking a high tension state (i.e., satiated for the major needs) will not learn any such link between stimulus and response. Although most of the studies have involved rats in a maze, a wide range of other organisms and stimulus contexts has been used. A number of studies even achieved the refinement of demonstrating that the speed and accuracy of learning increases with increases in the tension level. Until a few years ago, the literature on learning yielded the firm, secure conclusion that decreases in tension are of such value to the organism that he will orient his behavior toward bringing them about. Certainly, the import of these studies for our issue is in support of the contention that all behavior is concerned with tension reduction.

Unassailable though the body of findings just mentioned has seemed, a few dissonant studies gradually appeared. Some of these studies concerned what came to be called latent learning. It was discovered (see Hilgard, 1956) that if rats were left in a maze for some period of time, during which they were not in any particularly high tension state, and there was no opportunity to reduce tension states in any event, they would subsequently behave as if they had learned a good deal about the maze. When introduced into the maze on a later occasion with a high state of tension and the possibility of reducing that state by performing a particular response, they would learn that response faster than rats not having been given the earlier opportunity to explore the maze under tensionless conditions. So apparently learning can take place without the occurrence of decrease in tension.

Another set of dissonant studies concerned the phenomenon of spontaneous alternation, already discussed under the issue concerning whether dissonance is invariably unpleasant and avoided. In these studies, it become perfectly clear that even if a rat filled with tension had been able to reduce that tension through making a particular turn in a maze, he would be quite likely to turn the opposite way on the next trial (see Dember, 1961). The tendency mentioned before of an organism to give the response previously associated with tension reduction turns out to be an average tendency. In other words, over a set of trials, the organism will give the response associated with tension reduction more than any other response. But, if you look at the sequence of responses given during the set of trials, you will also see a tendency to alternate responses, even though this means accepting that tension reduction will not occur as often as the situation makes possible. One the basis of such findings, it would seem that not all behavior is in the service of tension reduction.

The final group of dissonant studies (e.g., Freeman, 1933, 1938, 1940; Yerkes & Dodson, 1908) challenged the conclusion that the greater the tension state, the more rapid and accurate the learning when giving the learned response ensures the experience of tension decrease. These studies employed tasks or contexts for learning that were more difficult than the admittedly rudimentary T maze. The striking conclusion was reached that for complex learning tasks, there is a level of tension beyond which learning becomes inaccurate and inefficient. In other words, moderate tension states lead to better learning than do intense ones, when the task is a complex one. This is so even though learning involves giving the response that leads to tension reduction. It would seem that the neat relationship between amount of tension reduction and speed of learning described earlier is true only in rudimentary learning situations.

While these dissonant studies were still only a trickle, behaviorists tried to shore up their brave conclusion concerning the necessity of tension reduction for learning to take place. Latent learning was considered an anomaly, difficult to understand, and not even clearly something to be called learning. Surely, the behaviorist argued, one would not want to make any sweeping revisions in such a heavily supported conclusion on the basis of a mere handful of studies, the meaning of which everyone agreed was unclear. By calling the findings of these few studies *latent* learning, the behaviorist was able to put them in a separate category than the main body of learning studies and thereby forget about them. Concerning spontaneous alternation, the behaviorist hit upon a formulation that rendered the findings consistent with his emphasis upon tension reduction. This interpretation was that along with the usually considered biological survival needs, there is also a need to explore, or manipulate. This manipulo-exploratory need can, like the others, contribute to the organism's level of tension. Spontaneous alternation is, then, the best strategy for the rat to employ in order to bring about the greatest overall reduction of tension through satisfying not only the biological survival need heightened by experimental manipulation but the need to explore as well. The upshot of this interpretation is that one can still conclude that all learning occurs in the context of tension reduction. Finally, the behaviorist attempted to account for the findings of studies utilizing complex learning tasks by suggesting that the effect of very high tension states in such situations is to render the organism unable to search out all the relevant information with which to learn, so insistent is his search for the wherewithal for tension reduction. Fallible though an organism thus conceived is, he still can be presumed to orient all his behavior toward tension reduction.

Even with such ingenious and spirited interpretations of the dissonant studies, it soon became apparent that the behaviorist's position was inadequate. The dissonant studies went from a trickle to a torrent, and, for a while, such studies seemed to be done simply for the fun of demonstrating once again the inadequacy of the behaviorist's position. As the dissonant studies reached torrent proportions, the underlying unity of their meaning became apparent. Not all learning requires tension reduction. Neither is all behavior in the service of tension reduction. In a brilliant speech voicing these conclusions, Harlow (1953) articulated what has become the modern view. He (Harlow, 1953) begins by giving rational arguments against the behaviorist's position:

> There are logical reasons why a drive-reduction theory of learning, a theory which emphasizes the role of internal, physiological-state motivation, is entirely untenable, as a motivational theory of learning. The internal drives are cyclical and operate, certainly at any effective level of intensity, for only a brief fraction of any organism's waking life. The classical hunger drive physiologically defined ceases almost as soon as food—or nonfood—is ingested. This, as far as we know, is the only case in which a single swallow portends anything of importance. The temporal brevity of operation of the internal drive states obviously offers a minimal opportunity for conditioning and a maximal opportunity for extinction. The human being, at least in the continental United States, may go for days or even years without ever experiencing true hunger or thirst.

Harlow is suggesting that the situation of strong tension is not common enough in the lives of most people to take it as the starting point for a motivational theory of learning. Not enough of the person's time can be considered to be spent in attempting to decrease high tension states. Much of the empirical evidence providing general support for these conclusions came from Harlow's laboratory (Harlow, 1950; Harlow, Harlow, & Meyer, 1950), in which studies of manipulatory behavior in primates had been taking place. It became apparent that primates are terribly intrigued by puzzles that they can manipulate, and will learn to solve these puzzles in the absence of biological drive reduction. Indeed, introducing food as a reward for solving the puzzle once it has been already learned has the effect of increasing the errors made in solution attempts. In other dramatic study, the major findings of which are shown in Figure 5–4, Butler and Alexander (1955) reported that monkeys will learn to open the door to their opaque aluminum cage merely in order to gain the opportunity to gaze out upon the activity in the laboratory and monkey colony. To judge from Figure 5–4, the monkeys hardly lost interest in observing the laboratory, though it may well have increased rather than decreased tension.

Summarizing these studies, Harlow (1953) says

> Observations and experiments on monkeys convinced us that there was as much evidence to indicate that a strong drive inhibits learning as

FIGURE 5–4

Mean response duration and mean number of responses as a function of days

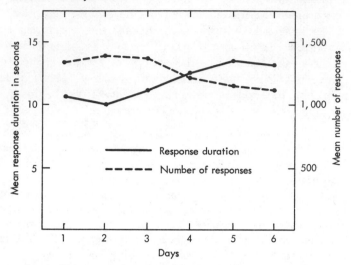

Source: R. A. Butler and H. M. Alexander, "Daily patterns of visual exploratory behavior in the monkey," *J. comp. physiol. Psychol.*, 1955.

to indicate that it facilitates learning. It was the speaker's feeling that monkeys learned more efficiently if they were given food before testing, and as a result, the speaker routinely fed his subjects before every training session. The rhesus monkey is equipped with enormous cheek pouches, and consequently many subjects would begin the educational process with a rich store of incentives crammed into the buccal cavity. When the monkey made a correct response, it would add a raisin to the buccal storehouse and swallow a little previously munched food. Following an incorrect response, the monkey would also swallow a little stored food. Thus, both correct and incorrect responses invariably resulted in S–R theory drive reduction. It is obvious that under these conditions the monkey cannot learn, but the present speaker developed an understandable skepticism of this hypothesis when the monkeys stubbornly persisted in learning, learning rapidly, and learning problems of great complexity. Because food was continuously available in the monkey's mouth, an explanation in terms of differential fractional anticipatory goal responses did not appear attractive. It would seem that the Lord was simply unaware of drive-reduction learning theory when he created, or permitted the gradual evolution of, the rhesus monkey.

Obviously, Harlow does not mean that the rhesus monkey is one single exception to the law that learning is mediated by tension reduction. Indeed, he goes on in the speech to cite evidence similar to that above concerning other primates, including man, and even rodents as well. One of the most striking studies mentioned is that of Sheffield and

Roby (1950), in which learning in rats was shown without biological drive reduction. Hungry rats learned to choose that arm in a T maze which lead to water sweetened with saccharine, a nonnutritive substance, in preference to the arm leading to plain water. The major results of this study are shown in Figure 5–5, which indicates that as days went by, the rats made more choices leading to the saccharine solution; they ran faster, and drank more. Harlow (1953) concludes:

> It may be stated unequivocally that, regardless of any relationship that may be found for other animals, there are no data indicating that intensity of drive state and the presumably correlated amount of drive reduction are positively related to learning efficiency in primates.
>
> In point of fact there is no reason to believe that the rodentological data will prove to differ significantly from those of monkey, chimpanzee, and man.

If such important behavior as that involved in learning is in some degree independent of tension reduction, then we are justified in concluding that not all functioning is in its service.

Harlow actually goes further than this to the suggestion that some behavior in learning situations brings about increases rather than decreases in tension. Such increases, if not intended, are at least tolerated. Harlow (1953) cites some evidence for this from studies conducted in his laboratory, and also includes one striking anecdote:

> Twenty years ago at the Vilas Park Zoo, in Madison, we observed an adult orangutan given two blocks of wood, one with a round hole, one with a square hole, and two plungers, one round and one square. Intellectual curiosity alone led it to work on these tasks, often for many

FIGURE 5–5

Acquisition in a T maze with saccharine solution (1.30 grams per liter) as reward

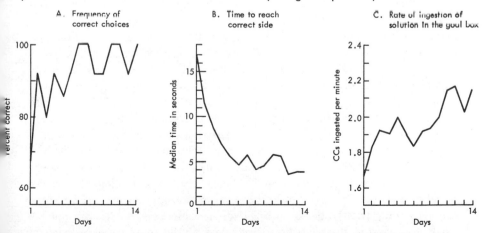

A. Frequency of correct choices   B. Time to reach correct side   C. Rate of ingestion of solution in the goal box

Source: F. D. Sheffield and T. B. Roby, "Reward value of a non-nutrient sweet taste," *J. comp. physiol. Psychol.*, 50.

minutes at a time, and to solve the problem of inserting the round plunger in both sides. The orangutan never solved the problem of inserting the square peg into the round hole, but inasmuch as it passed away with perforated ulcers a month after the problem was presented, we can honestly say that it died trying. And in defense of this orangutan, let it be stated that it died working on more complex problems than are investigated by most present-day theorists.

The suggestion made here is that once you study learning tasks of sufficient complexity to resemble the actual life experiences of organisms (T mazes clearly fall short of this) you find evidence on every side of behavior bearing little discernible relationship to any aim to reduce tension. Indeed, perhaps intriguing problems that spark the organism's curiosity may lead to persistent behavior that has the effect of raising tension, even to dangerous levels. Anyone who has become excited and stimulated at a party, or by an intellectual task, to such a degree that he has stayed up past his bedtime and expended lots of energy, without the slightest thought to how awful he would feel the next day, knows what Harlow means. Some of the most interesting behaviors definitely seem to arouse, rather than decrease tension.

In the years since Harlow's speech was made, more systematic studies concerning the possibility of tension increase as an aim have been done. Most of these studies have already been mentioned in discussion of the fourth issue. Perhaps the single most convincing body of work on the intent to increase tension is that involving sensory deprivation (e.g., Fiske, 1961). As I have mentioned already, these studies show that when you deprive the person of the usual levels of sensory stimulation, he goes to sleep (a sign of low-tension level), and when he awakens, experiences great discomfort and an intense wish for stimulation. It is even possible that the hallucinatory mentation mentioned by investigators in this field is the organism's attempt to manufacture stimulation and tension. Certainly, it has been clearly shown that the presentation of even the most banal stimulation (e.g., a recording of instructions) is greeted by subjects with enthusiasm and relief. Subjects will keep requesting such banal stimulation, and when all else fails, will leave the experiment in intense discomfort. It is not hard to conclude from such evidence that some behavior is in the service of tension increase. Also supporting this conclusion are the studies of Dember (1956) and Eisenberger, Myers, Sanders, and Shanab (1970) indicating that spontaneous alternation involves a positive interest in stimulus change, and Maddi and Andrews (1966) indicating that the people who produce novelty most are also most interested in it. These studies are relevant because novelty and change are undoubtedly tension-increasing occurrences.

Compelling though these findings seem, some behaviorists are not yet ready to abandon their position. But some of the most capable, such as Berlyne, have actually done so. Earlier, he (Berlyne, 1960) developed an ingenious behavioristic argument in which studies like those mentioned above would be explained as special cases of the attempt to reduce tension, strange though that may sound. Berlyne postulates that in the absence of external stimulation, the organism actually becomes very tense, due to spontaneously occurring internal stimulation. Subsequent attempts to increase external stimulation should therefore be understood as attempts to decrease the overall level of tension. Presumably, external stimulation has some inhibiting effect on spontaneous internal stimulation. First recognize what an extraordinarily complicated explanation this is. Sometimes external stimulation is talked about as if it increases tension, as when the laboratory rat is shocked and recoils in pain, and sometimes it is considered to decrease tension, as when the sensorily deprived subject is permitted to hear the instructions. An explanation of this type rises or falls on the compellingness of its treatment of whatever internal conditions are invoked to account for the two opposite effects of external stimulation. Even if there were not this theoretical difficulty, the notion that external stimulation actually decreases overall tension cannot adequately cover all the data. It must be remembered that it is typical of subjects in sensory deprivation experiments to fall asleep, and to remain groggy, lethargic, and unable to think even after awaking. None of this sounds like a high state of tension. And are the ulcers that killed Harlow's monkey to be understood as the result of tension decreases stemming from working on puzzles?

With the all too rare commitment to empirical knowledge of the true scientist, Berlyne (1967) has recently modified his position such that tension increase will now be recognized as rewarding along with tension decrease. Although he still believes that boredom may be a high-tension state, he does admit to a lack of experimental evidence for this view, and goes on to define classes of reinforcers that function because they increase tension. The first is ecological stimuli, that have presumably been important for survival and adaptation, and are therefore rewarding even though they increase tension. In this regard, he notes studies which have obtained introspective reports of pleasure accompanying painful sensations produced by pricks, pressures, and pinches. Another class of rewarding tension increasers are novel, complex, and surprising stimuli (called collative properties by Berlyne). The research evidence here has already been covered in discussion of the previous issue. Berlyne (1967) also notes that in the area of verbal learning in particular, increases in tension seem to be facilitative. Kleinsmith and Kaplan (1963, 1964) and Walker and Tarte (1963) have shown that the higher the level of arousal during learning, the greater the probability of long-term recall, though the smaller the probability of short-term recall. Berlyne, Borsa, Hamacher, and Koenig (1966) showed the same thing with white noise used to manipulate arousal. In other studies, even immediate recall has been improved by the application of various arousal-raising treatments during learning, such as white noise (Hoermann & Todt, 1960), tones (Schoenpflug & Schaefer, 1962), induced muscular tension (Courts, 1942), and physical exercise (Schoenpflug, 1964). In trying to explain these findings, Berlyne (1967, p. 69) says:

> We must therefore seek an alternative account of the effects of arousal on verbal learning. The one that emerges is . . . that verbal responses will be reinforced most effectively when arousal is at an intermediate level. Tests held some time after training—preferably 24 hours or more— give the surest measures of reinforcement. Immediate and short-term recall must depend on an interaction between the reinforcing effect of arousal and the effect of arousal on performance. We can expect these two effects to follow different inverted U-shaped functions.

He seems to be saying that moderate levels of arousal (or tension) are rewarding, whereas levels lower or higher than this are not. In some experimental settings, it may seem as if only tension reduction is rewarding, and in other settings, just the opposite. In reality, the difficulty is that the settings "reveal only one portion of the nonmonotonic [U-shaped] curve" (Berlyne, 1967, p. 69). In the years since Berlyne's statement, little has happened to provoke any change in conclusion. Apparently, agreement has been reached that tension increase is important to organisms, and empirical attention has settled on comparing the various theories to account for this phenomenon (see Eisenberger, 1972).

We are reaching the conclusion that not all behavior is oriented toward tension reduction, and that some behavior may even be oriented toward tension increase. This outcome of exploring the fifth issue tends to favor the fulfillment model, and the activation version of the consistency model. Not so supported are the conflict model and the cognitive dissonance version of the consistency model.

Sixth issue: Does personality show radical change after the childhood years have been passed?

Consistency and fulfillment positions are on one side of this issue, whereas conflict positions are by and large on the other. According to the pure psychosocial conflict model, there should not be radical change in personality once there is solidification of the defensive patterns established to avoid the anxiety which reflects underlying conflict. As these patterns are considered set by the time childhood has passed, conflict positions would not expect adulthood, or even adolescence, to be a time of radical personality change. What I have just said does not apply as much to the intrapsychic version of the conflict model, as it emphasizes the concept of defense only in nonideal functioning. But absence of radical change after childhood is clearly assumed by pure psychosocial conflict theorists such as Freud. In his theory, it is even typical to name the patterns of peripheral characteristics, or personality types, in terms of the early childhood stages of psychosexual development. In considering adolescence and adulthood to constitute only one developmental stage, Freud shows vividly his emphasis on the essentially unchanging nature of adult personality. Any changes taking place beyond puberty are not basic or radical. In contrast, fulfillment positions see personality as a rather continually changing thing, without any sharp difference in changeability between childhood, adolescence, and adulthood. This emphasis on fluidity is most apparent in Rogers and the other actualization theorists, who will not even consider the self-concept to be particularly stable. But the emphasis is also strong in some perfection theorists, like Allport, who sees life as a series of changes toward ever-increasing individuality. Perfection theorists tend to emphasize personality change in the direction of psychological growth, or simultaneously increasing differentiation and integration. Consistency positions also assume rather continual change in personality, having little recourse to a concept of defense. The cognitive dissonance version of the consistency model attributes to the person the frequent changes in personality that occur in the attempt to minimize the discrepancy between expectations and perceived occurrences. And the activation version of this model emphasizes the concept of psychological growth.

You may have noticed that I stated the issue in such a way that what is of interest is the occurrence of radical change in personality. It was necessary to do this because no sensible theorist, regardless of the model for theorizing he adopts, would dispute that certain unextraordinary changes in degree take place during adolescence and adulthood. If, let us say, a person with the kind of personality called anal by Freudians was stubborn in childhood, and became a bit less or more so in adulthood, no one would consider this theoretically disconcerting. In a literal sense, change will have occurred, but no special difficulty would have been created thereby for the conflict model. Radical changes in personality are a different matter. If a person's personality type shifted from oral, in childhood, to phallic, in adulthood, we would have a situation unexpected by Freudians. The only way Freudians could explain such a radical change in adulthood would be to postulate the intervention of an unusual and potent life context, such as psychotherapy or the trauma of catastrophe. If radical change in personality can be shown in the absence of such extraordinary occurrences, the psychosocial conflict model will not have been confirmed. Thus, in order to pinpoint the issue such that it really separates the various models, it is necessary to restrict ourselves to conditions or contexts that can be considered more natural and usual than participating in psychotherapy. These more natural conditions include such things as getting married, having children, going to college, changing jobs, and moving to a new location. You should also know that research relevant to whether there is any behavioral consistency at all will be discussed in Chapter 11 rather than here. However exciting the controversy produced by the attempt to explain behavior situationally may be, it is not really relevant to the sixth issue, which presumes that even radical changes will be expressive of personality.

On the face of it, the study of personality change is most adequately done by testing the same group of people at the beginning and at the end of the period of time under consideration—the so-called longitudinal study. Actually, there are few studies of this sort concerning adolescence and adulthood due to the obvious difficulties associated with having to wait long periods of time in order to obtain data. After the initial testing, subjects may move to dozens of locations, be no longer willing to participate, or even die. Such difficulties have led investigators to favor the cross-sectional study. In this kind of study a number of groups of subjects are employed with each group differing in age. Groups are tested only once and the differences between them are attributed to the effects of the span of years separating them.

Obviously, the cross-sectional study has the advantage of taking very little time and effort by comparison with the longitudinal study. But the cross-sectional study is also more risky, because it must be assumed that the various groups were similar in personality during the period of time ending with the age of the youngest group. Usually, there is no way to check this assumption. But suppose the span of years separating the adolescent and adult groups is large, say 30 years. In 30 years' time, it is rather likely that child-rearing practices would have changed enough to make it risky to assume similarity of childhood personality for all groups. And if the groups differed in personality during childhood, it may be no more than this fact that the investigator is observing and erroneously attributing to the effects of moving through adolescence.

Because of the greater definitiveness of longitudinal studies, I will consider them first. There are several longitudinal studies concerning the span of time from early adolescence to young adulthood. In a study that was rather precise quantitatively, Tuddenham (1959) interviewed 72 males and females the first time when they were adolescents and then again when they were in their early or middle adulthood. The interview material was rated for 53 personality variables, some of which were fairly descriptive and some inferential. Table 5–8 shows a sample of his findings concerning descriptive rather than inferential variables. The information concerning stability appears in the last two columns. Correlations between the earlier and later scores of subjects were generally positive, but quite low, the average being only .27 for men and .24 for women. These correlations are so low that one really could not predict effectively what a person would be like in young adulthood from his scores in early adolescence. The stability correlations may appear low due to such unfortunate factors as (1) the raters did not always agree strongly (see the first four columns of Table 5–8), and (2) the pair of

TABLE 5–8

Interjudge agreement and temporal stability of ratings: C. General (*i.e., manifest*) traits
(*N = 19 men, 17 women*)

Variable	Agreement 1940*		Agreement 1953†		Stability 1940–1953‡	
	Boys	Girls	Men	Women	Men	Women
Manifest traits (average)	.71	.65	.60	.57	.33	.35
1. Adjustment						
a. Social prestige	.84	.87	.50	.79	.25	.67§
b. Popularity with same sex	.75	.73	.48	.54	−.03	.48
c. Work	.78	.26	.68	.81	−.05	−.03
d. Heterosexual	.76	.78	.76	.80	.20	.47
e. Personality	.69	.86	.58	.82	.37	.15
2. Focus on internal versus external activities	.46	.33	.55	.28	.61	.30
3. Security feelings versus insecurity	.70	.59	.42	.52	.30	.33
4. Introspection versus absence of	.70	.15	.72	.46	.62§	.44
5. Egotism versus altruism	.76	.77	.60	.32	.45‖	.35
6. Creativeness versus mediocrity	.57	.80	.71	.52	.54‖	.37
7. Self-sufficiency versus dependence	.61	.51	.39	.61	.08	.55
8. Genuiness versus artificiality	.78	.72	.36	.58	.22	.37
9. Seriousness of efforts versus playfulness	.86	.23	.78	.26	.50‖	.56
10. Maturity versus immaturity	.63	.81	.59	.58	.30	.12
11. Strictness of super ego versus laxity	.47	.56	.64	.16	.34	−.03

* Agreement coefficients for 1940 are based on ratings of female judges F and G, corrected by the Spearman-Brown formula for two judges vs. two judges (See 1).

† Agreement coefficients for 1953 are correlations between a male and a female observer, based on independent two-hour interviews, corrected by the Spearman-Brown formula for two judges vs. two judges.

‡ Stability coefficients are correlations between the sum of the two 1953 ratings and the sum of two 1940 ratings.

§ Stability coefficient significant at 1 percent level (two-tailed test).

‖ Stability coefficient significant at 5 percent level (two-tailed test).

Source: Adapted from R. D. Tuddenham, "Constancy of personality ratings over two decades," *Genet. Psychol. Monogr.*, 1959.

raters working on the interview data for the first testing were different than the pair working on the second testing. Nonetheless, the evidence for substantial stability seems scanty.

In a less quantitatively-precise study, Jones (1960) compared subjects tested at 18 and 30 in a rather global, interpretive manner. His conclusion is that the rigidly controlled, well-ordered, compulsive people tended to continue in that pattern, whereas other types of people often changed dramatically, even to the point of becoming the opposite of what they were. In another global, interpretive study, Rohrer and Edmonson (1960) traced a large majority of the Negro adolescents described earlier by Davis and Dollard (1940). Rohrer and Edmonson conclude that after 20 years, these people showed a great diversity of adult life patterns, only partly predictable from observations made during adolescence. Although most investigators conclude that there are marked, even radical differences in personality in the process of going from adolescence to adulthood, there is an occasional exception. Symonds (1961), for example, studied 28 subjects ranging from 12 to 18 when first tested, and who were retested after an interval of 13 years. He found what he regards as high stability of personality, evidenced in correlations of the magnitude of .5 or .6 in such characteristics as general adjustment and aggressiveness.

The college years are a ready source of information about personality change following childhood. Although most such studies have been cross-sectional (see Jacob, 1957) there are a few that are longitudinal in design. Among these, the report by Freedman and Bereiter (1963) is notable not only for its carefulness but also because it extends even beyond the collegiate years. Their subjects were females from the classes of 1954, 1955, and 1956 of Vassar College, numbering 78, 74, and 79 people, respectively. These subjects had taken the Vassar Attitude Inventory (VAI), the Minnesota Multiphasic Personality Inventory (MMPI) and the California Personality Inventory (CPI) when they were freshman, again as seniors, and for the final time three to four years after graduation. There was evidence of systematic and important change during the college years, the nature of which is confirmed by other studies (e.g., Sanford, 1962). On the VAI, the subjects seemed to have become, as seniors, less ethnocentric and authoritarian while also becoming more expressive of impulses and rebellious independence. Changes in scores on the MMPI and CPI indicate a shift toward psychopathology, and away from conventional adjustment. But three to four years after graduation, these general trends had more or less been reversed. At the final testing, repression and suppression of impulses had increased on the VAI, scores on the psychopathology scales of the MMPI had decreased, and the picture obtained from the CPI was in the direction of conventional adjustment. Although the changes demonstrated in this study were not especially large, they did tend to reverse direction, and are therefore striking.

The studies mentioned thus far have all used test-retest agreement on the same measures as a procedure for determining the degree of personality stability or change. There are a few longitudinal studies, however, that have employed a more global, interpretive criterion of stability, based on the determination of analogous, rather than literally similar, behaviors at the different ages considered. These studies work at a genotypical level, whereas the others employ phenotypical analysis, to borrow a distinction from biology. Whether or not the genotypical approach is really more appropriate, you should recognize that it renders observation of change less likely, due to the abstract, interpretative level at which observation takes place.

In one genotypical study, Anderson (1960) tested all children in a Minnesota county who were enrolled in school from grades 4 to 12, and then tested them again five to seven years later, by which time some of them were in their twenties. He concludes that, of measures of intelligence and personality obtained at the first testing, only the former play an important role in predicting later adjustment. In spite of an approach not suited to focusing upon literal changes in behavior, Anderson reports that personality variables do not seem to be patterned by age.

Kagan and Moss (1962), in a major genotypical study, felt inclined to just the opposite conclusion. Twenty-one males and females were rated on a set of personality variables at four intervals during their childhoods and then again when they were in their twenties. Correlations were computed between certain childhood behaviors and their theoretically analogous adult behaviors. These results are presented in Figure 5–6, which also indicates the kinds of behaviors considered. Kagan and Moss (1962, pp. 266–268) concluded that:

> Many of the behaviors exhibited by the child aged six to ten, and a few during the age period three to six, were moderately good predictors of theoretically related behaviors during early adulthood. Passive withdrawal from stressful situations, dependency on family, ease-of-anger arousal, involvement in intellectual mastery, social interaction anxiety, sex-role identification, and pattern of sexual behavior in adulthood were each related to reasonably analogous behavioral dispositions during the early school years. . . . These results offer strong support for the generalization that aspects of adult personality begin to take form during early childhood.

FIGURE 5–6

Summary of relations between selected child behaviors (6 to 10 years of age) and theoretically similar adult behaviors

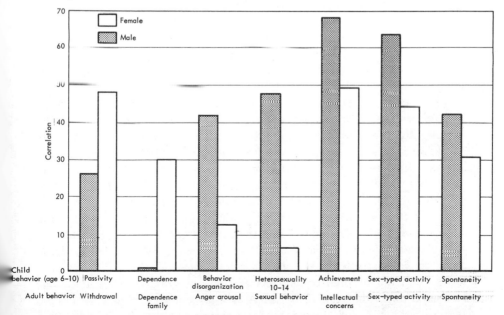

Source: J. Kagan and H. A. Moss, *Birth to maturity: A study in psychological development*. New York: John Wiley, 1962.

Actually, this seems to me rather unconvincing as a conclusion based on the findings in Figure 5–6. Even with an approach weighted toward the discovery of personality stability, we find that five of the seven correlations shown for boys and all seven for girls, are below .50. The average correlation is about .41 for boys and .31 for girls. To my mind, these findings show that there is more change than stability in personality, even when one adopts a genotypical approach!

Following their brave conclusion, Kagan and Moss made statements more consistent with the amount of change they observed. For example (Kagan & Moss, 1962, p. 269):

> Not all of the childhood reactions displayed long-term continuity. Compulsivity and irrational fears during childhood were not predictive of similar responses during adulthood. Moreover, task persistence and excessive irritability during the first three years of life showed no relation to phenotypically similar behaviors during later childhood.

And in another statement, these investigators (Kagan & Moss, 1962, p. 268) gave what seems to me the crux of the matter:

> However, the degree of continuity of these response classes was intimately dependent upon its congruence with traditional standards for sex-role characteristics. The differential stability of passivity, dependency, aggression, and sexuality for males and females emphasizes the importance of cultural roles in determining both behavioral change and stability.

Indeed, with results showing more change than stability, it would seem wise to conclude that whatever stability there is from childhood to adulthood occurs along the lines of sex-role definitions important to culture. When some aspect of personality is not intimately connected with what is defined as a sex role, it may well change enough in adulthood to be virtually unpredictable from childhood personality.

In a recent study of large scope, Block (1971) collected follow-up data in adulthood from subjects who had been extensively tested by other investigators during childhood and adolescence. The variety of data available included interviews, teacher and peer reports, self-reports and several structured and unstructured personality tests. Genotypic data concerning stability or change in personality was derived from these protocols by the ratings made by several psychologists. Mean correlations for the 171 subjects between junior high school and senior high school ages were .77 and .75 for males and females respectively. Between senior high school and adulthood they were .56 and .54 for males and females respectively. But the range of correlations was so great as to indicate that a number of subjects changed a good deal though some remained much the same. Block identified six female and five male types that differed not only in content of personality but also in degree of change from childhood to adulthood. Some of these types changed too much to be consistent with the contention that personality remains rather stable once the childhood years are past. Block's unusual approach of isolating types partly on the basis of changeability has provided findings that bear clearly on the issue under discussion.

Shifting our attention to the last half of life, from young adulthood through middle adulthood to old age, we find very few longitudinal studies to go by. There is the report by Terman and Oden (1959) following up on a group of gifted, extraordinary children studied years before who had now reached their forties. Originally, each child selected for study was in the top 1 percent of the population in intelligence quotient (IQ). The data on personality have not been systematically analysed, but in general, it appears that the superior child has become the superior adult. Although there is evidence of stability here, one must be careful in generalizing from this study both because it deals with such an unusual group of people and because its major concern is with intelligence rather than personality.

In another study, Kelly (1955) tested 300 engaged couples first when they were in their twenties and then again when they were in their forties. After correcting his correlations for attenuation, Kelly concluded that individual consistency was highest in the areas of values and vocational interests (correlations of approximately .50), and lowest with regard to self-ratings and other personality variables (correlations of approximately .30). Kelly points out that "Our findings indicate that significant changes in the human personality may continue to occur during the years of adulthood." This conclusion is even more likely to be accurate when you realize that the correlations of approximately .30 and .50 are only estimates of what would have been found if the measures employed had been more adequate. Actually, Kelly's obtained correlations must have been lower than the figures mentioned here.

In a recent study, Haan and Day (1974) obtained a picture of great change in their longitudinal study of personality in the period from adolescence to later adulthood. Their findings indicate that adulthood is a time of major reorganization in personality.

All in all, it seems clear that longitudinal studies concerning the years of adulthood and adolescence show so much evidence of change that it is reasonable to conclude that radical changes in personality must be going on. Sometimes later personality is virtually unpredictable from earlier personality; sometimes a developmental trend actually reverses direction. The conclusion I am reaching is rather consistent with the view of many experts in human development (e.g., Neugarten, 1964; Stevenson, 1957). For example, Neugarten (1964) is prompted to say concerning the research I have reviewed that:

> Whether the studies are test-retest or antecedent-consequent [genotypical] in design . . . the general picture with regard to consistency of adult personality can be summarized by saying that measures taken at

long time intervals tend to produce statistically reliable, but relatively low, correlations . . . The indication is that while there is continuity of personality measurable by present techniques, the larger proportion of the variance in the measures used (in the final testing) remains unaccounted for. Making allowances for the fallibility of measures with regard to reliability, the implication is that there is at least as much change as there is stability.

There is little in the findings of cross-sectional studies to contradict the conclusion that radical changes in personality take place beyond the childhood years. Because of this, and the less definitive status of cross-sectional studies, I will not consider them in any detail. They have been ably reviewed by Kuhlen (1945). In general, studies of interest patterns have shown large shifts from adolescence to adulthood. Among the most extensive and careful of such studies are those reported by Strong (1943), using the Strong Vocational Interest Blank, a test he devised which includes hundreds of items referring to tangible activities which the subject must indicate that he likes or dislikes. Analysing the interests of 2,340 men anywhere from 20 to 60 years of age, Strong obtained the kind of results shown in Table 5–9. This table shows the major interest changes that occur in two time spans; between 15 and 25, and between 25 and 55. Positive numbers in the two change columns signify change in the direction of liking the interest area involved, whereas negative numbers have the opposite significance. The columns listing ranks indicate the relative magnitude rather than the direction of the changes. Most interest areas show greater change from ages 15 to 25 than from 25 to 55, but there are some exceptions. Most change is in a positive direction from age 15 to 25, and in a negative direction from 25 to 55. Findings such as these prompt Strong to conclude that older and younger men do

TABLE 5–9

Major changes in interests from 15 to 25 years and from 25 to 55 years in percentage of likes

Classification of interests	N Items	Rank	Change, 15–25	Rank	Change, 25–55
People, desirable traits	13	1	+16.0	20	− 1.8
Amusements, general cultural	13	2	+15.3	18	+ 2.0
Occupations involving writing	9	3	+15.1	2	−10.2
School subjects	36	4	+14.4	9	− 3.8
Linguistic, primarily writing	23	5	+14.3	5	− 6.9
Possession of present abilities	25	6	+14.0	7	+ 4.1
Physical skill and daring	19	22.5	− 2.5	1	−17.0
Occupations involving physical danger, outdoors, mechanical pursuits, athletics, and travel	21	22.5	+ 2.5	3.5	− .70
Dislike of change	21	20	− 4.6	3.5	+ 7.0
Influencing others	19	7	+13.6	6	− 4.9

Source: Adapted from *Vocational interests of men and women* by E. K. Strong, Jr. (Stanford: University Press, 1943) Table 83 by Ann Roe in *The psychology of occupation* (New York: John Wiley, 1956) Table 7.7.

not have the same likes and dislikes. Older men like neither activities involving physical skill and daring, nor activities suggesting change and interference with established habits. In general, liking for linguistic activities declines with age, except for reading which is liked better. Interest in most amusements, excluding heavily cultural activities, declines with age. Summarizing, Strong (1943, p. 285) says that "interests change rapidly from those held at 15 years to those held at about 25, and then shift in the reverse direction much more slowly from about 25 years to 55 years." Once again, we see a general reversal of developmental trends.

Just to sample other domains of personality, I should point to studies like that of Terman and Miles (1936), in which it was found that early in maturity masculinity increased for both men and women, but then decreased after 30 years of age. Phillips and Greene (1939), studying 143 women teachers, found an initial rise in neuroticism (measured by the Bernreuter Personality Inventory) up to a peak at age 30, and a decline thereafter. There are many other studies showing some sort of reversal of developmental trend (see Kuhlen, 1945). Clearly there is ample basis upon which to conclude that radical changes in personality do take place beyond the childhood years.

Some of the changes that have been reported seem particularly relevant to the concept of psychological growth, which stresses concomitant increases in both differentiation and integration. Along with the decrease in activeness and range of interests mentioned by Strong, goes a decrease in the importance of sexual activity and vocational success (Kuhlen, 1945). At the same time there is a gradual increase in interest concerning philosophy, religion, and culture (see Kuhlen, 1945). These processes are well under way by the mid-1930s. Such increased introspectiveness and concern for the meaning of life may signify the elaboration of integrative principles assumed in the concept of psychological growth. In this view, the person becomes more able to organize and integrate the events of his experience as he ages.

It would be especially convincing to consider the increasing concern with a philosophy of life to indicate elaboration of integration processes if one could also point to increasing differentiation with age. In an obvious sense, such things as the decrease in range of interests with age that was observed by Strong, favor the possibility that differentiation is on the decline. There are certainly several recent studies (e.g., Brissette, 1967; Lehr & Rudinger, 1969) which show depression and general detachment to be a common accompaniment of old age. It is also possible, however, that as one gets older, differentiation becomes a primarily cognitive, rather than actional, process, too subtle to be well measured by gross procedures such as interest tests with their emphasis on tangible activities. Perhaps the increase in interest in reading and heavily cultural amusements that occurs with age signals an increase in the differentiation of personality on a perceptual, cognitive plane rather than an obvious actional one. Fortunately, there is a large body of evidence on perceptual differentiation that may be of help.

I refer to the series of studies by Witkin and his associates (Witkin, Dyk, Faterson, Goodenough & Karp, 1962; Witkin, Lewis, Hertzman, Machover, Meissner, & Wapner, 1954). They define *psychological differentiation* as the "degree of articulation of experience of the world; degree of articulation of experience of the self, reflected particularly in the nature of the body concept and extent of development of a sense of separate identity; and extent of development of specialized, structured controls and defenses" (Witkin et al., 1962, p. 16). The two things emphasized in this definition are the number of aspects or parts to the personality, and the separateness of the person from the world around him. These emphases square quite well with discussions of differentiation reviewed in previous chapters of this book. Witkin et al. (1962) also refer to integration, indicating its function in binding together and organizing the parts of personality discriminated from each other by differentiation. They present the intriguing point of view that integrative processes will determine the nature of the adjustment and degree of effectiveness that characterize the person, whereas differentiation bears little relationship to such matters. But they conduct no research on integrative processes.

In measuring psychological differentiation, Witkin and his associates put heavy reliance upon a number of ingenious tests of ability to be analytical in perceptual situations. Analytical perception ability is considered an indicant of psychological differentiation because it bespeaks a separateness of self and body from the world outside and a sensitivity to the parts of things in general. In the Embedded Figures Test, the person is presented a series of complex geometrical figures. The speed and accuracy with which he can detect previously seen simple figures that have been hidden within the complex ones is taken as a measure of psychological differentiation. In order to detect the embedded simple figure, the person must be able to analyze the complex figure into its component parts. The Rod and Frame Test presents the person with a rod surrounded by a square frame as the only visible things in an otherwise darkened room. The person is asked to adjust the rod to the upright position, which adjustment is complicated by the fact that the frame is tilted a certain number of degrees to either the left or the right. The average accuracy of rod adjustment to the upright position over a series of trials is taken as another measure of psychological differentiation. According to Witkin, accurate adjustment of the rod requires that the person disregard the cues provided by the surrounding frame, and use instead kinesthetic and proprioceptive cues stemming from the person's own body. Finally, in the Body Adjustment Test, the person sits in a seat placed within an experimental room where both seat and room can be tilted by the experimenter. The person's task is to adjust his seated body to the upright position from an initial starting point in which the chair is tilted either to right or left, and the room is tilted in the same or the opposite direction. Once again, the accuracy with which he adjusts his body to the upright position is taken as a measure of psychological differentiation because in order to be successful he must overlook visual cues from the external environment and rely upon his awareness of kinesthetic and proprioceptive cues signaling the positioning of his body. Scores on these three tests intercorrelate moderately, and show adequate reliability (Witkin et al., 1962, p. 40).

Although these investigators have concentrated on their perceptual tests, they have also employed more cognitive measures involving the person in composing stories about vague pictures (the Thematic Apperception Test), in indicating what inkblots look like to him (the Rorschach Test), and in drawing pictures of himself and others (the Draw-A-Person Test). In all these tasks, the aim is to detect the aspects of psychological differentiation such as articulateness of experience, and articulateness of body image. What is by now a large body of empirical evidence (Witkin et al., 1954; Witkin et al., 1962) indicates that these nonperceptual measures correlate with the perceptual ones in such fashion that it is sensible to consider them all to mirror some facet of the overall characteristic of psychological differentiation. Those of you who are familiar with Witkin's earlier (1954) emphasis upon the concepts of *field dependence* and *field independence* should take note of the fact that he (Witkin et al., 1962) shifted from these concepts to that of psychological differentiation largely on the basis of the empirical association between the original perceptual measures and the cognitive ones just mentioned.

Having given you a little of the background of Witkin's work, I can now describe the longitudinal studies relevant to determining what happens to the level of psychological differentiation during the life-span. Witkin et al. (1962, pp. 374–377) report two studies of special relevance. One involved a group of 26 boys and 27 girls, first studied at age 8 and restudied at age 13. The second group consisted of 30 boys and 30 girls, studied at ages 10, 14, and 17. With regard to the perceptual measures of psychological differentiation, the same trend was observed in both studies. In the words of the investigators (Witkin et al., 1962, p. 374), "The ability to determine the position of the body apart from the tilted room, to perceive the position of a rod independently of the tilted frame, to pick out a simple figure obscured by a complex design, tends to improve, on the whole, until about the age of 17." Thereafter, the rate in increase in psychological differentiation decreases, and, for females, may actually reverse slightly in direction. A parallel finding was obtained concerning articulateness of body concept, as measured in the figure drawings made by the boys and girls. Witkin et al. (1962, p. 376) conclude that "Children who showed a relatively articulated body concept at 10 showed it 7 years later as well, even though the drawings at the two ages gave evidence of a general change toward more sophisticated representation of the human body." Also reported (Witkin et al., 1962) are other studies concerning the period from infancy to age nine, and the period of the college years. The picture emerging from all these studies is essentially the same. Psychological differentiation shows a rapid increase from infancy through about the middle of adolescence, and a more gradual increase from that point on into young adulthood. In addition, the early differences between people in degree of psychological differentiation are maintained all the while everyone is increasing in the characteristic. Certainly, there is clear evidence that differentiation continues to occur beyond the childhood years.

One last observation from these studies bears upon the more general question of whether radical changes in personality occur following childhood. In connection with the attempt to study changes in body concept between the ages of 10 and 17, Witkin et al. (1962, p. 376) had occasion to consider not only articulateness, but also content of figure drawings, concluding that there were:

1. Vast changes in kinds of interests . . . which resulted in marked differences in content of drawings by the same child.
2. Marked decrease in drawing features suggestive of disturbance or pathology.
3. Changes in main conflict areas. Thus, the large and varied changes that occur in this period of life are reflected in the drawings; some of the changes are in content aspects of personality, others refer to nature of integration, still others to extent of differentiation.

Witkin believes that along with the gradual increases in differentiation (and presumably integration, though he does not study that), there occur radical shifts in the content (including conflicts) of personality.

Witkin's statement provides a basis for closing discussion of this sixth issue. There seems some evidence for radical changes in personality following the childhood years. In addition, there is also evidence suggesting that the dual processes of differentiation and integration that mark psychological growth continue into adulthood, though it is not clear if they diminish in old age. Perhaps the radical changes and reversals in the content of personality are occurring all the while that the complexity of the person, in the sense of differentiation and integration, is increasing gradually in a generally unidirectional way. These conclusions are not consistent with the pure psychosocial version of the conflict model. Perhaps most strongly supported are those models explicitly employing the concept of psychological growth.

CONCLUDING REMARKS

We have come a long, long way in Chapters 2, 3, 4 and 5, and are finally in a position to put together what we have learned. In considering the first two issues, we have formed an empirical basis for concluding that the concept of defense is tenable, and that some, but not all, behavior is defensive. These conclusions support all bases for core level theorizing except the pure psychosocial version of the conflict model, which assumes all behavior to be defensive, and the pure and variant cognitive dissonance versions of the consistency model, which essentially assume that no behavior is defensive. We reached the tentative conclusion, in pursuing the third issue, that the highest form of functioning is transcendent rather than adaptive. This conclusion supports the fulfillment model, and is contrary to the conflict model (at least in its psychosocial version), while failing to have any special significance for the consistency model. But we should not give much weight to this conclusion, as it is no stronger than our assumption that fulfillment and conflict theorists alike would designate the creative person to be the clearest embodiment of the highest form of functioning. Considering the fourth issue taught us that only large discrepancies from expectation (or dissonances) are unpleasant and avoided, whereas small discrepancies are actually pleasant and sought after. This conclusion actively favors two forms of the consistency model, the activation and variant cognitive dissonance versions, while not supporting the pure cognitive dissonance version of that model. The other models are not actively touched by this conclusion. We resolved the fifth issue by concluding that while some behavior aims at tension reduction, some behavior aims at tension increase. Favored are the activation and variant cognitive dissonance versions of the consistency model, and the fulfillment model in general. Contradicted are the pure cognitive dissonance version of the consistency model, and all forms of the conflict model, except perhaps for the variant of its psychosocial version. On investigation of the sixth issue, it became apparent that there are radical shifts in the content of personality during a time span extending through adulthood. In addition, there was evidence suggesting that psychological differentiation and integration continues beyond childhood. All in all, there is some support for the models emphasizing psychological growth as occurring throughout the life-span and some disconfirmation of models restricting the period of significant personality formation to childhood.

Merely by totaling the number of times a model has been supported or contradicted by our empirical analysis leads us to interesting and surprisingly clear overall conclusions. The only models which were never contradicted are both versions of the fulfillment model and the activation version of the consistency model. The only models that were never supported are the pure psychosocial version of the conflict model, and the pure cognitive dissonance version of the consistency model. The other models fall in between these two extremes, but are more frequently contradicted than supported.

It is interesting that the models most supported by our empirical analysis are also not at all incompatible logically. Although one could certainly adopt either version of the fulfillment model, or the activation version of the consistency model, one could also combine them without being logically inconsistent. In combining them, one would be assuming both a tendency to actualize potentialities of perfect living, and a tendency to minimize discrepancies between customary and actual levels of activation. That both assumptions could be harmoniously included in the same theory is suggested by the basic compatibility they share on fundamental questions regarding defensiveness, tension reduction and increase, and psychological growth. Though compatible, I believe them to stress different aspects of behavior, and hence, their combination might result in an even more comprehensive personality theory. But, at the moment, this is only speculation.

Lest you embrace these overall conclusions too completely, I must remind you that we have not yet considered the statements at the peripheral level of personality made by the various models. Perhaps one of the models falling between the extremes of support and disconfirmation with regard to core considerations will actually do a better job at the peripheral level than any other model. We must evaluate peripheral level statements before having a comprehensive basis for judging the relative value of the models.

Chapter 6 THE PERIPHERY OF PERSONALITY: CONFLICT MODEL

Statements about the core of personality depict the tendencies and characteristics that are present in all persons at all times, and that influence the overall directionality of life. In contrast, each peripheral aspect of personality is learned, present in some rather than all people, and specific rather than general in its effect upon behavior. Peripheral concepts of personality are the ones that relate most clearly, immediately, and obviously to the behavior constituting data (or that which is to be explained). The ideal theory of personality would include both core and peripheral statements. The core statements are important in understanding how people share a common psychological nature, and the peripheral statements are important in understanding behavioral or stylistic differences between particular persons. You should keep in mind, as you read this chapter, that there are two general kinds of peripheral characteristics. In Chapter 1, they were called *concrete peripheral characteristics* and *types*. The concrete peripheral characteristic is the smallest, most homogeneous unit of personality considered feasible by the theorist. It is what is used to explain the behavioral regularities that are observed in individuals. For example, a theorist may attribute the behaviors of calling people on the telephone, going to many parties, joining clubs, and talking a lot, to the trait of gregariousness. Gregariousness would constitute a peripheral characteristic of personality if it were considered something learned, and not present equally in all persons.

Personologists have often used the term *trait* for what I am calling a concrete peripheral characteristic. I have avoided such usage because, as you will see, some theorists postulate homogeneous particles of personality that have content inconsistent with the connotations of the trait term. Typically, a theorist will postulate a number of concrete peripheral characteristics, each of which can be present or absent in the personality of any given person. But when the theorist employs the type concept, he essentially groups together sets of concrete peripheral characteristics, thus forming larger, less-homogeneous units more vividly descriptive of the styles of living observed in people. The function of the type concept is to get at the "Johnian" quality of John.

In this chapter, I will consider the peripheral statements included in the various theories already covered in previous chapters. You should be prepared to find that some of the theorists do make an explicit distinction between periphery and core, whereas others either leave the distinction to be made by us, or else concentrate so much on the core that it is virtually impossible to determine what, if anything, they have to say about the periphery. In addition, among theorists who do actually consider the periphery, some emphasize the type concept and some emphasize the concrete peripheral characteristic.

CONFLICT MODEL: PSYCHOSOCIAL VERSION

Freud's position

It is fortunate that we consider Freud first, for his viewpoint provides a good example of the distinction between core and periphery of personality. He assumed that all persons have the same set of instincts, those concerning survival, sexuality, and death. Clearly this is an assumption concerning the core of personality, for it is inconceivable, theoretically, that one person should have only survival and sex instincts, but not the death instinct, whereas another should have only the death instinct, or only the sex instinct. All persons have all instincts, and these forces exert a continual, general influence on all functioning. For Freud, then, the id is clearly part of the core of personality.

The parts of the personality called ego and superego should also be considered part of the core, though the reasons for this are not as obvious as in the case of the id. Even though it has become fashionable in some psychoanalytic circles to talk of people with more or less ego and superego, it remains, nonetheless, that no one can be considered to be without ego or superego. The absence of ego is impossible, theoretically, because the ego comes into being by virtue of the existence of the id and the consequent necessity of satisfying instincts through interaction with the world. Without an ego there would no chance of consistent id gratification, and therefore, no chance of physical and psychological survival. Similarly, it is theoretically impossible to conceive of a person without a superego, because that part of personality is born out of the conflict between the person and the world, a conflict as inevitable as instincts which cannot be gratified independently of other people and things. It is the requirements of society that determine the superego, and, for Freud, individual life is inconceivable without the existence of society.

But to say that the ego and superego are core characteristics of personality, along with the id, is to mask an important difference between the first two and the last of these. Whereas all persons possess the same id, it is not true that the *content* of ego and superego is strictly constant for all people. For Freud, the ego consists of defenses and the concrete expressions of defenses in traits or consistencies of everyday functioning. Now, it is certainly true in his theory that all persons are defensive, but it is not at all true that they are considered defensive in the same ways. Psychoanalysts have distinguished quite a number of different defenses, and theorized about the developmental conditions determining which of these will appear in a particular person. In specifying the kinds of defenses that can be used, Freudians are making statements about the periphery of personality. That this is so is even more obvious when they begin detailing the concrete habits expressive of the various defenses, as we will see in a moment. Each defense is learned, and specific either to a particular person, or even to only a particular part of a person's behavior. Something quite similar is true for the superego. While it is present in all persons, its contents may vary depending upon the quirks of the particular parents bringing up the person. Consequently, the particular taboos and sanctions you recognize may be somewhat different from those of the next person. In considering the content of both ego and superego, we are dealing with the periphery of personality. The basic reason for this is that the content of ego and superego, in contrast to that of the id, is determined in large measure by the kind of people and things—the external environment— that is encountered.

Actually, the Freudian position on the periphery of personality is most vividly contained in the classification of *character types*. This can be clearly seen in Fenichel (1945, p. 467) who says:

> Character, as the habitual mode of bringing into harmony the tasks presented by internal demands and by the external world, is necessarily a function of the constant, organized, and integrating part of the personality which is the ego; indeed, ego was defined as that part of the organism that handles the communication between the instinctual demands and the external world. The question of character would thus be the question of when and how the ego acquires the qualities by which it habitually adjusts itself to the demands of instinctual drives and of the external world, and later also of the superego. . . . The term character stresses the habitual form of a given reaction, its relative constancy.

Later he (Fenichel, 1945, p. 468) indicates that character is not only the content of the ego, but of the superego as well:

The latest complication in the structure of the ego, the erection of the superego, is also decisive in forming the habitual patterns of character. What an individual considers good or bad is characteristic for him; likewise, whether or not he takes the commands of his conscience seriously, and whether he obeys his conscience or tries to rebel against it.

In these two quotes, it is clear that character is a learned pattern of fairly consistent ways of functioning, which pattern varies somewhat from person to person. In order to undercut the terribly abstract terminology used by Fenichel, let me encourage you to recognize that a person's character is the most obvious psychological thing about him—what you would be getting at if someone asked you to describe a friend.

Actually, it is possible to be more concrete, even in the structure of psychoanalytic terminology. A character type is a group of traits that is expressive of (1) particular underlying defenses, (2) a particular underlying conflict, (3) a particular response on the part of others to an underlying conflict, or (4) any combination of these. A trait, it turns out, can be primarily a pattern of thought, feeling or action, or, once again, some combination of these. Traits are concrete peripheral characteristics in our terms. All this may sound terribly complicated, but bear with me, and I think it will become more clear when we actually discuss the content of particular character types. In order to start on this discussion, you should have clearly in mind that the character type is learned, and represents the result of the interaction between the child, who is carrying out the core tendency of maximizing instinctual gratification while minimizing punishment and guilt, and the society, in the form of parents whose task is to uphold the requirements of corporate living. We will find that not only in this theory, but in all the others as well, the periphery is the fruit of earlier attempts to express the core tendency in a particular social and cultural context.

We have been saying that character types are the product of development, and hence, it is fitting that they bear the names of the various psychosexual stages, reflecting as they do, the Freudian position on development. The major stages of psychosexual development are the *oral, anal, phallic, latency,* and *genital.* Each stage has a particular concrete form of the sexual instinct, and arouses a particular range of reactions from parents. This amounts to saying that each stage is defined by a particular concrete version of the general conflict between the sexual instinct and society. It should not be surprising, then, that each stage has its own typical defenses, as the various defenses are differentially effective against different forms of conflict. And, as you will see, each of the stages but one has a particular character type associated with it. The concrete forms of the sexual instinct associated with the various stages of psychosexual development are summarized in their names. As you can see, there is an anatomical location designated in each name except that for the latency stage. Even conservative psychoanalytic thinkers are beginning to believe that the latency stage is not a true, inherent aspect of the sexual instinct, but rather, is a culturally determined period of developmental quiescence. This dubious status of the latency stage is reflected in the fact that it has no character type associated with it. Therefore, we will not concern ourselves with the latency period. It should not have escaped your notice that the psychosexual stages refer exclusively to the sexual instinct. What about the survival and death instincts? Are there developmental stages, and character types, associated with them? There are no developmental stages, and while some psychoanalysts have made attempts to designate relevant character types, there are not widely accepted and are often fragmentary and confusing in nature. The general state of affairs reflects the overwhelming importance, in Freudian thinking, of the sexual instinct. It is not at all inappropriate to say that the Freudian theory of personality hinges on sexuality as the basic human nature.

The oral, anal, phallic, and genital stages of development roughly cover, respectively, the first year of life, the second year, the third through fifth years, and the years from puberty onward. Obviously, one must go through the first three stages in order to reach the fourth. If the first three stages are successfully traversed, genitality is vigorously and fully entered upon. But if any of the developmental experiences in one or more of the three pregenital stages are destructive, then that stage or stages will have a lingering effect on later behavior. It is in order to indicate this lingering effect on the adult that three of the character types are named *oral, anal* and *phallic*. And, of course, the fourth character type is named *genital*. The fourth represents psychological maturity, whereas the other three represent different qualities of immaturity. To be more descriptive, each of the pregenital stages entails a particular form of childish sexual wish and impulse. In order for successful progress through that stage, the child must receive from parents and the world enough gratification so as not to feel hopelessly deprived and frustrated, and not so much gratification that it becomes too pleasant to remain in that particular phase of immaturity. If the child is either too frustrated or too indulged, he becomes *fixated* or stuck at that particular level of development. This means that in adulthood, he will show traits —thoughts, emotions, actions—characteristic of the particular conflict, defenses, or parental reactions defining that pregenital stage.

Now we are in position to examine the content of the various psychosexual stages of development. Starting at the beginning we find the *oral stage*, in which the anatomical location of the sexual instinct is the mouth. According to Freud, the development of the nervous system proceeds from the brain downward and outward, ensuring that the mouth region will be the first body orifice suited to the experience of pleasure and pain. To be sure, the survival instincts for food and water also ensure that the mouth shall be an important region in the experience of the organism. But Freud's emphasis is more upon the mouth as a tactually and gustatorily erotic area. In other words, the child is presumed to crave and enjoy stimulation of the mouth region through touch and taste and use of muscle. The craving and enjoyment are early forms of what will finally become mature sexuality in the genital stage

In order to understand the *oral character type*, you must recognize that the oral form of the sexual instinct leads to actions and fantasies involved in *taking* and *receiving*, and that, therefore, the conflicts salient at the oral stage are those precipitated by these selfish activities. (Fenichel, 1945, pp. 488–492). Freudians consider taking and receiving to be generalizations of the mouth activities of the first year of life. Receiving is the generalization of the earliest, passive (*oral incorporative*) situation in which the mouth is pleasurably stimulated by people and things in the process of being fed and caressed. Taking is the generalization of the slightly later, somewhat less-passive (*oral aggressive*) situation in which the child contrives to gain his own oral satisfaction through sucking, putting things in his mouth, chewing, biting, and even vocalizing.

There is, of course, an inevitable conflict between the child's unmitigated, selfish wish to receive and take, and the parents' own needs and duties, which do not permit unlimited time and attention to their offspring. The best that can happen is that the parents provide a modicum of instinctual satisfaction for their child. If they fall short of this modicum, by severely punishing the child for his need to receive and take, or by simply not having enough nurturance within them to make any difference, the inevitable conflict will be greatly intensified. This intensification will require especially strong and pervasive defenses, the employment of which are tantamount to a fixation, or arresting of growth. Once such defenses are instituted, change and development are impaired. The parents can also exceed the modicum of oral gratification by trying to be more nurturant than is consistent with their own needs and duties. This deviation from the ideal also leads to an intensification of the inevitable conflict because the nurturance will be only superficially satisfying, but will actually carry with it such resentment, and have so many strings attached, as to be counterfeit. Again the child will be frustrated and in pain, and have to institute defenses of such intensity and pervasiveness as to constitute fixation.

Having described how conflict is intensified, leading to oral fixation, it would be theoretically satisfying now to be able to present an exhaustive list of defenses and traits constituting the oral character. Unfortunately, psychoanalytic thinking is not that neat, although Abraham (1927a, 1927b) and Glover (1925, 1926, 1928) have made some beginnings. One can interpret their remarks to indicate that some traits recurring frequently in the oral character are *optimism-pessimism, gullibility-suspiciousness, manipulativeness-passivity, admiration-envy,* and *cockiness-self-belittlement.* It is common for Freudians to think in terms of traits having two opposing extremes, so-called *bipolar traits.* Both poles are considered to indicate fixation. It is tempting to think that one pole of the dimension expresses the fixation due to over-indulgence (e.g., optimism) whereas the other expresses the fixation of deprivation (e.g., pessimism). But it is difficult to determine how con-sistent such usage is with Freudian intent, as some Freudians suggest that people vacillate from one pole of a dimension to the other, now being optimistic, now pessimistic. In any event, the bipolar traits refer fairly directly to attitudes, initiated in the course of interacting on the oral level with the parents, concerning whether the world is a satisfying or depriving place, and whether or not you are capable of helping your-self to satisfaction. Optimism, pessimism and admiration are unrealistic estimates of the likelihood of being nurtured by other people. In manipulativeness and passivity, we see unconstructive tendencies to wrest satisfaction from the world or lie back and wait until it falls into one's mouth. Cockiness indicates an unrealistically affluent sense of one's own resources, whereas envy and self-belittlement indicate quite the opposite. The unrealistic quality of all these extremes is an indication of their defensive nature.

Having described some traits of the oral character, and having indi-cated their unrealistic nature, it would be theoretically satisfying to be able to list the defenses typical of the oral stage that find expression in these traits. But, as before, I must say that psychoanalytic thinking is un-fortunately not that neat, though a few beginnings can be considered. The defenses most usually mentioned as part of the oral character are *projection, denial,* and *introjection.* Projection is the process of being unaware of wishes, feelings, and impulses in oneself that might provoke punishment and guilt, and simultaneously misperceiving other people as having these same wishes, feelings, and impulses. Denial is the simpler process of not being aware of the presence of things, people, or events in the external world that could arouse anxiety either by provoking selfish instincts or signaling impending punishment. Finally, introjection is the process of incorporating another person—virtually be-coming that person—in order to either avoid the person's threatening nature, or avoid the threatening nature of one's own instincts. All three defenses are rather unsophisticated, and quite debilitating in that they grossly distort reality. Denial is the main determinant of optimism and pessimism, involving as they do attention to only some aspects of the world. Gullibility can also be attributed to the action of denial. Although denial may have some function in suspicion, this characteristic is more clearly an expression of projection, by attributing to others all those nasty manipulative and stingy tendencies that one fails to see in oneself. Manipulativeness and overgenerosity are most likely expressive of introjection, or the incorporation of overindulgent parents. The other traits can be explained as expressions of almost any of the three defenses.

Happily enough, we can be even more precise theoretically concerning the *anal stage and character* than was true above. The anal stage is marked by the shift in anatomical location of the sexual instinct from the mouth to the anal orifice. This shift is brought about, according to Freud, by the joint impact of nervous system development to the point where voluntary control of the anal sphincters is possible, and of intensified parental attempts to encourage excretory continence in the child. The child, for the first time, experiences the pleasurable and painful stimulation associated with eliminating and retaining feces, and begins to experiment with manipulating this stimulation through consciously eliminating and retaining.

To fully apprehend the anal character type, you should recognize that the anal form of the sexual instinct included actions and fantasies involved in *giving* and *withholding*. Giving and withholding are to be understood as generalizations of the anal activities of the second year of life. Giving (*anal expulsiveness*) is the generalization of the voluntarily controlled voiding of the bowels, and withholding (*anal retentiveness*) is the generalization of the voluntary decision not to void the bowels. Both activities are inherently pleasurable but also bring the child into inevitable conflict with his parents, who require that the giving and withholding be done according to schedule and propriety. Again, the best that can happen is that the parents permit a modicum of anal gratification, while still upholding the societally important rules of cleanliness and hygiene. If the parents are too punitive, and too disgusted at the child's messing, the inevitable conflict is greatly intensified. The conflict is also intensified if the parents are too indulgent, more indulgent than they can be for the child's own social and hygienic good, and for their own proprieties. As in oral overindulgence, anal overindulgence is really counterfeit. With the intensification of conflict come the extreme and pervasive defenses constituting fixation. This arresting of growth means that the adult personality will be anal in nature.

The traits and defenses of the anal character have been fairly precisely specified, both by Freud (1925a, 1925c, 1925d, 1925e) and others (e.g., Abraham, 1927c; Fenichel, 1945, pp. 278–84; Glover, 1926). Among the traits are *stinginess-overgenerosity, constrictedness-expansiveness, stubbornness-acquiescence, orderliness-messiness, rigid punctuality-tardiness, meticulousness-dirtiness,* and *precision-vagueness.* These traits express in thought process, interaction, and the general conductance of life, various concrete forms of the impulses to give and withhold, and the conflicts surrounding them, so characteristic of the anal stage of psychosexual development. As in the oral character, these anal traits show an unrealistic orientation at both poles. And, this unrealistic orientation is a sign of the defensive nature of the traits. The defenses considered characteristic of the anal stage and character are *intellectualization, reaction formation, isolation,* and *undoing.* In intellectualization, the person loses consciousness of the real, instinctual significance of his wishes and actions, and substitutes instead a fictitious reason that is much more acceptable to him and to society. The reasoning processes seemingly involved amount to rationalizations only. Reaction formation is the process of becoming unaware of your true wishes and impulses, and substituting instead awareness of the directly opposite wishes and impulses. In isolation, the connecting links normally present between the cognitive and affective components of wishes and impulses is severed, so that while something of the true nature of the wishes and impulses remains in consciousness, they no longer seem the source of unpleasant emotions, such as anxiety. Undoing is a defense whereby certain thoughts and actions take place with the true, but unrecognized significance of canceling out, or atoning for, other previous thoughts and actions of an anxiety-provoking nature.

While it is not possible to explicate precisely and exhaustively just how these defenses give rise to the traits of the anal character, some discussion along these lines is possible. Reaction formation leads to the renunciation of such socially unacceptable things as messiness, tardiness, and stinginess, and the assertion of yourself as quite the opposite, as meticulously clean, painfully punctual, and incredibly generous. This defense leads to the saintly qualities displayed by the anal character. These saintly qualities, plus such other characteristics as precision and stubbornness, are strengthened in their status as what the person considers true of himself by the operation of the intellectualization defense. It is the reliance upon isolation as well as the other defenses that permits glaring examples of the opposite of the saintly qualities, such things as messiness, and dirtiness, to be clearly shown in the person's behavior without constituting any particular source of discomfort and anxiety. Finally, the action of undoing is seen not only in such direct characteristics as orderliness, implying symmetry and organization, but also indirectly in the sometimes rapid shift from one pole to the other of the various traits mentioned above. You can avoid intense discomfort at an act of messiness if you can quickly atone for it with an extraordinary act of orderliness.

For vividness, I will close discussion of the anal character type with a striking description from the psychoanalytic literature (Rado, 1959, p. 326):

> A rough sketch . . . would depict him as highly opinionated and proud of his superior intelligence, avowed rationality, keen sense of reality, and "unswerving integrity." He may indeed be an honest man, but he may also turn out to be a sanctimonious hypocrite. He is the ultimate perfectionist. While very sensitive to his own hurt, he may, at the same time, be destructively critical, spiteful, vindictive and given to bitter

irony and to bearing grudges in trivial matters. Or, on the contrary, he may be overcautious, bent on avoiding any possibility of conflict. His "common sense" militates against what he views as fancies of the imagination: he is a "man of facts," not of fancies. He smiles condescendingly at people who are fascinated by mysticism, including "the unconscious" and dreams, but let him undergo some psychoanalytic treatment of the classical type, and he will switch to attributing oracular significance to slips of the tongue or the pen. As a "man of reason" he cannot admit even to himself that he is superstitious. His interest in fine arts is slight or pretended; his true admiration is reserved for mathematics, the exact sciences, technology, the new world of electronic computing machines. In contrast to the expressional, so-called hysterical type, he rarely has artistic gifts and conspicuously lacks genuine charm and grace. His amatory interests are laden with ulterior motivations and pretense.

This lucid, if somewhat impressionistic, description makes perfectly clear what a person with the kind of traits and defenses mentioned earlier would be like to encounter. The extremes of behavior depicted, and the pejorative language employed, make clear the presumed unconstructive, immature nature of the anal character.

Now let us consider the *phallic stage*, which is the last of the so-called pregenital, or immature, stages of psychosexual development. This stage is presumably brought about by the shift in anatomical location of the sexual instinct from the anus to the genitalia, though how this is to be explained in terms of nervous system development when the two regions are so close to each other remains one of the many obscurities in psychoanalytic thinking. Recognizing, then, that the anatomical basis for distinguishing an anal from a phallic stage is virtually absent, let us nonetheless consider a more general psychosocial basis for the distinction. By the time the child has reached the third year of life he begins to explore his body more systematically, and is also more alert to the bodies of others. That the genitalia become a major source of pleasure and pain for the first time is an assumption based on the observed increase in self-manipulation, or masturbation, in the manipulation and exploration of the genitalia of other boys and girls, and in the initiation of fantasies that have a frankly heterosexual quality. The child talks of marrying the opposite-sexed parent and of displacing the same-sexed parent. He talks of being a father or a mother. As you all must know, the phallic stage is the time of the Oedipal conflict, a thing of overwhelming importance in Freudian theory.

The key to understanding the *phallic character type* is recognition that this final pregenital form of the sexual instinct involves thoughts and actions concerning *the body as a frankly sexual thing* and *interaction between people as heterosexual* in nature. If the child's unabashed craving for stimulation of his genitals and for genitalized contact with parents and others is severely frustrated, out of the parents' own embarrassments, fears and secret fantasies, then the child will experience intense conflict. He will also experience intense conflict if his cravings seem to be overindulged, for the encouragement to replace the like-sexed parent in the opposite-sexed parent's affections inevitably runs afoul of the societal taboo against incest. Fixation is the result of both deprivation and overindulgence of craving for genital stimulation and genitalized relationships. As in the case of the oral and anal stages, some conflict is inevitable in the phallic stage, even if the parents give a modicum of satisfaction to the child. The inevitability of conflict is seen in that although the child must obtain enough gratification of genital cravings to develop a sense of himself as a worthwhile sexual being, he must also give up his selfish interest in the opposite-sexed parent as the object of his sexuality. As he gives up his interest in the opposite-sexed parent, he begins to long to be an adult (Freudians talk of this as a specialized part of the superego called the *ego-ideal*). But when the inevitable conflict is intensified by over- or underindulgence, the child experiences anxiety that takes the form of concern not only that he will lose the affections of the opposite-sexed parent but also that the same-sexed parent will retaliate for the competition by damaging the child's genitalia. The latter fear, so-called *castration anxiety,* and the former fear, so-called *separation anxiety,* both play an extraordinarily important role in Freudian thinking. Freud meant them very literally, although it has been common among later psychoanalysts to generalize their meaning.

The traits and defensive patterns of the phallic character have been described in detail by Reich (1931, 1933) and others (e.g., Abraham, 1927d). Among the traits are *vanity–self-hatred, pride-humility, blind courage-timidity, brashness-bashfulness, gregariousness-isolation, stylish-ness-plainness, flirtatiousness-avoidance of heterosexuality, chastity-promiscuity,* and *gaiety-sadness.* These traits are present in some degree in people with the phallic character, and represent either the genital craving directly, or the curtailment of the cravings due to fear of separation or castration. Some of the trait poles, such as blind courage and promiscuity, represent acting on the cravings in the face of the fears mentioned above. In general, the major defense underlying the phallic traits is *repression,* or the process of remaining unaware of the instinctual wishes and actions in order that anxiety not be experienced. While the superficiality involved in some of the poles of some phallic traits may well be understandable as the result of massive repression, it must be said that it is quite difficult to imagine how the complex traits mentioned above could all result from that one defense mechanism. But you should recognize that once the person has progressed to the phallic stage of development, he also has available to him the defenses of the earlier stages through which he has already gone. And it is similarly true of people in the anal stage that they have the defenses more typical of the oral stage available to them. There is no difficulty at all in understanding how the traits of the phallic character can come about if they can be considered expressive of not only repression but other defenses as well. But that the phallic, or for that matter the anal and oral, traits have the content they do can be traced to the form of psychosexual conflict dominant in that stage of development.

Putting the information of the last paragraph together into a concrete description of someone with a phallic character would go something like this: The person is preoccupied with his own beauty and extraordinariness, needing constant recognition of this on the part of others in order to feel comfortable. If he gets this support, and appreciation, he may well be delightful, interesting, provocative, spontaneous, and dramatic. If he is not greatly appreciated and sought after, he may slip into black thoughts of his worthlessness, ugliness, and incompetence, appearing to be a pale shadow of his other side. In general, he seeks the company of people of the opposite sex, enjoys enticing them and receiving their appreciation, but shies away from vigorous, deep, committed sexual relationships. In the male, the phallic character is either effeminate, or masculine in an obvious and inflexible way. The phallic character in a woman renders her an exaggeration of femininity—a Southern Belle, if you will. She may be chaste or promiscuous, but if promiscuous, will nonetheless give the impression of naïveté, childishness, and inner purity.

You have probably been wondering whether oral, anal, and phallic characters are to be considered psychopathological (mentally ill). They are not to be so considered, even though they do represent immaturity. That they are immature ways of being means that they carry the seeds of, or vulnerabilities to, psychopathology. But, in order for psychopathology to ensue, the person with a pregenital character structure must encounter environmental stress of sufficiently debilitating content and intensity to undermine him. Psychopathology is a breakdown of pregenital character structure. It is true that the nature of the pregenital character is considered a determinant of the nature of the psychopathological state. So, the breakdown of the oral character frequently leads to schizophrenia, and the breakdown of anal character leads to the obsessive-compulsive neurosis. Breakdown of the phallic character often leads to hysteria in women and homosexuality or perversion in men. This is not a book on psychopathology, and hence we cannot pursue these considerations further. They are important here simply to underline the fact that character types are not psychopathological states, even though the pregenital ones represent developmental immaturities.

All this brings us to the *genital stage* and *character,* representing as they do the pinnacle of development and maturity, according to Freudians. Although the genital stage is considered a true psychosexual stage, it is not easily distinguished from others on the basis of anatomical location of the sexual instinct, the relevant location being the same as for the phallic stage. But Freudians do point to the complete maturation of the sexual system, such that orgasm, ejaculation, and pregnancy become possible. Indeed, orgasm is considered to be the hallmark of satisfaction. But orgasm is combined with the erotic pleasures of the pregenital stages, yielding full adult expression of the sexual instinct. Although reaching the genital stage without any existing fixations at lower stages of development is the ideal condition, according to Freudians, this does not mean that genital functioning is free of conflict and nondefensive in nature. The person must still subscribe to societal sanctions and taboos in the expression of the sexual instinct, and hence there is conflict. But the conflict in minimal, and can therefore be resolved by that at once most mature and least rigidifying of defensive processes, *sublimation.* Sublimation involves changing the object of the sexual instinct such that it is more socially acceptable than the original or most obvious one, but in no other way disrupting or blocking the expression of the instinct. Of all the defenses, sublimation involves the least damming up of the libido, or energy, which is straining for expression. So instead of pursuing mother, as the boy is wont to do in the phallic stage, he pursues other females outside of the family, and in pursuing them accepts society's set of responsibilities and rules concerning heterosexual relationships. That all love is for Freud (1938) essentially "on the rebound" (the child having to give up his original attraction to the opposite-sexed parent), demonstrates once again the compromise nature of even ideal personality.

Although sublimation is clearly the defense associated with the genital character, it is difficult to specify any list of relevant traits. It is difficult because trait names of the genital character might sound too much like others already mentioned as pregenital to effectively convey what Freudians mean. What they mean is that the genital person is fully potent and capable in whatever he does. He is fully socialized, adjusted, and yet does not suffer greatly from this. He is courageous without the driven recklessness of the phallic character. He is satisfied with himself without the overweening pride and vanity of the phallic character. He loves heterosexually without the alarming neediness and dependence of the oral character. He works diligently and effectively without the compulsivity and competitiveness of the anal character. He is altruistic and generous without the sickening saintliness of the anal character. In short, he maximizes instinctual gratification while minimizing punishment and guilt.

As I have said many times before, one cannot help but be struck by the extraordinary emphasis given to sexuality by Freud. Nowhere is this more apparent than in the treatment of the character types, or peripheral characteristics of personality. It becomes perfectly clear that even the obvious differences between people are determined by various facets of the sexual instinct and attendant conflicts. Freudian thinking has often been criticized for its single-minded sexual emphasis. Although the criticisms seem cogent, we must recognize that they are made by modern persons, in societies grossly different from that in which Freud worked at the turn of the 20th century. In his day, enlightenment thought had gone peculiarly arid, with the result that it was not generally conceded that sexuality played an important natural part in living. The sexual act was for reproduction, not pleasure, and partial expressions of sexuality and sexual interest before physiological adulthood were not regarded as natural at all. It was an extraordinarily pristine atmosphere, an atmosphere in which Freudian thinking must have been a much needed if explosive corrective. In order to give you the full impact of this arid thinking, lest you doubt the picture I have painted, I will quote from an authoritative book, published in 1901, entitled *Maiden, Wife, and Mother: How to Attain Health, Beauty, Happiness*. This handbook is by Mary R. Melendy (1901), who was both an M.D. and a Ph.D., with seven or eight distinguished titles to her credit. In a chapter on being a good mother to boys, Melendy writes:

> Teach him that these [sexual] organs are given as a sacred trust, that in maturer years he may be the means of giving life to those who shall live forever.
>
> Impress upon him that if these organs are abused, or if they are put to any use besides that for which God made them—and He did not intend they should be used at all until man is fully grown—they will bring disease and ruin upon those who abuse and disobey those laws which God has made to govern them.
>
> If he has ever learned to handle his sexual organs, or to touch them in any way except to keep them clean, not to do it again. If he does, he will not grow up happy, healthy, and strong.
>
> Teach him that when he handles or excites the sexual organs, all parts of the body suffer, because they are connected by nerves that run throughout the system, this is why it is called "self-abuse." The whole body is abused when this part of the body is handled or excited in any manner whatever.
>
> Teach them to shun all children who indulge in this loathsome habit, or all children who talk about these things. The sin is terrible, and is, in fact, worse than lying or stealing! For although these are wicked and will ruin their soul, yet this habit of self-abuse will ruin both soul and body.
>
> If the sexual organs are handled it brings too much blood to these parts, and this produces a diseased condition; it also causes disease in other organs of the body, because they are left with a less amount of blood than they ought to have. The sexual organs, too, are very closely connected with the spine and the brain by means of the nerves, and if they are handled, or if you keep thinking about them, these nerves get excited and become exhausted, and this makes the back ache, the brain heavy and the whole body weak.
>
> It lays the foundation for consumption, paralysis and heart disease. It weakens the memory, makes a boy careless, negligent and listless.

It even makes many lose their minds; others, when grown, commit suicide.

How often mothers see their little boys handling themselves, and let it pass, because they think the boy will outgrow the habit, and do not realize the strong hold it has upon them! I say to you, who love your boys —"Watch!"

Don't think it does no harm to your boy because he does not suffer now, for the effects of this vice come on so slowly that the victim is often very near death before you realize that he has done himself harm.

The boy with no knowledge of the consequences, and with no one to warn him, finds momentary pleasure in its practice, and so contracts a habit which grows on him, undermining his health, poisoning his mind, arresting his development, and laying the foundation for future misery.

Do not read this book and forget it, for it contains earnest and living truths. Do not let false modesty stand in your way, but from this time on keep this thought in mind—"the saving of your boy." Follow its teachings and you will bless God as long as you live. Read it to your neighbors, who, like yourself, have growing boys, and urge them, for the sake of humanity, to heed its advice.

Right here I want to relate a fact that came under my observation. In our immediate neighborhood lived an intelligent, good and sensible couple. They had a boy about five years of age who was growing fretful, pale and puny. After trying all other remedies to restore him to vigor of body and mind, they journeyed from place to place hoping to leave the offending cause behind.

I had often suggested to the mother that "self-abuse" might be the cause, but no, she would not have it so, and said, "You must be mistaken, as he has inherited no such tendencies nor has he been taught it by playmates—we have guarded him carefully."

Finally, however, she took up a medical book and made a study of it and, after much thought, said, "I cannot believe it, yet it describes Charlie's case exactly. I will watch."

To her surprise, she found notwithstanding all her convictions to the contrary, that Charlie was a victim to this loathsome habit.

On going to his bed, after he had gone to sleep, she found his hands still upon the organ, just as they were when he fell asleep. She watched this carefully for a few days, then took him in her confidence and told him of the dreadful evil effects. Finding the habit so firmly fixed, she feared that telling him, at his age, what effect it would have upon his future would not eradicate the evil as soon as she hoped so, after studying the case for a time, she hit upon the following remedy. Although unscientific, literally speaking, it had the desired effect. Feeling that something must be done to stop, and stop at once, the awful habit, she said, "Did you know, Charlie, that if you keep up this habit of 'self-abuse' that a brown spot will come on your abdomen, light brown at first, and grow darker each week until it eats a sore right into your system, and if it keeps on, will eventually kill you?"

After Charlie had gone to sleep, and finding his hands again on the sexual organs, to prove to him the truth of her argument, she took a bottle of "Iodine" and, with the cork, put on the abdomen a quantity sufficient to give it a light brown color, and about the size of a pea. Next night, in bathing him, she discovered the spot, and said, "Look! Already it has come!" The boy cried out in very fear, and promised not to repeat it again.

The next night the mother put on a second application, which made the spot still darker and a trifle sore. Charlie watched the spot as he would a reptile that was lurking about to do his deadly work—and the mother was never again obliged to use the "Iodine."

You must remember that this harrowing excerpt is evidence of the nature of educated and sophisticated thought at the turn of the century. If Freud is right, how exacerbated would have been Charlie's Oedipal conflict! And, of course, one can find accounts in the same book concerning the evils of "self-abuse" in girls, and in general, a moralistic, punitive attitude concerning bowel training, and a depriving, rigidly regulated approach to early feeding. It is on this scene that Freud arrived to preach the naturalness of pregenital sexual cravings and actions, and the evils of excessive punitiveness and deprivation on the part of parents. Perhaps it is no wonder that his theory is so preoccupied with sexuality, when the times in which he found himself had so denied eroticism. But, especially if you feel convinced by what I have said, you must face the implications of the difference between modern times and Freud's day. In a real way, we have learned the lessons Freud taught. We accept and are constructive toward pregenital and genital sexuality to a degree that would have gladdened his heart. Indeed, we have changed so much that Freud's emphasis on sexuality seems almost to sidetrack us from the most important concerns of contemporary life.

Freud's extreme emphasis upon sexuality has seemed so unnecessary in our day that many personologists have begun developing the notion that he must have really meant general pleasure seeking. They contend that he used sex as nothing more than a metaphor for pleasure seeking. This interpretation clearly cannot be accurate to Freud's intent, for he is very explicit about his emphasis upon sexuality per se. After all, he did choose to distinguish the sexual instinct from other pleasure-oriented instincts. And he did name all of development psychosexual, not psychopleasurable. If further evidence of his intent were needed, one could point to his having disbarred certain psychoanalysts from his inner circle because they watered down the literal sexual message of his theory, thereby rendering it more palatable to nonbelievers (Jones, 1955). Substituting pleasure seeking for literal sexuality may make Freud's formulations more relevant to the problems of modern persons, but it does not illuminate the theorist's real intent.

Murray's position

Murray's major concrete peripheral characteristic is the *need*. Needs are motivational in nature, that is, they are tendencies to move in the direction of goals. But they are not like the Freudian instincts, which are also motivational in nature, because needs are largely learned, and involve goals and actions more concrete and close to everyday life than do the instincts. Given this concrete quality of goal definition, it should not surprise you to know that Murray postulates a large number of needs. Murray has in mind such needs as those for affiliation, achievement, power, succorance, and play. Even when Murray mentions the need for sex, it is clear that he refers to the narrow meaning that most people would endorse, namely, the attempt to achieve the goal of intercourse. Indeed, Murray's concept of needs is functionally closer to the Freudian concept of trait than to that of instinct. Different needs may be represented in different people, and hence, need analysis is useful in pinpointing individuality.

Since needs stand at the same level of personality analysis as do the Freudian traits, we might expect Murray to provide a scheme whereby needs are organized into psychologically meaningful patterns, such as the Freudian character types. Sure enough, Murray does talk of the oral, anal, phallic and genital types we have already discussed, and even adds to these the *claustral* and *urethral types* (Murray, 1938). The claustral type, or, as Murray prefers to call it, *complex*, stems from fixation during intrauterine life, and refers to a set of characteristics amounting to amorphousness and extreme passivity. The urethral complex, also talked about by some theorists more closely associated with Freud, involves fixation during the time when urinating actively and passively is a great source of pleasure, and refers to competitiveness, ambition, self-worship, and feelings of omnipotence. But nowhere in Murray's writings is it clear that he intends to use the six complexes or types as categories for subsuming or classifying the various needs he has delineated.

As you will recall, Murray, being basically a psychoanalytic thinker, also uses the concepts of id, ego, and superego. These three aspects of personality exist in all men, and hence, they should be considered part of the core of personality. But, as you will also recall, Murray has changed the meaning of all three concepts from that favored by Freud. Even more than in Freud, the content of superego and ego may differ from person to person, and hence, these contents are for Murray peripheral aspects of personality. In contrast to Freud, Murray finds the id also to vary in content from person to person. The id for Murray is not one unchanging set of instincts, but rather, the repository of any and all motivations, presumably even the needs I mentioned above. Hence, the id contents are in Murray also peripheral aspects of personality. But if contents of id, ego, and superego are peripheral, what are the characteristics of the core? Core characteristics become, for Murray, very abstract and contentless. They are the incessant motivatedness of the person, and his equally incessant attempts to reach his goals within the restrictions of his environment and his values and principles.

These conclusions suggest that Murray's needs are to be considered the content characteristics of the id, whereas you will recall that Freudian traits were considered content characteristics of the ego. But needs are not innate, according to Murray, and hence do not fit neatly into the meaning of the id, which meaning he at least partially endorses. Needs are too motivational in character to be considered the content of the superego. This leaves the ego, but the fit is no better here, as he (Murray & Kluckhohn, 1956, p. 26) has assumed the ego to be constituted of an elaborate set of functions. These functions are really *abilities* in the perceptual, apperceptual, intellectual, and affective realms of experience. To complicate matters even further, although his emphasis would seem to imply that the ego is to be considered a set of abilities, rather than the specific, learned, habitual styles of coping that constitute needs, Murray does at one point in his writing (Murray & Kluckhohn, 1956, p. 31) suggest in true psychoanalytic fashion that the general system of learned needs may well be part of the ego.

Elsewhere, I have discussed these complications and ambiguities at greater length than is possible here (Maddi, 1963). For present purposes it is enough to recognize that the question of the nature of the relationship between core and peripheral characteristics of personality is an important consideration in understanding a theory fully, and that Murray has not yet achieved a clear statement of his view of this relationship. A reasonable lead, which does not seem inconsistent with his general intent, would be to consider learned needs to be personality units that are formed out of the interaction between the core tendency of maximizing instinctual gratification while minimizing punishment and guilt, and the specific environmental contexts encountered in living. The learned needs would then exist as a more changeable, less-central, though more immediately expressed layer of personality. In such a scheme, id, ego, and superego would be different from needs, and indeed, would play, along with environmental contexts, a causal role in the development of needs. Adopting such a scheme would also be useful to more traditional psychoanalytic thinking, for the subsumption of traits into the ego is a dubious theoretical step, given the otherwise consistent emphasis upon the ego as a set of abilities or functions. The emphasis on ego as functions is actually as strong in psychoanalytic thinking as it is in Murray, regardless of the fact that Murray does not see all of these functions as defensive in nature. If Freudians adopted my suggestion, then character types would be considered a peripheral layer of personality that is more immediately expressed and more changeable than is the core level.

Actually, Murray's major contribution to personology has been his taxonomy of needs and his extensive and continuing attempts to collect systematic empirical evidence bearing on it. He is quite rare in his emphasis upon the careful delineation and study of concrete peripheral characteristics. It is worth our while, therefore, to dwell longer on the concept of need and its measurement. According to Murray (1938, pp. 123–124), the *need* is

> a construct (a convenient fiction or hypothetical concept) which stands for a force . . . in the brain region, a force which organizes perception, apperception, intellection, conation and action in such a way as to transform in a certain direction an existing, unsatisfying situation. A need is sometimes provoked directly by internal processes of a certain kind . . . but, more frequently (when in a state of readiness) by the occurrence of one of a few commonly effective press.

The way in which needs affect functioning is to produce perceptions, interpretations, feelings, and actions that are equivalent in terms of meaning or purpose. In order to diagnose a particular need as present in a person, you must observe equivalences of meaning in his (1) initiating or reacting inner state, (2) perception of the external situation, (3) imagined goal or aim, (4) directionality of concomitant movements and words, and (5) produced effect, if any (Murray, 1954, pp. 456–463). Take as an example the need for affiliation. The inner state may be specific cognitive and affective conditions best described as loneliness. This loneliness may be initiating in the sense that it exists regardless of whether the actual environmental circumstances are so affiliatively depriving. Or it may be reacting, in the sense that it must be aroused by affiliatively depriving circumstances. Regardless of whether the circumstances are or are not depriving, they must be perceived by the person as being so. The person must have as an imaginary goal a state of close and warm interaction with people. In addition, his plans, activities, and statements about what he is doing ought to show a consistent direction leading to closer contact with people. And, finally, if any effects follow from his actions, they ought to be those consistent with his goals and aims. When all these things are present, one can be sure that the person has a need for affiliation. In general, needs are not perceived as steady states. They are aroused by real or imagined deprivation. When aroused, they exist as tension states leading to instrumental behavior, which, if successful, brings about the goal state. Experience of the goal state brings satiation and a reduction in tension. A necessary concomitant of choosing the need construct as the basic peripheral characteristic is an emphasis upon the waxing and waning of directional behaviors.

Over the years, Murray has experimented with a number of apparently overlapping classifications of types and qualities of needs. But unlike the Freudian character types, Murray's classificatory schemes do not tie groups of needs together into consistent and recognizable kinds of people. Instead Murray's aim is to provide schemes for understanding the various kinds of needs that are possible. One of his classifications takes into account the degree to which the person's aim in his activity is intrinsic or extrinsic to the form of that activity. This leads to the distinction between *activity needs* and *effect needs*. Activity needs, or tendencies to "engage in a certain kind of activity for its own sake" (Murray, 1954, p. 445), are subdivided into *process needs*, involving performance, action, for the sheer pleasure to be derived from the exercise of available functions, and *mode needs*, which are satisfied by the excellence of activity rather than its mere occurrence (Murray, 1954, p. 446). It is significant that Murray is one of the few personologists to make a concrete attempt to conceptualize activity that occurs for its own sake. In contrast, effect needs are marked by attempts to bring about a particular desired effect or goal which is extrinsic to the activity engaged in, that activity serving a purely instrumental purpose (Murray & Kluckhohn, 1956, p. 15).

Another classificatory attempt seems to emphasize the origin of the need, and hence, the particular direction of activity that it imposes. In this attempt, *mental, viscerogenic*, and *sociorelational needs* are distinguished (Murray, 1954, pp. 445–452; Murray & Kluckhohn, 1956, pp. 13–21). The well-known viscerogenic needs (e.g., need for food) stem from tissue requirements and have very specific, easily recognizable goals. The mental needs are usually overlooked; they stem from the fact that "the human mind is inherently a transforming, creating, and representing organ; its function is to make symbols for things, to combine and recombine these symbols incessantly, and communicate the most interesting of these combinations in a variety of languages, discursive (referential, scientific) and expressive (emotive, artistic)" (Murray & Kluckhohn, 1956, p. 16). As the viscera have certain requirements, so too does the mind, and both sets of requirements stem from human nature. Mental needs do not have very specific goal states. Sociorelational needs arise from the inherently social nature of man (Murray, 1959, pp. 45–57) and include such specific dispositions as the *need for roleship*, the need "to become and to remain an accepted and respected, differentiated and integrated part of a congenial, functioning group, the collective purposes of which are congruent with the individual's ideals" (Murray, 1954, pp. 451–452). As described, the need for roleship seems to imply particular learning produced by the individual's experiences against the ever present background of his inherent sociorelational nature.

You must be getting the impression by now that the discussion of the core of personality according to Murray that was presented in Chapter 2 is a lot simpler and more psychoanalytic in flavor than the kinds of assumptions about human nature involved in this and other need classifications he has offered. Your impression is a true one. It is as if Murray transcended the narrow, sexually oriented conflict model, precisely when he turned to describing and organizing the needs apparent in people at the level of the behavior one immediately sees in their living. But though he transcended the Freudian model, Murray has never actually come to terms with the implications of having done so. This has lead to the rather chaotic quality of Murray's writings looked at from the point of view of formal personality theory. Assuming, in describing sociorelational needs, that human nature is inherently gregarious has implications contrary to the Freudian conflict model as we have described it. And yet, Murray nowhere discusses this complication. His is a mind in transition, resulting in theoretical writings that seem fragmentary, though provocative and intriguing. We will see a similar problem in the so-called ego psychologists.

In another discussion of need classification, Murray (1954, pp. 445–452) includes two additional types of needs that presumably cut across the mental, viscerogenic, and sociorelational, and seem to emphasize approach and avoidance tendencies. These are *creative needs*, which aim at the construction of new and useful thoughts and objects, and *negative needs*, which aim at the avoidance or termination of unpleasant, noxious conditions. Finally, his earliest and most famous taxonomy (Murray, 1938, pp. 152–226) distinguishes what are primarily effect needs, of a mental, viscerogenic, and sociogenic variety, on the basis of a much more fine-grained consideration of goals. These needs (Murray, 1938, pp. 152–226) appear below:

TABLE 6–1
List of needs for Murray

Need	*Definition*
n Abasement	To submit passively to external force. To accept injury, blame, criticism, punishment. To surrender. To become resigned to fate. To admit inferiority, error, wrongdoing, or defeat. To confess and atone. To blame, belittle, or mutilate the self. To seek and enjoy pain, punishment, illness, and misfortune.
n Achievement	To accomplish something difficult. To master, manipulate, or organize physical objects, human beings, or ideas. To do this as rapidly and as independently as possible. To overcome obstacles and attain a high standard. To excel oneself. To rival and surpass others. To increase self-regard by the successful exercise of talent.
n Affiliation	To draw near and enjoyably cooperate or reciprocate with an allied other (another who resembles the subject or who likes the subject). To please and win affection of a cathected object. To adhere and remain loyal to a friend.
n Aggression	To overcome opposition forcefully. To fight. To revenge an injury. To attack, injure, or kill another. To oppose forcefully or punish another.
n Autonomy	To get free, shake off restraint, break out of confinement. To resist coercion and restriction. To avoid or quit activities prescribed by domineering authorities. To be independent and free to act according to impulse. To be unattached, irresponsible. To defy convention.

TABLE 6-1—*Continued*

Need	*Definition*
n Counteraction	To master or make up for a failure by restriving. To obliterate a humiliation by resumed action. To overcome weaknesses, to repress fear. To efface a dishonor by action. To search for obstacles and difficulties to overcome. To maintain self-respect and pride on a high level.
n Defendance	To defend the self against assault, criticism, and blame. To conceal or justify a misdeed, failure, or humiliation. To vindicate the ego.
n Deference	To admire and support a superior. To praise, honor, or eulogize. To yield eagerly to the influence of an allied other. To emulate an exemplar. To conform to custom.
n Dominance	To control one's human environment. To influence or direct the behavior of others by suggestion, seduction, persuasion, or command. To dissuade, restrain, or prohibit.
n Exhibition	To make an impression. To be seen and heard. To excite, amaze, fascinate, entertain, shock, intrigue, amuse, or entice others.
n Harm avoidance	To avoid pain, physical injury, illness, and death. To escape from a dangerous situation. To take precautionary measures.
n Infavoidance	To avoid humiliation. To quit embarrassing situations or to avoid conditions which may lead to belittlement: the scorn, derision, or indifference of others. To refrain from action because of the fear of failure.
nNurturance	To give sympathy and gratify the needs of a helpless object; an infant or any object that is weak, disabled, tired, inexperienced, infirm, defeated, humiliated, lonely, dejected, sick, mentally confused. To assist an object in danger. To feed, help, support, console, protect, comfort, nurse, heal.
n Order	To put things in order. To achieve cleanliness, arrangement, organization, balance, neatness, tidiness, and precision.
n Play	To act for "fun" without further purpose. To like to laugh and make jokes. To seek enjoyable relaxation of stress. To participate in games, sports, dancing, drinking parties, cards.
n Rejection	To separate oneself from a negatively cathected object. To exclude, abandon, expel, or remain indifferent to an inferior object. To snub or jilt an object.
n Sentience	To seek and enjoy sensuous impressions.
n Sex	To form and further an erotic relationship. To have sexual intercourse.
n Succorance	To have one's needs gratified by the sympathetic aid of an allied object. To be nursed, supported, sustained, surrounded, protected, loved, advised, guided, indulged, forgiven, consoled. To remain close to a devoted protector. To always have a supporter.
n Understanding	To ask or answer general questions. To be interested in theory. To speculate, formulate, analyze, and generalize.

Source: *Explorations in Personality*, edited by H. A. Murray. Copyright 1938 by Oxford University Press, Inc. Revised 1966 by H. A. Murray. Reprinted by permission.

Associated with these needs are distinctions between certain qualities that they may possess. Needs can be proactive or reactive, diffuse or focal, latent or overt, conscious or unconscious (Murray, 1938, pp. 111–115; Murray, 1954, pp. 447–450).

I have gone into this much detail concerning these various schemes to point out that Murray's writings yield a bewildering array of overlapping classifications of needs. It is difficult to come by any one authoritative classification, and Murray has not addressed himself to the relationships between the available schemes in sufficient detail to make his thinking clear. While his shifting distinctions and the resulting ambiguities probably represent the difficulty of conceptualizing human complexities, they also stem from the extreme heterogeneity of functioning subsumed by the need concept. As you must have noted before as we discussed the example of need for affiliation, each need can be manifested in many internal and external ways, and Murray wishes to consider a great number of needs. It is not surprising that the influences upon functioning attributed to any particular need would tend to overlap with the presumed manifestations of other needs. Also, reasoning from behavioral observations to a great number and variety of needs, as Murray has done, precipitates a large and heterogeneous mass of assumed organismic requirements. No wonder that finding a basis for classifying needs that will keep them reasonably distinct in theory and in practice is difficult. Given the inherent heterogeneity of his need concept, Murray may be attempting a fineness of distinction between exemplars of the concept that is too great for classificatory neatness and clarity.

Such overrefinement of a basically heterogeneous concept should make for considerable difficulty in using or applying need analysis. If so, this would be a great problem, as peripheral concepts of personality are the ones that should relate most clearly, immediately, and obviously to the behavior that constitutes data. Murray (1938) was the guiding light in a massive attempt to find empirical evidence for the existence of his long list of needs. This research project was a pioneering effort, involving many personologists in the intensive observation and test of 50 college students. Murray and his collaborators provided detailed operational descriptions for each of the needs. But one is not reassured on reading these descriptions, for there seems too much overlap among the needs. One further suspects the great difficulty of making the fine distinctions in meaning that are required in order to distinguish one need from another. This difficulty is bound to be compounded in the typical research situation, where the investigator finds available only some, rather than all, of the possible manifestations of needs. It is understandable, then, that in this major attempt to employ Murray's list of needs, it was necessary to reach the diagnosis of particular needs by majority vote of a group of skilled investigators after considerable debate concerning their observations. This hardly bespeaks objectivity, and I would implicate the inherent heterogeneity of the need concept as the main culprit.

Perhaps because of this problem, Murray (1954, pp. 463–464) has moved in the direction of substituting the *value-vector* concept for the need. The *vector* principle refers to the nature of the directionality shown by behavior (e.g., rejection, acquisition, construction), and the *value* principle refers to the ideals that are important to people (e.g., knowledge, beauty, authority). A value-vector matrix is compiled in diagnosing what each person believes is worthwile, and the particular ways in which he moves to make those beliefs an actuality. At this early stage in its use, the value-vector system seems to involve less heterogeneity and fewer organismic assumptions than does the need system. The values and vectors listed currently are simple enough and few enough so that it should be more possible to reach agreement among investigators on their identification in functioning.

Until the value-vector system is further developed, the need concept must be considered the major concrete peripheral characteristic in Murray's theory. The need is by its nature something that waxes and wanes, that is strong during deprivation and weak under satiating conditions. Thus, the concept is best suited to the explanation of behavior that also increases and decreases, rather than remaining steady. But much of the person's behavior is steady and repetitive. In attempting to account for such behavior, Murray has recourse to the concept of *need-integrate* (Murray, 1938, pp. 109–110) which refers to the stable habits and attitudes developing out of the previous expression of needs. In the stability it implies, the need-integrate is more analogous to the trait concept used by other theorists than is the need. Unfortunately, Murray neither considers the possible content of major need-integrates, nor elaborates the concept in other ways that would alert us to its intended use.

Murray also details the various environmental events, called *press*, which can, by occurring in childhood, influence which needs develop with the greatest strength. A list of these press is shown in Table 6–2 (Murray, 1938, pp. 291–292). Once needs have been learned, press serve the function of triggering the need, which exists as a predisposition for certain actions. But the pressure referred to in the press concept can be either objectively real or only subjectively perceived. The subjectively experienced pressure is called *beta* press, and is to be distinguished from the objective pressure, or *alpha* press (Murray, 1938, pp. 115–123).

These considerations have led Murray to posit an interactional unit, the *thema*, or combination of a need and a press, to be basic for the personologist. But Murray is unclear as to whether the press component of the thema refers to an individual's own perception of the situational forces acting upon him or to their objective features. If it is the beta (subjective) press that is intended, this would suggest a belief on Murray's part that the internal factors governing people's perception must be accepted if behavior is to be understood. But it may well be the alpha (objective) press that is intended, because, as the need and need-integrate concepts already include certain influences upon perception, the beta press would seem to be superfluous as a component of the

TABLE 6–2

Press relevant in childhood

1. p Family insupport
    a. Cultural discord
    b. Family discord
    c. Capricious discipline
    d. Parental separation
    e. Absence of parent: father, mother
    f. Parental illness: father, mother
    g. Death of parent: father, mother
    h. Inferior parent: father, mother
    i. Dissimilar parent: father, mother
    j. Poverty
    k. Unsettled home
2. p Danger or misfortune
    a. Physical insupport, height
    b. Water
    c. Aloneness, darkness
    d. Inclement weather, lightning
    e. Fire
    f. Accident
    g. Animal
3. p Lack or Loss
    a. of nourishment
    b. of possessions
    c. of companions
    d. of variety
4. p Retention, withholding objects

5. p Rejection, unconcern, and scorn
6. p Rival, competing contemporary
7. p Birth of sibling
8. p Aggression
    a. Maltreatment by elder male, elder female
    b. Maltreatment by contemporaries
    c. Quarrelsome contemporaries
9. p Dominance, coercion, and prohibition
    a. Discipline
    b. Religious training
10. p Nurturance, indulgence
11. p Succorance, demands for tenderness
12. p Deference, praise, recognition
13. p Affiliation, friendships
14. p Sex
    a. Exposure
    b. Seduction; homosexual, heterosexual
    c. Parental intercourse
15. p Deception or betrayal
16. p Inferiority
    a. Physical
    b. Social
    c. Intellectual

Source: *Explorations in Personality*, edited by H. A. Murray. Copyright 1938 by Oxford University Press, Inc. Revised 1966 by H. A. Murray. Reprinted by permission.

thema. If the alpha press is intended, then Murray would seem to be calling for analysis and clarification of the objective demand characteristics of situations that force the person's behavior.

However intriguing the concepts just discussed may be, they are so unelaborated as to lead me to the conclusion that we must simply accept the need concept as the one we can work with, and await future theoretical developments. In closing, I should point out that Murray has also made some suggestions as to how needs may be related to each other. He includes discussion of the *unity-thema* (Murray, 1938, pp. 604–605), or need-press combination that is very pervasive because formed in early life. He also offers the concepts of *prepotency* (Murray, 1954, p. 452), which refers to the degree to which a need takes precedence over others when it is aroused, and *subsidiation* (Murray, 1938, pp. 86–88), which indicates that less potent needs can actually become instrumental to the satisfaction of other ones. To indicate that any particular behavior may express a number of needs at the same time, Murray (1938, p. 86) offers the notion of *fusion*. Murray is clearly toying with an hierarchical organization of needs, but has really done little more in this regard than point the way toward future theoretical development.

Erikson's position

The ego psychologist's position on the periphery of personality is, of course, similar to that of Freud. Where there is deviation from Freud is in the direction of seeing life as a series of developmental stages that continue on into adulthood. The position of ego psychology is most clearly seen in the theorizing of Eric H. Erikson.

Erikson delineates eight stages of human development, with a particular pattern of traits, or concrete peripheral characteristics, associated with fixation at each of the stages. The first four stages bear close relationship to the Freudian oral, anal, phallic, and latency periods, though Erikson is clearly more interested in their psychosocial significance than their biological nature. This emphasis permits him to include the latency period as a significant one for adult functioning, even though this period does not have a strong biological justification. And then, instead of one genital period, extending from puberty to death, Erikson delineates four more developmental stages which bear no relationship whatever to biological considerations of sexual instinct and libido. In Erikson, the Freudian emphasis on biological sexuality has been almost completely lost, or at least as lost as it could be while still retaining the importance of psychosexual conflicts surrounding feeding, eliminating, and such. As you should have expected from the discussion in Chapter Two of the status of ego psychology as a variant on the conflict model, Erikson's position is a peculiar, though intriguing, conglomerate of Freud and something more like a fulfillment position.

According to Erikson, the first ("oral") developmental stage involves the bases for *general trust* or *basic mistrust*. In this stage, the child is more helpless than he will ever be again, and it is other people who must nurture, protect, and reassure him. If these needs are filled, then the child will look on the world, and his own participation in it, with a generally trustful attitude, whereas if he is severely deprived, he will be distrustful. In later years, whether you are trusting or distrusting will make an extraordinary difference in the nature of your life. By trust and basic distrust, Erikson implies a group of traits—what is at least a good part of a character type—even though he does not detail them in any specific fashion. In this lack of detailing, characteristic of all the trait groups deriving from his eight stages, Erikson unfortunately falls short of fulfilling the task the personologist accepts when he theorizes about the periphery of personality. One cannot so easily proceed from Erikson's statements to the concrete behavior of people, knowing clearly just what one will look for in order to determine whether trust or distrust is part of the person's character. In any event, he does provide interesting descriptions of the overall emphasis of his position, such as in the following (Erikson, 1950, pp. 221–222):

> The firm establishment of enduring patterns for the solution of the nuclear conflict of basic trust versus basic mistrust in mere existence is the first task of the ego, and thus first of all a task for maternal care. But let it be said here that the amount of trust derived from earliest infantile experience does not seem to depend on absolute quantities of food or demonstrations of love, but rather on the quality of the maternal relationship. Mothers, I think, create a sense of trust in their children by that kind of administration which in its quality combines sensitive care of the baby's individual needs and a firm sense of personal trustworthiness within the trusted framework of their culture's life style. This forms the basis in the child for a sense of being "all right," of being oneself, and of becoming what other people trust one will become. . . . Parents must not only have certain ways of guiding by prohibition and permission; they must also be able to represent to the child a deep, an almost somatic conviction that there is a meaning to what they are doing.

In this vivid description of the ways in which parents help the child to progress through the first stage successfully to develop trust, or fail him by precipitating a fixation and subsequent distrust, Erikson makes perfectly clear how far this kind of thinking has shifted Freud's original emphasis in the direction of psychosocial rather than biological forces. The emphasis of the quote is on a loving mother-child relationship that is convincing in its deep, human meaningfulness.

The first stage of development lasts, as does Freud's oral period, for roughly the first year of life. Then we come to the second stage, coinciding with Freud's anal stage of the second year of life. Although Erikson (1950, p. 222) clearly means that there be this coincidence, saying "Anal muscular maturation sets the stage for experimentation with two simultaneous sets of social modalities; holding on and letting go," his emphasis is again on the social rather than biological implications of the stage. According to Erikson, successful passage through this second stage leads to later traits showing *autonomy*, whereas fixation leads to later expressions of *shame and doubt*. In explaining how this comes about, Erikson (1950, p. 222) stars by making clear that his is still basically a conflict position by stating that "As is the case with all of these modalities, their basic conflicts can lead in the end to either hostile or benign expectations and attitudes. Thus to hold can become a destructive and cruel retaining or restraining, and it can become a pattern of care: to have and to hold. To let go, too, can turn into an inimical letting loose of destructive forces, or it can become a relaxed 'to let pass' and 'to let be.'" For Erikson, the crucial development of this second stage is the psychosocial ability to make a choice for oneself. The child can choose to hold on or let go, with the bowel movement being a particularly vivid example of this, but no longer the basic defining characteristic of the stage. Continuing, Erikson (1950, p. 222) says

> . . . If denied the gradual and well-guided experience of the autonomy of free choice . . . the child will turn against himself all his urge to discriminate and to manipulate. He will overmanipulate himself, he will develop a precocious conscience. Instead of taking possession of things in order to test them by purposeful repetition, he will become obsessed by his own repetitiveness. By such obsessiveness, of course, he then learns to repossess the environment and to gain power by stubborn and minute control, where he could not find large-scale mutual regulation."

You see here the similarity in character traits attributed by Erikson and Freud to the second stage of development.

Erikson then clarifies why he thinks this second stage leaves the person with either autonomy or shame and doubt. If the social environment encourages the child to stand on his own feet, yet protecting him against meaningless and arbitrary experiences of shame and doubt coming about through excessive, unthinking punishment for attempts to exercise his own decision-making powers, then the seeds of later autonomy are sown. But when the child encounters a lot of punishment, which could easily happen, as his decision-making powers are just barely beginning to mature, and hence, will be unreliable, the seeds of later attitudes of shame and doubt are sown. Erikson thinks that shame is the rage felt at being punished for trying to be autonomous turned inward, against the self. It is not the punishers who are wrong, it is you, because you are inept and unworthy. This sense of shame goes hand in hand with self-doubt. Instead of learning to rely upon a gradually maturing decision-making prowess, the severely punished child doubts his own ability to function competently and independently. Such adults are constantly in doubt, and scurrying to hide themselves, lest they feel ashamed by the scrutiny of others.

Erikson's third stage, much like the Freudian phallic stage, roughly covers the years from three through five. True to his psychosocial emphasis, Erikson sees successful outcome of this third stage in traits expressing *initiative and responsibility*, while unsuccessful outcome leads in the direction of *guilty functioning*. Following his own words (Erikson, 1950, pp. 224–225), we find that this stage of infantile genitality adds to the inventory of basic social modalities

> . . . that of "making," first in the sense of "being on the make." There is no simpler, stronger word to match the social modalities previously enumerated. The word suggests pleasure in attack and conquest. In the boy, the emphasis remains on phallic-intrusive modes; in the girl it turns to modes of "catching" in more aggressive forms of snatching and "bitchy" possessiveness, or in the milder form of making oneself attractive and endearing.

The danger of this stage is a sense of guilt over the goals contemplated and the acts initiated in one's exuberant enjoyment of new locomoter and mental power: acts of aggressive manipulation and coercion which go far beyond the executive capacity of organism and mind and therefore call for an energetic halt on one's contemplated initiative.

As in Freud, we find here that the natural object of the child's initiative is the opposite-sexed parent, whom he wishes to capture and possess. The child, of course, must inevitably fail. If his parents have loved and helped him enough, however, he will learn by the failure to "turn from an exclusive, pregenital attachment to his parents to the slow process of becoming a parent, a carrier of tradition" (Erikson, 1950, p. 225). The basis for adult initiative and responsibility will have been achieved. But if the failure is exaggerated by unnecessary punitiveness, the child will experience considerable resignation and guilt, which experiences will form the basis for such things as acquiescence, feelings of unworthiness, and even irresponsibility, in later life.

Next, comes Erikson's view of the latency stage, full of development even if rather devoid of special psychosexual significance. Erikson's (1950, pp. 226–227) owns words are particularly worth quoting here:

> Before the child, psychologically already a rudimentary parent, can become a biological parent, he must begin to be a worker and potential provider. With the oncoming latency period, the normally advanced child forgets, or rather sublimates the necessity to "make" people by direct attack or to become papa and mama in a hurry; he now learns to win recognition by producing things. He has mastered the ambulatory field and the organ modes. He has experienced a sense of finality regarding the fact that there is no workable future within the womb of his family, and thus becomes ready to apply himself to given skills and tasks, which go far beyond the mere playful expression of his organ modes or the pleasure in the function of his limbs. He develops industry—i.e., he adjusts himself to the inorganic laws of the tool world. He can become an eager and absorbed unit of a productive situation. To bring a productive situation to completion is an aim which gradually supersedes the whims and wishes of his autonomous organism.
>
> His danger, at this stage, lies in a sense of inadequacy and inferiority. If he despairs of this tools and skills or of his status among his tool partners . . . he abandons hope for the ability to identify early with others who apply themselves to the same general section of the tool world.

According to Erikson, the successful completion of the latency stage leads to the traits expressing *industry*, whereas unsuccessful completion leads to the traits expressing *inferiority*.

In the discussion of the four stages thus far covered, we have seen much that is similar to Freud, though there is much more emphasis on the psychosocial significance of the stages. In addition, Erikson has the advantage over other psychoanalytic thinkers of being rather more explicit than they. For this reason, and because of his representative status among ego psychologists, I would certainly be justified to have spent considerable attention on him. But there is an even more important reason for scrutinizing his theorizing: he breaks up the period of adulthood into several segments and gives them the status of real developmental stages. In the general sphere of psychoanalytic thinking, it would not have been possible to achieve this view of developmental stages in adulthood without dropping Freud's great emphasis on the anatomy and physiology of the organism. Many people initially favorable to Freudian thinking have either broken away from it or remained uneasy about the short shrift given to adulthood without really doing anything about it. Murray was among the former, for in explaining the reasons for the course his career has taken, he said that he found Freud good as far as he went, but that he did not go far enough to fulfill the allegory, to record "the heroic adult and his tragic end" (Murray, 1959, p. 13). Well, in reserving four of his eight stages for the years following puberty, Erikson has certainly tried to improve upon Freud.

In approaching an understanding of the four remaining stages, you must keep in mind that each new stage is entered upon with the legacy of past stages. Weak points in character contributed by earlier fixations will influence, indeed, jeopardize successful development in the stage that is current. I think you must have surmised this characteristic of Erikson's theorizing while reading the quote from his description of the latency period, but if not, you should have it clearly in mind now.

The fifth stage is that in which *identity* or *role diffusion* occurs. Successful development leads to the bases of a clear adult identity, whereas unsuccessful development leads to a scattered, fragmentary, diffuse, shifting sense of who you are. In Erikson's (1950, pp. 227–228) words:

> With the establishment of a good relationship to the world of skills and tools, and with the advant of sexual maturity, childhood proper comes to an end. Youth begins. But in puberty and adolescence all sameness and continuities relied on earlier are questioned again, because of a rapidity of body growth which equals that of early childhood and because of the entirely new addition of physical genital maturity. The growing . . . youths . . . are now primarily concerned with what they appear to be in the eyes of others compared with what they feel they are, and with the question of how to connect the roles and skills cultivated earlier with the occupational prototypes of the day.
>
> The integration now taking place in the form of ego identity is more than the sum of the childhood identifications. It is the accrued experience of the ego's ability to integrate these identifications with the vicissitudes of the libido, with the aptitudes developed out of endowment, and with the opportunities offered in social roles. The sense of ego identity, then, is the accrued confidence that the inner sameness and continuity are matched by the sameness and continuity of one's meaning for others, as evidenced in the tangible promise of a "career."

According to Erikson, the task of settling on an identity is so hard, and so fraught with anxiety, that youngsters often overidentify, for protection, to the point of apparent loss of identity, with the heroes of cliques and crowds. Much of youthful "falling in love" can also be understood in this fashion. While such overidentifying is to be expected, if the task of finding an identity is too fraught with conflict due to lack of proper environmental support and understanding, the youngster may remain in this escape. When older, this will show up as role diffusion.

The sixth stage begins certainly by the time adolescence ends. This is the stage in which society expects the person to leave his parents and the other more protective societal institutions, such as school, and begin to function as a mature and able adult. According to Erikson, in order to reap the rewards available during the stage, the person must direct his functioning toward *intimacy*. If there is any inevitable conflict in this stage so undominated by parents and pregenital, pleasure-principle functioning, it is brought about by the tremendous difficulty in achieving intimacy in complex, impersonal societies. But I must say that it is perfectly apparent concerning this stage and subsequent ones that Erikson has, like other ego psychologists, transcended the pure conflict model. Even if my searching for a basis for conflict in societal complexity seems plausible, the inevitability of this basis is quite questionable. In any event, should the person fail to achieve intimacy, he will slip into *isolation*. As before, the person approaches this sixth stage with the legacy of earlier development. The more he has traversed earlier developmental stages successfully, the greater the likelihood of success in achieving intimacy.

Erikson's idea of intimacy is an elaboration of Freud's sage remark that one aspect of normalcy is the ability to love. Erikson (1950, pp. 230–231) lists the concrete capabilities that this implies as "(1) mutuality of orgasm, (2) with a loved partner, (3) of the other sex, (4) with whom one is able and willing to share a mutual trust, (5) and with whom one is able and willing to regulate the cycles of work, procreation, and recreation, (6) so as to secure for the offspring, too, a satisfactory development." As you can see, the characteristics of someone achieving intimacy would be very similar to the kind of thing other psychoanalytic thinkers have in mind when they speak of the genital character type. But in order to have the chance to achieve intimacy, the person must offer himself freely in situations that require a minimum of self-protection, such situations as sexual union and close friendship. If previous development has been unsuccessful, the person may not be willing to risk the pain attendant upon momentary failures in the search for intimacy. In that case, he will shrink into a deep sense of isolation and consequent self-absorption.

As adulthood progresses, the seventh stage of development opens. The particular focus of this stage is *generativity* versus *stagnation*. Interestingly enough, Erikson (1950, p. 231) calls this a nuclear conflict, although it is still not clear in the terms used in Chapter 2 that the conflict is inevitable. Be that as it may, let us recognize that Erikson (1950, p. 231) means by generativity

> . . . primarily the interest in establishing and guiding the next generation or whatever in a given case may become the absorbing object of a parental kind of responsibility. Where this enrichment fails, a regression from generativity to an obsessive need for pseudo intimacy, punctuated by moments of mutual repulsion, takes place, often with a pervading sense . . . of individual stagnation and interpersonal impoverishment.

Generativity and stagnation are certainly included in the intimacy or isolation of the sixth stage, but Erikson singles out this seventh stage because he feels that questions of generativity or stagnation become gradually more important as adulthood progresses.

The final stage of development is not clearly associated with any particular time in the life-span, but one may presume it to be something which begins about the period of middle age or perhaps a bit later. It is the stage in which the person will achieve *ego integrity* if he develops successfully, and *despair* if he is unsuccessful. Once again, the most direct way to Erikson's meaning is in his own words (1950, pp. 231–232):

> Only he who in some way has taken care of things and people and has adapted himself to the triumphs and disappointments adherent to being, by necessity, the originator of others and the generator of things and ideas—only he may gradually grow the fruit of these seven stages. I know no better word for it than ego integrity. Lacking a clear definition, I shall point to a few constituents of this stage of mind. It is the ego's accrued assurance of its proclivity for order and meaning. It is a post-narcissistic love of the human ego—not of the self—as an experience which conveys some world order and spiritual sense, no mater how dearly paid for. It is the acceptance of one's one and only life cycle as something that had to be and that, by necessity, permitted of no substitutions: it thus means a new, a different love of one's parents. . . . Although aware of the relativity of all the various life cycles which have given meaning to human striving, the possessor of integrity is ready to defend the dignity of his own life style against all physical and economic threats. For he knows that an individual life is the accidental coincidence of but one life cycle with but one segment of history; and that for him all human integrity stands or falls with the one style of integrity of which he partakes. . . . Before this final solution, death loses its sting.
>
> The lack or loss of this accrued ego integration is signified by fear of death; the one and only life cycle is not accepted as the ultimate of life. Despair expresses the feeling that the time is short, too short for the attempt to start another life and to try out alternate roads to integrity. Disgust hides despair.

Although his precise meaning is perhaps a little obscured by the dramatic intent of his writing, Erikson does provide some basis for our knowing what are the traits or peripheral characteristics of people with integrity or in despair. Clearly in this final stage, and to some extent in the one preceding it, we see a definite shift in the person's concerns from that which will happen in the future to that which has already happened.

This brings to a close our discussion of the eight stages of development. To have theorized about them is to have taken on a formidable task, as you must realize by now. Certainly Erikson's figurativeness and ambiguities must be regarded in the light of the enormity of the task. And actually, we can piece together a fairly clear typology of character. We have the person of integrity, who has such characteristics as an overall sense of what his life is about, who accepts that life, who does not fear death, and who is not typically in despair. These are all characteristics that could be measured, though Erikson comes nowhere near providing us with precise definitions of them. Such a person would also show the characteristics of successful development associated with the previous seven stages. The person who has failed the achievement of integrity would show the characteristics of one or more developmental failures in the previous stages. Continuing for a moment down the scale of development, we could say that a person who has achieved generatively would show a strong interest in public affairs especially as they influenced the future of the world, and a strong commitment to the upbringing of his own children. If the person showed these kinds of characteristics, and was too young for the stage of integrity versus despair to be relevant, we would expect to find the additional characteristics associated with successful development at earlier stages. But, if he was old enough for the eighth stage then he would show, in addition to generativity, either integrity or despair. If despair, then we would expect, along with generativity, some attributes of developmental failure at earlier stages. If integrity, then probably only the attributes of earlier developmental success. To complete this scheme, if the person showed the opposite of generativity—stagnation—then we would expect additional attributes signifying earlier developmental failures, and that when the person reached the age of the eighth stage of development, despair would be more likely than integrity.

It is probably not necessary for me to continue this statement of typology further. You can see by now that Erikson's position permits some reasonably clear statements to be made about the characteristics one can find in people depending upon their developmental parts. Indeed, you should also be able to see that the various types of peripheral personality patterns can be related to each other in the sense that one can predict, on knowing, let us say, that someone has achieved generativity, what his future and past development were probably like. This is a sign that the various character types are integrated into Erikson's theory, rather than simply representing descriptions of his observations of people. While his position has an unfinished quality, there being many loose ends, it is certainly a brave beginning.

CONFLICT MODEL: INTRAPSYCHIC VERSION

Rank's position

Rank's position seems both lucid and simple. This lucidity is based on deriving his view concerning the periphery of personality from the logical possibilities presented by his core level assumptions. The key to understanding Rank's statement of personality types is the simple recognition that once you postulate a force leading toward individuation and another toward unity, then there are three possibilities for stable patterns of functioning. These stable patterns can express individuality to the exclusion of unity, unity to the exclusion of individuality, or a blend of the two. Logically, there are no other possibilities. And concretely, these are the only possibilities focused upon by Rank.

Let us approach discussion of the personality types with a word about development. Birth disrupts the primitive unity of embryo with mother. From birth onward, there are many other separations between the person and his environment, separations as inevitable as life itself. Through these enforced separations, the person becomes more and more differentiated. The pressure toward unity can no longer take the primitive form of merging with the world, but must involve complex and subtle integrations of the parts of the person, and of the person with other things and people. As he grows in experience of this sort, the child comes to know his own self as a totality. From this point onward, the active form of his self, called *will* by Rank, is a serious force in the shaping of his life. Essentially, the will involves a sense of what one wants to accomplish, and who one is, in the context of the rest of the world.

The will has its beginning, according to Rank, as *counterwill*. As the child comes to learn that he can say no to adults and to his own impulses, he feels the sense of personal identity stemming from counterwill. Although immature, the expression of counterwill is an important accomplishment, as it presages, in normal development, the conscious, satisfying, active integration of person with the world that constitutes maturity for Rank. Munroe (1955, pp. 585–586) provides an especially clear discussion of the counterwill:

> The counter-will, developed *against* the parents and later representatives of external forces, against the "other" or "others," is thus wholesomely rooted in the basic human striving toward life and individualization. By itself, however, it tends to destroy the *union* which is equally necessary to the human spirit. Assertion of the counter-will, therefore,

tends to arouse feelings of "guilt." The profound distress implicit in the effort to be one's own self at the expense of the precious sense of union and support Rank calls *ethical* guilt. He contrasts this almost universal and potentially creative problem with *moralistic* guilt, which arises when one has committed an act disapproved by one's society or one's own socially developed code of behavior. Ethical guilt goes deeper. It may arise with *any* expression of the own will—and also with any compliance which, for the person, has involved an abrogation of such willing, even though correct from a moralistic standpoint. Ethical guilt, if I understand Rank aright, is his term for the tension between two poles of human experience—separation and union. . . . Resolution of this guilt becomes, for Rank, the human ideal and the goal of psychotherapy.

Ethical guilt can only be resolved through the achievement of simultaneous differentiation and integration, or psychological growth. Psychological growth is encouraged in the early years by a love relationship between child and parent. This relationship must, of course, include in its definition the child's need for succorance and support, even when he is expressing counterwill against the parents. Ideally, the parent accepts the counterwill of the child as a lovable part of its effort to establish its own self as an independent being, at the same time as responsibility is assumed for nurturing the child and teaching it the realities of the external world. If the child receives this kind of care, he will progress from the expression of counterwill to the expression of mature will or selfhood.

The ensuing personality type, called the *artist*, is the Rankian ideal. Rank does not use the term artist in its conventional meaning. Many painters, writers, and the like, would definitely not be artists by his definition. The artists is the person who has accepted both the fear of life and the fear of death, both the inevitable pressure toward individuation and the unavoidable longing for union, and achieved an integration of the two. His personal will is expressive of both differentiation and integration. Munroe (1955, pp. 585–586) gives something of the flavor of Rank's thinking on the artist:

> We have seen that this [psychological growth] requires an acceptance by the individual of his personal will as valuable—an acceptance begun in the counterwill. But this personal will cannot become truly constructive until it is accepted by another person. . . . Until the person can feel that his own willing is *right* (i.e., not guilty), until he can feel that it is accepted by "others," he cannot fully resolve the problem of separation with its counterpart of union. Rank's artist . . . does not stand alone on a pinnacle of individual worth. On the contrary "he who loseth his life shall find it." The act of separation is not enough, no matter how heroically accomplished. Neither is sacrifice of the self, whether it takes the form of heroic altruism and self-immolation or the unthinking compromise of the average man. These are the poles of experience, neither of which can fully express the human ideal. Rank's

choice of the term *artist* for the human ideal is an attempt to convey a
sense of creative integration as the highest goal of man. . . .

Rank has described what he means articulately enough to suggest some
of the relevant concrete peripheral characteristics. For example, the
artist type would certainly include people who showed a high degree of
differentiatedness and integratedness in their thoughts, feelings, and actions. In addition, they would show intimacy with and commitment to
other people without slavish loyalties or undue concern for social proprieties. In their work, they would be productive in the direction of
unusualness but also usefulness. In short, they show many of the signs
of transcendence associated with ideal personality as characterized by the
fulfillment model. But that Rank's position is still in the conflict tradition
is indicated by his insistence that a person cannot live ideally unless his
way is acceptable to at least some other people.

One of the remaining two personality types is called the *neurotic man*.
He is to be understood as expressing the tendency toward separation to
the exclusion of the tendency toward union. Like the artist, the neurotic
has committed himself to the pain of separation from the herd, but has
not won through to the artist's constructive integrations with the world.
Instead of expressing mature will or selfhood, the neurotic seems fixated
at the level of counterwill. In other words, he acts either against people,
or completely separately from them. In addition, though his personality
shows much differentiation, it is weak on integrating principles. His sense
of separateness is likely to be ridden by hostility and moralistic, rather
than ethical, guilt. Here there is a clue to the developmental handicap
culminating in neurosis. The handicap has to do with having been made
to feel wrong and unworthy at the time when the negativism implied in
counterwill was actually normal, with the results somehow precipitated
of an overcompensatorily strong embracing of counterwill. In adulthood,
the neurotic still shows counterwill as the only sign in his own selfhood.
Again, some of the concrete peripheral charcteristics embodying the
neurotic personality type can be discerned. The neurotic would be hostile,
negative, arrogant, isolationistic, critical of others, highly guilty, and so
forth.

The final personality type is that of the *average man*, or someone who
expresses the tendency toward union to the exclusion of the tendency
toward individuation. Although the neurotic is, in Rank's mind, clearly
inferior to the artist, the average man is inferior to both. The average man
is the most inferior because he has never even seriously entertained the
possibility of his own individuality. He acts as if the right of individuality,
guaranteed by the trauma of birth, were not there at all. Munroe (1955,
p. 585) once again provides a vivid description of what Rank had in
mind:

Every child develops something of a counter-will through the ordinary pains and frustrations of post-uterine existence. Many children, however, soon find it possible to so identify their own will with that of their parents as to avoid much of the guilt of separation and the pain of developing the own will further. Adaptation to the will of the parents and later to the dictates of a wider society is the keynote of these characters. Where there is no effort toward individuation, there is also no conflict about conformance. The person's life may be hard or dull, but as long as the person takes its external conditions for granted, so long as they seem really part of himself, he is spared the inner distress of guilt. Rank does not refer here to people who consciously conform for the sake of expediency. The average man is the man who naturally conforms to his society because he has never thought of doing anything else. His relations with his society are reminiscent of the symbiotic relationships between person and environment which prevailed in the womb. They represent the first and easiest solution to the problem set by birth. This essentially adaptive individual has a relatively harmonious relationship to his society, but only because he has never truly differentiated his own will from the significant surroundings. He is the prey of social change as victim or executioner. His truths are illusory, and his virtues may vanish overnight if the social configuration to which he belongs shifts its values.

The average man would be characterized by such concrete peripheral characteristics as conformity, dependability, superficiality, suggestibility, and lack of dissatisfaction. The emphasis here is on adaptation. The developmental handicap must have something to do with the kind of overwhelmingly negative response to the first expressions of counterwill that would lead the child to embrace for deal life the precise ways of his parents and the broader society.

This concludes my presentation of the personality types described by Rank. Intriguing and immediately identifiable in our own experience though these personality types are, I urge you to realize that there are, in Rank's position, only three kinds of people you can describe. This number cannot really be increased by considering mixed types, for the types offered are largely exclusive of each other. One cannot be both artistic and average, or even artistic and neurotic. You should consider carefully whether three personality types are enough to describe the full range of ways of life. We shall return to this point.

Jung's position

Jung (1933b) has offered an ingenious conceptualization of personality types, which is in some ways consistent and in others inconsistent with the rest of his thinking. The main distinction he makes is between the attitudes of *introversion* and *extroversion*. You can gain a preliminary grasp of these two attitudes as they are manifested in persons by Jung's (1933b, p. 412) statement that:

> The two types are essentially different, presenting so striking a contrast, that their existence, even to the uninitiated in psychological matters, becomes an obvious fact, when once attention has been drawn to it. Who does not know those taciturn, impenetrable, often shy natures, who form such a vivid contrast to those other open, sociable, serene maybe, or at least friendly and accessible characters, who are on good terms with all the world, or, even when disagreeing with it, still hold a relation to it by which they and it are mutually affected.

At the observational level, the extroverted person is concerned with the external world of things and people, whereas the introverted person is concerned with the internal world of his own ruminations. This useful observational distinction has been adapted by many psychologists and lay persons.

It is important to understand how Jung uses the distinction between introversion and extroversion not only in readily observed differences between people but in deeper lying elements of psychic life as well. In this regard, you should note that everyone, according to Jung, is capable of being both introverted and extroverted, even though these are actually opposite tendencies. This assumption is quite consistent with the intrapsychic conflict model—the personality is composed of intrinsically opposed elements. As the person grows to adulthood, one of the attitudes comes to be dominant, so that observationally he is either introverted or extroverted. This assumption implies that an attitude becomes dominant through some process of learning, though Jung does not specify what it is. It is mainly because we are dealing with a learned basis whereby persons differ from each other that the introversion—extroversion distinction is considered part of the periphery rather than core of personality.

Once an attitude becomes dominant, the person seems to be rather ruled by it. This does not mean, however, that the opposing attitude has no effect on him at all. The nondominant attitude does not evaporate, but becomes unconscious instead. As part of the personal unconscious, the nondominant attitude exerts a subtle effect, expressed in unexpected inconsistencies of behavior and vague longings to be other than one seems to be. Thus, a person in whom introversion is dominant will be generally ruminative, reflective, concerned with his own inner world, but will nonetheless experience a nagging wish to break out of his own mind into the world of action and interchange with others, and will actually show occasional gross and unexpected forays into extroverted behavior. Another sign of the potency of repressed extroversion in him may be that he will find overtly extroverted persons strangely attractive, even though they seem so different. Thus, when Jung speaks of an introverted person, he means someone in whom introversion is dominant and conscious and extroversion is nondominant and unconscious, but there as well. For the extroverted person, the opposite is true.

Jung (1933b) adds four additional distinctions between what he calls functional modes in developing his typology. These modes, which constitute general styles of experiencing, are called *thinking, feeling, sensing,* and *intuiting.* Thinking and feeling are grouped together as *rational,* in that they involve value-judgments. The valuation in the thinking mode involves classifying separate ideas or observations under general concepts and organizing these concepts systematically. This activity is generally referred to as determining what something means. In the feeling mode, the evaluation involved is that of determining whether the idea or observation constitutes something liked or disliked. However strange it may seem to consider feeling to be a rational function, you should recognize that Jung does this because feeling, as he defines it, shares with thinking the capacity to order and organize experience. Feeling does this by enabling the person to determine preferences.

In contrast, sensing and intuiting do not lead to establishment of order and involve no value-judgments. Therefore, they are considered *irrational* functions, though Jung does not mean this classification in any negative, disparaging way. In sensing, one simply experiences the presence and qualities of things, in an unevaluative, open way. Intuition involves apprehending the essential characteristics of something, in a manner that is immediate and unreflective. Whereas sensing concerns itself with literal recognition, intuiting involves grasping latent, underlying, or future possibilities.

As with introversion-extroversion, everyone has the capability for thinking, feeling, sensing, and intuiting, though typically one function becomes dominant through learning. According to Jung, the two rational functions oppose each other, as do the two irrational functions. Thus, if one of the rational functions achieves dominance, the other is relegated to the personal unconscious, there to exert a subtle, underground influence on experiencing. Further, if it is one of the rational functions that is dominant, the two irrational functions are subordinated to it, with the role of assisting the dominant function. Needless to say, the same sort of relationships hold if it is one of the irrational functions that achieves dominance. Concretely, if thinking is dominant, then feeling is unrecognized by the person, though it manifests itself in wishes and dreams, in occasional lapses into strong emotions, and in the attractiveness to him of persons in whom feeling is dominant. The functions of sensing and intuiting are conscious and active, but in the service of the thinking function. The person might well accumulate a wide range of sensations in order to operate on them with thought processes; and his intuitions might serve to initiate more systematic thought. With this example, you should be able to puzzle through the other combinations of functions

Jung (1933b) means too combine the introversion-extroversion distinction with the thinking-feeling and sensing-intuiting distinctions in arriving at what he calls *psychological types.* The types are *introversive-rational, introversive-irrational, extroversive-rational,* and *extroversive-irrational.* Of course, each type involving rational functions is further subdivided according to whether thinking or feeling is dominant, and each type involving irrational functions breaks down into sensing or intuiting dominance. This makes a total of 8 basic personality types.

Although Jung was explicit about his typology, he did not offer any systematic list of concrete peripheral characteristics to go along with it. From his descriptions of the types, one can derive some notions as to concrete peripheral characteristics, but it is difficult to be precisely sure. Nonetheless, it would appear that to the thinking introvert, theories and not facts are important, and he has a vague dread of the opposite sex. This latter occurs because sexual expression is in general both extroverted and concerned with feeling, and these tendencies have been repressed by the thinking introvert. The feeling introvert has a deep sense of God, freedom, immortality, and other values, but can be mischievously cruel because not only extroversion but also thinking have been repressed. The sensing introvert tends to be guided by what happens to him, without any operation of judgment, especially in regards to himself. To fill out the introverted types, the intuiting introvert discerns possibilities and pursues them wthout regard for himself and others, but cannot understand why he is undervalued by others. The latter takes place because of the repression of not only extroversion but sensing as well, producing a person who is not sensitive to what is going on around him.

To give examples of extroverted types, there is the thinking extrovert, whose ideas are banal and dull, and in whom the end justifies the means. These characteristics are understandable in someone who represses introversive tendencies and does not have a sense of what is proper and worthwhile due to the repression of feeling. The feeling extrovert displays extravagant though unbelievable feelings, and though he enjoys excellent rapport with others, hurts them by his tactlessness. The disadvantage of this type stems from the de-emphasis on logical and problem-solving thought inherent in repression of thinking and introversion. In the sensing extrovert, one finds a thoroughly realistic person, who is nonetheless rather slavishly bound to specifics and facts. This person never seems to get beyond the surface of things due to the repression of intuiting and introversion. Finally, the intuiting extrovert always seizes new things with enthusiasm, but is apt to become involved with unsuitable persons of the opposite sex. Though he capably discerns possibilities, the repression of sensing and introversion renders him rather unable to judge the results of his enthusiasms.

In each personality type, there are strengths according to what is dominant and conscious, and weaknesses due to what is nondominant and repressed. None of these types can be considered ideal, or even relatively better, according to Jung. Instead, Jung considers the attainment of self to be ideal. This process involves growing out of your personality type, as it were, so that none of one's human capabilities is submerged and unconscious. In attaining selfhood, a thinking introvert would have to become conscious of his feeling and extroversion capabilities, and integrate these into his everyday life. He would at the point of success not have a personality type at all. He would have fulfilled all his capabilities. It should be clear now that when one attains selfhood, one also loses individuality, for the personality types are, in Jung's system, the major basis for individual differences. In selfhood, one attains a universal personality, where the personal unconscious has shrunk to zero, and life's actions are a joint function of the ego and the collective unconscious. Each person attaining this selfhood would be like each other, regardless of differences in sex and other biologically determined considerations.

Jung's statements on peripheral characteristics of personality are consistent with his core statements in that all express the intrapsychic model, as was indicated earlier. The inconsistency between core and periphery concerns a failure on Jung's part to tell us how the personality types develop out of interactions between core and society. Clearly, the types are learned. But it is not so clear how, as a function of what one experiences, they develop. Certainly, to define a personality type in Jungian terms is simultaneously to make a statement about at least some of the content of the personal unconscious and ego. That which is dominant in a type is represented in the ego as conscious experience, and that which is nondominant in the personal unconscious as represssions. It is harder to know who the collective unconscious feeds into the personality types. One also misses reference to parent-child interactions, in any manner that could give some systematic ideas of the development of personality types.

Jung does say that personality types are developed early in life, and represent the major bases for behaving throughout young adulthood. But by the time the early forties are reached, there is a general shift in personality toward introspection and rumination. This is the time when the transition may be made from a personality type to selfhood. If the transition is not made, general despair and hopelessness may attend later adulthood. In order to successfully make the transition, it is necessary for everyone to become more conscious of his personal unconscious and to be attuned to the emanations into consciousness of the collective unconscious. What this will mean in content terms is more or less given by the personality type; the thinking introvert will have to become sensitive to feeling and extroversive tendencies in him, and so forth. In addition, everyone will have to accept and value the collective unconscious. This means, among other things, accepting experiences of the uncanny, of things going on which are beyond individual control. It also means

identifying with mankind and all living things in an uncritical, appreciative way. This part of Jung's view of the ideal is not very different from
Zen Buddhism. In psychotherapy, Jung has ingenious ways of aiding persons in the transition from specific personality types to selfhood. These
include spending time and effort at fantasy and imaginative activities,
such as painting and daydreaming.

Chapter 7 THE PERIPHERY OF
PERSONALITY: FULFILLMENT MODEL

At the core level, the differences between conflict and fulfillment models were readily apparent. By comparing the content of the last chapter with this one, it will be possible to determine to what degree the two models differ in conceptualizing the most tangible aspects of people.

FULFILLMENT MODEL: ACTUALIZATION VERSION

Rogers' position

As I implied earlier, a good heuristic device for detecting the parts of a personality theory that are peripheral in nature is to try to spot the points at which statements about the differences between people occur. In Rogers' theory, only one broad distinction between ways of living is made, this leading to the separation of people into two broad types. In core level terminology, these types comprise the people in whom the actualizing tendency is vigorously expressed, leading to the enhancement and enrichment of living, as opposed to the people in whom the actualizing tendency is protectively, defensively expressed, leading to the mere maintenance of living. Someone falling into the first type would be called a *fully functioning person* whereas someone falling into the second type would be considered *maladjusted* (Rogers, 1959). Of course, Rogers does not really believe that people fall so clearly into one type or the other. Rather, there are degrees to which people resemble one or the other extreme described by the type definitions.

If Rogers went no further in his theorizing, his position would be subject to the same criticism raised concerning Bakan. All one would be able to say about someone would be that he was either fully functioning or maladjusted. But fortunately, Rogers has elaborated the meaning of this core level distinction in peripheral level terms. He (Rogers, 1961, pp.

309

183–96) delineates a set of concrete peripheral characteristics pertaining to people who are fully functioning, thus giving this type the kind of specificity indispensable to usefulness in actually describing people. The first of these characteristics is *openness to experience,* intended to signify the polar opposite of defensiveness. According to Rogers (1961, pp. 187–188), in a person open to his experience,

> . . . every stimulus—whether originating within the organism or in the environment—would be freely relayed through the nervous system without being distorted by any defensive mechanism. There would be no need of the mechanism of "subception" whereby the organism is forewarned of any experience threatening to the self. . . . Thus, one aspect of this process which I am naming "the good life" appears to be a movement away from the pole of defensiveness toward the pole of openness to experience. The individual is becoming more able to listen to himself, to experience what is going on within himself. He is more open to his feelings of fear and discouragement and pain. He is also more open to his feelings of courage and tenderness, and awe. He is free to live his feelings subjectively, as they exist in him, and also free to be aware of these feelings.

Actually, it becomes clear on studying this statement that openness to experience is probably a group of concrete peripheral characteristics, rather than only one. If you think in the most concrete terms of how you would expect someone who is open to experience to be, you will recognize that a number of characteristics is involved. At the least, we can say that the person would be *emotional,* showing both positive and negative affects, and *reflective,* showing a richness of information about himself. These are clearly concrete peripheral characteristics because they would be used to describe only part of the behavior of any person, and to typify differences between people. Breaking down complex and heterogeneous concepts like openness to experience into their component parts can only render peripheral level theorizing more useful, as at the peripheral level you are, of course, concerned with the concrete business of understanding the most tangible aspects of people.

The next characteristic of the fully functioning person listed by Rogers, which he calls *existential living,* is even more clearly a set of interrelated characteristics. Existential living involves the nebulous quality of living fully in each and every moment. The subjective experience of so doing is that each moment is new and different from that which went before. In elaborating his existential quality, Rogers (1961, pp. 188–189) says:

> One way of expressing the fluidity which is present in such existential living is to say that the self and personality emerge *from* experience, rather than experience being translated or twisted to fit preconceived self-structure. It means that one becomes a participant in and observer of the ongoing process of organismic experience, rather than being in control of it.

Such living in the moment means an absence of rigidity, of tight organization, of the imposition of structure on experience. It means instead a maximum of adaptability, a discovery of structure *in* experience, a flowing, changing organization of self and personality.

Among the concrete peripheral characteristics discernible in Rogers' notion of existential living are *flexibility, adaptability, spontaneity,* and *inductive thinking.*

Another characteristic of the fully functioning person is what Rogers calls *organismic trusting.* It is not immediately apparent what meaning this concept has, and so I will quote at some length from Rogers' description (1961, p. 190):

> The person who is fully open to his experience would have access to all of the available data in the situation, on which to base his behavior; the social demands, his own complex and possibly conflicting needs, his memories of similar situations, his perception of the uniqueness of this situation, etc., etc. The data would be very complex indeed. But he could permit his total organism, his consciousness participating, to consider each stimulus, need, and demand, its relative intensity and importance, and out of this complex weighing and balancing, discover that course of action which would come closest to satisfying all his needs in the situation. An analogy which might come close to a description would be to compare this person to a giant electronic computing machine. Since he is open to his experience, all of the data from his sense impressions, from his memory, from previous learning, from visceral and internal states is fed into the machine. The machine takes all of these multitudinous pulls and forces which are fed in as data, and quickly computes the course of action which would be the most economical vector of need satisfaction in this existential situation. This is the behavior of our hypothetical person.
>
> The defects which in most of us make this process untrustworthy are the inclusion of information which does *not* belong to this present situation, or the exclusion of information which *does.*

Apparently, Rogers has in mind the ability to let a decision come to you, rather than trying to force it into existence, and trusting the decision as a worthy format for action even if its bases are not completely, unassailably apparent. This characteristic amounts to trusting your organism, of which, you will recognize, your consciousness is only one part.

There are two final characteristics that are really implied in those already discussed. The first is *experiential freedom,* and by it Rogers means the sense that one is free to choose between alternative courses of action. Rogers does not really want to assume that man has free will, in the old philosophical sense. All he means is that the fully functioning person experiences himself as choosing freely, regardless of the sad fact that his actions may indeed be determined in the sense of being somewhat predictable on the basis of his past experiences. The fully functioning person has the marvelous, exuberant feeling of personal power that comes with believing that anything is possible and what happens really depends on you. The final characteristic is *creativity*, or the penchant for producing new and effective thoughts, actions, and things. You can see that if a person has available to him all of his organismic capabilities and experience, and is also characterized by flexibility, he is quite likely to be a consistent producer of new and useful entities.

Put all these qualities together, and you have the fully functioning person, truly actualization theory's gift to the human race. The composite picture is one of great richness, as is so clearly seen in these words (Rogers, 1961, pp. 195–196):

> One last implication I should like to mention is that this process of living in the good life involves a wider range, a greater richness, than the constricted living in which most of us find ourselves. To be a part of this process means that one is involved in the frequently frightening and frequently satisfying experience of a more sensitive living, with greater range, greater variety, greater richness. It seems to me that clients who have moved significantly in therapy live more intimately with their feelings of pain, but also more vividly with their feelings of ecstasy; that anger is more clearly felt, but so also is love; that fear is an experience they know more deeply, but so is courage. And the reason they can thus live fully in a wider range is that they have this underlying confidence in themselves as trustworthy instruments for encountering life.
>
> I believe it will have become evident why, for me, adjectives such as happy, contented, blissful, enjoyable, do not seem quite appropriate to any general description of this process I have called the good life, even though the person in this process would experience each one of these feelings at appropriate times. But the adjectives which seem more generally fitting are adjectives such as enriching, exciting, rewarding, challenging, meaningful. This process of the good life is not, I am convinced, a life for the faint-hearted. It involves the stretching and growing of becoming more and more of one's potentialities.

There is a clear difference in emphasis upon what is ideal in living between Rogers and such psychosocial conflict thinkers as Freud and Sullivan. I trust the difference will not have escaped your attention. The psychoanalytic ideal is one of responsibility, capability, commitment, effectiveness and adaptation to social "realities," whereas the Rogerian ideal stresses experiential richness, range of living, flexibility, spontaneity, immediacy, and change. This difference, which shows up so clearly when one reaches the level of peripheral characteristics of personality, is traceable primarily to psychoanalytic theory being a psychosocial conflict position and Rogerian theory being a fulfillment position, with the consequent emphasis in the former position on compromise and defense, and in the latter position on expressing potentialities.

Having covered the peripheral characteristics defining one of the two great Rogerian types, it remains to discus the other. This is quite easily accomplished, as the other—the emphasis of which is upon maintaining, rather than enhancing living—is nothing more than the opposite of the fully functioning personality. The person who is maintaining rather than enhancing living is *defensive* rather than open to experience, *lives according to a preconceived plan* rather than existentially, and *disregards his organism* rather than trusts it. More or less in consequence of these things, he feels *manipulated* rather than free, and is *common* and *conforming* rather than creative. These characteristics of the maladjusted person all follow from the existence of *conditions of worth,* which, as I mentioned in Chapter 3, are the kind of sanctions learned from significant others in the person's life who, because they respected only some of his potentialities, led him in turn to the same pattern of differential or partial self-acceptance and respect. Conditions of worth, like Freud's superego, are the bases for defense.

However engaging and true to your own experience these two personality types may be, I encourage you to recognize that they are only two. Rogers does not even permit any basis within his own writing for considering various combinations of the set of concrete peripheral characteristics comprising fully functioningness or maladjustment. You have no formal theoretical justification for expecting, let us say, that one person might be high in openness to experience while being low in existential living, for being high in one brings with it the expectation that the other will be strongly represented as well. Although Rogers is more concrete than Bakan concerning the peripheral level of personality, it is nonetheless true that Rogerian theory permits you to say only two kinds of things about people. This is particularly surprising because Rogers shows such humanistic emphasis upon individuality. This interest in the many different ways in which people can live is shown in passages such as this (Rogers, 1963, p. 9):

> Perhaps it should be stressed that these generalizations regarding the direction of the [actualization] process in which [people] are engaged exist in a context of enormously 'diverse specific behaviors, with different meanings for different individuals. Thus, progress toward maturity for one means developing sufficient autonomy to divorce himself from an unsuitable marriage partner; in another it means living more constructively with the partner he has. For one student it means working hard to obtain better grades; for another it means a lessened compulsiveness and a willingness to accept poorer grades. So we must recognize that the generalizations about this process of change are abstractions drawn from a very complex diversified picture.

This passage, in which Rogers is discussing how patients come closer to the fully functioning life, sounds fine until you scrutinize it. On reflection, it becomes apparent that any behavior—some act or its opposite—

can express fully functioningness. As we recognized before, such a position is elastic, *post hoc,* and quite untestable. One cannot determine whether it is true or false.

In my opinion, the difficulty stems from Rogers' obvious interest in a comprehensive understanding of living which inevitably means taking seriously such concrete behavior patterns as leaving or staying in a marriage, even though he gives you the formal theoretical apparatus with which to make only a few general distinctions. The difficulty can be traced to Rogers' position being first and foremost a theory of psychotherapy and only secondarily a theory of personality. It is certainly appropriate for a theory of psychotherapy to concern itself with only two basic things, maladjustment and the fullest utilization of potentialities. But once you theorize about personality, you take on the task of understanding all there is about a person that has any regularity. This inevitably leads you to consider many specific differences among people, too many for proper understanding by a theory recognizing only two personality types. Now I am not for a moment denying that Rogerian theory can be developed so as to be more comprehensive, so that, for example, it will be theoretically possible to understand why fully functioningness would take the form of leaving a marriage in one person and staying in another. I am simply saying that such development, though needed, has not currently been accomplished. For vividness, recognize that Erikson's position permits many more distinctions between personality types than does that of Rogers. The criticism I have made of Rogers applies with only slightly less force to Rank, who postulates merely three personality types.

In concluding, I wish to point out that Rogers' theory, like the others, makes personality types and concrete peripheral characteristics a function of the interaction between core tendencies and environmental encounters, or in other words, development. For Rogers, if the core tendency of actualizing potentialities is met with unconditional positive regard from significant others, then the person will show the peripheral characteristics of the fully functioning type. In contrast, if the core tendency is met with conditional positive regard, conditions of worth and the other signs of maladjustment will ensue. But unlike the emphasis found in Freud, Erikson, and even Sullivan, the Rogerian personality types do not refer to particular periods of life. Rogerian theory does not utilize the idea of stages of devleopment.

Maslow's position

Although Maslow, the other actualization theorist, names many concrete peripheral characteristics in his discussion of personality, he is not at all systematic about the delineation of personality types. He names characteristics more for illustration than to provide a set, dependable scheme whereby one can identify and understand various patterns of living. In this, Maslow's writing is particularly deceptive, because it is so rich in vivid, illustrative references to courageousness, humor, spontaneity, and the like.

The only personality type that Maslow concerns himself with sufficiently to describe in the kind of concrete terms necessary at the peripheral level of analysis is that which bespeaks complete psychological maturity. In core terms, these are people who have fully actualized themselves through vigorous expression of potentialities, search for knowledge, and interest in beauty. Maslow (1955) informally collected together information about such a group of men, for the purpose of understanding their concrete peripheral characteristics better. Among the persons he included in his group were Lincoln, Jefferson, Walt Whitman, Thoreau, Beethoven, Eleanor Roosevelt, Einstein, and some of his own friends and acquaintances! The common features, or traits of these people turn out to be (1) *realistic orientation,* (2) *acceptance* of self, others, and natural world, (3) *spontaneity,* (4) *task orientation,* rather than self-preoccupation, (5) *sense of privacy,* (6) *independence,* (7) vivid *appreciativeness,* (8) *spirituality* that is not necessarily religious in a formal sense, (9) sense of *identity with mankind,* (10) feelings of *intimacy* with a few loved ones, (11) *democratic values,* (12) recognition of the *difference between means and ends,* (13) *humor* that is philosophical rather than hostile, (14) *creativeness,* and (15) *nonconformism.* Although this list is long and heterogeneous enough to escape easy integration into an organized picture of personality, it is certainly consistent with Maslow's general emphasis, and is similar in many respects to Rogers' description of the fully functioning person. We can certainly take these 15 characteristics as the starting point for a delineation of the mature personality type according to actualization theorists, even though a number of the designations would require additional elaboration and definition in order to be really useful in the description of people.

Maslow presents little else that can pass as a personality type, as he is so overwhelmingly interested in fostering the growth of a humanistic psychology. If you recall his notion of hierarchy of needs, however, you will see that the possibility of fixation at some developmental point below full self-actualization is implicit in his position, with the resultant logical capability of describing different sorts of immature personality types. Although Maslow himself does not explore these implications of his position, we should note the possibility that there could be personality types oriented toward the satisfaction of (1) physiological needs, (2) safety needs, (3) needs for belongingness, and (4) needs for esteem. The potentiality for a typology of personality at the peripheral level of analysis is greater in Maslow than in Rogers, though at present Maslow must also be criticized for providing so little concrete basis for understanding different ways of life.

FULFILLMENT MODEL: PERFECTION VERSION

Adler's position

Adler's viewpoint on the periphery of personality is carried in his concept of *style of life* (Ansbacher & Ansbacher, 1956). Ansbacher (1967) has provided an illuminating account of the developmental course of Adler's thinking leading up to this concept. A person's style of life, or type, in our terms, is the pattern of interrelated concrete peripheral characteristics that find regular expression in him and that determine his individuality. The rudiments of style of life are established by the time five years of age are past, and there is no basic change thereafter, except on the occasion of such special intervention as psychotherapy. The relationship between periphery and core of personality is clearly specified by Adler (Ansbacher & Ansbacher, 1956) when he indicates that he indicates that a person's style of life is the concrete result of the course taken by the core tendency of striving for perfection in the context of existing and imagined inferiorities and the particular family situation involved. Real and imagined inferiorities stem primarily from *organ weaknesses* and the specifics of *family constellation* (Dreikurs, 1963). The idea of organ weakness is clear enough, I suppose, regardless of the ticklish problem of diagnosis. An organ weakness can be anything from overly small hands to a heart with leaky valves.

By family constellation, Adlerians generally mean the person's status with regard to his siblings. Adler (Ansbacher & Ansbacher, 1956) emphasizes the roles of oldest child, second child, youngest child, and only child. In brief, the oldest child must be "dethroned," must give up the position of undisputed attention and affection when another sibling is born. Because of this, the oldest child cannot escape some feelings of resentment and hatred toward his siblings and parents. A second child is in a more advantageous position. He never received undisputed attention, and hence, does not feel bereft at the birth of a younger sibling. And the presence of an older sibling, or "pacemaker" (Ansbacher & Ansbacher, 1956, p. 379), is a challenge to develop rapidly. The youngest child has many "pacemakers" to goad development, and never has the experience of losing attention to a "successor." Whereas the oldest child reveres the past and views his siblings with alarm, and the second child accepts the realities of sharing attention, the youngest child can concentrate all his energies on catching up to his elders, feeling secure in the affection lavished on him by everyone in the family. The other family constellation discussed by Adler is that in which all siblings are of the same sex, in which case, one has a special problem of sexual identity.

Birth order partially determines the network of inferiorities felt in a family. This situation is added to by real inferiorities, the prototype of which are organ weaknesses. By the interaction of these things, a complex set of rivalries and alliances are formed. For example, an oldest child with strong intellectual capabilities may arouse rivalry in a younger child, which rivalry might be expressed in direct intellectual competition or in an avoidance of the intellectual domain in favor of some other areas less dominated by the older child. Or a youngest child, indulged and helped by everyone else in the family may respond to the pacemaking function of older siblings by excelling beyond them all (Ansbacher & Ansbacher, 1956, p. 381).

A person's sense of his inferiorities, and his means of circumventing or transcending them, are properly understood as expressive of the core tendency of striving for superiority. But there is more to be said than this. The style of life will evolve from the content of real and imagined inferiorities, and from the manner in which they are transcended or circumvented. This manner of dealing with inferiorities will be greatly influenced by the *family atmosphere,* or general values, attitudes, and action-patterns of family members, notably parents. If the atmosphere established by the parents is one of cooperation, mutual trust, respect, help, and understanding, then the child will be encouraged to express his attempt to overcome inferiorities in a manner that is constructive for him and for others. In such an atmosphere, an oldest child, for example, will respond to being dethroned not with disobedience and criticality but with an attempt to nurture and develop his younger sibling. But, if the family atmosphere is one of competition and distrust, or neglect, or even pampering (Ansbacher & Ansbacher, 1956, pp. 369–375), the child will be destructive in trying to overcome inferiorities. Whether the child will be active or passive in these attempts will be influenced by whether the family atmosphere is such that he is encouraged to give and initiate, as well as receive. Thus, the two distinctions out of which Adlerians formulate a typology of style of life are *constructiveness-destructiveness,* and *activeness-passiveness.*

I have made it sound as if family atmosphere provides a complete accounting of the constructiveness-destructiveness, activeness-passiveness of styles of life. While this is indeed the position that makes most sense to me in the framework of Adlerian thought, I must point out that some eminent Adlerians (e.g., Dreikurs, 1963) make this only part of the story, with the rest involving free will. According to them, the person has free choice, uninfluenced by past experience, over the nature of his orientation toward his inferiorities. Dreikurs (1963, p. 247) says:

> This asserts the child's ability to decide what to do with an obstacle he encounters, although such a decision does not take place on the conscious level, for the child may not have developed more than a

rudimentary verbal capacity when such a decision is required. Adler's contention of such freedom of choice was—and still is—incomprehensible to most students of psychology. They want to know what induces one child to give up, another to compensate, and still another to over-compensate. They cannot believe there is nothig that "makes" a child do it; that it is his own conclusion, his own response, his own evaluation of the situation which is influential. It is a creative act, which in itself is a phenomenon that our deterministically oriented contemporaries find difficult to comprehend.

If "creative acts" refer to something godlike, something that has no antecedents in past experience or the personality itself, then Dreikurs has surely left the scientific fold. But if "creative acts" can themselves be explained as the end results of a particular pattern of past experience, then there is little problem, except the confusion fostered by using words such as free will. I have assumed that Dreikurs really means this latter view, and that his confusing terminalogy can be traced to a zealous attempt to convince readers that the child does indeed have a structure and substance. I make this assumption on the basis of statements by Adler (1964, p. 36), such as the following, which seem inconsistent with unmitigated free will:

> No soul develops in freedom. Each one is in mental, emotional and nutritional dependence upon his immediate environment on the earth and in the cosmos, yet so far independent that he must take up these relations seriously: he must answer them as the questions of life.

If it is only consciousness and not free will that is meant, then family atmosphere is the only concept necessary for explaining the means by which the child will learn to strive for superiority.

As you can surmise from preceding discussions, four types of peripheral personality, or life-style, have been suggested by Adlerians. They are the *active-constructive, passive-constructive, active-destructive* and *passive-destructive* styles. These styles are established in childhood and it is assumed that they do not change much thereafter. The constructive-destructive distinction refers mainly to the direction of social interest, while the active-passive distinction tends to concern the more individualistic implications of striving for perfection. Actually, Adler (1964, p. 79) considers the active constructive style to epitomize mental health:

> It is almost impossible to exaggerate the value of an increase in social feeling. The mind improves, for intelligence is a communal function. The feeling of worth and value is heightened, giving courage and an optimistic view, and there is a sense of acquiescence in the common advantages and drawbacks of our lot. The individual feels at home in life and feels his existence to be worthwhile just so far as he is useful to others and is overcoming common instead of private feelings of inferiority. Not only the ethical nature, but the right attitude in aesthetics,

the best understanding of the beautiful and the ugly will always be founded upon the truest social feeling.

This passage emphasizes the importance of a cooperative connection with others and society, even so far as to say that the healthiest form of inferiority feelings is that which links you with the failings of all men. In the following passage, Adler (1964, pp. 47–48) emphasizes the active, or more individualistic, aspects of healthy living:

> Courage, an optimistic attitude, common sense, and feeling of being at home upon the crust of the earth, will enable [the healthy person] to face advantages and disadvantages with equal firmness. His goal of superiority will be identified with ideas of serving the human race and of overcoming its difficulties with his creative power.

The passive destructive style is considered to epitomize psychopathology, as you may have imagined. But in order to understand the emphasis intended, you should recognize that passivity need not involve inertia, or doing nothing. It can, and usually does, involve a concerted unwillingness to solve one's problems and assume one's responsibilities, blaming others instead. With this in mind, Adler's (1964, p. 81) words are illuminating:

> In the investigation of a neurotic style of life we must always suspect an opponent, and note who suffers most because of the patient's condition. Usually this is a member of the family, and sometimes a person of the other sex, though there are cases in which the illness is an attack upon society as a whole. There is always this element of concealed accusation in neurosis, the patient feeling as though he were deprived of his *right*—i.e., of the center of attention—and wanting to fix the responsibility and blame upon someone. By such hidden vengeance and accusation, by excluding social activity whilst fighting against persons and rules, the problem-child and the neurotic find some relief from their dissatisfaction.

Of the remaining two styles, the passive-constructive should be more healthy than the active-destructive. This is because the constructive-destructive dimension (having to do with social interest) is somewhat more important than activeness-passiveness in determining what is ideal. But here we meet an ambiguity, signaled by the absence of descriptions in the Adlerian literature of the passive-constructive style. Probably, this style does not really exist in the minds of Adlerians, because even the activeness-passiveness dimension is bound up with considerations of social interest, and constructiveness is not really thought of in passive terms.

For further clarification, it would be useful to focus more concretely on how these four (or are they three?) styles are actually concretized in specific behavioral terms. Here there is not too much to go on, as concrete behaviors expressive of life-styles are regarded by Adlerians to vary widely. Of relevance is the notion that each of these styles comprises a set of goals or finalisms. But these finalisms are arbitrary and subjective, and are therefore considered fictional. Despite the striking nature of the term, *fictional finalism*, it seems to me that Adlerians are simply stressing the motivational character of the entities or attributes constituting styles of life.

Dreikurs (1963) has specified the fictional finalisms associated with the four life-styles mentioned above. But it should be kept in mind that Dreikurs was originally attempting to explicate ways in which children could misbehave, and hence, the life-styles he details had little to do with constructiveness. But he has attempted to generalize his position such that we can consider it to have some relevance to constructiveness without too much risk of distortion. The four goals he considers are (1) the attainment of *attention* and *service*, (2) the abrogation of *power*, (3) the achievement of *revenge*, and (4) the bid to be *left alone*. Actually only the first kind of goal applies to the two constructive styles of life. You can understand why this should be by recognizing that the constructive styles involve cooperation and respect for others as well as for self. Hence, considerations of power, revenge, and isolation are irrelevant. The hallmark of the active constructive style of life is *ambitiousness*, or orientation toward success, whereas that of the passive-constructive style is *charm*, or receiving special attention for what one is rather than for what one does. As implied above, all four kinds of goals are relevant in the case of the two destructive or competitive and distrustful styles. In the active-destructive style, the attention-getting goal takes the form of being a *nuisance*, whereas the power, revenge, and isolation goals take the forms of *rebelliousness, viciousness,* and *denigration*, respectively. The attention-getting, power, revenge, and isolation goals in the passive-destructive style take the concrete form of *laziness, stubbornness, passive aggression,* and *despair*, respectively.

A hypothetical consideration of the manner in which the organ inferiority mentioned earlier, overly small hands, would be oriented toward in each of the four styles of life may be an aid to understanding at this point. The person with an active-constructive style of life might try to overcome smallness of hands in a direct, uncompromising and socially useful fashion. He might, if he had musical talent and interest, attempt to be a concert pianist in spite of his small hands, relying upon dexterity and practice to achieve excellence. Overcoming the organ inferiority would take place in the context of ambitiousness and success. In contrast, the passive-constructive person might beautify his hands in some manner, so that the very things which were inferior to begin with would now become the object of admiration. He would have achieved superiority through charm. The active-destructive person might be a nuisance by nagging people to remember his handicap, and seek power, revenge, and denigration by manipulating people with normal hands to feel guilty and irresponsible for being so well endowed and self-satisfied. Finally, the passive-destructive person might show laziness through not working because of his handicap, and indicate his stubbornness, passive aggression, and despair, by refusing charity and other attempts to help him. Although my examples involved actual organ inferiority, the same kind of thinking is appropriate even if you start with an imagined, or psychologically determined, inferiority. I also ask you to note something that was mentioned previously. It is the destructive-constructive distinction that carries the major implications of mental health and illness for Adlerians. The two destructive orientations are psychopathological, whereas the two constructive ones are healthy. If the attempt to attain superiority is engaged in at the expense of others, it is pathological, whereas if it proceeds in cooperation with, and in the context of, other people, it is healthy.

Dreikurs (1963) originally developed his typology for use with children and adolescents, though it could readily be applied to adults as well. Another attempt at a typology, engaged in by an Adlerian (Mosak, 1971), was frankly concerned with adults, and should be mentioned here. Unfortunately, there is little attention on Mosak's part as to how the types he identifies fit into the Adlerian dimensions of constructiveness-destructiveness and activity-passivity. Mosak (1971) mentions (1) the "getter," who exploits and manipulates life and others by actively or passively putting others into his service; (2) the "driver," whose over-conscientiousness and dedication to his goals rarely permit him to rest; (3) the "controller," who either wishes to control life or ensure that it will not control him; (4) the "good man," who prefers to live by higher moral standards than his contemporaries; (5) the "victim," who always loses; (6) the "martyr," who attains nobility through "dying" for causes or principles; (7) the "baby," who finds his place in life through charm, cuteness, and exploitation of others; and (8) the "excitement seeker," who despises routine and revels in commotion. Several other types mentioned are not so easy to outline briefly. One disconcerting feature of Mosak's typology is that it seems to refer rather exclusively to negatively toned styles. It is therefore unclear what his stand is on ideal personality.

Although Adlerian attempts at typology can hardly be considered developed enough to convince us that they can be objectively applied and studied, a beginning has certainly been made. The goals discussed, especially by Dreikurs, are generally the kind one would expect given the overall emphasis of the Adlerian position on the painfulness of inferiority and the striving to overcome it. And certainly, the attributes of everyday life considered by this theory are somewhat different—and therefore especially interesting—from the well-known ones considered by Freudians and Rogerians.

Incidentally, and in closing this section, you should recognize that although Adler's position makes of the periphery of personality something established through learning during the first few years of life, it does not, in contrast to Freud, distinguish personality types on the basis of developmental stages. Rather than stages, Adler uses family configuration, inferiorities, and family atmosphere as the bases of distinguishing types. This is consistent with Adler's wholistic or global emphasis, in which the fine discrimination of the second year of life from the third, or the fourth, would seem unfruitful. For Adler, things such as family atmosphere would not be likely to change enough so that one could attribute particular forms of adult personality to developments during brief periods of early childhood.

White's position

White does no more than give us a sketch of the lines along which he might develop a position on the periphery of personality. These lines involve *competence* as opposed to *incompetence,* and *sense of competence* as opposed to *shame.* In the normal course of events, expression of the core tendency—need to have an effect upon the world—leads through practice of capabilities to actual competence and also to the subjective experience of a sense of competence. But if parents thwart and punish expressions of effectance motivation, actual incompetence and the subjective experience of shame is the result. White (1960) makes a neat distinction between shame and guilt, the former being the experience of shortcoming or failure to reach a valued goal through lack of ability, whereas the latter implies touching or transgressing a moral boundary. Shame is connected with incompetence. In contrast, guilt does not imply that one is unable to do something; it signifies that one has done, or is thinking of doing, something within one's power that is forbidden. Guilt is connected with conscience, not competence. In any event, if White were to develop the implications of his position for the peripheral level of personality he would undoubtedly offer a typology of people based on their specific competencies and incompetencies, and on the contents of their shame and sense of competence.

Actually, the overall form that such a classification would take may be inferred from White's (1960) great sympathy for Erikson's version of ego psychology. Erikson's view of the eight stages of man, discussed earlier in this chapter, is for White a very discerning picture in developmental terms of the periphery of personality. Where White disagrees with Erikson is on the centrality of the psychosocial conflict model proposed by Freud. According to White, Erikson fails to recognize that most aspects of the character types and developmental stages he considers are better understood by a competence model than by a conflict model. Although Erikson has certainly, like other ego psychologists, championed a view of the ego as independent of the id, rather than merely an extension of it, he is still too wedded to his early psychoanalytic beginnings for White.

In order to communicate his view, White (1960) provides an excellent discussion of the psychosexual stages of development in which he tries to show that the conflict model, though clearly relevant to some of the things going on in development, is inadequate to explain most of the modes of functioning, or character traits, detailed by Erikson. Concerning the anal stage, he (White, 1960, pp. 118–119) says:

> The bowel training model is wrong, I think, in two ways. First, it concerns a function that is governed by the autonomic nervous system, that never comes under direct voluntary control, and that does not carry the experience of initiative that goes with voluntary action. The child may be proud when he can meet parental expectations, but it will be pride in meeting a somewhat mysterious demand by a somewhat mysterious process of habit formation, not the pride of mastering things directly by trial and by effort expended, as when one learns to throw or to bat a ball. Second, it is a situation in which cultural requirements inevitably prevail. Every child is bowel trained. This is a far greater victory for authority than generally prevails elsewhere; in other matters the child preserves more freedom to resist, plead, cajole, and force compromises on his surrounding adults. In short, the bowel training model all but eliminates the initiative and versatility on the child's part that is an essential aspect of any true autonomy. The best outcome of the bowel training problem is that the child will come to will the inevitable.

White points to what he considers a mismatch between Erikson's emphasis on autonomy as the result of successful completion of the anal stage, and his choice, with Freud, of the bowel-training situation as the major vehicle whereby autonomy can be learned.

Similarly, White (1960, p. 125) points out the difficulty in considering the Oedipal conflict of the phallic stage prototypic for initiative:

> And it seems to me that the Oedipal prototype falls short as a general model for the phallic stage in just the way toilet training failed for the anal stage. Once again Freud selected as his central image a hopeless situation, one where defeat for the child is inevitable. The child must learn to renounce the whole Oedipal wish, just as he must learn to renounce any thought of not being bowel trained. I submit the idea that if these were the true and determinative models it would be quite a problem to explain the survival of any sense of initiative. These models help us to understand why we have shame and guilt, but they do not give us much reason to suppose that we could emerge with autonomy and initiative. The competence model is not so harsh, though it certainly is not intended to gloss over the tragic features of childhood.

White follows through on his sense of the logical mismatch between Erikson's view of development and the Freudian conflict position by incorporating the genital stage into the general criticism presented above. According to Freudians, the sexual act, and more specifically, the orgasm, is the prototype of maturity or genitality. But while the orgasm is well suited logically to serve as the prototype for love in a more general sense, it is not at all well suited for understanding work. Working and loving can be used as summary terms for most of what Erikson and other psychoanalytic thinkers typify as successful adult living. Love, like the orgasm, involves intense, sporadic, and impulsive emotions, thoughts, and actions. But working is quite the opposite in its emphasis upon stability, persistence, and self-control. For White, the competence model is much more appropriate for the understanding of the many aspects of adult functioning that have to do with work and productivity than is the Freudian conflict position.

The thrust of White's remarks is that while the Freudian position is not exactly irrelevant to what is happening in development, it is not nearly as central as has been supposed. White accepts Erikson's chronology and classification of character traits or types, but finds them more naturally suited to an explanatory model that is of the fulfillment, rather than conflict type, and that stresses effectance motivation and competence, rather than sexuality per se. Although he cannot make the kind of basic criticism of considering orality prototypic of the first year of life that he did concerning the anal, phallic, and genital stages, White nonetheless has accumulated many observations of behavior during this first year that are not readily understood in oral terms. He (White, 1960, pp. 110–111) says:

> Somehow the image has gotten into our minds that the infant's time [during the first year] is divided between eating and sleep. Peter Wolff (1959) is now showing that this is not true even for newborn infants, who show distinct forerunners of what will later become playful exploratory activity. Gesell notes that at four weeks there is apt to be a waking time in the later afternoon during which visual experience begins to be accumulated. At 16 weeks this period may last for half an hour, and the times increase steadily up to one year, when Gesell's typical "behavior day" shows an hour of play before breakfast, two hours before lunch, an hour's carriage ride and another hour of social play during the afternoon, and perhaps still another hour before being put to bed. At the age of 12 months the child is already putting in a six-hour day of play, not to mention the overtime that occurs during meals and the bath.

Clearly there is a lot of activity during the first year of life that is difficult to understand as oral, or even as a generalization form an oral prototype. And then, of course, White makes hay with the latency stage, a time that psychoanalysts have never pretended to be able to understand in terms of their sexual conflict position. White finds the name latency a complete misnomer, for the period is one of intense activity relative to social and work competence.

In his criticisms of the Freudian conflict position as an explanation of Eriksonian character types, White implies a developmental theory of effectance motivation, and a specific set of social consequences of this development. During the first year of life, the child does not act as an integrated unit, displaying instead rudimentary, discrete examples of effectance motivation. The rudimentary nature of the child's capacities at this time is shown in the involvement of mainly hands, mouth, and voice in the attempt to produce effects in the world, and in the easy distractability that gives his attempts their playful, unimportant appearance. Actually, the attempts are very important, for by the end of the first year the child has gained some of his later basis for competence in interacting with the inanimate and social worlds. According to White, it is the physical maturation enabling walking, and the cognitive maturation enabling a sense of yourself as an organized entity that marks the next developmental stage. In this stage, effectance motivation is expressed in a more concerted, organized, persistent way, building upon the competencies gained during the first stage, and expanding to include locomotion.

In the social domain, the child experiences himself and is experienced by others as much more of a force than previously. The battle of the toilet is one result of this, but is only an example, rather than a prototype, of a more general negativism that is to be understood as the beginning of assertiveness. Continuing, White suggests that what is called the phallic stage, and initiated according to psychoanalytic thinkers by genital eroticism, is really a stage of development marked by great increases in three spheres of competence: locomotion, language, and imagination. Locomotion reaches the point of being a serviceable tool rather than a difficult stunt. Language likewise reaches a state at which it can support wider understanding and social exchange. Concerning imagination, this is the time when the child can first maintain the fantasy of an imaginary companion. He also begins to dramatize himself in adult roles. White believes that this growth in competence leads to intrinsic emotional and interpersonal crises having little to do with sexuality. He (White, 1960, pp. 124–125) argues that

> Perhaps the best way to make this clear is to imagine for the moment a child in the phallic stage who is normal in every way except that no increase in genital sensitivity takes place. This child would still make locomotor, linguistic, and imaginative progress, would become interested in being like adults, would make comparison as to size, would be competitive and subject to defeats and humiliations, would be curious, ask endless questions and encounter rebuffs, would have had dreams and guilt feelings over imagined assertive or aggressive actions, would learn about sex roles, would struggle to understand his relation to other family members, and might very well ask about marrying one of the parents. All of these things arise inescapably from progress in the growth

of competence. They all have important emotional consequences. In all these situations there is a chance to maintain and strengthen a sense of initiative; in all there is also a chance that the environment will act so as to impose a burden of guilt.

According to White, by the time the child has reached the latency period, he has progressed in competence and in the maturation of his organism to the point where he is no longer satisfied with exploration, play, and make-believe. In line with his interest in being an adult, he needs to feel useful and to be able to make things and deal with things that have significance in the adult world. And, of course, he goes from this state to that called genital, in which he really begins to assume the roles and responsibilities of an adult.

In closing this section on White, it is important that you recognize his endorsement of the developmental stages and character types suggested by Erikson, and his spirited argument that they are more naturally derived from a fulfillment model stressing effectance and competence than from a conflict model stressing sexuality and compromise. Although Adler and White have similar views of the core of personality, White has a more elaborate, differentiated view of the periphery of personality. In arriving at a set of peripheral characteristics, White has relied upon an elaboration of his core tendency involving differentiation into developmental stages. In contrast, Adler does not pattern expression of his core tendency developmentally, preferring instead to derive peripheral characteristics by differentiating kinds of organ inferiorities, family constellations, and family atmospheres.

Allport's position

Allport, like Murray, has given considerable attention to the problem of what is the best way to conceptualize concrete peripheral characteristics. But reaching a rather different conclusion than Murray, Allport has chosen for his major concrete peripheral characteristic something resembling a trait or grouping of habits. Originally, he (Allport, 1937), called his concept the *personal trait*, but later called it the *personal disposition* (Allport, 1961, p. 273), defined as ". . . a generalized neuropsychic structure (peculiar to the individual), with the capacity to render many stimuli functionally equivalent, and to initiate and guide consistent (equivalent) forms of adaptive and stylistic behavior." In order to gain greater understanding of this concept, a number of its implications will be discussed. In the discussion, I will compare the personal disposition to Murray's need concept, as Murray is the other personologist considered thus far who takes the concrete implications of his peripheral concepts seriously enough to offer careful definitions and detailed descriptions.

First let us consider the presumed effects of personal dispositions upon the person's functioning. Allport indicates that the personal disposi-

tion operates by producing equivalences in function and meaning between perceptions, interpretations, feelings, and actions not necessarily
equivalent in the natural world. In discussing this influence, Allport
(1961, p. 322) develops the following example. While Russians, college
professors, liberals, peace organizations, and antisegregationists may
seem different to many observers, to a person with the personal disposition *fear of Communism,* all of these stimulus configurations may be
equivalent in their perceived "Communist" properties. Such a personal
disposition would also engender response sequences that are equivalent
in their function of reducing the perceived threat of Communism. The
person might advocate war with the Russians, be suspicious of teachers,
vote for extreme right-wing persons and policies, join the Ku Klux Klan,
and so forth. Stimulus and response equivalences are diagnosed on the
basis of perceived meanings and related coping behaviors, rather than on
any necessarily obvious similarities. Although similar to the personal
disposition in some respects, the need concept stresses much more the
directional organization of behavior, with a sequence of acts that are
instrumental to reaching a goal followed by acts that involve the
consummation of the goal.

Another way of stating this difference between the personal disposition and the need concepts is to say that the latter is more motivational
than the former. For the need, the equivalences of functioning produced
are closely tied to the goal the person is trying to achieve, to what might
be called the "why" of behavior. Hence, need-produced behavior shows
waxing and waning corresponding to whether the need is aroused or
satisfied. In contrast, the personal disposition, like other trait concepts, is
a steady, unvarying entity, exerting a continuous influence upon functioning. There is little waxing and waning, because there is not, properly
speaking, any goal to be striven for and reached. The personal disposition
concept seems to give a larger place to the "what" and "how" of
behavior than does the need concept. But care must be taken not to
conclude that Allport is uninterested in motivation. Actually, he (Allport, 1961, p. 370) considers all personal dispositions to be motivational
to some degree in that they cause behavior. And even more important, he
distinguishes between those personal dispositions having greater or less
intention included within them, calling them *dynamic* and *stylistic,*
respectively (Allport, 1961, pp. 222–223). All in all, dynamic personal
dispositions are reminiscent of needs, whereas stylistic dispositions may
be somewhat like need-integrates.

The next difference concerns the disposition of tension. The need
functions according to some variety of the tension-reduction principle,
virtually by logical necessity, whereas most personal dispositions are
considered not to have tension reduction as an aim. This difference is
not to be construed as indicating that Allport's concept lacks motivational
significance of necessity, however, as motivation is for him in its most

important or propriate sense rather synonymous with conscious intent rather than tension state (Allport, 1961, pp. 222–225).

Having covered some of the implications of the personal disposition concept, we can now turn to an emphasis of overwhelming importance in Allport. He believed that each personal disposition is unique to the person studied. Actually, Allport (1961, p. 349) includes in his peripheral theorizing the less-important concept of *common trait* to account for the similarities attributable to possession of a common human nature and a common culture. But the common trait, though an admissible and useful concept, is for him an abstraction arrived at by generalizing across people, and hence will necessarily miss the actual dispositions of each person to some degree. The real personality is only considered to emerge when personal dispositions are assessed, and this requires intensive study of a person's past, present, and anticipated future functioning, though the use of such techniques as the case history and content analysis of personal documents (Allport, 1961, pp. 367–369, 1962). Allport (Allport & Odbert, 1936) has been unwilling to narrow the number of dispositions any further than the combinations that would be possible using the 18,000 or so common trait names in the English language.

Given the emphasis upon uniqueness, it is not at all surprising that Allport nowhere offers any list of typical personal dispositions. The closest he comes to specifying the typical content of personal dispositions is to suggest two bases for classifying them. One classification (Allport, 1961, p. 365) involves the pervasiveness and consistency with which personal dispositions influence functioning. Distinctions are made between *cardinal, central,* and *secondary* dispositions. Cardinal dispositions, if they exist in a personality, will set the entire pattern of a person's life. Central dispositions, possessed by virtually all people, are significant stabilizing features of functioning. Secondary dispositions produce relatively transient organization. The other classificatory principle is less clear, and bears some resemblance to that just described. It refers to the degree to which a disposition is at the core of a person's being (Allport, 1961, p. 264). Application of this principle leads to the Lewinian distinction between the *genotypical* and *phenotypical* disposition, the latter, though it involves some consistency in functioning, being less a reflection of the essential nature of personality than is the former. But Allport's discussion is sketchy, and it is not entirely clear what difference there is between genotypical and cardinal dispositions, on the one hand, and between phenotypical and central dispositions, on the other hand. You should also recognize that what little attempt Allport has made to organize or categorize personal dispositions is not for purposes of delineating types or styles of living. This absence of emphasis upon types may also be due to his extreme position on uniqueness.

If one man's personal dispositions may be entirely different from those of other men, how can you make lists of dispositions and organize them into types? And yet, while Allport is being true to the logic of his assumption concerning uniqueness in not offering lists of dispositions and a typology, he has certainly delivered into our hands a viewpoint on the periphery of personality that is very difficult to employ in any concrete way. About all Allport really gives you to go on in using his position is the notion that dispositions can be identified by the fact that they produce stimulus and response equivalences. But this is hardly enough. Human functioning is complex enough so that, without benefit of more concrete guidelines, stimulus and response equivalences can be found at many different livels, in many different ways. Each investigator is thrown completely upon his own artistry in each diagnosis of a disposition. He cannot derive much assistance from the diagnoses made by other investigators, or even from his own prior diagnoses. And he certainly cannot predict in advance of observation what any person's dispositions will be like. Nor can he be entirely sure that he is even using the personal disposition concept in the manner Allport may have intended.

But Allport, like Murray, must at least be given credit for having carefully delineated the nature, if not the content, of his concrete peripheral characteristic and having attempted to describe the manner in which it influences functioning. Such theoretical care concerning concrete peripheral characteristics is a valuable thing on the personological scene. It is the kind of care that could lead to viewpoints so well developed and specified as to make their use and empirical test really possible. But, unfortunately, Allport's theoretical efforts have fallen short of this goal of usability and empirical test because of his extreme emphasis upon the uniqueness of personal dispositions. Certainly, then, we should consider carefully the reasons for his extreme emphasis, in an attempt to determine whether it is really necessary. But I shall defer this consideration until Chapter 9.

What remains for discussion here is the nature of the relationship between personal dispositions (the periphery of personality) and propriate functions (the core of personality). Allport virtually never discussed this relationship directly, so I shall have to piece together what seems like relevant implications. In his earliest statement of the proprium, Allport (1955, pp. 41–56) made quite clear that it was to comprise general, pervasive functions or capabilities that were common to all men and had little in the way of structure or fixed content. If this is so, then personal dispositions are clearly not to be considered part of the proprium per se, representing as they do structural bases for lumping together certain stimuli and certain responses in a manner particular to one person alone. But later, Allport (1961, pp. 110–138) leaves one uncertain as to whether or not the proprium includes structural considerations. If the proprium is to include structure considerations, then it is possible to imagine that cardinal and genotypical dispositions, which are so general, might actually be part of the core of personality. But this is not likely to be

Allport's true intent, for he also seems to suggest that personality structure is formed out of the interaction between propriate functions and
environmental contexts.

A much more likely and useful position would be to consider that the
propriate functions, which comprise the core tendencies and characteristics, are not themselves combinations of dispositions, but rather the
major forces precipitating and combining with the person's life experiences to form dispositions. For example, propriate striving would
refer to the universal propensity for phenomenally important intention-
ing, or more simply, for working hard to reach goals that seem personally
significant. Because of propriate striving, it would be possible to develop
cardinal and central dispositions having dynamic properties. Cardinal,
and for that matter even genotypical dispositions would not, then, stand
at the core of personality, but rather would be the most general and
pervasive of a person's dispositions. No matter how general and pervasive, however, dispositions would be peripheral by comparison with
propriate functions. In this manner, cardinal and genotypical dispositions
could be put to their intended use of pinpointing individuality, because
if considered part of the periphery they would not have to be common
to all persons.

A personality theory is a changing, growing thing, and it may well be
that Allport was moving in the direction I have suggested above. He
was attempting to conceptualize components of personality that seem to
be sets of personal dispositions which reflect the qualities of propriate
functioning. Examples of this type of unit are his characteristics of
maturity (Allport, 1961, pp. 275–307) such as specific, enduring *extensions of the self,* techniques for *warm relating to others* (such as tolerance), stable *emotional security* or self-acceptance, habits of *realistic
perception, skills* and *problem-centeredness,* established *self-objectification* in the form of *insight* and *humor,* and a unifying *philosophy of life*
including particular *value orientations,* differentiated *religious sentiment,*
and a generic, *personalized conscience.* If I see his movement accurately,
Allport was, in describing the characteristics of maturity, breaking out
of the trap of an overemphasis on uniqueness. The end result of so
doing might have been a classification of personality types achieved
along content lines, and reflecting the concrete ramifications in behavior
of the core tendency of propriate functioning.

As personal dispositions are clearly learned, it is important to ask how
this learning takes place. It is relevant, first, to recognize that personal
dispositions are expressive of propriate functioning, if for no other reason
than that they describe individuality. But initially the infant's functioning is opportunistic rather than propriate. Opportunistic functioning is
regulated by, and in the service of needs of a biological nature. At this
level of functioning the infant has little freedom of choice, reacting to
pressures rather than being himself a force in the world. If the child

receives the support, love, and nourishment he needs at this early stage, he will begin to develop the kernels of selfhood. This means that there will be a shift from opportunistic to propriate functioning, and as you know, propriate functioning is proactive rather than reactive, being regulated by the person's own psychological goals, values, and principles. These goals, values, and principles must be the stuff of personal dispositions.

Probably, early opportunistic striving provides the basis for what will later become personal dispositions. Allport suggests that the original opportunistic strivings are expressed in certain patterns of action that come into being because they are useful in satisfying these strivings. But, once the person has matured a bit, and been sufficiently nurtured and supported by other people, opportunistic goals recede in importance because they can be satisfied readily and their existence is not a source of anxiety. The instrumental action patterns do not necessarily atrophy, however, even though they are no longer needed since the opportunistic goals have receded. Some of the action patterns become *functionally autonomous* (Allport, 1961, p. 229) of their origins, and continue to exist as personal dispositions. The action patterns that remain in this fashion are probably those that articulate best with the general propriate functions, which, as you may recall, include such things as self-identity and self-extension.

In his famous phrase, functional autonomy, Allport wished to convey his belief that action patterns including values, opinions, and goals, are not limited in importance simply because they may have started out in the service of some biological need that is no longer central. But Allport has often been criticized for vagueness in delineating the concept of functional autonomy. How does it work? What are its implications? What is the organismic basis for such an idea? Allport has recently attempted to clarify and specify the concept somewhat. He suggests that propriate functional autonomy comes about because the presumed energy potential possessed by the human is in excess of that contributed by survival needs, and hence there is an ongoing tendency to utilize this excess by increasing competence and pressing toward a unification of life (Allport, 1961, pp. 249–253). Allport's thinking remains somewhat vague concerning specific mechanisms whereby functional autonomy takes place, and thus provides a number of bases for controversy. He has not circumvented the repeated criticism that functional autonomy is more of an assertion than an explanation, although he does suggest that an extremely critical reception indicates an already closed mind when he says that his concept

> is merely a way of stating that men's motives change and grow in the course of life, because it is the nature of man that they should do so. Only theorists wedded to a reactive, homeostatic, quasi-closed model of man find difficulty in agreeing (Allport, 1961, pp. 252–253).

Fromm's position

Fromm is one of the most sophisticated and perhaps the most complete of the personologists on the nature of the periphery of personality.
His concrete peripheral characteristic is the *character trait,* and he has
described *orientations* or character types which comprise sets of interrelated traits. Having been profoundly influenced by Freud, Fromm
(1947, p. 57) tends to compare and contrast his own view with that of
the conflict theorists:

> The theory presented . . . follows Freud's characterology in essential
> points: in the assumption that character traits underlie behavior and
> must be inferred from it; that they constitute forces which, though
> powerful, the person may be entirely unconscious of it. It follows Freud
> also in the assumption that the fundamental entity in characters not the
> single character trait but the total character organization from which a
> number of single character traits follow. These character traits are to be
> understood as a syndrome which results from a particular organization
> or, as I shall call it, orientation of character.

You may recognize that not only Fromm and Freud, but also Adler
and Erikson, are in rather explicit agreement on the assumptions stated
so clearly above. In addition, such personologists as White, Murray, and
Allport would probably agree, though their emphases on particular
traits or needs rather than on types lead to some uncertainty. The note
in the quote from Fromm that sounds new to our discussion is the
recognition that there is a difference between a character trait and the
behavior it is used to explain. As I will argue in Chapter 9, it is important for a personologist to recognize this, because so doing will lead
him to focus upon what are the data, after all, that he wants to explain.
Any theorist should take this matter seriously, but the personologist
often does not. Fromm makes clear what must be true for all personologists, namely, that the peripheral characteristic of personality is an
explanatory concept—something the theorist devised—rather than a mere
description of the observational facts.

Now to the content of Fromm's position on the periphery of personality. His character types are four *nonproductive orientations,* and
one *productive orientation.* In the nonproductive classification, there are
the *receptive, exploitative, hoarding,* and *marketing orientations.* In
Fromm's (1947 pp. 62–63) words, the person with a receptive orientation

> . . . feels "the source of all good" to be outside, and he believes that
> the only way to get what he wants—be it something material, be it af-
> fection, love, knowledge, pleasure—is to receive it from that outside
> source. In this orientation the problem of love is almost exclusively that
> of "being loved" and not that of loving. Such people tend to be in-
> discriminate in the choice of their love objects, because being loved by
> anybody is such an overwhelming experience for them that they "fall for"

anybody who gives them love or what looks like love. . . . Their orientation is the same in the sphere of thinking: if intelligent, they make the best listeners, since their orientation is one of receiving, not of producing, ideas. . . . They show a particular kind of loyalty, at the bottom of which is the gratitude for the hand that feeds them and the fear of ever losing it. . . . It is difficult for them to say "no," and they are easily caught between conflicting loyalties and promises. . . .

They are dependent not only on authorities for knowledge and help but on people in general for any kind of support. . . . . This receptive type has great fondness for food and drink. These persons tend to overcome anxiety and depression by eating and drinking. . . . By and large, the outlook of people of this receptive orientation is optimistic and friendly; they have a certain confidence in life and its gifts, but they become anxious and distraught when their "source of supply" is threatened.

Fromm has added to this vivid description, a concrete list of the traits comprising the receptive orientation. These traits have a positive and a negative pole, i.e., they sound more admirable at one pole than the other. Fromm includes both poles because he feels that the more deeply is the person's personality of the nonproductive, receptive type, the more will the negative poles of the traits describe his behavior. But if the receptive orientation is mitigated by some degree of a more productive orientation, then the positive poles of the traits will be more accurate. I will return to this point after we have viewed all the orientations. For the moment, we should focus on the list of traits, which is as follows (Fromm, 1947, p. 114):

Receptive orientation

Positive aspect	*Negative aspect*
accepting	passive, without initiative
responsive	opinionless, characterless
devoted	submissive
modest	without pride
charming	parasitical
adaptable	unprincipled
socially adjusted	servile, without self-confidence
idealistic	unrealistic
sensitive	cowardly
polite	spineless
optimistic	wishful thinking
trusting	gullible
tender	sentimental

You can probably imagine what Fromm means by the *exploitative orientation*. He describes it this way (Fromm, 1947, pp. 64–65):

The exploitative orientation, like the receptive, has as its basic premise the feeling that the source of all good is outside, that whatever one wants to get must be sought there, and that one cannot produce anything oneself. The difference between the two, however, is that the exploitative type does not expect to receive things from others as gifts, but to take them away from others by force or cunning. . . . In the realm of love and affection these people tend to grab and steal. They feel attracted only to people whom they can take away from somebody else. . . . We find the same attitude with regard to thinking and intellectual pursuits. Such people will tend not to produce ideas but to steal them. . . . They use and exploit anybody and anything from whom or from which they can squeeze something. . . . This orientation seems to be symbolized by the biting mouth which is often a prominent feature in such people.

A list of character traits is also included for the exploitative orientation (Fromm, 1947, p. 115):

Exploitative orientation

Positive aspect	*Negative aspect*
active	exploitative
able to take initiative	aggressive
able to make claims	egocentric
proud	conceited
impulsive	rash
self-confident	arrogant
captivating	seducing

The third nonproductive style of life is the *hoarding orientation*. Once again, Fromm (1947, pp. 65–66) describes this orientation vividly:

While the receptive and exploitative types are similar inasmuch as both expect to get things from the outside world, the hoarding orientation is essentially different. This orientation makes people have little faith in anything new they might get from the outside world; their security is based upon hoarding and saving, while spending is felt to be a threat. They have surrounded themselves, as it were, by a protective wall, and their main aim is to bring as much as possible into this fortified position and to let as little as possible out of it. Their miserliness refers to money and material things as well as to feelings and thoughts. Love is essentially a possession; they do not give love but try to get it by possessing the "beloved. . . ." Their sentimentality makes the past appear as golden; they hold on to it and indulge in the memories of bygone feelings and experiences. . . . One can recognize these people too by facial expressions and gestures. Theirs is the tight-lipped mouth; their gestures are characteristic of their withdrawal attitude. . . . Another characteristic element in this attitude is pedantic orderliness. The hoarder will be orderly with things, thoughts, or feelings, but again, as with memory, his orderliness is sterile and rigid. . . . His compulsive cleanliness is another expression of his need to undo contact with the outside world.

The list of character traits comprising the hoarding orientation is as follows (Fromm, 1947, p. 115):

Hoarding orientation

Positive aspect	Negative aspect
practical	unimaginative
economical	stingy
careful	suspicious
reserved	cold
patient	lethargic
cautious	anxious
steadfast, tenacious	stubborn
imperturbable	indolent
composed under stress	inert
orderly	pedantic
methodical	obsessional
loyal	possessive

It should not have escaped your attention that the three orientations described thus far are similar in some ways to Freudian character types. Both the receptive and the exploitative orientations are reminiscent of the oral character type. And indeed, if one follows some psychoanalytic thinkers, such as Abraham (1927a, 1927b), who distinguish between oral-incorporative and oral-aggressive character types, then the fit becomes even closer. Oral-incorporativeness seems like the receptive orientation, and oral-aggressiveness seems like the exploitative orientation. In addition, the hoarding orientation is quite reminiscent of the anal character type. These similarities should not surprise you, for Fromm started out as a psychoanalytic thinker, though he gradually developed a very different view. The existence in his theory of the first three orientations indicates that Fromm found some Freudian statements concerning the periphery of personality to be warranted. But, as you will see below, he docs include some orientations that have no counterpart in psychoanalytic thinking. If you add to this the fact that Fromm is very different from Freud at the core level of personality, you will see that it is a mistake to consider Fromm to be a psychoanalytic thinker. Even though he admits the value of some of Freud's statements concerning character types, Fromm explains their development on grounds that have nothing to do with psychosexuality.

I will consider Fromm's developmental views in a moment, but for now, let us return to a consideration of the remaining orientations. The final nonproductive style of life is the *marketing orientation,* and in delineating, it, Fromm expresses much of his originality as a personality theorist. Fromm takes the modern marketplace as the model for this orientation, which involves man being reduced to a commodity (Fromm, 1947, pp. 68–72):

The modern market is no longer a meeting place but a mechanism characterized by abstract and impersonal demand. One produces for this market, not for a known circle of customers; its verdict is based on laws of supply and demand; and it determines whether the commodity can be sold and at what price. . . . The character orientation which is rooted in the experience of oneself as a commodity and of one's value as exchange value I call the marketing orientation.

In our time the marketing orientation has been growing rapidly, together with the development of a new market that is a phenomenon of the last decades—the "personality market.". . . The principle of evaluation is the same on both the personality and the commodity market: on the one, personalities are offered for sale; on the other, commodities. Value in both cases is their exchange value, for which use value is a necessary but not a sufficient condition. . . . However, if we ask what the respective weight of skill and personality as a condition for success is, we find that only in exceptional cases is success predominantly the result of skill and of certain other human qualities like honesty, decency, and integrity. Although the proportion between skill and human qualities on the one hand and "personality" on the other hand as prerequisites for success varies, the "personality factor" always plays a decisive role. Success depends largely on how well a person sells himself on the market, how well he gets his personality across, how nice a "package" he is; whether he is "cheerful," "sound," "aggressive," "reliable," "ambitious"; furthermore what his family background is, what club he belongs to, and whether he knows the right people. . . . Like the handbag, one has to be in fashion on the personality market, and in order to be in fashion one has to know what kind of personality is most in demand. . . . Since modern man experiences himself both as the seller and as the commodity to be sold on the market, his self-esteem depends on conditions beyond his control. If he is "successful," he is valuable; if he is not, he is worthless. The degree of insecurity which results from this orientation can hardly be overestimated. If one feels that one's value is not constituted primarily by the human qualities one possesses, but by one's success on a competitive market with ever-changing conditions, one's self-esteem is bound to be shaky and in constant need of confirmation by others. Hence one is driven to strive relentlessly for success, and any setback is a severe threat to one's self-esteem; helplessness, insecurity, and inferiority feelings are the result. If the vicissitudes of the market are the judges of one's value, the sense of dignity and pride is destroyed.

The marketing orientation underlies the problem of alienation that has been so vivid in the minds of contemporary social critics (e.g., Sontag, 1961), sociologists (e.g., Simmel, 1950), and personologists (e.g., Schachtel, 1961). This orientation is clearly different from anything Freud considered, and yet seems so valid in contemporary life. The character traits comprising the marketing orientation are as follows (Fromm, 1947, p. 116):

Marketing orientation

Positive aspect	Negative aspect
purposeful	opportunistic
able to change	inconsistent
youthful	childish
forward-looking	without a future or a past
open-minded	without principle and values
social	unable to be alone
experimenting	aimless
undogmatic	relativistic
efficient	overactive
curious	tactless
intelligent	intellectualistic
adaptable	undiscriminating
tolerant	indifferent
witty	silly
generous	wasteful

Having discussed the four nonproductive orientations, we come now to what Fromm considers to be the ideal character type, the productive orientation. As you will see, the productive orientation bears similarity to the Freudian genital character, and to the fully functioning or self-actualizing personalities of Rogers and Maslow, as well as to the active-constructive style of life of the Adlerians, and the mature personality according to Allport. Once again, I will let Fromm speak for himself in describing the *productive orientation* (Fromm, 1947, pp. 83–97):

> In discussing the *productive character* I venture beyond critical analysis and inquire into the nature of the fully developed character that is the aim of human development and simultaneously the ideal of humanistic ethics. . . . The "productive orientation" of personality refers to fundamental attitude, a *mode of relatedness* in all realms of human experience. It covers mental, emotional, and sensory responses to others, to oneself, and to things. Productiveness is man's ability to use his powers and to realize the potentialities inherent in him. If we say *he* must use *his* powers we imply that he must be free and not dependent on someone who controls his powers. We imply, furthermore that he is guided by reason, since he can make use of his powers only if he knows what they are, how to use them, and what to use them for. Productiveness means that he experiences himself as the embodiment of his powers and as the "actor"; that he feels himself one with his powers and at the same time that they are not marked and alienated from him. . . . Productiveness is man's realization of the potentialities characteristic of him, the use of his *powers*. . . . How is man related to the world when he uses his powers productively? . . . The world outside oneself can be experienced in two ways: reproductively by perceiving actuality in the same fashion as a film makes a literal record of things photographed . . . and *generatively* by conceiving it, by enlivening and recreating this new material through the spontaneous activity of one's own mental and emotional

powers. . . . Human existence is characterized by the fact that man is alone and separated from the world; not being able to stand the separation, he is impelled to seek for relatedness and oneness. There are many ways in which he can realize this need, but only one in which he, as a unique entity, remains intact; only one in which his own powers unfold in the very process of being related. It is the paradox of human existence that man must simultaneously seek for closeness and for independence; for oneness with others and at the same time for the preservation of his uniqueness and particularity. As we have shown, the answer to this paradox—and to the moral problem of man—is *productiveness.*

One can be productively related to the world by acting and by comprehending. Man *produces things,* and in the process of creation he exercises his powers over matter. Man *comprehends the world,* mentally and emotionally, through love and through reason. His power of reason enables him to penetrate through the surface and to grasp the essence of his object by getting into active relation with it. His power of love enables him to break through the wall which separates him from another person and to comprehend him. Although love and reason are only two different forms of comprehending the world and although neither is possible without the other, they are expressions of different powers, that of emotion and that of thinking, and hence must be discussed separately.

Fromm lists no set traits which comprise the productive orientation. This is partly because he feels that the truly productive person would not be predictable enough so that one could specify fixed traits. By productiveness, after all, he does not mean sticking to a job, or acting in a repetitive way, but rather something more like creativity and transcendence. But there are certainly some traits, such as imaginativeness, that one could list for the productive orientation, so the reason of unpredictability cannot be sufficient to explain why Fromm chooses not to offer a list of traits. The rest of the reason lies in the relationship he suggests between the productive and nonproductive orientations. According to Fromm, it is very unlikely that anyone would show a completely developed productive orientation. In this, Fromm is much like Rogers, who indicates that the fully functioning person is an ideal characterization of life, not actually achieved *in toto* by anyone. What one normally finds, according to Fromm, is some combination of productive and nonproductive orientations. This is why Fromm bothered to include positive aspects along with negative aspects for the traits comprising the nonproductive orientations. The more the productive orientation is combined with a nonproductive one, the more will the postive aspects of the traits comprising the nonproductive orientation be accurate. Thus, the positive aspects of the traits listed under nonproductive orientations can characterize the productive qualities of a person's style of life.

As I mentioned in introducing discussion of the productive orientation, it bears resemblance to the ideal peripheral personality of a number of other theorists. You can probably see now what I meant. The emphasis on actualizing one's capabilities and being creative is similar to Rogers and Maslow. The emphasis on concrete productions, and the orientation toward production and perfection is similar to White and Adler. The emphasis on reason and love is similar to Allport's discussion of psychological maturity. And, although the quotes I selected do not play it up, there is similarity to Freud in the fact that mature sexuality, in the senses of orgasm and progeny, are also considered productive. That Fromm's views are similar not only to other fulfillment theorists, but to some conflict theorists as well, reflects at the peripheral level the classificatory problem we had with him at the core level (see Chapter 3). Although Fromm is primarily a fulfillment theorist, he incorporates elements of the conflict emphasis as well.

Before leaving Fromm, we should consider his view of development, or the way in which the various orientations can come about through the interaction between expression of the core tendency and the environmental contexts that are encountered. As I indicated before, Fromm's view of development is very different from that of Freud. First, the core tendency is different. For Fromm, man's life is basically an attempt to realize his human nature, which includes, you will remember, such needs as those for relatedness, transcendence, and identity. Psychosexuality plays a small part in all this. The second divergence from Freud is in the nature of the parent-child interaction that is considered important in understanding the resultant peripheral personality types. For Fromm, the three important types of interaction are *symbiotic relatedness, withdrawal-destructiveness,* and *love* (Fromm, 1947, pp. 107–108). In the symbolic situation,

> . . . the person is related to others but loses or never attains his independence; he avoids the danger of aloneness by becoming part of another person, either by being "swallowed" by that person or by "swallowing" him.

Being swallowed by parents, as it were, leads to the masochistic patterns of behavior culminating in the receptive orientation. This whole pattern is encouraged by parents who render the child dependent upon them, but in the specially violating way that entails laying oneself bare to be used by others in one's search for satisfaction. But if the reverse situation occurs, if the parent's abnegate authority to the child by catering to his every whim and encouraging him to use them, the pattern that will develop is more like sadism. This sadism in the child will culminate in the exploitative orientation, expressing as it does dependence upon others for purposes of violating them.

The symbiotic relationship is one of closeness to and intimacy with the other person, though at the expense of freedom and integrity. In contrast, the withdrawal-destructiveness type of parent-child relationship is characterized by *distance*. According to Fromm (1947, pp. 109–110):

> In the phenomenon here described, withdrawal becomes the main form of relatedness to others, a negative relatedness, as it were. Its emotional equivalent is the feeling of indifference toward others, often accompanied by compensatory feeling of self-inflation.

This withdrawal pattern, which will culminate in the marketing orientation, is encouraged by parents who are destructive toward the child. In other words, they will not simply frustrate his needs, but will attempt to subjugate and destroy him. In the face of such an onslaught, the child copes with the sense of powerlessness by retreating and becoming indifferent. But the destructiveness that engenders withdrawal need not be on the part of the parents. Indeed, if the parents are indifferent and withdrawn from the child, he may well develop the pattern of destructiveness, which according to Fromm (1947, p. 110) is the active form of withdrawal. The resulting pattern of assertiveness will culminate in the hoarding orientation.

As you have undoubtedly anticipated, when the parent-child relationship is one of love, with all its implications of mutual respect, support, and appreciation, then the child will develop in the direction of productive orientation. Loved by his parents, the child will love himself, and have no reason not to love others.

It is as members of their culture that parents affect their children, and hence, one may expect each of the various orientations to be prominent under a particular set of cultural conditions. Fromm feels that the receptive, exploitative, and hoarding orientations were especially characteristic of the 18th and 19th centuries, though they are by no means absent now. He dates their prominence thusly because they require a form of society in which one group had an institutionalized right to exploit another group. Since the exploited group has no power to change, or any idea of changing its situation, it will tend to look up to its masters as its providers. Hence, the receptive orientation. The societal model for the exploitative character goes back to piratical and feudal ancestors and goes forward from there to the robber barons of the 19th century who exploited the natural resources of the Continent. "The hoarding orientation," according to Fromm (1947, p. 81), "existed side by side with the exploitative orientation in the eighteenth and nineteenth centuries. The hoarding type was conservative, less interested in ruthless acquisition than in methodical economic pursuits, based on sound principles and on the preservation of what had been acquired." Fromm associated the hoarding orientation with the Protestant Ethic. But the marketing orientation has reached a position of predominance only in the 20th century, with its emphasis upon the modern marketplace and its materialistic, superficial values. And as you might expect, the societal model consistent with the productive orientation has not yet emerged on the world scene, according to Fromm. It is describable, however, and would, in a phrase, suit the human needs of man, rather than of the marketplace. It would be truly a *sane* society (Fromm, 1955).

It is with a sense of disquietude that I conclude this discussion of Fromm's position on the periphery of personality. Of the theorists thus far covered, he alone has been so explicit and complete concerning what he does and does not mean by traits and orientations. No one else has endeavored actually to list the traits that comprise the character types he wishes to consider. While it is true that Murray and Allport have given more care to the delineation and definition of their concrete peripheral characteristics of need and personal disposition, Fromm surpasses them in organizing traits into types. And one has the feeling that someone could easily provide precise definitions for the traits he employs. All this pleases me greatly about Fromm. It should be possible to determine the empirical fruitfulness of Fromm's position because he has gone a long way toward the theoretical formalism necessary to make a position really usable. But for all this I also find myself somewhat disappointed, and hence the disquietude. I am not particularly enlightened or convinced by his account of development. Sometimes he suggests that the child will develop in a manner opposite to the way he has been treated by the parent. This is seen in the notion that parents who swallow up their children will produce children who ask the world to swallow them. But at other times, he suggests that the child will develop in a manner similar to that of the parent, or the society, of which the parent is, after all, the representative. This seems implicit in such notions as that the existence in society of a downtrodden class was necessary as a model for the receptive orientation. This may all sound very reasonable, but let me pinpoint my difficulty. If you are a member of this downtrodden class, for example, would you, according to Fromm, swallow up your child, or encourage him to swallow you? Common sense suggests the latter, and yet, knowledge that classes tend to perpetuate themselves suggests the former. And Fromm himself seems unable to decide. I do not want to make too much of this criticism, as the difficulty can, after all, be resolved. It is a matter for future theoretical effort. All in all, I commend Fromm's position to you as an excellent example of peripheral theorizing, regardless of whether it turns out to be supported by empirical evidence.

Existential psychology

Although there are implications in existential thought which could lead to a position on peripheral personality, existentialists differ as to whether such theorizing is worthwhile. Binswanger (1963) and Boss (1963), at one extreme, say very little that is explicit, systematic, or formal about development, types, and concrete peripheral characteristics.

To be sure, their discussions of authentic as opposed to inauthentic being definitely imply two general ways of operating or styles. But they nowhere explicate these implications, probably believing, with the actualization fulfillment theorists, that to do so would be inconsistent with their overall emphasis upon freedom. Less extreme is Keen (1970) who, though not offering a position on peripheral personality per se, does indicate something of the form development takes in early life. At the other extreme in Maddi (1967, 1970) who elaborates two personality types which he sees as consistent with the kind of core theorizing engaged in by existential psychologists, and has some fragmentary notions of the developmental history linking core to periphery. What follows will be based largely on the writings of Keen and Maddi, but you are cautioned to recognize that though they believe themselves to be working in the spirit of existentialism, there are others in that tradition who would disagree.

As you will recall from Chapter 3, existential psychologists emphasize the difference between facing ontological anxiety and guilt squarely and lying to yourself. When you lie, you act as if life were not a series of decisions which you have the responsibility for making, relying instead upon the erroneous belief that certain forces acting upon you constitute necessities. But if you remain honest or authentic, you realize that these forces are actually only possibilites which you can choose to be affected by, or to transcend. This process of creating your own life heavily involves the use of mental powers in what Gendlin (1965–66) calls the explication of experience. The two personality types Maddi (1967, 1970) proposes essentially state the differences between authentic and inauthentic being as styles or habitual predispositions, though his terminology is sometimes a little different from that above.

At the core level, Maddi (1967, 1970) postulates the presence of biological, social, and psychological needs, considering this consistent with the conceptualization in existential theorizing of Umwelt, Mitwelt, and Eigenwelt. It is the psychological needs—for symbolizing, imagining, and judging—that carry the uniqueness of the human being, both as a species and as an individual. The more you symbolize, imagine, and judge, the greater and more unusual will be your storehouse of (1) categories with which to recognize, (2) ideas about desired change, and (3) values and preferences. But, since biological and social needs are also parts of human nature, the best life will be that which vigorously expresses all three sets of needs.

The personality type expressing inauthentic being comes about when the psychological needs have been defended against. The person makes minimal use of symbolization, imagination, and judgment, which means that his thoughts are few, gross, and stereotyped. He does express biological and social needs, but shows the simplest, least subtle forms of them, due to the relative absence of psychological expression. Maddi

(1970) considers this personality type to show biological and social reductionism, and labels it *conformism*. Why it is conformism is apparent in the self-definition (sense of identity) and the world view it entails. The conformist's *sense of identity* is as nothing more than a player of social roles and an embodiment of creature needs. The difficulty is not that the human is not these two things, but that what he is in addition finds little representation in the conformist's self-definition.

Let us focus on social reductionism for a moment. If your Mitwelt is such that you view yourself as nothing more than a player of social roles, you are in effect accepting the idea that the social system is a terribly potent force in living. Society appears to be institutions and laws that transcend individuals and have a life of their own. This inclines you to the belief that the current content and form of the social system is its necessary and unchangeable nature and that individuals have no choice but to conform to its pressures. In the long run, conforming to social system pressures even comes to appear morally worthwhile. This takes the form of the conviction that it is the social system, as currently constituted, that protects everyone against chaos, and therefore we all ought to do our share to support its institutions, however restricting they may be. The way to give this support is to play adequately the social roles that are given to you as a responsibility of citizenship.

There are parallel implications of biological reductionism. If your Umwelt is such that you view yourself as nothing more than an embodiment of creature needs, you obviously come to believe that such needs as those for food and water are terribly important and real forces in living. Physical survival seems unquestionably of paramount importance, and hence, the degree to which biological needs are satisfied is taken as the hallmark of adequate living. It becomes difficult to imagine justifying deprivation of these needs under any circumstances. Any alternative to direct, immediate, and constant expression of these needs, if an alternative could be construed as possible, would be unwise because it would constitute a violation of all that is important.

The person whose Umwelt and Mitwelt are characterized by biological and social reductionism must necessarily feel powerless in the face of social pressures from outside, and powerless in the face of biological pressures from inside. Creatureness and social roles seem like givens, like causal factors independent of his puny power to influence. He will not experience life as a series of decisions he willingly makes. Indeed, he would never seriously reject a social role or change it. He would never think to question just how important physical survival is anyway. Soon he will become his social roles and biological needs—there being no longer any act of consciousness worth speaking of to mark the fact that his identity is not the only one possible. There will be little basis for raising abstract questions about the nature of existence.

The generalization of his identity into a world view potentiates his difficulties on a grand scale. This *world view* is based on pragmatism and materialism. The pragmatism comes primarily from viewing not only yourself but everyone else having to play the assigned social roles. The only relevant question becomes how good the people are in enacting these roles. Materialism comes primarily from the belief that not only you, but others as well, are no more than the embodiments of biological needs. This leads to coveting not only the goods that are objects of the needs (e.g., clothes to make one attractive), but also the processes instrumental to obtaining these objects (e.g., making money). The pursuit of material things is elevated to the status of a natural process.

With this self-definition and world view, it is easy to see how the conformist would be often in conflict. The conflict is that inherent in the likelihood that social roles and creature needs will lead in different, if not incompatible, directions. This potentiality for conflict arises from the fact that while social roles become institutionalized along the lines of what is socially acceptable, biological needs are defined in terms of animalistic urges, without regard to propriety. The only self-consciousness the conformist ever feels consistently has to do with his inability to satisfy both aspects of his identity with the same set of actions. He will try to assuage biological and social pressures at different times, or in different places, keeping possible incompatibilities from the eyes of others and from direct confrontation in his own awareness. His being-in-the-world will be fragmentary, disunified, a pastiche of bits and pieces.

The conformist's relationships with others are contractual rather than intimate. If you and everyone else are considered bound by certain rules of social interaction and in need of certain material goods for satisfaction and survival, relationships will tend to be based on the economic grounds of who is getting what from whom, when, and for how much. The conformist will not be willing to just let an interaction go in whatever direction that develops, nor will he be willing to continue or terminate it on the basis of how interesting or stimulating it is. Rather, he will want it structured in advance, and it will have to be clear all along what is in it for him in terms of social status or material advance. And once he gets what he wants, there will be no further reason for contact. Bonds of affection, loyalty, camaraderie, and love will not tend to develop in any full-blown sense of these terms. The conformist's relations will tend to be rather cold-blooded, even though the absence from them of intimacy and spontaneity will leave a nagging sense of loneliness and disappointment.

However unappetizing conformism seems, Maddi (1967, 1970) does not regard it as frank psychopathology, but rather predisposition to psychopathology. Conformity is too common and livable to be regarded as sickness, though it has its own characteristic sufferings and limitations. The main disadvantage of conformism, according to Maddi, is that it renders the person vulnerable to certain stresses, the occurrence of which can precipitate existential sickness. The stresses are those that can disrupt his being-in-the-world by disconfirming his self-definition as a player of social roles and an embodiment of biological needs. The three such stresses Maddi (1967, 1970) lists are the threat of imminent death, gross disruption of the social order, and the repeated confrontation with the limitations on deep and comprehensive experiencing produced by conformity. The first of these has its disconfirming effect by demonstrating human finitude to someone who has, in stressing the paramount importance of physical survival, forgotten that he will die. The second disconfirms the belief in society as absolute to someone who has assumed it cannot change. The third is a direct disconfirmation of the conformist's being-in-the-world, usually occasioned by the strenuous objections of someone close to him that is suffering because of his superficiality. The sickness resulting from such disconfirmations is called existential because in all its forms it reveals a breakdown in the ability to consider life meaningful and worthwhile (Maddi, 1967, 1970).

As you will expect, the personality type epitomizing authentic being is the opposite of conformism. In this ideal type, there is vigorous expression of psychological needs along with biological and social needs. This leads to biological and social experiencing showing considerable taste, subtlety, intimacy, and love, due to the humanizing, organizing effects of symbolization, imagination, and judgment. This personality type is called *individualism* because the vigorous expression of psychological needs involves an extensive and unusual cognitive mass (Maddi, 1967, 1970).

True to what has been said, the individualist is presumed to define himself (*sense of identity*) as someone with a mental life through which he can understand and influence his social and biological experience and urges. Although he recognizes and accepts social and biological pressures, he does not feel powerless in the face of them and experiences considerable room to maneuver in the process of finding just the right life for himself. He believes he is capable of choice and has freedom, though he is not so naïve to think that there are no constraints upon him, no necessities. His stance is one which questions whether things that seem constraints really are recalcitrant to influence.

Understandably, in his *world view*, he sees society as the creation of persons, properly in their service, and believes the human to be unique among living things because of his extraordinary mental powers which make it possible for him to be master of his own fate. Certainly the individualist will be realistic enough to recognize that social systems are not always responsive to their publics, and that persons often act as if they believe themselves no different from the apes. But he will consider such social systems and such persons to be less than ideal, to have fallen short of what it is within human power to achieve. The value of this judgment is that it provides the individualist with a format for action.

He may decide to withdraw from such inhuman societies and persons. Alternatively, he may try to convince the people that they are wrong and influence the social system through political action.

This ideal personality type is called the individualist not because it connotes a steely aloofness and indifference to others. Such a person is an individualist only because his actions and thoughts are relatively uncommon and expressive of psychological needs. Actually, he will relate to others more deeply than the conformist, substituting intimacy for contract. Just because the individualist's life will be a frequently changing, unfolding thing should not suggest lack of discipline or persistence. Do not be misled by the emphasis on subtlety, taste, intimacy, and love. More than anyone else, the individualist will have standards, know what he wants, and be willing and able to pursue his desires with rigor and self-reliance. He could even perform unpleasant tasks gracefully if they are definitely related to reaching the desired goals. And he would show the courage to face ontological anxiety born of a belief in his own power and dignity.

Certainly the individualist sounds like a fine fellow. But beyond this attractiveness, his value inheres in not being vulnerable to stress. Neither the threat of imminent death nor gross disruption of the social order would disconfirm the individualist's self-definition. The accumulated sense of superficiality in living would simply not occur, and so would never be a problem. All in all, his being-in-the-world would be very hardy indeed.

Like Rogers and Maslow, Maddi has postulated two personality types only, even though his general position emphasizes individuality so much that one would have expected more types to be proposed. To be sure, the individualist type does embody the emphasis on individuality, but it must still be considered a drawback that the formal theorizing permits only two kinds of people to be distinguished. Probably, there are several subtypes of individualists and conformists, though it is not immediately apparent how they could be generated from the assumptions that have been made. Perhaps one root would be to subdivide the conformist type along lines of whether biological or social needs are paramount in expression. And perhaps the individualist type could be divided into those who are primarily symbolizers or imaginers or judges. This separation of mental styles is a bit reminiscent of Jung's peripheral theorizing. Another drawback of Maddi's peripheral statement is that although types are proposed, there is no formal consideration of concrete peripheral characteristics. Several are implied, and perhaps could be more explicitly stated in the future.

As is common among existential psychologists, Maddi is quite sketchy about development. Existentialists generally assume that being-in-the-world is learned, but do not take you beyond this truism to precise consideration of just how a particular style or some other develops. What

Maddi (1967, 1970) does say is that individualism requires (1) respect and admiration of the child (something like Rogers' unconditional positive regard) as someone who will develop into a unique person, and (2) encouragement to exercise symbolization, imagination, and judgment with regard to one's biological and social experiences. This encouragement can be in the form of direct ideological communication, or by being a thinking parent as a model for the child. In any event, it is important that the psychological needs not appear as unimportant or threatening to the parents.

If the parents do feel threatened by psychological needs, or if they fail to recognize their importance, there will be no encouragement of the child to develop symbolization, imagination, and judgment. According to Maddi (1967, 1970) this is rather consonant with devaluing and disrespecting the child, because the psychological needs define what is human about the human being. Out of this complex of parental influences will come conformism, with its emphasis on biological and social reductionism.

Aside from some clarifying examples, Maddi goes no further. There is no consideration of developmental stages, and little elaboration of who are the significant persons in the child's development, beyond the assumption that not only parents but also teachers are of note. Keen (1970) presents four developmental stages, which though not tied to Maddi's personality types, are quite consistent with the general existential emphasis. The first stage is *fusion*, in which the distinction between subject and object has not been made by the child. The second stage is *separation*, which begins at that point during the first year when oneself is experienced as different from the rest. In the third stage, or *satellization*, "the child's experience of subjectness and objectness reverse themselves" (Keen, 1970, p. 41) and he falls into orbit around his parents. Where he had been the triumphant center of gravity in the separation stage, the child must give ground to the superior judgment and power of adults, which amounts to emphasizing what Keen calls being-for-others. But in return, the child gains considerable security. And here Keen makes the interesting point, reminiscent of the Freudian position on how parents can avoid instilling fixations, that to stimulate the child's being-in-the-world, it is useful to apply mild punishment. While severe punishment renders him unwilling to explore possibilities, and no punishment does not stimulate him to recognize them, mild punishment actually broadens his sense of alternatives and decreases his acceptance of parentally endorsed options. The final stage then emerges as *similarity*, in which by age seven or so the child is beginning to assess accurately the degree to which he and others (parents, siblings, peers) are alike and different.

This, of course, is a sound developmental course, culminating in authentic being or an individualistic style. But the major developmental hazards are pressures leading toward lying. Although Keen is clear about how lying to others and oneself jeopardizes authentic being, he is unfortunately ambiguous about what brings this lying about. Presumably, it is anything in parents and other significant adults that will interfere with the ideal developmental course mentioned above. Of perhaps most significance, according to Keen, is too severe or insufficient punishment during the satellization stage, so that the child never emerges from dependence upon the wishes and beliefs of others.

Chapter 8 THE PERIPHERY OF
PERSONALITY: CONSISTENCY MODEL

It became clear in Chapter 4 that at the core level of personality the consistency model does not emphasize content. What remains to be determined is the model's disposition toward content at the periphery of personality. Interestingly enough, we shall see that of the three theories considered here, one fails to specify the content of peripheral characteristics, another is quite eclectic, and the third considers the kind of content that could well be learned in the pursuit of consistency.

CONSISTENCY MODEL: COGNITIVE DISSONANCE VERSION

Kelly's position

Kelly's basic unit of personality is the *personal construct*. Personal constructs are organized into *construction systems*, which comprise the personality. As you will recall from Chapter 4, Kelly offers the general definition of a construct as an idea or abstraction that is dichotomous in nature. He also gives some notion of the manner in which constructs are organized into systems, this manner being basically hierarchical. These statements are all at the core of personality, for they do not differentiate one man from another. In order to have a position on the periphery of personality, Kelly would have to specify the content of the sets of personal constructs believed to comprise the commonly encountered construction systems. Nowhere does he do this. Like Allport, Kelly is adamant on the uniqueness of people, and the attendant uselessness of attempting to specify what they may be like in advance of actually encountering them. Each person is so different from the next, in his view, that the most a theorist can do is to provide a consistent set of notions about what the common units of personality are like, and how these units are organized. To presume that these units and organizations have typical content is to

349

do violence to human uniqueness. Indeed, if Allport's recent specification of the contents of characteristics of psychological maturity does indicate, as I have suggested, the first step in the development of a typology of character, then Allport has actually become less insistent on individuality than is Kelly. Furthermore, Rogers, who also emphasizes individuality, is less extreme on this point than is Kelly. After all, Rogers does specify the general content of the character type called the fully functioning person, and its opposite, the maladjusted person.

The closest that Kelly comes to developing a position on the periphery of personality can be seen in two aspects of his theorizing. These aspects are (1) the specification of different types of constructs, not in terms of their content, but rather in terms of their logical and functional properties, and (2) the specification of techniques for diagnosing the content of a person's constructs once you have him concretely before you. As to the first point, many of the different types of constructs have already been mentioned in Chapter 4. You will recall the distinctions between such things as *constellatory, propositional,* and *preemptive constructs.* In addition, Kelly (1955, pp. 532–533) suggests that constructs can be *preverbal* (having no consistent word symbols to represent them), *comprehensive* (subsuming a wide variety of events), *incidental* (subsuming a narrow variety of events), *superordinate* (including other constructs as one of their elements), *subordinate* (being included as an element of other constructs), *tight* (leading to unvarying predictions), or *loose* (leading to varying predictions while still maintaining their identity). In addition, Kelly (1955, p. 533) specifies what he calls *dimensions of transition,* which refer to functioning over time, the main direction of which is change in constructs or organization of construction systems. Among these dimensions of transition are some familiar emotions, such as *anxiety* (the awareness that the events with which one is confronted lie outside the predictive potentialities of one's construction system), and *aggressiveness* (the active elaboration of one's perceptual field). There are, in addition, some dimensions of transition that refer more to the successive use of different types of constructs, rather than to emotional states. An example is the *creativity cycle,* in which one starts with loosened constructions and terminates with tightened constructions. In all this, Kelly is clearly trying to deal with a number of content considerations usually considered important by personologists. It is hard to avoid the feeling, however sympathetic you may be to Kelly's kind of theory, that these matters are given short shrift. Is creativity simply the process of starting with loose constructs, which are ones that lead to diverse predictions, and ending with tight constructs, which are ones that lead to specific predictions? Is anxiety nothing more than the awareness that you have encountered something you do not understand? Kelly's position is spirited and ingenious, but tells only part of the story of personality, leaving the drama of peripheral characteristics undisclosed.

The other point at which Kelly comes closest to explicating the periphery is in his specification of the manner of diagnosing construct content. I have already covered part of this in Chapter 4, where it was made clear that the Role Repertory Test is the most definitive manner of determining the content of the person's constructs. Not only will this test disclose content, but it will also give information as to how the various existing constructs are organized in the person's construction system. In addition to all this, Kelly (1955, pp. 452–485) also offers guidelines for diagnosis based on less-definitive information than that available in the Role Repertory Test. Such information is typically found in interviews, but personal documents, such as diaries, can also be used in diagnosis. Although less definitive than the Role Repertory Test, interviews and personal documents can be useful if the personologist remains sensitive to what the person is actually saying, and is credulous concerning it. Through the adoption of attitudes of credulousness and perceptual literalness, Kelly believes the personologist can discover the constructs a person uses, and the way in which these constructs are organized. The actual diagnosis of constructs will require perception of recurring regularities, both involving imputed similarities and differences among events. But you can imagine how hard the identification of such regularities would be as soon as you are dealing with human experiences of any real degree of complexity. Indeed, when Kelly (1955, pp. 319–359, 1962) has tried to show how this kind of diagnosis actually gets done, the reader is left with a sense that the statements made about constructs are only among those that could be made, rather than being definitive. In addition, one is hardly convinced that the statements about constructs give insight into the essential features of the person's character or style of life. It is hard to avoid the conclusion that Kelly's position would be more meaningful if he offered some inklings as to typical, common types of character.

McClelland's position

McClelland, like Allport and Murray, has concerned himself extensively with precise definition of concrete peripheral characteristics. He does not just toss off concepts like trait or style leaving questions of what is really meant to others. His concern with the proper, clear definition of the concrete units of personality that differentiate one person from another bespeaks special emphasis upon the periphery. Unlike the other theorists thus far considered, McClelland assumes not one, but three kinds of concrete peripheral characteristic. They are *motive, trait,* and *schemata.* Each characteristic has a separate definition, process of development, and type of effect upon functioning.

Let us turn first to a consideration of the motive concept, as it is the most important of the three in McClelland's thinking, and follows most naturally from his conceptualization of the core of personality. McClelland (1951, p. 466) defines a *motive* as ". . . a strong affective association, characterized by an anticipatory goal reaction and based on past association of certain cues with pleasure or pain." Although you might not be willing to believe it, the essential meaning of this rather opaque statement is very straightforward. What McClelland means is that whenever some cue arouses in you the anticipation of some change in state that will increase either pleasure or pain, you have a motive. Anything from a ringing doorbell to a fast beating heart can serve as a cue, as long as it serves as a signal that some change in state is imminent. Stimuli become cues on the basis of past experience. The anticipated change in state also comes out of past experience, and may have any specific content from the expectation that you will be successful to the expectation that you will enter into close contact with other people. And finally, the anticipated change in state must have associated with it the expectation of an increase in either positive or negative affect, if one is to properly invoke the motive concept for what is happening. To paraphrase, then, a motive is a state of mind aroused by some stimulus situation that serves as a signal that some change in situation is imminent that will be either pleasant or unpleasant. McClelland assumes that the person will act on his motive such as to bring about the anticipated pleasure, or avoid the anticipated displeasure, as the case may be. The anticipated change in state including positive affect is considered an *approach motive,* in that the person tries to act in such fashion that his anticipation will indeed become a reality. In contrast, the anticipated change in state including negative affect defines an *avoidance motive,* in that the person works to keep his anticipation from becoming a reality.

This division of motives into two broad classes is the first step McClelland takes in specifying the content of the motives he believes people can have. The second step is essentially that of endorsing Murray's extensive list of needs that includes such examples as the needs for nurturance, compliance, and so forth. Of the needs on this list, McClelland has focused upon three, the needs for achievement, affiliation, and power, with the first of these receiving the lion's share of attention. In relating this list to the distinction between approach and avoidance motives, McClelland seems to intend that we consider there to be an approach and an avoidance version of each need. The avoidance version of need for achievement is called *fear of failure,* to indicate that in the person possessing it, a cue that a competitive situation exists, brings to mind the anticipation of failure and attendant negative affect, leading to attempts to avoid the situation. The approach version of need for achievement involves reacting to a cue that a competitive situation exists with anticipation of success and attendant positive affect, and attempting to thrust oneself actively into the fray. Although McClelland's meaning is clear, he often slips into the confusing position of calling this approach version of the need for achievement nothing different than the *need for achievement*. It would be much less confusing to call it something like *hope for success*, as does an associate of McClelland (Atkinson, 1957), and thereby preserve a verbal basis for distinguishing approach and avoidance versions of some common motivational characteristic. In any event, McClelland presumes that there are approach and avoidance versions of other needs, such as that for affiliation and power, although he has not attempted to specify them.

There are two additional considerations to be discussed in regard to motives. One is their effect upon behavior, and the other is their process of development. As to effects upon behavior, it is presumed that the arousal of motives increases the amount and intensity of behavior. This effect is observable not only in overt actions, but in thought processes as well (McClelland, 1951, p. 482). When there is a task to be addressed, increased motivation leads to increased output on the task. Another general effect of motives is the achievement of interrelatedness between diverse aspects of the person's behavior (McClelland, 1951, pp. 485–486). Motivation is believed to organize responses, introduce trends into behavior, producing orientation and direction. According to McClelland, it is this capacity of the motive concept to make sense out of varied responses which distinguishes it from any other explanatory concept of personality and makes it so useful. The final effect of motivation is that of sensitization (McClelland, 1951, pp. 448–489). People in a state of motivation seem more sensitive to some kinds of environmental cues than to others. There seems to be a lowering of perceptual if not sensory thresholds to the specific kinds of stimulation especially relevant to the motive.

Although McClelland assumes that the effects of increase, interrelation, and sensitization of behavior take place in the case of both approach and avoidance motives, there are subtle differences traceable to these two motivation classes. Thus, though both approach and avoidance motives lead to increases in the amount of behavior, approach motives do so by augmentation of effective, efficient behavior, whereas avoidance motives do so by augmentation of ineffective, obsessive behaviors. In imagination, for example, approach motives lead to anticipations of the satisfaction of success and concern with how best to plan for adequate task performance. In contrast, avoidance motives would lead to imagination obsessed with the obstacles to reaching the goal and unrealistic thought of magical satisfaction. And, to carry through our analysis, although both kinds of motive would lead to behavioral interrelatedness, approach motives would achieve organizations focused on effective instrumental actions and achievable goals, whereas avoidance motives would achieve organizations stressing passive expressions of need and frustration. Finally, in producing sensitization, approach motives would render salient cues associated with challenge and satisfaction, whereas avoidance motives would render salient cues associated with threat and dissatisfaction. So, approach and avoidance motives can be considered to have similar gross effects upon behavior with clear and distinct differences in behavioral effects at a more subtle level of analysis.

We can turn now to the process whereby McClelland believes motives develop. In considering this, it will be possible to see the relationship between core and peripheral levels of personality in this theory. You will recall that the core tendency according to McClelland is the maximization of small discrepancies, and the minimization of large discrepancies, between expectation and occurrence. Small discrepancies result in positive affect, whereas large discrepancies result in negative affect. It is McClelland's view that if a particular domain of living is characterized by small discrepancies for the person, he will come to learn an approach motive, whereas if the domain is characterized by large discrepancies, he will learn an avoidance motive. If the domain yields little in the way of discrepancy at all, if it is completely predictable, the person will come to be indifferent to it altogether. Now that I have said this, it should begin to become apparent to you why McClelland defines motivation as he does. In simple terms, what McClelland means is that if you have enough pleasant emotional experiences in a certain area of functioning, then you will learn to expect, each time you get some cue that the area is relevant to your living, that pleasant experiences will ensue through approaching the situation. In contrast, if you have had sufficient unpleasant experiences in that area, then you will learn to expect unpleasant experiences whenever some cue is present, and therefore attempt to avoid the situation.

In order to make McClelland's meaning more vivid, I will quote from his account of the development of the achievement motive (McClelland, Atkinson, Clark & Lowell, 1953, p. 62):

> A concrete example involving the development of the achievement motive may help explain its implications in practice. Suppose a child is given a new toy car for Christmas to play with. Initially, unless he has had other toy cars, his expectations . . . as to what it will do are nonexistent, and he can derive little or no positive or negative affect from manipulating it until such expectations are developed. Gradually, if he plays with it (as he will be encouraged to by his parents in our culture), he will develop certain expectations of varying probabilities which will be confirmed or not confirmed. Unless the nonconfirmations are too many (which may happen if the toy is too complex), he should be able to build up reasonably certain expectations as to what it will do *and confirm them*. In short, he gets pleasure from playing with the car. But what happens then? Why doesn't he continue playing with it the rest of his life? The fact is, of course, that his expectations become certainties, confirmation becomes 100 per cent, and we say that he loses interest or gets bored with the car; he should get bored or satiated, according to the theory, since the discrepancies from certainty are no longer sufficient to yield pleasure. How-

ever, pleasure can be reintroduced into the situation, as any parent knows, by buying a somewhat more complex car, by making the old car do somewhat different things, or perhaps by letting the old car alone for six months until the expectations about it have changed (e.g., decrease in probability). So, if a child is to continue to get pleasure from achievement situations like manipulating toy cars, he must continually work with more and more complex objects or situations permitting mastery, since, if he works long enough at any particular level of mastery, his expectations and their confirmation will become certain and he will get bored.

Here McClelland is clearly talking about the approach version of the achievement motive. After this kind of early experience, one would certainly expect that each time the person recognized a cue indicating the existence of a mastery situation, he would experience a sense of challenge and the anticipation that reaching the goal of mastery would lead to emotional satisfaction. McClelland et al. (1953, p. 65) also describe the development of an avoidance version of the achievement motive.

> In the second place, there are limits placed on the development of n achievement by the negative affect which results from too large discrepancies between expectations and events. Thus Johnny may develop expectations as to what a model airplane or a solved arithmetic problem looks like, but he may be unable to confirm these expectations at all, or only very partially. The result is negative affect, and cues associated with these activities may be expected to evoke avoidance motives. To develop an achievement approach motive, parents or circumstances must contrive to provide opportunities for mastery which, because they are just beyond the child's present knowledge, will provide continuing pleasure. If the opportunities are too limited, boredom should result and the child should develop no interest in achievement (and have a low n achievement score when he grows up). If the opportunities are well beyond his capabilities, negative affect should result and he may develop an avoidance motive as far as achievement is concerned.

After an early history of large discrepancies between expectation and experience in mastery situations, the person would learn an avoidance version of the achievement motive. This would mean that each time he recognized a cue that a mastery situation existed, he would experience threat and the anticipation that he would fail.

The core tendency concerning discrepancy size and its relation to affective experience refers, of course, to any area of functioning, not only that concerning mastery. Therefore, the person can learn approach or avoidance versions of many different motives, depending upon the specific experiences he encounters in the world. As you can see from the quotes included above, the parents serve the very important role in McClelland's theory of influencing, if not determining, the degree of discrepancy characterizing the various areas of functioning over at least the period of time when the child is rather dependent. McClelland indicates that most motives are learned in childhood, though he does not provide very specific periods for the learning of particular motives. There is no sign in his writing that he means to adopt a theory in which stages of development are important, and indeed, the postulation of stages generally requires more emphasis upon inherent attributes and capabilities of the human than is present in consistency theories. McClelland et al. (1953, pp. 68–74) do detail the basis in development for different degrees of a motive, but such detail is beyond my purpose here. Nonetheless, it should have caught your attention by now that this theory is clearly the most detailed and precise of those we have considered concerning concrete peripheral characteristics.

Before we turn from McClelland's motive concept to his views concerning the other two concrete peripheral characteristics, I would like to introduce you to his unorthodox position concerning the biological drives, such as those for food and water. It is best to quote his (McClelland et al., 1953, pp. 81–84) own words here:

> Now according to our theory, how could we explain the fact that the longer an animal is deprived of food the more motivated he appears to become? Since most psychologists have been accustomed to thinking of biological need states as the primary sources of motivation, this is a very important question for us to discuss. In the first place, it is clear that in terms of our theory food deprivation does not produce a motive the first time it occurs. The lack of food in a baby rat or a baby human being will doubtless result in diffuse bodily changes of various sorts, but these do not constitute a motive until they are paired with a subsequent change in affect. More specifically, if the organism is to survive, the cues subsequent to food deprivation must always be associated with eating, and eating results in two types of affective change—pleasurable taste sensations, and relief from internal visceral tensions. Thus internal (or external) cues resulting from food deprivation are associated very early and very regularly in all individuals with positive affective change, and thus they become capable of arousing the hunger *motive* with great dependability.

McClelland then goes on to an explanation of why the motive gets stronger as food deprivation is increased. We do not need to go into this. It will suffice to recognize that for McClelland, there are no motives at birth, even though there are physiological needs that can render the organism uncomfortable in a diffuse way. A motive involves a concrete, tangible set of goals and instrumental actions relevant to reaching the goals. Hence a motive must be learned on the basis of relevant experience. One can only speak of motives in regard to physiological needs when these ends have, through learning, come to be represented psychologically as anticipations, goals, and instrumentalities. This kind of learning is mediated for McClelland by affective experience, and that is tied to discrepancies between expectations and experiences. For all these reasons, biological needs cannot be considered the basic building block of personality for McClelland.

Remaining to be discussed are the other two peripheral characteristics, traits and schemata. After presenting an extensive and excellent analysis of what other personologists have meant by the term *trait*, McClelland (1951, p. 216) concludes that it should be defined as ". . . the learned tendency of an individual to react as he has reacted more or less successfully in the past in similar situations when similarly motivated." In other words, when someone is faced with what he perceives to be the same situation with the same variety and intensity of motivation that he has encountered in the past, he tends to perform the type of response which satisfied the demands of the situation and motivation before. By McClelland's definitions, a trait and a motive are actually very different. A motive is a set of anticipations of what will happen, these anticipations taking the concrete form of goals and emotional involvement, and a commitment to whatever course of action is likely, given the nature of the situation that exists, to lead to the fulfillment of these anticipations. Very likely, responses expressive of the need for achievement, for example, will differ considerably over time, as the situations in which this motive will be aroused may differ widely in their characteristics. A motive leads to consistency of intent, but not necessarily of actual responses.

In contrast, a trait is no more than a collection of habits having nothing of the goal-directedness of the motive. If you have the trait of expansiveness, for example, it leads you to act expansively every time a situation comes up that is similar to the ones in which you learned to be expansive. According to McClelland, the learning of a trait takes place because a certain style of functioning is rewarded consistently in a certain kind of situation, but this is not the same as saying that the trait has motivational properties. Perhaps people laughed and listened to you whenever you happened to be expansive in their presence, and so now you have the habit or trait of expansiveness in social situations. For McClelland, if your expansiveness has the status of a trait you will act this way in social situations because you are used to doing so, and without any act of consciousness of intent. If, however, expansiveness had the status of a motive in you, or was part of an instrumental course of action leading to a goal, then you might be expansive in a social situation on the basis of intent to act that way, rather than simply because it felt natural and familiar to you. A motive can often lead you to do unfamiliar, untried things, whereas a trait can never have this function.

This distinction McClelland is celebrating by defining motive and trait as he does is so clear in our own experience that it is amazing to me that virtually no other personologist has made it in any precise way. Generally speaking, those who rely on the concept of trait include in it both intentional and habitual behaviors, and the same is true of those who tend to rely only on the concept of need. According to McClelland, however, both concepts are needed, because of clear differences between intentional and habitual functioning. The trait concept can explain response repetition, whereas the motive concept can explain sequentially arranged series of responses, where each of the responses is actually different. As you may have surmised, I think that Murray, in distinguishing needs and need-integrates, and Allport, in distinguishing dynamic and stylistic traits, were recognizing what McClelland makes explicit.

McClelland sees reason for yet another distinction, for which he employs the concept of schema. Unfortunately, he does not offer any concise definition of the schema (plural schemata), but he definitely means it to be a unit of cognition or mentation. Actually it is a symbolization of past experience—it stands for the past experience, rather than being it, and is inevitably a simplification (McClelland, 1951, p. 254). Words and language generally are good examples of schemata. But, obviously, McClelland means to emphasize not any old schemata that may exist, but rather those that characterize the particular person you are trying to understand. For this, it would be much more important to know the person's effective vocabulary, for example, than it would be to know the full range of words available in the language. Examples of schemata recognized by McClelland (1951, pp. 239–282) are ideas, values, and social roles. Whereas motives are learned on the basis of the typical degree of discrepancy between expectations and occurrences, and traits are learned on the basis of the acts that are consistently rewarded, the learning of schemata is more directly representative of cultural transmission. The particular peculiarities of parents and significant others strongly affect motive and trait learning. In contrast, such things as ideas, values, and social roles are determined in the main by the nature of the culture in which the person exists. Ideas, values, and social roles are often communicated rather directly, in verbal terms, with the units of communication being social institutions, such as family, school, church, rather than individuals per se. McClelland believes that schemata have a general, pervasive influence on the processes of perception, memory, and thinking. Obviously, the possibilities you can imagine, the observables that will be salient enough for you to notice, the things you will remember, and even the thoughts you can have will be limited and influenced by the set of ideas, values, and social roles you have internalized.

Although the identification of three separate classes of concrete peripheral characteristics may strike you as a breath of fresh air at this point, following all the fuzziness we have encountered in previously considered theories, it is probably not entirely clear that motives, traits, and schemata are really that different. Perhaps we can get greater insight into McClelland's meaning if we consider the nature of the presumed relationship between these three entities, for related they must surely be. But such consideration is difficult, for most of what McClelland has to say on the matter is scattered through his writing and not really summarized in any one place. Nonetheless, we should make an attempt. You will recall that the motive has as its primary characteristic *intent*, and can be described as a directional force. In contrast, the trait is primarily an habitual basis for performing as one performed before when situation and motivation repeat themselves. And finally, a schema is primarily a cognitive unit referring to some aspect of the shared definitions whereby men in the same society live. The schema is not intentional in any strict sense, though ideas, values, and roles do often include prescriptions for action.

With this as introduction, let us take a concrete example from the achievement domain, and follow through some of the distinctions that can be made. You will recall that the definition of a motive involved the arousal of the intention by a cue. The perception of aspects of the environment as cues that an achievement, or success-failure, situation is present requires the presence of achievement schemata in the form of ideas concerning achievement. But one could certainly have such achievement schemata without also possessing an achievement motive. If one had no such motive, one would be able to recognize the existence of an achievement situation and simply not participate in it. But if the achievement motive were also present, then one would get involved in the sense of attempting to bring about success or avoid failures. So the trigger for the achievement motive are the achievement schemata. The content of these schemata can influence where and when the achievement motive is displayed, though the vigor and imaginativeness of attempts to reach success or avoid failure are clearly determined by the intensity of the motive itself. The eventual effectiveness of attempts to reach success or avoid failure is a function of achievement traits. Such traits are habits of persistence, and they are not strictly speaking a product of motive intensity or existence of achievement schemata. They are separate entities in themselves. Such traits as persistence could be in the service of an achievement need, as in this example, but they could function quite separately from it as well. If we generalized from this extended example, in hopes of arriving at some preliminary statement of the differences and interrelation between McClelland's three peripheral concepts, it would go something like this: schemata form the general frame of reference for living, and determine the concrete possibilities available for each life; motives are the basis for personal, rather than culturally shared, intentions, and determine the content and intensity of directional activity; traits form the style of a person's functioning, and determine his routine, habitual behaviors.

The discussion thus far should have given you some abstract sense of what McClelland means by traits, schemata, and motives. He becomes more concrete too, in detailing the contents of these three kinds of characteristics. But before turning to that, I would like to point out a problem concerning the relationship of the core and peripheral levels of personality in McClelland's theory. As traits, schemata, and motives are clearly at the peripheral level of personality, they should be presented as formed out of the interaction of the core tendency with the external world. But the core tendency as described by McClelland is really only relevant to the development of motives. Traits and schemata seem to be formed in some other way than as the result of maximizing small discrepancies between expectations and occurrences while minimizing large discrepancies. The statements made by McClelland about the learning of traits and schemata suggest other assumptions about the core of personality that go beyond that mentioned above. But he is not explicit about this. There is little for us to do at the moment but live with the confusion resulting from the inconsistency between his core and peripheral statements. I suggest that we consider the usefulness for understanding observable behavior of not only motives, but traits and schemata as well, even though the latter two concepts currently exist disinherited from the core.

Having recognized this confusion, we can turn to consideration of the content of motives, traits, and schemata. For motives, McClelland adopts the list offered by Murray (1938) which includes such things as the needs for achievement, affiliation, power, succorance, and change. There are 40 such needs, and though they need not be listed here, I would like you to recognize that they are fairly concrete and mirror the common-sense, everyday concerns of people. If you asked people what motivated them, they would very likely say that they wanted achievement, affiliation, power, and so forth. McClelland offers no particular list of traits, being inclined to accept whatever habits other psychologists may implicate as important. So there is no specification of trait content that is as precise as that for motives. Finally, McClelland suggests two kinds of content for schemata. The first kind refers to ideas and values, and constitutes an endorsement of the classification offered by Spranger (1928). That classification includes ideas and values concerning economic, aesthetic, social, political, religious, and purely theoretical realms of life. The second kind of schema content refers to social roles, and here McClelland endorses the classification offered by Linton (1945). This classification breaks down roles into those involving age, sex, family position, occupation, and association group membership. This means that different role behavior is expected of people of different ages; of people of different sex; from fathers, sons, sisters, brothers, aunts, cousins; from lawyers or unskilled laborers; and finally, from Liberals, Methodists, and Boy Scouts. As McClelland develops his analysis of the content of roles, it becomes quite clear that they are culturally patterned sets of traits. Indeed, McClelland's (1951, p. 293) definition of role is "a cluster of traits (or pattern of behavior) which serves as the culturally normal or modal solution to recurrent, usually social problems peculiar to a particular status or position in society." Although roles are clusters of traits, the role characteristic is something expressing a rather universalistic social problem and cultural solution. In contrast, traits which are not parts of roles have been learned on the basis of experience peculiar to the particular family environment in which a person has been reared, and do not express any cultural or societal universal. Actually, it seems to me that roles must also include motives, insofar as the accomplishment of certain goals, regularly and recurrently, is necessary to validate one's occupancy of a culturally defined position. I will discuss this implication of the schema concept in the next chapter.

One of the most striking things about the content McClelland gives to his motive, trait, and schema concepts is its eclecticism. In this, he exemplifies the point I made in Chapter 4 that consistency theories tend to be eclectic with regard to personality content. This tendency stems from minimal assumptions concerning the content and inevitability of inherent attributes of man. As I have already indicated, his theory includes two peripheral concepts, schemata and traits, that are not even derived from the one core tendency he offers. And now we see that the content attributed to the three peripheral characteristics does not stem from the overall fabric of his theory. Instead, McClelland has culled from the available psychological, anthropological, and sociological literature the lists that seem most complete and least tied to any particular theoretical assumptions. This is clear evidence of the eclectic emphasis of consistency theories. So eclectic is his theorizing concerning content that McClelland does not even consider whether the implications of the lists endorsed for schemata, traits, and motives are consistent. I do not mean to suggest that they are inconsistent, but rather that the question of consistency is not important to McClelland.

Actually, McClelland's theory is, in terms of precision concerning concrete peripheral characteristics, virtually a model for the personologist. Not only has he provided careful definitions of his three concepts—definitions that at last attempt to clarify the similarities and differences among them—but he has also offered guidelines as to the measurement of their content. In other words, he has gone one step beyond the offering of lists as a means of specifying content. That step involves indicating how best the items in the lists are to be measured. The technical way of putting this is that McClelland has offered operational definitions to supplement his theoretical definitions. Operational definitions tell you what operations you must perform in order to determine the existence and intensity of the entity you want to know about. An operational definition of body temperature, for example, is mercury level on the calibrated scale of a thermometer. Of all the personologists considered thus far, McClelland and Murray are alone in having attempted this at once tedious, difficult, and indispensable step in theorizing. Without operational definitions of concrete peripheral characteristics, you, as the user of a theory, can never be sure you are working with what the theorist intended in his lofty abstract writing.

I cannot hope to give a detailed accounting to the actual nature of the operational definitions here, but some examples should give you the flavor of what has been offered. Since a motive involves so much intent to reach a currently absent goal, it is only reasonable that one not measure it in conditions where the environment is so structured and familiar as to call up old, habitual ways of doing things, or where the socially proper things to do are so clear that only these ways of functioning will be aroused. The attempt to be socially appropriate is behavior determined by schemata, and habitual behavior is determined by traits. Motives refer more to very personal desires. It is therefore thoroughly understandable that McClelland would specify fantasy as the raw material in which to search for motives. In order to elicit fantasy in some sort of standardized way he specifies a set of ambiguous pictures of people to be presented to subjects with instructions to compose stories about what has happened, is happening, and will happen. The pictures are ambiguous enough, and the task is unusual enough, that one may be reasonably sure that neither traits nor schemata will be major determinants of behavior. The stories are then scored for the presence or absence of motives.

Take the need for achievement as an example. The operational definition of this need is *competition with a standard of excellence*, with the approach form of it stressing hope for success, and the avoidance form stressing fear of failure. So, when scoring the approach form, you look for aspects of the story indicating the concrete wish for success, anticipation of success, the overcoming of obstacles to success, and positive affect in connection with statements of competition with a standard of excellence. In contrast, when scoring the avoidance form, one looks for the concrete wish to avoid failure, worry about failure, the specification of seemingly insurmountable obstacles to success, and negative affect in connection with statements of competition with a standard of excellence. McClelland et al. (1953) have formalized what I have said in terms of scoring rules for imaginative stories.

If one were interested not in the need for achievement, but rather in schemata concerning achievement that might exist in the person, one would, on the basis of what I mentioned earlier, stress what the person says in describing himself when the situation is publicly defined as relevant to achievement. For the measurement of achievement schemata, McClelland suggests, the operational format of a set of achievement related questions which the person answers as true or false of himself. McClelland is perfectly willing to have schemata measured by any standard questionnaire concerning values, such as the Allport-Vernon-Lindzey (1951) test called *A Study of Values*. This test attempts to measure Spranger's value orientations on the basis of true-false questions. You can by now predict what McClelland would specify as the operations whereby achievement traits can be measured. He would put the person into familiar situations and observe to see the pervasiveness of such behaviors as persistence. He would not ask the person whether he is persistent, or scrutinize his fantasy, so much as actually watch him performing in familiar achievement-related situations such as studying for tests.

One final matter should be touched on briefly. You will recall that many personologists organize the concrete peripheral characteristics they specify into personality types. Like Allport and Murray, McClelland has not gone far in this direction. The concrete traits, schemata, and motives he specifies remain more or less separate from each other. He has told you how to measure them, so you could do just that, and let their interrelationships emerge from your empirical work. But there is certainly little theoretical specification of probable interrelationships. This is again very understandable in a consistency theorist, who would have little reason for predicting one organization of peripheral characteristics as more likely than another possible one. About as far as McClelland (1961) has gone in specifying personality types is to summarize in theoretical terms the empirical fruits of a large-scale research attempt to determine the influence of achievement motives, and to a lesser extent, achievement traits and schemata, on the behavior of people taken as individuals and as members of a society. We will be discussing his research in Chapter 10, and hence need not go further here.

CONSISTENCY MODEL: ACTIVATION VERSION

Maddi's position

Elaborating upon the core theorizing he and Fiske have offered, Maddi and his students have developed a view of the periphery of personality, including an emphasis upon both concrete peripheral characteristics and their organization into types of personality. Although the activation view of the periphery of personality has an unfinished quality, it should be kept in mind that it is a very recent development within personology. The fortunate aspect of its recency of development is that it has been possible to profit from the earlier theoretical efforts of other personologists. In order to understand the derivation of concrete peripheral characteristics and personality types from the core aspects of activation theory, you must keep in mind three basic kinds of similarity and difference among people (Maddi & Propst, 1971), to be discussed in the paragraphs that follow.

The first consideration is the characteristic curve of activation. Here, the core statement of similarity among people is that they all have such a curve that takes the general shape of Kleitman's cycle of existence. In other words, activation customarily rises sharply after waking, then more gradually to some point in the middle of the day, then begins to decline gradually, and finally declines more rapidly as sleep is approached. But Maddi and Propst (1971) hold out the possibility that there may be differences among people concerning the sharpness of rise and fall, and the point during the day when the shift from rising to falling takes place. Individual differences in the shape of the customary curve of activation may well help in the explanation of so-called night and day people. Surely, we have all encountered people who are most alert and effective early in the morning or late at night, with the middle of the day being somewhat indifferently placed between the two extremes. People who have an unusually high early morning or late night characteristic level of activation should, by comparison with more usual people, show more intense impact-increasing behavior in the early morning or late evening, respectively. Unfortunately, Maddi and Propst do not follow up this intriguing suggestion. Made in passing, their suggestion represents one of the only references by a personologist considered in this book to the possible importance of differences among people in the patterning of activities during a single day.

The second basic consideration of similarity and difference between people involves the average height of a person's characteristic curve of activation. The core statement is that everybody has a characteristic curve of activation that varies over some range of values between zero and the absolute maximum. But the statement of individual difference, leading to a position on the periphery of personality, is that the range of values covered by any person's activation curve need not be the same as that of another person. These differences can be pinpointed by a comparison of the averages of each person's range of characteristic activation values over the course of a day (or several days of precision). This brings us to the basic distinction offered by Maddi and Propst (1971) in developing a typology of peripheral personality. It is the distinction between *high-activation* and *low-activation* people. At the most obvious level, this distinction refers to the assumption that the average of the characteristic curve of activation is higher for some people than for others. But if you recall the discussion of Fiske's and Maddi's position from Chapter 4, you will recognize that this distinction must subsume many points of difference between these two kinds of people. High-activation people will spend the major part of their time and effort pursuing stimulus impact in order to keep their actual activation levels from falling too low, whereas low-activation people will spend the major part of their time and effort avoiding impact so as to keep their actual activation level from getting too high. In order to obtain a more concrete understanding of the peripheral personalities of these two kinds of people, it is necessary to consider the third basic kind of similarity and difference among people.

This third consideration involves the anticipatory and correctional techniques used for maintaining actual activation at the characteristic level. At the core level, it is assumed that all people are similar in that they employ anticipational and correctional techniques for increasing or decreasing stimulus impact in a manner consistent with the shared necessity of minimizing discrepancies between actual and customary levels of activation. But the theory also provides a basis for understanding individual differences in these anticipational and correctional techniques by explicating the many contributants to impact. You may recall that impact is considered a joint function of the intensity, meaningfulness, and variety of stimulation from interoceptive, cortical, and exteroceptive sources. Impact, of course, determines actual activation level. Maddi and Propst (1971) have outlined some of the implications of the definition of impact for differences among people in peripheral personality. First, a person may favor or find salient one of the three attributes of stimulation (i.e., intensity, meaningfulness, variety) in his anticipational and correctional strategies. The high- and low-activation personality types are both subdivided into three parts reflecting this distinction concerning preference for particular stimulus attributes. High-activation people who favor intensity, meaningfulness, or variety are considered to have an *approach motive* for *intensity, meaningfulness,* or *variety*, respectively. Low-activation people for whom intensity, meaningfulness, or variety is most salient are considered to have an *avoidance motive* for *intensity, meaningfulness,* or *variety*, respectively. The terms approach and avoidance motivation are used in much the same manner as in McClelland's position, with the approach motives often called *needs* and the avoidance motives often called *fears*. At this point, it should be clear that Maddi and Propst are offering a typology of peripheral personality including three high- and three low-activation types, with the three subdivisions of each major type bearing content resemblances. So, for example, the *high-activation-need for meaningfulness person* would spend most of his time and effort in instrumental behavior aimed at the goal of increasing the meaningfulness of his experience, with this concrete directionality serving the overall function of keeping his actual activation level from falling too low. Just the opposite would be true for the *low-activation fear of meaningfulness person*. Orientations toward particular stimulus attributes are considered motivational because it is these attributes that can actually augment or diminish impact. The three approach and three avoidance motives represent concrete peripheral characteristics, in the terminology of this book.

In order to gain further understanding of the activation theory position on peripheral personality, it is necessary to introduce additional distinctions. One has to do with the favored source of stimulation. Here Maddi, Propst, and Feldinger (1965) collapse the three distinctions offered by Fiske and Maddi into two, the internal and the external. As the distinction between cortical and interoceptive sources postulated by Fiske and Maddi will undoubtedly be quite hard to make in practice, the simplification suggested by Maddi et al. (1965) seems reasonable. In any event, it is considered important to know whether the person is oriented toward internal or external sources of stimulation. This distinction recognizes that one way of regulating impact is to look to sources of stimulation essentially outside the body (anything from thunderclaps or wind to music or pictures) whereas another way is to turn within the organism (focusing on anything from thoughts or daydreams to pains or dizziness). The former orientation is called the *external trait* and the latter the *internal trait*, with the term trait being used in the manner of McClelland to emphasize habitual rather than motivational behavior. In finding internal or external stimulation salient, the person is not raising or lowering impact necessarily. The distinction being made is similar to Jung's regarding introversion-extroversion. It is only when the person begins to manipulate stimulation, be it external or internal, by pursuing or avoiding intensity, meaningfulness, or variety, that he shows the goal-directedness of motivation. The external and internal traits are simply habits of emphasis, and, of course, represent concrete peripheral characteristics in our terminology. The distinction as to salient source of stimulation must be made within each of the 6 personality types already mentioned, raising the overall number of kinds of people considered to 12.

As if this were not complication enough, Maddi, Charlens, Maddi, and Smith (1962) offer yet another distinction that must be taken into account in understanding the activation position on peripheral personality. It is the distinction between the *active* and the *passive trait*. The emphasis here is much the same as in Allport's distinction between proactive and reactive functioning. The person with the active trait has the habit of initiative, such that he influences his external and even internal stimulus environment, whereas the person with the passive trait is habitually indolent, permitting himself to be influenced by internal and external stimuli over which he has no subjective sense of control. The activeness-passiveness distinction is especially important in understanding differences among people in the proportion of their time spent in anticipational as opposed to frankly correctional behaviors. An active person will anticipate his activation requirements well, because he is self-reliant and an initiator. We should expect to see in such a person the fruits of anticipational functioning. As I will elaborate later, these fruits will include such things as psychological differentiation and integration. In contrast, the passive person will not anticipate his activation requirements well, and will frequently be in the position of having to correct for actual activation levels that have already become too high or fallen too low.

There will be a "last-ditch stand" quality to the passive person that Maddi and Propst (1971) have suggested involves distorting reality. Although the activeness-passiveness distinction is not firmly attached to the rest of activation theory, Maddi et al. (1962) seem to consider it important, and hence we should consider it, recognizing that it represents an inconsistency in theorizing. We noted a similar inconsistency in McClelland's peripheral theorizing, and can give this one the same interpretation. Consistency theorists de-emphasize core assumptions involving specified content to such a degree that there is a tendency in them to be eclectic at the peripheral level. Nonetheless, the distinction as to activeness or passiveness must be made within each of the 12 personality types we already have, making the staggering total of 24 in all!

Lest you rush to criticize activation theory too harshly for postulating such a large number of personality types, let me point out some things that may not yet be completely explicit in your minds. First, some theorists, such as Allport and Kelly, are apparently willing to entertain an unlimited number of personality types, such is their emphasis on individuality. Infinity is surely a larger value than 24. Furthermore, some theorists, such as McClelland, Murray, and Erikson, may end up with quite a sizable number of personality types when their peripheral level theorizing becomes complete and explicit enough for us to entertain a count. After all, Murray and McClelland have postulated a huge number of concrete peripheral characteristics, and Erikson has only sketched out a typology, not bothering to consider the subtypes implicit in his theorizing. In this context, activation theory can at least say that the 24 types it proposes are all that are likely given the nature and number of its core level assumptions. And this brings us to a final point, which is that the actual number of types considered important by activation theorists may well dwindle as time goes on. After all, the theory has barely been used in practice, and there has been little opportunity for the relevant empirical evidence to ride herd on the play of reason.

My presentation of the typology has been very abstract, and I would not be surprised to find it lacking vividness for you. Let me therefore try to describe the types a little more fully now. In this description, you will also gain insight into what kinds of behavior the concrete peripheral characteristics and typology are meant to explain. Most of the description that follows will indeed concern the kinds of observable phenomena that activation theorists feel it is important to explain.

The high-activation person with active and external traits will be a "go-getter," seeking out challenges to meet in the physical and social environment. He will be energetic and voracious in his appetites. Interested in a wide range of concrete, tangible events and things, he will be a hard man to keep up with. Although he will not be especially hampered by pressures toward conformity, he will tend to be a man of facts, not fancies. He will not spend much time in rumination or daydreaming. He will be straightforward and not complex and subtle so much as extensively committed and enthusiastic. He will want to encounter people and things rather continuously. If he also has a high need for meaningfulness, he will be a pursuer of causes and problems, a statesman, businessman, or journalist, rather than a scholar. But if he has a high need for intensity, he may pursue action and tumult per se, being an athlete or soldier or bon vivant. And if he has a high need for variety, he will show curiosity about causes and mechanisms governing men and things, being adventurer, explorer, or world traveler.

Now switch to a high-activation person in whom the active trait occurs with the internal rather than external trait. He will show little outward evidence of the pursuit of impact. Perhaps the most one would notice externally is a wealth of knowledge and similar fruits of an active orientation toward internal processes. He will be a thinker, a daydreamer, responding to the challenges posed by the limitations of mind and body, without much regard to the tangible affairs of the outside world. He will be subtle and complex, showing depth and considerable cognitive and emotional differentiation. He will not be especially social, though he may have some close, intimate friends. In general, he will not be interested in the obvious, surface manifestations of people and things. If he also has a high need for meaningfulness, he will lead the life of the mind, engaging in scholarly, ruminatory, philosophical pursuits. If, instead, he has a high need for intensity, he will pursue sensations and emotions, perhaps as poet, or lover. Should he have a high need for variety, however, he will strive for novelty and originality in some sort of creative or imaginative endeavor.

By way of sharp contrast, let me turn now to the personality types involving low activation. The low-activation person with active and external traits will be the eternal conservationist, bent on heading off social and physical disorganization and conflict through negotiation, control, and integrative attempts. He will tend to be a conformist and an advocate of stability at any cost. Though reasonably energetic, he will tend to be simple in his tastes and involvements. If he also has a high fear of meaningfulness, he will express his organizational and integrational interest in a manner involving the simplification of problems and the avoidance of ambiguities. Should he have a high fear of intensity instead, he will tend to exert a dampening effect on vigorous, potentially disorganized external conditions, becoming perhaps an efficiency expert. If he has a high fear of variety, he will seek to force routine on the environment, preferring the familiar and the predictable to the new.

The person low in activation, with a combination of active and internal traits will be somewhat different. He, too, will be a conservationist, but with special emphasis upon his own organism. In other words, he will be an advocate of the golden mean, being careful to avoid excesses and indulgences of any kind. He will avoid putting any kind of strain upon his person, be it a pleasant or unpleasant experience. His personality will be simple, uncomplex, devoid of inconsistencies—in short, integrated and dependable. If he has a high fear of meaningfulness, he will show special absence of detailed and diverse thoughts and daydreams, tending instead toward stable and recurring cognitive themes the function of which is to render any given experience similar to what has gone before. If he has a high fear of intensity, he will have an ascetic emphasis about him, naturally avoiding sensation for its own sake. And if he has a high fear of variety, he will force himself to function consistently and stably, giving a picture of dependability and constancy devoid of flamboyance.

Thus far, we have considered the personality types including the active trait. As you can see, the various types differ depending upon other considerations than activeness. There is even the implication that the high-activation types are more extraordinary and interesting people than the low-activation types. Certainly the high-activation types are at least more vivid and describable. But the essential difference between high- and low-activation types is not that between the ideal and non-ideal forms of living. According to activation theorists, this distinction overlaps much more with that concerning the active and passive traits. All personality types including the active trait are rich in anticipational techniques. This means that they provide a successful basis for selecting the kinds of experiences that will minimize discrepancies between actual and customary levels of activation. As people falling into these types do not therefore experience discrepancies often, they feel reasonably satisfied with their lives, experience little frustration and negative affect, and are, in truth, effective in their own ways. You may like the high-activation types better, feeling them to be more interesting and important, but they are no different in ability to fulfill their view of the good life than are the low-activation types. In contrast, the personality types including the passive trait are rather chronically frustrated and ineffective. It is these types, to be described now, that are considered nonideal by activation theorists.

The high-activation person with external and passive traits will have the standards, attitudes and goals of his counterpart with the active trait, but will not have available to him the action habits with which to bring about his own satisfaction. To be sure, he will profess an interest in challenges, voraciousness of appetite, and a wide range of interests. But he will do little about all this. He will have the same emphasis on concrete, tangible, external realities as does his more action-oriented counterpart. But he will have few anticipational techniques for avoiding the situation wherein his actual level of activation will be lower than that which is characteristic for him. About the only anticipational technique he will have is the passive one of preferring situations that have been associated with high impact in the past. But he will have little concrete way of even bringing about these preferred situations, depending instead upon their "natural" occurrence. He will be a dilettante, a consumer rather than producer of impact. With regularity, he will be in the uncomfortable position of correcting for an actual level of activation that is already too low. The emergency nature of this position will contribute to his behavior its defensive or distortional quality (see Chapter 4). Depending upon whether he also has a high need for meaningfulness, intensity, or variety, the distortional corrections will take the form of artificially augmenting the meaning, intensity, or variety of what is happening in the environment. Something banal may be seen as pregnant with meaning, something simple as complex, and something monotonous as subtly new. Such distortions may sometimes involve gross, paranoid suspiciousness toward other people, and the imputation of human or even supernatural attributes to the inanimate environment.

Next is the high-activation person with internal and passive traits. Once again, this person will profess many of the interests and activities expressed by his more action-oriented counterpart without, however, carrying through on what he professes. He will be frequently dissatisfied, and frequently faced with the emergency task of correcting for actual activation levels that have fallen too low. His personality will not show the degree of differentiation and complexity one would imagine from hearing him talk. Nor will he actually spend much time in true exploratory and imaginative thought. He will be frequently bored, uninvolved, and dissatisfied, and frequently faced with the emergency task of correcting for actual activation levels that have fallen too low. The particular way in which he distorts the reality of his internal stimulation in order to bring about the correction will, as usual, be understandable in terms of whether the need for meaningfulness, intensity, or variety is strongest in him. Because the distortion involves internal more than external stimulation, the end result of the process may even include such phenomena as hallucinations and delusions.

Let us turn to the types involving low activation. When a person combines low activation with external and passive traits, he will sound like a conservationist, but somehow not be able to protect himself from high impact through controlling and ordering the social and physical environment. In his simplicity and ineptitude, he will frequently be swamped by stimulation that leads to excessively high levels of activation for him. Rather than interact actively with the environment in order to bend it to his impact requirements, he will renounce it. His best protection from the regular experience of excessive activation will be to shrink from the world, becoming a hermit, a tramp, or even a schizophrenic. Of course, the quality of the withdrawal from the world will be influenced by whether it is meaningfulness, intensity, or variety that he especially fears.

Finally, we come to the personality type including low activation, and both internal and passive traits. Once again, such a person would appear to be much like his more active counterpart. He would advocate the golden mean, and deplore excesses of any kind. His personality would indeed be simple and uncomplex. But he would not be especially effective in anticipating the imminent possibility of excessive impact, and hence would find himself faced with the need to reduce it fairly regularly. Being oriented toward internal sources of stimulation, he would tend to employ what are usually called the desensitizing or repressive defenses. In this fashion, he would render ineffective the organismic sources of impact. The particular defenses employed could be at least partially understood on the basis of whether the fear of meaningfulness, intensity, or variety was especially strong in him.

Hopefully, this brief description has lent some vividness to the personality typology offered by activation theory. There is little more to say except to note that some developmental assumptions have definitely been made in arriving at this typology. It has been assumed that the characteristic curve of activation becomes solidified early in life, after which time it changes little. Also, some learned basis has been assumed for the activeness-passiveness and external-internal traits, as well as for the needs for or fears of meaningfulness, intensity, and variety. None of these assumptions are sufficiently detailed in developmental hypotheses by this as yet incomplete personality theory. Some rudimentary developmental statements concerning the characteristic curve of activation have already been reviewed in Chapter 4, and Maddi (1961b) has offered some suggestions concerning how high and low needs for variety may be learned. Nothing more is available. Nonetheless, it must be said that activation theory has been articulated in such fashion as to lead to a definite and usable position not only on the concrete peripheral characteristics but also on the types comprising peripheral personality.

It seems clear now that activation theory is rather different in emphasis from most kinds of personality theory (though, of course, it is closest to other consistency theories). While activation theory can claim to address some phenomena (e.g., activity level, boredom) not emphasized elsewhere, it might well have difficulty explaining phenomena that are easy for other approaches. For example, it is not immediately apparent how activation theory would explain such universally accepted human events as guilt and self-condemnation.

Chapter 9 RATIONAL ANALYSIS
OF PERIPHERAL CONSIDERATIONS

In the three preceding chapters, I reviewed many points of view on the periphery of personality. It is time now to consider the similarities and differences among these views, so that we can better appreciate the essential features of what personologists consider to be the concrete ways of living that you can find in people. An understanding of these essential features will be useful in approaching the empirical analysis in Chapter 10, the aim of which is to identify the kinds of peripheral assumptions that seem most fruitful in the light of available evidence.

The first section of this chapter will compare, contrast, and analyze the various kinds of concrete peripheral characteristics that appear in peripheral theorizing. The next section attempts similar discussion of the conceptualizations of personality types. These two sections will not be organized around the three models of personality, as the formal issues arising from different peripheral conceptualizations are rather independent of the models involved. Bear with these sections, even if they seem a bit disorganized, for certain fairly definite conclusions are reached in the end. The final section of this chapter analyzes the content of peripheral statements by comparing and contrasting the particular theories as expressions of the three models.

THE VARIOUS KINDS OF CONCRETE PERIPHERAL CHARACTERISTICS

In beginning discussion of the concrete peripheral characteristics that have been postulated, I will focus first upon their nature and function. Despite the many differences in terminology and emphasis that we encountered in the peripheral theories, only three basic kinds of concrete peripheral characteristic seem to emerge. One kind concerns goals and instrumental strategies, another concerns unselfconscious habits of performance, and the third concerns ideas, values, and principles of thought. Examples of the first, or motivational, unit are the *need* (Murray), *motive* (McClelland, Maddi), *dynamic disposition* (Allport), *fictional finalism* (Adler), and *defense* (Freud). If it seems strange to list defense with the others, just recognize that defenses have the goal of avoiding anxiety, and in this are not very dissimilar to avoidance motives. The major example of the kind of concrete peripheral characteristic involving un- selfconscious habits of performance is the *trait*, as used by McClelland, Maddi, Adler, Fromm, and Freud. Also relevant, however, are the *need- integrate* (Murray), and *stylistic disposition* (Allport). Finally, the kind of concrete peripheral characteristic emphasizing principles of thought is exemplified by the *schema* (McClelland), *personal construct* (Kelly), and perhaps *condition of worth* (Rogers). Jung's functional *modes* also seem to emphasize thought, though they may be too broad for considera- tion as concrete peripheral characteristics.

Not only are there basically just three kinds of concrete peripheral characteristics, but, interestingly enough, no one of them seems particu- larly frequent in one of the models for personality theorizing as opposed to the others. Some explicit form of a motivational concept and an ex- plicitly cognitive concept appear in examples of the conflict, fulfillment, and consistency models. The trait concept is by all odds the most popular, and it appears in the theories exemplifying all three models. Actually, the trait concept is sometimes so broadly defined as to include a cognitive or motivational emphasis along with a habit emphasis. It can hardly be said that the nature and function of the concrete peripheral characteris- tics appearing in a theory follow in any precise fashion from the per- sonality model it represents.

Probably, the major factor in a theorist's decision as to the form and nature of the concrete peripheral characteristics he will employ is a sense of what will be necessary in order to explain the behavioral phenomena that seem important. After all, the models seem broad enough in their logical possibilities to permit any and all of the three kinds of concrete peripheral characteristic. The models may well put constraints on the content emphasized at the periphery of personality, but I will not discuss this possibility until later. For the moment, we should delve further into the tie I have suggested between the kinds of concrete peripheral characteristics one employs and the behavioral phenomena one feels it is important to explain.

Motives and traits

The most common distinction among kinds of concrete peripheral characteristics leads to an entity emphasizing motivation and another emphasizing habit. Of the personologists, McClelland is most insistent on this distinction, defining motive and trait as mutually exclusive. Maddi is in complete agreement, having adopted McClelland's usage. Although Adler does not discuss the matter at any length, he must be in essential agreement, as he distinguishes sharply between the fictional finalisms (motives) and the traits that comprise character. Murray, with his distinction between needs and need-integrates, and Allport, who distinguishes dynamic and stylistic dispositions, show substantial similarity to McClelland. But they hardly agree with him completely, being unwilling to define motivational and habit concepts in mutually exclusive fashion. Although it may not seem so at first, Freud also offers a basis for the distinction, in postulating not only traits but also the more motivational defenses as components of character types. Clearly, he does not separate the two completely, as defenses are at a high level of generality and tend to subsume, or at least produce the learning of, traits.

To be sure, the remaining personologists who engage at all in peripheral theorizing do not offer any explicit basis for distinguishing motives and traits. But it is difficult to determine whether the absence of such a distinction occurs because the theorists actively consider drawing it a mistake, or more simply because they are rather unconcerned about the precision and completeness of peripheral theorizing. Working in terms of the overall spirit of the theorizing, I would surmise that Erikson, Sullivan, Rank, and Fromm would not be against the distinction in principle. After all, they tend to rely upon an extremely broad and flexible definition of the trait in their peripheral theorizing, all the while they are also describing the person in strongly motivational terms. It is more difficult to say how the few remaining personologists would react to the possibility of distinguishing motives and traits. Only Rogers (1963) has gone on record in a fashion suggesting opposition to the distinction, asserting that the motive concept is unnecessary in what we would call peripheral theorizing.

Taking all the positions into account, it seems clear that the distinction between motive and trait is an important one in the peripheral theorizing of at least half, if not a majority of the personologists we are considering. Those who are most explicit in drawing this distinction make clear that they do so because of the conviction that there are two different classes of behavior to be observed in people. So different do these classes of behavior seem that it appears natural and appropriate to explain them through different kinds of concrete peripheral characteristics. You will recall from the discussion of McClelland's peripheral theorizing that the two classes of observed behavior were called directional and repetitive. Let us dwell further on the distinction between these classes, in order to ensure that the personologist's bases for employing the motive and trait concepts are clear.

Repetitive behavior is very simple. Whenever a situation comes up that is similar to what you have experienced before, there will be a tendency in you to function as you have before. This tendency to repeat old behaviors will be automatic in the sense that you do not have to make a decision about it. Indeed, you may well not have any awareness of these old behaviors that you are repeating. Automatic, habitual behavior is not expressive of the intellect, so much as it is mechanical; a situation comes up and it provokes in you previously learned behavior that is so familiar that you do not even notice yourself performing it. A great deal of behavior is of this sort. One person may have a particularly characteristic choice of words or pitch to his voice in public, social situations, another person may have a particularly aggressive way of driving a car, another may dress according to a particular color scheme, another may be expansive when confronted with people of the opposite sex. If you pointed out these behaviors to the people performing them they might well be surprised, perhaps even to the point of doubting the veracity of your observations. And if you asked them to tell you about their personal goals, they would not include expansiveness, particular choice of words, and so forth.

Goal-directed behavior is as different as it can be from the stylistic behavior just described. Obviously, in goal-directed behavior you have an explicit goal, something that can be put into words and that you work toward. The task of reaching the goal requires that you be ingenious in finding and performing just those instrumental acts that will be successful in the environment in which you find yourself. If you have the goal of feeding yourself because you are hungry, and you are in the environment of a modern American home, the most probably successful instrumental acts will be those involved in finding and searching the refrigerator and pantry. But if you have the same goal and find yourself in the environment of a forest, you would employ the different instrumental acts of trying to find a stream where there might be fish to be caught, or of stalking land game, or of searching out edible vegetation. Which of these possibilities you carried out, and in what order, would likely be determined by the particular characteristics of the forest as they presented themselves to you. Although the goal in home and forest examples is the same, the directional behavior aimed at reaching the goal is different because it must be suited to the characteristics of the environment. If you pointed out to the person what kinds of actions you observed, he would hardly be surprised. Indeed, he would explain to you that he was doing those things in order to try to gain food in the particular circumstances he had encountered. The obviously different actions in the two examples are rendered functionally equivalent by the existence in the person of the same goal of getting food. Goal-directed behavior thus appears to be intelligent rather than mechanical in nature. What this means is that the person pursuing a goal must assess the nature of the environment, make a decision as to the best strategy to follow, and embark upon that strategy flexibly enough so that he can change his mind if he encounters additional information unavailable originally. There is too much self-consciousness and decision-making in this kind of behavior to consider it mechanical. It involves the operation of intellect.

Although the distinction we are discussing seems clear, I can imagine some psychologists saying that it really cannot be drawn in practice, for behavior has a unitary quality. From the standpoint of this holistic position, the distinction mentioned above is a false one, however rational it may sound, because all aspects of behavior are so interdependent as to be inseparable. I do not find this argument convincing. If the opposition is to any separation of behaviors into classes, then the holistic position borders on an evasion of the psychologist's difficult but unavoidable task of deciding what he is supposed to explain. To say that all behavior is to be explained, and not to classify behavior into various categories, is to structure the explanatory task in a manner that must lead to failure. To avoid classification would be like a physicist asserting that his task was to explain the universe, without being willing to discuss the various physical entities comprising it.

But the holistic argument might be directed against the particular distinction between repetitive and directional behaviors, rather than against all possible distinctions. To be sure, the decision as to whether one was observing repetitive or directional behavior would be difficult to make in practice. But it pays to have an open mind and to explore the distinction further, especially because so many personologists seem to have adopted some form of it. How could we structure observation so as to enter into the spirit of the distinction? Certainly, if you permit yourself to do no more than observe the overt behavior of a person in some unspecified situation it may well be unclear whether what you are observing is behavior which repeats old habits or behavior which is directed toward future goals. But nobody advocating the distinction between repetitive and directional behaviors would be that naïve as an observer. In order to try to distinguish these two categories of behavior, you would first of all have to observe the person repeatedly over a wide range of situations. To discern repetitive behavior, you would look for recurrences that did not seem to be parts of sequences and that seemed tied to the repetition of situations. To discern directional behavior, you would look for discrete actions that seemed to bear sequential relationship to each other, and that were not restricted in occurrence to repetitive situations. The identification of sequences of action would be greatly facilitated by the person's verbal statements concerning his personal goals. Such verbal statements would certainly be obtained by anyone wanting to distinguish repetitive from directional behaviors. If you accept the importance of distinguishing repetitive and directional behaviors, it will seem natural and appropriate to explain the former with some sort of habit or trait concept, and the latter with some sort of motive concept.

To the rescue of the concept of motivation

One definite implication of adopting some form of the motive and trait concepts in peripheral theorizing is that not all behavior is motivated! All behavior can be considered caused, for the trait is as much a cause of mechanical, repetitive behavior as the motive is of intellective, directional behavior. Nonetheless, a trait is not a motive. Some personologists would have difficulty accepting a theoretical formulation which suggested that not all behavior is motivated. Invariably, these are personologists who have attributed motivational significance to their postulated core tendencies. Certainly, if the core tendency is motivational, then by virtue of the fact that it is considered to infuse all functioning, there cannot be some functioning that is without motivation. Some theorists who attribute motivational properties to their core tendency, such as Rogers and Maslow, do not make an explicit distinction between motive and trait at the peripheral level. As they do not assume a basically nonmotivational entity at the periphery, there is no inconsistency between their core and peripheral theorizing. But other theorists who tend to attribute motivational significance to their core tendency, such as Freud, also fall into the logical inconsistency of using the trait concept in discussing the periphery. Fortunately, I think there is a simple way out of this logical dilemma that does little or no violence to the real intent of the various personality theories, and may at the same time render more clear and precise the nature of the motivation concept.

Greater clarity and precision in the use of the motivation concept would certainly make it more intellectually appealing than it currently seems to many psychologists. We have reached the bewildering point where virtually any sort of behavior will be called motivated by some psychologist. Birds flying, bees buzzing, ladies sweating, babies playing, monkeys solving problems, rats hoarding, cockroaches crawling, and men sleeping, will all be described in a diverse array of motivational terms. So loosely is the concept used, and so huge are the differences of opinion from psychologist to psychologist, that it would not be surprising to find people turning away from motivational explanations altogether. A trend in that direction may well be under way, to judge from the fact that a number of psychologists of eminence (e.g., Kelly, 1955; Skinner, 1950) can gather followings for approaches to understanding behavior that profess to exclude the motivation concept.

But as most personologists consider the motivation concept too valuable to abandon, it seems wise to work toward clarity and precision in its use. The distinction drawn between motive and trait, which involves restriction of the relevance of the motivation concept to identifiably directional behaviors, seems a step toward clarity and precision. This view, apparently based on the intent of many personologists, is very close to that of Peters (1958) who, in an excellent logical analysis of the motivation concept, concludes that it is best suited to explain behavior involving the existence of a personal goal and instrumental strategies relevant to achieving that goal. Recently, Kagan (1972) and Dember (1974) have adopted similar views. As anything that can properly be called a personal goal will be really rather concrete and specific, it seems to me that the motivation concept is most appropriately applied at the peripheral level of personality. A core tendency is simply too general and universalistic to achieve representation in the person's mind as a goal and attendant instrumental strategies.

So one way out of the logical dilemma of assuming all behavior to be motivated at the same time that one of the concepts you employ at the peripheral level is essentially nonmotivational is to deny motivational significance to your core tendency. This way recommends itself to us because it would encourage clarity and precision in the use of the motivation concept. But before adopting this solution, we must consider what would be lost by divesting core tendencies of motivational significance. The major reason why some personologists attribute motivational significance to core tendencies is to emphasize that these tendencies are meant to describe requirements of the organism and overall directionalities that are so basic as to be common to all people. I am prepared to grant that if core tendencies did not refer to these basic requirements and directionalities, they would not be fulfilling their intended theoretical purpose. The question is whether they can fulfill this purpose without being accorded motivational status. If we can find an affirmative answer to this question, then we can accept the solution to the dilemma posed at the beginning of this paragraph.

In pursuing the answer to the question, we should consider the core tendencies, as postulated by personologists, that do not seem heavily invested with motivational import. McClelland's theorizing is a good example. According to him, it is common to all persons to experience negative affect when the discrepancy between expectation and occurrence is large, and positive affect when it is small. Negative affect leads to avoidance behavior, and positive affect to approach. As we would expect of any proper core statement, the positive and negative affects disclose certain organismic requirements, and the approach and avoidance behaviors indicate directionality. But in neither affect nor behavioral adjustment to it is there evidence of proaction or intellect. There is little choice, decision making, or flexibility (at least before considerable learning has occurred). Rather, the approach and avoidance behaviors are automatic, almost reflexive organismic adjustments to comfort and discomfort. Such behavior is more like a tropism than anything else. Something happens and you are drawn to it, something else happens and you are repelled by it. There are no personal goals, instrumental strategies, choices, or manipulation of the environment, and hence, no motivational significance.

In McClelland's theorizing, the core tendency is the core tendency, not a motivation. Or if you prefer another name, the core tendency could be referred to as a *drive*, once again distinguishing that from a motive. Actually, the distinction between drive and motive is often made in the psychological literature. A drive is more biological and/or mechanical, and less self-conscious and/or intellective than a motive. Drive-induced behavior may lead to experiences whereby motives are learned, but what is learned may bear little concrete relationship to the underlying drive. Thus, the drive to approach small and avoid large discrepancies between expectation and occurrence may lead to a strong achievement motive. But it is only when the concrete standards (goal) of excellence and competitive strategies for attaining them are present in the person's mind that McClelland will talk in motivational terms.

Maddi's theorizing agrees in this respect with that of McClelland. The core tendency to maintain activation at the characteristic level is not motivational because it merely represents the organism's requirements and whatever automatic adjustments to them that are available. Maddi only attributes motivational significance to the goal-oriented, intellective attempt to either increase or decrease the variety, meaningfulness, or intensity of stimulation. It is certainly true that in pursuing any of these motives, activation level may well change in the direction of the organism's requirements. But the person's intent is still not directly that of producing such activation changes.

We have learned from considering the theorizing of McClelland and Maddi that it is possible to postulate a core tendency which expresses organismic requirements and overall directions without at the same time being motivational. In order to do this, you must couch your core tendency in terms of mechanical, reactive, driven behaviors existing prior to learning. Motives emerge clearly as learned units comprising goals and proactive, intellective behaviors that, though very likely consistent with the organismic requirements, do not express them directly. Let us try to apply these principles to other personality theories, in order to determine what is gained and what is lost.

The principles fit Rogers' theory easily. He describes his actualizing tendency in terms that indicate it to be the organism's natural, inherent requirement to develop along the lines of its potentialities. The process of actualization is nothing that involves conscious intent, awareness, or decision. Actualization simply goes on because it is an expression of the nature of the organism. Indeed, attempts to use the intellect and be proactive about the business of actualization usually misfire, and are looked upon skeptically by Rogers. This is as clear a nonmotivational statement of core tendency as there is in the personological literature.

In spite of this Rogers often refers to the actualizing tendency as a motive. As you may recall from Chapter 3, Rogers imputes the actualizing tendency not only to humans, not only to animals, but to all other living things as well. I quoted Rogers in that chapter as referring to a giant seaweed actualizing itself all the while it was buffeted by the surf. Poetically forceful though this example is, it makes perfectly clear that Rogers cannot mean to consider the actualizing tendency to be motivational and still be convincing on logical grounds. If the actualizing tendency is a motive, we would have to agree that seaweed assumes its size, shape, color, and other attributes because it is motivated to do so! This clearly cannot be. Seaweed becomes what it becomes because it is equipped with a genetic blueprint and the tendency to actualize that blueprint. No choice and no manipulation of the environment is involved. What is operating are organismic requirements and drives, not motives. Similarly, when Rogers applies this same actualizing tendency to humans, it is not a motive.

My analysis does not doom Rogers to go forever without a concept of motivation. He could, if he so desired, develop a motivational concept at the peripheral level of personality emphasizing learned goals and instrumental strategies. This peripheral motivation might even be structured as the development, through learning, of more psychological forms of the actualizing tendency. Perhaps Rogers' *need for positive regard* and *need for positive self-regard* are where motivation should be considered to inhere. For that matter, even a concept like need for achievement might be considered the concrete, peripheral resultant of expressing the actualizing tendency, when an existing inherent potentiality happened to find best expression competitively, and the environment supported competition. I cannot help but note that this kind of development of and emphasis on the peripheral level of personality would be welcome in Rogers' theory, as it currently has very little to say there. Unfortunately, Rogers (1963) has clearly stated a disbelief in the value of theorizing about specific motives in the manner of McClelland. This disbelief simply does not change the fact, however, that Rogers' imputation of motivational significance to the actualizing tendency itself seems rather poetical and inconsistent with the most precise use of the motivation concept.

Other personologists, such as Adler, Freud, Erikson, White, Fromm, and existentialists also tend to attribute motivational siginficance to their core tendencies, but describe them in ways indicating more proaction and intellect than does Rogers. It may seem at first as if these theorists have adhered to the cannons of clarity and precision concerning the motivation concept that I advocated earlier, and still found a way to apply the concept at the core level. If this is really true, then we should simply accept that personologists can, with equal logical rigor, assume that all or only some behavior is motivated. But I for one still find it difficult to endorse attributing motivational characteristics to core tendencies because organismic requirements are at such a high level of generality as to be unconvincing as personal goals. Let me express my meaning gradually by considering a few of the personologists just mentioned.

Adler, for example, sees the tendency toward perfection as underlying all functioning and as being motivational in nature. He does not imput this "great upward drive" as he puts it to inanimate living things, and he does describe it in terms that indicate the existence of personal goals and concern with appropriate instrumentalities. Out of a sense of inferiority, the person will develop a compensatory goal, and then organize his energies and attention toward attaining this goal. All this certainly sounds as if it is an admissible motivational explanation of directional, proactive behavior. But let us look more closely at the personal goal. This will take the form of what Adler calls a *fictional finalism*. A fictional finalism might be wanting to be beautiful, or charming, or famous, or respected, or intelligent, or generous, but it would be very unlikely to be wanting to be perfect. In other words, the actual goal a person has will be more specific, limited, and peculiar to him than is the universalistic core tendency. It is in the fictional finalism, and associated strategies of instrumental action, that motivation inheres. The overall core tendency toward perfection, while it provides an explanation of what is the directional community of all persons, is not properly understood as a motive, for it is probably too ubiquitous to achieve direct representation in the mind as a personal goal. This kind of core tendency, though more unique to organisms that can have personal goals than is that of Rogers, is still better considered an organismic requirement than a motive. The motives in Adler are the fictional finalisms, which are, of course, at the peripheral level of personality.

As I indicated earlier, something that the organism requires can very well be called a *need*, and the attempt to satisfy that need can well be called a *drive*. So we can even agree with Adler's designation of his core tendency as a drive, if we are careful to recognize that drive and motive are different in their implications. In Adler, drive (tendency toward perfection) gets translated into motive (fictional finalism) through learning and development. It may sound to you as if I have done little more than change some words around and insist on a rigor of usage that borders on intellectual preciosity. I do not think this is true. Recognize that once we accept that Adler's core tendency may be an organismic drive, but is not a motive, and that motivation is a peripheral consideration, then it becomes possible to believe that not all behavior is motivated without giving up a belief in Adlerian theory. Indeed, one can even recognize, in addition to fictional finalisms, concrete peripheral characteristics that are not motivational in nature without causing rational damage to the theory. And certinly Adlerians do seem to want to include in the style of life traits, such as charmingness, that explain repetitive behavior. Accepting my analysis means that you do not have to defend the inclusion of traits in the periphery of personality all the while you are trying to cast your core tendency in motivational terms, with the disconcerting result of a logical requirement that all behavior be motivated.

The conclusions reached above can also be applied to the other person-ologists. Allport apparently does not consider his core tendency toward psychological maturity to be motivational, and that is a good thing. It is unlikely that this tendency would actually achieve representation in the mind as a personal goal. More likely, one would have much more con-crete goals, such as becoming a good physician or father or friend or lover. These personal goals might well represent the results of the core tendency, but are themselves peripheral manifestations. They are reason-able examples of what Allport might call *dynamic traits.* In Maslow's case, it can also be said that the core tendency of self-actualization is un-likely to appear as a personal goal in people. Much more likely is the appearance of more concrete goals. Fromm's core tendency of attempting to express human nature is another case in point. Fromm does break down this general tendency into a number of parts, such as the need for rooted-ness. And it is more likely that these relatively concrete aspects of the core tendency will achieve mental representation as personal goals. But probably one must become even more concrete before the kinds of things that are commonly considered goals are encountered. So too with White's point of view. It is unlikely that people do all the things they do because they are imbued with the single motivation to be competent. All the things they do may well add up to a tendency toward competence in the theorist's mind, but this is a different thing. Similarly, the existential-ist's emphasis on authentic being is also probably too broad and en-compassing to be motivational, though the particular decisions with which one is faced in life could well be. With regard to all these theorists it can be said that the core tendency is most clearly considered not a motive but an organismic requirement or even drive. This permits saving the motivation construct for the kind of concrete, goal-oriented behavior found at the periphery of personality. And this means that such theories could then easily incorporate the possibility that not all behavior is motivated.

Let us turn now to the psychoanalytic thinkers, Freud, Murray, and Erikson, whose shared position can be treated in much the same manner as the theorists already considered. The core tendency of maximizing in-stinctual gratification while minimizing punishment and guilt is probably at too high a level of generality to achieve concrete representation as goal states and attendant instrumentalities. Happily, however, psychoanalytic theory provides a built-in basis for being more specific concerning the locus of motivation. Let us consider the instinctive (pleasure principle) and defensive (reality principle) parts of the core tendency separately. The instincts not only have a source in and energy from, organismic re-quirements, they also have aims and objects. Indeed, the major psychic or mental significance of the instincts is in the form of objects and the wish to obtain them. Psychoanalytic thinkers use the term object in much the same manner as we are using the term goal or goal state. Generally speaking, people learn to recognize and pursue whichever of the relevant objects that are available in their environment. This is not so different from saying that people learn personal goals and attendant instrumental strategies. Psychoanalytic thinkers would come most of the way toward adopting the motivational view we are considering in this section by using the term motivation to refer only to the objects and possibly the aims of the instincts, leaving their source and energy to be accounted for as organismic requirements and drives.

A matching concretization and restriction of imputed motivational significance would be helpful also concerning the defensive part of the core tendency. It is unlikely that the abstract, ubiquitous attempt to avoid all punishment and guilt registers in the mind as a personal goal. But it is very likely that people have specific avoidance goals leading them to shun the very situations expressive of the specific objects and aims of their instincts. Such an avoidance goal might be to avoid being hit by mother (when the instinctual object and aim of stealing money, let us say, is aroused). The specific defense instituted to realize the avoidance goal can, in our terminology, be considered an instrumental strategy. Interestingly enough, although Freud considers the defenses to operate unconsciously, he describes them in the terminology of intellect and choice (Peters, 1958). All in all, specific avoidance goals and attendant defensive instrumentalities can with clarity be considered motivational.

In this section, I have tried to sketch how, with little loss in explanatory power, the various personality theories could be adjusted where and when necessary to permit a use of the motivation concept that is clear, precise, consistent, and readily acceptable from the standpoint of reason. This usage involves considering core tendencies and characteristics to represent organismic drives and requirements, saving the motivation concept to apply to the peripheral level, with its personal goals and intelligent strategies for reaching them. Of all the theories, only the psychoanalytic one appears to lose much of its original impact, which depended so much on the notion of unconscious motivation. What does this new use of the motivation concept do to the unconscious contents of the mind?

The problem of the unconscious

Perhaps some of you have been becoming rather disconcerted on reading the last few pages. It must be clear that in stressing personal goals as the hallmark of motivation, I am taking the position that nothing which cannot easily register in a person's awareness as something he wants really has motivational significance. I seem to be embracing a phenomenology of motivation. What the person says he wants is what we, as personologists, would have to agree that he wants. This must seem to do violence to those of you who believe in unconscious motivation, for that position requires, by definition, that there be some goals toward which the person works of which he will be unaware. Even if you cannot imagine me to be enough of a Freudian to be disturbed by your discomfort, you have read Chapter 5, in which I presented a strong empirical case for the existence of defense in some people at least, and in which I tried to translate defense theory into something more palatable to reason. Therefore, I must have some belief in the existence of unconscious processes. You could conclude that I am just being inconsistent in also taking the position I have taken in the last few pages. Let me hasten to indicate that this is not the case.

In my position on motivation, it is only necessary that the personal goal have been conscious at one time. If this condition is met, then you are sure that you are dealing with a genuine personal goal, rather than some goal merely imputed to the person by the personologist. But a personal goal, though conscious at first, need not stay that way. If it precipitates personal conflict (e.g., I really want to hug mother but if I do, father will get angry and punish me) then it may well be defended against and hence drop out of consciousness. My position can well accept the possibility that a personal goal that is defended against because it precipitates a personal conflict can continue to affect behavior even though no longer available to awareness. The behavior thus affected would still show decision making, and instrumental sequences of acts, though all of these might be a little less well organized by virtue of the absence of conscious appreciation of the goal that is being pursued. What my position excludes is the possibility that what I am calling organismic requirements are unconscious motives. Be clear that this possibility is excluded only because I believe such organismic requirements to be too general, ubiquitous, and universal to ever achieve mental representation as personal goals, not because I do not believe in unconscious motivation. If something never was a personal goal, it can hardly be defended against.

Actually, I think my position to be very close to Freud's real intent, granting the existence of some semantic differences and some confusions. Freud concerned himself in the main with unconscious motives that would, in his estimation, have been conscious except for the action of defenses. These unconscious motives seem close to what I am talking about. But Freud also made occasional and to my mind uneasy reference to a part of the unconscious that had never been, and could never be, conscious. He thought this might be the collective or racial unconscious emphasized by Jung. Freud was not always sure it really existed in the mind as, of course, the unconscious should in his view. I think I know what Freud was getting at. Might he not have been recognizing, however tentatively and imperfectly, that the most universal, general organismic requirements do not achieve mental representation as goals, even though they do exert a broad influence on behavior? I think this likely because, after all, it really makes little sense to talk about an unconscious that has never and can never be conscious as still somehow in the mind. In any event, I think my position on motivation does not do great violence to the notion of unconscious motivation in psychoanalytic thinking. And certainly, it must do even less violence to other personality theories which utilize the concept of defense, for they are much less specific concerning the necessary content of conflicts than is psychoanalytic theory.

But you must recognize that even as the acceptance of my position makes of motivation a peripheral characteristic, therefore leading to the conclusion that not all behavior is motivated, so too does it lead to the notion that not all behavior has a component of unconscious motivation. Primarily behaviors stemming from a personal goal that has been forced from awareness by defenses can be considered unconsciously motivated. This conclusion accords nicely with the discussion of defensiveness in Chapter 5, which found that not all behavior is defensive. But accepting this conclusion will require a shift in thinking on the part of some people of psychoanalytic inclination. Some people of this inclination believe that all behavior is at least partially determined by unconscious motivation. Perhaps it will help to recognize that all behavior might well be influenced in a very general way by the organismic requirement of maximizing instinctual gratification while minimizing punishment and guilt, even though the precise explanation of the particular aspects of behavior you see now or another time will be achieved primarily with peripheral constructs which will only sometimes involve unconscious motivation. Actually, what I am suggesting accords well with Freud's original intent in theorizing, which was to find an explanation for the oddities and paradoxes of behavior.

As Peters (1958) points out, Freud wanted to explain slips of the tongue, dreams, hypnotic dissociation, and this clearly colored his development of the notion of unconscious motivation. In other words, Freud developed the concept of unconscious motivation to explain those things that people did, or omitted doing, for which they had no adequate explanation themselves. These things were clearly not accidental, as some theorists thought at the time, for the people to whom they happened were displeased by their inability to understand, and the occurrences were so directional and predictable that they seemed motivated. Peters (1958) makes a very good point here. If Freud had been convinced by explanations people could give of these oddities of behavior, he would never have developed the notion of unconscious motivation. Peters generalizes from this to say that it is only when the explanation a person gives for his behavior does not convince us that we should look to the possibility of unconscious motivation. This is what Freud would have done, and what we should do too.

Thus, imagine that we see a person suddenly stop in the process of walking down the street, veer, and walk to the other side of the street. If we ask him why he did this and he says that he spied a tobacconist's shop on the other side of the street, and went toward it because he needed tobacco, there is nothing to stop us from being convinced. The behavior is directional and appropriate to a personal goal of which the person is aware (i.e., to get tobacco). There is no call here for invoking the concept of unconscious motivation. There is no oddity. But suppose everything else were the same, save that the man ran rather than walked across the street. If he gave the same explanation as above, we would still be left wondering why he ran. If there were no cars around, and if the store were not obviously about to close, running would be an oddity. If the man could tell us nothing more than he wanted tobacco, we might well suspect that his actions were at least in part influenced by unconscious motivation.

It seems to me that the position I am taking on motivation has the advantage, in consideration of unconscious motivation, of getting us back again to the kind of thing Freud had in mind. Unconscious motivation is an explanatory construct that should be employed only when it seems relevant, that is, when a person's own account of his goals is unconvincing as an explanation of his behavior. This use of the concept of unconscious motivation is more defensible from the point of view of reason than is that which makes all behavior somehow an expression of unconscious motivation. The latter approach only seems understandable to me if the theorist has some investment in second-guessing people, or in convincing them that he knows them better than they know themselves, or in rendering them pessimistic and distrustful concerning themselves and others.

Jung's case is complicated by his assumption of both a personal and a collective unconscious. The personal unconscious formed by the action of defenses, can be handled as in Freud as a special case of motivation. But, according to the position I have been developing, the collective unconscious, having never been conscious at all, does not qualify as motivation. Do not be troubled by this, for it is not even clear that Jung meant the collective unconscious to be motivational in the precise sense of determining directional as opposed to repetitive behaviors. The collective unconscious emphasizes thought structures—typical problems and solution attempts—that are especially common for the human species. Only the derivatives of these essences or archetypes ever even become concrete enough to achieve or affect consciousness, according to Jung. It does not seem likely that he would have objected to considering the archetypes to express organismic requirements, saving the term motivation for the learned goals and aims developing in persons as the result of complex interactions among the various aspects of personality and between them and the environment.

Schemata

Thus far, I have taken the position that it is sensible for a peripheral theory of personality to include two types of explanatory construct—

motive and trait. In taking this position, I have followed McClelland closely. But what of his schema concept? Is this too a useful ingredient in peripheral level theorizing? You will recall that I advocated including both motive and trait concepts because they seemed useful in explaining two different categories of observable behavior—directional and repetitive. If we feel that classifying all behavior as either directional or repetitive is comprehensive enough and differentiated enough to do little violence to the meaning of behavior, then we will find little cause to advocate a schema concept. After all, what would it explain then? But should we feel that this dual classification of behavior is so gross that it does violence to our sense of what is happening in our own lives and those of the people around us, then we would find additional classificatory categories helpful. And perhaps then the schema concept would seem a welcome explanatory device.

With this in mind, let us examine the schema concept more closely. McClelland defines schemata as cognitive maps or units, primarily taking the concrete form of values, and social roles. In addition, he feels that schemata represent a shared cultural, rather than personal, level of experience. What he had in mind was distinguishing between behavior that involves the pursuit of personal goals and behavior that involves the pursuit or upholding of societal goals. For, after all, what are values and social roles but mutually agreed upon standards for behavior in aggregations of people? McClelland is actually suggesting that the motive construct be used to explain behavior directed at attainment of personal goals, whereas the schema concept be used to explain behavior directed at attaining or maintaining societal goals. When a person acts in order to be socially appropriate or moral, he is being determined by the sense of social roles and values he has incorporated from his culture. When he acts in order to reach a goal that refers to his own advancement or satisfaction, he is being determined by his motives. And when he acts in an automatic, unreflective manner he is being determined by his traits.

What are the implications of this discussion of schemata for our classification of behavior as directional or repetitive? Essentially, schema-determined behavior will be directional in nature. It will exhibit the same qualities of intelligent functioning found in motivated behavior, namely, decision making, and flexible tuning of instrumental actions to the particular characteristics of the environment that is encountered. But the goal worked toward will be one agreed upon by the members of the relevant society to be important and worthwhile in relations between people. The goal of a motive is not defined by consensus, nor does it necessarily regulate group behavior.

Schema-determined behavior is not repetitive in nature. In order to see this, take generosity as an example. A man may act generously without intending to, in other words, in an automatic, repetitive way, or he may actively and self-consciously attempt to act generously. In the first instance, we would be observing the *trait* of generosity, whereas in the second the *schema* of generosity. It would be possible for someone actively trying to be generous to have the *motive* of generosity, but only in a culture that did not make generosity a value or a role. If you can recognize the possibility of analyzing behavior into two broad categories called repetitive and directional, with the directional category subdivided into that which is associated with personal goals and that which is associated with societal goals, then you can conclude that it is useful to include in theories of the periphery of personality the concepts of trait, motive, and schema.

Theories of the periphery that employ only one concept, or even two, are not as likely to be clear, precise, and comprehensive as those which employ all three. This is especially true when the theory specifically restricts the consideration of behavioral categories to less than the three mentioned. So, when Kelly's consistency theory employs only cognitive explanatory constructs and construes behavior as though it were little more than mental activity, we may be left with a feeling of incompletion because not all that is important in behavior is considered. Actually, however, many theories of personality contain the rudiments of the triadic characterization of the periphery I have been advocating. In psychoanalytic theories, such as those of Freud, Erikson, and Murray, there is not only an id but a superego as well. The content of the superego is essentially social goals. The process of satisfying id and placating superego could very reasonably lead the theorist to incorporate both motive and schema concepts at the peripheral level. And yet, interestingly enough, two out of three of these psychoanalytic theories employ only the concept of trait, which is the least predictable of the three from the core assumption of existence of id and superego! But in looking at the list of things called traits by these theorists, it is easy to imagine reclassifying them as either traits, motives, or schemata. This same reclassificational possibility exists in other theories as well, notably those of Fromm, Maslow, and Rogers. Finally, the universalistic social emphases of Adler and Jung suggest that their peripheral positions, if developed further, might find utility in the schema concept. The existentialists would seem to be a dissenting voice, for though they emphasize cognition, so do they emphasize the individualistic use of it.

THE PERIPHERAL CONCEPT OF TYPE

Until this point, we have concentrated upon the concrete peripheral characteristics. These are the supposedly indivisible, and therefore basic, building blocks of peripheral theories of personality. But by themselves, they are too concrete to give much sense of the actual flavor of a person's life. They are the trees in the forest, and although a careful study of individual trees will yield much understanding of the nature of trees, it will not by itself clarify the overall dimensions of the forest to any great extent. Lest we lose the forest for the trees, let us turn our attention to another kind of concept relevant to peripheral level theorizing. This concept occurs at a higher level of generality, and has the function of subsuming and grouping together the concrete peripheral characteristics into meaningful patterns. An analogous concept in physics would be compounds, which represent the meaningful combination of elements into more complex units.

For Freud, Fromm, Maddi, Rank, and Jung this more complex, organizational characteristic is *character* or *personality type*. Adler is getting at the same thing when he offers the concepts of *style of life*. And so is Murray in his concept of *complex*, though he fails for some mysterious reason to subsume formally his more concrete concept, *need*, under this more general one. The other personologists do not really offer an organizational concept. In some cases, notably Rogers, Maslow, and existential psychology, the distinctions made between types of people are too few to require such a concept. These positions only distinguish between people succeeding and failing in vigorous expression of the core tendency. These theorists need do no more, therefore, than name these two kinds of people in terms of the content of their personalities. So, Rogers talks of the *fully functioning* and the *maladjusted* persons, and Maslow, though less-terminologically consistent, is similar in emphasis, while Maddi considers individualism and conformism. No more abstract designation for types of people is needed in the way that would be so if more than two types were considered.

Other personologists, notably Allport and Kelly, are so insistent concerning the importance of individuality that they not only fail to offer type concepts, but also avoid designating the possible contents that will be found in their concrete peripheral characteristics. These are related omissions, for organizing the concrete peripheral characteristics into types must largely be done along content lines, and hence, in order to offer a type concept the theorist must have committed himself to specifying the common content of personality. Allport, more than Kelly, does provide a possible basis for theoretical development leading to delineation of the content of peripheral traits in his nicely detailed propriate functions. Thus, one might explore the theoretical yield of considering some people to show concrete peripheral characteristics indicating a personality type stressing *rational coping*, or *propriate striving*, and so on.

Finally, there are personologists, notably McClelland, whose omission of a type concept is more difficult to understand. McClelland certainly specifies both kind and content of his concrete peripheral characteristics, and in so doing indicates a fine-grained interest in comprehensiveness. But he does very little in terms of organizing these concrete peripheral characteristics into types. Perhaps this omission stems from his deep eclecticism concerning personality content. Since McClelland derives the content of his motive, trait, and schema concepts from the work of many different people, it is difficult to put it all together into meaningful patterns. And, of course, his core tendency is relatively contentless, so no help can be looked for from that quarter.

It should be quite clear from this summary that the type concept does not provide any particular basis for distinguishing among conflict, fulfillment, and consistency positions. This is not really surprising, since we have already seen that the kinds of concrete peripheral characteristics are not specific to the three models, and types are combinations of these characteristics. It does not even seem that the omission of the type concept is specific to one or two models, as it occurs in examples of all three.

We have encountered three reasons why personologists, in their peripheral level theorizing, omit reference to coherent patterns of concrete characteristics for which the type concept is appropriate. The reason in McClelland's case does not really represent a theoretical conviction obviating specification of types as much as it does a consequence of his eclecticism with regard to personality content. McClelland would never argue that the concept of personality type is unworthwhile. Indeed, his own work on personality factors leading to economic development (McClelland, 1961), in which he seems to be developing a type of personality involving achievement traits, motives, and schemata, indicates that he has nothing against the notion of types. He simply is in the position of having little formal theoretical basis for postulating them.

But the other two reasons for avoiding the type concept have more ideological commitment behind them. In one of these two cases (e.g., Rogers, Maslow, and existentialism), we find that only two kinds of person are considered important enough to specify in content terms, rendering elaboration of a type concept superfluous. One cannot criticize a theorist for failing to be superfluous. But one can question whether in considering only two kinds of people, he is really being complete enough. Such theorists seem to believe that the only important thing to know about someone is whether or not he is actualizing himself or becoming authentic. It is through a commitment to this view that they have not offered formal theoretical bases for additional behavioral distinctions. It is surely a paradox that theorists who stress individuality as much as they do offer peripheral statements describing only two kinds of people. I hope that if this book has convinced you of anything it is that such theorizing is not complete enough to do justice to the complexity of life.

The other ideologically bolstered reason for omission of the type concept is the general emphasis upon individuality. We will have to talk more about the problem of individuality in a moment, but for now you should realize the severe limitations upon a theory made by its dedication to the proposition that all persons are unique. You will have noticed that the theories of Allport and Kelly could not even be discussed in any detail in this chapter, they are so unspecific concerning the peripheral level of personality. The same extreme emphasis on individuality is found in some existential psychologists. These positions can really only be used to understand data you already have in hand. They provide little or no basis for predicting what kinds of people you are likely to encounter. As such, they do not even improve upon common sense.

The problem of individuality

Personologists differ in the degree to which they stress individuality. Those who tend to believe that people are similar enough to be understood adequately by grouping them into a small number of types include Freud, Sullivan, Rank, Adler, Fromm, Jung, and Maddi. Another group of personologists is substantially in agreement with this position, though they have less to say about types. These personologists are best described as believing that there is some small set of dimensions or variables that can be applied to all men with profit from the point of view of understanding. Included in this group would be Erikson, White, and McClelland. In contrast to the personologists already mentioned is a group that is rather militant concerning individuality. Regardless of whether or not their theories do justice to their beliefs, these personologists have a steadfast ideological commitment to the idea that people are more different from each other than they are similar. Included in this group are Rogers, Maslow, Allport, Kelly, and the existentialists.

It will be instructive to consider the point of view of the most ideologically committed and verbally forceful of the individualists, Gordon Allport. For him (Allport, 1955, p. 22), "each person is an idiom unto himself, an apparent violation of the syntax of the species." In explicating this position, Allport (1955, p. 22) focuses upon the apparently limitless range of potential behavior available to the human by virtue of a big brain and a relative absence of instincts, and ventures the opinion (Allport, 1955, p. 23) "that all of the animals of the world are psychologically less distinct from one another than one man is from other men." All this is strong medicine that could kill the patient—psychology—already in a fever over the struggle for general laws that psychologists believe would make its scientific status indisputable. To anyone engaged in this struggle, Allport's position must seem cruel heresy, and hence, further consideration of it is in order.

Allport (1937, p. 4) argues that the major task of personology is to understand and predict the individual case, rather than the contrived average case. Concepts and relationships aimed at predicting the average case are called *nomothetic*. A concept such as McClelland's need for achievement would be considered nomothetic by Allport. It is nomothetic because of the belief that many people can be given a score on need for achievement. According to Allport, it is only by distorting each person's behavior somewhat that the concept of need for achievement can be applied. The distortion is invariably considered to involve disregarding important qualitative differences among people in favor of describing them all in similar, average terms. Now if nomothetic concepts and laws, derived from and applicable to the data of aggregates of people, were completely adequate for predicting each individual case, there would be little purpose in Allport's championing of the inviolacy of individuality. In practice, however, perfect prediction and understanding using nomothetic concepts and laws is never achieved. Indeed, there is often a sizable minority of cases to which the nomothetic concept and general law do not seem to apply. For example, most people characterized as high in need for achievement will work harder than most people characterized as low. But some people called high will not work, whereas some people called low resemble beavers. This is not surprising to Allport (1961, pp. 332–356), who believes that nomothetic concepts are merely convenient fictions that are only useful insofar as they may resemble the true personality of some people. If a moderate degree of understanding and predictive accuracy is sufficient to satisfy the investigator, then Allport is not seriously opposed to the nomothetic approach. But the paramount goal of the personologist requires a greater approximation to the truth.

In the attempt to achieve this goal, it will be necessary, according to Allport, to develop concepts and laws that are derived from and applicable to the data of each individual case alone. At first he called such theorizing *idiographic* (Allport, 1937, pp. 3–23), and seemed to take such an extreme view that virtually no generalization across persons would be possible (Allport, 1942, p. 57). Whatever organization of behaviors into classes that is attempted is considered properly done only within persons; not across people. Thus, if the need for achievement were used as an idiographic concept, it would refer to a class of behaviors in one person only, and would not really be used on anyone else. More recently he (Allport, 1961, pp. 257–361, 1962) has substituted the term *morphogenic* for idiographic, and seems to be formulating a position that is less extreme, permitting the use of concepts that are not in principle restricted in applicability to only one person. The emphasis is still overwhelmingly on concepts and laws that reflect the individuality of the person studied, but it is at least considered possible that those concepts and laws would turn out to apply to some other people as well. Allport makes a strong plea for freedom from the restricting and nomothetic mold of other sciences, which he believes have not been confronted with uniqueness on a grand scale, and has recently (Allport, 1962) offered a number of suggestions for concrete morphogenic methods of study.

Allport is posing an alternative to the traditional view of science that he believes will lead to the highest level of prediction and control. Although the morphogenic approach should certainly be tried in research, it raises a keen sense of futility when couched as a replacement for an approach encouraging generalizaiton across persons. Must knowledge of individuals remain as unrelated, odd bits of information? How can significant systematization of knowledge be achieved? It should be established with certainty that nomothetic methods have been adequately tested before they are discarded on the grounds that they typically leave some individual cases unexplained.

Whether or not other sciences have been faced with overwhelming individuality, they certainly do recognize the necessity for deduction, from the general law and the characteristics of the situation involved, of explanations and predictions that apply to the individual case. For this to be done well, the general law must provide exhaustive specification of the conditions under which it does and does not apply, and the investigator must have sufficient knowledge of the concrete prediction situation in order to determine whether or not he should use the law. For example, the law contending that need for achievement leads to hard work might only be applicable in conditions of permissiveness and opportunity rather than authoritarianism or lack of resources. Furthermore, complex phenomena may well call for the application of more than one law, and hence, the relationships between laws must be clearly specified. For example, in addition to the law relating need for achievement to hard work, there may be laws determining whether the person will approach or avoid permissive situations. You would have to be able to apply these latter laws to a person in order to understand whether or not his need for achievement level was readily expressed in work intensity. Only if all this information is available will it be possible to evaluate the explanatory adequacy of nomothetic methods, and even then, particular general laws may turn out to be incorrectly formulated without this constituting a demonstration of the inadequacy of the methods they represent. The degree of theoretical and methodological care and precision involved in the adequate application of nomothetic methods is not often recognized as important or attempted in psychology, and hence, the development of really useful nomothetic concepts and laws may be stifled, and individuality may loom overly large as an explanatory problem. Certainly, a strong case for the inadequacy of nomothetic methods in personology cannot presently be made.

It is by no means clear that any personologist believing in individuality must reject the nomothetic approach in order to be true to his belief. To the contrary, the nomothetic approach is so natural to science that it seems straightforward to use it in the absence of evidence showing it to be inadequate. What the personologist believing in individuality should do is use the nomothetic approach in the manner most calculated to do justice to individuality. Let me be more specific about what constitutes the nomothetic approach. Essentially, it involves specifying not only the kinds of concepts at the peripheral level of personality but their content as well. I emphasize specification of content in peripheral level theorizing because it is so much more to the point than is core level specification of content. The latter is nice to have, but speaks to what is common to all persons, and therefore is not useful in understanding individuality. It is the specification of peripheral content that is crucial because in doing this you designate the classes of behavior in people that your theory will recognize. This means that even though you may recognize differences between particular people, you nonetheless expect to achieve understanding of them with a standard, unchanging set of concepts. You are assuming that while individuality may exist, true uniqueness does not. The differences that exist between people are relative, not absolute.

Even with this assumption, it is possible to use the nomothetic approach in a manner facilitating the understanding of individual differences. This involves postulating as many different kinds of concrete peripheral characteristics and types as seems practical and intuitively accurate. Clearly, the more concrete peripheral characteristics you have and the more ways they can be combined to yield types, the more differences between people your theory will recognize. In other words, the nomothetic approach should be used complexly in order to permit an understanding of individuality. In what I have said you should recognize a strong argument for the kind of theorizing about concrete peripheral characteristics found in McClelland, who offers the most categories of concept (motive, trait, schema) and a goodly number of content distinctions (e.g., needs for achievement, affiliation, power, and so forth) within each category. Fromm's theory is another example of complex use of the nomothetic approach. While he offers only the trait concept for the base unit, he nonetheless lists some 47 traits. And while he organizes these traits into only five types, he does indicate that there are many combinations or mixtures of types, at least some of which he specifies. Maddi's activation approach exemplifies the complex use of the nomothetic approach at the level of the type concept. He suggests 24 types of peripheral personality.

THE CONTENT OF PERIPHERAL PERSONALITY

My emphasis to this point has been on the various kinds of concept one finds in theorizing about the periphery of personality. In this section, I will shift emphasis to the content of this theorizing, giving no regard to the kind of concept in which this content is found. In the content of peripheral personality, we can get a more vivid picture of what the theorist thinks characterizes life than would be possible in considerations of the fine points of the form of concepts. One can certainly quibble about whether the theorist has expressed his views in the most elegant and precise form, but in the final analysis differences and similarities between peripheral level theories will be carried primarily in matters of content or substance. And peripheral level content is more useful in understanding the concrete ways in which adults lead their lives than is core level content, the latter being not concerned with particular types of people.

Although the three models for personality theorizing that we have been considering did not appear to be a determining influence on the kinds of peripheral concepts employed, they do have definite implications for the content emphasized. In pinpointing these content implications, I have found it useful to use the distinction between the ideal and non-ideal peripheral personalities.

The conflict model

You will recall that, at the core level, the essence of the conflict model is expressed in the inevitable opposition of two great forces. In the psychosocial form of this model, one of the forces expresses the human as an individual while the other expresses the human as a member of society. As society is more powerful than individuals, this version of the conflict model makes all behavior defensive. The person will only try to get what he wants if he can find a way of doing it that is consistent with the corporate good, for fear of what would happen otherwise. One would expect such theories, at the peripheral level, to stress ideal functioning indicative of socialization (dependability, adaptation, adjustment to social pressures, attitudes and values consistent with and justifactory of the social order), and nonideal functioning indicative of social immaturity (irresponsibility, competitiveness, impulsivity, withdrawal, rebelliousness, conformity).

Sure enough, in the pure psychosocial conflict theory of Freud, we see much that conforms to the expectations stated above. The ideal or genital type is someone who can truly love and work. But remember that loving and working occur on the basis of a defensive process, sublimation, and hence, even this highest form of living does not transcend societal regulations. It is not too inaccurate to say of this theory that it explains adults as loving on the rebound (having had to give up the original love object —the opposite-sexed parent), and working as a way of channeling anti-social instincts into acceptable behavior. Hence, the giving and receiving of love at biological, social, and psychological levels, and the commitment to regular, productive enterprise, will both involve stability, dependability, and adjustment to pressures. There will be generosity, responsibility, and predictability more than flamboyance and impulsivity. The picture is of solidity in whatever one does. In contrast, the nonideal or pregenital types are bogged down in self-preoccupation with how, when, why, and if to take and receive, give and withhold, and heterosexualize living. The task-oriented process of straightforward, dependable, productive living is interrupted frequently by these signs of insecurity, self-preoccupation, selfishness, and rigidity. The pregenital person is too concerned with himself to be a good citizen. Freud's content emphases at the periphery come consistently out of his emphases at the core.

The two variants on the psychosocial conflict model, Murray and Erikson, generally show the expected peripheral content emphases in considering nonideal functioning. Murray endorses, with some elaboration, the pregenital types of Freud. So does Erikson, although he also adds some additional nonideal emphases such as identity-diffusion, social isolation, stagnation, and despair. But as you can see these additions are quite in character with the psychosocial conflict model. With regard to the characteristics of ideal functioning, Murray and Erikson are only partially expressive of this model. In addition to the solid virtues designated by Freudians, Murray and Erikson consider the possibility of at least some degree of imaginativeness, originality, and changeability. These additional emphases have not always seemed convincingly articulated with core assumptions. You will recall, for example, that White criticized Erikson's view of ideal peripheral characteristics as being too optimistic in their socially transcendent implications for a conflict model with its inevitable subjugation of the individual to society. Further, I called to your attention in Chapter 6 the odd fact that Murray's peripheral theorizing, emphasizing needs and need-integrates, did not seem to fit, or be fitted by him, into the core characteristics of id, ego, and superego. Perhaps the most meaningful conclusion to reach is that the theories of Murray and Erikson are in transition away from the psychosocial conflict model.

In the intrapsychic version of the conflict model, the inevitably opposed forces all emanate from within the person. As there is no assumption of powerful society bent on detecting and thwarting the individual, ideal functioning does not emphasize defensiveness. This is not to say that the relationship between the individual and his society is irrelevant. It is always relevant, because one of the opposing forces leads in the direction of individuation, and isolation, whereas the other leads in the direction of dependence, and gregariousness. The best that can be accomplished is a compromise in which both forces are expressed. Thus, at the peripheral level, ideal functioning should show a commitment to being an individual in some fashion that can be respected by those around you, and to associating yourself with people and ideas without hampering your own growth. These adjustments will be made with flexibility and awareness, as there is little defensiveness. Nonideal functioning should express the defensive negation either of the force toward individuality or the force toward union. The first alternative would stress rebelliousness and rejection of other people, whereas the second alternative would stress anxious conformity. Both alternatives would involve inflexibility, because they are defensive in nature. As you can perceive, nonideal functioning in both intrapsychic and psychosocial conflict theories is similar. Ideal functioning is a bit less steady and un-flamboyant in the intrapsychic version. Actually, the intrapsychic version comes quite close to the variant of the psychosocial version.

Of the intrapsychic conflict theories, only those of Rank and Jung have an extensive statement concerning peripheral personality. The content emphases of Rank conform very well to expectation. The two nonideal types are the average person (emphasis upon conformity, passivity, and dependence) and the neurotic (emphasis upon rebelliousness, and in-sistent alienation from people). The ideal type, or artist, transcends con-ventional society, but in a fashion that can be respected by others and therefore permits him to retain his commitment to them. He is essentially a hero. What he does is extraordinary, but he does not do it simply for himself.

At first blush, Jung's position does not seem to conform so well to expectation. The ideal for him is to achieve selfhood, which involves de-veloping a kind of universal personality, not individualistic as much as expressive of that which is in us all. Consciousness is only one aspect of selfhood, and must make way for acceptance and expression of the collec-tive unconscious, if the ideal is to be achieved. But, in a way, Jung is agreeing with the other intrapsychic conflict theorists. After all, the ego, or seat of consciousness, is an individualistic force. It is that force with which the person navigates in the external world of events and affairs and outcomes. He needs to incorporate the collective unconscious into his day-to-day functioning in order that it temper the individualistic ego with the accumulated, shared wisdom of mankind. Thus, in achieving selfhood, the person strikes a balance between individualistic and com-munal tendencies. The other personality types, in that they do not involve a sufficient role for the collective unconscious, can be interpreted to be too individualistic to be ideal. But it must be admitted that Jung's posi-tion is less clearly expressive, at the peripheral level, of the intrapsychic conflict model than is that of Rank.

The fulfillment model

The fulfillment model postulates only one great force, thereby avoid-ing the assumption that conflict is inevitable. But the one force does ex-press the person's individuality, and hence, he may come in conflict with society. This happens only when he has been failed by society, but the consequence for him is, nonetheless, nonideal functioning. As society is stronger than the individual, nonideal functioning is defensive.

At the core level, the actualization version of the fulfillment model stresses the humanistic belief that the content of the great force is the person's inherent potentialities and the inexorable attempt to realize them in tangible form. One need do nothing more, to be ideal, than give one-self over to one's genetic blueprint and follow it wherever it leads. The intentional, self-conscious actions one might wish to take will corrupt expression of the actualizing tendency. At the peripheral level, the actualization version of the fulfillment model should stress spontaneity, changeability, unselfconscious acceptance of self and others, simple confidence, sensitivity, imaginativeness, and impulsivity. In contrast, nonideal functioning should involve premeditation, an evaluative attitude, planfulness, anxious conformity, lack of confidence, and an overwhelming sense of obligation to a monolithic duty.

The peripheral statements of Rogers, the pure actualization theorist, conform almost exactly to these expectations. The fully functioning, or ideal, person will show openness to experience, existential living, organismic trusting, creativity, and congruence between his view of himself and what his potentialities really suit him to be. In contrast, the nonideal or maladjusted person will show strong preoccupation with how, when, why, and what he is or what he should do. These rigidifying concerns introduce a constraint in the direction of conformity and fixity that interferes with the more mature process of continually enlarging and experiencing your own capabilities. Maslow, the variant on the actualization version of the fulfillment model, shares these emphases with Rogers, but adds to them certain ideological considerations. The ideal person according to Maslow, also possesses democratic and humanitarian values, and these presumably also guide his behavior. The nonideal person possesses authoritarian and materialistic values. In this emphasis upon values, both ideal and nonideal, Maslow seems to be approaching the perfection version of the fulfillment model.

In the perfection version, there is little concern with inherent potentialities as a basis for individuality. Instead, there is a conception of what perfect life, or essential human nature, is like. It is this goal toward which the human is impelled, often regardless of real or imagined inferiorities. At the peripheral level, perfection theorizing should emphasize evidence of transcendence over one's own limitations and the limitations of society, guided always by ideals and principles that are superordinate to man. In contrast, nonideal functioning should stress concern with mere biological survival and satisfaction, anxious conformity, and the avoidance of risks. As you can see, the content implications of actualization and perfection versions of the fulfillment model are quite similar. The mild differences between the positions show the actualization version emphasizing intuitive functioning, sensitivity, spontaneity, and impulsivity, whereas the perfection version stresses rational functioning and consistent striving toward goals that have little to do with either inherent potentialities or societal pressures. These differences all stem from the actualization emphasis upon a genetic blueprint and the perfection emphasis upon the best in living regardless of endowment.

Happily, the perfection theorists include much in their peripheral theorizing that matches what I have said above. In Allport's emphasis upon maturity as the presence of a consistent philosophy of life, a religious sentiment, and a generic conscience, we see how ideals are expected to infuse ideal functioning. Nonideal functioning, for Allport, is opportunistic, erratic, impulsive, pleasure-seeking, defensive, and conforming. In more rudimentary form, one sees similar implications in Adler, whose peripheral position is unfortunately not very elaborate. Taking the active-constructive and passive-constructive styles of life as indicative of the ideal, we emerge with a view stressing ambition to reach certain goals and charmingness with regard to other people. Adlerians may intend in such emphases to imply transcendence of self and society in the service of ideals, but this will not be entirely certain until their peripheral theorizing is further clarified. White's emphasis upon consistent, perfectionistic striving and rationality can be seen in his adoption of the peripheral theorizing of Erikson, with its concern at the ideal level with ego integrity, generativity, intimacy, and identity, and at the nonideal level with despair, stagnation, isolation, and identity diffusion. It is interesting that White should have explicitly borrowed Erkson's theorizing. Not only is Erikson a variant on the conflict model moving toward the fulfillment model, but White may also be an incipient fulfillment variant with something of the conflict theorist in him. I say the latter because, in an important paper on competence and the psychosexual stages of development, White (1960) does seem to accept that there is some value to the psychosocial conflict model, even though it must be supplemented by his fulfillment emphasis.

The key to understanding Fromm is that he indicates ideal functioning should be defined as the most constructive aspects of the nonproductive (nonideal) orientations. Generally speaking, from the receptive orientation, one would derive tolerance, acceptance, trust, and the ability to be dependent; from the exploitative orientation, initiative, impulsivity, and effectiveness in grappling with external pressures; from the hoarding orientation, conservation of resources, loyalty, and a sense of the value of things; and from the marketing orientation, adaptability, curiosity, changeability, and openmindness. Fromm includes both the qualities of spontaneity and openness of the actualization position and the striving and sense of industry of the perfection position. As I pointed out in Chapter 3, this combining of emphases is also apparent in his core statements. The opposites of the qualities mentioned above define nonideal functioning, which strongly emphasizes conformity, pleasure-seeking, and concern with biological survival, for Fromm.

Ideal functioning, in existential psychology, is called individualism, and stresses the development of sufficient consciousness so that the true nature of life as a series of decisions can be properly understood. With this understanding comes the ability to make decisions well, evaluating ontological anxiety against ontological guilt, and taking responsibility for what is done. The emphasis here is on rationality, self-reliance, independence, and honesty. Nonideal functioning, or conformism, is the opposite. In conformism, consciousness is not highly developed, and the stereotypes and conventionalities of society are clung to in the vain attempt to avoid making decisions. Clearly, existential psychology well expresses in its peripheral statements what we would expect of the perfection fulfillment model.

The consistency model

As this model makes minimal content assumptions at the core level, there is little that can be formulated by way of expected content at the peripheral level. Any or no specification of peripheral content would be understandable. If content is specified, however, it should at least reflect the procedures whereby people can insure maximal consistency.

Turning to the actual theories, we find that the pure cognitive dissonance theorist, Kelly, specifies no peripheral content. The variant on this position, McClelland, does specify content, but it is an eclectic, omnibus specification. As such, it does not deviate from what we would expect. The activation theorist, Maddi, specifies content in a less omnibus fashion than McClelland. Virtually all the content in Maddi's peripheral theorizing refers to specialized procedures for anticipating activation requirements or correcting discrepancies between actual and customary levels of activation. This is true for tendencies to approach or avoid intensity, meaningfulness, and variety of stimulation, and for the development of differentiation and integration of functioning. The content emphases of the activation version of the consistency model do not appear as important considerations in the other models. The major basis in Maddi's thinking for differentiating ideal from nonideal functioning is the activeness-passiveness trait. This trait is at the same time not strictly derivable from the core assumptions of the activation position, and yet similar in emphasis and implications to the bases for distinguishing ideal from nonideal that appears in the perfection version of the fulfillment model.

Chapter 10 EMPIRICAL ANALYSIS
OF PERIPHERAL CONSIDERATIONS

In the end, any conceptualization is only as adequate as its empirical support. It would be of no use to have a theory beautiful from the standpoint of reason which did not account for the relevant facts or was contradicted by them. We should hasten, therefore, to consider the empirical studies that bear on peripheral theorizing. An analysis of empirical studies could give evidence concerning which of the postulated concrete peripheral characteristics really exist, and how they actually organize themselves into larger units, or types. Empirical analysis can also indicate the amount of behavior (data) explained by each of the existing concrete peripheral characteristics. Having all this information, it would be easy to decide upon the relative fruitfulness of the various peripheral theories and the models they represent.

From what I have said, you can see that an empirical analysis could do great things. In the analysis we will actually conduct, however, it will only be possible to reach more modest conclusions, many of which will be tentative at that. Although it is possible to specify the kinds of studies that would permit the strong conclusions mentioned in the previous paragraph, such ideal studies have not been done in the main. Nonetheless, I will outline the studies that should be undertaken, organized in the form of a strategy with three steps. If you comprehend this ideal strategy, and the kinds of inferences it would permit, you will have no difficulty understanding why the actual studies we will subsequently consider are relevant. And who knows, when you see the discrepancies between the conclusions we can and might have reached, you may find yourselves motivated to conduct studies more closely approximating the ideal.

401

THE IDEAL STRATEGY

Step one: Measuring concrete peripheral characteristics

In approaching the adequate empirical analysis of peripheral theorizing, the first step is to attempt the development of an empirical measure for each concrete peripheral characteristic specified in the various theories under consideration. Arduous though this is, there is no way around it. An attempt must be made to measure all the traits mentioned by Freud, all the needs of Murray, and so forth down the list of personologists. Here and there on the list, you will encounter some theorists, such as Allport, and Kelly, who literally offer nothing upon which a measurement attempt can be based. Others, like Sullivan, are so murky in describing personality types, that much guess work will be involved in deciding what concrete peripheral characteristics they consider important. Here is striking demonstration of the drawback of lack of theoretical elaboration at the peripheral level. How are you supposed to measure something if it is not clear what it is? Whoever attempts to carry out the first step of this ideal strategy will sigh in relief and gratitude whenever he encounters a personologist who is explicit concerning the form and content of concrete peripheral characteristics.

In any event, in attempting to measure the various concrete peripheral characteristics that have been postulated, you must be guided not by what you think a characteristic really means, but rather by what the personologist under consideration thinks about it. Only in this fashion can the success or failure of the measurement attempt be considered a reflection on the adequacy of his theorizing. We have little trouble in being guided by the theorist's meaning when he has provided us with an *operational definition* of the postulated characteristic. An operational definition, if you do not already know, is a literal specification of what you have to do in order to observe the entity under consideration. Unfortunately, only McClelland, Murray, and Maddi even try to provide operational definitions, with McClelland's being a little more useful, because less ambiguous. And even McClelland offers thoroughly complete operational definitions only for some motives.

To see the value of operational definitions, recall McClelland's discussion of motives. In Chapters 8 and 9, you read that, in a formal sense, a motive is a personal goal and the instrumental capability flexible enough to permit pursuit of the goal in a wide variety of situations. In discussing measurement operations, McClelland (1961) recognizes the formal attributes of motives that distinguish them from traits and schemata. A motive involves a personal goal, and therefore, the measurement operation must elicit mentation, rather than merely actions. But not just any mentation will do. The goal to be measured is personal, not social, and hence one must favor measurement operations that do not suggest to the person that his behavior will be judged as to its social desirability. As soon as you start asking the person questions about his goals, or actions, you are too likely to get responses in terms of what is considered socially appropriate. Such questioning may be useful in the measurement of schemata, but is misleading for motives. Taking the requirement of personal mentation into account, McClelland concludes that the best measurement operations involve eliciting fantasy from the person in the form of stories composed about pictures of fictitious people, and then to analyze the content of the stories for evidence of goals and predispositions to instrumental behavior relevant to the goals. The meaning of the pictures should be ambiguous enough, and the task of making up stories unstructured enough, to render it unlikely that people will respond with socially desirable, rather than personal goals. Further, since the human content of the pictures arouses mentation about what the fictitious people are doing, and may want, one is likely to get information about motives, rather than traits, as the latter are so habitual as to be virtually unrepresented in the composition of stories. Some of you may recognize the task described here as Murray's (1943) famous *Thematic Apperception Test.* Regardless of the existence of this technique prior to McClelland's attempt to measure motives, it is extremely well suited to his operationalization. And anyway, Murray devised the test primarily for the measurement of his very similar need concept, though he never provided the compelling operational rationale available in McClelland's theorizing. It is to Murray's credit that McClelland had his groundbreaking work to build upon.

McClelland (1961) is almost as precise about the manner in which the form of schemata is to be measured. If you want to know about a person's social goals, defined by his values and sense of social roles, you might as well just ask him straightforwardly. It matters little if he spruces up his answers because he thinks he will be evaluated by society, for it is just his sense of what society stands for that you want to measure. Questionnaires concerning the directionalities and goals in people's behavior tend to elicit schemata, in comparison with fantasy, or so-called projective tasks, which tend to elicit motives. Finally, from a formal standpoint, traits are to be measured by creating familiar circumstances in which action is called for, and then observing the regularities in people's functioning.

My summary of McClelland's operational attempts is of necessity brief, but I want you to appreciate that no other personologist comes close to him in precision. Indeed, going beyond the formal attributes, McClelland even offers very workable operational definitions for the content of the motives he has emphasized the most (achievement, affiliation, and power). For example, the operational definition for the achievement motive is *competition with a standard of excellence* (McClelland et al., 1953, pp. 110–112). Along with this overall definition, you are provided with a carefully devised scoring system with which to analyze fantasy for evidence of interest in competition with a standard of excellence (McClelland et al., 1953, pp. 107–138). With varying emphases and degrees of precision, Murray and Maddi provide measurement specifications in similar fashion to McClelland.

Once you leave McClelland, Murray, and Maddi, you are on your own in measuring the concrete peripheral characteristics offered by personologists. The best you can find are vivid descriptions of the application of a characteristic to life events. If such descriptions are extensive enough, you can form an impression of what the theorist means that is sufficiently precise to help in deciding upon measurement operations. Once having decided upon the appropriate measurement operations for the entire set of concrete peripheral characteristics, the tedious but unavoidable and important job of attempting to provide adequate measures can go forward. Assuming that the measure already has theoretical adequacy (or face validity) by virtue of the careful selection of measurement operations, it remains to be seen whether it can be demonstrated to have empirical existence.

In major part, a concrete peripheral characteristic will be considered to have empirical existence if its measure has adequate *reliability*. There are two kinds of reliability, called *internal consistency* and *stability*. In order to appreciate internal consistency, you must keep in mind that a measure almost always has a number of parts. For example, if you are measuring need for achievement with a scoring system to be used on fantasy productions, the different categories in the scoring system will be the parts of the measure. If your measure is a questionnaire, then each of the questions will be a part of the measure. Internal consistency refers to the degree to which the parts of the measure, presumably put there for theoretical reasons, really do seem to go together at an empirical level of analysis. On a questionnaire, this will involve determining the likelihood that a person answering one of the questions in a particular way will answer the other questions in similar fashion. On a scoring system applied to fantasy, internal consistency will be expressed as the tendency to apply the various scoring categories the same way on a given person's productions. If you demonstrate sufficient internal consistency, you have found empirical support for the contention that your measure gets at some genuine entity. The entity is genuine in the sense that its postulated parts really do seem to hang together. But exactly how internally consistent a measure should be before you conclude that it reflects something real is a ticklish question. For some concepts, like the trait, you would expect a high degree of internal consistency because, theoretically, the range of behaviors comprising it should be small and very similar to each other. But a concept like need or motive is inherently more heterogeneous, comprising as it does not only goals but instrumental sequences of action as well, all of which wax and wane. In short, even though concrete peripheral characteristics are supposed to be the basic unit of peripheral personality, we should recognize that the degree of internal consistency we should require of such characteristics depends partially upon their postulated nature. Nonetheless, unless a measure has at least moderate internal consistency, there is little empirical ground for considering it to reflect a genuine entity.

When you assess the stability of a measure, you are determining the likelihood that you will get the same result with it when applying it to the same people on two or more similar occasions separated in time. Generally speaking, the closer the results from the different testing sessions, the more you will feel justified in considering your measure to get at some genuine entity. This is because concrete peripheral characteristics are assumed to be reasonably stable in life. But exactly how stable we should require a measure to be is once again a partially theoretical question. In theory, some concrete peripheral characteristics, like Rogers' openness to experience, and McClelland's need for achievement, should be less stable over time than some others, like Freud's stinginess. If you are open to experience, you will be literally different from moment to moment, and your need for achievement should be high when it is frustrated but low when it is satisfied. So, the degree of stability that we require as evidence of empirical existence is partially determined by how the theorist describes the nature of the characteristic assessed by the measure. But, as with internal consistency, there must be at least moderate stability before one has empirical grounds for considering the measure to reflect a genuine entity.

From an empirical point of view, a measure must be made up of parts that are homogeneous and that work the same way more than once. If these two things are not true, then it may well be that the rational, or theoretical adequacy of the concrete peripheral characteristic being measured was more apparent than real. We want concrete peripheral characteristics that are convincing not only rationally, but also empirically. If the attempt to measure a characteristic has been capably undertaken, and internal consistency and/or stability is found to be lacking, then you can be sure that there is a heretofore unrecognized theoretical problem to blame. A common theoretical problem in such cases is the choice of concrete peripheral characteristics that are not really as irreducible as they might have seemed (Fiske, 1963). If a concrete peripheral characteristic can be subdivided further, then when you attempt to measure it, you will find a lack of internal consistency because the measure incorporates disparate parts. If you build your theory of personality on concrete peripheral characteristics that turn out to be inconsistent at the empirical level, you are building on shifting sands.

The failure of attempts to develop reliable measures can well be the occasion for a theorist returning to the drawing board. He can revamp a concrete peripheral characteristic in hopes of making it more homogeneous, or he can undertake a more sweeping reconsideration of all his peripheral level theorizing. Clearly, evidence as to the reliability of measures of currently postulated concrete peripheral characteristics can aid us in empirically evaluating the theories of personality they represent. We may find that one or another theory, or model for theorizing, seems to do a better job from the point of view of this initial empirical criterion of a reliability of measures. If so, we will be justified in reaching the tentative conclusion that this theory or model for theorizing is more empirically genuine. The conclusion would be tentative, because assessment of the reliability of measures is only the first step in the ideal strategy for empirical analysis of peripheral level theorizing.

Step two: Interrelationships among measures

The completion of the first step in the empirical analysis of peripheral level theorizing should leave you with measures of those concrete peripheral characteristics that indeed lend themselves to reliable measurement. Some concrete peripheral characteristics postulated by some theorists would undoubtedly have fallen by the wayside. In other words, they will not have met the empirical criterion of reliable measurement. Indeed, it is possible that most of some unfortunate personologist's peripheral theory will not have survived the first step of empirical analysis.

The second step begins with the surviving concrete peripheral characteristics, and concerns peripheral level theorizing about types. Take all the reliable measures you have been able to develop, and determine the relationships among them. You would do this by applying the measures to the same group of people, and then analyzing the results with available statistical techniques for determining *correlation*. Actually, the best technique for what I have in mind is *factor analysis*. This technique not only determines how strongly related to each other a number of measures are, but also organizes those that are interrelated most highly into clusters, called factors. Factor analysis is a very powerful and important technique in the empirical assessment of peripheral level theorizing. Take Fromm's peripheral level theorizing as an example for explaining the value of factor analysis. Assume that all of the traits that he presents under the five character orientations have been reliably measured, and that the measures have all been applied to the same group of people. Then one thing a factor analysis will tell us is if these traits cluster together in the manner predicted by his theory. There should be clusters of trait measures (factors) corresponding to the receptive, exploitative, hoarding, marketing, and productive orientations. If there is nothing like this, then we can say that there is no empirical support in the clustering of traits for Fromm's peripheral level theorizing about types of people. Whatever organization the traits show does not conform to the theory. Alternatively, one could find that Fromm's theorizing is quite strongly supported by empirical evidence, or even that it is only moderately supported.

An additional thing of importance about this second step is that all measures could be applied to all people studied. Hence, it becomes possible to determine the correlations and factor clusterings not only of the concrete peripheral characteristics of one theory, but of all theories under consideration. This is an ideal empirical procedure for determining the overlap among theories. We no longer have to rely upon our rationality alone to determine whether, for example, what Fromm talks about as the hoarding orientation is essentially what Freud meant by the anal character type.

Step three: The construct validity of peripheral theorizing

The third, and final step in the ideal strategy for the empirical analysis of peripheral theorizing concerns the validity of concrete peripheral characteristics. Obviously these characteristics are meant to be used in the explanation of something. It would be trivial for them to explain nothing more than their own measures, for these measures are, after all, only the empirical form of the concept. It is important for you to grasp the idea that each concrete peripheral characteristic has been theoretically developed so as to serve as the explanation for a particular set of human behaviors (other than the measure of the characteristic). For example, take McClelland's need for achievement and its measure involving fantasy behavior. In general, a characteristic like this one would be used to explain such entities—call them variables—as competitive social relationships, an interest in accumulating money, a driven commitment to work, an uneasiness with leisure time, and so forth. These variables can be said to be explained by the need for achievement. The higher a person is on this need, the more intense should such variables be in his everyday life.

The hypothesized relationships between the need for achievement and these other variables can be tested empirically, due to the existence of a measure for the need that involves behavior radically different than that involved in the variables. If data obtained from a group of subjects showed that the fantasy measure participated in a network of relationships with the relevant variables, then we would be in a position to conclude that the construct, need for achievement, had validity. Actually, to be careful, we would also want to demonstrate that the fantasy measure did not correlate with variables bearing no theoretical relationship to it.

What I have described comes very close to the assessment of construct validity, as formulated by Cronbach and Meehl (1955). It is not the only kind of validity, but seems the most relevant to the empirical analysis of peripheral theorizing. Other forms of validity investigation are more appropriate when the measure under consideration is intended to predict one variable to a very high degree (e.g., the measure of high school grades as a predictor of college success). In contrast, each concrete peripheral characteristic is usually conceptualized as influencing a reasonably wide variety of variables of human behavior. And the degree of influence is usually considered only moderate, as can be seen from the fact that personologists believe that in order to fully explain any one behavioral variable, a number of concrete peripheral characteristics acting simultaneously must be invoked. Taking this seriously, it becomes clear that one can consider a concrete peripheral characteristic to be valid if its measure shows moderate intercorrelation with a set of theoretically relevant variables (convergent validation) and an absence of intercorrelation with theoretically irrelevant variables (discriminant validation). For further discussion, see Campbell and Fiske (1959).

Thus far, I have discussed only the validation of single characteristics. A further goal within the third step of our strategy is to determine whether the entire list of concrete peripheral characteristics offered by a theorist really does account for all the variables of human behavior. Although each concrete peripheral characteristic, taken by itself, is not intended to account for all behavior, the entire list offered really should do this job. Virtually all personologists say, at one place or another in their writing, that they accept the goal of explaining all behavior. So two criteria, namely, that each concrete peripheral characteristic actually explain only the variables it was postulated to explain, and that the entire set of characteristics offered by a theorist explain all variables, define the assessment of empirical validity.

In order to carry out this step, we will need to know a good deal about what are to be considered the variables of human behavior. Here we encounter extraordinary difficulty. Of the personologists considered in this book, only Murray even touches the question of data categories. He offers the data designations of *proceedings* and *serials* (see Maddi, 1963; Maddi & Costa, 1972). A proceeding is a psychologically meaningful unit of behavior, having a specifiable beginning and end, and some duration in time. Examples of a proceeding might be anything from a conversation, to solving a problem in your head, to writing a paper. Proceedings can be more or less social, more or less action-oriented, as long as they are meaningful to the person engaging in them. A serial is a number of proceedings organized in a sequential fashion. Examples might be a marriage, or a college career. It is proceedings and serials, Murray argues, that are to be explained by concrete peripheral characteristics. Murray gives us no help, unfortunately, in deciding how we are to identify proceedings and serials. There is only the hint, in the insistence that they be meaningful to the person, that they are to be phenomenally, or introspectively, defined. In other words, the person will virtually define them for himself.

Generally speaking, the other personologists offer no more along the lines of a data language than the notion that a theory of personality ought to explain all behavior. Actually, when you try to understand just what might be meant by this statement that is so excessively general as to be

arid, you discover what I have already said in Chapter 1. By all behavior, personologists tend to mean behavior that has regularity and
continuity in time. If the person is competitive, or generous, or idealistic
over a range of situations and time, then the personologist is interested.
As you can see, this position is even more vague than is that of Murray.
How in the world are we to proceed on the third step?

Probably, the most feasible thing to do is read the descriptions and
examples of life made by personologists when they are discussing the
peripheral level of personality. In this reading, you should remain alert
for indications of the variables considered relevant to particular concrete
peripheral characteristics, and, in a more general vein, the full range of
variables discussed. Even from the descriptions quoted in Chapters 6
through 8 you can get an idea of what I am suggesting. Recall, for
example, the vivid description of the anal personality type by Rado
(1959, p. 326), and Fromm's (1947, pp. 68–72) descriptions of marketing
and other orientations, so replete with behavioral references separate
from those which you would use as measures of the relevant concrete
peripheral characteristics. In addition, the behaviors relevant to the need
for achievement mentioned in an example earlier in this chapter are
straight from McClelland's descriptions. According to what I am suggesting, all the variables recoverable from close reading of the life descriptions offered by the personologists we are considering, would constitute
the behavior we have to work with in our empirical analysis. Perhaps it
would be helpful to adopt, as a heuristic device facilitating alert reading,
the distinctions in the preceding chapter between repetitive behaviors
and directional behaviors having personal or social goals. These distinctions are implied in the writings of many personologists.

With this large group of variables in hand, we could in principle
proceed with the empirical analysis of validity. It would be best to have
available the same group of people on whom the second step of our
analysis was performed. It would be necessary to agree upon how best
to identify the existence and intensity of the variables constituting data
in each of the people being studied. Perhaps, for this purpose, they could
be asked to give extensive descriptions of their own behavior, and these
descriptions could be scrutinized by the investigators. Even better, though
more cumbersome, would be to observe these people over some period of
time in many different situations, and to use these observations as estimates of the intensity of the variables. Or the two possibilities could be
combined. Such a combination was tried by Murray (1938) in his path-
finding attempt to understand personality.

Then one could combine in the same factor analysis not only variables
but measures of concrete peripheral characteristics as well. What would
be expected is that clusters composed of theoretically appropriate variables plus measures would emerge from the analysis. If, for example, the
measure of need for achievement appeared in the same cluster with (1)

competitive actions, (2) the sense of time as important, and (3) a commitment to hard work, we could conclude that there is convergent validational evidence for McClelland's theorizing. Of further support would be the finding that the need for achievement measure did not appear on any other cluster, thus indicating discriminant validation. Although factor analysis is usually considered an exploratory technique, what I am suggesting here amounts to using it deductively to test hypotheses concerning the relationship of certain concrete peripheral characteristics to certain behaviors.

Clearly, if a theorist's concrete peripheral characteristics are to have empirical validity, they must show a relationship with the variables he has indicated as being relevant. In an overall sense, if his peripheral level theorizing is to be considered complete by empirical standards, then there should also not be any large proportion of variables unrelated to one or another of his concrete peripheral characteristics. This is so, incidentally, even if the unrelated behavior is not of the kind he has referred to in his theorizing, because the personologists included here have committed themselves to the explanation of virtually all behavior. If they say that personality explains all behavior, without being more specific, then they must account for all viable behavioral variables, even those that they do not specifically mention in their descriptions. What one says as a theorist is important, so one should only say what one means.

A word of practicality

The strategy just described seems to me rather ideal for determining which of the postulated concrete peripheral characteristics is homogeneous and stable enough to be considered genuine, for discerning the nature of the organization of these characteristics into types, and for specifying the validity of peripheral theorizing. Although the strategy has a potentially great yield for personology, carrying out its procedures would be extraordinarily difficult and time consuming. Clearly, the scoring and analyzing of the data on the huge scale advocated could only be done with the help of the giant computers now becoming available, and the financing of large foundations supporting basic research in psychology. Also necessary would be the services of a large staff, which could count on the cooperation of many personologists not directly involved in the work. As to the results, it must be expected with such large amounts of initial data that some of the factors obtained in the third, and perhaps even the second step of the strategy would be virtually impossible to interpret in an intellectually satisfying manner. These uninterpretable factors would reflect such irrelevant things as common but theoretically unimportant procedures for measuring variables, and even accidental similarities of data. To be sure, all large-scale research in the personality area is likely to uncover some results that are ambiguous or irrelevant to personality theorizing. If one avoided panicking, it would be possible to simply accept that some factors would be uninterpretable, and still carry out the strategy rather effectively by requiring that those which are interpretable conform to what would be expected in one or another of the theories. Nonetheless, it must be at least mentioned that the ideal strategy may be difficult to carry out in a practical manner at this time because of its massiveness.

It will be valuable to keep the strategy in mind, however, so that it may serve as a goal toward which simpler, more feasible efforts can be pointed. For example, it may be more practical at this time to focus upon single theories of peripheral personality, rather than all of them at once. But in focusing upon a single theory, the various steps in the strategy could still be employed. Such a program of research would include only the variables and measures relevant to the particular theory in question, with the results clarifying which of these variables, concrete peripheral characteristics and types, if any, were most empirically viable. And if different groups of investigators were working on different theories, it would not be very long before one could begin to gain an overall view of the most fruitful approaches to peripheral theorizing from a comparison of the results of these various research projects. Even such approximations to the ideal strategy would be a big improvement over current research practice. As Carlson (1971) pinpoints ably in her review, broad to say nothing of comprehensive efforts to measure personality, are virtually absent from the contemporary research literature.

Having discussed a proposed ideal strategy and one more practical version of it, I would like to move on now to procedures that are actually practiced in personology. As you may have surmised, the empirical evidence available on the basis of current practice falls short in various ways of the evidence required in the ideal strategy. Nonetheless, we must turn to what is available, in hopes of gaining some increased knowledge concerning the peripheral theories. Perhaps having discussed a conceptualized ideal strategy will have the effect of alerting you to the shortcomings of the work we will be considering. But lest I arouse too much cynicism in you, let me point out that some of the work reviewed in the following pages is striking, dramatic, and important. Without it, the personality field would be much less vital.

FACTOR ANALYTIC STUDIES

As you will recall, the third step of the ideal strategy called for employing factor analysis in determining the intercorrelations among a large group of variables and measures of concrete peripheral characteristics. The characteristics would be considered empirically validated when their measures correlated only with theoretically relevant variables. Although I advocated a particular use of factor analysis, you should recognize that it is a general procedure for determining the empirical clustering of any variables based on their intercorrelations. It is not at all necessary that measures of concrete peripheral characteristics be included along with other variables. Indeed, such measures have almost never been included in the available factor analytic studies relevant to personality. Typically, the investigator obtains data on a group of variables, performs a factor analysis upon them, and then attempts to interpret the meaning of the clusters or factors obtained. It might be concluded that the factors expressed some particular concrete peripheral characteristics described in the personological literature. Going further, it would be possible to perform another factor analysis on the factors already obtained. The result of this would be a set of so-called second-order factors, describing the way the original factors grouped themselves into larger units. It would then be possible to try to interpret these larger units as expressive of particular personality types described in the personological literature.

The procedure just described can constitute an inductive strategy for empirical evaluation of peripheral theorizing. It is inductive mainly because no measures of concrete peripheral characteristics are included, so you cannot really test hypotheses concerning the relationship of such characteristics to behavioral variables. The best you can do with the inductive use of factor analysis is arrive at clusterings of behavioral variables that suggest, but only suggest, the relevance of particular concrete peripheral characteristics. This may sound acceptable, but believe me, once you include in the factor analysis a sufficient number of variables to do justice to even a small number of theories, you obtain factors so complex and ambiguous as to meaning that the task of interpreting just which concrete peripheral characteristics and types they express becomes much more tenuous than you might think. One of the most vulnerable points of inductive factor analytic studies has been the almost inevitably intuitive, crude nature of the interpretation of factors. The aura of empirical rigor and objectivity attending the inductive use of factor analysis is more apparent than real. In contrast, the deductive use of factor analysis advocated in the ideal strategy involves much more straightforward interpretation of factors. Only when a factor includes both the measure of a concrete peripheral characteristic and the major variables deemed expressive of it theoretically, is that characteristic to be considered empirically valid.

Most factor analytic studies currently available have been of the inductive type. Indeed, virtually all of these studies have fallen short of the ideal procedure in yet another way. They have not started with all the variables that seem to crop up in the writings of all personologists. To be sure, it would be acceptable, in the interest of practicality, for a study to concern itself with all of the variables in one theory alone. At least then it could be said that the study comprehensively treated that theory. Fortunately, some available studies have approximated this goal. But sometimes, the variables included in a study are not really specifiable in some intellectually satisfying way (such as comprehensively treating a theory). The investigator, perhaps out of an atheoretical bias or theoretical naïveté, will include some heterogeneous array of variables, not concerning himself with the implications of so doing. The outcome of such factor analytic studies is of dubious value, for to consider the resulting evidence comprehensive or even representative with regard to life in general or some particular theory is erroneous and often badly misleading. You only get out of a factor analysis what you put into it, and therefore, it is never acceptable to be ignorant of the implications of the variables you have decided to consider. The set of variables considered should either be comprehensive, or at least specifiable in a theoretically meaningful way. Fortunately, the naïve use of factor analysis is decreasing in psychology.

Cattell, Guilford, and Eysenck

Among factor analysts, the work of three men, Cattell, Guilford, and Eysenck, is especially pertinent to empirical evaluation of peripheral theorizing. First I will describe something of their procedures, leaving communication of their results for later.

The factor analytic work of Raymond Cattell approximates closely the inductive procedure mentioned in the preceding section of this chapter. He has attempted to obtain comprehensive behavioral information so that his results will reflect upon the question of what concrete peripheral characteristics it is most fruitful to postulate. Actually, like many factor analysts, Cattell has been much concerned with the building of comprehensive, valid tests of personality. This task is not really very different from that of clarifying the concrete peripheral characteristics that should be represented in personality theory. In an effort to obtain behavioral observations comprehensively, Cattell (1946, 1957) began by assembling all personality variable names occurring in the dictionary (as compiled by Allport & Odbert, 1936) or in the psychological literature. This list was first reduced to 171 variable names by combining obvious synonyms. Then a sample of 100 adults from many walks of life was selected. Associates of these people, who knew them well, were asked to rate them on these 171 variables. Intercorrelations and factor analyses of these ratings were followed by further ratings of 208 men on a shortened list of variables. Factor analyses of the latter ratings led to the identification of what Cattell described as "the primary source traits of personality." Cattell and his associates then set out to build a personality test that would give evidence of these source traits. The end result of considerable investigation is the *Sixteen Personality Factor Questionnaire* (Cattell & Stice, 1957), which is made up of many items concerning life activities that the respondent must indicate that he likes or dislikes. Twelve of the

16 factors, which have been obtained through factor analyzing the answers to these items given by many people, are similar to those obtained in the earlier work with ratings, while 4 appeared only on the test.

In considering the findings most relevant to the task of empirical evaluation of peripheral theorizing, we should focus on the 16 factors of Cattell's test. Each factor can be considered to reflect a concrete peripheral characteristic. Cattell has also factor analyzed the 16 primary factors, or source traits as he calls them, deriving from this analysis 7 second-order factors which link the first-order factors together. The second-order factors might be considered to reflect the organization of concrete peripheral characteristics into types.

Before turning to the actual substance of Cattell's findings, a brief summary of the procedures of Guilford and Eysenck is in order. In finding behavioral data upon which to perform factor analyses, Guilford and his associates (Guilford, 1959; Guilford & Zimmerman, 1956) collected together the items from a number of tests of personality that were already in common use. These tests had, by and large, been constructed along rational, theoretical lines, rather than by some empirical clustering procedure like factor analysis. Guilford had a sample of people answer all of the items from these tests, a task mainly requiring them to indicate whether or not they liked the various kinds of activities presented. The answers to items were then intercorrelated and factor analyzed. Through a long process of refining, pruning, and interpreting the resulting factors, a number of personality tests were constructed. The final of these is the most authoritative. Called the *Guilford-Zimmerman Temperament Survey* (Guilford & Zimmerman, 1949), it includes a large number of items to be endorsed as being liked or disliked and yields 10 factors. These factors, as those in Cattell's test, can be considered to reflect concrete peripheral characteristics. Guilford does not provide information concerning second-order factors.

Of the three factor analysts being considered, Eysenck samples the possible range of behavioral observations least widely. Although his work is therefore less valuable to us than that of the others, it is nonetheless capable of teaching us something. In his first study (Eysenck, 1947), the sample was 700 neurotic soldiers. The behavioral data of the study included some answers given by the soldiers to factual questions about themselves, and also some ratings of the soldiers made by psychiatrists. The total number of items of information upon which the factor analysis was performed was only 39. Eysenck finds two factors, or concrete peripheral characteristics, to be sufficient to describe the clustering of items. Subsequently, Eysenck (1947) has added more subjects to this original sample, in an attempt to determine whether these two factors are still sufficiently descriptive of people to be considered basic. The final sample totaled roughly 10,000 normal and neurotic subjects, and the information available concerning them varied from responses on test items to behavior in performance situations. He has reported that the same two factors found to describe the original 700 neurotic soldiers continued to be descriptive of the larger sample.

We are in a difficult position in evaluating the relevance of Eysenck's work to our present concerns. He has, *in toto*, included more kinds of behavioral observation in his studies than have the other two factor analysts, who rely primarily upon responses to test items. But, following the original study, Eysenck has used a procedure called *criterion analysis*, which is essentially deductive rather than inductive (Anastasi, 1961). In criterion analysis, you already have a hypothesis in mind as to what the important factors are, and so you plan your study in order to test that hypothesis. One thing this means is that you select your behavioral observations in order to be theoretically relevant to the factors you assume of importance. The second thing it means is that you design your study to include criterion groups, groups that should possess discriminably different degrees of the hypothesized factors. The end result of this procedure is that you get information largely relevant to your hypotheses only, rather than more general information. Since the two factors that have preoccupied Eysenck were originally found descriptive of neurotic soldiers, a rather unusual group of people, then all the generalization of these results to other people may mean is that some evidence of these two factors can be found in people in general. It does not at all mean that these two factors are as basic in describing people in general as they might have been in describing neurotic soldiers. The conclusion that people in general can be adequately and comprehensively described by two factors alone may be quite spurious. Actually, one might wonder whether these two factors alone would have seemed so adequate for describing even the neurotic soldiers if more than the original 39 behavioral observations had been included. After all, Guilford included hundreds of items, and Cattell included 171 trait names in their studies. It is not surprising that the less information you put into your factor analysis, the less information you get out of it!

Number of factors

In turning to a consideration of the findings of Cattell, Guilford, and Eysenck, we will do best to pose a number of questions concerning the relationship between them and peripheral level theorizing. The most obvious question is whether the number of factors resulting from factor analytical research indicates to us the number of concrete peripheral characteristics it is fruitful to assume. If so, then we would want to evaluate theories of personality making concrete proposals concerning the periphery as to how close is the number of characteristics they offer to the number of factors obtained in research.

As you already know, the work of Cattell suggests 16 factors, that of Guilford 10, and that of Eysenck only 2. And of the 16 factors offered by Cattell, 4 only appear on his test, so the most conservative estimate of his research would place the number of factors close to that of Guilford. Of course, we must remember that Cattell reduced the number of variable names he began with in the not quite empirical manner of deciding that many of them were obvious synonyms. While this procedure for reducing variables can be questioned as not necessarily reflecting anything more than his own judgment, I do not think anyone would argue seriously that two variable names very similar in meaning might in reality be different at an empirical level. In all probability, even if Cattell had religiously included the entire original list of variable names in his studies, it would have in effect been reduced by the raters anyway. After all, if two variable names seem synonymous to a rater, he will use them both in the same way. Cattell's number of factors is not likely to be an underestimate on the grounds that he erroneously reduced the original list of variable names. In support of this conclusion is the work of Guilford, in which no reduction of data took place before the factor analysis, and yet only 10 factors seemed to emerge.

But there is another reason why the number of factors obtained by Cattell and Guilford might be an underestimate of the number actually needed in order to account for the clustering of all behavioral variables considered relevant by personologists. Simply put, neither Cattell nor Guilford has sampled widely enough to ensure representativeness with regard to that body of variables. Remember the criticism I just made of Eysenck. The two factors he offers can only be said to be a comprehensive description of neurotic soldiers upon whom a very modest amount of variables is available. The more extensive and heterogeneous are the variables you include, and the larger and more heterogeneous is your sample of people, the greater will be the number of primary factors you obtain. To be sure, there must be some upper limit of useful factors, beyond which the rule just stated will not hold. But certainly Eysenck has not reached that limit, and neither have Cattell and Guilford in all probability.

Certainly, neither Cattell nor Guilford, to say nothing of Eysenck, has included sufficient variables to do justice to all the personality theorists we are considering. It is true that Cattell started with all the variable names he could find, an admirably inclusive undertaking. But it must be borne in mind that, in his test, he measures variables solely by obtaining the person's answers to questions posed for him by the experimenter. The same is true for Guilford's test. Even when the questions concern remembrances of fantasies and performed acts, it must be said that questionnaires do not tap actual fantasizing and actual performance of acts. In test responding, all you have are data of people trying to describe themselves as best they can remember and as frank as they wish to be in terms of questions posed by someone else. To appreciate the severe limitation on variables that is involved, recognize that the questionnaire technique taps information that someone like McClelland would see as most relevant to determining schemata, but little relevant to motives and traits. If information concerning fantasizing and actual performance of acts were included by Cattell and Guilford, we might well see an increase in the number of factors necessary to describe empirical clustering of data.

In fairness to Cattell, we must remember that he devised his questionnaire in order to see whether the factors originally obtained in analyzing ratings made of people by their associates would also be found in self-descriptions. And he feels he has found considerable agreement between the two kinds of data. It is certainly true that ratings made of you by others need not bear any clear relationship to your fantasies and actual actions, but at least Cattell can claim some generality for his 16 factors beyond the measurement operation of questionnaires alone. This is more than Guilford can do. But let us look closely at just how far we would be willing to generalize from Cattell's data, for ratings made by others and self-descriptions bear a particular kind of similarity to each other. It is quite likely that ratings made by others and self-descriptions both tend to reflect culturally shared meaning, the stuff of schemata. Cattell would counter at this point by indicating that by now it seems clear that his 16 factors are recoverable from other kinds of data as well, notably observations of social behavior, and expert descriptions of pathological behavior. That these claims are not completely convincing, however, is indicated by the following quote from Anastasi's (1961, pp. 509–510) book on psychological testing:

> Factors identified through the correlation of ratings may reflect in part the influence of social stereotypes and other constant errors of judgment, rather than the subject's trait organization. Cattell maintains that his identification of primary personality traits is corroborated by the findings of other studies by himself and other investigators, using not only ratings but also such techniques as questionnaires and objective tests. Some of the alleged similarities in trait descriptions, however, appear forced and not too convincing. It should be recalled that an element of subjectivity is likely to enter into the identification of factors, since the process depends upon an examination of these measures or items having the highest loadings on each factor. . . . Hence the cross-identification of factors from different investigations using different measures is difficult. Despite the extensive research conducted by Cattell and his associates over a period of nearly twenty years, the traits proposed by Cattell must be regarded as tentative.

Although this statement refers most directly to the content of Cattell's results, the criticism actually applies as well to the number of factors he has found.

We should conclude that Eysenck's small number of factors is quite invalid for our purposes, whereas the somewhat larger number found by Cattell and Guilford is probably an underestimate due to the exclusion in their studies of data comprising fantasy and actual performance. Indeed, a recent factor analytic study by Cattell and Delhees (1973) suggests the identification of seven additional factors. But the underestimation may well not be so great as to justify the theorizing of those personologists, such as Murray, McClelland, and Fromm, who have postulated a great many concrete peripheral characteristics. A perusal of the content designations of their lists of characteristics suggests that at least some of them are too synonymous to be considered separately. You may recall that I suggested this first in discussion of Murray's peripheral theorizing concerning needs (see Chapter 6). Given the relatively heterogeneous nature of the need construct, and the great number of needs postulated, there is bound to be overlap between them at the empirical, or observational level. This difficulty will, of course, also be found in McClelland's position, since it adopts Murray's list of needs. And to convince yourself that Fromm has included some synonyms in his clusters of traits, simply go back and read them in Chapter 7. So one thing factor analytic studies teach us is that the number of concrete peripheral characteristics, though larger than 16 in all probability, is not necessarily very much greater than that.

But the clearest conclusion to be reached on the basis of factor analytic studies is that the number of concrete peripheral characteristics is certainly no lower than ten. Among the theorists who are specific concerning the periphery, two—the conflict theorist, Erikson, and the fulfillment theorist, Adler—seem to suggest fewer than ten characteristics. In Erikson's case, this is not actually true, for, as you will recall, his eight designations referring to developmental stages are intended as summarizations of clustered concrete peripheral characteristics. In the nomenclature of factor analysis, therefore, these eight designations refer to second-order, rather than primary factors. Unfortunately, Erikson has not disciplined himself to specify concrete peripheral characteristics. Nonetheless, it cannot be said that his position is disproved by the findings of Cattell and Guilford concerning the number of primary factors. Although one suspects a similar state of affairs for Adlerians, who would probably not really want to defend the position that there is only one concrete peripheral characteristic associated with each of the constructive orientations, they are less clear on this matter than is Erikson.

Finally, I should say a word about the implications for theorizing about personality types of Cattell's analysis of second-order factors. Originally, he offered only two, but has subsequently recognized five other less-pervasive, though nonetheless, clear factors. So, the number of second-order factors ranges somewhere between two and seven. Two second-order factors will permit consideration of four types of personality, namely, people high on both factors, low on both factors, high on the first but low on the second, and low on the first but high on the second. Seven second-order factors suggest 196 personality types. All of the personologists having developed positions concerning personality types postulate something between 4 and 196 such entities. Therefore, Cattell's analyses of second-order factors give us no aid in evaluating personality theories on the basis of the number of types they recognize.

The kinds of factors

Factor analysts tend to label their factors *traits,* though on closer scrutiny it becomes clear that they do not mean this in the narrow sense of habitual behaviors alone. They use the term trait broadly enough to be synonymous with our usage of the term concrete peripheral characteristic. When one looks at the content of their factors, it becomes apparent that distinctions could be made between habitual behaviors (or traits in the narrow sense), cognitive behaviors (or such things as values), and motivational behaviors. Indeed, one factor analyst, Cattell (1950), even offers the distinction between dynamic and nondynamic traits, calling the former *ergs* and the latter *traits.* This is very close to McClelland's distinction between motive and trait. These distinctions will be discussed along with the content of the factors.

The content of factors

The last way in which I will consider factor analytic studies is in terms of the empirical evidence they provide concerning the content of concrete peripheral characteristics. Let me begin by listing the 16 factors of Cattell, going from there to the 10 of Guilford, and the 2 of Eysenck. Then I will tell you about the second-order factors found by Cattell.

The 16 factors included in Cattell's test are bipolar in nature. They are called *Schizothymia* (aloof, cold) v. *Cyclothymia* (warm, sociable); *Dull* (low-intellectual capacity) v. *Bright* (intelligent); *Low-Ego Strength* (emotional, unstable) v. *High-Ego Strength* (mature, calm); *Submissiveness* (mild) v. *Dominance* (aggressive); *Desurgency* (glum, silent) v. *Surgency* (enthusiastic, talkative); *Low-Super Ego Strength* (casual, undependable) v. *High-Superego Strength* (conscientious, persistent); *Threctia* (timid, shy) v. *Parmia* (adventurous, thick-skinned); *Harria* (tough, realistic) v. *Premsia* (sensitive, effeminate); *Inner Relaxation* (trustful, adaptable) v. *Protension* (suspecting, jealous); *Praxernia* (conventional, practical) v. *Autia* (Bohemian, unconcerned); *Naïveté* (simple, awkward) v. *Shrewdness* (sophisticated, polished); *Confidence* (unshakable) v. *Timidity* (insecure, anxious); *Conservatism* (accepting) v. *Radicalism* (experimenting, critical); *Group Dependence* (imitative) v. *Self-Sufficiency* (resourceful); *Low-Integration* (lax, unsure) v. *Self-*

Sentiment Control (controlled, exact); *Low-Ergic Tension* (phlegmatic, composed) v. *High-Ergic Tension* (tense, excitable).

If you think you are having difficulty getting the meaning of these factors, picture poor Cattell having to interpret and name them! He concluded that the best thing to do, by and large, was to give them names out of his imagination, along with a few adjectives indicating the flavor of the thing, waiting for future research to clarify their psychological meaning. The kind of research he thinks will help involves getting people's scores on these factors by having them take his test, and then determining the actual behavioral differences between people high and low on each of the factors. While such research will certainly help, we must unfortunately proceed at the moment with what is available. I cannot but suggest, however, that if Cattell had followed the ideal strategy, involving the development of measures of postulated concrete peripheral characteristics for inclusion in factor analytic studies along with other variables, his findings would have been more immediately understandable. Be this as it may, let us see how his findings bear on peripheral level theorizing.

In attempting this, it will also be best to summarize the findings of Guilford and Eysenck, so that we can see how much they agree or disagree with those of Cattell. The 10 factors of the *Guilford-Zimmerman Temperament Survey* are also bipolar in nature, though they are given names broad enough to refer to both poles. The factors are called *General Activity* (hurrying, liking for speed, liveliness, vitality v. slow and deliberate, easily fatigued, inefficient); *Restraint* (serious-minded, deliberate, persistent v. carefree, impulsive, excitement loving); *Ascendance* (self-defense, leadership, bluffing v. submissiveness, hesitation, avoiding conspicuousness); *Sociability* (having many friends, seeking social contacts and limelight v. few friends and shyness); *Emotional Stability* (evenness of moods, optimistic, composure v. fluctuation of moods, pessimism, daydreaming, feelings of guilt, worry, loneliness); *Objectivity* (thick-skinned v. hypersensitive, self-centered, suspicious); *Friendliness* (toleration of hostile action, acceptance of domination, respect for others v. belligerence, hostility, resentment, desire to dominate); *Thoughtfulness* (reflective, observing of self and others, mental poise v. interest in overt activity and mental disconcertedness); *Personal Relations* (tolerance of people, faith in social institutions v. faultfinding, critical of institutions, self-pitying); and *Masculinity* (interest in masculine activities, not easily disgusted, hard-boiled v. interest in feminine activities, easily disgusted, fearful, romantic, emotionally expressive).

In considering the similarities between this list of factors and that of Cattell, I am struck by some obvious correspondences. Guilford's General Activity factor seems similar to the Low-Ergic Tension v. High-Ergic Tension and the Desurgency v. Surgency factors of Cattell. Guilford's Restraint, and Cattell's Low-Superego Strength v. High-Superego

Strength factors seem similar. Continuing down Guilford's list, his Ascendance factor is clearly similar to Cattell's Submissiveness v. Dominance and Group Dependence v. Self-Sufficiency factors. There is correspondence between Guilford's Sociability and Cattell's Schizothymia v. Cyclothymia factors. And what Guilford calls Emotional Stability finds a concordant note in Cattell's factors of Low-Ego Strength v. High-Ego Strength, and Low Integration v. Self-Sentiment Control. Guilford's Objectivity factor has similar meaning to Cattell's Threctia factor. And where Guilford refers to Friendliness, Cattell finds Inner Relaxation v. Protension. There is no ready counterpart for Guilford's Thoughtfulness factor on Cattell's list, though one might suggest a combination of Dull v. Bright, and Naïveté v. Shrewdness. What Guilford calls Personal Relations is probably mirrored in Cattell's Praxernia v. Autia, and Conservatism v. Radicalism. And finally, Guilford's Masculinity factor bears similarity to Cattell's Harria v. Premsia factor.

These striking similarities can be taken as empirical evidence that an adequate peripheral theory of personality must recognize in its concrete peripheral characteristics content concerning a number of areas of human functioning. One area is clearly that concerned with culturally patterned values and beliefs regarding social roles and institutions. There are two content themes in this area. One is the degree to which the person does or does not possess a set of values bearing on the regulation of personal, perhaps selfish, goals and impulses (this is the matter of conscience). The second theme is the strength of commitment to the existing social system, reflected in degree of tolerance for or criticism of people acting in social roles, and of social institutions themselves. These content areas represent what we have been calling schemata.

The other large content area does not refer so much to values and principles, though it is difficult to determine whether it comprises traits (in the narrow sense), motives, or both. Factor analysts have neglected to investigate whether they were dealing with instrumental, goal-directed functioning or merely habitual functioning. Although I cannot specify whether they be traits or motives, the content themes that seem separate from values per se appear clear enough. They can be subdivided into those specifically involving interaction with other people, and those that are more general than that. The more general themes that a peripheral theory should include are a person's general activity (perhaps activation) level, and his degree of cognitive-actional differentiation or complexity. In addition, a theory should consider of importance how strong is the person's emotional stability or instability, where stability refers to dependability and predictability, whereas instability refers to impulsivity and changeability. The final themes of a general nature that a peripheral theory should address are the degree to which the person is reflective, or inward turning, as opposed to action-oriented, or outward turning, and the degree to which he expresses masculinity or femininity. Femininity includes sensitivity, vanity, and aestheticism, whereas masculinity is the opposite of these things. Turning to the content themes more specifically interactional in nature, we find represented the strength of a person's tendencies to be gregarious or socially aloof, cooperative and accepting or competitive and critical, and dominant and independent or submissive and dependent.

Although these conclusions concerning the content themes that a peripheral theory should address have been reached on the basis of the work of Cattell and Guilford alone, there is nothing in Eysenck's more fragmentary work that is in violation of them. His two factors are introversion-extroversion, and what he calls neuroticism. The introversion-extroversion emphasis is seen in not only the social themes above, where the person is described as either seeking contact with others or not, but in the more general emphasis upon inward turning v. outward turning. By neuroticism, Eysenck means something very much like what I have summarized as emotional stability or instability.

Recently, Cattell and Gibbons (1968) have performed a complicated factor analysis on responses given by 302 undergraduates to slightly abbreviated forms of both the *16 Personality Factor Questionnaire* and the *Guilford-Zimmerman Temperament Survey*. The main purpose of this study was to determine whether the factors obtained from a combination of these two tests are similar to those obtained from each test alone. Of the 14 factors which were included from the *16 Personality Factor Questionnaire*, and the 15 from the *Guilford-Zimmerman Temperament Survey*, 14 and 9, respectively, emerged in the composite factor analysis. The two tests seem to share a good deal of common content concerning personality, and there seems little reason in this study to change any of the conclusions reached earlier.

Comrey and his associates have also attempted of late to determine the number and content of factors necessary to describe personality as measured by questionnaire items. In one study, by Comrey and Duffy (1968), the responses of 326 subjects to the tests of Cattell, Eysenck, and others were factor analyzed. Results indicated the importance of at least the factors of neuroticism, shyness, empathy, hostility, and general activity. There was also some evidence for compulsion and socialization, but dependence, which has appeared in earlier studies, seemed absent. In a similar study, Duffy, Jamison, and Comrey (1969) factor analysed the responses of 259 subjects to Guilford's test. The factors that emerged were shyness, dependence, empathy, neuroticism, compulsion, hostility, general activity, thoughtfulness, and masculinity. As you can see, the number and content of the factors obtained shifts around a bit depending upon the tests that are employed. Nonetheless, the conclusions reached earlier, which were rather conservative, are hardly disconfirmed by these results. In a sense, it is surprising to find as much consistency as there seems to be, through all the differences in sampling of items, subjects, and analysis techniques.

What can we do with the list of content emphases developed out of the initial work of Cattell and Guilford, now that we know it to be fairly reliable? How can we use the content emphases to evaluate existing peripheral theories of personality? In approaching this question, there are two things you must keep in mind. One is that the list comprises things that a peripheral theory can be expected to address, but is not exhaustive of the things that might be important. It is not exhaustive because, as indicated earlier, not all kinds of behavioral observations specified as important by one or another of our personologists have been sampled by factor analysts. Therefore, if a content theme on our list is not included in a theory, we may criticize it, but if it includes some content themes not on our list, we cannot conclude that a theoretical error has been made. The other point to keep in mind is that considerable interpretation goes into designating the meaning of a factor in words. And I have heaped interpretation upon interpretation by trying to identify similarities in the factors arrived at by the three factor analysts. Therefore, it is very difficult to fault an existing peripheral theory of personality as long as a content theme it considers comes at all close to something on our list.

You will recall from Chapter 9 that conflict and fulfillment positions do not differ generally in the content of their peripheral level theorizing. The difference between them is in what content is considered ideal and nonideal. The ideal in conflict theories stresses adjustment, dependability, and stability, whereas the ideal in fulfillment theories stresses transcendence, voluntary commitment, and changeability. Each position stresses the opposite of its ideal in delineating the nonideal orientations. From this rendition of conflict and fulfillment theories, you can easily see that the findings of factor analytic studies provide no empirical bases for favoring one position over the other. Factors have been found referring at one pole to adjustment, dependability, and stability, and at the other pole to transcendence, voluntary commitment, and changeability. There is little in the factor studies, as presented so far, that would lead you to interpret one pole of these factors as nonideal and the other pole as ideal. Therefore, we must conclude that the adaptation-transcendence content of factor analytic studies constitutes empirical support for both conflict and fulfillment models. The content themes specifically concerning social interaction are also understandable from the standpoint of both models. What is difficult for both models to explain precisely is the factorial content concerning activity or drive level.

Turning to the consistency model, I would remind you that it leads in peripheral theorizing either to eclecticism of content or to content expressing the maintenance of consistency. Certainly, peripheral content specification that is as comprehensive and eclectic as that of McClelland can hardly be disproved by our factorial evidence. But neither can it really be supported, for the results of factorial studies could be virtually anything without disproving such a position. If a position cannot be disproved by findings, neither can it be proved. In contrast, Maddi's emphasis on activation, and on impact increasing or decreasing behaviors engaged in for purposes of consistency maintenance, finds support in the factorial evidence of themes concerning activity, and adaptation or transcendence. The peripheral content themes in the activation version of consistency theory are at the same time fewer and more articulated with core assumptions than are those of the cognitive dissonance version of that model. Indeed, the activation version is precise enough to permit realization that it cannot easily explain the factorial evidence concerning social interaction.

Interestingly enough, for a full explanation of all the content themes represented in factorial research, a combination of the activation version of the consistency model, and either the conflict or the fulfillment model may be most fruitful. Perhaps you recall the conclusion reached in Chapter 5, that on the basis of empirical evidence bearing upon core assumptions, some combination of the fulfillment model and the activation version of the consistency model would be most advantageous. The present facet of our empirical analysis of peripheral considerations yields very similar results.

But before leaving factorial studies altogether, let us consider one final aspect of content as contained in Cattell's second-order factors. Cattell labels his two major second-order factors *High Anxiety* v. *Low Anxiety*, and *Introversion* v. *Extroversion*. In order to score high on *Anxiety*, a person must show *High* rather than *Low-Ergic Tension* (be tense and excitable rather than phlegmatic and composed), *Timidity* rather than *Confidence* (insecurity rather than unshakableness), *Protension* (suspecting, jealous) rather than *Inner Relaxation* (trustful, adaptable), *Low-Ego Strength* (emotional, unstable) rather than *High-Ego Strength* (mature, calm), and *Low-Integration* (lax, unsure) rather than *Self-Sentiment Control* (self-sufficiency). In order to score low on *Anxiety*, a person must reverse the pattern. A high score for *Introversion* is obtained by scoring high on *Schizothymia* (aloof, cold) rather than *Cyclothymia* (warm, sociable), *Desurgency* (glum, silent) rather than *Surgency* (enthusiastic, talkative), *Threctia* (timid, shy) rather than *Paramia* (adventurous, thick-skinned), *Autia* (Bohemian, unconcerned) rather than *Praxernia* (conventional, practical), and *Self-Sufficiency* (resourceful) rather than *Group Dependence* (imitative). Needless to say, one scores high on Extroversion by reversing this pattern.

These two second-order factors suggest four personality types. The first type, *High-Anxiety-Introversion*, is tense, excitable, insecure, suspecting, jealous, emotional, unstable, lax, unsure, and in addition, aloof, cold, glum, silent, timid, shy, Bohemian, unconcerned, and resourceful. The second type, *Low-Anxiety-Introversion,* is phlegmatic, composed, confident, unshakable, trustful, adaptable, mature, calm, and self-sufficient, in addition to being aloof, cold, glum, silent, timid, shy, Bohemian, unconcerned, and resourceful. The third type, *High-Anxiety-Extroversion,* is tense, excitable, insecure, suspecting, jealous, emotional, unstable, lax, unsure, and also, warm, sociable, enthusiastic, talkative, adventurous, thick-skinned, conventional, practical, imitative and dependent. The final type, *Low-Anxiety-Extroversion,* is phlegmatic, composed, confident, unshakable, trustful, adaptable, mature, calm, and self-sufficient, and also, warm, sociable, enthusiastic, talkative, adventurous, thick-skinned, conventional, practical, imitative, and dependent.

Do these personality types seem strikingly in line with any theory under consideration here? Some theories, like that of Murray, Kelly, and McClelland do not postulate personality types, and need not be considered further. Others, like Erikson, White, and Allport, are so nebulous concerning personality types, that it is not really feasible to evaluate their positions with regard to the factorial information presented above. Among the remaining theories, those of Freud, Rogers, Maslow, and Fromm are not strikingly confirmed by the factorial evidence concerning personality types. Here and there, a bit of one of these theories seems to match one of the types presented above. So, for example, the *Low-Anxiety-Extroversion* type seems somewhat similar to Freud's *genital character,* and there is some, but less, correspondence between the *Low-Anxiety-Introversion* type and the fully functioning person of actualization theory. But neither Freud nor the actualization theorists have provided peripheral theorizing capable of rendering the other factorial types easily understandable.

The only peripheral theories fitting the types derived from factorial studies very well are those of Adler, Maddi, and, to some extent, Jung. It seems to me that the *Low-Anxiety Extroversion* and *Low-Anxiety-Introversion* types bear much similarity to Adlers' *active constructive* and *passive-constructive* styles of life, respectively. Further, the *High-Anxiety-Extroversion* and *High-Anxiety-Introversion* factorial combinations are reminiscent of Adler's *active-destructive* and *passive-destructive* styles of life, respectively. From the descriptions of the factors given above, it seems clear that High and Low Anxiety are much like high and low activation. Further, Extroversion and Introversion suggest the external and internal traits emphasized by Maddi. Although the emphasis on introversion-extroversion is quite accurate for Jung, it is not clear how low and high anxiety would fit his position. So, once again we find the empirical support tending toward the fulfillment model and the activation version of the consistency model.

Although the theories of Maddi, and of Adler, seem most actively supported by the evidence just presented, we must keep in mind that Cattell has also found five other second-order factors. These five are less pervasive and striking than the original two, but they have nonetheless been named. They have content considered reflective of *creativity, independence, tough poise, neuroticism,* and *leadership*. By the time all 47 personality types possible with 7 second-order factors have been scrutinized, it is doubtful that we would feel much support for one as opposed to another peripheral theory. Recognizing the inconclusive, though somewhat suggestive, nature of our consideration of factorial studies, let us move on to other research bearing upon the empirical analysis of peripheral considerations.

OTHER STUDIES OF PERIPHERAL PERSONALITY

The studies just reviewed did not involve selection of the behavioral variables constituting data so as to coincide with those considered important by any one theory. In general, they included a sampling of variables that was broad and eclectic enough so that the factors emerging from the data analysis were not more likely simply on sampling grounds to support one kind of theory or another. The virtue of inductive factor analytic studies, when they sample broadly, is that they aid us in determining the relative fruitfulness of different approaches to peripheral theorizing. To be sure, the studies reviewed in the last section showed some restriction in data sampling (witness the absence of fantasy and performance data). Nonetheless, they sampled more broadly than is typical in personological research, and are therefore probably the most useful of the available studies to us.

Remaining to be discussed here are the studies that restrict their concerns explicitly or implicitly to only one peripheral theory of personality. In order to be included here, such single-theory studies will have to focus primarily upon the measurement of one or more concrete peripheral characteristics or types, and also be concerned with the assessment of construct validity for the entities measured. Not emphasized will be studies in which concrete peripheral characteristics or types are used as explanatory concepts, but not measured. We cannot cover everything, and such studies are simply less relevant to whether particular concrete peripheral characteristics and types exist than are the studies focusing upon measurement and construct validation. In the main, I shall also exclude frankly developmental studies, even when they reflect a theoretical emphasis present in this book. Generally speaking, developmental studies do not focus upon the measurement of concrete peripheral characteristics and types, and also frequently study youngsters. For both these reasons, developmental studies are of secondary relevance to empirical evaluation of peripheral theorizing. Indeed, some personality theorists do not even detail the presumed basis upon which their peripheral concepts are derived through learning and development.

In addition, I shall emphasize only studies that are reasonably rigorous in their measurement attempts, systematic in their sampling of subjects, and knowledgeable in the data analyses undertaken. These restrictions are necessary in order to have any chance of obtaining a clear empirical analysis of peripheral considerations. There are many studies in the literature that are either so methodologically poor or so theoretically indirect and ambiguous, as to be better left unchronicled here.

Even with the restrictions suggested, it must be said at the outset that the studies to be considered are simply not as useful in evaluating the various approaches to theorizing as are the comprehensive studies reviewed in the previous section. The major reason for the limited utility of single-theory studies, whether or not they use factor analytic techniques for analyzing data, is that they focus upon one and only one peripheral theory of personality. Usually, these single-theory studies have a partisan flavor, i.e., they are performed by investigators who already believe the theory. One probable effect of such partisanship is to give the theory the benefit of the doubt, when findings can be interpreted more than one way. All things considered, it would not be surprising to find some solid empirical evidence for each of the peripheral theories, given the fact that these theories have all been devised by especially sensitive, serious, and intelligent personologists.

Of major value in the empirical evaluation of peripheral considerations are studies pitting the various theories against each other by comparing their explanatory capabilities. But failing enough carefully devised studies of this kind to make a difference, we will have to make do with what we have. Do not be too ready to give the laurel wreath to a theory, even if it is the one you secretly believe, just because a few limited studies seem to lend it some empirical support. Look instead for a heavy accumulation of empirical support, for many studies pointing in the same direction, and for studies that truly impress you as to their relevance to living.

One implication of my sermon is that a peripheral theory should really be shunned if it cannot even boast empirical support from partisan research. This would be a logical conclusion if we could be sure that personologists had attempted to conduct empirical studies stemming from that theory, and had failed to turn up any support. But we cannot conclude that a peripheral theory is unfruitful if, though reasonably clear, it has simply never been the focus of research efforts. All in all, the best policy to adopt in reading the following pages is to be duly impressed when there is formidable empirical support for a peripheral theory, while keeping an open mind concerning theories which do not have such support, unless it is clear that research attempts in their behalf have been mounted but have failed.

I will organize the following discussion in the simplest way—by particular theories. But the studies to be covered all involve one or more of three basic ways of measuring concrete peripheral characteristics and types. Perhaps it will aid understanding for me to mention these three ways of measuring beforehand. The first is self-description, which involves presenting the subject with a set of questions or adjectives and instructing him explicitly to depict himself by his responses (this is the approach most common in the factorial studies covered earlier). What characteristic of the subject the investigator hopes to glean from the responses need not be apparent, but the subject must know that he is describing himself in some way. The second measurement technique is the analysis of fantasy. Obtaining the fantasy productions involves providing the subject with an ambiguous, unstructured stimulus that he is to render clear and structured through an act of imagination. The presumption is that the subject's fantasy will disclose the characteristics of his personality. The final measurement technique is the rating of performance or action. This technique involves the investigator in classifying and quantifying the subject's behavior on some explicit and structured task he has been given. The task requires action and choice but depends little upon fantasy. With this bare introduction to the basic measurement techniques, let us plunge in.

Freud's position

In order to be considered especially pertinent, research must involve measurement of the traits or defenses presumed to form the oral, anal, phallic, and genital character types. The subjects should be old enough to at least have attained puberty. By and large, the single traits comprising the types are not so specific to Freudian theory alone that their study is definitive to someone interested in testing that theory. Understandably, we should only prick up our ears when a study includes clusters of traits representing one or more types. Also of some interest are studies that, while they focus on only one trait, have singled out one that is fairly unique to the Freudian tradition (e.g., castration anxiety).

Having established these specifications, what comes immediately to mind are the studies concerning the Blacky Test (Blum, 1949). The stimuli in this test are 12 cartoons, portraying the adventures of a dog named Blacky, his mother, father, and a sibling. The cartoons were carefully devised in order to pose familial situations reminiscent of the psychosexual themes and conflicts considered important in psychoanalytic theory. The subject is asked to compose stories in response to the pictures, this constituting fantasy data. After doing this, he is asked to answer a series of multiple-choice and short answer questions pertaining to the psychoanalytic theme or conflict presumably posed in the picture. Finally, the subject is asked whether he likes or dislikes each of the cartoons. The final two sorts of data resemble self-description. Blum (1949) has offered a scoring procedure for these three sources of data, the end result of which are scores for the subject reflecting the intensity of his disturbance on 13 dimensions. The content of these dimensions is shown in Table 10–1. You should realize that these dimensions do not actually reflect either the traits or the defenses listed in Chapter 0 under the various character types. Rather, some of the dimensions seem indicative of the character types (or possibly subtypes) themselves (e.g., oral eroticism, and anal retentiveness). Other dimensions seem to refer to general qualities transcending any particular character type, but probably indicating the overall degree of defensiveness and conflict (e.g., guilt feelings, sibling rivalry). In theoretical terms, it is certainly clear that the content of the dimensions is germane to Freud's position, though their precise status as concrete peripheral characteristics, types, or conglomerates of these, is unclear.

Consistent with this ambiguity is the necessity of global, intuitive scoring of the so-called dimensions. But even with intuitive scoring, Blum (1949) reports acceptable levels of agreement between himself and another psychologist working independently on the same protocols. As can be seen from Table 10–1, the percentages of agreement on the various dimensions range from 76 to 100, with an average of 92.6. In major part, the scoring procedure involves deciding whether a story shows a strong or weak emphasis upon the dimension being considered.

TABLE 10–1

Spontaneous story scoring agreement

Dimension	*Obtained percent scoring agreement*	*Percent expected by chance*
Oral eroticism	100	56
Oral sadism	96	61
Anal expulsiveness	84	43*
Anal retentiveness	96	44*
Oedipal intensity	96	53
Masturbation guilt	84	50
Castration anxiety (males)	100	56
Penis envy (females)	76	53
Positive identification	100	79
Sibling rivalry	92	56
Guilt feelings	80	51
Positive ego ideal	100	92
Narcissistic love-object	92	54
Anaclitic love-object	100	85

	Obtained	*Expected by chance*
Mean	92.6%	59.5%
Median	96.0%	55.0%
Range	76%–100%	43%–92%

* These two dimensions were scored on a four-point scale instead of a two-point scale. Hence the chance expectancy of agreement is somewhat lower.
Source: G. S. Blum, "A study of the psychoanalytic theory of psychosexual development." *Genet. Psychol. Monogr.*, 1949.

For example, Blum (1949) lists the following story, to a card showing Blacky nursing, as strong on oral eroticism:

> Blacky has just discovered the delightful nectar that Mama can supply—it is an endless supply and she is enjoying it. She doesn't know where it comes from, but she doesn't care. Mama is pacific throughout it all—she doesn't particularly like this business of supplying milk, but she is resigned to it. It is a pretty day and they are both calm and happy.

For contrast, consider a story to the same card that is considered weak on oral eroticism (Blum, 1949):

> Blacky, a male pup of a few weeks, is having his midday lunch. Mama is bored with the proceedings but as a mother with her maternal interests is letting Blacky have his lunch to Blacky's satisfaction.

In this story, there is none of the elaboration so indicative of lingering oral conflict seen in the first story.

Having encountered at least some evidence that well-trained investigators can agree on scoring the stories, we should now turn our attention to the question of whether the dimensions of the test have sufficient internal consistency and stability to be considered empirically genuine. Charen (1956) reports stability correlations for the 13 dimensions that range from a high of .52 through very low positive and even some negative values. The implication of low negative correlations is that people's responses changed almost completely from the first to the second testing. But we are justified in looking into the matter of reliability further, for Charen's study involved a period between testing of four months, which is long enough that one might expect certain real changes in personality not indicative of test inadequacy. The possibility of real personality change is heightened by the fact that in that four-month period, the subjects were recovering from a serious illness, tuberculosis.

Granick and Scheflen (1958) have reported a study concerning stability, internal consistency, and interscorer agreement for the Blacky Test. Their results on interscorer agreement, which ranged on the 13 cards from 58 to 95 percent, with an average of 77.5 percent, are poorer than those obtained by Blum, but still somewhat acceptable. In considering stability and temporal consistency, these investigators adopted an unorthodox approach that is not really very relevant to the 13 dimensions as used. For internal consistency, they apparently considered it sufficient to demonstrate persistence from story to story in level of verbal fluency and articulation of the card theme with the composed story. For stability, they offer evidence that records obtained from the same subjects at different times can be matched at a better than chance level by the investigator, and that the thematic content of the stories written by the same subjects at two points in time are more frequently similar than are the stories written by a group of subjects and their matched controls. If there were no other evidence concerning the reliability of the Blacky dimensions, we should have to conclude that we cannot be sure of their empirical genuineness, because the approach of Granick and Scheflen is simply too far from the intended use of the dimensions. Fortunately, Berger and Everstine (1962) have studied stability in a more direct fashion. With an interval between testings of four weeks, they obtained stability correlations on 50 college males for the 13 dimensions that ranged from .20 to .54, with an average of .44. The stability of the dimensions seems quite modest, especially for a theory that considers significant development and change to be largely over by the time puberty is reached. The difficulty, of course, may lie in the test rather than the theory. After all, the so-called dimensions do have the heterogeneity and ambiguity mentioned before. An analysis of internal consistency could help in determining whether this is the source of the difficulty. Unfortunately, there do not seem to be extensive studies on internal consistency. I suggest that we push on to consider studies of validity, keeping in mind that in these dimensions, we are hardly working with the stable characteristics envisioned by psychoanalytic theory.

First, we should consider two factor analytic studies performed on the same set of data. The data were originally obtained by Blum (1949) by administering the Blacky Test to 119 male and 90 female college students. On the basis of scores obtained by these subjects, Blum computed the intercorrelations among the dimensions, separately by males and females, and felt that he had uncovered strong support for psychoanalytic theory. But instead of going over his results and conclusions, I will give attention to two factor analytic studies done by other investigators on Blum's data, because the statistical procedures they employed are more sophisticated than were his. The aim of both factor analytic studies was to clarify the clustering of dimensions. If the dimensions really represented concrete peripheral characteristics, then such studies would yield evidence as to whether the psychoanalytic view on the subsuming of characteristics into types was accurate (think of the second step of the ideal strategy). But an air of ambiguity is lent to the enterprise by virtue of the difficulty in determining whether the dimensions are unitary enough to represent concrete peripheral characteristics. Nonetheless, let us push on.

The first factor analytic study was done by Neuman and Salvatore (1958) and the second by Robinson and Hendrix (1966). Neuman and Salvatore obtained six factors for males that corresponded reasonably well to the oral, anal, phallic, latency, and genital characters. But the six factors they extracted for females seemed contradictory to psychoanalytic theory. They could not stretch their conclusions to grant any more than partial confirmation to the theory of character types. Working with the same data, Robinson and Hendrix applied a factor analytic technique deemed more sophisticated and accurate than that employed in the earlier study. The factor matrices they obtained are reproduced for males in Table 10–2 and for females in Table 10–3. As you can see, the 13 dimensions appear down the side of the table, whereas the factors obtained are listed across the top. The term in parentheses under the factor number represents the interpretation the investigators deemed best suited to the results appearing in the body of the table. In order to follow these interpretations, you should know that the numbers in the body of the table are correlations, and that the higher they are (whether positive or negative) the more the dimension involved is a defining attribute of the factor.

Considering the results obtained by Robinson and Hendrix for males, it would seem that the first factor represents orality, because of the high positive contribution to the factor made by *oral eroticism* and *oral sadism*. The negative contribution made by *anal retentiveness* adds support to this interpretation, though the positive loading of *oedipal intensity* is, strictly speaking, a complication. The third factor is characterized by positive loadings for *oral eroticism, anal expulsiveness,* and *castration anxiety*. This seems to represent a developmental situation that in psychoanalytic terms would span from the oral through the phallic stages, and hence, can only roughly be considered to express the anal character. But, Fenichel (1945) does point to the frequency with which castration anxiety is intermingled with anal-sadistic fears, and hence, there is some justification for the interpretation offered by Robinson and Hendrix. The fifth factor is characterized by positive loadings for *anal expulsiveness, masturbation guilt,* and *sibling rivalry*. Except for *anal expulsiveness*, contributing dimensions are accurate to the psychoanalytic view of the

TABLE 10–2

Principal component-varimax analysis of 13 Blacky dimensions for 119 males

	Factors						
Dimensions	*I* (Oral)	*II* (Latent)	*III* (Anal)	*IV* (Genital)	*V* (Phallic)	*VI* (Guilt)	h^2
Oral eroticism...........	59†	−10	50*	−22	−15	−10	71
Oral sadism.............	75†	01	05	−32	19	14	71
Anal expulsiveness.......	20	04	57*	−09	54*	−16	65
Anal retentiveness.......	−54*	−34	04	17	−32	00	54
Oedipal intensity........	79†	−30	−12	24	−09	−06	74
Masturbation guilt......	−10	08	−04	17	83†	−01	70
Castration anxiety.......	−15	−06	91†	08	04	14	88
Positive identification....	09	30†	−03	14	−08	−04	68
Sibling rivalry..........	18	−22	11	−08	65†	09	54
Guilt feelings...........	04	−07	04	01	02	97†	95
Positive ego ideal........	−17	−16	−30	87†	01	−08	91
Narcissistic love-object...	28	−83†	03	21	−01	06	80
Anaclitic love-object.....	−02	08	21	86†	07	09	79

* Significant at .05 level.
† Significant at .01 level.

Source: S. A. Robinson, & V. L. Hendrix. "The Blacky Test and psychoanalytic theory: Another factor-analytic approach to validity." *J. proj. Tech. pers. Assessment,* 1966.

TABLE 10–3

Principal component-varimax analysis of 13 Blacky dimensions for 90 females

	Factors					
	I	II	III	IV	V	
Dimensions	*(Anal)*	*(Phallic)*	*(Genital)*	*(Guilt)*	*(Oral)*	*h²*
Oral eroticism....................	42	05	00	31	57*	60
Oral sadism.....................	−09	−21	−21	40	54*	54
Anal expulsiveness...............	83†	04	−13	03	03	71
Anal retentiveness...............	−73†	31	−12	11	07	66
Oedipal intensity................	71*	06	04	07	04	51
Masturbation guilt...............	16	01	−17	90†	−13	88
Penis envy......................	−10	72†	13	14	08	57
Positive identification...........	−04	−09	−08	22	−83†	76
Sibling rivalry...................	46	12	32	13	−59*	69
Guilt feelings...................	17	−12	−47	−56*	−10	59
Positive ego ideal................	−19	36	74†	−17	−09	74
Narcissistic love-object...........	09	85†	−08	−11	−12	76
Anaclitic love-object.............	26	−27	80†	−01	−10	79

* Significant at .05 level.
† Significant at .01 level.
    Source: S. A. Robinson, & V. L. Hendrix. "The Blacky Test and psychoanalytic theory: Another factor-analytic approach to validity." *J. proj. Tech. pers. Assessmnt,e* 1966.

phallic stage. But, once again, even more accurate to the results would be some conglomerate of anal and phallic character types. The second factor includes a positive loading for *positive identification,* and negative loadings for *narcissistic love-object* and *anal retentiveness.* Robinson and Hendrix suggest that this represents something like a latency character type, because the latency period is supposed to be one in which the child is trying identifications with various adults and social roles, and relinquishing the selfish loves of the phallic period. The fourth factor is characterized by positive loadings on *positive ego ideal* (or personal aspirations and values) and *anaclitic love-object* (choice of a love-object resembling the person on whom the individual was dependent for comfort in infancy). If you had to call this factor anything, then in the light of the other factors, one might conclude that it represented the genital period. But, in all seriousness, it should be recognized that the two strong positive loadings are somewhat contradictory. Finally, the sixth factor for males seems clearly expressive of *guilt feelings.*

    The results for females are rather similar to those for males. The fifth factor is clearly oral, with its positive loadings of *oral eroticism* and *sadism,* and its negative loadings of *sibling rivalry* and *positive identification.* The first factor is defined positively by *anal expulsiveness, sibling rivalry,* and *oedipal intensity,* but shows a negative loading for *anal retentiveness.* If anything, this factor seems a conglomerate of anal and phallic periods, but even in such an interpretation, the negative contribution of *anal retentiveness* is difficult to understand. But the second factor, defined by positive loading on *penis envy* and *narcissistic love-*

object, does conform reasonably well to the phallic character type in women. Interestingly enough, no factor was obtained for women that seemed relevant to the latency period. This finding seems consistent with the belief of many psychoanalysts that the latency period is a cultural artifact. Finally, the fourth factor seems to express *guilt feelings.*

In the results reported by Robinson and Hendrix, more than in those of Neuman and Salvatore, there is reason to believe that the theory of character types has some empirical viability. But a note of caution is necessary, because the so-called dimensions are probably not the bedrock, fundamental, irreducible, minimally interpretive, concrete peripheral characteristics upon which the theory of character types is built. Instead, the dimensions seem to be general, perhaps rather heterogeneous, conglomerates, in the scoring of which considerable interpretation is necessary. It may be that in the highly interpretive act of scoring the dimensions, the results of factor analyses such as those described above are predetermined. If the scoring of dimensions involves acting as if the theory of character types is true, then the ensuing factor analysis may be doing little more than celebrating the scorer's acumen in putting his belief in the theory of character types into action. Were the dimensions of the Blacky Test less general and interpretive, one could well be impressed by results showing them to group themselves into types in a manner consistent with psychoanalytic theory.

Let us turn now from the factor analytic studies to studies investigating the construct validity of the 13 dimensions of the Blacky Test. Blum and Hunt (1952) have reviewed much of the early work of this nature. I will concentrate on studies testing psychoanalytic hypotheses concerning peripheral personality. In one such study, Aronson (1950) focused upon the Freudian theory of paranoia. He administered the Blacky Test to 30 paranoid schizophrenics, 30 nonparanoid schizophrenics, and 30 normal control subjects. The three groups were comparable in age, intelligence, occupation, religion, and status as veterans. The basis for distinguishing paranoid schizophrenics from nonparanoid schizophrenics was the presence of delusions (common in paranoid people).

In the psychoanalytic theory, paranoia and schizophrenia are considered breakdown products of the anal and oral character types, respectively. Consequently, Aronson hypothesized that the paranoid schizophrenics would show greater intensity of *anal retentiveness, anal expulsiveness, oral sadism,* and *oral eroticism* than would the normal subjects. Further, the paranoid schizophrenics would be stronger than the nonparanoid schizophrenics on only *anal retentiveness* and *anal expulsiveness.* The results supported his hypotheses in all instances except *anal expulsiveness,* indicating considerable support for the Freudian position. But Aronson also found the paranoid group to show greater evidence of *masturbation guilt,* conscious attempts at denial of strong underlying *castration anxiety;* a consistent tendency toward feminine identification; severe superego conflicts, and a preference for narcissistic types of love-object choice. Many of these differences could not have been precisely predicted from psychoanalytic peripheral theorizing.

There are a number of other studies (e.g., Blum & Kaufman, 1952) investigating scores on the Blacky Test of people with certain psychological disorders. In the main, these studies are less pertinent than that of Aronson for illuminating the empirical validity of Freudian peripheral theorizing. Actually, the explicit intent of these studies is often to develop, rather than test, a psychoanalytic explanation of the disorder under consideration. Such studies assume the adequacy of the test and the validity of the theory, actually clarifying neither. In what is probably the most rigorous of these studies, Linder (see Blum & Hunt, 1952) administered the Blacky Test to 67 male sexual offenders, and 67 nonsexual offenders matched for age, race, IQ, education, socioeconomic and marital status, length of sentence, and previous convictions. Analysis of the data showed that the sexual offenders were significantly higher (more disturbed) on 9 of the 13 Blacky dimensions. Although this study may provide evidence that sexual offenders are very sick people, it does not really clarify psychoanalytic peripheral theorizing.

In a radically different study, Swanson (1951) attempted to use the Blacky Pictures in testing certain psychoanalytic predictions about the interpersonal behavior of groups of people. Scores on the Blacky dimensions were obtained on the 20 members of each of two training groups at the National Training Laboratory for Group Development at Bethel, Maine. The aim of the members of such groups is to come to know each other and themselves in a deeper fashion through the meetings. Swanson predicted that high scores on *oral sadism, anal expulsiveness, oedipal intensity, sibling rivalry,* or *guilt feelings,* would raise the total amount of a person's actual participation in permissive groups like those at the Training Laboratory. Swanson used the pattern of a person's scores on the Blacky dimensions just mentioned to reach an overall judgment concerning the likelihood of his participation in the interaction of the group. These judgments were then correlated to several measures of actual participation. In general, these were sufficient positive correlations obtained in both groups to indicate that Swanson's judgments had validity. It is quite difficult, however, to see how this study bears on the validity of psychoanalytic theory except in an indirect fashion.

There is a very pertinent study by Adelson and Redmond (1958) concerning the anal character type. They obtained the Blacky Test scores on *anal retentiveness* and *anal expulsiveness* for 61 college women. The hypothesis was that anal retentive subjects should have greater ability to recall verbal material than anal expulsive subjects. The basis for this hypothesis is clearly in the Freudian belief that fixation occurs later in the anal period for retentive than for expulsive subtypes. The later the anal fixation occurs the greater the emphasis upon "holding on" rather than "letting go." Of the 61 subjects, 32 were classified as expulsives, 18 as retentives, and 11 as neutral. Subjects read two prose passages, each of several hundred words. One passage included sexual and aggressive themes whereas the other was innocuous. Subjects were asked to reproduce the passages immediately after presentation and again one week later. As you can see from Table 10–4, the retentives showed greater recall under all conditions. In general, neutral subjects scored midway between the other two groups. Adelson and Redmond also presented evidence that these differences in verbal recall cannot be accounted for by differences in intellectual capacity. This very clear and rigorous study provides strong support for the construct validity of the psychoanalytic notion of anal expulsive and anal retentive subtypes of the anal character.

TABLE 10–4

Differences between expulsives and retentives in verbal recall
(expulsives $N = 32$; retentives $N = 18$)

Tests	Group	M	SD	t	P
Innocuous passage—Immediate recall..............	Expulsive	19.9	12.84	2.25	.05
	Retentive	28.3	12.08		
Innocuous passage—Delayed recall...............	Expulsive	9.9	6.00	2.60	.02
	Retentive	15.1	8.66		
Disturbing passage—Immediate recall*..........	Expulsive	21.6	9.59	2.68	.02
	Retentive	28.7	12.29		
Disturbing passage—Delayed recall*.............	Expulsive	11.1	5.92	3.66	.001
	Retentive	19.3	8.94		

* The mean scores for the disturbing passages refer to thought units.
Source: J. Adelson, & J. Redmond. "Personality differences in the capacity for verbal recall." *J. abnorm. soc. Psychol.*, 1958.

In another study, Kline (1968) attempted to determine the relationship between obsessional traits (which are considered expressive of extreme anality) and characteristics of toilet training (the conditions under which an anal fixation would have occurred). He used the Blacky Test and four obsession scales to measure anality, attempting to correlate them with information about toilet training. Although his results are ambiguous and indicate the importance of sex differences, there is some small support for the hypothesis. Tribich (1974) put 107 male students in a group situation where the task was to judge the magnitude of apparent movement of a light. Confederates of the experimenter, with the status of authority figures, were members of the group and tried to influence the students' judgements. Students with an oral character, as measured by the Blacky Test, were positively influenced by the "authority," whereas those who were anal reacted against the attempted influence. This result appears to be solid support for Freudian peripheral theorizing.

This sampling of studies using the Blacky Test will have to suffice.

Annotated bibliographies for the test are now available (Schaeffer, 1968; Taulbee & Stenmark, 1968), and there is even a form for females (Robinson, 1968).

There are, of course, studies pertinent to Freudian peripheral theorizing that have not employed the Blacky Test. Although I cannot hope to be complete in reviewing them, I shall try to be representative. In presenting the studies, I shall cover the various character types in their presumed developmental order.

Concerning the oral character type, there is an occasional study like that of Goldman (1948), who secured self-descriptions on 19 traits from 115 young adults. The list of traits included most of those specified as part of the oral character. With few exceptions, the presumed oral traits did show empirical intercorrelation. It was possible to isolate 20 subjects who showed the positive pole of orality (characterized by optimism, trust, and expansiveness), and 20 subjects who showed the negative pole of orality (characterized by pessimism, distrust, and conservatism). In criticizing this study, Sears (1950) says, "It is a misfortune that these rather significant findings were not presented with sufficient clarity and explanation of the mathematical devices used that some confidence might be placed in them." In a subsequent study, Goldman (1951) attempted empirical validation of the interpretation that the clustering of traits represented the oral character. The results do indicate that subjects showing the pessimistic clustering of presumed oral traits had experienced earlier weaning from the breast than had subjects exhibiting the positive clustering. But the relationship is a weak one, and many other predicted relationships were not supported. It can hardly be said that there is strong evidence of empirical validity.

Sarnoff (1951) has reported a study concerning the defense mechanism of identification (or introjection), which is a primitive technique for avoiding anxiety generally attributed to the oral stage of development. More specifically, he focused upon identification with the aggressor, a notion found nowhere else but in Freudian theory. This defense involves becoming more like the person who is hurting you in order to avoid the anxiety associated with the threat of pain to you and the threat of your own destructive anger. Sarnoff reasoned that anti-Semitism among Jews was prima facie evidence of identification with the aggressor, and proceeded to construct a questionnaire to assess it. Jews receiving a high score on this questionnaire "were regarded as having taken, toward their own Jewish group, the same anti-Semitic attitudes that are expressed by majority group bigots in our society" (Sarnoff, 1951). On the basis of this questionnaire, 100 Jewish college students were divided into two groups of 45 high in anti-Semitism and 55 low in anti-Semitism. Several personality tests were also administered to these subjects in order to measure the personality differences between the two groups. The results, shown in Table 10–5, are offered by Sarnoff in support of hypotheses from

TABLE 10–5

Differences between the number of highs and lows on each of the personality variables

Personality Variables	Number of Highs*	Number of Lows*	p†
Death of mother, father, and parents-as-a-group............. 25		13	.01
Disparaging remarks about mother........................ 19		11	.04
Disparaging remarks about father......................... 12		6	.05
Derogatory remarks about home and home life.............. 8		5	.13
Fear of parental disapproval............................. 6		2	.05
Favorable comments about mother........................ 16		32	.09
Favorable comments about father......................... 5		11	.15
Favorable comments about home and home life............. 8		19	.08
Self-negation... 15		6	.01
Fear of the future...................................... 5		1	.04
Fear of rejection by others.............................. 12		5	.03
Admission of psychic stress.............................. 21		13	.05
Self-derogatory remarks................................. 20		21	.34
Self-assertion... 0		4	.05
Absence of fears....................................... 2		7	.09
Favorable remarks about the self........................ 5		11	.15
Passivity in response to aggression....................... 20		12	.05
Suppression of desires to retaliate against aggression.......... 3		0	.05
Turning hostility against the self......................... 9		4	.05
Active retaliation in response to aggression................. 14		31	.06

* For the variables based on the Thematic Apperception Test, these differences represent a comparison between 43 Highs and 54 lows. Three of the 100 TAT protocols were either lost or had to be omitted from the analysis because subjects did not adhere to the instructions. All of the other differences, those based on the Sentence Completion, involved 45 Highs and 55 Lows as previously stated.

† Since all of our specific predictions were made on an a priori basis which took into account the direction of the differences, only one half of the probability curve is used in determining levels of significance. The level of significance of these predicted results was obtained by reducing by one half the probabilities reported to the conventional "t" tables since these tables use both halves of the probability curves.

Source: I. Sarnoff. "Identification with the aggressor: some personality correlates of anti-Semitism among Jews." *J. Pers.*, 1951.

Freudian theory. In the study, anti-Semitic Jews (highs) were likely to be insecure, chronically fearful people who had been severely rejected by their parents. They tended to dislike themselves through having experienced parental dislike. They also hated their parents. Being unable to accept themselves, these Jews seemed obliged to search for devious means of increasing their adequacy and, at the same time, fulfilling the urge to reject themselves. In Sarnoff's (1951) words, "In becoming anti-Semitic, these Jews may be vicariously appropriating the power position of the majority-group chauvinists and simultaneously achieving a vehicle for perpetuating the negative images of themselves and their parents." Although this study provides some evidence for the validity of the concept of identification with the aggressor, it does not tie down this personality characteristic to the oral stage of development.

Another defense mechanism associated with the oral stage is projection, which involves attributing to others characteristics that are really your own, in order that you can remain unconscious of their presence in you, and therefore free of anxiety. Remaining alert to this precise meaning will aid us in what follows, for projection is often given the general meaning of simply expressing the characteristics of one's personality in external situations, especially if they are ambiguous. This general meaning is really not what Freud meant.

One relevant and intriguing study was done by Sears (1936). He obtained from nearly a hundred college fraternity men character trait ratings of themselves and each other. The traits rated were stinginess, obstinacy, disorderliness, and bashfulness. The degree of a given trait attributed to others by a subject was compared with the amount attributed to him by the others. No clear relationships were found. But when a rough measure of insight was taken into account, it was found that those men who possessed more than the average amount of a trait tended to attribute more than average amounts to others, provided insight was lacking. In essence, this means that projection of these character traits appeared to be a function of lack of insight. This finding is not inconsistent with the concept of projection, which includes not only the attribution of one's own characteristics to others, but also the debarment from consciousness of those characteristics in oneself. The latter aspect of projection may have been tapped by Sears's insight measure. Although the study provides no information as to whether the four traits involved were indeed undesirable to the subjects, it is fairly safe to assume that they were, as they are generally undesirable. In addition, the traits are relevant to the psychoanalytic notions concerning psychosexual stages of development (as you noted in Chapter 6, stinginess, obstinacy, and disorderliness are anal traits, while bashfulness is either oral or phallic). The great difficulty with this study as evidence for projection is that Sears also found that subjects very low on a trait would attribute lowness to others if insight was lacking. But being low on an undesirable trait should not lead to projection, theoretically, because there is no personal basis for conflict with the superego and subsequent guilt and anxiety. This latter finding throws into serious question whether the prior finding is adequately interpreted as projection. Of course, one could say that for some people, because of particularly peculiar early life experiences, an absence of these traits is a potential source of guilt, and that both findings were obtained because these kinds of people existed in the sample alongside the more usual ones. But the study provides no information with which to check this possibility, and it seems rather farfetched anyway.

Actually, the methodology Sears used has come under considerable criticism (see Holmes, 1968) because the manner in which he measured "insight" essentially forced the negative correlation he then interpreted as evidence of projection. The subject was considered to lack insight if his peers rated him high on a trait but he placed himself below the rating he assigned to the group. That these subjects attributed a greater amount of that trait to other people than did the subjects possessing an equal amount of the trait but having insight, becomes a statistical artifact of method! The negative correlation reported by Sears would have been found regardless of whether the subject was insightful or not. An insightful subject (who by Sears's definition would have given himself a higher rating than his peers) would have to see others as low on the trait.

Rokeach (1945) attempted to replicate Sears's findings, only to discover that the correlation supporting the hypothesis of projection only occurred when the data were analyzed in the erroneous manner mentioned above. When the data were analyzed in a fashion that did not force the predicted relationship, it did not occur. Since then, the absence of relationship has been found by several investigators, such as Lemann (1952), and Wells and Goldstein (1964). In other studies by Murstein (1956), and Page and Markowitz (1955), what appeared evidence for projection was thrown into considerable doubt by the existence of groups in whom the attribution of traits also occurred, but with the subject being conscious of it.

In an intriguing attempt to demonstrate projection, Wright (1940) took care to create conditions that would provoke guilt in his subjects. A pair of toys, one preferred and the other nonpreferred, were given to the subjects, who were eight-year-old children. Then the children were asked to give away one of the two toys to a friend. Immediately after this they were asked which toy they thought the friend would have given away. Control group children were asked this question, without first having been asked themselves to give away one of the toys. The proportion of times that the friend was considered generous (giving away the preferred toy) was much less after the conflict situation, in which the child himself was forced to give away a toy, than it was under the control condition. This indicates that stinginess is projected when the person feels guilty about his own stingy thoughts.

While this study certainly seems consistent with projection as a defense, it is a little weak in that it cannot be demonstrated that the attribution of stinginess occurred without any conscious relationship to one's own stingy thoughts. If one's own stinginess was consciously appreciated, then attributing stinginess to a friend would be generalization more than defensive projection. It appears that whenever a study avoids being plagued by statistical artifacts, the only thing suggestive of the projection it demonstrates is something that may well take place with full awareness of the subject. This has led Holmes (1968) to contend that a simple generalization explanation of the phenomenon is superior to that of projection. Here and there, studies of projection are reported (Ahler, 1967; Katz, Sarnoff, & McClintock, 1956; Sarnoff & Katz, 1954), the design of which makes it difficult to determine whether subjects had awareness of their presumed defense. In light of what has been said above, it is difficult to know what to make of these studies.

Let us turn now to research on traits rather than defenses associated with the oral character. A particular oral activity, smoking, is easily measured, and has received considerable research attention of late. This research has mainly sought to determine the nature of general differences between smokers and nonsmokers. Matarazzo and Saslow (1960) have concluded from a careful review of 44 such studies that, despite much speculation about the relationship between early nursing experiences and smoking, no clear-cut pattern of personality peculiar to smokers has yet emerged from the literature. Although smokers seem to be more extroverted, which sounds plausible as an oral trait, they are also more anxious than nonsmokers. In a particularly extensive study, Schubert (1959a, 1959b) tested hypotheses derived from Freud and Fenichel, concerning smoking as expressive of oral fixation, only to find that the smokers among his 1,500 college students showed as much evidence of being arousal or activation seekers as of being oral in character. It seems fair to conclude that if striking empirical support for the concept of oral character is to be found, it should not be sought in the literature on smoking.

More supportive of Freud's position is a study by Masling, Weiss, and Rothschild (1968), which tested the hypotheses that oral-dependent persons need support and approval from others. Subjects were introduced into a type of conformity experiment invented by Asch, in which a pseudo subject actually in the employ of the experimenter, insists on an apparently wrong judgment of some perceptual phenomenon (such as the length of a line). The true subject may or may not conform to the confederate's erroneous response. Masling et al., accumulated 23 undergraduate males who conformed, and 21 who did not. On scrutinizing their performance on the Rorschach Test, a fantasy method of assessing personality, they discovered that the conforming subjects tended to show evidence of an oral character type. Also promising is the work of Cooperman and Child (1969), who utilized 115 undergraduate males in determining the relationship between aesthetic preference and food preference. Certain hypotheses they derived from psychoanalytic theory were confirmed when 8 of the 12 oral personality variables they studied correlated significantly with the aesthetic preference score.

Turning to the anal character type, we encounter another study by Sarnoff (1960). His aim was to investigate the empirical validity of the defense mechanism of reaction formation, which is a cornerstone of the Freudian position on the anal character. Sarnoff reasoned that warm, accepting, loving feelings toward others are anxiety provoking because socially unacceptable in our crass, market-oriented society. Therefore, when such warm feelings are aroused, people who tend to use the defense mechanism of reaction formation, should show an increase in cynical, critical feelings toward others. In order to test this hypothesis, Sarnoff gave his 81 male undergraduates one of two experimental manipulations. One of these manipulations, designed to arouse strong feelings of affection, involved listening to a live presentation of a portion of William Saroyan's play, *Hello out There*. The other manipulation involved listening to a taped version of the same thing, and was supposed to arouse only mild feelings of affection. Before hearing the portion of the play, all subjects filled out questionnaires yielding measures of cynicism and of reaction formation. Following the play, subjects again filled out the cynicism questionnaire. The results showed, contrary to expectation, that regardless of the strength of the tendency to use reaction formation and of the degree of affection arousal, all subjects decreased in cynicism. It is true that people tending toward reaction formation decreased least in cynicism, but this is very meager support for the hypothesis. This study can be attacked on a number of grounds, not the least of which is the theoretically unconvincing assumption that feelings of affection are disapproved of socially. In addition, the measurement of defensive tendencies through self-description in the form of answers to questions is not really in the spirit of Freudian thinking. After all, one is not supposed to be aware of one's defenses.

Nalven (1967) compared 30 subjects who relied upon repression with 30 who relied on intellectualization (which is a defense mechanism often associated with the anal character type) on a task of some complexity requiring perceptual decisions. The measurement of repressive and intellectualizing defenses was accomplished using a sentence completion test (which taps primarily fantasy). As one would expect from psychoanalytic theory, the intellectualizers could formulate more alternatives in the decision-making task than could the repressers. Although this study certainly supports Freud's position, it should be pointed out that an important basis for deciding that subjects were repressers was sparsity of response on the sentence completion test. It is the same sparsity that was looked for on the perceptual decision task. Thus, someone of a different theoretical persuasion could insist that no more has been demonstrated than a difference between the groups in productivity. To be convincing, studies of defense mechanisms must provide some basis in their design for believing that the mechanism under consideration has indeed been aroused. But putting the findings of this study together with those on sensitizing defenses already reviewed in Chapter 5 makes the existence of such mechanisms a reasonable surmise. Of course, there is little if anything in any of this research that demonstrates sensitizing defenses to be strongly associated with the anal character.

Turning from defenses to the traits of the anal character, we encounter an interesting study by Pettit (1969), concerning attitudes toward time. He constructed a time scale of 40 items to ascertain the ways in which time has special meaning and serves to organize a person's experience. This scale was administered to 91 undergraduates along with two questionnaire measures of anality and one of spontaneity. As one would expect from Freud's position, the preoccupation with time as an organizing principle correlated positively to the measures of anality and negatively to the measure of spontaneity. While it is likely that one feature of the anality measures is time concern, the correlations obtained would seem to be too high to be explained away in this fashion.

Centers (1969) tested the hypothesis that persons with an anal character type would express tough attitudes in regard to the mischievous behavior of teen-agers and the dependence of social welfare recipients. A sample of 562 adults answered his attitude questionnaire and two questionnaires he devised to reflect anality. Modest support is reported for the hypothesis. In a similar study, Koutrelakos (1968) tested 100 males on the Authoritarianism (F) Scale and a questionnaire concerning perceptions of and attitudes toward their fathers. As will be discussed later, the Authoritarianism Scale is an instrument in general use that would be interpreted by Freudians to indicate the severe conscience and aggressiveness of anality. As predicted, highly authoritarian subjects perceived their fathers as more authoritarian and more similar to their ideal person than did subjects low in authoritarianism. Although both these studies provide support for the Freudian position, it must be said that the measures employed may well overlap on methodological (not theoretical) grounds. Hence, some amount of relationship found may be spurious. In addition, the measures (e.g., Authoritarianism Scale) are sufficiently general in content to be claimed as relevant by other personality theories besides that of Freud.

There are few studies of the clustering of traits constituting the phallic character. But one finds some studies concentrating on one of the defenses or traits that has been considered relevant. The studies of defenses concern repression, and have already been reviewed in Chapter 5. As a totality, they are rather convincing, even though many of them can be strongly criticized. Of the studies concerning single traits, the most uniquely relevant to Freudian theory are those of *castration anxiety, castration wish,* and *penis envy,* all matters that are supposed to derive their importance in the adult personality from events during the phallic stage of development. Virtually all of these studies have employed fantasy measures of the various castration and envy themes. This kind of measurement is clearly appropriate, as such themes are supposed to be unconscious. Blum (1949) found significantly more responses to the Blacky Test indicative of castration anxiety among males than females, a finding that obviously supports Freudian thinking. Schwartz (1955, 1956) devised a method of scoring thematic apperception tests for castration anxiety, and found that male homosexuals displayed significantly more castration anxiety than normal males. In addition, males obtained higher castration anxiety scores than females. In the only self-descriptive approach to measurement, Sarnoff and Corwin (1959) used a multiple-choice questionnaire about castration anxiety in showing that males with high-castration scores have significantly greater increase in fear of death than low-castration males after having been exposed to sexually arousing stimuli. This finding supports Freudian thinking in that the sexually arousing stimuli should lead to guilt and fear of punishment most in those males having experienced fixation during the phallic stage through harsh punishment of their sexual desires for their mothers. Castration anxiety is presumably indicative of the harshness of such punishment. Intriguing though this finding is, it has required considerable interpretation and assumptions in order to be construed as support for Freud's position.

Finally, Hall and Van de Castle (1965) looked for evidence of castration anxiety, castration wish, and penis envy in reported dreams. Their study was particularly careful. The scoring system for *castration anxiety* involved such themes as difficulty with the penis, the changing of a man into a woman, and threatened or actual damage to or loss of part of the body. The criteria for *castration wish* were the same except that the events do not occur to the dreamer but rather to another person in his dream. The scoring system for *penis envy* includes the changing of a woman into a man, admiration of man's physical characteristics, and the acquisition of male objects. As scoring dreams for such characteristics involves some interpretation, it is important to demonstrate that the scoring systems can be used with adequate agreement by different investigators. Hall and Van de Castle report interscorer agreement that is higher than 95 percent on each of the three scoring systems. The subjects were male and female college students, who reported their recent dreams as part of a class assignment. The results of this study show that there is more evidence of castration anxiety among men than women, and that women show more penis envy and castration wish than do men. The findings of this and the other studies mentioned above are quite in line with Freudian thinking concerning the phallic character type. But it must be said that there is nothing that could testify to the accuracy of the Freudian viewpoint on development.

I am at a loss for what to say concerning research relevant to the genital character type. Freudians do not themselves seem to do such research, probably because this type represents an ideal to them. There are virtually no fully genital people, according to Freudians. In addition, the concrete peripheral characteristics of the genital character are hardly peculiar to Freudian theory, and hence, research concerning them would not provide vivid support or disconfirmation of the position. Personologists not of Freudian persuasion, particularly actualization theorists, have conducted research that bears on the kinds of emphases to be found in descriptions of the genital character. But these researches are more appropriately presented elsewhere in this review.

Before concluding this section, I should mention research themes involving the development of two paper and pencil tests of defensiveness.

In both tests, several defenses are involved, and hence several character types are implied. One of the tests, the *Defense Mechanism Inventory,* was introduced by Gleser and Ihilevich (1969) in an attempt to measure the relative intensity of five major groups of defenses. The test is composed of 12 brief stories (2 for each of the conflict areas of authority, independence, masculinity, femininity, competition, and situational) each followed by four questions regarding the person's actions, fantasy, thoughts, and feelings in the situations involved. Five responses exemplifying the five sets of defenses are provided for each question and the person selects the one most and the one least representative of his reactions. The five sets of defenses are *Turning Against Object* (displacement and identification with the aggressor), *Projection, Principalization* (intellectualization and isolation), *Turning Against Self* (masochism and autosadism), and *Reversal* (denial, reaction formation, and repression). Although Gleser and Ihilevich indulge a confusing tendency to relabel defenses well known by different names, their inventory appears at face value to have much bearing on Freudian theory.

Gleser and Ihilevich report internal consistency correlations that are comparable for males and females and range from $-.31$ to $.83$. Even if the two lowest (and quite unacceptable) correlations are omitted, the range is still large, from $.57$ to $.83$. These unimpressive findings suggest that at least some of the defensiveness scores are too heterogeneous as presently measured to be convincing as to empirical existence. The test fares better with regard to stability over a one-week interval, with correlations ranging from $.85$ to $.93$, and an average of $.89$.

As to validity, Gleser and Ihilevich report that psychologists were quite able to match stories with conflict areas and responses to questions with defense mechanisms. So the test appears to fit accepted beliefs of experts concerning defensiveness. It was also found that subjects who relied mainly on global defenses (Turning Against Self and Reversal) were more field dependent than subjects who relied on differentiated defenses (Turning Against Object and Projection). Not only would there be disagreement among psychologists concerning the interpretation of this last finding, but its relevance to Freudian thinking is far from clear.

Gleser and Sacks (1973) reported a further validational attempt in which the Defense Mechanisms Inventory was administered to 85 college students after they had been exposed to a conflict situation in which they were led to believe their scholastic ability had proved deficient. There were several measures included of the effects of this conflict on mood and estimates of self-worth. In general, subjects with a tendency to defend by Turning Against Self reacted to the conflict with self-depreciation, anxiety, and depression. In contrast, subjects with a tendency to defend by Reversal but not by Turning Against Others showed no decrease in self-worth or increase in anxiety and depression. But there were some sex differences in this study, and the results were far from conclusive. Clearly, the Defense Mechanisms Inventory will require more reliability and validational evidence before we can rest easy with adopting it as strong evidence for Freudian thinking.

The other test of defenses enjoying research attention of late is the *Repression-Sensitization Scale,* introduced by Byrne (1961b) and later revised (Byrne, Barry, and Nelson, 1963). Considerable research has been done with this scale, as indicated in several reviews (e.g., Byrne, 1964; Chabot, 1973). Originally devised to measure the same dimension on a paper and pencil test that is involved in perceptual defense and vigilance, the scale is best considered to incorporate several defenses at each of its two poles. The scale is constructed out of items from the Minnesota Multiphasic Personality Inventory, and has proven acceptable in internal consistency and stability.

Various studies (e.g., Altrocchi, Parsons, and Dickoff, 1960; Axtell and Cole, 1971; Bergonis, Lloyd, and Johansson, 1973; Byrne, Steinberg, and Schwartz, 1968; Merbaum, 1972; Pagano, 1973; Schill, 1969) have contributed construct validational evidence that repressors are different from sensitizers in theoretically interesting ways in such areas of functioning as self-ideal discrepancy, physical illness, free associative sex responses to double entendre words, effects of task familiarity on stress responses, and various cognitive skills. But some nagging problems have also emerged. For example, the high correlation between the Repression-Sensitization Scale and Welsh's anxiety factor on the Minnesota Multiphasic Personality Inventory (.97 for males; .96 for females) that has been reported by Gleser and Ihilevich (1969) raises serious question as to whether it is defenses or merely anxiety that is being measured. In addition, Chabot (1973) amasses evidence that there are a number of unresolved procedural and sampling problems surrounding the Repression-Sensitization Scale, and alerts us to equivocal areas, such as sex differences, in which available findings are anything but clear. It would be difficult at this time to argue persuasively that this scale provides strong empirical validation for Freudian theorizing.

Now we can leave Freud's position, and go on to other personologists. You should keep in mind that the studies we have covered tend to support Freudian theory in a general way, sometimes falling short of the comprehensiveness and incisiveness we should expect.

Murray's position

Murray (1938) pioneered the modern emphasis upon empirical measurement and validation of the concrete peripheral characteristics present in a peripheral theory of personality. He and a capable staff of personologists collected huge amounts of data relating to his list of needs (e.g., for achievement, affiliation, power, nurturance, succorance, change) on a small group of college males. Over a period of six months or so, these investigators employed all methods of measurement—self-description, fantasy, and behavior ratings—toward the end of understanding the peripheral personalities of these young men.

To read the results of this extraordinary undertaking today is to invite a mixture of awe at the pioneering zeal of this group and a definite sense of the unsophisticated manner in which the business of measurement actually went forward. Instead of ensuring sufficient objectivity to the measurement techniques that they could be used with high agreement by different investigators working independently, Murray instituted a diagnostic counsel. In this counsel, debate would ensue as to what was actually being observed in a subject, and finally, a conclusion would be reached by majority vote. Laudably democratic though this procedure is, it is not very objective in the scientific sense of different people being able to observe the same thing independently. It is very difficult for me to be critical, however, because I sincerely believe that Murray's approach was the most constructive thing that could be done at the time. The measurement of personality had not had sufficient time and experience to become sophisticated. Murray's procedures were brave beginnings, even if his findings cannot be taken as demonstrating the empirical existence and validity of his concepts. A gauge of his influence is that some of the techniques he and his colleagues invented, such as the *Thematic Apperception Test* (Murray, 1943) are still very much in use.

Another gauge of his influence is that his peripheral theory has had by far the greatest impact of any on the personologists whose major function it is to develop tests for assessing personality. Murray's list of needs has been a ready starting point for many investigators wanting to provide a comprehensive test of concrete peripheral characteristics. Dramatic though this fact is, one must be careful not to conclude in the absence of additional information that Murray's theorizing is necessarily more accurate to reality than that of other personologists. The popularity of his needs is probably as much as anything a function of their common-sense appeal and of Murray's care in trying to define them operationally. We must see how fruitful tests built on his needs are before concluding anything.

A recent test influenced by Murray's thinking is the *Activities Index* of Stern (1958). This text is composed of more than 300 items describing activities for which the person is supposed to indicate preference or dislike. Embedded in the test are 30 of Murray's needs, each measured by 10 of the items. Stern gathered the original items for the test on the basis of reading Murray's own descriptions of the needs, and used a number of procedures, including factor analysis to pare down the items to only those concerning each need which intercorrelated highly and were relatively separate from those relevant to other needs. The resulting need measures have adequate internal consistency and stability. It can therefore be said that most of the needs postulated by Murray in his peripheral theory of personality have some claim to empirical existence.

But this conclusion needs to be qualified in certain ways. First is the disconcerting fact that a number of the need measures correlate fairly highly with one another. This could call into question whether the needs postulated are really so different from each other. The second qualification involves the fact that Stern's test uses only self-description in the form of answers to questions. Although Murray has advocated the use of self-description in measuring needs, he has also insisted that relevant fantasy and even performance be also used in order to obtain the most accurate picture. Stern's decision to use only self-description reflects the test developer's bias that such information is more objective and quantifiable than is fantasy. If McClelland is right in presuming that self-description elicits schemata more than motives, then we would expect Stern's test to fail in that it reflects culturally appropriate images of the person more than is accurate to his true personal goals. Indeed, the current testing literature is replete with evidence that self-description used as a method of obtaining information about traits and motives suffers from the effects of what have been called response styles (e.g., Jackson & Messick, 1958). The most pervasive response style seems to be the tendency on the part of the test taker to respond to the items in socially desirable fashion (e.g., Edwards, 1957). There is no guarantee whatsoever that people taking Stern's test are responding in terms of their actual personal goals rather than their views of what goals it is proper and socially constructive to have.

Were the *Activities Index* the only empirical evidence of the tangible measurability of Murray's needs, we could not conclude strongly that there was evidence of their empirical reality. But there is another test based on his needs that, though also employing the self-description format, does so in a manner aimed at obviating the hazard of socially desirable responding. This test is the *Edwards Personal Preference Schedule* (Edwards, 1953). Edwards started with 15 needs drawn from Murray's list, and prepared sets of items whose content appeared to fit each of these needs. At first he presented these items to a group of college students in the same form used by Stern, namely, as descriptions of activities they were to indicate they liked or disliked. Being alert to the problem in assessing personal goals of the tendency to respond in socially desirable fashion, Edwards also had other people judge each of the items for its social desirability. He found an extremely high correlation (.87) between the frequency with which the college students indicated preference for items and their judged social desirability! As a result of this disturbing finding, Edwards adopted what is called the forced choice format for the presentation of items. In other words, he presented items not singly but in pairs, with care to ensuring that each item in a pair was similar in judged social desirability. Then respondents were asked to choose which item in each pair they preferred. The estimate of need strength gained through totaling the number of times items relevant to it were chosen, is presumably free of influence due to socially desirable responding. The resulting need scores were correlated with a separate scale, developed at another time, for purpose of measuring the strength of the tendency in people to respond in socially desirable fashion. The correlation between the need scores and socially desirable responding was quite low, indicating the success of Edwards' procedure.

Table 10–6 shows that the 15 need measures on this test have reasonable internal consistency (split-half correlations from .60 to .87), and stability (test-retest correlations from .74 to .88). Also, Table 10–7 shows that the intercorrelations of the need measures are satisfactorily low, the highest being .46 and the lowest close to zero. Later studies (e.g., Waters, 1967) have reported various stability and internal consistency estimates, but this is to be expected when samples and testing conditions vary. In particular, evidence has accumulated that the scale scores may vary with shifts in the instructions given subjects. This, of course, is to be expected, and is only a problem if too gross. But there is evidence in at least some studies (e.g., Weigel & Frazier, 1968) to indicate some stability of scores despite instructional changes. It may be reasonably

TABLE 10–6

Coefficients of internal consistency and stability for the PPS variables

	Variable	Internal consistency* r_{11}	Stability† r_{11}	Mean	SD
1.	Achievement	.74	.74	14.46	4.09
2.	Deference	.60	.78	12.02	3.68
3.	Order	.74	.87	11.31	4.45
4.	Exhibition	.61	.74	14.43	3.67
5.	Autonomy	.76	.83	13.62	4.48
6.	Affiliation	.70	.77	15.40	4.09
7.	Intraception	.79	.86	17.00	5.60
8.	Succorance	.76	.78	12.09	4.59
9.	Dominance	.81	.87	15.72	5.28
10.	Abasement	.84	.88	14.10	4.96
11.	Nurturance	.78	.79	14.04	4.78
12.	Change	.79	.83	16.17	4.88
13.	Endurance	.81	.86	12.52	5.11
14.	Heterosexuality	.87	.85	15.08	5.66
15.	Aggression	.84	.78	11.55	4.57
	Consistency Score		.78	11.59	1.78
	N	1,509		89	

* Split-half, based on 14 items against 14 items, corrected.
† Test and retest with one week interval. Means and standard deviations are for first testing.
Source: A. L. Edwards. "Edwards Personal Preference Schedule." New York: Psychol. Corp., 1953.

TABLE 10–7

Intercorrelations of the variables measured by the PPS (N = 1,509)

Variable	2. Def	3. Ord	4. Exh	5. Aut	6. Aff	7. Int	8. Suc	9. Dom	10. Aba	11. Nur	12. Chg	13. End	14. Het	15. Agg	Consistency score
1. Achievement	-.17	-.05	.03	.14	-.33	-.09	-.14	.19	-.28	-.30	-.14	.07	.02	.09	.10
2. Deference		.26	-.22	-.30	.08	.10	-.09	-.22	.16	.05	-.09	.22	-.28	-.31	-.12
3. Order			-.21	-.15	-.16	-.06	-.08	-.16	.02	-.16	-.18	.33	-.16	-.16	-.06
4. Exhibition				.09	-.08	-.22	-.02	.11	-.18	-.17	.12	-.27	.12	.11	.00
5. Autonomy					-.33	-.10	-.21	.07	-.26	-.36	.15	-.13	.09	.29	.11
6. Affiliation						-.01	.09	-.12	.09	.46	.06	-.15	-.21	-.33	-.04
7. Intraception							-.16'	-.12	-.01	.07	-.10	.03	-.19	-.20	.06
8. Succorance								-.22	.11	.16	-.18	-.31	.07	-.01	-.05
9. Dominance									-.34	-.20	-.11	-.16	.04	.21	.02
10. Abasement										.23	-.11	.07	-.29	-.25	-.05
11. Nurturance											-.12	-.12	-.21	-.33	.00
12. Change												-.14	-.07	-.08	.00
13. Endurance													-.27	-.22	-.06
14. Heterosexuality														.15	.01
15. Aggression															.05

Source: A. L. Edwards. "Edwards Personal Preference Schedule." New York: Psychol. Corp., 1953.

concluded, then, that there is empirical evidence in Edwards' test for the existence of many of Murray's concrete peripheral characteristics. It would still be valuable, however, to attempt measurement of the needs utilizing the person's fantasy. I say this not simply out of insistence that if Murray thought fantasy an important means of measuring his needs, that it should be tried. More importantly, it is apparently not entirely clear that Edwards' procedure avoided socially desirable responding completely. Anastasi (1961, pl. 516) raises the possibility that the social desirability of items changes when they are paired, and cites research actually indicating just this:

> Edwards, however, did not recheck the [social desirability] scale values of his statements when presented in pairs. Later research suggested that the [social desirability] values do change under these conditions. Not only are there significant differences in [social desirability] scale values of paired items, but a correlation of .88 was found between the redetermined scale values of paired items and their frequency of endorsement. It is also relevant to note that studies on faking indicate that scores on the [Edwards Personal Preference Schedule] *can* be deliberately altered to create more favorable impressions, especially for specific purposes. The latter possibility, of course, exists in any forced-choice test in which items were equated in terms of general social norms only. On the whole, it appears that the social desirability variable was not as fully controlled in the [Edwards Personal Preference Schedule] as had been anticipated.

Perhaps the best way of summarizing the attempts of Stern and Edwards to develop tests of peripheral personality utilizing Murray's list of needs is to say that especially with the corrections for socially desirable responding employed by Edwards, there is empirical evidence that entities having the content referred to by Murray do indeed exist in people. This conclusion is supported by a similar test devised by Jackson (1967) in order to be less vulnerable to response biases than the others. Whether these measured entities have the status of needs is still unclear. It is unclear not simply on the rational grounds suggested by McClelland, and partially agreed to by Murray, that motivational entities are best measured in fantasy productions, but also on the empirical grounds of the pervasive influence upon self-description of such response styles as socially desirable responding. From McClelland's point of view, the arousal of tendencies toward socially desirable responding by the testing procedure that requires respondents to answer questions about what they are like is very understandable, this procedure being best suited to the measurement of schemata. Therefore, no more precise conclusion is possible here than that there is empirical evidence for the existence of entities having the content specified by Murray, leaving open the matter of the kind of entities they may be.

Even though the operations employed in reaching measures of these entities is not as solidly in the spirit of Murray's theorizing as might be managed, it could still be that the entities are indeed primarily motivational in nature. And, in principle, one could garner additional information relevant to an empirical conclusion on this question of motivation by a vigorous attempt to determine the construct validity of the measures. Please note that this is like the third step of the ideal strategy suggested earlier. But we do not have much to go on in assessing construct validity. The manuals describing both the tests of Edwards and of Stern report such meager investigation of validity as to be literally inconsequential. It is true that since the publication of these tests, they have been used extensively in research. Rarely, however, has the aim of the research been to investigate the validity of the various measures. Rather, their validity has been more or less assumed, with the aim of the research banking on the adequate measurement of the range of needs specified on the test. For this reason, it is very difficult to determine the status of the various measures from the point of view of validity. Nonetheless, the weight of indirect evidence is sufficient to suggest the probable validity of at least some of the needs measured on the two tests.

In a representative example of a study (Bernardin & Jessor, 1957) concerning the *Edwards Personal Preference Schedule,* people were put through three experimental task situations requiring the explicit demonstration of dependent or independent behavior. As shown in Table 10–8, people who had scored high on the need for deference and low on the need for autonomy (called Dependents) showed more reliance on others for approval and for help than did people low on the need for deference and high on the need for autonomy (called Independents). No relationship was found, however, between these need measures and conformity to the opinions and demands of others. This finding suggests that the measures of needs for deference and autonomy on Edwards' test are sufficiently free of the influence of schemata to be interpretable as motivational in nature. As you can imagine, however, other conclusions are also possible, and hence, an airtight case cannot be made.

Recently, studies have been reported which attempt to compare the

TABLE 10–8
Differences between dependents and independents in both suggestion and corroboration scores

	Suggestion Score		*Corroboration Score*	
	Independents	*Dependents*	*Independents*	*Dependents*
Mean...............	.95	3.50	1.45	10.90
SD................	1.24	2.31	1.63	7.53
H value...........	12.42		22.98	
p level...........	<.01		<.01	

Source: A. C. Bernardin & R. A. Jessor. "A construct validation of the Edwards Personal Preference Schedule with respect to dependency." *J. consult. Psychol.*, 1957.

need scores obtained on the *Edwards Personal Preference Schedule* with other tests of the same needs. Poe (1969) administered to a sample of 132 male and female undergraduates an adjective checklist and both the standard form and a normative modification of the Edwards test. Following the validational criteria formulated by Campbell and Fiske (1959), Poe attempted to determine whether scores for a particular need agreed more closely across tests than with scores on other needs within tests. This joint criterion of so-called convergent and discriminant validation was satisfied to a minimal extent.

In a similar study, Megargee and Parker (1968) employed first one sample of 70 adolescent delinquents, and then another of 86 female Peace Corps trainees. It is of special interest that they compared Edwards's questionnaire test with ratings made of Thematic Apperception Test stories. In general, they found that the thematic apperception and questionnaire methods of measuring Murray's needs cannot be considered equivalent or parallel. They contend that "Investigators who study these variables using one of these tests as their operational definition should be cautious in generalizing the results to the construct as operationally defined by the other instrument." At first encounter, findings such as this may well produce skepticism as to the very existence of the needs Murray has postulated. And, insofar as he accepts that they should be measurable not only in fantasy but in self-description questionnaires as well, this skepticism is justified. But, as I will detail later, in a position like that of McClelland, which presents a strong theoretical rationale for fantasy being the only appropriate basis for assessing needs, the findings just mentioned represent little challenge. We shall have to consider once again in this chapter whether self-descriptive tests are measuring motivational entities.

Erikson's position

Erikson's theorizing has informed a fair amount of research in recent years. Most of it, however, is not really relevant here, for either of two reasons. In one instance, you find research concentrating on childhood and adolescence. While it is understandable that such research gets done, for much of Erikson's emphasis is on the early years of life, it is the period of adulthood that concerns us most here. The other kind of study, which is irrelevant, attempts to tie together a mass of findings by referring in some vague, *post hoc* fashion to Erikson's peripheral theorizing. This is a far cry from planning a study for the purpose of testing the empirical adequacy of his position. At the least, for a study to be valuable to us, it would have to try to measure the subject's status on the psychosocial stages of development, and use this information to understand his adult functioning. Such studies are few, compared to the many which make reference to Erikson in one manner or another.

Certainly, the studies discussed as relevant to the Freudian position on peripheral personality are also relevant here. To be sure, Erikson's theorizing is less biologically oriented, even for the childhood years. But the Freudian conceptualization of oral, anal, and phallic character types bears resemblance to the types covered by Erikson in the first three stages of man. Erikson's position, then, receives the same general but somewhat unincisive support that we found for Freud's position. But, Erikson's unique contribution to peripheral theorizing concerns adolescence and adulthood. Therefore, only if there is empirical support for these aspects of his position can we seriously say that fruitfulness has been demonstrated.

Of the few studies available, I will review several that are particularly sound and relevant. The first, done by Peck and Havighurst (1960), has the advantage of comprehensiveness. It involved following the character development of youngsters in the period from age 10 to age 17. The traits or groups of traits studied showed consistent development during this period such that the youngsters tended to keep their rank order in the group. This suggests that whatever determined the rank order in the first place must have occurred sometime before 10 years of age. Fortunately, parental behavior that might have set the youngster's traits had been examined three years before the beginning of the study. Meaningful relationships were obtained between themes of parental behavior and certain traits in the youngsters. Ego strength and moral stability in the youngsters were most closely related to mutual trust and consistency within the family. Superego strength was most highly related to parental consistency; friendliness to familial trust and democracy. A pattern of hostility and guilt in the youngsters was highly related to parental behaviors displaying severe discipline, lack of trust, and lack of democracy. Apparently, if a child receives warmth and love from his parents, and is both trusted and permitted to exercise his own processes of choice, he will appear more psychologically vigorous and affluent as a youngster than will be true if he experiences the opposite parental attitudes. This study suggests the empirical validity of Erikson's conceptualizing the first two stages of man as involving trust versus mistrust, and autonomy versus shame and doubt.

In contrast to this broad, somewhat vague study with many loose ends is one by Bronson (1959) which concerns itself with the period of adolescence designated by Erikson as relevant to the development of firm identity versus role diffusion. Bronson focused upon the attempt to determine whether a group of concrete peripheral characteristics, referring at one pole to a firm sense of identity and at the other to identity diffusion, had actual empirical existence. Starting with a sensitive reading of Erikson's (1956) descriptions of identity and diffusion, Bronson decided upon four such characteristics for measurement. They are (1) to be certain or uncertain that there is a relationship between one's past and current notions of oneself; (2) to show a low or high degree of internal tension or anxiety; (3) to be certain or uncertain about which are one's dominant personal characteristics; and (4) to be stable or fluctuating in one's feelings about oneself. Bronson correctly hypothesized that significant positive intercorrelation among these bipolar characteristics would constitute support for Erikson's conceptualization of the fifth stage of man (identity versus role diffusion).

The subjects were 46 college students, mainly female. Bronson measured the first two characteristics mentioned above through ratings made by investigators of the behavior of the subjects during a 20-minute interview. The investigators were three trained clinical psychologists, and the average of their ratings was used as the data. A self-descriptive procedure was used to measure the final two characteristics, with the procedure being repeated after a four-week interval in order that the estimate of stability or flux required in the fourth characteristic could be made. As can be seen in Table 10–9, the correlations among the four measures ranged from .47 to .71, and all were highly significant from a statistical point of view. Apparently, there are some adolescents who are anxious, do not perceive a relationship between who they are now and who they were before, are not sure what their dominant attributes really are, and change their minds about these matters as well. These people show identity diffusion. That some adolescents have a firm sense of identity is shown by the existence of a type with the opposite characteristics.

In another relevant study, Yufit (1969) attempted to determine whether the behavioral expressions of persons classifiable as intimate relaters were different from those classifiable as isolates. You will recall that intimacy versus isolation is the sixth of Erikson's eight ages of man. A large battery of paper and pencil tests plus interviews were collected

TABLE 10–9

Correlations among measures relating to aspects of identity diffusion

	1 *Continuity* *with past*	*2* *Freedom from* *anxiety*	*3* *Certainty of* *self-conception*
1. Continuity with the past (interview rating)...............	—		
2. Freedom from anxiety (inter- view rating)....................	.59†	—	
3. Certainty of self-conception (semantic differential measure)....	.71†	.47*	—
4. Temporal stability of self-rating (semantic differential measure)....	.53*	.47*	.54†

Note: N = 18 for the correlations involving the interview measures; N = 46 for the remaining value.

* $p < .05$, two-tailed test.
† $p < .01$, two-tailed test.

Source: G. W. Bronson. "Identity diffusion in late adolescents." *J. abnorm. soc. Psychol.*, 1959.

on 61 undergraduates, who were classified as "intimates," "isolates," or controls (i.e., neither one nor the other). Complex and sometimes intuitive scoring procedures were employed on interviews and other tests. Then the data were factor analyzed. The emerging factors tended to suggest the value of thinking of persons as "intimates" and "isolates" in understanding their behavior.

In an unusual study employing fairly rigorous methodology, Waterman, Buebel, and Waterman (1970) addressed themselves to Erikson's hypothesis that a positive outcome in any stage of development is rendered more likely by positive outcomes in earlier stages. In the first part of their study, Waterman et al., employed a questionnaire concerning whether one believes the events of one's life are determined personally or by the force of external circumstance (the *Internal-External Locus of Control Scale* of James, 1957) as an index of whether autonomy or shame and doubt had been the outcome of the second stage of development. They also used questionnaire methods to assess whether trust or distrust had taken place in the first stage. Their dependent variable was outcome in the identity versus role diffusion stage, something they also measured by questionnaire. As predicted, identity went along with internal locus of control (autonomy), and role diffusion with external locus of control (shame and doubt). But the hypothesized relationships linking identity with trust and role diffusion with distrust did not occur. In the second part of their study, these investigators employed a self-concept measure to test the predicted relationships mentioned above. This procedure produced more consistent support for Erikson's view. But it should be noted that, in this part of the study, one source of data was employed to measure several characteristics, raising the possibility that the relationships are somewhat spurious reflections of overlap of method.

Constantinople (1969) has developed a 60–item self-rating scale called the *Inventory of Psychosocial Development*. This scale is based methodologically on a previous technique offered by Wessman and Ricks (1966) and theoretically on Erikson's stages. Constantinople reported a median stability correlation of .70 on 150 subjects with a six-week interval between testings. Although reliability is by no means overwhelming, it is sufficient to entertain the notion that this scale measures successful and unsuccessful development at the stages of *trust v. mistrust, initiative v. guilty functioning, autonomy v. shame and doubt, industry v. inferiority, identification v. role diffusion,* and *intimacy v. isolation.* Information concerning the validity of this scale is developing slowly. In a particularly relevant study, Reimanis (1974) reasoned that unsuccessful resolution of conflicts in psychosocial development should give rise to feelings of anomie or social disorganization. To test this prediction, he administered both the Inventory of Psychosocial Development and a commonly used anomie scale to two samples (100 male veterans, and 141 male and female students). Table 10–10 shows the resulting correlations. As expected, unsuccessful psychosocial development tends to be associated with anomie, whereas successful psychosocial development tends not to be. These findings are similar to those of Constantinople (1969, 1970) who found successful development to be associated with happiness.

Marcia (1966) has elaborated Erikson's stage of ego identity v. role diffusion, which is certainly the most heavily emphasized period. According to Marcia, it is possible to distinguish no less than five orientations in Erikson's thinking about this period: *identity achievement,* persons who have experienced the crisis and are committed to an occupation and an ideology; *moratorium,* persons currently in the crisis with only vague commitments to occupation and ideology; *foreclosure,* persons who, while committed to an occupation and ideology, seem to have experienced no crisis, their commitments being largely parentally determined; *identity diffusion,* persons who may or may not have experienced the crisis, but who exhibit no commitment; and *alienated achievement,* persons who have experienced the crisis and exhibit no commitment but have a worked out ideology condemning the social system. Determination of a subject's identity status is made by rating his responses to a standardized interview according to rules provided by Marcia (1966). Interscorer agreement on ratings has hovered between 80 and 90 percent in several studies (e.g., Toder and Marcia, 1973; Orlofsky, Marcia, and Lesser, 1973). Apparently, no internal consistency or stability in-

TABLE 10–10

Correlations between anomie and the inventory of psychosocial development

	Srole scale measurement of anomie		
Inventory of psychosocial development item	*Veterans Administration members*	*College males*	*College females*
Basic trust	−.17	−.17	−.28*
Mistrust	.31*	.21	.25*
Initiative	−.08	−.05	−.36*
Guilt	.31*	.40*	.25*
Autonomy	−.14	.26	−.14
Shame and doubt	.28*	.40*	.13
Industry	−.17	.06	−.36*
Inferiority	.16	.44*	.29*
Identification	−.10	−.14	−.35*
Role diffusion	.24*	.43*	.22*
Intimacy	−.06	−.24	−.28*
Isolation	.42*	.29*	.16

Note. Veterans Administration members $N = 74$, college males $N = 55$, college females $N = 86$.
* $p < .05$.
Source: Adapted from G. Reimanis, "Psychological Development." *J. pers. soc. Psychol.,* 1974.

formation is available, so we cannot be sure that the statuses have solid empirical support.

Orlofsky et al. (1973) studied the relationship of the various identity statuses described above to measures of intimacy, isolation, social desirability, affiliation, and heterosexuality, in an attempt to determine whether difficulties in identity would jeopardize later development. As expected from Erikson's theorizing, *foreclosure* and *identity diffusion* subjects had the most superficial and stereotyped interpersonal relationships. *Moratorium* subjects were the most variable. And whereas *identity achievement* subjects were characterized by social intimacy rather than isolation, it was actually the *alienated achievement* subjects who were most marked in this regard. The last finding is a bit surprising, but the investigators reasoned that the capability of *alienated achievement* subjects indicates that they have foregone the identity crisis in favor of the intimacy crisis. This is an intriguing notion, but not one readily derivable from Erikson's present theorizing.

Toder and Marcia (1973) studied the role of identity status in the response to conformity pressure by placing 64 college females into a task situation where confederates of the researchers would attempt to mislead the subjects in the judgments they were asked to make. Females with identity statuses that might be regarded as stable (*achievement* and *foreclosure*) conformed to the pressure less than those with unstable statuses (*moratorium* and *diffusion*). While not unequivocally supportive of Eriksonian thinking, this study and the previous one represent a beginning that bears further attention.

The studies I have reviewed suggest the fruitfulness of Erikson's peripheral theorizing. But more carefully planned work will have to be conducted before the position can be comprehensively evaluated from an empirical standpoint. I might mention that some investigators (e.g., Neugarten, 1964), especially concerned with the aging process, believe Erikson's emphasis upon such conflicts of maturity as ego integrity versus despair to be very helpful in ordering research findings dealing with the problems of old people. There are currently several studies charting the increase in depression as age advances (e.g., Brissette, 1967; Grant, 1969; Lehr & Rudinger, 1969; Zung, 1967), and the possibility that a commitment to useful work may stem the tide (e.g., Rybak, Sadnavitch, & Mason, 1968). In general, however, these studies do not attempt to measure ego integrity versus despair, so much as use it as an explanatory construct.

Rank's position

Although Rank's peripheral personality types are clearly delineated, his theorizing has hardly provoked much research. Of all the professionals for whom personality theory is important, it is psychologists who have the sophistication and inclination to conduct rigorous empirical research on a regular basis. And among psychologists, Rank's theorizing has never become popular. I am frankly unable to understand why this is so. Nonetheless, it is by no means true that Rank's position has been insufficiently pruned and developed to warrant the attempt at empirical analysis. Far from it.

There is one large-scale research program that indirectly suggests the empirical promise of Rank's peripheral theorizing. MacKinnon (1965) has conducted a complicated study of creativity in architects. Admittedly at a loss for a theory which would pull together his numerous findings in some coherent fashion, MacKinnon rediscovered Rank and found him very useful. MacKinnon feels that his group of creative architects displays the acceptance of their own individuality coupled with the interest in and involvement with other people that Rank considered so characteristic of the type he called the artist. MacKinnon's ordinary achitects seemed much like Rank's common man, with his emphasis upon conformity and mediocrity. Finally, MacKinnon even found an intermediate group of respected, productive, but not highly creative architects that resembled Rank's descriptions of the neurotic man, replete with a commitment to his own individuality at the same time that he is unwilling to risk rejection.

Recently, Helson (1973a; 1973b) has reported parallel studies focusing on the personalities of male and female creative writers. Utilizing interviews with the writers, and various ratings of their works, she abstracted through cluster analysis personality types reminiscent of Rank's artist, neurotic, and average person. The most creative of the writers tended to display the artist's temperament and life-style.

There are also a few studies attempting to evaluate Bakan's constructs of agency and communion. Agency is sufficiently similar to the Rankian fear of death, and communion to fear of life, that these studies are of interest here. In one of them, Brown and Marks (1969) administered a questionnaire concerning these two tendencies to 150 maladjusted subjects and 150 normal subjects, with the intent of determining whether unmitigated agency was higher in the former group, as Bakan would expect. The results provided some support for this expectation.

Carlson (1971a) studied sex differences in agency and communion in two ways. The first way involved obtaining, from 18 male and 23 female undergraduate subjects, descriptions of seven remembered instances of intense emotion considered to be of importance to them. The instances were rated by judges to be agentic, communal, or mixed, and the interscorer agreement was a high 93 percent. As Bakan would expect, 60 percent of male responses were coded agentic, as compared with only 40 percent of female responses. Also, when each subject was classified as either agentic or communal on the basis of the predominance of his responses, 10 of the 14 males emerged as agentic, as compared with only

5 of the 20 females (this finding achieved statistical significance). It was also possible to determine whether "unmitigated agency" represents an undesirable thing (as Bakan contends) by determining whether agentic responses tended to be unpleasant emotions (e.g., fear, anger), whereas communal responses tended to be pleasant emotions (e.g., joy, love). The results supported this contention.

Carlson's second procedure was a bibliographic study, in which she employed data already collected by others for other purposes. She looked at 100 studies in which differences between males and females could have been found, with a view toward determining whether such differences conformed with Bakan's general views on agency and communion. Although his results overwhelmingly support those views, they must be taken with a grain of salt. When, for example, studies show that females are more accepting, cooperative, and emotionally expressive than males, this is taken as evidence for greater communion in females. But, if Bakan's concepts are to have any value, they must be *explanations* of such observations, not merely tacked on as an afterthought. Carlson's second procedure is dangerous insofar as it may lull us into believing that notions of agency and communion have been precisely, and fruitfully demonstrated when all that has happened is that already recognized sex differences have been pointed to once again.

There is very little else by way of rigorous research that is sufficiently relevant to Rankian thought to be mentioned here. And what has been reviewed tends either to end by recognizing the utility of Rank's conception of types rather than beginning to test it, or to involve another though admittedly related theorist. It is premature, therefore, to evaluate Rank's peripheral theorizing empirically, though there are some interesting leads to be followed.

Jung's position

Believers in Jung's theory do not themselves seem to do much research. But there have been intriguing studies performed by others. Notable among them is Stephenson's (1950), which considered not only extroversion versus introversion and the thinking, feeling, sensing and intuiting modes, but consciousness versus unconsciousness of these characteristics as well. He considered the 16 combinations of these aspects of personality that would be of interest to Jung (e.g., conscious-thinking introvert, unconscious-intuitive extrovert), and set about finding descriptions of them in that theorist's writings. He selected five descriptive sentences for each of the 16 combinations. This led to a pool of 20 descriptive sentences for each of the modes, 40 for each level of consciousness, and 40 for each of introversion and extroversion. This approach is of special interest because it employs a theorist's own words in measuring the peripheral considerations he is defining.

Armed with these descriptive sentences, how does one measure a subject's peripheral personality? Stephenson had each descriptive sentence written on a card, and asked subjects to determine for each statement whether it applied to him (1) very definitely, (2) not at all, or (3) somewhere in between. The subject does this by sorting the cards into the three relevant piles. This technique came to be known as the *Q-sort*. When the subject is done, it is possible to determine, by counting the sorted cards, how much he is introverted, or extroverted, or conscious, or thinking, and so forth. The Q-sort procedure is extremely flexible in that not only is it possible for a subject to describe himself, but he can be instructed to describe others as well.

Stephenson chose for study Jung's contention that differences in personality type cause misunderstandings among persons. For data, Stephenson described himself by a Q-sort, and then had several judges supposedly familiar with him describe him by the same procedure. In addition, the judges also described themselves. By Stephenson's own Q-sort, he is an extrovert. Five of the judges were introverts (by their self-sort), and their Q-sort of him correlated with his own .46, .45, .61, .59, and .61, for an average of .54. Two of the judges were extroverts, and their Q-sorts of him correlated with his own only .47 and .40, for an average of .44. Contrary to Jung's expectation, the extroverts were certainly not superior in perceiving a fellow extrovert. This conclusion is strengthened by evidence that the extroverted judges were drawing on their own personality characteristics to a much greater degree than the introverts in attempting to describe Stephenson. Correlations between judges' self-sorts and their sorts of Stephenson were, on the average, .23 for the introverts and .50 for the extroverts. Unfortunately, this study does not seem to have been followed up, and it employed a very small sample. Nonetheless, it does raise questions as to whether it is personality types which differ that misunderstand each other.

Actually, the introversion-extroversion dimension has led to considerable research, but with neither the procedure nor the hypothesis presented above. The work I shall now describe was inspired by the eminent English psychologist, Hans Eysenck (1947), whose personality questionnaire, called the *Maudsley Personality Inventory*, was devised to measure not only introversion-extroversion, but neuroticism as well. Many of the studies relevant to the Jungian types were actually done by followers of Eysenck. In addition, Raymond Cattell (Cattell & Stice, 1957), in his *16 Personality Factor Questionnaire* (mentioned earlier), found evidence for a first-order factor of introversion-extroversion, and a second-order factor which he thought even closer to what Jung had in mind. The studies I will review have, in the main, employed one or the other of these measures.

First, let us consider works directed toward the adequacy of these measures. Marshall (1967), though he reports no new data of his own, cites existing evidence for the validity of Cattell's first- and second-order factors of introversion-extroversion as measures of Jung's distinction of the same name. Once this correspondence is established, the construct validation work on Cattell's factors is relevant to Jung's theory as well. It has been found that, on the average (Cattell, 1957), introversion is high among researchers, artists, and planning executives, as well as in creative workers in both art and science. In contrast, extroversion is high in mechanical occupations (e.g., engineers) and those requiring alertness (e.g., cooks, firemen). Among teamsters, those high in introversion are accident-prone. Introversion is also slightly correlated with certain psychopathological symptoms, particularly depressive reactions. Finally, women are higher than men in introversion, though there is no change in the average value of this characteristic over the age range from 16 to 60 years. As you would expect, the second-order factor of introversion-extroversion operates similarly to the first-order factor.

It has also not escaped investigators that there might well be some relationship between the introversion-extroversion scales offered by Cattell and by Eysenck. Crookes and Pearson (1970) compared scores on the two procedures obtained from 60 maladjusted subjects. Correlations between the separate measures of introversion-extroversion "are all very similar and quite substantial."

Several normative studies suggest that more needs to be known about the meaning of the questions and testing situations used for both these tests. For example, McQuaid (1967) reports that on the basis of a sample of 1,733 Scottish subjects compared with available U.S. norms for Cattell's measure, that there is a definite trend toward greater extroversion among Americans. Both Salas (1967) and Skinner, Howarth, and Browne (1970) report that Eysenck's measure of introversion-extroversion can be shifted by instructional set. When subjects are asked to simulate a "nice personality," extroversion scores go up, and the opposite is true when they are asked to fake being "bad." It is at present difficult to determine how much of a problem is involved.

Eysenck's measure does seem to have some validity in terms of the self-perceptions of subjects. Kramer (1969) administered the measure to 242 undergraduates, who had previously rated themselves for (1) how extroverted they felt they really were, (2) how extroverted they felt they appeared to others, and (3) the ideal amount of extroversion one should have. The first two ratings correlated with Eysenck's measure of extroversion .46 and .48, respectively. The 243 undergraduates used by Harrison and McLaughlin (1969) first took Eysenck's measure and then were read descriptions of the typical introvert and extrovert. Following this, they rated themselves on these two dimensions. Introversion-extroversion scores correlated .72 with the self-ratings of the same characteristics. It would seem that measures like that of Eysenck and, for that matter, Cattell, provide convenient ways of determining a person's level of introversion and extroversion.

The remaining studies to be discussed here concern the relationship between extroversion-introversion and various behaviors other than self-rating. As Carrigan (1960) has indicated, the body of research involved has produced ambiguous and even contradictory results over the last 30 years. Some of this may be a function of the extreme generality of the theorizing behind introversion-extroversion. This generality has permitted investigators to work with particular corners of the theorizing which may not coincide with what other investigators are doing. But, in addition, it may be that other variables moderate the effect of introversion-extroversion such that its relationship to behavior is only clear when they are controlled. Wallich and Gahm (1960) introduced the use of moderator variables to good advantage, and their approach has been adopted by some investigators working with introversion-extroversion.

Taft (1967) attempted to determine the effects of introversion-extroversion on the expressive behavior involved in writing. He used 86 undergraduates who took Eysenck's test and also gave a sample of handwriting. It was found that extroverts wrote either larger or smaller than introverts, but that in order to understand whether it would be larger or smaller, one had to take anxiety or neuroticism level into account. Extroverts low in neuroticism wrote largest, whereas extroverts high in neuroticism wrote smallest.

Some studies bear on the affiliative behavior of introverts and extroverts. On the basis of Jung's theorizing, Bieler (1966) hypothesized that extroverted persons should prefer paintings in which humans are present, whereas introverts should prefer those without humans. He too employed Eysenck's test, and he too discovered that in order to make sense out of his data, it was necessary to use anxiety or neuroticism level as a moderator variable. He found that extroverts low in neuroticism do indeed prefer paintings including people, and introverts low in neuroticism prefer paintings devoid of people. But there was no difference between highly neurotic introverts or extroverts.

Shapiro and Alexander (1969) have done a careful investigation following Bieler's lead. They chose another measure of introversion-extroversion, the *Briggs-Myers Type Indicator* (Myers, 1962), a questionnaire specially devised to yield information not only on Jung's introversion-extroversion dimension, but on the four modes of thought as well. The final sample was 130 undergraduates, all of whom not only took the Briggs-Myers Type Indicator but also were led to believe that they were to receive electric shocks. Anxiety was strongly aroused in some subjects, who expected the shocks to be painful, and only minimally aroused in others, who were told that the shocks would be quite mild. They were also told that there would be a brief waiting period before the shocks, during which they could elect to either talk with other subjects or remain alone. Choosing to be with others was considered evidence of an affiliative behavior. Several checks on the effectiveness of the procedure for arousing anxiety, carried out following the experiment, yielded positive results. The principal results concerning the effects of introversion and extroversion on affiliative behavior moderated by anxiety appear in Table 10–11. As you can see, highly anxious extroverts showed the strongest affiliation tendencies, whereas highly anxious introverts showed the weakest affiliation tendencies. This difference was statistically significant. But the difference between introverts and extroverts low in anxiety was not large enough to achieve significance. The last two studies taken together suggest that the potential differences between introverts and extroverts in affiliative behavior are only actualized in anxiety-producing circumstances or when neuroticism exists. Perhaps neuroticism is a chronic state of anxiety.

Before turning to other matters, I should mention a group of studies exploring the origins of introversion-extroversion. These studies employ one or more of the measuring instruments for introversion-extroversion mentioned above, and focus either upon parent-child relations or heredity. The most consistent conclusion is that accepting, loving, positive parents frequently have extroverted children, whereas rejecting, cold, negative parents have introverted children (see Siegelman, 1968). Studies attempting to determine the relationship between birth order and introversion-extroversion differences yield contradictory results (see Siegelman, 1968). Finally, there seems clear evidence of hereditary differences in introversion-extroversion from studies of identical and fraternal twins, and these differences have been shown to persist over considerable periods of time (see Siegelman, 1968). As Jung's position concerning the origins of introversion-extroversion is not clear, it is difficult to determine what role these studies should have in evaluating his theory.

Carlson and Levy (1973) have reported an intriguing set of studies in which predictions concern the effect of Jungian personality types on

TABLE 10–11

Relation of induced anxiety and E-I to intensity of affiliation for males

	I		*E*	
	Mean	*N*	*Mean*	*N*
High anxiety......	−4.80	(25)	4.42	(21)
Low anxiety......	3.36	(13)	1.18	(11)

Interaction: (Anxiety x *EI*)F = 4.9, df = 1, 62; p = .03

Note. The higher the score, the higher the affiliation tendency. Isolation scores subtracted from affiliation scores for intensity. Means collapsed across birth order.

Source: K. J. Shapiro and I. E. Alexander. "Extroversion-introversion, affiliation, and anxiety." *J. Pers.* 1969.

memory, social perception, and social action. The Myers-Briggs Type Indicator was taken by all the female college students serving as subjects. As predicted, the results of the first study showed that introverted-thinking types performed best on a memory task involving impersonal stimuli (numbers), whereas extraverted-feeling types performed best when the stimuli were social and emotionally-toned (faces in various expressions). The second study replicated the first, utilizing a task that was comparable in structure for both types of subjects. The task in the third study was to interpret (rather than merely remember) emotions from facial expressions. A series of pictures of the same person, differing in emotional expression, were shown to subjects (the emotional expressions had previously been labeled with a high level of agreement by 100 judges). Results showed that intuitive perceptive types were significantly more accurate in interpreting emotional expressions than were sensing judging types, a finding predicted by Jung. In the final study, the predicted tendency for social service volunteers to be extroverted intuitive types was confirmed by comparing the Myers-Briggs Type Indicator scores of such volunteers with a control group.

The research discussed in this section provides general support for the Jungian emphasis upon introversion-extroversion, which seems a seminal dimension for understanding human behavior. But I must caution you, because there are many more studies yielding negative or conflicting results than could be mentioned here. The studies reported by Carlson and Levy (1973) represent an extremely important direction for research to take. It is through such an emphasis upon the Jungian types (not only introversion-extroversion but also the modes of thinking, feeling, sensing and intuiting) that precision in evaluating Jungian peripheral theorizing will be achieved.

Rogers' position

Although Rogers' position on the periphery of personality is hardly elaborate, it does have some fairly definite empirical implications. In order to see this, you should recall that the fully functioning person has five groupings of concrete peripheral characteristics referred to as *openness to experience* (including emotionality and reflectiveness), *existential living* (including flexibility, adaptability, spontaneity, and inductive thinking), *organismic trusting* (including congruence between what you believe yourself to be and what you believe to be worthy), *experiential freedom* (a sense of free will and personal control over life), and *creativity* (a penchant for producing new things). The groupings of concrete peripheral characteristics comprising the maladjusted person are the opposite of these, namely, *defensiveness, living according to a preconceived plan, disregard of organism, feelings of being manipulated,* and *conformity*. There are two ways in which empirical study could permit evaluation of this theorizing. Study could focus upon whether or not the concrete peripheral characteristics postulated for each personality type really do show evidence of covarying. Study could also focus upon one or more of the postulated characteristics, with the aim of determining whether they are associated with successful living, if they are part of the fully functioning type, or unsuccessful living, if they are part of the maladjusted type.

Although there is much research that seems from its topic as if it should be relevant to the second focus, little of it has actually been done with particular Rogerian emphases in mind. What I cover here will be selected so as to be as close to his emphases as possible. Needless to say, however, some research mentioned elsewhere because it seems to fit there best, might also be construed as lending some general support to Rogerian emphases. This will be true of many of the fulfillment positions.

In a study done to evaluate Rogerian theory directly, Pearson (1969; 1974) concerned herself with the existence and interrelationship of openness to experience and organismic valuing as concrete peripheral characteristics. Each characteristic was conceptualized as comprising several parts. The parts or phases of openness to experience were considered to be (1) attention, or symbolizing the recognition of affective cues in a significant event, (2) reaction, or symbolizing the personal impact or significance of the event, and (3) exploration, or differentiating and symbolizing the personal impact or significance of the event. These phases were measured by paper and pencil performance tests (not questionnaires), carefully developed, and with adequate reliability. The phases of organismic valuing were construed as (1) information collection, relevant to eventual decision; (2) information appraisal; (3) decision making, or choosing among formulated alternatives; and (4) decision implementation. These phases were measured by three paper and pencil tests, two of performance and one a questionnaire on decision making. Once again, these measures were carefully devised and showed adequate reliability. The scores obtained from 90 male and female undergraduates showed that the various phases of each characteristic did intercorrelate, indicating support for their existence. But contrary to what Rogerians would expect, openness to experience and organismic trusting scores did not correlate. This rigorously done study suggests that the various concrete peripheral characteristics postulated by Rogers do not organize themselves neatly into his two personality types. This may even provide a basis for considering the existence of subtypes, thereby rendering his formal theorizing more capable of dealing with individuality (see Chapter 7).

There have been other attempts to develop measures of openness to experience as well. Tittler (1974) has offered a 38-item questionnaire, with the item content drawn from encounter and sensitivity group protocols. Scores on these items from 105 undergraduates were subjected to factor analysis. The result was 9 openness to experience factors, 4 of which seemed to have construct validity in the sense of negative correlations with measures of dogmatism and conventionality. In a similar approach, Coan (1972) administered theoretically-relevant questionnaire items to 383 college students and factor analysed the resulting scores. Sixteen factors resulted, many of which seemed reasonably valid on the basis of correlations between them and a battery of personality tests. In an attempt at cross-validation, Coan repeated this study on 219 college students, using a combination of original and fresh items. The end result is an openness to experience instrument containing 83 items, which yields 7 factors corresponding very closely to the original 16. This instrument, called the *Experience Inventory*, contains scales concerning (1) aesthetic sensitivity, (2) openness to hypothetical ideas, (3) constructive utilization of fantasy, (4) openness to unconventional views of reality, (5) indulgence in fantasy, (6) unusual perceptions and associations, and (7) deliberate and systematic thought. Although it is too early in our empirical knowledge of these measures to be anything like sure that they are reliable and valid indicators of the Rogerian concept of openness to experience, their emergence signifies growing interest in this concept.

In a more general vein, Rogers contends that for the fully functioning person, the self-concept undergoes continual change and has distinct dimensions or parts, whereas the self-concept of the maladjusted person is just the opposite. There are a few studies indicating that the self-concept does not undergo major changes (e.g., Block, 1962; Havener & Izard, 1962), but disagreeing as to whether self-consistency is a positive or negative indicator of effective adjustment. Concerning the possible dimensionality of the self-concept, Akeret (1959) provides evidence that it includes at least four major divisions, defined by academic, interpersonal, sexual, and emotional content. He finds that these four dimensions are not highly intercorrelated. The trouble with this study is that it does not bear on Rogers' contention that the self-concept is unitary only in the maladjusted person. Although the studies mentioned in this paragraph have the ring of relevance to Rogers' theory, they are actually not very helpful in evaluating that position.

The aspect of fully functioningness that has received extensive research attention is that of organismic trusting. According to Rogers, a fully functioning person will have faith in his organism, in the intuitive, even impulsive urges to action he experiences, because he will not have developed the conditions of worth that could dictate which aspects of him are valuable and which are to be shunned. In contrast, the maladjusted person lives a life controlled so as to pass the muster imposed by his conditions of worth. The operational clue to understanding the research effort concerning these matters is that in organismic trusting, there would be little difference between how the person described himself and what he would like to be, whereas the difference between these two frames of reference would be great for the person with conditions of worth. Virtually all the studies I will review below concern the magnitude of the difference between descriptions of the perceived self and the ideal self. Moreover, the typical means of measuring the so-called self-ideal discrepancy is to present the subject with a list of statements taken from actual verbalizations made by patients in Rogerian therapy, and to ask him to sort them into a set number of categories running from very inaccurate to very accurate as descriptions of him. Then he sorts the very same group of statements into categories running from very inaccurate to very accurate as expressions of his ideals for himself. As you may recognize, this is a variant on the Q-sort technique (Stephenson, 1953) described earlier, which yields information that can be factor analyzed to produce a quantitative index of the discrepancy between the perceived and ideal selves. This operationalization of organismic trusting and conditions of worth is very much in the spirit of Rogers' theory.

The first and most widely quoted study employing the self-ideal discrepancy measure is that of Butler and Haigh (1954). They measured self-ideal discrepancy in a group of patients both before and after receiving therapy, and also at a number of follow-up times. On the average, the size of the discrepancy decreased over time. Matched control groups started out with a smaller discrepancy, but did not decrease as time went by. The decrease in discrepancy shown by the patient group was considerable, and for the most part, involved a movement of the self-description toward the ideal description. These results are presented in detail in Tables 10–12 and 10–13. It is not clear that the findings support Rogers' viewpoint. Certainly, the closer the person is to fully functioningness, the smaller should be the discrepancy between self and ideal. To be sure, psychotherapy should bring people nearer to fully functioningness. But statements of ideals are operational representations of conditions of worth, and surely, the function of therapy should be to remove these aspects of maladjustment. Ideals would be considered beneficial from the standpoint of a perfection theory, but not an actualization theory. In this context, it is unfortunate for the Rogerian position that Butler and Haigh found the reduction in self-ideal discrepancy occurring as a function of therapy to be brought about primarily by a movement of self-description toward ideals. My interpretation of the results of this study as not really consistent with Rogerian theory is bolstered by the report that the ideal descriptions tended to be fairly uniform, indicating a shared cultural context. Ideal descriptions seem the stuff of conditions of worth, i.e., socially imposed beliefs as to what is important.

The difficulty I have mentioned has led to a modified Rogerian view

TABLE 10–12

Self-ideal correlations in the client group

Client	Pre-counseling r	Post-counseling r	Follow-up r
Oak.	.21	.69	.71
Babi.	.05	.54	.45
Bacc.	−.31	.04	−.19
Bame.	.14	.61	.61
Bana.	−.38	.36	.44
Barr.	−.34	−.13	.02
Bayu.	−.47	−.04	.42
Bebb.	.06	.26	.21
Beda.	.59	.80	.69
Beel.	.28	.52	−.04
Beke.	.27	.69	−.56
Bene.	.38	.80	.78
Benz.	−.30	−.04	.39
Beri.	.33	.43	.64
Beso.	.32	.41	.47
Bett.	−.37	.39	.61
Bico.	−.11	.51	.72
Bifu.	−.12	−.17	−.26
Bime.	−.33	.05	.00
Bina.	−.30	.59	.71
Bink.	−.08	.30	−.20
Bira	.26	−.08	−.16
Bixy.	−.39	−.39	.05
Blen.	.23	.33	−.36
Bajo.	.16	.29	.47
Mean z.	−.01	.36	.32
Corresponding r.	−.01	.34	.31

Source: J. M. Butler, & G. V. Haigh. "Changes in the relation between self-concepts and ideal-concepts consequent upon client-centered counseling." In C. R. Rogers and R. F. Dymond (eds.), *Psychotherapy and personality change.* Chicago: Univer. of Chicago Press, 1954.

concerning self-ideal discrepancy. Some Rogerians (see Shlien, 1962) have considered large discrepancies to represent poor adjustment, and moderate discrepancies to reflect vigorous functioning. And extremely small discrepancies are suspected to be defensive statements made by maladjusted people (Chodorkoff, 1954a, 1954b). The thinking behind such statements is that a very large self-ideal discrepancy can only come about if the self-description is viciously critical, and a very small self-ideal discrepancy requires that the person be twisting his view of himself to conform to what is socially desirable. Perhaps both large and small discrepancies signify strong conditions of worth. Then only moderate self-ideal discrepancies would signify the absence of maladjustment.

Of direct importance to the empirical evaluation of this modified Rogerian viewpoint are the studies determining the relationship between self-ideal discrepancy and general adjustment and happiness. Brophy

TABLE 10–13

Self-ideal correlations in the control group

Client	Pre-counseling r	Follow-up r
Aban.....................	.80	.50
Abor.....................	.00	.30
Acro.....................	.86	.89
Agaz.....................	.75	.83
Akim.....................	.84	.86
Akor.....................	.48	−.03
Ajil.....................	.49	.45
Afit.....................	.73	.71
Abul.....................	.58	.77
Adis.....................	.42	.65
Abri.....................	.35	.30
Abbe.....................	.35	.36
Acme.....................	.80	.65
Abco.....................	.65	.76
Abet.....................	−.01	.43
Adir.....................	.30	.07
Mean z..................	.66	.68
Corresponding r..........	.58	.59

Source: J. M. Butler & G. V. Haigh. "Changes in the relation between self-concepts and ideal-concepts consequent upon client-centered counseling." In C. R. Rogers and R. F. Dymond (eds.), *Psychotherapy and personality change.* Chicago: Univ. of Chicago Press, 1954.

(1959) collected from 81 female nurses self-reports of general satisfaction, vocational satisfaction, adjustment and values, and occupational and life roles. The results suggest that congruence between perceived and ideal selves is necessary for general happiness and for satisfaction in specific life areas. Turner and Vanderlippe (1958) obtained a broad range of information relating to effectiveness and satisfaction with life from 175 college students on whom they also had self-ideal descriptions. The range of information obtained included measures of general health, extracurricular participation, sociometric indices, scholastic adjustment, and a test of temperament. Subjects with low self-ideal discrepancy needed fewer days in the hospital, and less frequent visits to the clinic. Further, the lower the self-ideal discrepancy, the greater the tendency to be preferred as a companion. Finally, the results of the temperament test, which are shown in Table 10–14, indicate that people with low self-ideal discrepancy tend toward general activity, ascendance, sociability, emotional stability, and thoughtfulness. The authors (Turner & Vanderlippe, 1958) conclude that

> The emergent composite picture of the college student high in self-ideal congruence (as contrasted with the student low in self-ideal congruence) is that of one who participates more in extracurricular activities, has a higher scholastic average, is given higher sociometric ratings by his

TABLE 10–14

Correlations between self-ideal congruence
expressed as Z values and traits measured by the
Guilford-Zimmerman Temperament Survey

Trait	Correlation with self-ideal congruence
1. General activity	.50*
2. Restraint	−.10
3. Ascendance	.58*
4. Sociability	.36*
5. Emotional stability	.36*
6. Objectivity	−.03
7. Friendliness	−.16
8. Thoughtfulness	.41*
9. Personal relations	−.25
10. Masculinity	.10

* Significant at the .01 level.
Source: R. H. Turner, & R. H. Vanderlippe, "Self-ideal congruence as an index of adjustment." *J. abnorm. soc. Psychol.*, 1958.

fellow students, and receives higher adjustment ratings on . . . certain traits.

A similar picture is presented by Rosenberg (1962) in a study relating self-ideal discrepancy to the various scales of the California Personality Inventory. This personality test includes such variables as sociability, dominance, flexibility, and achievement. Rosenberg found that the greater the self-ideal discrepancy, the lower the score on 15 of the 18 variables of this personality test. What this means is that people with large self-ideal discrepancies are generally inept in the kinds of interests and capabilities relevant to successful living. A contribution to the merging picture is made by studies concerning the tendency to agree with statements regardless of their content. This acquiescent response style is most marked in people having a large self-ideal discrepancy (Murstein, 1961). As another study (Schulberg, 1961) suggests that acquiescent responding occurs in people who seem to be smiling on the outside while jeering on the inside, we can take Murstein's findings as indicating yet another dimension of the ineptitude for living that accompanies a large self-ideal discrepancy. Similarly, Mahoney and Hartnett (1973) found that male and female subjects high on a self-actualization measure had much smaller self-ideal discrepancies than did subjects low in self-actualization. All in all, the modified Rogerian notion that not only large, but also small, self-ideal discrepancies would be indicative of maladjustment rather than fully functioningness does not seem to have empirical support.

There is a final group of studies stemming from another implication of the notion of organismic trusting. According to Rogers, if one has accepted oneself, i.e., if the self-ideal discrepancy is small, then one will also accept, respect, and value other people. As you will recall from Chapter 3, this expectation reflects the assumption made by actualization theorists that there is nothing in the basic nature of man that is necessarily selfish and hostile. In this assumption, actualization theories are very different from psychosocial conflict theories. Suinn (1961) proceeded to test whether male high school seniors who accepted themselves would show a generalized acceptance of their fathers and male teachers. On a set of adjectives, his subjects described their perceived and ideal selves, perceived and ideal fathers, and perceived and ideal male teachers. Suinn found that the smaller the self-ideal discrepancy, the smaller the father-ideal and teacher-ideal discrepancies. This supports the contention that if you accept yourself you also accept other people.

Medinnus and Curtis (1963) studied the relationship between self-acceptance and child-acceptance in mothers. Their 56 mothers filled out a questionnaire and a semantic differential scale, each of which yielded a measure of the degree to which self and ideal were different. There was also a semantic differential measure of the general degree to which their children were accepted by them. Medinnus and Curtis found that the two measures of self-acceptance intercorrelated, as you would expect, and that both of them were positively related to the measure of child acceptance. So, not only do male high school students who accept themselves accept their fathers and male teachers, but also mothers who accept themselves accept their children. The relevant literature includes other studies supporting the notion that self-acceptance occurs in the context of acceptance of others (e.g., Berger, 1953, 1955; Rosenman, 1955; Sheerer, 1949; Stock, 1949). Even though some of these studies are methodologically less relevant to the Rogerian frame of reference, they yielded results similar to the previously detailed studies. The substantial evidence that people who accept themselves also accept others supports not only Rogerian theory, but that of Maslow, Fromm, and existential psychology as well. Of course, it is possible that the tendency to respond in socially desirable fashion may have contaminated the studies just considered, thereby weakening our conclusion.

Another Rogerian research theme involves the *Experiencing Scale*, developed by Gendlin and Tomlinson (1967). Experiencing is described as ". . . the quality of an individual's experiencing of himself, the extent to which his ongoing, bodily, felt flow of experiencing is the basic datum of his awareness and communications about himself, and the extent to which this inner datum is integral to action and thought" (Klein, Mathieu, Gendlin, & Kiesler, 1969, p. 1). As you can see, the organismic trusting characteristic of fully functioningness is heavily involved here as it is in the self-ideal discrepancy already mentioned. Though the name might imply it, the Experiencing Scale is not a questionnaire filled out by the subject. Rather, the subject verbalizes in some manner, usually in psychotherapy, about anything of interest or importance to him. Then the verbalizations are rated by the psychologist as to the degree of "experiencing." There are seven stages of experiencing, running from the lowest, in which the subject seems distant or remote from his feelings, through the middle range, in which the subject gets his feelings into clearer perspective as his own and may even be able to focus upon them as his inner reality, to the highest, in which feelings have been scrutinized and explored such that they become a trusted and reliable source of self-awareness. Klein et al. (1969) provide a scoring manual for the Experiencing Scale, and report adequate interscorer reliabilities after practice.

Most of the research involving this scale had concerned patients' progress through psychotherapy, and is not, as such, of great relevance here. Suffice it to say that there is evidence to the effect that patients who are judged by their Rogerian therapists to have improved during treatment have moved up the stages of experiencing (see Klein et al., 1969). There is also some evidence that the Experiencing Scale may be an adequate measure of organismic trusting, construed as a concrete peripheral characteristic (as a predisposition that persists over time and stimulus situations). For example, it has been found (see Klein et al., 1969) that successful therapy patients start, continue, and end therapy at a higher level of experiencing than do less successful patients. Once you conclude that those who profit most from psychotherapy are those who needed it least to begin with, you are dealing with the kind of behavioral regularity signifying the presence of a concrete peripheral characteristic. In other studies amplifying this theme, neurotics showed higher levels of experiencing than schizophrenics, who would, of course, be considered the sicker of the two groups (see Klein et al., 1969). Also of note, though not specifically directed at a test of some Rogerian hypothesis, is the study of Gorney and Tobin (1969), in which it was shown that as persons make the transition from adulthood to old age, their level of experiencing drops. The Experiencing Scale would seem to be an intriguing tool with which Rogerian notions could be tested.

Another promising beginning on translating Rogerian theorizing into manageable empirical observations has been made by Wexler (1974), who reasoned that the self-actualizing process can be discerned in mental content as progressively greater differentiation and integration, and in verbal style as a vivid, focused quality not unlike the higher levels of experiencing mentioned above. In considering verbal style, Wexler was influenced by the prior work of Rice and Wagstaff (1967). Using a sample of undergraduate males and females, Wexler demonstrated that there is a positive correlation between degree of differentiation and integration, and degree of focused voice style during the subjects' description of emotional episodes. Further, both of these variables correlated positively with another purported test of fully functioningness. But you will see later, there are additional studies that lend general empirical support to Rogers' position, though these studies are even more directly relevant to other theories.

Maslow's position

Maslow's position is sufficiently similar in empirical implications to that of Rogers that anything supporting the latter also tends to support the former. There is, however, a cognitive emphasis in Maslow that is less explicit in Rogers. This is the emphasis upon democratic values as part of the self-actualizing person, as opposed to authoritarian and traditionalistic values in the nonactualizing person. While Rogers would probably agree, he does not stress such matters. But Allport, Fromm, and the existentialists clearly agree with Maslow. The body of personological research on the authoritarian personality (Adorno, Frenkel-Brunswik, Levinson & Sanford, 1950), though planned independently, is especially relevant to Maslow's emphasis on this subject.

Adorno et al. developed a fascism or *F* scale, for purposes of assessing the degree to which people have authoritarian values. As is proper for studying values, the scale derives from self-descriptions obtained through giving the subjects a list of relevant questions to answer. Examples of the items appearing on the *F* scale are "obedience and respect for authority are the most important virtues children should learn" and "familiarity breeds contempt," with "yes" answers considered authoritarian. The first version of the *F* scale had internal consistency of .74, but removal of some poor items increased reliability to .90. Adorno et al. set about determining the kinds of behavior and attitudes that occur in people high and low on the *F* scale. Their large group of subjects included a majority of white, native-born, middle-class Americans functioning as students in universities, public school teachers, public health nurses, prison inmates, psychiatric patients, and labor union and other club members. The results revealed a fairly coherent group of correlates for the *F* scale. The person high in fascistic values is also ethnocentric in the sense that he is not only opposed to other cultures, but attributes correspondingly high importance to his own. He is hostile not only toward minority groups, but also toward everyone that has different ways or values from his own. Further, he is hostile toward and contemptuous of anything that is weak. This was shown not only in the dislike of weakness, but indirectly in the admiration and valuing of power and strength, as exemplified by money, masculinity, and age-status authority. Also, the person high in fascistic values is essentially a conformist, a moralist with absolute values. He is intolerant of ambiguity in such social roles as those of parent-child, sex, and teacher-child. Finally, he sees the world as a dangerous place, full of chaos and unpredictability, with uncontrollable catastrophe imminent.

Also included in the study by Adorno et al. were interviews and unstructured tests of fantasy. By and large, the results obtained with these procedures corroborated the other findings. But the interviews and fantasy tests are seriously flawed methodologically (see Hyman & Sheatsley, 1954). To be sure the *F*-scale findings have also been criticized, mainly on the grounds that the sample may not have been fully representative of the general population, and that the test items may have been contaminated by response sets. Although these criticisms have some justification, attempts to explain away the attributes of the authoritarian personality as presented above have not been very convincing.

Since the appearance of the work of Adorno et al., a huge number of studies tracing the correlates of the fascism scale has been done. Many of these studies have complemented and extended the findings reported above. For example, in a study unusual for having been conducted in a "real life" context involving performance rather than self-description, Vroom (1959) showed that among supervisors in a large delivery company, authoritarians were affected less positively by the opportunity to participate in company decisions than were nonauthoritarians. Presumably, people high in fascistic values feel most comfortable in authoritarian work situations, even when they are not in power.

There are, of course, some studies using the *F* scale that yield equivocal results. It has been suggested that this situation may be due to a lack of purity in the fascism scale such that it is measuring not only authoritarian values but many unintended things as well (see Peabody, 1966). One such unintended thing may be the tendency to agree or disagree in answering questions regardless of their content. And another unintended characteristic may be our old friend, socially desirable responding. To date, a great deal of effort has been expended in the attempt to purify the fascism scale of such contaminations (see Peabody, 1966). But the purified scales that are now available do not seem to be providing a clearer picture of the effect on living of possessing authoritarian values. I am not especially surprised by this state of affairs, as it has never been clear to me that an authoritarian value orientation can be measured accurately if the tendencies to acquiesce and to respond in socially desirable fashion are excluded. After all, the authoritarian person deeply believes in the importance of acquiescence and conformity. Perhaps we will come closer to clarity by assuming that the authoritarian orientation can be expressed not only in fascistic values, but also in acquiescent and conforming traits. Once you adopt this point of view, you are not likely to hasten to exclude acquiescent and conforming tendencies from a measure of authoritarianism.

In similar but less criticizable research, Rokeach (1960) has demonstrated that dogmatism as a characteristic of values and attitudes has such far-reaching effects as to rigidify the process of solving intellectual problems. There seems striking evidence not only for the existence of authoritarian values, but also for their occurrence in people whose lives are quite describable as lacking in self-actualization. And, of course, since the studies are correlational, there is also evidence that the absence of authoritarianism occurs along with behavioral manifestations that seem more like descriptions of self-actualization.

In the last two decades, many studies have been performed tracing the effects of dogmatism upon various behaviors. Ehrlich (1955, 1961a, 1961b) compared the performance of 57 undergraduates enrolled in a sociology course on precourse and postcourse tests, separated by 10 weeks, and on a follow-up several months later. The higher the dogmatism scores, the poorer the performance on all three sociology tests, even when academic aptitude skills were controlled. Five years later, Ehrlich (1961b) obtained, from many of the original subjects, dogmatism scores, sociology test scores, and their reported final grade-point averages on graduation. Essentially the same results were obtained as before. But Costin (1965) attempted to replicate Ehrlich's findings and was unsuccessful. Baker (1964) performed a similar study on 56 student nurses, with the measure of performance being the number of correct identifications of definitions for 20 psychological concepts they were supposed to have learned. Oddly enough, he found that the higher the dogmatism scores, the better the performance! To make matters worse, Costin (1968), employing a design similar to his earlier work, obtained results indicating that dogmatism correlated positively with the students' retention of psychological misconceptions he had purposely given them but not with their acquisition of basic psychological principles that were also taught. The contradictory nature of these findings suggests the action of important variables that were not measured (Ehrlich & Lee, 1969).

The studies reported above all occurred in classroom settings, where it was not possible to control situations and experiences very well. Under more rigorous laboratory conditions, a consistent picture of the effects of dogmatism on learning begins to become apparent. Adams and Vidulich (1962) compared the 18 highest and lowest dogmatism scorers in the number of errors made while learning two lists of 15 belief-congruent word pairs (e.g., ball-round) and 15 belief-incongruent word pairs (e.g., ball-square). As expected, the high-dogmatism subjects made more errors in learning the belief-incongruent list. But they also, unexpectedly, made still more errors learning the belief-congruent list. That there may still be some tendency among high-dogmatism subjects to learn only belief-congruent or personally interesting materials well is indicated in studies by Kleck and Wheaton (1967) and Pyron and Kafer (1967). Consistent with this is the research of Restle, Andrews, and Rokeach

(1964), which found that low-dogmatism subjects were able to solve a difficult problem faster than high-dogmatism subjects when the solution always involved choosing an odd, unusual alternative rather than a usual one. The implication that dogmatic persons do not learn well when operating in a novel situation or when the solution is novel is supported by further studies done by Rokeach, Swanson, and Denny (1960), Mikol (1960), Zagona and Zurcher (1965), and Jacoby (1967).

Not only is the dogmatic person unable to learn effectively in conditions of novelty, he is also swayed in his judgments by the contradictory judgments of high-status persons. Vidulich and Kaiman (1961) tested 30 high- and 30 low-dogmatism undergraduates in a situation requiring perceptual judgments (how far a spot of light had moved in a darkened room). All subjects were tested in the company of the experimenters' confederate, whose task it was to try to sway judgments. Sometimes the confederate was introduced as a college professor and sometimes as a high school student. The results indicated a tendency for high-dogmatism subjects to acquiesce to high-status judgments. Support for this finding is found in research by Powell (1962) and Mikol (1960), among others. The implications of conformity on the part of dogmatic persons were authenticated by Zagona and Zurcher (1964) in observational evidence, gleaned over four months of contact, to the effect that in small groups, dogmatic persons are leader oriented, unspontaneous, and prefer lectures to class discussion. That the conforming effect of dogmatism is not merely a cognitive or attitudinal thing is suggested by Clark (1968), who investigated the relationship between dogmatism scores and the ability to discern a previously observed simple figure embedded in a more complex one (*field dependence-independence*). In his sample of 523 undergraduates dogmatism was negatively correlated with this ability.

There is support in the research on dogmatism and authoritarianism for Maslow's contention that democratic, liberal values are part of the self-actualizing person. It should be noted that this body of work also provides general support for the positions of Rogers, Allport, Fromm, and existentialism.

In recent years, a general questionnaire aimed at measuring the various facets of self-actualization has been devised in strict adherence to Maslow's theorizing (Shostrom, 1965, 1966). Called the *Personal Orientation Inventory* (POI), this test consists of 150 paired, opposing statements. In each instance, the subject must choose one of the two as most relevant to him. The test is scored as two major scales, *inner-directedness* and *time competence,* and 10 complementary scales, *self-actualizing values, existentiality, feeling reactivity, spontaneity, self-regard, self-acceptance, nature of man, synergy, acceptance of aggression, and capacity for intimacy.* An adequate degree of reliability is reported for the scales (Ilardi & May, 1968; Klavetter & Mogar, 1967; Shostrom, 1966).

Thus far, the POI displays considerable construct validity (see Fox, Knapp & Michael, 1968; Guinan & Foulds, 1970; Shostrom, 1966). One facet of this validity concerns behavioral ratings made by trained personologists. Various POI scales correlate positively with the degree to which subjects are rated as self-actualizing (McClain, 1970; Shostrom, 1965). POI scales also correlate negatively with alcoholism (Zaccaria & Weir, 1967), felony (Fisher, 1968), and hospitalization for psychopathological symptoms (Fox, Knapp, & Michael, 1968). The relationship of the POI to other personality tests has also been studied. All POI scales correlate negatively with Eysenck's neuroticism score (Knapp, 1965). Also, the inner-directed scale of the POI correlates positively with the autonomy scale and negatively with the abasement scale of the Edwards Personal Preference Inventory (Grossack, Armstrong, & Lussieu, 1966). Positive correlations have also been found between POI scales and various tests of creativity (Braun & Asta, 1968; Damm, 1968). Finally, there have been some studies involving actual performance. The main scale scores of the POI are positively related to academic achievement (LeMay & Damm, 1968; Stewart, 1968). In addition, high scores on the POI are associated with teaching and therapist effectiveness (Dandes, 1966; Graff & Bradshaw, 1967). Also relevant is the finding that subjects scoring high in self-actualization seek novelty more than those scoring low (Schwartz and Gaines, 1974).

Several studies have investigated whether responses to the POI are seriously effected by the tendency to present oneself in a socially-desirable light. Fisher and Silverstein (1969) and Foulds and Warehime (1971) found that instructions to fake responses in a favorable direction actually produced lower self-actualization scores in subjects! This is in striking contrast to other tests, which appear so vulnerable to putting one's best foot forward. Also, it has been shown that the POI scales are actually negatively related to measures of the tendency to respond in socially-desirable direction (Warehime and Foulds, 1973), and of conformity behavior (Crosson and Schwendiman, 1972). Perhaps subjects who dissimulate on questionnaires do so in terms of cultural stereotypes of ideal behavior. If self-actualization is different from such stereotypes, then it is understandable that encouragement to present oneself in a good light would have no or even adverse effects upon POI scores.

In an attempt to determine just how resistant to faking the POE is, Warehime, Routh and Foulds (1974) presented subjects first with instruction concerning the content of the self-actualization concept. They reasoned that, given this clue, subjects high in the tendency to respond in a socially-desirable direction would be able to increase their self-actualization scores. Although they used 276 subjects, they were unable to demonstrate this effect. Only when they combined instruction about the self-actualization concept with practice in answering some of the very items on the POI was there some tendency for subjects bent on appearing socially-desirable to increase their self-actualization scores. And the tendency was very small at that. It seems likely that the POI is remarkably resistent to faking. This strengthens its claim to construct validity.

Lest we become too enthusiastic, I should point out that there have also been failures to establish the validity of this test (see Fox et al., 1968; Guinan and Foulds, 1970). A particularly interesting finding that is difficult to rationalize with Maslow's thinking was reported by deGrace (1974). Using 30 subjects, he demonstrated that there is no difference in level of anxiety between high and low self-actualization scorers on the POI. Nonetheless, the POI seems a promising lead in investigating broad patterns of functioning clearly associated with the positions of Maslow and Rogers.

There are several recent studies stimulated by Maslow that have not employed the POI. Leith (1972) obtained scores on three verbal creativity tests from 106 subjects immediately after they had been subjected to two kinds and degrees of stress that should have constituted a threat to needs at the lower end of Maslow's hierarchy. Oddly enough, the effect of stress seems to have been to increase the number and originality of responses. According to Maslow, the opposite should have taken place, because unsatisfied or frustrated lower needs should render higher needs unsalient, and creativity is an expression of higher needs. Graham and Balloun (1973) attempted to show that in any pair of needs at different levels in the hierarchy postulated by Maslow, satisfaction of the lower need should be greater than of the higher need. Of the three scores derived from interviews to test this prediction, one produced the expected results, one did not, and the other yielded equivocal findings. Adding to this, the scanty information that was provided concerning the interscorer agreement and the reliability of the ratings made from interviews, made it difficult to conclude that there was support for Maslow's thinking as claimed by the researchers. Finally, Ebersole (1972) interviewed students about their peak experiences, and found that in 55 percent of such instances, the experiencer regarded its effect on his life to be transitory. Although Ebersole regards this as supporting evidence for Maslow's position, it could as easily be taken the opposite way. And besides, 55 percent is barely a majority.

Adler's position

When we turn to the first perfection theorist, Adler, we are struck by the adsence of research relevant to his peripheral theorizing in general. I believe the theorizing on life-styles, fictional finalism, and traits to be clear enough for meaningful research to have been done. Perhaps the Adlerian view has simply not been popular enough among psychologists for it to have captured their research attention. The one notable exception to what I have said is in regard to birth order, which as you will recall, is an important determinant of life-style, according to Adler. Since Schachter's (1959) intriguing research on birth order and affiliative tendencies in females, there has been a virtual flood of related studies. Here we see another instance, to go along with Eysenck's stimulation of Jungian research and Rokeach's of Maslowian, of how a primarily research-oriented personologist can capture the imagination of others like him in the service of broader theoretical concerns. And we shall see this again.

In that path-breaking study, Schachter (1959) observed that, under stress, firstborn college girls tended to seek the company of others while later born girls tended to withdraw into themselves. As part of the same large study, he also offered evidence that the general preference for affiliation and withdrawal when experiencing stress on the part of firstborn and later born children, respectively, permitted understanding of such diverse behaviors as combat flying effectiveness and alcoholism. With such dramatic findings, it is not surprising that researchers were attracted to the area. A general search for the correlates of birth order began.

One consistent finding concerns attendance at college. Schachter (1963) concluded, on the basis of reviewing earlier studies, that eldest children are more likely to become eminent than later born children. Soon it became apparent that 50 to 65 percent of the student bodies in many colleges around the country, such as Columbia University (Schachter, 1963), Dartmouth College (Bender, 1928), Kansas State University (Danskin, 1964), Reed College (Altus, 1966), University of Florida (Hall & Barger, 1964), and many more, were firstborn children. These percentages are larger than one would expect from the corresponding figures in the population at large (Schachter, 1963). This seems striking confirmation of Adler's contention that being born first precipitates ambition.

Although firstborn children more often go to college, there is no firm evidence that they do better there than later born children. Campbell (1933) found no differences between these two groups in achievement. But Pierce (1959), Elder (1962), and Schachter (1963) did find that the firstborn children had higher grade-point averages. Although there is some evidence that these children have a higher need for achievement than later born children (Sampson, 1965), it is known that this need is not a good predictor of grades (McClelland, 1961). In light of the general evidence that families place greater demands upon firstborn children and expect them to reach greater heights (Bossard & Boll, 1955; Dittes, 1961; Rosen, 1961), it would seem that their going to college expresses the ambition mentioned above, whether or not this eventuates in excellent grades.

But the ambition suggested in firstborn children does not have the connotation of independence. Indeed, Sears (1950), and Schachter (1964) found that firstborn children are actually more dependent on others and more easily influenced than those born later. That later born children are more accepted by their peers (Sells & Roff, 1963) suggests a more relaxed attitude in them. In this regard, Dimond and Munz (1967) found later borns more able to break through social barriers by self-disclosure. But it does seem that when expected to undergo painful electric shock, firstborn females have a stronger desire than later born females to await the experience in the company of others (Gerard & Rabbie, 1961; Schahter, 1959). Zucker, Manosevitz, Langon (1968) have found evidence of the same effect in a naturally occurring catastrophe. This again suggests that the apparent ambition of firstborn children is dependent enough to constitute a wish for approval rather than success in personal terms. Consistent with this interpretation are the results of Radloff (1961), who designed a study in which he was able to make some of his female subjects believe that their opinions were at variance with those of a large majority of their peers. Among firstborn females, those in presumed conflict with their peers expressed a stronger desire for further discussion than did those in agreement with their peers. This effect did not appear for later born females. Similarly, Koenig (1969) found that firstborns give consensual or group-related answers when asked to describe themselves. Other studies are consistent with these (e.g., Wrightsman, 1960), though it is possible that the picture for males is more complicated (Connors, 1963; Dember, 1964; Sampson, 1962).

There is also some intriguing information concerning birth order and psychopathology. Although the contention that firstborn children are more resistant to alcoholism than later born children (Schachter, 1959) has not held up in later study (Smart, 1963), they do seem more prone to being "problem children" (Rosenow & Whyte, 1931), and are more apprehensive about dangerous situations (Longstreth, 1970). Actually, the highest proportion of delinquents seem to be middle children (Sletto, 1934). There is some rather inconclusive evidence that later born children (at least females) are more prone to schizophrenia than those born earlier (Schooler, 1961). Last-born children also seemed to have lower social competence in general (Schooler, 1964). Although some studies find later born children to be more creative (Staffieri, 1970), others report the opposite (Eisenman & Schussel, 1970). The picture is simply not clear as yet. To make matters worse, Hall (1965) has reported that male only children have high divorce rates, whereas female only children have low divorce rates! It will take some careful sampling and measurement to sort out the confusion elements in what is admittedly an exciting and booming research area.

Worthen and O'Connell (1969) have done one of the rare studies directly concerned with Adler's concept of social interest. As they are

TABLE 10-15

Correlations between the social interest index score and 18
California psychological test (CPI) scores

CPI attribute	r^a	r^b	r^c
Dominance	.27‡	.20†	.35‡
Capacity for status	.27‡	.25‡	.26†
Sociability	.27‡	.24‡	.27‡
Social presence	.07	.08	.08
Self-acceptance	.16†	.09	.20*
Sense of well-being	.36‡	.27‡	.36‡
Responsibility	.39‡	.29‡	.32‡
Socialization	.39‡	.31‡	.28‡
Self-control	.19†	.10	.26†
Tolerance	.26‡	.17*	.27‡
Good impression	.21‡	.14*	.35‡
Communality	.40‡	.37‡	.18*
Achievement via conformance	.35‡	.25‡	.35‡
Achievement via independence	.13*	.05	.14
Intellectual efficiency	.33‡	.24†	.30‡
Psychological mindedness	.09	−.02	.34‡
Flexibility	−.22‡	−.27‡	−.17*
Femininity	.29‡	.03	.08

ᵃ Total N = 344.
ᵇ Males n = 189.
ᶜ Females n = 155.
* $p < .05$.
† $p < .01$.
‡ $p < .001$.
Source: K. B. Greever, M. T. Tseng, & B. U. Friedland, "Development of the Social Interest Index." *J. consult. clin. Psychol.*, 1973.

referring to the cooperative (rather than competitive) form of this
tendency, which form can develop through learning, their study concerns Adler's peripheral statement and is relevant here. Constructive
social interest was measured by a test of values constructed by the first
author, and humor appreciation by a test constructed by the second
author. A positive correlation was obtained between social interest and
humor appreciation. It remains to be seen how close to Adlerian construals are the measurement operations.

Recently, Greever, Tseng, and Friedland (1973) have developed a
paper and pencil test called the *Social Interest Index* for determining
the degree of positive social interest in four areas of life (work, friendship, love, and self-significance). On the basis of agreement among three
prominent Adlerians, 32 items were selected, each of which was responded to by subjects on a five-point scale of personal relevance. It
was demonstrated that these items did not correlate with a scale of
socially-desirable responding. Internal consistency was .81 and stability
over a 14-day period was .79.

Having tested 228 male and female subjects, Greever et al., found that
social interest scores are higher for females than males, increase with
age, and grade point average, but are unrelated to socioeconomic level.

With the possible exception of the finding concerning grade point average, the results are consistent with Adlerian thought. The results of correlating the Social Interest Index with a standard, comprehensive test of personality, the California Personality Inventory, are shown in Table 10–15. A claim to construct validity is made because the Index shows correlates referring to communality, responsibility, socialization, sense of well-being, and achievement via conformance. This test seems worthy of additional empirical study.

White's position

As White's peripheral theorizing is the same as that of Erikson, everything I said concerning the ego psychologist is relevant here. There is surprisingly little research to go on, rendering us unable to assess the position from an empirical standpoint. In one study, Wherry and Waters (1968) administered a 150 item questionnaire about usual feelings involving individual, social, and accomplishment states to 235 undergraduates in an attempt to find an objective approach to measuring motivation. Through a factor analysis, they obtained factors best described as competency motivation and general satisfaction. Accordingly, they believe White's position to be supported. Also, Smith (1966) reports the results of a factor-analytic study of Peace Corps volunteers as indicating that an important difference among people is whether or not they have a basic attitude of self-confidence and self-reliance. This finding provides support for a number of fulfillment positions in addition to that of White, as results reviewed elsewhere can be construed as general support for his.

Goldfried and D'Zurilla (1969) have begun development of an inventory, the *Survey of Problematic Situations,* which attempts to determine mine the subject's level of competence. The Survey consists of a series of situations sampled from academic and social incidents provided by college freshmen, staff and faculty, and from clinical folders. Responses to these situations were obtained from a group of college freshman and high school seniors, and then evaluated as inferior, average, or superior by teachers and counselors. These evaluations provided the scoring rules with which to assess competence. Although Goldfried and D'Zurilla have made an interesting beginning, there is simply too little information available about this inventory at this time to make any judgement about its adequacy empirically or its theoretical relevance to White's position.

Although it is also too early to tell in the case of the work of Good and Good (1973), they are developing a test called the *Fear of Appearing Incompetent Scale.* Comprised of 36 True-False items, the reliability of this scale was tested on 355 undergraduate subjects, with a resulting internal consistency correlation of .89. It is possible that this scale will prove relevant to White's emphasis on *sense* of competence (Good and Good may be measuring its opposite), whereas Goldfried's and D'Zurilla's inventory assesses *actual* competence.

Allport's position

It would be quite possible to pass over Allport without any attention, as he is so nonspecific concerning the periphery of personality. Nonetheless, he does give us some inkling of a peripheral viewpoint in stating his criteria of maturity. Research could be done, even at this rudimentary stage in his peripheral theorizing, to determine whether these criteria of maturity occur in people whose lives are successful, proactive, and propriate, rather than unsatisfactory, reactive, and opportunistic. Although research has not been explicitly directed to such matters, there are some findings in the literature than can be interpreted as relevant. For example, the research on dogmatism and authoritarianism cited for Maslow is relevant here as well. So is the work on the self-concept reviewed in connection with Rogers. The studies on internal versus external locus of control, which will be covered when we get to existential psychology, could also be considered to clarify the existence and nature of proactive as opposed to reactive behavior, a distinction dear to Allport's heart.

But there are two considerations more nearly unique to him that should be mentioned here. One concerns the sense of humor, which Allport incorporated into his criteria of maturity. Actually, as he also believed it was mature to have a philosophy of life and stable bases for social intimacy, the study by Worthen and O'Connell (1969) just reviewed for Adler could as well have appeared here. In any event, O'Connell (1960) has also reported results suggesting that a sense of humor is indeed associated with successful living. Working with 332 college student subjects for whom self-ideal discrepancies were available, he found that those with small discrepancies appreciated humor more than those with large discrepancies. In addition, those with small discrepancies tended to appreciate nonsense wit, whereas those with large discrepancies tended to appreciate hostile wit.

The other consideration involves Allport's emphatic peripheral statement that there exist not only dynamic (motivational) traits but also expressive (stylistic) traits. This statement may have even stimulated McClelland's distinction between motives and traits. In any event, Allport and Vernon (1933) did a pioneering study of performance (rather than self-description or fantasy) aimed at determining whether there was sufficient consistency to expressive movements to justify the belief in the importance of expressive traits. In one part of this large program of research, a group of 25 subjects was tested in three different sessions, each separated by about four weeks. During each session, the subject responded to a large number of different tests providing measures of speed of reading and counting; speed of walking and strolling; length of stride; estimation of familiar sizes and distances; estimation of weights; strength of handshake; speed and pressure of finger, hand and leg tapping; drawing squares, circles, and other figures; various hand-writing measures; muscular tension; and so forth. In addition, observer ratings were obtained for various measures, such as voice intensity, speech fluency, amount of movement during natural speech, and neatness of appearance.

First, Allport and Vernon assessed the stability of the various expressive measures over the three testing sessions. In general, these estimates of reliability were reasonably high, and compared favorably to stability for self-descriptive measures of personality. It would seem that expressive characteristics have claim to empirical existence. Next, Allport and Vernon examined the relationship between scores for the same tasks performed by different muscle groups, such as left and right side of the body, and arms and legs. Strikingly enough, they found about the same level of consistency as had been reported for the same muscle groups over time. This important finding suggests a general or central integrating factor that produces a consistent style no matter what peripheral manifestation is observed.

The final analysis attempted in this study was the intercorrelation of the major variables from all the tasks. A total of 38 measures was inter-correlated by a form of cluster analysis roughly comparable to factor analysis. Three factors seemed to emerge, as indicated in Table 10–16. The first, or *areal factor,* included such variables as area of total writing, area of blackboard figures, area of foot squares, and length of self-rating checks. Motor expansiveness is what seems to be involved here. The second factor (called centrifugal-centripetal by the investigators) seems to involve *extroversion-introversion,* including such measures as overestimation of distance from body, and underestimation of weights. The third factor, called the *factor of emphasis,* included such measures as voice intensity, movement during speech, writing pressure, tapping pressure, and pressure of resting hand. In this kind of research is the basis for determining the content of expressive traits that should be included in peripheral theorizing. Subsequent studies of expressive characteristics (e.g., Allport & Cantril, 1934; Estes, 1938; Huntley, 1940) are not very useful in this regard, having focused upon the degree to which people can predict other features of a person's personality from his expressive movements. These studies seem to make the assumption that the expressive movements are not themselves aspects of personality.

Fromm's position

As I have already indicated, the studies cited under discussion of Rogers on the relationship between self-acceptance and acceptance of others also provide support for the emphasis in Fromm upon the in-

TABLE 10–16

Three factors based on expressive movements

Areal group factor	
Area of total writing	.69
Total extent of figures	.67
Area of blackboard figures	.64
Slowness of drawing	.52
Area of foot squares	.48
Overestimation of angles	.45
Ratings on movement during idleness	.39
Length of self-rating checks	.38
Length of walking strides	.37
Centrifugal group factor	
Overestimation of distance from body with legs	.66
Overestimation of distance from body with hands	.55
Extent of cubes	.53
Underestimation (reverse of overestimation) of weights	.53
Verbal speed	.34
Underestimation of distances toward body with hands	.33
Ratings on speech fluency	.33
Group factor of emphasis	
Ratings on voice intensity	.71
Fewness of parallel lines	.65
Ratings on movement during speech	.53
Writing pressure	.52
Overestimation of weights	.46
Finger pressure on stylus	.45
Tapping pressure	.42
Underestimation of distances between hands	.42
Verbal slowness	.38
Ratings on forcefulness	.38
Overestimation of angles	.36
Pressure of resting hand	.32
Unoccupied space in drawing figures	.31

Source: Adapted from G. W. Allport & P. E. Vernon, *"Studies in expressive movement."* New York: Macmillan, 1933.

extricably intermingled destiny of individuals and groups. In an even more general sense, other studies discussed in relation to fulfillment theorists lend indirect support for Fromm's position. But none of this bears on the receptive, exploitative, hoarding, marketing, and productive character types themselves. It is true that the first three types bear considerable similarity to the oral incorporative, oral aggressive, and anal types postulated by Freudians. Therefore, much of the research already discussed for Freud bears on Fromm's position as well. You will recall that there was some empirical support for the Freudian oral and anal types.

There is one large-scale field study (Fromm & Maccoby, 1970) which bears directly on the hoarding, receptive, and exploitative character types. This is a naturalistic, anthropological study of a Mexican village, far from urban life. The coauthors came to know and help the villagers over a period of years, studying them all the while. The part of this large and interesting project of most relevance here concerns a long, detailed questionnaire they administered to the villagers in hopes of obtaining information about character types which could aid in their understanding of day-to-day behavior and the social forces shaping it. Three questions are listed here as examples (Fromm & Maccoby, 1970, pp. 240–241):

14. Describe your idea of a good mother.

· · ·

16. When you were a child, did you fear the anger of your father more, or that of your mother?

· · ·

47. Should women have the same rights as men? Why?

Although these questions may appear easy to fake, let me remind you that Fromm and Maccoby knew their subjects well and had reason to believe they could be trusted.

The questionnaire was scored for 406 adult villagers, or 95 percent of the adult population. The scoring attempted to disclose which character types were present in a protocol, and which of them was dominant. In attempting to accomplish this, the various traits Fromm (1947) has listed under the types were used. The areas of concern were mode of assimilating experience, mode of relatedness, sociopolitical relatedness, parental centeredness, and other behavioral traits. In addition to the supposedly nonideal character types, an attempt was made to score for productiveness directly. The scoring was inevitably somewhat global, and the scorers had to steep themselves in Fromm's position and the procedures involved. Nonetheless, reasonably adequate interscorer reliability was achieved for work of this kind (percentage of agreement ranged from 72 to 100). In addition the Thematic Apperception and Rorschach tests were employed in a subsidiary way, yielding some interesting agreements and disagreements with the primary measure, the questionnaire (Fromm & Maccoby, 1970, pp. 271–291). Finally, the scored questionnaires were subjected to a factor analysis, in order to determine whether the emerging factors conformed to character types. As you can see, this procedure conforms well to the first two steps of the ideal strategy discussed at the beginning of this chapter. Scores for traits relevant to Fromm's types are factor analyzed to see whether those types do in fact emerge. Of course, the scoring was rather interpretative, and the investigators can be presumed to have already believed in the value of the types. Nonetheless, emerging evidence for the position can be taken seriously.

The factors obtained include ones well interpreted as receptive, exploitative, hoarding, and productive orientations. True to expectation, the last of these relates to the others, such that one can speak of productive or nonproductive versions of them. Although an age factor accounted for the biggest slice of the sample's behavior, productiveness-unproductiveness, exploitativeness-nonexploitativeness, and hoarding-receptivity followed in that order. In addition, there was a masculinity-femininity factor, and also one for mother-father centeredness. Needless to say, none of the factors other than character types are inconsistent with them in Fromm's theory. It is interesting to note that Fromm's marketing orientation did not seem to emerge. The investigators contend that this orientation was simply not present in this rather traditional, rural village. This is also consistent with Fromm's position, which makes the marketing orientation a product of modern industrialization and urbanization.

In interpreting the results, the investigators make some interesting and persuasive interpretations of how the existing orientations reflect long-standing cultural, social, and political realities of Mexican society. For example, the receptive orientation was found to be less often associated with productiveness than either the hoarding or the exploitative orientations. Considering the authoritarian tradition of the wealthy landowner and his serfs that has existed in Mexico for centuries, it is not surprising that villagers would be pushed into developing receptive orientations of an unproductive variety (they succumbed to excessive dependency on their masters). But the hoarding orientation is more likely to occur in a productive mode because it was also possible, given the sociopolitical situation, for some few villagers to own their own tiny plot of land, which would provide them with a slim but possible means for independence. That they had to hold onto this valuable parcel of land for dear life, as it were, encouraged a hoarding form of productiveness. Finally, some with an exploitative orientation were able to achieve a productive mode due to the social changes taking place in Mexico, which are opening up the possibility for entrepreneurship among villagers who would otherwise be damned to poverty and dependence. My conclusion is, that, with all its faults, this comprehensive study provides general, if not the most precise, support for Fromm's position. Studies of its sort should be mounted with regard to the other positions.

Understandably, no information emerged concerning the marketing orientation. This is unfortunate, as it is the part of Fromm's peripheral theorizing most unique to him. There is some available research, however, that bears on the phenomenon of alienation, central to the definition of the marketing personality. Unfortunately, work on alienation is often more polemical than scientifically rigorous. Exemplary of the alienation research on adults is the work of Keniston (1966), in which 12 college males were studied intensively via repeated interviews, tests, and observations concerning their life situation and values. Unfortunately, Keniston does not see fit to include careful discussion of his procedures for selecting subjects, scoring their responses, and conducting statistical analyses of the data. These omissions are consistent with Keniston's preference for intuitive, impressionistic portraits of people, used as examples to elucidate his theoretical views. In any event, Keniston contends that there is an alienated personality type, which includes such concrete peripheral characteristics as a futile quest for positive values, possession of a pessimistic existentialist orientation, a distrust of commitment, and a disaffection for adulthood. His students emerge as people who know what they are not, but have little conviction as to what they are. Although the general emphasis in Keniston's work is consistent with the marketing orientation, it can hardly be said that his research is rigorous enough to have unequivocally demonstrated the empirical validity of Fromm's theorizing. There do not seem to be more rigorous studies of the marketing personality in adults.

Indeed, Keniston (1966) thought he was providing a basis for understanding alienation in Freudian or at least ego psychology terms. He suggests that his alienated males had unresolved oedipal conflicts, stemming from their being mother's darling in the context of either literal absence of father, or his extreme detachment and unimportance in the home. As such, Keniston's research would not really be so supportive of Fromm's position. But Keniston's Freudian explanation is very nebulous. It is not at all clear how or if the data bear him out in it. In this context, the research can be interpreted by us conservatively to indicate the existence of a pattern of personality not unlike Fromm's marketing orientation. For that matter, these data are also generally relevant to existential psychology.

There are a few studies (e.g., Benson, 1966; Klein & Gould, 1969; Reimanis, 1966) concerning children in school situations indicating the existence of such characteristics as fatalism, meaninglessness, and powerlessness. While these studies are rigorous enough in their measurement procedures and sampling, it is not clear what relationship their results bear to the adult personality. After all, the childhood school years may normally be ones characterized by a sense of powerlessness, without this auguring an adult personality of the marketing type.

Existential psychology

Although Maddi's (1967, 1970) peripheral theorizing might not be acceptable to those existential psychologists who prefer such an extreme position on the individuality issue that no such theorizing is considered useful, we shall work with it nonetheless. The alternative would be to find very little research of any relevance to existentialism. In specifying his two personality types as individualism and conformism, Maddi fits into a good deal of ongoing research in psychology. Some of this research might have been mentioned in other places, for it is certainly relevant to other theories. But it is perhaps most specifically relevant here.

First is the burgeoning literature on whether people believe their life to be controlled by them (internal locus of control) or by society and others (external locus of control). This research theme was pioneered by Julian Rotter (1954), who did not aim to provide any special support for existential psychology. Nonetheless, the findings are relevant here, insofar as the individual perceives himself as having a mental life through which he can understand and influence his experiences, and treats life as a series of decisions he must make responsibly (Maddi, 1970). This would clearly involve an internal locus of control. In addition an external locus of control would bespeak the social reductionism of the conformist, who perceives his life as manipulated by social forces uninfluenceable by him.

After several refinements, an *Internal v. External Locus of Control (I-E) Scale* was made available for general use (Rotter, Seeman, & Liverant, 1962). This scale consists of 23 items from which the following have been chosen:

> I more strongly believe that:
> 6. a. Without the right breaks one cannot be an effective leader. (External)
>   b. Capable people who fail to become leaders have not taken advantage of their opportunities. (Internal)
>
> . . .
>
> 9. a. I have often found that what is going to happen will happen. (External)
>   b. Trusting to fate has never turned out as well for me as making a decision to take a definite course of action. (Internal)
>
> . . .
>
> 17. a. As far as world affairs are concerned, most of us are the victims of forces we can neither understand, nor control. (External)
>   b. By taking an active part in political and social affairs, the people can control world events. (Internal)

Reliability for this scale seems quite adequate (Rotter, 1966). By now, several other similar measures have been developed (e.g., Bialer, 1961; Crandall, Katkovsky, & Crandall, 1965).

The first group of construct validation studies concerns the ramifications of belief in internal as opposed to external control of events on characteristics of primarily personal as opposed to socially relevant behavior. Crandall et al. (1965) found that schoolboys high in internal control beliefs spend more time in intellectual free play activities, and scored higher on both reading and arithmetic achievement tests. Similarly, Seeman (1963) and Seeman and Evans (1962) found differential learning between internals and externals in two field settings. The latter investigators reported that among hospitalized tuberculosis patients, those believing in external control had obtained less knowledge about their own conditions than those believing in internal control.

This finding was not attributable to socioeconomic or hospital-experience factors. Controlling for intelligence and the novelty of stimulus materials presented for learning, Seeman (1963) demonstrated that prison inmates scoring low in externality were superior to those scoring high in retention of information presented to them concerning procedures relating to achieving parole successfully. As might be expected, it has also been shown that subjects high in externality tend to be conformists, both when conformity is measured by questionnaire (Odell, 1959), and by performance (Crowne & Liverant, 1963).

Consistent with the general picture of competence emerging from the studies mentioned above are findings concerning risk taking. In a situation where subjects were required to bet on the outcome of 30 trials of dice throwing, with the alternatives having objective probabilities, Liverant and Scodel (1960) showed that the more the subjects believed in an internal locus of control the more they would choose bets of intermediate probability and avoid low-probability bets. Similar results reported by Lefcourt (1965) also indicated that internally oriented subjects tend to regulate their performance in terms of the realistic constraints contained in the probabilities. The only deviation from this conclusion concerns the observation made by Liverant and Scodel (1960) to the effect that internally oriented subjects never seemed to select an extremely high or low probability bet. In reflecting upon the meaning of the risk-taking findings, it is perhaps valuable to consider Butterfield's (1964) study concerning anxiety, the results of which are presented in Table 10–17. Using questionnaire measures of anxiety, he found that the stronger the sense of external control, the more evidence was given that anxiety has a debilitating rather than facilitating effect upon the person (see rows 5 and 6 of Table 10–17). Perhaps the seemingly unrealistic behavior of the highly external person in risk-taking situations reflects the debilitating effects upon him of anxiety concerning evaluation. In addition, Table 10–17 (row 4) indicates that the more external a person is, the less constructive is his reaction to frustration. Additional support for this position is provided by the studies of Platt and Eisenman (1968) and Feather (1967).

The general theme that internally- and externally-oriented persons are sharply different in perception and performance is amplified by several recent studies. Using 98 male and female subjects, Alegre and Murray (1974) demonstrated that externally-oriented persons are more susceptible to verbal conditioning, which, of course, utilizes extrinsic reinforcements. That this may indeed reflect the generally greater experience of possibility or choice enjoyed by internally-oriented persons is suggested by the findings of Harvey and Barnes (1974), who presented their subjects with choice situations in which the two options differed as to attractiveness, or were either both attractive or both negative. Characteristically, internally-oriented subjects experienced a greater sense

TABLE 10–17

Intercorrelations of measures

Measures	1	2	3	4	5	6	7	8	9	10	10	11	12	13
1. Locus of control	—													
Frustration reactions														
2. Intropunitive	184	—												
3. Extrapunitive	149	135	—											
4. Constructive	−366*	623*	−042	—										
Anxiety reactions														
5. Debilitating	233	−081	267	−050	—									
6. Facilitating	−677*	−206	−139	488*	−766*	—								
Academic aspirations														
7. Range	398*	287	252	133	098	132	—							
8. Lowest grade	368*	044	722*	458*	199	123	027	—						
9. Actual grade	−073	063	−159	130	220	−035	−090	684*	—					
Fear of failure														
10. Satisfaction	246	−073	−019	−223	299*	−172	−475*	−415*	−075	—				
11. Satisfaction difference	064	093	020	−341	675*	−339*	010	−496*	187	888*	888*	—		
12. UE-LS	248	−033	149	−336*	014	126	218	−492*	124	277	277	−022	—	
13. (UE-LS) range	207	112	008	−342*	096	114	−419*	−463*	024	250	250	−020	093	—
Intelligence														
14. WAIS vocabulary	−174	210	037	601*	−429*	466*	091	−453*	387*	469*	469*	−367*	−055	042

* p < .05.

Source: Adapted from E. C. Butterfield, "Locus of control, test anxiety, reactions to frustration, and achievement attitudes." J. Pers., 1964.

of personal choice when the options were similar in attractiveness. Cherulnik and Citrin (1974) induced their 100 male and female subjects to express preferences for objects promised to them at a later time, and then failed to make good on the promise. They found that internally-oriented subjects increased in preference for the preferred and un-delivered object when the reasons for its not being delivered were made personally meaningful. In contrast, preference for the undelivered object increased for externally-oriented subjects when the reason given was impersonal and arbitrary. It would seem that externally-oriented persons feel more comfortable in arbitrary, uncontrollable conditions, whereas the opposite is true for internally-oriented persons. Internally-oriented persons appear to approximate the existential ideal, in the sense that they regard life to be a series of decisions which they can influence. There is ample evidence accumulating that these internally-oriented persons are activistic and effective in their functioning.

Let us turn now to some studies comparing various socially significant groupings of people as to the external or internal nature of their beliefs concerning control. In one of a series of studies on racial or ethnic group-ings, Battle and Rotter (1963) found that lower class blacks were sig-nificantly more external (measured by the Children's Picture Test of In-ternal-External Control) than lower class whites or middle-class blacks and whites. Using adult subjects, Lefcourt and Ladwig (1965, 1966) re-ported higher rates of belief in external control among black than among white prison inmates. In a third ethnic group investigation, Graves (1961) adapted the *I-E* Scale for high school students and found whites to be most internal, followed by Spanish-Americans, and then American Indians. Concerning males enrolled in a southern black college, Gore and Rotter (1963) found that subjects scoring most in-ternal (*I-E* Scale) signed statements expressing the greatest amount of interest in social action concerning civil rights. That these statements did not represent empty commitments is shown by Strickland (1965) who found that actual black activists have a stronger belief in their own power than do blacks who do not take part in the civil rights move-ment. Similar results were obtained by Coleman, Campbell, Hobson, McPartland, Mood, Weinfeld, and York (1966) in their study of 645,000 pupils in grades 3, 6, 9, and 12 in 4,000 American public schools. In summarizing this amazing study, they (Coleman et al., 1966, p. 23) say:

> . . . A pupil attitude factor, which appears to have a stronger relation-ship to achievement than do all the "school" factors together, is the ex-tent to which an individual feels that he has some control over his own destiny. . . . The responses of pupils to questions in the survey show that minority pupils, except for Orientals, have far less conviction than whites that they can affect their own environments and futures. When they do, however, their achievement is higher than that of whites who lack that conviction.

In all of the ethnic studies, groups whose social position is lowly either by class or race tend to score higher in the external-control direction. And to judge from the already reported attitudinal and action correlates of the belief in external control, it is easy to see why disadvantage due to class or race tends to perpetuate itself. Supporting the dire implication of the ethnic studies are the findings of Cromwell, Rosenthal, Shakow, and Kahn (1961) to the effect that schizophrenics have a stronger belief in external control (using three measures) than do normals. If, as Maddi (1967, 1970) has contended, some proportion of people diagnosed schizophrenic are actually suffering from existential sickness, then this result lends some support to the contention that conformity is the premorbid state for this sickness.

The investigators whose work I have summarized obviously want to reach the conclusion that the belief that reward is externally or internally controlled has a causal influence on actions. To be sure, this seems a sensible position, especially with regard to some of the studies, such as that of Coleman et al. (1966), where beliefs concerning locus of control seem intimately related to school achievement. But all of the studies discussed are correlational in nature, making conclusions of causality highly inferential. It could be, for example, that it is actual experiences of competence and effectiveness that incline one to the belief in the internal control of rewards, rather than the other way around. In defense of their interpretation of belief as that which causes action, Rotter and his associates have marshaled experimental rather than correlational evidence. For example, Phares (1957) had two groups of subjects perform the same task of predicting a sequence of events. One group was told that success on the task was due to skill in deciphering the ordering of events, whereas the other group was told that success was due to chance, there being no rational ordering. Despite the fact that both groups received the same number and sequence of reinforcements, subjects with skill instructions changed expectancies more frequently and more in the direction of previous experience than did subjects with chance instructions. The differences in action between the two groups seemed understandable on the basis of whether subjects did or did not believe that they could influence their own destiny. Analogous findings have been obtained concerning perceptual thresholds for nonsense syllables (Phares, 1962), and resistance to extinction (Holden & Rotter, 1962; James & Rotter, 1958; Rotter, Liverant, & Crowne, 1961). The evidence from these studies indicating that people who believe they can influence the occurrence of reward through their own skill act differently from people not having this belief certainly strengthens the inference made concerning the direction of causality in the correlational studies.

But before leaving the *I-E* Scale, I should point out that several recent studies have questioned its homogeneity. Collins (1974) administered the test to 300 college students, and factor analyzed the scores. He found a common theme running through the items, but was also able to abstract four fairly distinct and unrelated factors. The factors seemed to distinguish the belief in the world as (1) a difficult place, (2) an unjust place, (3) a place governed by luck, or (4) a politically unresponsive place. Abramowitz (1973) separated the *I-E* Scale items into those of a political nature and those of a more personal nature. Utilizing 166 male and female subjects, he found that the political items correlated positively with membership in sociopolitical action groups, whereas the personal items did not. Through studies of this sort we may learn more about what is admittedly an intriguing test.

Turning from the *I-E* Scale, we find a gradually developing body of studies quite relevant to, and for the most part inspired by, existential theorizing. For example, Houston, and Holmes (1974) subjected their subjects to conditions of threat involving temporal uncertainty. Some of the subjects were induced to avoid thinking about the threat by immersing themselves in distracting activities, whereas the other subjects were left to their own devices. Physiological measurement showed that the subjects engaging in avoidance thinking actually experienced a greater stress reaction to the threat than the other subjects. Through interviews, it was determined that the subjects who did not engage in avoidance activities spent the time thinking about the threat and reappraising it as less serious than originally believed. Insofar as a temporal uncertainty is not very different from ontological anxiety, this study provides support for the existential belief that accepting such anxiety rather than avoiding it is consistent with personal growth. Liem (1973) permitted some students in an undergraduate course to choose the type of recitation section they preferred, and granted them considerable choice in the ongoing conduct of the section, but denied such choice to other students in the course. Subjects who were permitted choice performed better than the others on a course examination, and give higher ratings of satisfaction with their sections than did subjects not permitted choice. This is another demonstration of the value for personal comfort and growth of control over one's own life.

Some interest is developing in devising ways of measuring the sense of meaninglessness that results from an accumulation of ontological guilt. Crumbaugh and Maholik (1964) and Crumbaugh (1968) have offered a questionnaire, called the *Purpose in Life Test*, aimed at assessing Frankl's concept of existential vacuum. Although their study of the reliability of the questionnaire is quite incomplete, they do report an estimate of internal consistency of .85 with 120 subjects. The construct validation of the instrument is also scant, but there is a correlation of .44 with the Depression scale of the Minnesota Multiphasic Personality Inventory, and another of .48 for males and .32 for females with a measure of anomie. Sharpe and Viney (1973) administered the

Purpose in Life Test to 58 college students, and also interviewed them concerning their world view. Then three judges rated the interviews for indications of meaninglessness. Subjects showing existential vacuum on the *Purpose in Life Test* had world views that were negative, lacking in purpose, and devoid of transcendent goals. Although this test is probably of value, much more care must be given to its development than has taken place thus far.

Another related test, called the *Existential Study,* is under development by Thorne (1973), Pishkin and Thorne (1973), and Thorne and Pishkin (1973). The 200-item questionnaire has been produced factor analytically to yield seven scales on self-status, self-actualization, existential morale, existential vacuum, humanistic identification, existence and destiny, and suicidal tendency. In one study, the test was administered to 193 felons, 89 alcoholics, 153 adherents to Ayn Rand's rational philosophy, 336 unwed mothers, 159 students, and 338 schizophrenics. The followers of Rand were highest in existential morale, with students and felons next, alcoholics and unwed mothers demoralized, and schizophrenics disintegrated. However interesting this test may be, it should be recognized that (1) little information regarding internal consistency and stability is available, (2) not must has been done to determine its construct validity, and (3) it has not been guided by a consistent and definite set of existential ideas (e.g., self-actualization is not really an existential concept).

Maddi (1975) has devised a 60 item questionnaire, called the *Alienation Test,* assessing the powerlessness, adventurousness, nihilism, and vegetativeness aspects of meaninglessness that appear in his theorizing. Each of these dimensions can be measured across relationships to work, persons, social institutions, family members, and self. The internal consistency of the dimensions and relationships ranges from .62 to .96 with an average of .86. Stability figures range from .54 to .87 with an average of .80. Relevant to discriminant validation are the findings that that *Alienation Test* is uncorrelated to intelligence or sex, though it does show a small and understandable relationship to socioeconomic class and age. A beginning on convergent validation has been made in that the scales of the *Alienation Test* show negative correlation of varying degree with a measure of creative attitudes toward living. Also, persons scoring high on meaninglessness in interpersonal relationships describe themselves as enjoying time spent alone. Once again, additional study is needed before the value of this test can be determined.

There is also a growing body of research on the regular tendency of some persons to conform by trying to be socially desirable. This literature is clearly important for the existential position, though it is also relevant for Rogers, Maslow, and Allport.

But at the outset, I should address a ready criticism. Much of the research in which conformity is measured on some performance task suggests that conforming tendencies are situation specific (e.g., Hollander & Willis, 1967). This could be taken as evidence that no conformist personality type exists. But such a conclusion seems premature, however mystifying the performance results may be. There is, after all, a considerable body of research suggesting that indeed the tendency to conform may be quite general. I refer to the research employing questionnaire measures of socially desirable responding and internal versus external locus of control.

Crowne and Marlow (1960) have reported an extensive attempt at construct validation for their carefully developed Social Desirability Scale (M–C SDS). On the face of it, the tendency to respond in a socially desirable direction should express conformity and an emphasis on social role playing. By and large, the empirical findings bear this out. In an extensive research program (Crowne & Marlowe, 1960) it was determined that persons scoring high, compared to low, in socially desirable responding show greater attitude change after delivering an appeal for an attitude they did not originally endorse (thereby resolving cognitive dissonance); express higher need for affiliation; and terminate psychotherapy sooner (perhaps out of unwillingness to face themselves). In addition, the higher the M–C SDS score, the greater the tendency to give common word associations and fewer, more concrete responses on the Thematic Apperception, Rorschach, and sentence completion tests. In their fantasy productions, high M–C SDS scorers are especially rejecting of people, but tend to underestimate the extent to which their friends really reject them. The highest thresholds in a perceptual task requiring the recognition of obscene words belong to these high social-desirability scorers.

There is also a group of findings concerning socially desirable responding and performance of simple laboratory tasks. Subjects high on the M–C SDS generally perform better on the pursuit rotor (Strickland & Jenkins, 1964) and do more skillfully a motor steadiness task (Strickland, 1965) and other simple motor tasks (Willington & Strickland, 1965). Although the results may indicate superior motor ability in these subjects, it seems more likely that we are observing the heightened attentiveness provided by a wish to appear socially desirable. Consistent with this interpretation is the finding (Crowne & Marlowe, 1960) that subjects high in M–C SDS are less likely to rate a monotonous spool-packing task as dull.

In general, the picture emerging is of a personality type characterized by intense interest in appearing attentive, consistent, competent, and acceptable, in the context of conformity, and showing superficial interest in, but lack of deep commitment to, others and a general unwillingness to face these facts. The implications of defensiveness are supported by Conn and Crowne (1964), who found that high M–C SDS scorers selected euphoria as an alternative to the expression of anger in a manner suggestive of reaction formation. Similarly, Fishman (1965) found that subjects high in M–C SDS expressed less verbal aggression toward the experimenter when he imposed nonarbitrary frustration (whereas arbitrary frustration did not differentiate high from low M–C SDS scorers). Apparently, the person high in socially desirable responding can only express anger when he can give himself justification (or rationalization) for it.

Any information concerning the relationship of M–C SDS to psychopathology should be of interest, as Maddi (1967, 1970) has contended that conformism is the premorbid state for existential sickness. Even though the M–C SDS was specifically designed to be independent of frank psychopathology, there is some research indicating that this is not so. Katkin (1964) reports the correlations between the M–C SDS and the MMPI scales commonly used to assess psychopathological trends. Eight of the 10 correlations reached significance, raising the possibility that conformity predisposes toward sickness. That the strongest correlation was between the M–C SDS and the Schizophrenia Scale is noteworthy, as Maddi (1967, 1970) assumes that many persons diagnosed schizophrenic are actually suffering from existential sickness.

The research reviewed thus far has concerned the aspect of conformity emphasizing social reductionism in the definition of life. Maddi and Costa have collected some unpublished information concerning this phenomenon that is presented here merely in the spirit of exploration. They devised a Biological Reductionism Scale (BR Scale) that, after piloting and psychometric analysis, consists of 10 items. The reliability of the scale is .75. Examples of items are "Man's ability to think makes him different in kind, not just degree, from the other animals" and "Sexuality in man is more an expression of affection than a biological need."

Scores on the BR Scale were obtained from a sample of male and female college students numbering 60. Also obtained on these subjects were scores on measures of imagination, originality, interest in variety, stimulus-seeking, judgment, divergent thinking, and internal versus external locus of control. With the exception of the BR Scale, the other measures are already in the literature. Although this simplified our task at the outset, it complicated the attempt to clarify the meaning of the results, for the measures often turned out on empirical analysis to be something slightly different than expected. In any event, the results do show promise.

It was surmised that the BR Scale would correlate positively with the *I-E* Scale on the grounds that one form of reductionism ought to occur generally with the other. The correlation was not significant, but further analysis of the internal consistency of the *I-E* Scale showed that on the sample at least there are two distinct components involved. One component contains items concerning the person's beliefs about his ability to influence the events of his personal life (e.g., "People's misfortunes result from the mistakes they make"), whereas the other component deals with control over more distant social system or political events (e.g., "By taking an active part in political and social affairs the people can control world events"). Treating these two components separately led to the uncovering of a correlation of .24 ($p < .03$) between the social system component of the *I-E* Scale and the BR Scale. This lends support to the contention that someone who sees himself as an embodiment of biological needs will also consider social role-playing of importance.

The BR Scale also showed a correlation of $-.0.26$ ($p < .02$) with a composite measure of imagination composed of the Plot Titles, Symbol Production, and Remote Consequences Tests from the divergent thinking battery (Guilford, 1967) and the Novelty of Productions Score derived from Thematic Apperception Test stories (Maddi, Propst, & Feldinger, 1965). Further, there was a correlation of $-.23$ ($p < .04$) between the BR Scale and a composite of the three need-for-variety-measures scored from Thematic Apperception Test stories (Maddi et al., 1965). Finally, the BR Scale and a measure of stimulus seeking (Zuckerman, Kolin, Price, & Zoob, 1964) showed a correlation of $-.24$ ($p < .03$). The general implication of these findings is that persons who define themselves as embodiments of biological needs tend not to be imaginative, original, or interested in novelty or stimulus-seeking. This suggests that biological reductionism is properly considered an aspect of conformism.

Kelly's position

Kelly, the consistency theorist, says virtually nothing substantive concerning the periphery of personality. Consequently, there is virtually nothing we can do in the attempt to determine the empirical viability of his position. Using Kelly's Role Constructs Repertory Test (see Chapter 4), Bieri (1961) has shown that people differ in the number of bipolar constructs they have available to them. But these differences in psychological complexity or differentiation do not really bear on the peripheral point of view that is explicitly Kelly's. They are potentially of importance, however, to any theory conceptualizing differences of differentiation in peripheral personality (e.g., Allport, existential psychology).

There is an intriguing, though admittedly inductive rather than hypothesis testing study by Sechrest (1968), in which two samples of 57 and 67 nursing students participated. They all filled out the Role Constructs Repertory Test, and also took the Minnesota Multiphasic Personality Inventory (MMPI), and a sociometric instrument requiring them to specify how pleasant they thought each member of their group was. Sechrest determined that the personal constructs of intelligent-unintelligent, anxious-nonanxious, and friendly-unfriendly were among the most common in the group. His attempt, then, was to determine whether the personal constructs one employs are expressive in some sense of the realities of one's existence. This hypothesis, while not strictly derivable from Kelly, is consistent with the general emphasis in his approach on a kind of rational trial and error in finding the best bases for navigating life. Sechrest also had available to him his subjects' linguistic ability score on the American Council on Education Test (a kind of intelligence measure). He tried to evaluate scores on this against reliance upon intelligence-unintelligence as a construct. From the Minnesota Multiphasic Personality Inventory, he extracted an anxiety score (the Psychasthenia scale) to evaluate against reliance on the anxious-nonanxious construct. For similar purposes with regard to the friendly-unfriendly construct, he utilized a number of sociometric nominations as a friendly person. His (Sechrest, 1968) results appear in Table 10–18.

As you can see, moderately intelligent subjects are more likely to use intelligence as a personal construct than highly intelligent ones. At the lowest level, there is no difference. Those subjects who employ anxious-nonanxious as a construct are likely to be either extremely high or low on the MMPI measure of anxiety. But the findings concerning the low end of the scale on Sample 1 are washed out on Sample 2. The safest conclusion is that highly anxious subjects use anxious-nonanxious as a

TABLE 10–18

Relationships between employment of certain personal constructs and corresponding personal characteristics

Personal characteristic measuring instrument	Score	Personal construct			
		Sample 1 (N = 57)*		Sample 2 (N = 67)	
		Nonuse	Use	Nonuse	Use
		Intelligent-unintelligent			
ACE aptitude test					
L score	70+	15	4	16	9
	60–69	6	11	8	14
	–59	12	9	10	10
	x^2	7.02; p < .05		3.57; p < .20	
		Anxious-nonanxious			
MMPI					
Pt raw score	20+	2	13	2	12
	10–19	15	15	18	21
	–9	1	9	7	7
	x^2	8.66; p < .02		5.03; p < .10	
		Friendly-unfriendly			
Nominating					
No. of nominations	10+	6	22	5	25
	–9	14	15	15	22
	x^2	4.52; p < .05		4.52; p < .05	

* For personal construct "anxious-nonanxious" N = 55 only.
Source: L. Sechrest, "Personal constructs and personal characteristics," *J. Indiv. Psychol.*, 1968, 24, 162–166.

construct. Similarly, subjects relying on friendly-unfriendly in their construct system receive a large number of nominations as "most pleasant." This study provides evidence of correspondence between the way one construes the world and the way one behaves in it. It is not possible, however, to specify which comes first. Although the use of such presumably uninfluenceable variables as intelligence suggests that construals follow objective features of experience, this inference is not convincing with regard to anxiety and popularity.

Nonetheless, more work of this sort should be done. Perhaps the work of Adams-Webber (1970) on the discriminant validity of various forms of the Role Constructs Repertory Test suggests an increase in interest concerning personal construct study. Recently, Guertin (1973) employed a procedure for computer analyzing data describing the important persons in a subject's life using his own constructs as variables. Factor analysis yielded personal, people, and cultural factors.

McClelland's position

Fantasy techniques for measuring personality present the person with an ambiguous or incomplete stimulus, requiring that he structure or complete it by exercise of his own imagination. In utilizing his own fantasy to structure or complete the stimulus, he is presumably displaying his personality. Although fantasy techniques have been criticized for being so uncontrolled that it is truly difficult to determine the real meaning of any responses by the person, they have the great advantage over self-descriptive techniques of being more likely to circumvent response styles. There are no right or wrong answers on a fantasy task, and the investigator encourages the subject to realize this. If it is not clear what the investigator is trying to find out, it is unlikely that the person being tested will find some basis for being acquiescent or responding in socially desirable fashion. This is why McClelland has considered fantasy measures the most relevant to the motive construct, with its personal rather than societal goals. The technique of eliciting fantasy he has relied upon is the *Thematic Apperception Test* (Murray, 1943), with its ambiguous pictures, about which the subject must compose a story with a beginning, middle, and end.

The first motive concentrated on was the need for achievement (McClelland, Atkinson, Clark & Lowell, 1953). McClelland et al., first devised a scoring system for thematic apperception suiting his definition of the need as goal-directed fantasy expressing competition with a standard of excellence. After reading a story composed by someone, the investigator applies the first, or general component of the scoring system. This component calls for the overall judgment as to whether the story includes imagery *definitely relevant* (scored 1), *doubtfully relevant* (scored 0), or *definitively irrelevant* (scored −1) to competition with a standard of excellence. If the story is scored definitely relevant, then the second (or specific) and third (or weighting) components of the scoring system are employed. The second component involves scoring for the presence (1) or absence (0) of each of the specific categories of goal-directed functioning. These categories are achievement *wish, instrumental activity* toward an achievement goal, *block* or obstacle to reaching the goal, *goal anticipation,* and associated *goal affect.* The third component is for weighting purposes, and involves giving an additional point to a story which is completely devoted to an achievement theme. All of the stories composed by the person are scored in this fashion, with the intensity of need for achievement indicated by the algebraic sum of the scores.

As you know from the ideal research strategy previously discussed, the first thing to consider is the reliability of this measure of the need for achievement. Since fantasy measures require considerable judgment on the investigator's part, one kind of reliability that is important is that between two independent users of the scoring system. It has been repeatedly demonstrated (Atkinson, 1958; McClelland et al. 1953) that two experienced scorers working independently can obtain need for achievement scores from the same protocols that agree to the tune of correlations exceeding .90. This is excellent interscorer reliability. The situation concerning the internal consistency and stability of the need for achievement measure is not nearly as satisfactory. Correlations range from .22 to .54 for stability (Haber & Alpert, 1958; Lowell, 1950) and are approximately .65 for internal consistency (Atkinson, 1950). Recognizing that we might conclude that there was no compelling empirical evidence here that the concrete peripheral characteristic, need for achievement, really exists, McClelland (1958) has pointed out that validity is much more important than reliability, especially in a fantasy measure. After all, fantasy tests by their nature involve considerable measurement error, as the investigator cannot be sure in any particular instance that he has properly understood the respondent's real meaning. McClelland recommends that we consider the internal consistency and stability results to indicate that the reliability of the measure is somewhere above zero, and proceed with all haste to an assessment of validity.

A great many studies have been done investigating the construct validity of the fantasy measure of the need for achievement. One of these studies is experimental in nature, whereas the others are correlational. The experimental study and most of the correlational studies concern the effects of high and low levels of the need for achievement on the behavior of individual people, whereas the remainder of the correlational studies concerns the effects of the need on the social system phenomenon of economic growth. Let us consider first the studies concerning individuals.

The experiment of McClelland, Atkinson, and Clark (1949) launched the study of individuals. It had as its major aim demonstration that an investigator could arouse the need for achievement by experimental manipulation of a theoretically relevant sort. There were two groups of male college students included, both of which groups were given a series of tasks to perform. In the experimental group, the tasks were introduced as tests of intelligence that are often used to select people of high administrative capacity for positions in Washington. There was further elaboration of the ability of the tasks to disclose a person's capacity to organize material, to evaluate crucial situations quickly and accurately, and to be a leader. In short, the instructions given to the experimental group were calculated to arouse a high level of need for achievement. In contrast, the control group was given the same tasks to perform but with neutral, relaxing instructions stressing that the investigator just wanted to try out some tests of uncertain utility. Following the brief, but difficult tasks, the people in both groups were asked to compose stories about four ambiguous pictures showing human beings in work situations.

The important data of the study are these expressions of fantasy. There were striking, and theoretically reasonable differences in the stories composed by the two groups. To make the differences vivid, I shall quote one story from the control group and one from the experimental. Both stories were composed in response to a picture of a boy sitting at a desk with a book open in front of him. First, the control group story:

> A boy in a classroom who is daydreaming about something. He is recalling a previously experienced incident that struck his mind to be more appealing than being in the classroom. He is thinking about the experience and is now imagining himself in the situation. He hopes to be there. He will probably get called on by the instructor to recite and will be embarrassed.

Nothing in this story deals with achievement or with standards of excellence, but compare it with an experimental group story:

> The boy is taking an hour written. He and the others are high-school students. The test is about two-thirds over and he is doing his best to think it through. He was supposed to study for the test and did so. But because it is factual, there were items he saw but did not learn. He knows he has studied the answers he can't remember and is trying to summon up the images and related ideas to remind him of them. He may remember one or two, but he will miss most of the items he can't remember. He will try hard until five minutes is left, then give up, go back over his paper, and be disgusted for reading but not learning the answer.

Thinking in terms of the scoring system mentioned earlier, this story certainly qualifies as *definitely relevant* to competition with a standard of excellence under the first component. As to the second component of the scoring system, there is evidence for *obstacle* of a personal variety ("he saw but did not learn"), *instrumental activity* ("trying to summon up the images and related ideas to remind him of them"), *goal anticipation* ("He may remember one or two, but he will miss most of the items he can't remember"), and *goal affect* ("and be disgusted for reading but not learning the answer"). Clearly, this story would also be wighted under the third component of the scoring system, because there is nothing but an achievement theme represented.

To be more precise about the results of this experiment, I should report two things to you. First, the average intensity of need for achievement, relying upon total score attributed to each protocol through use of the entire scoring system, was significantly greater in the experimental group than in the control group. In addition, each of the specific categories of goal-directed fantasy comprising the second component of the scoring system was significantly greater in the experimental than in the control group. These results provide evidence of the validity of the fantasy measure of need for achievement. But some of you may be wondering, since reading the high need for achievement story quoted above, whether obstacles that are not surmounted, instrumental activity that is unsuccessful, and negative affect concerning the goal, have a proper place in a measure of the need for achievement. Should not such a measure include only fantasy positively oriented toward achievement? From the beginning, McClelland and his associates have contended that fantasy reference to obstacles, instrumental activity, goal anticipation, and goal affect referring to competition with a standard of excellence are relevant regardless of the pessimism or optimism of their content. Pessimistic and optimistic content may well define the avoidance and approach versions of the need, respectively, but both are relevant. Some empirical support for this distinction between approach and avoidance versions of the need for achievement is to be found in the experiment we are considering. The experimental group was subdivided into a group that experienced failure on performing the tasks following the achievement arousing instructions, and a group that experienced success. In the former subgroup of the experimental group, pessimistic content in achievement-relevant fantasy was more common than it was in the latter subgroup. Recently, Atkinson (1960) has interpreted many findings of the performance of people high in test anxiety as indicating fear of failure, rather than the more positive need for achievement.

Over the last 15 years, a great deal of correlational work has been done in an attempt to determine whether the fantasy measure of need for achievement predicts the sorts of actions and life patterns that one would expect. I cannot possibly review all the studies here, nor would that be necessary. It will suffice to summarize major findings in such fashion that the significance for living of need for achievement becomes apparent.

First, there is a group of findings suggesting the social and intellectual significance of high or low levels of the need for achievement. American males with high need for achievement come more often from the middle class than from the lower or upper class, have better memory for incompleted tasks when the situation is arranged such that everyone must complete and fail to complete an equal number of tasks, are more apt to volunteer as subjects for psychological experiments, are more active in college and community activities, choose experts over friends when asked who they want as partners to work on difficult problems, and are more resistant to social pressure to conform (Atkinson, 1958; McClelland et al., 1953).

Of even more theoretical importance is a group of findings concerning how people high and low in need for achievement actually perform when confronted with a work situation. Lowell (see McClelland, 1961) presented people with a task requiring them to unscramble many scrabbled words, and recorded how many words a person unscrambled in each of five consecutive periods of four-minutes duration. As you can see in Figure 10–1, people high and low in need for achievement started at about the same level of performance, but, as time went on, those with high levels of the need did progressively better than those with low levels. The people high in need for achievement appear to be concerned enough

FIGURE 10–1

Mean output of scrambled words per four-minute period for subjects with high and low *N* achievement scores

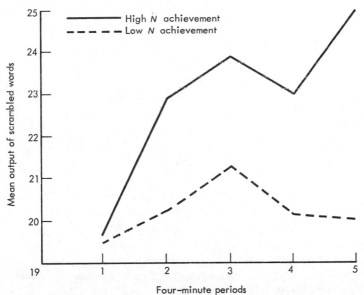

Source: D. C. McClelland. *The achieving society.* Princeton, N.J.: Van Nostrand, 1961.

about doing the task well to learn how to do it better as they go along. But you should not assume that these people will do better at any kind of task. Indeed, at a routine, ordinary task, where one cannot learn to do better as one proceeds—crossing out the *s*'s in printed material, for example—there is no difference in the performance of people with high and low need for achievement. Similar results were obtained by French (1955) using a decoding task, presented under instructional conditions encouraging relaxation. Indeed, another group of people performed the decoding task under instructional conditions relevant to other motives than the need for achievement. The instructions indicated that those people doing the work fastest would be allowed to leave the room, whereas the others would have to continue working. Under these instructional conditions, the people low in need for achievement actually do a little better than the others, indicating that the possibility of getting out of work is what appeals to them the most. All these results together suggest that high need for achievement will lead a person to perform better when he perceives that he can display significant excellence through his attempts. If the task is routine or if finishing it sooner implies cooperating with someone or getting some nonachievement reward like time off, subjects low in need for achievement (and presumably high in some other needs) will perform better.

That people high in need for achievement are challenged by situations in which they can display significant excellence is echoed in studies concerning risk taking. McClelland (1958) reports that people high in need for achievement will choose to take moderate risks, in a ring-toss game permitting the person to stand as close to the ring as he wants, whereas those low in need for achievement will take either large or small risks. You can convince yourself of this by observing, in Figure 10–2, that the biggest differences between the curves for high and low need for achievement groups occurred in conjunction with moderate probability of success. McClelland suggests, ingeniously, that taking both large and small risks has the function of removing the outcome from implication for your own skill and excellence. Success or failure is then either ensured, or a matter of chance. But in taking a moderate risk, you are trying to be successful in a context that properly tests your skill. It is the high need for achievement person who would be challenged by such a possibility.

Summarizing thus far, it seems clear that it is possible to develop a fantasy measure of the concrete peripheral characteristic need for achievement, which though not distinguished from the point of view of internal consistency and stability, operates in a theoretically meaningful fashion in both experiment and correlation study.

Convincing though these studies are, there do exist some perplexing results as well (see Katz, 1967; Klinger, 1966). Notable among the perplexities are questions about the generality of the fantasy measure,

FIGURE 10–2

Percentage of throws made by five-year-olds with high and low "Doodle" N achievement at different distances from the peg and smoothed curve of probability of success at those distances. 26 S's, 10 throws each. Plotted at midpoints of intervals of 11 inches beginning with closest distance stood (4"–14", 5"–15", etc.)

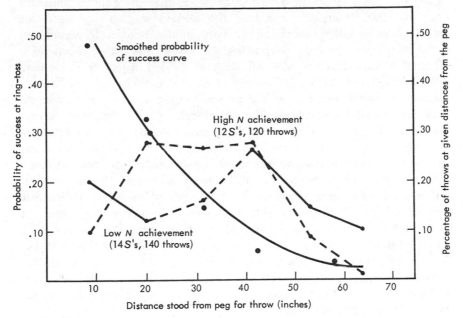

its applicability to females, and its openness to contamination by other variables. The answers to these questions should be sought in future research. Having found a measure that has brought us this far, we can ask the more precise question of whether it is clear that the measure has motivational status. There are three things one would expect of a measure if it had motivational status in McClelland's terms: that it refer to striving toward a goal, that it reflect at least momentary satiation when the goal is reached, and that it concern personal rather than societal goals. The first expectation is shown in the results already covered. Not only does the measure itself indicate striving toward a standard of excellence, but so too do its work relevant correlates. The evidence concerning momentary satiation, though not extensive, is very intriguing. In an attempt to understand the reliability of the measure better, Atkinson (1958) correlated the need for achievement score obtained on each story with that of each other story. The results of this indicate a kind of saw-toothed effect, in which writing a story high in need for achievement seems to satiate one momentarily, leading to the immediately following story being low in the need. The story immediately following this will be high again, and so forth. This effect occurs in most persons, regardless of their overall score on need for achievement. The effect is just what you would expect in a motive measure, and helps us to take a more sophisticated view of the low reliability of the fantasy measure. The low reliability is partly an inevitable result of actually measuring a motive, which is, after all, a waxing and waning thing.

The final requirement of a motive measure is that it tap personal rather than societal goals. There is evidence that the fantasy measure does just this. It seems clear that the fantasy measure of need for achievement is either unrelated or very mildly related to structured self-descriptive measures purporting to assess the same need (De Charms, Morrison, Reitman, & McClelland, 1955; Lindzey & Heineman, 1955; McClelland, 1958; McClelland et al., 1953). Whereas the fantasy measure is based on those of the person's thoughts that are unencumbered by societal restrictions, the structured self-description measures are based on the degree to which the person subscribes to universalistic achievement sentiments posed by other people. As such, the latter measures should tap achievement values or schemata more than motives, with the opposite being true of the fantasy measure. The absence or mildness of correlation between the two types of measure is therefore understandable. This interpretation is strengthened by the nature of the correlates obtained for the two kinds of measure. De Charms et al. (1955) found that whereas the fantasy measure was correlated to behaviors involving memory and performance, a structured self-description measure involving achievement values was not related to such behaviors but was related to the tendency to be influenced by the opinions of experts in an ambiguous situation.

The fantasy measure seems to tap an achievement motive in McClelland's sense, and the structured self-description measure may well tap an achievement schema. This conclusion requires discussion of the position put forward by Campbell and Fiske (1959) to the effect that one must be able to measure a concrete peripheral characteristic by more than one method in order to be sure that it exists. If the characteristic shows up on only one measurement operation, then there is too much risk that one is measuring no more than a peculiar attribute of that type of operation, and nothing of substantive significance for personality. Although this seems a position with much soundness, results like those mentioned in the previous paragraph alert us to the need for greater precision. For example, to require that attempts to measure the need for achievement in fantasy and in structured self-description agree before concluding that the need really exists would be directly contradictory of theoretical formulations of the nature of the need. The only form of Campbell's and Fiske's position warranted here is that one might want to develop two fantasy measures of need for achievement, in order to ensure that the current measure is not somehow an artifact of the thematic apperception task. In general, attempts to measure peripheral characteristics by more than one method should be guided by theorizing concerning the nature of the characteristic. One should not require a characteristic to show generality across any old measurement operations.

I shall turn now to the correlational studies linking the need for achievement to the social system phenomenon of economic development. These studies constitute the most exciting demonstration of the effects of personality on society that exist in the social science literature, however much one may criticize fine points of methodology and interpretation. The theoretical impetus for considering the need for achievement to be a determinant of economic development comes from the classical sociologist, Max Weber (1930). In his view, it was the impact of Protestantism upon people that spurred industrialization and capitalism. As a sociologist, he sought causes for social system phenomena in the social system itself. Protestantism is a social institution of a religious nature, and as such, is not an attribute of individuals. The explanation thus obtained is bound, therefore, not to cover each person one can find. Indeed, the explanation is too gross to hold even for all societies. Although the most important societies that became industrialized were predominantly Protestant in religion, there are definite exceptions. Belgium, for example, had as vigorous an industrial revolution as any northern European country, even though the orthodox religion there was Catholicism. And Venice achieved a form of capitalism that was perhaps more pure and vigorous than any seen in modern times, all the while it was officially Catholic. Such observations lead the personologist to speculate that Weber was right insofar as his social system "cause" mirrored an underlying psychological or individual cause. An even more accurate version of the supposed cause than Protestantism might be protestantism, or the existence of a set of values in people stressing the importance of hard work, excellence, and self-reliance. These values generally overlap with Protestantism as a religious form, but need not always do so. McClelland theorized that values such as these lead parents to create the kinds of experience for their children leading to high levels of the need for achievement, in much the same manner already described in Chapter 8. If enough parents in a society bring up their children this way, then there will eventually be many citizens choosing a way of life involving the challenge of competition with a standard of excellence. Following Weber, McClelland contends that this challenge is most vivid and salient in entrepreneurial activity, which activity is basic to economic development.

Utilizing this general theoretical framework, three extraordinary studies have been performed. In the first of these, Berlew (1956) attempted to determine the relationship between the modal level of need for achievement and economic growth in ancient Greece. Following accepted historical belief, Berlew considered three time periods for this society: the period of growth, from 900 B.C. to 475 B.C.; the period of climax, from 475 B.C. to 362 B.C.; and the period of decline, from 362 B.C. to 100 B.C. In each of these time periods, he tried to measure both need for achievement and economic development. For the first, Berlew decided to use as raw material surviving literature, and to analyze this in much the same manner I described previously for the analysis of thematic apperception stories. From each of the time periods, he selected literature in the following categories: Man and his gods, farm and estate management, public funeral celebrations, poetry, epigrams, and war speeches of encouragement. These categories were selected in an attempt to sample widely literature that was imaginative more than realistic or descriptive. Because of its imaginative nature, one could expect this literature to be expressive of the personal motives of the writers. These writers were all famous and excellent men, a fact which Berlew feels increased the likelihood that in measuring their need for achievement level he was obtaining a representative picture of the modal level of this need in the society at large. If these men were so valued by their society, they must have mirrored it fairly accurately. Finally, the number of lines in each category of literature and in each time period was the same, in order to ensure that there was no bias in the measurement of need for achievement. In this manner, Berlew was able to obtain average levels of the need associated with each of the three time periods.

The measurement of economic development was, if anything, more difficult to obtain. After considering and rejecting as unfeasible the most obvious measure, Berlew decided upon a measure that is intriguing though somewhat indirect. To understand its significance, you must remember that the economic life of the Greek city-states was organized around agriculture and overseas trade. Above all, it was maritime commerce which brought prosperity, and Athens and its seaport, Piraeus, were at the very center of Greek commerce. What Greece had to trade was largely surplus wine and olive oil. These were sent overseas to trade for grain from Sicily, rugs from Persia, the perfumes of Arabia, foodstuffs, and basic metals and other materials. Olive oil and wine were carried in large earthenware jars which remained in the cities of delivery even after their contents were consumed. These jars, many of which were made by potters in or near Athens, have been found in regions all around the Mediterranean and many of them dated at least within the century of their production and use. From the anthropological literature concerning the location of these vase remains, Berlew was able to calculate the area of Greek trade in millions of square miles. He contends that, especially for Greece, whose prosperity depended so much on commerce, extensiveness of trade area is a plausible measure of economic development.

Now I can tell you about the results of this groundbreaking study. In the periods of growth, climax, and decline, the average levels of need for achievement were 4.74, 2.71, and 1.35, respectively, a trend that is statistically significant. The levels of economic growth associated with these three time periods were 1.2 million square miles, 3.4 million square miles, and 1.9 million square miles. Depicted in Figure 10–3, these dramatic results lead Berlew to the conclusion that the high level of need for achievement in the period of growth had the effect of spurring economic development, as shown by the sharp increase in trade area from this period to the period of climax. In addition, the decrease in level of need for achievement in the period of climax determined a decrease in economic growth, as shown by the sharp decrease in trade area from this period to the period of decline.

In truth, these results, however striking they are, can be criticized on many methodological grounds. One might almost commend the investigator on his courage in attempting to demonstrate the effect of personality factors on societal phenomena in a historical situation. But the results obtained and the conclusions formulated are upheld in equally striking fashion by two similar studies concerning different societies. One study (Cortes, 1960) involved Spain in the late Middle Ages. Cortes

FIGURE 10–3

Average *N* achievement level plotted at midpoints of periods of growth, climax, and decline of Athenian civilization as reflected in the extent of its trade area

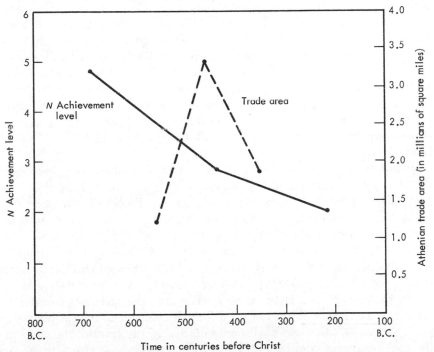

Source: D. E. Berlew. "The achievement motive and the growth of Greek civilization." Unpublished bachelor's thesis. Middletown, Conn.: Wesleyan Univer., 1956.

identified periods of economic growth, from 1200 to 1492 A.D., climax, from 1492 to 1610 A.D., and decline, from 1610 to 1730 A.D. The measure of modal level of need for achievement was very similar to that of Berlew. Literary catgeories of fiction, verse, history, and legends were sampled with the same precautions used in the previous study. The measure of economic growth was shipping cleared from Spain for the New World in thousands of tons per year. The results of this study are strikingly similar to those of Berlew. Cortes found a level of need for achievement that was highest in the period of growth, and lowest in the period of decline. Economic growth, in contrast, was highest in the period of climax, and quite low in both of the other periods.

The final study indicating that modal level of need for achievement in a society will exert an influence on subsequent economic activity is that of Bradburn and Berlew (1961) concerning England from Tudor times to the Industrial Revolution. The investigators divided this span of time into 50-year segments. For purposes of measuring need for achievement, they sampled the literary categories of drama, sea voyages, and street ballads, again with the same precautions employed by Berlew. Their measure of economic development was gains in coal imports at the port of London above and beyond what would have been expected on the basis of past figures. The procedure for estimating gain is complex. Suffice it to say that using gain estimates rather than gross amounts is a more sophisticated measure economically speaking. The results of the study are shown in Figure 10–4. The average level of need for achievement continues fairly stable from 1500 through 1600, then declines sharply to a low point at 1650 which is maintained through 1700, and finally increases sharply from that time on to a high point in 1800. Strikingly enough, the measure of economic activity follows a very similar course, but 50 years later in time. This study improves upon the previous two because it shows for the first time that level of need for achievement can go up as well as down, and that economic activity will follow these vicissitudes fairly precisely.

Important though the three studies just described are, they are dwarfed by the magnitude and importance of a similar study done by McClelland (1961). Taking the world as his frame of reference, he endeavored to determine the influence of need for achievement on economic development. Needing raw material available on all nations in which to search for need for achievement, McClelland decided upon stories appearing in the readers used in the education of children. These stories are fictional and imaginative, sometimes even articulating with the mythology of the society. As such, they are appropriate raw material for the measurement of level of need for achievement in the people composing them. But they are also representative of the level of the need in the society, argues McClelland, because the society has decided to use them as instructional material for its children. Thus, the level of need

FIGURE 10–4

Averaged *N* achievement levels in English literature (1550–1800) compared with rates of gain in coal imports at London 50 years later

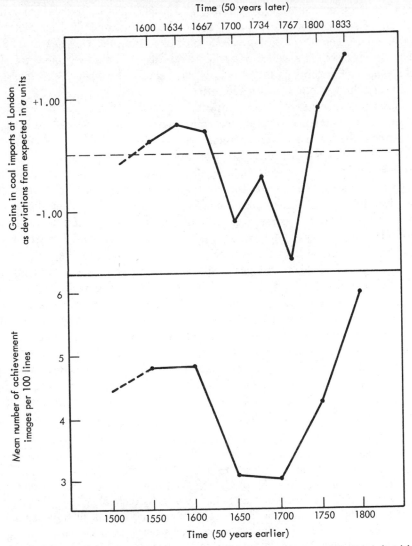

Source: N. M. Bradburn & D. E. Berlew. "Need for achievement and English industrial growth." *Econ. Develpm. cult. change*, 1961.

for achievement obtained in children's readers can be considered modal for the society. McClelland was able, though with considerable difficulty, to obtain 21 stories from the children's readers used in 23 countries in 1925, and 21 stories used in 40 countries in 1950. The 23 countries of the 1925 sample also appeared in the 1950 sample. All the stories were translated into English and mixed together so that scorers would have no clues as to their origin. The original form of the need for achievement scoring system was employed (McClelland et al., 1953), with the usual high level of interscorer agreement, and unusually high internal consistency. Estimates of internal consistency based on the split-half method corrected for length of test in 1925 and 1950 samples was .75 and .80, respectively. This is a very adequate reliability in a fantasy measure. In addition, McClelland found virtually no relationship between level of need for achievement and story length.

Obtaining a measure of economic development that could be applied to so many countries at the same time was even more difficult than measuring the need for achievement. After much consideration and investigation, McClelland decided upon two economic measures. The one first offered by an economist (Clark, 1957) involves international units of income. Obviously income is the best gauge of economic development, but the difficulty is that money has different value in different societies. In an attempt to overcome this difficulty, Clark advocated translating into international units of income, each unit being taken as the quantity of goods exchangeable in the United States for $1 over the average of the decade from 1925–34. In this way, all currencies can be translated into a scale having the same meaning. Although there are certain difficulties with this measure of national income, McClelland adopted it as one of the few permitting comparisons across many nations. Because of the difficulties, however, he decided to include another economic measure as well. This one was the amount of electricity produced in a given country. Conveniently enough, there is a standard unit for measurement of electricity, the kilowatt-hour, used by the whole world. In justifying the theoretical utility of the kilowatt-hour as a measure of economic growth, McClelland (1961, pp. 85–96) says:

> We have argued that economic growth, in its most unambiguous sense, is growth in the production, service, and use of the most modern technology ("hardware") known to society at a given moment in history. Certainly in our time the production and use of electricity in a country should be highly diagnostic of the level of its technology, since it is the form into which most of the energy is converted which runs our complex civilization. Though the sources of energy may be quite varied (water power, animal power, wind, coal, oil), electricity has become the *form* in which energy is most economically stored and transmitted.

Armed with two reasonably adequate measures of economic growth, McClelland next faced the problem of determining whether or not a country made gains in the period from 1925 to 1950 that were remarkably big. Some manner of determining the *rate* of growth seemed proper, for the absolute size of gains did not seem useful. The trouble with absolute size of gain is that it is highly correlated with the initial level of development. In other words, a society relatively high in kilowatt-hours per capita in 1925 would show more absolute gain from 1925 to 1950 than would a society relatively low in 1925. After considering many faulty methods of obtaining a measure of rate of economic growth, McClelland settled on a procedure that involves predicting from the regression line which best fits the overall relationship between initial level and gain, the amount of gain that is to be considered normal. Gain exceeding or failing to meet this amount is considered extraordinary. It is extraordinarily high or low economic gain that is to be related to level of need for achievement.

Let me pass over much of the interesting and complex results of this huge study, to the overall findings most directly relevant to our discussion of the economic effects of need for achievement. As indicated in Table 10–19, McClelland (1961, p. 92) found that the higher the need for achievement level in a country in 1925, the greater its rate of economic growth from 1925 to 1950 as measured by both international units of income ($r = .25$) and kilowatt-hours of electricity per capita ($r = .53$). Strikingly, there was virtually no relationship between need for achievement level in 1950, and the measures of economic growth from 1925 to 1950. These results, obtained from a study with a truly grand scale, lead to the same conclusion suggested by the three studies described previously. The level of need for achievement in a society is a clear influence on the subsequent rate of economic development. It is equally apparent that the influence does not take place the other way around. More than any other psychological studies, those inspired by McClelland render in tangible form the contribution to the understanding of social system phenomena that can be made by the personologist. Neither economists, nor any other social scientists besides personologists, would have seriously pursued in research the possibility that a motivational variable could have a causal role in the explanation of economic growth. I assume that the far-reaching implications of McClelland's work for international economic and political policy are apparent. In terms of our more immediate concern in this chapter, it is clear that the need for achievement has motivational status and should be included in peripheral level theorizing about personality.

McClelland's work with the need for achievement has stimulated

TABLE 10–19

Correlations of reader N achievement scores with deviations from expected economic gains

n Achievement level by year	I.U./Cap 1925–50 N = 22	Kw-hr./Cap 1929–50 N = 22	Both combined N = 21
1925	.25	.53, $p < .01$ pd	.46, $p < .02$ pd
1950	−.10	.03	−.08

pd = predicted direction.
Source: D. C. McClelland. *The achieving society.* Princeton, N.J.: Van Nostrand, 1961.

similar studies of the needs for affiliation and power. These studies are not as extensive or convincing as those cited above. Fantasy in the form of stories composed about pictures also served as the raw material for the measurement of the needs for affiliation and power, the scoring systems for which were patterned after that described above for the need for achievement. The scoring or operational definition of the need for affiliation in thematic apperception involves evidence of concern in one or more of the characters over establishing, maintaining, or restoring a positive affective relationship with another person. This affective relationship is most adequately described by the word friendship. In contrast, the scoring definition for the need for power stresses concern in the characters of the story with control of the means of influencing a person, expressed in such ways as pleasure in situations of dominance, and reference to dominance and persuasion activities. Although the interscorer agreement associated with both scoring systems is high (generally correlations of .85 to .90), the internal consistency of these two scoring systems appears to be even lower than that for the need for achievement. Reliability estimates are in the neighborhood of only .43 and .32 corrected to full test length for the needs for affiliation and power, respectively (McClelland, 1961, pp. 161 and 168). But if we were willing to rely upon the validity studies of the need for achievement measures as a gauge of the acceptability of its underlying concept, then why not do so for these two measures as well?

Heyns, Veroff, and Atkinson (1958) conducted an experiment in order to determine whether the need for affiliation could be measured as higher using this scoring system in a group of people in whom the need was aroused as compared to a group in which no arousal took place. The 31 college fraternity brothers in the arousal or experimental group performed a sociometric task before composing stories about pictures of people. The sociometric task consisted of (1) ranking a given set of traits according to the degree to which possession of the trait would make a person likable, (2) description of self and the other members of the group in terms of these traits, and (3) choice of at least three persons as the most desirable personal friends in the group. Heyns et al. felt that this task would arouse a high level of the need for affiliation. A control group of 36 college males was simply drawn from a psychology class without experiencing any arousal condition before composing stories about the same pictures used in the experimental group. The results show that the overall need for affiliation score is considerably higher in the experimental group than the control group, and that the various subcategories of the scoring system also tend to discriminate the groups in this direction. So it can be concluded that the measure of need for affiliation operates as it should experimentally, and therefore has a claim to construct validity. There are also a few correlational studies indicating that the measure has empirical validity. Atkinson and Walker (1958) indicate that people high in need for affiliation tend to be approval seeking, and to be especially sensitive to faces when they are presented along with other stimuli in a perceptual task. The perceptual task involved having subjects decide which of four simultaneous stimuli, presented tachistoscopically at speeds too short for complete perception, was a face. People high in the fantasy measure of need for affiliation picked out the face more accurately than people who were low. McClelland, Sturr, Knapp, and Wendt (1958) also report that people high in the need for affiliation are generally considered likely to succeed by their peers. That this reflects the strong interpersonal commitment these people have made is suggested by French's (1956) evidence that people high in the need for affiliation choose friends over experts to work with them on a performance task, even though skill is important in completing the task with the greatest reward. In addition, Atkinson, Heyns, and Veroff (1954) found that persons scoring high in need for affiliation were considered unpopular by their peers on a sociometric rating. This result has been confirmed in similar circumstances by Groesbeck (1958), and Byrne (1961a). DeCharms (1957 found that under cooperative task instructions those high in need for affiliation perform best, whereas under competitive instructions, they perform more poorly than those low in this need. Additional studies are reviewed by Mehrabian and Ksionzky (1970).

There is less research available on the fantasy measure of need for power. In developing the scoring system, Veroff (1958) tried to perform a natural experiment that would show the scoring system to be sensitive to a situation of high-power motivation. This arousal situation involved people who were candidates for election as student leaders at their college. The candidates had to petition for their candidacy, and following this declaration, were given one month for campaigning before the actual election. After two days of balloting, the candidates congregated at the pools to see what the balloting had decided. At least two hours elapsed after they had congregated before the results of the election were known, and in this time period, the candidates were asked to compose stories about pictures of people in the manner of previous studies. Veroff reasoned that whatever other motives would be aroused in these candidates, the need for power would certainly be high. The control group consisted of 34 college males from the same school merely asked to compose the stories as part of their activities in a psychology course. The average need for power score, based on the entire scoring system, was higher in the experimental group than in the control group. In addition, most of the subcategories of the scoring system discriminated the two groups in the same direction. There are also two other measures of need for power available (Uleman, 1965; Winter, 1971), both derived from arousal experiments, and the latter claiming to emphasize the positive wish for power rather than the negative fear of powerlessness.

Construct validational research has now become available on the need for power. McClelland, Davis, Kalin, and Wanner (1971) report, primarily from Winter's (1971) findings, that men with a high drive for personal power tend to drink and gamble more, to own prestige items (such as power cars and credit cards), and confess to more aggressive impulses (such as wanting to walk out on a date and to yell at someone in traffic). These seem various ways of feeling big and important. Failing them, a tendency toward alcoholism may develop, which is interpreted as being powerful in one's fantasy, without the usual requirement of consistent, effective social action. If the inclination of power motivation is tempered by a sense of social responsibility, it tends to express itself more in political and social commitments and actions (McClelland et al., 1971).

McClelland (1961) included measures of need for affiliation and need for power in his previously mentioned large-scale study of social system phenomena. Even though his primary focus concerned the relationship between need for achievement and economic growth, he felt it valuable to include these other measures for two reasons. The first is that it should be only the need for achievement, and not other motives such as affiliation and power, that relates to economic development. If it could be shown that affiliation and power motivations bear little on economic growth, then the case for the relevance of need for achievement would be all the stronger. The second reason had to do with notions of to what at the social system level these other two needs would be relevant other than economic development. In the process of obtaining information concerning economic development, much other social system information was obtained as a matter of course, and this information was put to use in assessing the empirical value of the other motive measures.

The results concerning need for affiliation indicate that it bears a complex relationship to population growth, a matter that should not be too surprising. The need for affiliation is positively related to birthrate in 1950 ($r = +.41$) and negatively related to birthrate in 1925 ($r = -.41$). But why should high need for affiliation lead to having more children in 1950 and fewer children in 1925? McClelland's reasoning is complex, and will only be summarized here. Generally speaking, there seems evidence that prior to the introduction of large-scale public health measures, the birthrate appears to have been largely controlled by the death rate. But whereas the correlation between birthrate and death rate is high prior to 1950, by that time it has been significantly reduced by modern public health measures. Perhaps the meaning of the positive relationship between need for affiliation and birthrate in 1950 is that people determine how many children to have by how many they want, without fear that many will die. But the negative relationship between need for affiliation and birthrate in 1925 is more difficult to understand. It will help to know that even though there is a general positive relationship between birthrate and death rate in 1925, there turns out to be a negative relationship between need for affiliation and death rate at that time. This negative relationship does not appear in 1950. Putting all these pieces together suggests that in the pre-public health era, how many children survive of those born depends more on how much care and attention their parents give them than is true in contemporary times. McClelland (1961, p. 163) concludes that in 1925:

> The parents with higher need for affiliation care more for their children, fewer of them die, and there is therefore less need for "excess" children to take the place of those who die off. In other words, those countries with a high [need for] affiliation have a lower infant mortality rate, and a lower birth rate.

Although it can hardly be claimed that this indirect, but plausible and intriguing, chain of reasoning really substantiates the validity of the need for affiliation measure, further research seems worthwhile.

The final matter of relevance from McClelland's study concerns both the needs for affiliation and power. It turns out (McClelland, 1961, p. 168) that a combination of high need for power and low need for affiliation is very closely associated with the tendency of a nation to resort to totalitarian methods of governing its people. Strikingly enough, every one of the notorious police states (e.g., Germany, Japan, Spain, Russia, Argentina, Portugal, Republic of South Africa) in the sample showed this particular pattern of the two motives! I take it that the meaning is clear that in countries where many people are personally motivated to dominate others and avoid warm relationships with them, political forms will tend in the direction of a denial of equality and individual freedom.

McClelland (1971) has recently prepared an especially useful discussion of the intertwining of needs for affiliation, achievement, and power in both personal and socially relevant behaviors. Notable among recent studies on such matters is that of LeVine (1966) in which the percentage of achievement dreams in the Yoruba and other tribes of Northern Nigeria is used as a basis for understanding their social patterns and interrelationships. Also, Donley and Winter (1970) have coded the inaugural addresses of American presidents from Theodore Roosevelt to Richard Nixon for the needs for achievement and power. These scores seem surprisingly accurate in predicting administrative decisions of these men while in office. These results are schematically presented in Table 10–20.

What do these intriguing findings tell us concerning peripheral level theorizing? Even though their reliabilities are poor, the measures of need for affiliation and need for power act empirically in a theoretically sound manner in relating to both individual and social system phenomena. It would appear that peripheral level theorizing ought to include these two needs.

This conclusion is further strengthened by the recent appearance of an important book (Winter, 1973) on the need for power. In this book,

TABLE 10–20

Motive characteristics of American presidents and associated trends in office

President	*High* n *achievement*	*High* n *Power*	*Associated trends in office*
T. Roosevelt.............. 6.2		8.3	Strong and active presidents,
F. Roosevelt.............. 5.2		6.3	attempting to accomplish much,
Truman.................. 4.1		7.3	quite willing to use political in-
Kennedy................. 6.8		8.3	fluence and expand government
Johnson................. 7.5		6.8	to gain ends
	Low n *achievement*	*High* n *Power*	
Wilson.................. 3.0		5.4	Stubborn desire to impose his will, even at cost of accomplishments [George & George 1956]
	High n *achievement*	*Low* n *Power*	
Hoover.................. 4.0		3.0	Stress on accomplishing more at less cost, smaller government involvement, willing to sacrifice political influence for goals of economy and efficiency
Nixon................... 8.5		5.1	
	Low n *achievement*	*Low* n *Power*	
Taft.................... .9		2.0	Relatively inactive, not trying to achieve major accomplishments or use the power potential of office of the President
Harding................. 2.3		3.4	
Coolidge................ 1.7		3.1	
Eisenhower.............. 2.8		4.1	

Source: Adapted from R. E. Donley & D. G. Winter. "Measuring the motives of public officials at a distance: An explanatory study of American presidents," *Behav. Sci.*, 1965, 3, 85–86.

Winter has amassed an enormous amount of empirical information concerning how this need, as measured in fantasy, influences personal and social action. It is impossible to recount these vast findings here, so an example or two will have to suffice. Following from the proposition that persons high in need for power want to control the existing social system, whereas those high in need for achievement want to change it, Winter and his associates predicted that among student activists members of the Black Power Movement would be high in *n* power but members of the New Left Movement would be high in *n* achievement. This prediction was confirmed with various student samples. These results are seen as consistent with those concerning the average level of *n* power among persons in various occupations. The highest average is in business management, followed by teaching, psychotherapy, and the religious vocation. Although these findings would not in all instances be expected by the assumptions it is common to make, they are consistent with McClelland's peripheral theorizing.

In an overall sense, there is no more striking evidence of the empirical fruitfulness of postulated concrete peripheral characteristics than that offered by McClelland and his associates. But the great bulk of characteristics designated in the peripheral theorizing has not been touched. And the numerous characteristics are not organized into a few types that could manageably be studied empirically. The soundest conclusion to reach is that though there is support for some of the theory, most of it has not been tested.

Maddi's position

Most of the research directly relevant to Maddi's peripheral theorizing has concentrated on the need for variety and the traits of activeness-passiveness and internal-external orientation. In this research, Maddi and his associates followed McClelland in utilizing thematic apperception as the raw material for measurement. They did this because the need for variety is considered a motive, and they were swayed by McClelland's arguments concerning the proper measurement of such entities. In addition, they conceptualized different forms of the need for variety, depending upon the trait characteristics occurring with it. Because of this, they considered it of potential value to have a rich, multifaceted source of information such as fantasy. They turned to the analysis of thematic apperception with the idea in mind that the need for variety would take *active-internal, active-external, passive-internal,* and *passive-external* forms. As you will recall from Chapter 8, these forms of the need for variety actually constitute four of the personality types supposedly characterized by high-activation requirements.

Attempts to devise measures of these four motivational types evolved over a number of studies. In the first of these, Maddi, Charlens, Maddi, and Smith (1962) selected the two types that would have the most obvious kind of expression in thematic apperception. Clearly a person could compose stories about pictures of people which imbued them with a sense of boredom and dissatisfaction with the status quo, coupled with interest in the possibility that something more unusual might happen. But it would be equally possible for a person to simply compose stories that are themselves novel and unusual, thereby producing his own variety. Scrutiny of some sample stories inclined Maddi et al. to the belief that the former orientation toward novelty is passive and external, whereas the latter is active and internal.

So, without further ado, Maddi et al. defined two scoring systems to be studied for construct validity. The scoring system for the passive-external form of need for variety was patterned after those pioneered by McClelland. Called *desire for novelty,* it refers to the extent to which stories reflect dissatisfaction with the status quo because of its boring nature, and an appreciation of externally caused novel occurrences. The scoring system has the same three components as that for the need for achievement, and can be used by different scorers with a high level of agreement (correlations range from about .80 to about .90; Maddi & Andrews, 1966;

Maddi & Berne, 1964; Maddi et al., 1962; Maddi, Propst, & Feldinger, 1965). Estimates of internal consistency have ranged from .31 to .41 (Maddi & Andrews, 1966; Maddi et al., 1965), and an estimate of stability was .47 (Maddi & Andrews, 1966). If anything, these reliability results are better than those reported for the need for achievement measure.

Maddi et al. (1962) also developed a scoring system for the active-internal form of need for variety. Called *novelty of productions,* the scoring system concerns how unusual or novel are the stories themselves, regardless of how much goal-directed striving toward novelty is attributed to characters. The scoring system includes three aspects each of character treatment and plot treatment. The categories of plot treatment are *unusual event, unusual interpretation* (scored when a story is strange, humorous, or ironical), and *unexpected ending* (scored when the end of a story violates a definite expectation built up by the preceding narrative). The categories of character treatment are *unusual role designation* for characters actually pictured in the stories (such designations as spy and diplomat), *unusual role designation* for characters the subject introduces into the story, and *uncommon naming.* That the agreement in the use of this scoring system is high is shown by estimates of interscorer reliability that range from .84 to .92 (Maddi & Andrews, 1966; Maddi et al., 1962; Maddi et al., 1965). Also high for fantasy measures are estimates of internal consistency of the scoring system, which have ranged from .63 to .80 (Maddi & Andrews, 1966; Maddi et al., 1965). The sole estimate of stability is adequate, being .65 (Maddi & Andrews, 1966). It would seem as if the tendency to infuse fantasy with a desire for novelty and the tendency to fantasize in unusual ways are distinct, and homogeneous, entities in people.

Maddi et al. (1962) performed an experiment to see whether the scoring systems would be sensitive to conditions which should arouse the need for variety. People in the aroused, or experimental group, were bored by being required to attend to a tedious recording of the physical characteristics of a town delivered in monotonous tones with much repetition. Following this experience, the people composed stories about four pictures of people in the standard manner. There were two control groups. In one of them, the period of time prior to composing stories was taken up by whatever the people chose to do that could be accomplished in a classroom setting. In the other control group, a novel, unusual, and somewhat humorous recording was played prior to the story composition task. Maddi et al. reasoned that in neither control group should there have been much arousal of the need for variety. The experimental treatment was expected to arouse not only the need for variety, but also the trait of passivity. The tendency to be passive should have been strong because the subjects were asked to give their full attention to the recording. They could only comply with these instructions by relinquishing the many active procedures (e.g., tapping feet, daydreaming, walking out) whereby people avoid monotonous situations. Thus, people in the experimental group should have shown, on the thematic apperception task, an increase in passive expressions, and a decrease in active expressions, of the need for variety. The results of this experiment conformed to expectation: the aroused group showed a higher level of desire for novelty and a lower level of novelty of productions than did either control group. In addition, the control groups did not differ from each other in desire for novelty or novelty of productions. In the control groups, desire for novelty and novelty of productions were negatively correlated, and this relationship was even stronger in the aroused group. Maddi et al. concluded that their arousal condition had the joint effects of arousing the need for variety, and the trait of passivity.

Although it is certainly plausible to consider novelty of productions and desire for novelty to be active and passive measures of the need for variety, respectively, there is at least one major alternative to this view. That alternative questions whether novelty of productions is motivational at all. Certainly, this measure does not include the obviously goal-directed fantasy characteristic of other motive measures. Perhaps novelty of productions is a stylistic expression of a flexible, original, creative turn of mind. Further, perhaps desire for novelty is the only actual measure of the need for variety. It it is also true that flexibility and originality require, for their vigorous expression, freedom from strong motivational states, then the negative relationship between desire for novelty and novelty of productions, and the effects upon both measures of the experimental manipulation would be very understandable: When the need for variety, or any motive, is strong, flexibility and creativity will be low. The alternative explanation to that of Maddi et al. is reminiscent of White's contention that the expression of effectance motivation in exploration of the world only occurs when the major survival needs have been satisfied, and Harlow's (1953) demonstration that the hunger drive interferes with puzzle solution in the monkey. Maddi and Berne (1964) did a correlational study to determine which of the two interpretations of the desire for novelty and novelty of productions measures was most adequate. In this study, they obtained from the thematic apperception of a group of people, scores on not only these two measures, but the needs for achievement, affiliation, and power as well. They reasoned that if the alternative explanation considered above is accurate, then there would be a negative correlation between novelty of productions and each of the motive measures, whereas if the interpretation of Maddi et al. is accurate there would be only the negative correlation between novelty of productions and desire for novelty. The latter result was obtained, clearly supporting the position that novelty of productions and desire for novelty are alternative forms of the need for variety.

The next step for Maddi and his associates was a series of correlational studies (Maddi, 1968a; Maddi & Andrews, 1966; Maddi et al., 1965) aimed at determining the construct validity of the two posited measures of need for variety. Indeed, at this point a third measure was devised. Also involving analysis of thematic apperception, this measure, called *curiosity*, reflects the degree to which stories are infused with the asking of questions and the posing of problems with concomitant interest in obtaining new, additional information with which to resolve the perplexities. On rational grounds, it was presumed that this measure is an active expression of the need for variety, as is novelty of productions, but is different from that measure in reflecting an external rather than internal trait. In other words, in the active pursuit of variety, novelty of productions involves favoring internal sources of stimulation, whereas curiosity involves favoring external sources. The curiosity measure, like the other two, can be used with adequate agreement by different scorers (.83 to .90) and has sufficient reliability to permit considering it further (internal consistency = .50 to .68; stability = .39).

The correlational studies support the claim of the novelty of productions and desire for novelty measures to construct validity, but suggest a different interpretation of the curiosity measure than that postulated above. Some of the findings of these studies are presented together in Table 10–21. Working down the first column, you can see that the higher a person is in novelty of productions, the less he will explore the objects

TABLE 10–21

Selected correlates of novelty of productions, curiosity, and desire for novelty

	Fantasy variables			
	Novelty of productions	*Curiosity*	*Desire for novelty*	*Number of s's*
Performance variables				
Time spent exploring a room.........	−.42†	.38†	.11	62
Introspective productivity...........	.27*	.06	−.07	62
Complexity of line-drawing completions.....................	.39†	−.05	−.20	62
Original uses for common objects.....	.42†	−.05	−.22	42
Self-description variables				
n Change.........................	.31*	−.26	.44*	42
n Order..........................	−.27	.42†	.27	42
Conjunctivity-disjunctivity..........	−.32*	.36*	.11	42
Impulsivity.......................	.21	−.10	−.34*	42
Rigidity factor....................	−.38*	.38*	.20	42
n Understanding...................	−.02	.25	−.41†	42
Reflectiveness....................	.33*	−.02	−.36*	42
Exteroception....................	−.48†	.27	.18	42
n Sentience......................	.13	−.01	−.43†	42
Energy..........................	.12	−.03	−.50†	42

* significant at .05 level.
† significant at .01 level.
Source: Adapted from S. R. Maddi, B. Propst, & I. Feldinger, "Three expressions of the need for variety." *J. Pers.*, 1965; S. R. Maddi, & S. Andrews, "The need for variety in fantasy and self-description." *J. Pers.*, 1966; and S. R. Maddi, "The seeking and avoiding of variety." Unpublished manuscript, Chicago, 1968.

in a room with which he is unfamiliar, but the more he will explore his internal environment through introspection. A high degree of novelty of productions also predisposes people to complete fragmentary line drawings in a complex way, and to be original in thinking up uses for common objects. The active, internal search for novelty indicated in these performance characteristics is also shown in self-description. People high in novelty of productions describe themselves as being interested in change, disjunctive thinking, and contemplative activities. In complimentary fashion, they are not interested in order, in appearing rigid, or in the practical external world of affairs (exteroception). The performance correlates of the fantasy measure of novelty of productions suggest that it reflects behavior indicative of striving toward variety and its self-descriptive correlates clarify that variety is indeed a personal goal.

In contrast, the desire for novelty measure has shown no performance correlates to date, a fact that would cause alarm concerning its empirical validity were it not for the reasonable argument that something measuring passivity should not, after all, reflect such active tendencies as performance that actually creates novelty. People high in desire for novelty should be appreciative of novelty when they encounter it, but not be active creators of it themselves. They are consumers rather than producers of novelty. Indeed, as shown in the third column of Table 10–21, people high in desire for novelty do describe themselves as interested in change, and give insight into their passivity by also describing themselves as without initiative, interest in understanding, contemplativeness, sentience, energy, or anything else that might aid in pursuit of novelty. You may ask what good is motivation that does not provide a format for action? But that is another question, the answer to which may lead to the study of psychopathology. For the moment, it can well be concluded that there is empirical support for viewing desire for novelty to be a passive form of the need for variety.

The original conceptualization of the fantasy measure of curiosity has not received empirical support. It is true that people high in curiosity do actively explore the objects in a room with which they are unfamiliar. But that this finding should not be construed as indicating an active, external form of the need for variety is disclosed by the self-descriptions of people high in curiosity. As you can see in the second column of Table 10–21, these descriptions indicate an interest in order, conjunctivity of thought, and rigidity. Inadvertently, Maddi and his associates seem to have developed a measure of the active tendency to fear variety rather than revel in it! Once again we are alerted to the wisdom of McClelland's distinction between approach and avoidance versions of each of the needs. People with fantasy high in curiosity seem to be concerned with variety because it is a threat to them, and wish to avoid the threat by ordering their experience so as to minimize or at least dampen novelty and change.

Especially because the novelty of productions and curiosity measures deviate from the usual format stressing obviously goal-directed fantasy, Maddi and his associates planned a further demonstration of the motivational nature of these measures. A definite implication of the motivation construct is that you can manipulate the person to learn something if learning it leads to satisfaction of his motive. The stronger the motive, the more you can manipulate him to learn. Thus, if novelty of productions and desire for novelty are really approach versions of the need for variety, then people high in one or the other of them ought to learn something, when rewarded by novelty, more effectively than people low on these measures. Further, if curiosity really measures an avoidance version of the need for variety, then people high in it ought to learn less well for novelty rewards than people low on that measure.

Feldinger and Maddi (1968) did an experiment to test these predictions. First they obtained thematic apperception stories from a large group of people, and through applying the scoring systems, were able to isolate groups high and low on each of the three measures. All groups were given the learning task, which consisted of viewing cards presented one at a time. Each card had on it two pairs of lines, one pair being parallel and the other unparallel but symmetrical. The person was asked to choose one pair of lines from each card. For half the people in each group, choosing parallel lines led to viewing a line drawing of a usual object. But when they chose the nonparallel lines, they viewed a line drawing showing an unusual version of the usual object. The only difference in procedure for the people in the other half of each group was that choice of the nonparallel lines led to seeing the usual object, whereas choice of the parallel lines was associated with the unusual object. There were 45 cards with parallel and nonparallel lines on them, and the measure of learning employed was the number of choices leading to viewing unusual or novel objects. For novelty of productions, the high group showed more choices that led to viewing novel objects than did the low group. There was a similar trend in the high and low desire for novelty groups. The people high in curiosity made fewer choices leading to novelty than did the group low in curiosity. These results, taken along with those of the correlational studies reviewed above, are thoroughly consistent with considering novelty of productions and desire for novelty to be measures of approach versions of the need for variety, and curiosity to be an avoidance version.

The combination of high need for variety, with active-internal or passive-external traits, defines two of the high-activation types postulated by Maddi. Also, the combination of high fear of variety with active-external traits, constitutes one of his low-activation types. Strictly speaking, it would be important in assessing the construct validity of the position to determine whether the activation requirements of people high in novelty of productions, desire for novelty, or curiosity conform to the theoretical expectations. Such research has not been attempted due to the difficulty in determining customary level of activation in any reasonably direct and convincing manner. There is a scale offered by Zuckerman, Kolin, Price, and Zoob (1964) indicating the degree to which a person seeks stimulation, a tendency of obvious relevance to customary level of activation though hardly exhaustive of its meaning. In pilot data obtained in Maddi's laboratory, this Sensation-Seeking Scale shows a sizable positive correlation with novelty of productions, a small positive correlation with desire for novelty, and an absence of correlation with curiosity. These findings suggest the promise of devising a more adequate measure of characteristic level of activation, so that relation to the fantasy measures may be studied.

A recent study by Thayer (1967) bids fair to have solved the problem of simple measurement of customary level of activation. He devised the Activation-Deactivation Adjective Check List, composed of a number of adjectives relevant to activation which the subject endorses in the manner most descriptive of him. The self-descriptions of 221 male and female college students were factor analyzed, with four of the resulting factors clearly indicative of activation. Thayer lists the factors and the adjectives loading highest on each of them as follows: *general activation* (lively, active, full of pep, energetic, peppy, vigorous, activated); *high activation* (clutched up; jittery, stirred up, fearful, intense); *general deactivation* (at rest, still, leisurely, quiescent, quiet, calm, placid); *deactivation sleep* (sleepy, tired, drowsy). According to Thayer, these factors roughly constitute four points on a hypothetical activation continuum running from sleep to anxious tension. Although complete reliability information is unavailable, estimates of stability were obtained for some of the adjectives, and range from .57 to .87, with a median of .75.

Thayer attempted two kinds of validation of these factors as points on an activation continuum. The first kind involves other self-descriptions, and the second involves physiological recordings of autonomic nervous system activity. One of the validation attempts involving self-description was based on the conceptualization of characteristic curve of activation as being low on awaking, rising to a peak near the middle of the day, and falling thereafter until sleep occurs (see Chapter 4). In one study (Thayer, 1967), subjects filled out the adjective checklist in the middle of the day and again in the evening. As expected, general activation and high-activation scores went down, while general deactivation and deactivation-sleep scores went up from one testing to the next. In a similar study (Thayer, 1967), subjects took the checklist four times, at roughly 9:00 A.M., 12:30 P.M., 5:00 P.M. and 11:00 P.M. As shown in Figure 10–5, general activation and high-activation scores went from low to high to low again, while general deactivation and deactivation-sleep scores did just the opposite. These findings provide striking evidence that the adjective checklist is measuring characteristic level of activation and that

FIGURE 10–5

Mean scores of four AD-ACL factors at four diurnal periods

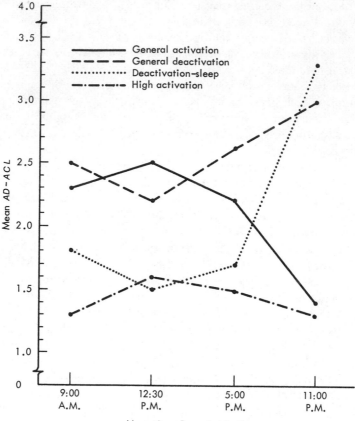

Source: R. E. Thayer, "Measurement of activation through self-report." *Psychol. Rep.*, 1967.

the four factors do represent points on a continuum of characteristic activation. Further, support for this conclusion is found in studies involving physiological correlates of the adjective checklist. Thayer (1967) obtained recordings of heart rate and degree of sweating (skin conductance, as you may recall from Chapter 5) on a small number of undergraduates who had also filled out the adjective checklist. The four activation factors were correlated with heart rate and sweating measures taken singly, and also combined into a composite indicator of autonomic activity. In three separate studies, the composite indicator of autonomic activity correlated with the four activation factors in such fashion as to indicate that the factors represent points on a continuum of activation. The heart rate and sweating measures, taken singly, correlated less strongly and dependably with the activation factors, but did not yield any contradictory information to that already presented. All in all, Thayer's work seems to have demonstrated the reasonableness of theorizing about a customary level of activation, and provides the opportunity to further evaluate the construct validity of Maddi's peripheral theorizing by determining whether the two approach and one avoidance orientations to variety described earlier really do have the activation characteristics expected for them.

Costa (1970) attempted such a demonstration in the course of a large-scale investigation of the interrelationships between measures of activation, need for variety, originality, and other cognitive abilities. He administered many tests to a group of 60 male and female undergraduates, and subjected the data to an elaborate procedure of analysis (not unlike factor analysis) permitting the test of hypotheses concerning interrelationships. His results indicated little support for Maddi's position, in that customary and actual levels of activation (measured by Thayers' adjective checklist) did not relate to thematic and questionnaire measures of personality types expressive of novelty orientation. But neither the novelty nor the cognitive measures intercorrelated among themselves in the fashion which has emerged in previous studies, raising the question of whether the testing situation or subjects somehow contributed to the negative findings. Also, perhaps it was too optimistic to surmise that such a physiological variable as activation level could be adequately measured by an adjective checklist. Nonetheless, this study must be regarded as a sobering one for Maddi's position.

Further evidence of the value in assuming that there is a characteristic level of activation with implications for under- and overactivation is suggested by Zuckerman, Persky, Miller, and Levin (1969). In their study, they measured anxiety and activation (adrenocortically), and manipulated stimulation. Their 22 male subjects were tested first on two control (normal) days, and then on one understimulation day and one overstimulation day. Understimulation consisted of confinement in darkness and silence; overstimulation consisted of an eight-hour, multichannel, multimedia program. The overstimulation condition resulted in greater autonomic and adrenocortical activity than the understimulation condition. In contrast, the understimulation condition produced greater increases in anxiety, depression, and feelings of unreality. In both under- and over-stimulation, subjects showed greater activation adrenocortically than they had on the control (normal) days. To some degree, under- and over-stimulation seem to have comparable effects on the body.

There are by now several other measures of variety seeking that involve questionnaire technique rather than fantasy (e.g., Garlington & Shimota, 1964; Zuckerman, Kolin, Price, & Zoob, 1964). These are less relevant to Maddi's position, and hence, will not be discussed at length here. In an attempt to provide normative data on three of these questionnaire measures, McCarroll, Mitchell, Carpenter, and Anderson (1967) found them to overlap considerably. Pearson (1970) has compared questionnaire and fantasy measures directly, and found the former to be more reliable and differentiated than the latter.

Mehrabian and Russell (1973) regard the various questionnaires mentioned above to be sufficiently in agreement concerning underlying assumptions about activation level, and sufficiently overlapping without being comprehensive, to warrant attempting to derive from them one overall measure. Through a careful process of excluding the items from this large pool that were either unrelated to the others or tainted with the tendency to respond in socially-desirable fashion, a final questionnaire of 40 items was devised. This measure of arousal seeking tendency has internal consistency of .87 and stability of .88 with a seven week interval between testings. Information concerning construct validity shows that the test correlates negatively with anxiety and neuroticism measures, and positively with extroversion, affiliation, and preference for arousing situations. It is unclear at this moment whether this test measures activation per se or a conglomerate of novelty and intensity preferences, though subsequent empirical work should provide further clarification.

CONCLUDING REMARKS

We have reached the end now of the empirical analysis to be attempted. The time has come to integrate the conclusions reached in this chapter and in Chapter 5. With regard to this chapter, it must be admitted that the studies performed under the aegis of the various theories are of limited value in the empirical analysis of peripheral considerations. There is danger of deciding that a theory is empirically sound for no better reason than that it is championed by personologists who are especially energetic and capable concerning empirical inquiry. At most, we should use the results of the essentially partisan research just reviewed to supplement the other empirical conclusions reached in this chapter and in Chapter 5.

Recall that we found considerable empirical support in Chapter 5 for both versions of the fulfillment model and the activation version of the consistency model. There is nothing in this chapter to change that view. Both the factor analytic studies presented earlier and the more partisan studies that followed suggested empirical support for the peripheral theorizing associated with these models. It is true that there was not much research associated with some of the fulfillment theories, but this should not be held against them, as it does not seem as if research effort was mounted. And the research listed under each theory has been to some extent arbitrary. Little research has been done in the personality field that is so specific to a particular theory that it is relevant to that theory and no other. More frequently than not, theories near to the one under consideration in the sense of belonging to the same class, are also supported by the findings.

From the analysis of core considerations presented in Chapter 5, it emerged that the only models rather unsupported are the pure psychosocial version of the conflict model and the pure cognitive dissonance version of the consistency model. Although the review of factor analytic studies conducted earlier in this chapter seems to support conflict as well as fulfillment models, it should be kept in mind that this may be in part due to the generality and ambiguity of the factorial studies. In addition, the partisan studies show spotty but intriguing support for Freudian peripheral theorizing. While the evidence in this chapter is not persuasive enough to change the conclusions drawn in Chapter 5, there is certainly cause for wishing that more research of a relevant sort would be done.

One vexing problem (to which I hope you are now alert) when a field is dominated by research that concerns only one small corner of one particular theory is that all, or at least many, theories seem to have reasonable empirical support, even though you have a vague, disquieting suspicion that the theories have not been tested at all. There is great need for research in personology that stems from a comparative analytic orientation. Such research, whether on a specific point, or more comprehensive than that, will yield evidence of the relative fruitfulness of the theories involved. The problem of lack of comparative orientation is further aggravated when the research does not even follow in any precise way from any particular theory. Because this is true of most of the research reviewed in the latter part of this chapter, it has been difficult to reach definite conclusions concerning whether the theories are really supported empirically. This is not to say that the research is uninteresting or even necessarily unrigorous. But even if the research considered here as relevant to single theories had been more partisan, as long as that expressed itself in concern for precise relevance to the theory, then definite conclusions might have been drawn. And think of what might have been accomplished with more comparative analytic studies.

Chapter 11 THE BEHAVIORISTIC ALTERNATIVE

From the early days of this century to modern times, the movement known as behaviorism has exerted an enormous influence on psychology. This is not to say that exactly what behaviorism entails has been so apparent. Even a highly regarded behaviorist, Berlyne (1968), is provoked to say

> It is extremely difficult to say exactly what "behavior theory" is and to delineate its boundaries. Is it a branch of psychology, a school of psychology, a theoretical position, a methodological approach? It is certainly not quite any of these, and yet it is all of them to some extent. What is the relation of behavior theory to the rest of psychology? All sorts of answers to these questions have been put forward at one time or another. There are those who have felt that behavior theory is destined to assimilate more and more of psychology as time goes on, so that everything in psychology will eventually be marked with its stamp, and the sooner the better. Others, of course, have felt that behavior theory is a transitory aberration whose pernicious influence will soon be seen for what it is and annihilated. Some have maintained that all psychologists are behavior theorists, but that some realize it and some do not; the implication is that those who are aware of what they are doing will do it better.

When ranking behaviorists themselves make such statements, I could with some justice have excluded behaviorism from consideration here, on the grounds that its form and content are not yet sufficiently clear. But such an exclusion would be unfortunate, as behaviorism, for all the confusion as to what it really is, has penetrated every fiber of psychology today. Actually, for all the ambiguity about the boundaries of behaviorism, its main thrust has been clear all along, and has not changed. This thrust concerns learning, the increase or decrease in frequency of overt, easily discernible movements (which are called responses), when they are fol-

lowed by stimuli that act as positive or negative reinforcers. Berlyne
(1968, p. 629) is quite definite about this emphasis of behaviorism on
learning:

> The term "behavior theory" has been used fairly interchangeably
> with the term "learning theory." "Learning theory" seems to have come
> into use rather earlier, and some writers, notably Mowrer, have favored
> it. Hull and Spence have preferred to speak of "behavior theory." There
> have been some not very happy attempts to distinguish between the
> theory of learning and "behavior theory" as the theory of performance,
> but, although, according to most theories, there are differences between
> the principles that determine the acquisition of habit-strength and those
> that determine the probability and vigor of responding, it is certainly
> impracticable to separate the two completely, let alone to assign them
> to two distinct bodies of theory. The term "behavior theory" is perhaps
> to be preferred, on the grounds that "learning theory" has came to en-
> compass much more than a statement of the principles that govern
> learning.

It is only to be expected that a theory of learning would have ramifications into many areas of psychology. What does need careful scrutiny is
the nature and extent of the impact behaviorism has had on these areas.
In the personality area, we should identify what is of relevance, and
determine its similarities and differences to the other theories in this
book. In this regard, we should consider whether behaviorism represents
a frank alternative to personality theory as an explanation of behavior.

As I have said many times now, a personality theory must include
statements about a core, a periphery, and a developmental process linking the two. The core statement concerns assumptions about the unchangeable nature of man, the peripheral statement concerns the life-
styles that it is possible for men to acquire, and the developmental statement shows how each peripheral style derives from the interaction of
the core with the environment. As the developmental statement heavily
involves learning, behaviorism should be of importance in this aspect of
personality theorizing. This is all the more so because many personality
theorists merely assume some process of learning that is capable of linking the core with the periphery, focusing their attention on those instead.
Actually, it is hardly inaccurate to say that behaviorism does just the
opposite, namely, focusing on the process of learning without much
emphasis on core and peripheral considerations. Behaviorists are loath
to make pronouncements about the unchangeable nature of man, and are
almost equally unwilling to elaborate styles. For the behaviorist, considering man's inherent nature is to stray too far from tangible observations, and assuming styles is to overemphasize predispositions to behave
that are not a function of the stimulus characteristics of situations.

From what I have said, it should not be surprising to find behaviorism
less concerned with the personality domain than with other areas of psy-

chology. It is my impression that this is indeed so. Berlyne (1968, p. 638) seems to agree when he says, "It can hardly be overlooked that problems of personality have figured much less prominently in the writings of the behavior theorists than in psychological literature as a whole." He does lay some responsibility for this on ambiguity as to what personality is and is not, but recognizes that the primary factor is the differing emphases of behaviorism and personology. Whatever else it considers, personology must concern individual differences. It concerns both when individuals act differently under the same stimulus conditions, and when an individual acts similarly under several different stimulus conditions. Behaviorism has little to say about such individual differences, understandably, because it has sought general laws stating invariant relationships between stimuli and responses (Berlyne, 1968). If the responses of two individuals differ, the most likely explanation, according to behaviorists, is that the stimuli having elicited or reinforced the responses also differed. And if an individual responds the same way twice, the most likely reason is, according to behaviorists, that the stimulus situation was also the same. But in order to get a more differentiated view of behaviorism as it relates to personality, it will be necessary to go into greater detail.

MODERATE BEHAVIORISM

In understanding the behaviorist movement, one should recognize that it has not been a wholly uniform thing. The moderate, as opposed to the radical, form of the position has been fashioned by such psychologists as Clark Hull (1943) and Kenneth Spence (1948). Hull's work at Yale University stimulated such similarly inclined associates as Dollard & Miller (1950). At Iowa State University, Spence's colleagues included Farber (1948), and Taylor (1951, 1953). These psychologists, along with many others (e.g., Berlyne, 1960; Brown, 1961) have continued over the years to produce a corpus of research and theorizing that represents a reasonably distinct form of behaviorism. It derives in essence from the pioneering work of Ivan P. Pavlov (1927).

In explaining learning, moderate behaviorism has focused upon stimulus-response, or S-R, bonds. One speaks of an *S-R bond* when a particular stimulus regularly elicits a particular response from the organism. With an occasional exception, moderate behaviorists have contended that the strength of an S-R bond is increased when the occurrence of the response in question is followed by a reward, and decreased when followed by punishment. In other words, the stimulus comes to elicit the response dependably because the response obtains for the organism something of positive value. In order to pinpoint just what this positive value is, moderate behaviorists have theorized about the nature of organisms. They have assumed the existence of drives, such as hunger, thirst, and sex, which have the status of biological imperatives in that they support physical survival. So, if an organism is thirsty, it can be taught to emit a particular response in the presence of a stimulus if the response is regularly followed by something to drink. The organism will learn that the stimulus is a reliable sign that it can reduce its drive if it performs in a particular fashion.

Although the main thrust of moderate behaviorism is clearly on learning, the various assumptions mentioned above can be considered to frame a position on the core and periphery of personality. The core tendency is *the attempt to reduce the tension of biological drives.* The drives having received most emphasis are *hunger, thirst, sex, activity, curiosity,* and *pain.* Since increments in each of these drives are experienced bodily as tension, it is possible to speak of *general drive,* or the total amount of tension across all the aroused drives at any given time. The core characteristics are the appropriate goals or *rewards* corresponding to the various drives. *Food* is the reward for the hunger drive, as the removal of food is the punishment. The reward for thirst is liquid; for sex, sexual experience; and for activity, exercise. In order to discern what the presumed reward is for the curiosity drive, remember that all drives are uncomfortable tension states that must be reduced. The tension of curiosity (or perhaps uncertainty would be clearer) is reduced by *information* (Berlyne, 1960). There is ambiguity concerning the pain drive. In one sense, it is nothing more than another way of stating the core tendency of tension reduction. In another sense, it refers to a particular source of tension, namely, physical injury, and has associated with it the reward of *safety.* In any event, as in the example concerning removal of food, the opposite of the reward in the case of each drive is the punishment. All the drives mentioned are inherent and unlearned. For this reason, moderate behaviorists call them *primary drives,* and their corresponding goals *primary rewards.*

Moderate behaviorism also has something to say about the periphery of personality. After all, a strong S-R bond, or *habit* (Dollard & Miller, 1950) is in our terminology a concrete peripheral characteristic. The habit is learned on the basis of expression of the core tendency in the stimulus environment, and is suited to the discussion of individual differences. Certainly two persons encountering the same stimulus conditions and response contingencies for reward or punishment will learn identical habits. But if the learning history of two persons is different, then their habits will differ even though their core drives are the same. Once learned, habits persist for sometime (this is called *resistance to extinction*) even if reward no longer follows the emission of the response. Someone who had learned to be intimidating toward women because that led frequently to their having sexual intercourse with him, would continue in his ways at least for a while even if times had changed such that gentility would have been more valued. This is one way in which moderate behaviorism could recognize that a person's behavior sometimes imposes itself on the stimulus surround rather than being controlled by it. But if the reward for responding in a particular way continues to be absent, the habit will eventually extinguish. The number of trials to extinction of a no longer rewarded habit is one measure of its strength.

From its inception, behaviorism was appealing in large part because it promised a simple, clear, understanding of learning. The stimuli serving as signals for responses, and the rewards or punishments contingent upon the responses were all observable, concrete aspects of the external environment. Indeed, the aspect of behavior chosen for study —the response—was a movement, rather than a thought or feeling, and therefore also clear and observable directly. It is true that influential behaviorists, such as Hull, recognized all along that if a depiction of the learning process of such simplicity as the S-R bond was to be adequate, certain complications concerning individual differences would have to be taken into account. He believed that individual and species differences existed, but need not jeopardize the search for general laws governing learning in all organisms. If such general laws are possible, then individual differences can be considered no more important than something to be taken into account in the application of the laws to everyday life. Bridge designing is, for example, governed by general laws, even though the building of any particular bridge involves problems of application unique to it. So, for Hull (1945), it was important to search for general laws, by "assuming that the forms of the equations representing the behavioral laws of both individuals and species are identical, and that the differences between individuals and species will be found in the empirical constants which are essential components of such equations." In other words, the researcher should cancel out or neutralize individual and species differences by adding those constants (which are, after all, arbitrary numbers) to his equations as will help to make learning data seem to be identical across the individuals and species studied. Once you do this, of course, you run the risk of missing individual and species differences in the nature of learning because your method of study is not suited to highlighting them. The only way you can have any sort of test of the validity of the assumption that there are general laws governing learning is to observe how easy or difficult it actually is to find and manipulate the constants that must be employed to yield up general laws.

In this regard, it must be admitted that the elegant emphasis on S-R bonds has been an oversimplification. Berlyne (1968, p. 642) summarizes much research and theorizing by saying that:

> Contemporary . . . behavior theorists make copious use of "intervening variables," as we have noted. These are essentially mathematical devices to make cumbersome relations between inputs (stimulus-variables) and outputs (response-variables) conceptually manageable.

There must be some sort of correspondence, but not necessarily a one-to-one correspondence, between values of these variables and conditions within the organism that are not directly observable. Spence recognizes this and mentions two additional types of psychological laws, the one (O-R laws) identifying response variables as functions of "organic variables" (i.e., measurements of neuroanatomical or neurophysiological properties of the organism") and the other (S-O laws) identifying organic variables as functions of stimulus variables. Most psychological laws must surely be placed in a final category, containing what we may call "S-O-R laws," stating how response variables are determined jointly by stimulus and organic (i.e., intervening) variables.

Berlyne has said that it is necessary to include organismic variables, which are internal and therefore unobservable, in formulations of the stimulus control of behavior. He goes on to list five classes of organismic variables: (1) *transient intervening variables,* whose values change within a matter of minutes or hours (e.g., emotional state, motivational condition); (2) *age as a variable,* which focuses upon how stimulus-response relationships change over long periods of time; (3) *variables, the values of which can remain fixed* over long periods of time (e.g., habits); and (4) *constitutional or congenital predispositions* to particular kinds of behavior. It seems to me that when one has indeed filled out Berlyne's outline of what is needed, a theory will have been devised that has considerable relevance to the understanding of individual differences, and that could easily be considered to have personality as an important subject matter. The statement about learning as being inviolately constant will have so many exceptions, will be shored up by so many intervening variables, as to have lost its position of centrality and elegant simplicity. Moderate behaviorism will then be even closer to personality theory.

Actually, developments in this direction have been taking place, mainly in the attempt to apply behaviorism to human beings, who are obviously so much more complex than lower animals. The initial emphasis on responses as tangible, directly observable movements, and stimuli as manipulatable aspects of the external environment, has been modified considerably. Now behaviorists will consider thoughts and feelings as responses along with movements. Such internal, relatively unobservable states as thoughts and feelings may even be considered implicit or incipient movements in an attempt to save the old emphasis on that which is tangible. Perhaps more striking is the declaration that internal events (e.g., thoughts, feelings, metabolic states) can be considered stimuli with potential for influencing responses. In recent times, it is common to see, inserted between the old S and R of the S-R bond, s's and r's standing for the internal and unmeasured stimuli and responses that have been assumed.

In addition, the moderate behaviorist's position on drives has undergone considerable elaboration. It became too cumbersome and unconvincing to try to explain the myriad forms of human behavior as attempts to reduce the tension of some few biological drives, such as hunger and thirst, and rewards, such as food and water. So, the concepts of *secondary drive* and *secondary reward* were devised. In contrast to the primary drives and rewards, these are learned and changeable. According to Berlyne (1968, p. 664), "The principle of *secondary* reinforcement postulated that neutral stimuli accompanying primary rewards (i.e., conditions in which primary drives are reduced) would acquire a conditioned reward-value in their own right." So, if a person always ate his food in a blue room, the color blue would have a pleasant, comforting effect on him even when he encountered it in a noneating context. Blue would have become a secondary reward.

A secondary drive is assumed to be evoked as "a consequence of conditioning by any stimulus (warning signal) that has habitually preceded or accompanied pain" (Berlyne, 1968, p. 664). So, if a person was locked in a blue room without any food available, the pain of his mounting hunger would become associated with the color blue. Subsequently, on encountering blue in another context not related to food deprivation, he would experience discomfort, or anxiety. If some stimulus such as blue is associated with primary drive increase, it becomes a secondary drive. In order to continue functioning as a secondary drive or reward, a stimulus such as blue must at least occasionally be paired once again with the primary drive or reinforcement from which it derived its power. Consistent with the notion of secondary (nonbiological) drives is Miller's (1951) currently accepted assumption that any strong stimulus functions as a drive.

Because they are learned and changeable, secondary drives and rewards qualify as concrete peripheral characteristics in the terminology of this book. They, along with habits, constitute the statement on peripheral personality that can be derived from moderate behaviorism. Secondary drives and rewards play a major role in the behaviorist's attempt to understand human behavior. Thus, such diverse goals as money or fame or truth can be conceptualized as secondary rewards, linked by past association with such primary rewards as food or water. And such uncomfortable states as anxiety and aggression can be considered secondary drives learned by association with the primary drives. Since the learning histories of persons are likely to differ, secondary drives and rewards can show considerable variation from individual to individual. The same, of course, is true of habits.

Anxiety research

Moderate behaviorism has produced an enormous amount of research. Most of it is experimental, focuses upon learning, and employs subhuman organisms as subjects. Despite the emphasis upon learning, much of this research supports the assumption that biological needs exist, and that tension reduction is rewarding. Thus, an organism deprived of food or water will learn an S-R bond more rapidly the greater the deprivation, at least when the learning task is relatively simple, but when the learning task is relatively complex, there may actually be a level of drive too great for effective learning (e.g., Farber & Spence, 1953; Yerkes & Dodson, 1908). Although the bulk of the research has concerned the hunger and thirst drives, or the more general avoidance of pain, more recent work has also indicated that the postulated curiosity drive exists. Various organisms will perform work in order to obtain information (e.g., Berlyne, 1960), or experience stimulus change (e.g., December, 1961). Even though most of the research has employed subhuman subjects, enough of it has been done with humans to suggest that one can safely conclude the existence of various biological drives in them as well.

Of course, the existence of such drives is hardly surprising. Also, as they would be relevant to a behavioristic theory of personality as core characteristics, they would have little role to play in explaining those persisting individual differences which are at the heart of the personological enterprise. Further, the putative core tendency of moderate behaviorism, which makes tension reduction the aim of all functioning, is not so unassailably supported by research. The research both supporting and questioning the tension-reduction assertion has already been reviewed in Chapter 5.

A representative theme in behavioristic research that is especially relevant here is that concerning manifest anxiety. This research has focused exclusively on human beings, and concerns itself with individual differences. There is ambiguity, however, in the conceptualization of anxiety among behaviorists. In the main, anxiety has been viewed as an expression of general drive or tension. But it is also possible to consider anxiety a secondary drive, learned through association with primary drives. The latter formulation, though less common in the literature, would actually be more consistent with the focus on individual or group differences in the research, and the implication carried in many of the measurement operations employed, that it is truly anxiety and not just tension that is being studied.

Much of the voluminous research on anxiety involves the *Manifest Anxiety Scale* (Taylor, 1953). This questionnaire is devised of items (from the Minnesota Multiphasic Personality Inventory), to be answered true or false, by which the subject describes himself with regard to such matters as insecurity, lack of confidence, and physiological symptoms. Examples of items are "I have very few headaches" and "I am very confident of myself," with other items having to do with diarrhea, constipation, and social apprehension. The initial selection of items for this scale was made by a number of clinicians who judged them relevant to anxiety. Taylor (1953) reported adequate reliability for the items actually included in the scale, and found them to yield higher scores in psychiatric patients than in normal subjects. Although it was assumed that the score on this test is closely related in humans to general drive level, which should wax and wane as a function of deprivation of rewards, the logic of rendering the test reliable suggests that it is persisting individual differences in anxiety level that are of concern. There should not be any persisting individual differences in general drive level, but rather only the transitory differences expressing the waxing and waning of the primary drives we all share. The implication that it is indeed individual differences that are of concern definitely suggests a view of the variable as a learned or secondary drive.

Spurred by the development of the Manifest Anxiety Scale, other psychologists constructed questionnaire measures of a more circumscribed nature. There are by now measures of anxiety in test situations, social situations, and children (Bendig, 1956; Dixon, de Monchaux & Sandler, 1957; Lykken, 1957; Mandler & Sarason, 1952; Sarason, 1958; Welch, 1952, 1956). Recently, Endler, Hunt, and Rosenstein (1962) have even devised a measure that permits you to assess the degree of subjective anxiety the person has in any of a number of environmental contexts.

Following from the assumption that anxiety functions like general drive is the prediction that high anxiety should facilitate learning in simple tasks but disrupt it in complex tasks. A number of studies (e.g., Farber & Spence, 1953; Spence, Farber, & McFann, 1956; Taylor & Spence, 1952) have supported this prediction. To give you the flavor of the research, let us concentrate on Spence et al. (1956), who employed a paired-associates learning situation. In this type of learning task, the subject is first exposed to a list of paired associates. After this, one stimulus from each of the pairs is shown to him and he must attempt to supply the other member of the pair. Spence, et al. constructed two lists of paired associates. In the list used in the first experiment, the items in each pair were highly similar in meaning (e.g., adept-skillful), whereas in the list used in the second experiment, the items in each pair were rather dissimilar to each other (e.g., undersized-wholesome) and actually more similar to items in other pairs. The learning task for the first list is simple, because when the subject is presented one item in a pair, he is aided in remembering the other by the similarity among them. In contrast, the second list makes for a harder learning task, because the subject is actually hindered in responding correctly if he uses similarity as a clue. The results of the first learning experiment done by Spence et al. (1956) are reproduced in Figure 11–1, and indicate that, as expected, subjects high in anxiety on the Manifest Anxiety Scale take fewer trials and make fewer errors in learning a simple task. But, in their second experiment (as shown in Figure 11–2), it became apparent that subjects

FIGURE 11–1

Paired-associates learning as a function of anxiety under conditions of minimal interpair competition and high initial stimulus-response associative strength

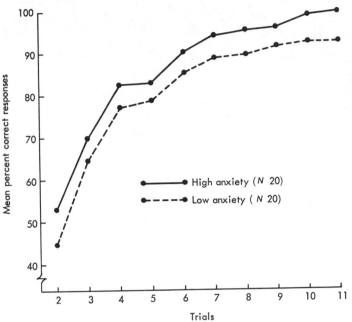

Source: K. W. Spence, I. E. Farber, & H. McFann, "The relation of anxiety (drive) level to performance in competitional paired associates learning." *J. exp. Psychol.*, 1956.

high in anxiety require more trials and make more errors in learning a complex task. In Figure 11–2, the pair of curves labeled as "low assoc." refer to those items employed in the second experiment that were borrowed from the first list and added to the second.

But there are also a number of studies (e.g., Bindra, Paterson, & Strzelecki, 1955; Kamin & Clark, 1957) that either do not support or actually contradict the interpretation of anxiety as an expression of general drive. Some of these studies, such as that of Bindra et al. (1955), involve the prediction that anxiety facilitates and disrupts learning on simple and complex tasks, respectively. Spence and Spence (1966) contend that these negative studies are in the minority, and that they indicate the heretofore unrecognized importance of sex of subject. This recognition of the importance of an individual difference variable is the sort of thing that raises the question as to whether learning is well described by general laws; perhaps males and females learn in a different manner. But another interpretation of the contradictory results mentioned above is offered by Sarason (1957a), who believes that some studies of

FIGURE 11–2

Paired-associates learning as a function of anxiety under conditions of high interpair competition. Word pairs of both high- and low-association value were interspersed within the same training list, but were analyzed separately.

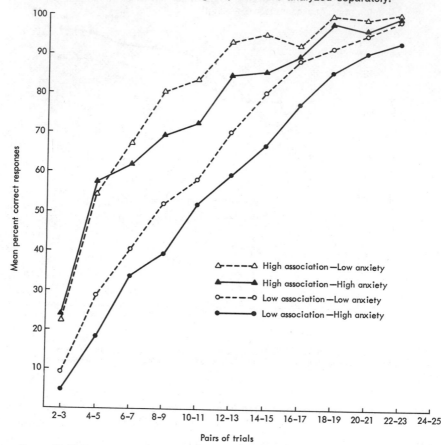

Source: K. W. Spence, I. E. Farber, & H. McFann, "The relation of anxiety (drive) level to performance in competitional and non-competitional paired associates learning," *J. exp. Psychol.*, 1956.

simple and complex learning failed to yield the expected results because the response to be learned was nondefensive rather than, as is typical of the studies with positive results, a protective response to stress. In a number of learning tasks, the simplicity of the situation has been confounded with its stressfulness. Korchin and Levine (1957) have actually interpreted task complexity as little more than a stress variable. More theoretical attention should be given to whether there exists a distinction between task complexity and stressfulness.

Another general prediction concerning manifest anxiety is that it ought to show a positive relationship to physiological indices of emotionality or tension level. Although it must be said that this expectation has been neither fully nor sophisticatedly researched, the available findings are generally negative. Questionnaire measures of anxiety do not seem to relate consistently to physiological variables, such as sweating (e.g., Berry & Martin, 1957; Raphelson, 1957). But these negative findings do not unequivocally demonstrate the lack of construct validity of manifest anxiety measures because it has been typical to use only one or at most two measures of physiological functioning in any study, even though it is well known that subjects show wide individual differences in mode of physiological expression (Lacey, 1950).

As suggested above, one should expect highly anxious persons to be more disrupted in their functioning by personal threat or stress than low anxious persons. Numerous studies have tested this expectation, with stress usually created by means of verbal instruction; e.g., leading the subject to believe that he is about to take an intelligence test. Although some investigators (e.g., Farber & Spencer, 1956; Taylor, 1958) have not been able to support this expectation, most of the available findings indicate that highly anxious subjects show relatively poor performance under conditions of stress (e.g., Korchin & Levine, 1957; Nicholson, 1958; Sarason, 1957a). An example of this phenomenon is provided by Sarason (1957b) whose results are shown in Figure 11–3. In his simple nonsense syllable learning task, highly anxious subjects did best under neutral instructions, but under instructions stressing the importance of

FIGURE 11–3

Mean number of correct anticipations for high-, middle-, and low-anxious groups on List B, Day 1, under neutral, subject-oriented, and experimenter-oriented instructions

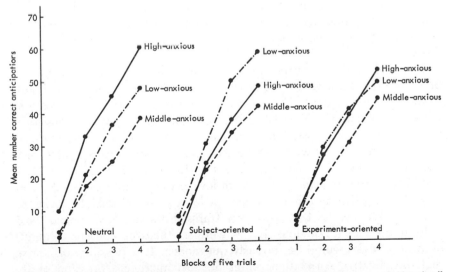

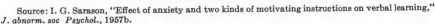
Source: I. G. Sarason, "Effect of anxiety and two kinds of motivating instructions on verbal learning," *J. abnorm. soc Psychol.*, 1957b.

success for self-esteem, low anxious subjects performed best. When instructions emphasized merely the experimenter's attempt to develop a test, there was little difference among subjects with different levels of anxiety.

These studies on vulnerability to stress suggest that the highly anxious person is generally insecure, self-depreciatory, and lacking in self-confidence. Indeed, many studies (e.g., Cowen, Heilizer, Axelrod, & Sheldon, 1957; Trapp & Kausler, 1958) have disclosed high anxiety subjects to be too self-preoccupied, and generally less content with themselves than are low anxiety subjects. These findings, taken together with those concerning vulnerability to stress, have led to an interpretation of anxiety (e.g., Mednick, 1957) as leading, when high, to self- (rather than task-) oriented, personalized responses in the face of stress.

From the general thrust of these findings and interpretations, one would expect the highly anxious person to tend more toward psycho-pathology than would the less anxious person. That this is accurate is suggested by the very high relationship between the Manifest Anxiety Scale and the Psychasthenia (obsessiveness) Scale of the Minnesota Multiphasic Personality Inventory (e.g., Erikson & Davids, 1955). Although the items in the two scales overlap somewhat, the relationship between them is too high to be explained in this manner alone. The implications of rigidity of thought carried by this finding are borne out by the fact of a positive correlation between the Manifest Anxiety Scale and various measures of authoritarianism (e.g., Siegal, 1954). There are also studies showing positive correlations between anxiety scales and both indices of general maladjustment and ratings of anxiety made by clinicians (e.g., Lauterback, 1958; Taft, 1957). In addition, some findings suggest that high anxiety may result in a greater susceptibility to persuasion and opinion change, and to greater sensitivity to reinforcements provided by the experimenter in learning situations (e.g., Fine, 1957; Janis, 1955).

It would hardly be surprising, given the emerging composite picture of self-doubt, vulnerability to stress and persuasion, to find the highly anxious person particularly concerned with pleasing others and avoiding negative evaluations. What is surprising is that the opposite seems to be true! Many anxiety questionnaires have been found to correlate very highly but negatively with measures of the tendency to respond to personality test items in a socially desirable direction (Edwards, 1957). It would seem that it is the person with low anxiety who is especially concerned with pleasing others. Perhaps a high score on anxiety scales reflects a willingness to be particularly frank and open, or a special sensitivity to one's own reactions. If this were so, then the construct validity of anxiety scales would be seriously questioned. It is possible, of course, that the negative correlation represents just another expression of the highly anxious person's inability to be task-oriented and to respond appropriately, being bound instead to a ruminative self-preoccupation that does not permit social appropriateness in an obviously public and evaluative testing situation. It is quite important to know which of the two interpretations is correct, as one is consistent with the other findings already reviewed, whereas the other is not.

As you can tell from the preceding paragraphs, the Manifest Anxiety Scale and other similar anxiety questionnaires have been employed in numerous studies which go beyond the specific predictions stemming from the concept of general drive alone. The correlation of anxiety scores with scores on other performances constitute the makings of R-R (response-response), rather than S-R, laws, in the terminology of moderate behaviorism (Spence, 1948). In searching for R-R laws, the investigator is trying to determine invariances in the relationship among responses, without tying the responses in any rigorous way to antecedent stimuli. It is my impression that when moderate behaviorists become interested in human behavior per se, they tend to abandon strict emphasis upon the stimulus control of behavior, focusing instead upon how the various facets of behavior go together. This seems understandable given the enormous complexity of human as opposed to subhuman behavior. If I am accurate in my perception, research themes such as that concerning manifest anxiety show an implicit distinction in moderate behaviorism between subhuman and human behavior, even though in explicit, formal theorizing, no such distinction is assumed.

Moderate behaviorism and psychoanalytic theory

There are several other research themes that have traditionally been considered part of the behavioristic movement. For example, there is the research which stems from the proposition that frustration breeds aggression. Although Berlyne (1968) lists this research as concerned with aggression construed as a secondary drive, it is not clear in behavioristic theory just how this interpretation can be made. As in the case of manifest anxiety, one could as easily consider aggression to be a primary, or unlearned drive, because the tie between frustration and aggression is considered invariant. Other investigators loosely in the behavioristic tradition (e.g., Berkowitz, 1962) have considered aggression as a learned drive by detaching it from any necessary connection with frustration. In general, these investigations focus upon how experiences of success and failure in fighting lead to learned patterns of dominant and submissive behavior. In effect, they are saying that one is aggressive if one has learned to be so (Ulrich & Azrin, 1962). The ambiguity as to the best theoretical stance to take toward the phenomenon of aggression seems to stem at least in part from a peculiar affinity between behaviorism and psychoanalytic thinking.

This affinity becomes even more apparent in research themes within the behaviorist movement that appear to bear an uncertain relationship to behavioristic thinking. An example is conflict, a subject that has provoked considerable study among moderate behaviorists (e.g., Berlyne, 1964; Brown & Farber, 1951; Miller, 1959). Although one might, by doing theoretical handstands, derive this interest in conflict from behavioristic thinking, it does not seem to follow from it naturally and simply. I do not think behaviorists would have emphasized conflict so much, had it not been for the impact upon them of psychoanalytic theorizing. I feel similarly about the study of defenses, which has been mounted with great energy by behaviorists (e.g., Farber, 1948; Miller & Dollard, 1941; Mowrer, 1940, Sears, 1943; Whiteis, 1956). In general, these studies have employed subhuman subjects, and focused upon observable responses without regard to underlying mentation.

Indeed, the behaviorists who have done most to elaborate the position so as to account for individual differences in human behavior (e.g., Dollard & Miller, 1950) explicitly consider themselves to be dealing with the same range of phenomena important to Freud. From their viewpoint, Dollard and Miller were focusing upon those aspects of Freud most amenable to operationalization and empirical test, and by dispensing with the rest, improving upon psychoanalytic formulations. In the main, they have dispensed with the mentalistic aspects of Freud, and his theoretical statements about the necessarily incompatible nature of individuals and society. What they have emphasized instead are the most biological aspects of his thinking, and tangible movements rather than thoughts.

In my estimation, behaviorism only seems to resemble psychoanalytic theory, while in reality being quite different from it. Although it is true, for example, that Freud would have endorsed the behaviorist's assumption of primary drives, such as hunger, thirst, and sex, he would not have agreed to defining them as devoid of mentality and therefore similar to what is present in lower animals. Freud saw the instincts as *wishes and attendant emotions*, present in the mind, and though derived from metabolism, not merely biological phenomena. In addition, he considered the importance of instincts to be in large measure their incompatibility with the social requirement of maintaining the common good. From this assumption, as you know, derives Freud's emphasis upon conflict and defense. But, for him, conflict is not merely the presence of incompatible response tendencies. Conflict also, and more importantly, involves a mental dilemma in which guilt and fear of punishment are inevitable participants. Defensiveness, for Freud, is a mental operation, denoting conscious and unconscious mentation, only one small expression of which is in some actual movement or response.

On the basis of these differences in theoretical emphasis, Freud would have justifiably disagreed with the behaviorist's reliance upon subhuman subjects for experimentation. Further, he would not have accepted such experimental designs as that of Mowrer (1940), mentioned in Chapter 5, in which the measure of defensive behavior is the substitution of a weaker habit for a stronger one in the face of stress. The defense mechanism of regression, which Mowrer thought he was demonstrating, makes no sense in Freud's thinking unless it derives from his conceptualization of psychosexual stages of development. It is neither clear that rats have psychosexual stages of development, nor how, if they do, the pushing of a bar or rearing on one's hind legs articulates with such stages in any important fashion.

Strictly speaking, research emphasis upon conflict and defense is most understandable if one has a theory such as that of Freud, replete with the very assumptions that behaviorists have found objectionable. In addition, the frustration-leading-to-aggression hypothesis follows much more readily from Freud's thinking concerning the anal stage of psychosexual development than it does from moderate behaviorism. Even the study of manifest anxiety has, among behaviorists, involved more focusing upon mental content (e.g., socially desirable responding, experienced lack of self-confidence, obsessive thinking) than they can easily justify. It is not enough for a behaviorist to insist that he is studying what Freud believed important when the changes in psychoanalytic thinking that have been made radically alter its emphases.

I am drawn to the conclusion that the rudimentary theory of personality contained in moderate behaviorism is either a pseudo-conflict theory, with the assumptions rendering conflict inevitable very implicit but there nonetheless, or a kind of fulfillment theory, in which the story of human behavior is to be understood as nothing more than the styles each person learns for the reduction of tension from drives. If it is to be the former, then a more full-bodied embracing of Freud's mentalistic and social assumptions would lead to research of greater relevance. If it is to be the latter, then one would probably want to spend less research effort on such topics as conflict and defensiveness.

RADICAL BEHAVIORISM

Radical behaviorism derives from Watson (1924) more than from Pavlov, and finds its contemporary expression in Skinner (1938, 1953, 1957), and those he has influenced (e.g., Krazner & Ullman, 1965; Lundin, 1969; Verplanck, 1954). Like moderate behaviorism, it focuses upon the way in which stimuli control actions, and considers the laws of learning whereby this control takes place to be invariant across individuals and species. But what makes radical behaviorism radical is an unwillingness to make assumptions about the existence and importance of drives, primary or secondary, and the insistence that even the minimally mentalistic concept of habit is unnecessary for understanding. Apparently, there are not, in radical behaviorism, even the rudiments of a position on the core and periphery of personality. And yet, radical behaviorism claims to be able to predict, control, and understand all behavior. As such, it should represent a frank alternative to personality theorizing (and, for that matter, any other kind of theorizing in psychology).

Radical behaviorists have championed many useful concepts and distinctions in understanding learning, and in this have influenced all areas of psychology including moderate behaviorism. Speaking for all radical behaviorists, Skinner asserts that the only appropriate criterion for scientific explanation is prediction and control. To accept an explanation merely because it seems to make sense or has coherency (i.e., intuitive and rational knowledge) is to be deluded. The extreme emphasis upon prediction and control leads to a preoccupation with changing behavior. You must be able to change behavior in order to demonstrate the ability to control. Thus, the first break with personality theorizing is the radical behaviorist's disinterest in behavior that remains the same over many different situations.

The distinctions radical behaviorists make concerning stimuli and responses are all aimed at providing a basis for understanding how responses change by increasing or decreasing in frequency. At the outset, it should be recognized that for an event to be classified as a stimulus it must be observable and manipulatable. And for an event to be classified as a response it must be observable and quantifiable. There are two classes of response. In Frankel's (1971, p. 447) words:

> When a response is regularly elicited by a stimulus as the result of the inherited characteristics of the organism, it is called an *unconditioned respondent*. If we were to change the diaper of an infant and accidentally stick him with a pin, he would probably start crying. Since the response of crying when pin-pricked is not the result of previous experience but the consequence of the inherited structure and capacities of the infant, it is an unconditioned respondent. When a previously neutral stimulus can elicit a response, it is called a *conditioned respondent*. The process whereby neutral stimuli function as conditioned eliciting is called *respondent conditioning*. Thus the sight of the pin may now cause the infant to cry.

Respondent conditioning was heavily emphasized by Pavlov (1927), and forms much of the basis of moderate behaviorism. Because it was recognized earlier, respondent conditioning is often called classical. Emotional behaviors often have respondent components. For example, a slap in the face may elicit crying from a child. The respondent components of our emotions (i.e., their unlearned tie to particular eliciting stimuli) may well underlie the feeling of helplessness we have about our moods (Frankel, 1971).

But much more important than respondent conditioning for radical behaviorism is *operant conditioning*. Although some of our behaviors are reflexive in nature, most of what we do usually passes as voluntary. These responses are called *operant* to emphasize that they "operate" upon the environment, and the shaping or control of them is achieved by *operant conditioning.* In Frankel's (1971, pp. 447–448) words:

> Opening a refrigerator is an operant response insofar as it is a function of subsequent stimuli (food). If the refrigerator were always empty we would not open refrigerator doors. The presence of the food increases the strength of the operant response. When a stimulus following an operant response increases the strength of the operant, it is called a *reinforcing stimulus.* The difference between a reinforcing stimulus and an *eliciting stimulus* is that the former always follows an operant response whereas the latter always precedes a respondent.
>
> A reinforcer is said to be positive when the effect of the operant response is experimentally observed to "produce" the reinforcing stimulus. Food is therefore a *positive reinforcer* for opening refrigerator doors. In contrast, whenever the effect of an operant response is experimentally observed to "eliminate" a stimulus, that stimulus is called a *negative reinforcer.* Let us suppose that the infant is now six months old, and he has not forgotten that we stuck him with pins. If we discover that whenever we enter the room the infant turns to the wall, we might hypothesize that we were an aversive stimulus that negatively reinforced facing the wall. By regularly facing the wall in our presence, the child eliminates us from his visual field.

Thus, the organism performs an operant (or voluntary) response in order to bring about a positive reinforcing stimulus or eliminate a negatively reinforcing stimulus. If the investigator wishes to increase the frequency of an operant response, he must wait until it occurs, and then follow it with either the presence of a positive reinforcer or the absence of a negative reinforcer. An increase in the frequency of an operant response indicates that learning (operant conditioning) has taken place.

Radical behaviorists also distinguish between *unconditioned* and *conditioned* reinforcers. When it is not the past training of the organism that has produced the ability of a reinforcer to increase the rate of an operant response, the stimulus is considered an unconditioned reinforcing stimulus. Examples are food and water, which are presumed to be intrinsically reinforcing. But we also seek stimuli that are not immediately relevant to food and drink. For example, adults work for money and students work for grades, though we are not born with needs for money or grades. A neutral stimulus (money or grades) may subsequently function as a conditioned reinforcer when it has been present during the occurrence of an unconditioned reinforcer. Unconditioned and conditioned reinforcers are similar to the primary and secondary rewards (or punishments) of moderate behaviorism.

A final class of stimuli are those which supply information rather than elicit or reinforce responses. Information is provided by *discriminative stimuli,* which in large measure control our lives. In our society some people's functions are advertised by their uniforms, for example. The uniforms are discriminative stimuli. Frankel (1971, p. 449) gives a clarifying example about how the classifications offered by radical behaviorists are used in understanding complex human behavior:

> A stimulus may function as a discriminative stimulus at one point in time and as conditioned reinforcer at another. In the presence of our mother (a discriminative stimulus) we may ask (an operant response) for money (a conditioned reinforcer). With the money in our hand (a discriminative stimulus) we may go (an operant response) to the grocer (a discriminative stimulus) for candy (an unconditioned positive reinforcer).

You will note from this example that the discriminative stimulus must precede or accompany the operant response, whereas the conditioned reinforcer always follows the operant response. It should also be kept in mind that radical behaviorists (and their more moderate counterparts agree) emphasize stimulus and response generalization. A response associated with a particular discriminative stimulus may occur, through *stimulus generalization,* in the presence of some similar discriminative stimulus that was not involved in the original learning. *Response generalization* refers to the tendency of very frequent (strongly learned) responses to occur in the context of other stimulus conditions than those in which they were learned. The concepts of stimulus and response generalization carry a distinct possibility for personalistic exploration; some responses occur in other stimulus circumstances than those which were learned.

Schedules of reinforcement and the extinction process

Radical behaviorists have been especially adept at determining the effects upon the strength of a learned response of various contingencies of reinforcement. When an operant response is reinforced every time it is emitted, this is called a *continuous schedule of reinforcement.* But especially in the natural world outside the laboratory, reinforcements are more often intermittent. *Intermittent reinforcement* can occur according to a *ratio schedule,* in which a relationship exists between the number of responses emitted and the number of reinforcements taking place (e.g., every third response is reinforced), or an *interval schedule,* in which reinforcement occurs after a certain period of time regardless of the number of responses that have occurred. There are many other reinforcement contingencies that have been recognized. Suffice it to say that each reinforcement schedule has a different effect on the acquisition, maintenance, and weakening (extinction) of an operant response. Frankel (1971, pp. 452–453) gives evidence of this in an extended example that is close to everyday life:

A child asks his father for money to buy bubble gum. Whenever he makes this request, he is given the money for the gum. Suppose that in the course of two months the child has received money two hundred times. When reinforcement follows an operant every time, the schedule is one of continuous reinforcement. Imagine now that another child makes the same requests for the same time period and the same number of times, but his father does not always grant the request. This is an intermittent schedule of reinforcement. Suppose the dentist subsequently tells both parents that their children must stop chewing bubble gum. The parents agree, and from that day on they refuse to grant the requests of their children. In operant terms, a previously rewarded operant response (asking for bubble gum) will undergo *extinction* as a result of non-reinforcement. Extinction refers to the procedure of continuous non-reinforcement which results in a lowering of response rate. Both children on discovering that their requests were going to be refused (non-reinforced) would suddenly begin asking more frequently. At first, non-reinforced trials result in a rise in the frequency of the operant. This observation has been confirmed in hundreds of experiments. It is also not uncommon in our experience to find ourselves trying harder after frustration. However, as the non-reinforcement of the operant response continues over trials, the weakening of the response manifests itself in lower and lower rates of responding, until finally it returns to its initial level (prior to the first reinforcement), or disappears altogether. In our example, both children will gradually stop asking their parents for bubble gum. However, the child who had been reinforced on a continuous schedule will extinguish faster than the child who had been reinforced on an intermittent schedule. If we observe an individual seemingly struggling in vain, and we wonder how someone can work so hard when achieving so little reinforcement, we may speculate that a history of intermittent reinforcement for that individual effects the present drawn-out extinction process. Ironically, the very perserverance of an individual who has refused to give up and has inspired us with a sustained effort despite repeated failures may be at that moment undergoing extinction.

Apparently, intermittent reinforcement schedules can produce response patterns that are difficult to unlearn even when no further reward is forthcoming. Here too is something of personalistic relevance: some response patterns continue unchanged even if they do not lead to reinforcement.

There is little point in inquiring as to whether there is empirical support for the various tenets of radical behaviorism. Those tenets are largely the result of research of a painstaking and rigorous variety. There is, of course, the problem shared with moderate behaviorism, namely, that lower organisms such as pigeons and rats are subjects much more often than humans. As long as one is willing to assume that the laws of learning are universal, this emphasis on subhuman species is no special limitation. But it arouses the skepticism of personologists, who are loath to make that assumption, even about learning. Some psychologists (e.g., Köhler, 1925; Tolman, 1948) believe that learning in humans takes place much more cognitively, through processes labeled insight and the like, than behaviorism would ever admit. Indeed, one criticism of behaviorism mounted on cognitive grounds appears in Chapter 12 of this book. Nonetheless, it must be said that, within its own set of assumptions, radical behaviorism has amassed considerable empirical support.

The absence of core and periphery in radical behaviorism

As indicated earlier, the moderate behaviorist's emphasis on primary and secondary drives, and habits, can be construed as a rudimentary position on the core and periphery of personality. There is not even this much of a position on personality in radical behaviorism. According to Skinner, the organism should be treated as a black box, which though it may not be empty, need not be peered into in order for understanding of behavior to be achieved. The responses constituting behavior are tangible and can be controlled by manipulating the external stimulus environment, and that is that. Of course the emphasis of such a position would be on behavior modification or learning. But radical behaviorists disapprove of their moderate counterparts for diagrams linking external stimuli to observable responses by way of a series of internal stimuli and responses.

Do radical behaviorists really deny the existence of common, unchangeable aspects of human nature? No, but they will not speculate about them and consider them unimportant in behavior modification. Any enduring, relatively unmodifiable behavior that might stem, say, from a particular genetic constitution, would not be of interest. Skinner (1957, p. 371) puts it this way:

> Even when it can be shown that some aspects of behavior is due to season of birth, gross body type, or genetic constitution, the fact is of limited use. It may help us in predicting behavior, but it is of little value in an experimental analysis or in practical control because such a condition cannot be manipulated after the individual has been conceived. The most that can be said is that the knowledge of the genetic factor may enable us to make better use of other causes. If we know that an individual has certain inherent limitations, we may use our techniques to control more intelligently, but we cannot alter the genetic factor.

It should be recognized that in his single-minded emphasis upon behavior modification, Skinner is disagreeing to some extent with the personologist over what is to be explained. The personologist would include as important data behavior that does not change, as long as it characterized individuals or the human species as a whole.

But what of the drives that moderate behaviorists and virtually everyone else in psychology recognize as important influences on behavior? Here surely are inherent or core characteristics that can have a variable influence on behavior (e.g., when hungry one may be more active than when satiated). In general, radical behaviorists abhor concepts referring to unobservable, internal states construed as causes of behavior. What virtually every personologist does is thus regarded as unscientific. To radical behaviorists, theorizing about unconscious motivation, or defenses, or life fear, or will to power, or achievement motivation, or even hunger drive, is to admit ignorance of the external stimuli controlling the various behaviors supposedly explained in this fashion.

Although the primary drives of the moderate behaviorist are less abhorent because more believably biological than these other concepts, the radical behaviorist still does not consider them useful explanatory devices. For the radical behaviorist, one gains nothing of scientific value in "explaining" that a person eats at one time and not at another by saying that he was hungry at first and not subsequently. One gains nothing because it is then necessary to determine the mechanism governing the waxing and waning of whatever it is that is called hunger. This turns out to be number of hours since last having eaten. It is this tangible, observable, external stimulus situation that governs eating behavior. To talk of a hunger drive is at best superfluous (if we know the external stimuli controlling the responses to be explained) and at worst misleading (by dulling our curiosity to find the external stimuli if we do not yet know them).

It is instructive to observe how radical behaviorists attempt to maintain this unwillingness to assume the existence of internal motivating states. All experimenters know that animals are more active when deprived of food or water, and an active animal is easier to train. So, radical behaviorists do indeed deprive their subjects of food and water. But in describing their experimental procedure, they do not say that the animal was hungry or thirsty. At most they will refer to the effects of deprivation on the body. A pigeon will be described as at "eighty percent of its free-feeding weight." The more active the animal is, the greater the likelihood that he will emit the desired operant response along with others. When the desired operant occurs, it can be reinforced with the same food or water that had been withheld before the beginning of the experimental task. Soon enough, the food or water reinforcement will increase the rate at which the operant in question is emitted, and learning is said to have occurred. But once again the effectiveness of the food or water will not be discussed as having to do with its drive-reducing properties, as would be so in moderate behaviorism. For the radical behaviorist, a stimulus qualifies as a reinforcement if it increases the rate of an operant, and nothing else need or should be asked.

To me, the handstands radical behaviorists must do in order to avoid the mentalistic, personological implications of the learning process are, in the final analysis, unconvincing. One problem is the definition of reinforcement as that stimulus which increases or decreases the rate of emission of an operant response. But the reinforcement concept is also a major part of the explanation of learning. How do we know that learning has taken place? Because an operant response has changed in rate through the action of a reinforcement. How do we know that a stimulus has reinforcing properties? Because it can change the rate of an operant response. With all their rigor and concern for science, radical behaviorists have fallen into a serious circularity here. Moderate behaviorists have avoided this circularity by defining a reinforcing stimulus in terms of the drive or tension it reduces, rather than the change in response rate it may produce. With reinforcement defined in terms of tension-reducing capability, it becomes an empirical question whether a reward or punishment affects response rate. Hence, the use of reinforcement as an explanation of such rate changes is not circular in moderate behaviorism.

Of course, radical behaviorists do not think they deny the existence of physiological processes that might be called drives. Rather, they prefer to refer only to observable and manipulatable things, hence the emphasis on body weight rather than hunger. But then why not tie the definition of reinforcement to such body states as weight, rather than to the very data (operant rate) that reinforcement is supposed to explain? Because radical behaviorists insist that physiological processes such as drives do not affect learning, but rather only activity level. One reduces the body weight of a subject only because the ensuing high-activity level means that many operant responses are being emitted, so it is easier to focus upon one of them for conditioning purposes. To define reinforcement in terms of bodily states would be to admit that they too affect learning.

But not only would it be more scientific to define reinforcements in other terms than what they are to explain, such as bodily states, it would also be thoroughly consistent with common sense, or intuitive knowledge. The radical behaviorist is coming perilously close to functionally decorticating himself (Murray, 1959), in his concern for scientific purity. Are we really supposed to believe that the procedure of decreasing the subject's body weight by depriving him of food was just hit upon by empirical exploration alone, and was not assumed all along to increase activity level because of its effect on hunger? Are we really supposed to believe that food qualifies as a positive reinforcer merely because it has been observed to affect the rate of operant responding, without any tie to already known nutritional requirements of organisms? Why was food tried as a possible reinforcer in the first place? Do not we all know that it was tried because we all accept the fact that food-deprived subjects want food, and will do almost anything to get it? Did we need all the elegant experiments of the radical behaviorist to tell us that? And is not the substitution of rigorous-sounding terminology (e.g., 80 percent of free-feeding body weight) for the commonsense terms covering the same phenomena a sleight of hand intended to convey that some grand new knowledge has been obtained?

But I must admit that some empirical knowledge deriving from radical behaviorism is striking and useful. In particular, I would point to the research showing the differential effects of various schedules of reinforcement on acquisition, maintenance, and especially extinction of operant responses. It is of considerable value, in the attempt to explain human behavior, to know that something learned according to an intermittent schedule of reinforcement extinguishes more slowly than if a continuous schedule had been involved. I suspect even here, however, that the plan for the radical behaviorist's research comes from his intuitive knowledge, which heavily includes the very speculations concerning what is inside the black box that are supposedly inadmissible in psychological science. If that is so, then the radical behaviorist is really not doing anything so different from the moderate behaviorist, who is, as indicated before, not unwilling to make assumptions constituting personality theory.

If it is true that intuition and common sense play a greater role in the radical behaviorist's enterprise than is admitted or should be expected from his noninferential terminology, then one might expect to find little slips of the tongue, as it were, that belie the rigor. Frankel (1971) believes he has found evidence of one such slip, in Skinner's explanation of superstitious behavior. As you know, it is common for personologists like Freud (1960) to refer to such mentalistic considerations as repressed hostile feelings projected onto others, in explaining superstitious (excessively fearful) behavior. Thus, one thinks of the world as dangerous because of one's own projected anger. Skinner, of course, will have none of this, preferring to search instead for the external, manipulatable stimulus conditions producing superstitious behavior.

In offering a laboratory demonstration of superstitious behavior, Skinner (1961) starts with a pigeon maintained at 75 percent of its free-feeding body weight, and places it in an experimental chamber arranged so that food is presented every five seconds no matter what the pigeon is doing (fixed interval reinforcement). In such a situation, if the "clock is arranged to present the food . . . at regular intervals *with no reference whatsoever to the bird's behavior,* operant conditioning usually takes place" (Skinner, 1961). Skinner (1961) goes on to describe the results of such conditioning:

> One bird was conditioned to turn counterclockwise about the cage, making two or three turns between reinforcements. Another repeatedly thrust its head into one of the upper corners of the cage. A third developed a "tossing response," as if placing its head beneath an invisible bar and lifting it repeatedly.

These responses involved orientation to some aspect of the environment rather than a mere execution of movements. He interprets these findings as the development of superstitious behavior. Apparently, such superstitious behavior is very resistant to extinction. With learning taking place according to a time interval of 15 seconds between presentations of food, one conditions an operant response which will then be emitted 10,000 times despite the absence of food (Skinner, 1961)! In accounting for this superstitious behavior, Skinner does not have recourse to covert stimuli and responses such as impulses, emotions, repression, or projection, relying instead on an analysis of the stimulus conditions under which an organism will behave as if his actions were effective in determining the reinforcing consequences.

What makes it possible to call this superstitious behavior is that *Skinner and we all know that the pigeon's responses are not really effective* in bringing about the reinforcement, which occurs only after some time interval regardless of what responses are being made. Frankel (1971, p. 455) asks:

> How did Skinner know that the bird was superstitious? Presumably because Skinner was outside the pigeon's universe, and thus was able to know that the ritualistic behavior . . . was not instrumental in getting the pellet of food. But is it really possible to call one behavior superstitious and another behavior unsuperstitious within the framework of the operant model?

In elaborating upon the challenge in the last sentence, Frankel (1971, pp. 455–458) presents a lengthy but pithy parable:

> Let me make the point clearer through the use of a pigeon parable. Imagine that one of the pigeons, Max, begins to wonder whether it is necessary for him to walk in circles in order for the food to arrive. Max decides to perform an experiment and walks to another section of the cage, only to discover that the food is delivered. Shall he conclude that the reinforcement is unrelated to his behavior? He might also conclude that there are two behaviors related to the delivery of food. Max may try another experimental excursion to another part of the cage and once again discover that a pellet of food is delivered. He then might conclude either that his behavior is unrelated to the delivery of food or that three behaviors are related to the food. Suppose Max now decides to see whether doing nothing leads to the same result. He discovers that again food is delivered and again he is faced with the dilemma of deciding whether the *behavior of doing nothing* is related to food delivery or whether food delivery is unrelated to behavior. Suppose Max had access to a philosopher pigeon, whom he asks for advice. He may say to the philosopher, "Food is a life and death matter and it comes at intervals so long as I am doing something. When I purposely do nothing it also comes. Must I worry about it or think about it at all?" The philosopher may reply, "The ways of the world are strange. Life is given and life is taken (reinforcement)

both in the experimental chamber and back in the cage (present reinforcement and historical reinforcement contingencies), and it is difficult for us to comprehend the ways of our Lord, B. F. Skinner. Sometimes he is benevolent in the experimental chamber and sometimes he is
not. It is a question of deciding ultimates. If what we do is irrelevant
to life and death, then it becames a problem to decide what is relevant
to behavior and if anything can be "relevant" in the context of a
universe that remains ultimately beyond reach. The teachings of Skinner
are clear about this—Man must assume control and behave as if his
behavior is relevant to important goals. One of our prophets has developed a system whereby it would have been possible to kill many
German men and women—because German men and women killed
many Polish men and women. Thus the prophet, an American, developed a missile system carrying one of our own species to eventual
destruction. The judgment of Skinner (1961, p. 426.02), as related in
the book, is simply: 'The ethical question of our right to convert a
lower creature into an unwitting hero is a peacetime luxury.' It is clear
that Skinner is concerned with our species and more concerned with us
than he appears to be with German men and women. So, in practical
matters, one must assume there is a meaning, a reinforcement, to which
our operants are directed."

Max may reply: "Philosopher, I take it you are not an atheist, but
that you do believe that there is a God, called Skinner, though his ways
are inscrutable." The philosopher answers, "Yes, I do believe." "Are
you not merely superstitious?" asks Max. The philosopher replies:
"You come to me with a problem and I provide you with a solution
which implies that inscrutability need not eliminate meaningfulness—
go about your daily affairs as if things mattered, as Skinner suggests."
Max walks away from the philosopher and ponders the solution. He
doesn't want to be superstitious. He doesn't want to live as if anything
he does matters, if it does not, in fact, matter. Max then hits upon a
clever idea. "If my behavior is irrelevant (no God—no Skinner) then
I may as well commit suicide or do nothing. However, if my behavior
is relevant, then I must commit myself accordingly. It is also true that
life would be better if behavior mattered. Since I will never understand,
even if he 'is,' I will never know the solution to my problem. However,
it makes sense to choose the alternative that would be better if true,
and that alternative is to act *as if* my behavior were relevant to the
consequences." Max then returns to his experimental chamber and
continues his walking in circles.

Are we not all like Max insofar as we are inhabitants of a Skinner
box? As inhabitants of a Skinner box, can any of us discover whether
a given behavior is superstitious or non-superstitious? Skinner, the
scientist, informs us that through the operation of contingencies of reinforcement our behavior is controlled. Skinner also informs us that the
only relationship necessary to establish the effectiveness of a reinforcer
is the "order and proximity of response and reinforcement." Such a
formula does not allow for distinctions such as right and wrong,
superstitious or non-superstitious unless these refer to receiving rein-

forcement after a response. Clearly, the pigeons accomplish this. They do get reinforced; therefore, they are as correct as they can be within the confines of an operant conditioning paradigm. Since reinforcement will always take place when the organism is doing one thing or another, there is no way for it to decide the relevance of its behavior to reinforcement.

The best the organism can hope to accomplish is to discover that the reinforcement is delivered on a certain time schedule, but this would require that the organism leave his universe and consult with the controlling network outside of his universe. By definition, this is not possible. At best, one may infer, deduce, or extrapolate that there must be a universal clock (interval schedule of reinforcement), and indeed, such deductions, inferences, and extrapolations on the parts of priests, medicine men, and philosophers take place. This is what Skinner calls superstitious behavior. He seems to think that science is free from such superstitions. If so it is also uninvolved in the nature of that "universal clock" that regulates the reinforcement schedule. In fact, scientists are as superstitious as anyone else. It is the scientist who has developed the extraordinary ritual of the scientific method in an effort to understand the nature of the universe, or, as in the case of our pigeons, the nature of Skinner.

The scientist is searching for meaning in the form of laws. But what proof is offered that a law has been discovered? For the behaviorist, the ultimate criterion as to whether we know anything is contingent upon reinforcements. A law must be proven to have reinforcing consequences. To say we will discover other laws is to do nothing more than express the faith that we shall find behaviors that lead to reinforcing consequences. Of course, the Pope will also undoubtedly tell us that belief in Christ has reinforcing consequences, and further religiosity will lead to behaviors that lead to other reinforcements. We have already seen that "persevering" may become an interpretation of another person's behavior when he does not extinguish a response. If he is on an extinction schedule of non-reinforcement, then we would know whether such a response is right or wrong, but we can never know that unless we could get outside our universe. Thus, like our pigeons, we require *faith* to believe that behavior is relevant to the universal clock.

When Skinner writes an essay concerning the ways in which the world operates and the ways in which it should operate, he is presuming to have an insight into the nature of that clock as a result of his scientific background. Skinner's statement (1961, p. 4) "Let us agree to start with, that health is better than sickness, wisdom better than ignorance, love better than hate, and productive energy better than neurotic sloth" ignores the implications of his own writings. It was Skinner who argued that one reinforcement is not better or worse than another. Reinforcements simply reinforce behavior. To say love is better than hate is to say nonsense, unless he adds that it is better to love X reinforcement than to hate Y reinforcement. This is absurd because loving or hating a reinforcement is contingent upon a history of other reinforcements or present contingencies. Thus, to hate or love a reinforcement is to love or hate the law of gravity. Yet Skinner writes as though knowledge of reinforcement effects the law of reinforcement.

Of course, Skinner is careful to put superstitious in quotes, on the grounds that he will not interpret behavior or make value judgments about it. Because of his own assumptions, he knows he cannot know anything more than what he observes. Actually, here and there (e.g., Skinner, 1961), he also uses drive names such as hunger, again in quotes. But, as Frankel (1971, p. 458) aptly charges, words like "hunger" or "superstitious" are interpretations of behavior, not mere descriptions. And interpretations are miniature theories insofar as they purport to describe the "meaning" of what is seen. Although Skinner considers theory to be explanatory fiction at worst, and irrelevant at best, he is in fact theorizing when he interprets movements as if he knew their meaning. That the interpretations make good common sense should not dull our perception that he is theorizing nonetheless.

What Frankel has pinpointed is hardly unimportant. Consider another ramification of the radical behaviorist's theorizing intuitively without admitting that so doing affects his actions and conclusions. Skinner has provided a powerful technology with which to change and control behavior, so it is not surprising to find his approach utilized in psychotherapy (e.g., Ayllon & Azrin, 1968; Goldiamond & Dyrud, 1967). But especially in something so crucial as psychotherapy, it becomes necessary to consider what behavior shall be changed, and in what direction change shall be implemented. Skinner asserts again and again that his is merely a technology for behavior modification, which is all the more scientific for carrying no value judgments within it. And when behavioristic psychotherapists discuss cases, they refer to the curing of stuttering, or autism, or some such gross abnormality the correction of which is such an unquestioned good that no value judgment seems to be involved.

When pressed further on just what changes should and should not be made, the behavioristic psychotherapist is likely to say that he brings about specifically those changes that the patient wants. The therapist is not so much a manipulator as a helper. But suppose that a patient came to the radical behaviorist's office asking for aid in becoming courageous enough to assassinate the President. What would the therapist say or do? He might turn the patient away, indicating disinterest or even opposition to such an aim. If he did this, he would be admitting that his behavior modification technology is in the service of his theory as to what is good and bad, constructive and unconstructive. Alternatively, he might engage the patient in conversation, on the expressed or private presumption that the stated aim was not the real one. Perhaps the patient just wants to feel more effective, or change his life substantially. In choosing this alternative, the radical behaviorist would be showing the subjugation of technology to a theory no less than by turning the patient away.

It is only by aiding the patient to gain courage to murder that the therapist would be true to his nonevaluative position. And yet, we all know he would not do that. Once again, we see the operation of theory—rife with value judgments, and not dissimilar to that forming the corpus of personology—in the decisions, plans, and conclusions of the radical behaviorist.

The upshot of all this is that radical behaviorism, as an alternative to personality theorizing, is not so pure as it purports to be. There is the distinct possibility that insofar as it is relevant to the understanding of complex human behavior, it is so by virtue of implicit, intuitive theorizing not dissimilar to what takes place more explicitly in moderate behaviorism. To refer to "hunger," and to maintain subjects at some fraction of body weight at the same time as one chooses food as a reinforcer, is to be assuming the existence of hunger as a primary drive, and the effectiveness of the reinforcer as a tension reducer. To try to explain the resistance to extinction of "superstitious" behavior is to admit that there are learned traits or habits which affect behavior rather directly, even though the stimulus justification of such behavior in the environment may not be particularly apparent. And, for that matter, to turn patients away or to become convinced that they do not know their own minds, is to have a theory of psychopathology and mental health. If radical behaviorism does indeed contain the intuitive seeds of a personality theory, such ought to be brought to flowering, so that its strengths and weaknesses can be clearly judged in the marketplace of ideas.

If it still be insisted that radical behaviorism includes no theorizing having implications for core and peripheral statements on personality, then the sorts of slips and therapeutic decisions discussed above should be strictly weeded out. The radical behaviorist ought to behave as if he really believed the presently stated tenets of his position. He is a describer and manipulator of physical movements and nothing more. If the radical behaviorist adhered strictly to this, then Frankel's (1971, p. 459) words are well worth noting:

> One can wonder what Skinner's appeal would be if he described only movements and did not add theoretical projections. Would the reader have the patience to project his own interpretations upon the movements or would he read someone like Freud who at least makes systematic projections? Skinner and Freud are similar in that both have an ingenious ability to take a unit of behavior and establish its meaning. Freud interprets dreams. Skinner interprets movements. The *undemonstrable conjectures* of Freud are perhaps no worse than the *meaningless movements* of Skinner.

To say that all behavior is the result of learning, and then to say nothing about developmentally common themes as to what is learned, is to do very little in the attempt to understand human life. To say that learning is dependent upon reinforcers, and to give no basis for discovering or identifying reinforcers except as learning actually occurs, is to damn us to a minute analysis of every event of human life that amounts to searching for a needle in a haystack. To insist that we need not speculate about the contents of that black box we call the organism, is to force us to act as if those wonderfully simplifying and organizing inferences about the true nature of complex phenomena we wish to understand, which have produced rapid advance in every other science, are somehow irrelevant in ours.

Toward a rapprochement

Until recently, the debate between radical behaviorists and personologists was quite intense. But a spirit of reconciliation is developing now, in which the personality theories becoming most influential are those that give weight to the situation as one determinant of behavior, and behaviorism is recognizing its implicit theorizing about human core and peripheral characteristics. For behaviorists, this shift is most apparent when attempts at psychotherapy are made. According to those "card-carrying" behaviorists, Hunt and Dyrud (1968, pp. 149–150):

> . . . the innate proclivities of man have an important bearing on behavioral modification. They can lie waiting as traps or can be employed as powerful allies. . . . There is no reason why we cannot devise methods to play into man's ethology, to turn the apparent rigidities of innate tendencies to our advantage. . . . In a sense, the important part of the modification would consist of putting the individual into a position in which "nature would take its course," in a new and better direction.

In another statement, Hunt (1975) admits implicit theorizing among behaviorists far beyond core characteristics alone:

> Identification of the effective reinforcers for a particular person and his particular behavior can be quite difficult, requiring shrewd guesses based on personal experience and empathy, clinical knowledge and dynamic theory, plus a good green thumb for behavior—in-context.

It is understandable that in the act of finding reinforcers that will work for the client, the behavior therapist's implicit personality theory will be shown.

Hand-in-hand with the growing willingness to make implicit personality assumptions explicit is increasing self-criticism among behaviorists. Where earlier there was an optimistic, almost incautious attitude of invincibility, there is now a more sober appraisal of the whole approach. Hunt (1975) provides a good example of this evaluative attitude. He identifies three related weaknesses in behaviorism as a scientific approach and as a psychotherapy that are beginning to gain wide discussion.

First is the problem of unexpected side-effects. It is apparent now, that schedules of reinforcement may have unintended but important and systematic effects on behavior other than the behavior that is the target of the treatment or shaping. Examples are (1) aggression as a side-effect of aversive conditioning (e.g., Ulrich, Dulaney, Kucera, and Colasacco, 1972), (2) behavioral "contrast," where changes in the re-inforcement schedule in one segment of a session changes behavior in another segment, though the schedule there remains unchanged (e.g., Reynolds, 1968), and (3) "auto-shaping," in which even pigeons seem to acquire an operant-pecking response without their having been direct reinforcement of it (e.g., Jenkins, 1973).

The second or ethological weakness of radical behaviorism is its scant ability to deal with species-specific behaviors, especially the differences between lower organisms, higher primates, and the human being. Spe-cifically, it is the human's symbolization and his active use of this to control his own and other's behavior that creates havoc with attempts at behavior shaping (Hunt, 1975). Not only the therapist and the ex-perimenter can shape behavior but so can his client and subject! Related is the accumulating evidence (e.g., Medin, 1972) that even in monkeys "reward can function to decrease as well as increase the probability of choosing an object," thus casting doubt upon positions based on an automatic strengthening function of reinforcement. There are also humorous examples of animal research in which strange "misbehavior" results from the shaping of responses not a natural part of the relevant organism's repertoire (e.g., Hinde and Stevenson-Hinde, 1973).

The third weakness in their approach that is gaining increasing atten-tion from behaviorists is the difficulty in accounting rigorously for self-regulation of behavior. Just what this mysterious self is that can control its actions is a vexing problem in a position that has been as situational as radical behaviorism (Hunt, 1975). According to Hunt and Dyrud (1968), an entirely new set of assumptions may be necessary to under-stand human symbolization, instead of the earlier attempt to generalize from lower organisms with rudimentary mentation. The experimental evidence is consistent with this clinical conclusion in showing that human adults do not seem to learn without awareness of so doing. Du-lany (1962, 1968), Spielberger (1962) and Bandura (1969) have dem-onstrated convincingly that for learning to occur in humans, it is not only necessary for the person to be able to verbalize the relationship between the target response class and the reinforcement but also to verbalize the intention to cooperate with the learning task! In situations where it may be presumed that this cooperative attitude does not exist, it has been shown (e.g., Calder and Staw, 1975a, 1975b) that extrinsic reinforcement (the usual kind recognized by behaviorists) does not add to, but rather interacts with, intrinsic reinforcement (the inherent value in the task), decreasing overall performance.

Early in his presidential address before the American Psychological Association, Bandura (1974, p. 860) said:

> After individuals discern the instrumental relation between action and outcome, contingent rewards may produce accommodating or oppositional behavior depending on how they value the incentives, the influencers and the behavior itself, and how others respond. Thus reinforcement, as it has become better understood, has changed from a mechanical strengthener of conduct to an informative and motivating influence. . . . Theories that explain human behavior as the product of external rewards and punishments present a truncated image of man because people partly regulate their actions by self-produced consequences.

For Bandura, recent research developments of the sort we have been discussing have shifted the emphasis of behaviorism from the study of response learning to analyses of memory and cognition. The rest of his address theorizes about these mental functions. In this new emphasis, Bandura is being joined by other behaviorists (e.g., Boneau, 1974; Dember, 1974; Mischel, 1973). Even Skinner (1971) seems somewhat willing. This movement toward matters of concern to personologists, such as individual differences in perception and choice, coupled with the increasing influence of personality theories sharing similar concerns, such as fulfillment approaches, promises a productive rapprochement.

CONCLUDING REMARKS

It is important, in considering the relative merits of personality theorizing and the behavioristic approach to recognize that to some extent they have been oriented toward different empirical phenomena. In data terms, the emphasis of behaviorism on the learning process means that it orients toward behavior that changes. In contrast, personology emphasizes behavior that remains the same, or at least that changes only slowly. The main concepts in behaviorism concerning stable behavior are stimulus and response generalization, and resistance to extinction. These concepts are not the heart of behaviorism. In addition, personology emphasizes individual and species differences, whereas behaviorism attempts to hold them constant in order to attempt specification of that which is universal in the learning process. In a sense, it is the constants in learning formuli that refer most to the personologist's concerns, and these constants could hardly be construed as central in behaviorism.

But, though their emphasis lies elsewhere, behaviorists do accept that some aspects of behavior are at least relatively stable. Insofar as this is true, it becomes worthwhile to consider how much their theorizing about behavioral stability resembles what the personologist does. We have seen that moderate behaviorism makes assumptions which can be construed as statements about the core and periphery of personality. Radical behaviorism, in contrast, attempts to explain behavior without recourse to such organismic variables as primary and secondary drives, tied definitionally to primary and secondary rewards. Nor does radical behaviorism use such terms referring to life-styles as habit. But it does seem extraordinarily difficult to maintain this extreme purity from interpretations based on the contents of what is within the skin, or black box. If such purity were strictly adhered to, behaviorism might even be too cumbersome, too dependent upon empirical study of each and every minute external stimulus and manipulatable movement, to be of much practical use. While the risk of being wrong is certainly present once one theorizes what is important, that risk is minimized if theorizing is careful enough to lead to hypothesis testing. Fortunately, even radical behaviorists now seem more willing to theorize explicitly.

What remains an unanswerable question at this time is just what kind of personality theorizing will go on in behaviorism. The persistent reference of behaviorists to Freud, and the choice of such research topics as conflict and defense, suggests that they are utilizing the conflict model. But the exclusion from the behavioristic formulation of the dynamic aspects of Freudian theory, such that defenses become habits learned as the result of certain reinforcement schedules rather than ego operations rendering certain thoughts unconscious, suggests that the very things making psychoanalytic formulations expressive of the conflict model are disputed. And recent emphases in behaviorism have been on human choice, memory, and perception. In the final analysis, it may be that behavioristic personality theorizing follows the fulfillment model, with life being understood as the general attempt to satisfy primary, biological drives through cognitive effort and intention.

Understood this way, behaviorism is not so much a frank alternative to personology. Rather, it is an approach to understanding learning which, in some of its statements, is not so different from the enterprise framing this book.

Chapter 12 THE RISE OF SOCIAL LEARNING THEORY

Recently, an emphasis called "social learning theory" has been gaining considerable centrality in psychology. It has implications for the study of personality, and should therefore be considered here. Initially an offshoot of moderate behaviorism, the social learning position seems to have emerged in response to the difficulty human behavior has posed to learning emphases developed in laboratory experiments on rats and other lower organisms. Human beings are so complex that their behavior often seems different in kind, not just degree, from that of other animals. Faced with this problem, some behaviorists have clung steadfastly to their simple, S-R, associationistic emphases, shoring up their theories with an additional assumption here and there, and attempting wherever possible to translate apparent human complexity into the simple response repertoires of their rats and pigeons. But other behaviorists have chosen instead to develop more complex theoretical approaches that, though retaining something of the flavor of behaviorism, provide understanding of human complexity without seeming to explain it away. It is from the work of this latter group of behaviorists that social learning theory arose. As the name given to this approach suggests, there is still emphasis upon learning rather than inherent characteristics, and upon the social surround rather than internal dispositions as the determiner of behavior.

The main architects of social learning theory are Joseph Wolpe (1958, 1969), Albert Bandura (1969), Richard Walters (Bandura & Walters, 1963), Julian B. Rotter (1954), Walter Mischel (1968, 1971), and to some extent, Hans J. Eysenck (1957). Although there are certainly differences among their views, the substantial similarities have begun to define a consistent approach to understanding and influencing human behavior.

THE BREAK WITH PSYCHOANALYTIC THOUGHT

You will recall from Chapter 11 that moderate behaviorism has had a fascination with psychoanalytic theory. This has taken the form of trying to purge psychoanalytic theory of its most metaphysical features, such as the unconscious and defenses, by translating everything possible into the behavioristic concepts of habit and drive. Although it can fairly be questioned whether what emerged from this translation is psychoanalytic theory anymore, behaviorists were nonetheless cheered that they could appear to retain the clinical insights of Freud without doing violence to their view of scientific rigor.

It is significant that the social learning theorists have explicitly detached themselves from psychoanalytic theory even though they are, if anything, more interested in abnormal or neurotic behavior than the general run of moderate behaviorists. Why should this be happening? Mainly because social learning theory emphasizes cognition, or information processing, or thought that is rational and logical. Although Freud certainly emphasized mental functioning, it was unconscious wishes, impulses, and conflicts that emerged as the major determinants of behavior. One cannot engage in vigorous rational trial and error if unconscious mental processes are paramount. One is left with rationalization, or that which appears to be rational but is really not.

It is the intent on the part of social learning theorists to emphasize a rational process of learning from experience that prompts Eysenck and Rachman (1965, pp. 9–10) to say:

> How does our theory compare with the psychoanalytic one? In the formation of neurotic symptoms, Freud emphasized the traumatic nature of the events leading up to the neurosis, as well as their roots in early childhood. . . . The Freudians' stress seems to be rather misplaced in allocating the origins of all neuroses to this period. It is possible that many neurotic symptoms find their origin in this period, but there is no reason at all to assume that neurotic symptoms cannot equally easily be generated at a later period, provided conditions are arranged so as to favor their emergence.
>
> The point, however, on which the theory here advocated breaks decisively with psychoanalytic thought . . . is in this. Freudian theory regards neurotic symptoms as adaptive mechanisms which are evidence of repression; they are "the visible upshot of unconscious causes." Learning theory does not postulate any such "unconscious" causes, but regards neurotic symptoms as simply learned habits; there is no neurosis underlying the symptom, but merely the symptom itself. *Get rid of the symptom (skeletal and autonomic) and you have eliminated the neurosis.*

In attributing psychopathology to certain learned habits alone, social learning theorists are also rejecting Freud's emphasis on the inherent conflict between instincts and society or superego. Where Dollard and Miller (see Chapter 11) retained an intuitive reliance upon this conflict formulation, all the while trying to divest Freud of seemingly untestable metaphysics, the social learning theorists want to make their break complete.

But it must be recognized that some social learning theorists, especially Eysenck and Wolpe, are very close to their moderate behaviorist ancestors. These theorists recognize the existence and importance of the primary drives (see Chapter 11). Their main emphasis is upon the drive for avoidance of pain, and the anxiety they see as at the heart of neurotic symptomatology is considered a secondary drive deriving from this primary one. Anxiety is a conditioned reaction, brought about by the conjunction on one or more occasions of an initially neutral stimulus with a painful event. This emphasis on habits and secondary drives rather than conflicts and defenses stems in part from research evidence. It is common for psychoanalysts to refer to Masserman's (1943) classical studies of "neurosis" in cats as justification for a conflict explanation of psychopathology. Masserman trained cats to receive food at a given location and later shocked them at that location. They developed what looked like intense anxiety reactions, which were explained in terms of conflict over whether to approach or avoid the location. Wolpe (1958) repeated Masserman's experiment but added another group of animals. This additional group was shocked in the experimental apparatus, but had not had the prior approach training with food that was given to the conflict group. The "anxiety responses" observed were similar in both groups, suggesting that pain but not necessarily conflict is the essential ingredient in anxiety reactions.

If anxiety is simply a learned reaction, it should be removable, however persistent it has become, by some process of new learning that cancels out the old S-R bond. This statement underlies the psychotherapeutic efforts of the branch of social learning theory closest to moderate behaviorism. Wolpe (1958), for example, employs what he calls *systematic desensitization therapy,* in which the person is encouraged to think of anxiety-provoking thoughts while relaxing. As soon as anxiety occurs, he is to think of something else. He tries this over and over until he can contemplate the previously anxious thoughts without this emotion. As you can see, this is very far from the psychoanalyst's encouragement to his patient to free associate and thereby rediscover suppressed experiences from the past.

When systematic desensitization therapy and other behavioristic techniques of psychotherapy became available, there was an initial flood of enthusiasm for them. They promised a simple and quick antidote for nagging symptoms that clients seem capable of talking about forever without any behavioral change. By now, however, sobriety is replacing overenthusiasm. One has only to read relevant case histories to recognize that even direct attempts to remove symptoms without any concern for underlying problems is long, arduous, and not invariably successful.

For example, Wolpe (Krasner & Ullman, 1966) reports the use of systematic desensitization therapy with a woman suffering with an intense fear that she would be involved in a collision whenever she was driving in a car. Wolpe regards this phobia to have developed when there was indeed a collision while her husband was driving. It took more than 60 sessions of concentrated, arduous attention to nothing more than this symptom to get it to go away, and at that, Wolpe regards her as fortunate, indicating that sometimes fears simply cannot be treated effectively by this approach. An additional vexing problem with this case (and many others like it) is that despite Wolpe's insistence that it is systematic desensitization therapy that finally produced symptom remission, many psychoanalytically-inclined readers will find considerably signs to suggest otherwise. Wolpe mentions near the end of his discussion that as the woman was questioned further, it became clear that her fear was more generalized than it seemed originally. In addition, the only two men besides her husband whom she had loved were her first fiancé, who died in an airplane crash just before they were to marry, and her father, who had died some time after that; in the same year that she married her present love. It might well be that behind what seemed a simple phobia deriving from an accident is the deeper fear of abandonment by loved males. If one was so inclined, it would be easy to implicate the Oedipal triangle as an abandonment she had never fully resolved. Further, Wolpe's claim that systematic desensitization therapy must have produced symptom remission, because no transference was permitted to develop, is also a bit less than convincing. The therapist even went riding in a car with the client at one point in his attempt to help her overcome her fear. Events of this sort would be regarded by psychoanalysts as definitely courting transference.

It is probably too early in our experience with behavioristic psychotherapies to evaluate them fully and well. Suffice it to say that they are not the dramatic end to all our searching for methods to alleviate human suffering, if any psychotherapy ever could be. And the claim made for them that they do not implicitly employ techniques deriving from more dynamic, mentalistic theories of personality has not been proven definitely. What we can be sure of is that psychotherapy research seeking to study outcome could profit from an explicit comparative analytic stance. I do not mean anything so simple as to compare proportion of cures across various psychotherapies, though this is certainly a useful step in accumulating information with which to evaluate. At some point very soon, it will be necessary to determine whether therapists employing a particular technique use it and no other, and if they do, whether that single technique leads to more or less symptom remission than other single techniques. We cannot rely for this determination on what the therapist says he did and did not do. There seems no alternative to detailed and painstaking observational studies of ongoing psychotherapy sessions.

In any event, to summarize: Wolpe's approach, which is in its assumptions very similar to Eysenck's position, conceptualizes learning as S-R bonds cemented by reinforcement, with primary and secondary drives providing the motive force for activity. In this regard, the positions are similar to the older moderate behaviorism mentioned in Chapter 11. The core tendency is still tension reduction, and the core characteristics are still the primary drives and rewards. The peripheral characteristics are habits and secondary drives and rewards.

COGNITION AS PARAMOUNT

It is common to regard Bandura, Rotter, and Mischel as moderate behaviorists. But, in them, the notion of social learning has reached a kind of peak that virtually removes them from the behaviorist camp. This seems to me true for two reasons: (1) the assumption that learning can take place without the person emitting a response and receiving positive or negative reinforcement for it, and (2) the paramount importance in learning that is attributed to cognition (which is, after all, internal and not directly observable).

Turning first to Bandura (Bandura & Walters, 1963; Krasner & Ullmann, 1966) we find that he emphasizes what might be called S-S (stimulus-stimulus) laws, in contrast to the S-R laws of behaviorism. He believes that one need not actually emit a response in the presence of a stimulus cue, with a reinforcement following the response, for learning to take place. For him, it is possible for a person to observe someone else behaving in a particular way in response to a particular stimulus and learn just by seeing what happens to him. Then, when the person who has observed is himself in such a situation, he is likely to behave the same way he observed. The person observed has served as a *model* for imitative learning on the part of the person observing.

In this view, modeling behavior is the most common and important form of learning in humans. In making this point, Bandura (Krasner & Ullman, 1966) argues that

> . . . one does not employ trial-and-error or operant conditioning methods in training children to swim, adolescents to drive an automobile, or in getting adults to acquire vocational skills. Indeed, if training proceeded in this manner, very few persons would ever survive the process of socialization. It is evident from informal observation that the behavior of models is utilized extensively to accelerate the acquisition process, and to prevent one-trial extinction of the organism in situations where an error may produce fatal consequences.

Going further, Bandura (Krasner & Ullmann, 1966) contends that operant conditioning is not only a less common but also a less effective procedure for learning at the human level. He quips that if a child had no occasion to hear the phrase "successive approximations," or any other combination of unusual words, it is doubtful whether such a verbal response could ever be shaped by differential reinforcement of the child's random utterances. This frontal assault on radical behaviorism would probably produce the rejoinder that verbal behavior is not sufficiently universal across animal species to warrant granting it such importance for purposes of theorizing about the learning process. Anticipating this, Bandura (Krasner & Ullmann, 1966) concludes that such a position ". . . simply highlights the inadvisability of relying too heavily on infrahuman organisms for establishing principles of human behavior." He is incredulous that we would actually be asked to believe that verbal communication in humans is unimportant merely because no researcher has ever succeeded in teaching a rat to talk in a recognizable language. Instead, we might be well advised, according to him, to conclude that modeling procedures are superior over operant conditioning procedures in promoting learning. He suggests that we relegate the role of operant conditioning in humans to that of regulating performance of behavioral sequences once they have been already learned through modeling.

To get a vivid sense of what is being said, consider one of the many research studies (see Bandura & Walters, 1963; Mischel, 1968) supporting learning by imitation. Bandura (1965) had his subjects, who were children, watch a film of an adult who displayed novel aggressive responses, such as hitting and kicking a Bobo doll. The subjects were split into three groups on the basis of what the consequences of the adult's behavior were in the film. In one group, the adult's aggression was punished, in another it was ignored, and in the third it was rewarded. When tested after the film, children who had observed aggression punished expressed less aggression in their behavior than children who had observed it either ignored or rewarded. But, in subsequent testing, when children were offered attractive incentives to reproduce the adult's behavior, the differences between the groups vanished! Presumably, all of the subjects learned the observed aggressive behavior. The effect of punishing the observed behavior seems to have been merely to inhibit its performance in the children. On this basis, it is argued that reward and punishment does not increase or decrease what is learned, but rather the likelihood that it will be expressed in performance.

Cognition, or information processing, or thought must be very active and important, even in the child, if it is possible for him to learn by observing others, and then to decide whether to express what has been learned on the basis of presumed outcomes. Giving such a major role to cognition is definitely not found in moderate behaviorism, even when it makes some concession to mentalistic matters in considering the human being.

In what sense, then, is the position of Bandura and his colleagues a behaviorism at all? It does not consider rewards and punishments important in learning, and emphasizes cognition as much if not more than action. According to Mischel (1968), whose own position is quite similar, Bandura is a behaviorist in that though he emphasizes cognition he does not assume elaborate motivations, impulses, conflicts, and the like, to be underlying the behavior that is observed. Mischel and the others attempt to explain expectations and imitative (heavily cognitive) learning in terms or a relatively uninterpretive analysis of the observable stimulus conditions that are occurring. This new body of theory is, according to him, truly a "social learning" position, in that it attempts to explain thoughts and actions in terms of concrete social, functional realities. Mischel (1971) sees social learning theory as an alternative to other personological approaches, which seem to emphasize either traits (broad, cross-situational consistencies in behavior) or motivational states (which underlie many, apparently dissimilar behaviors).

In discriminating the social learning approach from positions emphasizing traits, Mischel (1971, p. 75) considers the case of a woman who seems hostile and fiercely independent some of the time, but passive, dependent and feminine on other occasions. His position is that the woman is all of these seemingly contradictory things, but with each behavior being tied to the particular stimulus conditions which elicit it. This seems a very reasonable position. But Mischel contends that trait theorists would have difficulty understanding the woman, because traits are general dispositions presumably finding expressions across a great many unspecified stimulus situations. But surely it is a vague use of the trait concept that Mischel criticizes, rather than any use one would want to defend. I grant that some personality theorists name traits and then leave hem hanging there, as if there were no limits to their influence upon behavior. But if this were not mere sloppiness, why would a theorist ever postulate more than one trait? He postulates many because he at least implicitly recognizes that the sphere of influence of each is limited. Traits are, after all, used primarily in the explanation of individual differences. In personology, one can certainly point to a use of the trait concept rigorous enough as to be hard to distinguish from what Mischel advocates. Allport (see Chapter 7), for example, considered personal dispositions to render a definite delimited range of stimuli and responses functionally equivalent. Also, McClelland (see Chapter 8) defines a motive as a predisposition which only becomes active in the presence of certain motivational cues. Murray (see Chapter 6) shared this view, taking pains to implicate both subjectively and objectively perceived situation cues (alpha and beta presses) arousing the trait. It is my impression that when the trait concept is used carefully, it is very similar to Mischel's emphasis.

This becomes even more apparent when Mischel (1971, p. 77) stresses that social learning theory is interested in ". . . the functional relations between what [one] does and the psychological conditions of [one's] life." Clearly, he does not want to be restricted to a mindless listing of the links between particular cognitions and particular stimulus situations. He wishes to consider how these links go together into larger functional units relevant to the main enterprises of life. How different, I ask you, is this from Allport's intent?

How different is it, for that matter, from the intent of theorists emphasizing underlying motivations for observed behaviors? I certainly grant that many personality theorists have used the motivation concept loosely. But, once again, we must distinguish loose usage from rigorous usage, for it is only the latter that is a proper target for Mischel, if he would demonstrate the *inherent* superiority of his position. In carving out the relevant domain of social learning theory, Mischel (1971, pp. 78–79) emphasizes "covert representation" (for learning which is unexpressed externally), the whole matter of "the individual's interpretation of events and experiences," and the occurrence of "mediation." In discussion mediation, he (Mischel, 1971, p. 81) emphasizes the importance of the human as an active organism, who "evaluates, judges, and regulates his own performance," and who "in addition to being rewarded and punished by the external environment. . . . [learns] to monitor and evaluate [his] own behavior and to reward and punish [himself], thus modifying [his] own behavior and influencing [his] environment." Is there any personality theorist who would find this emphasis different from what he thought was his own? Hardly, unless it be those who so stress unconscious motivation that the self-deterministic ring of Mischel's words would be objectionable. But then, at the very least, Mischel might do well, at this early stage in the development of social learning theory, to oppose it to theories of unconscious motivation alone, rather than to all motivational emphases.

Indeed, from the examples and cases he raises, Mischel does seem to have psychoanalytic theory as his main objection. A notable case in point concerns Pearson Brack, an American pilot during World War II, whose famous problem is discussed by two psychoanalysts, Grinker and Spiegel (1945, pp. 197–207). During a bombing mission, Brack's plane was severely damaged by flak which also rendered him unconscious. The plane began to dive, and Brack barely regained consciousness in time to right it before it crashed. Seriously injured, Brack was hospitalized for a month. After this time he seemed fully recovered, and was returned to duty. But on his next two missions, he fainted when the plane reached about 10,000 feet, the elevation at which the original flak damage had occurred.

After intensive interviewing, the psychoanalytically-oriented psychiatrist at the hospital concluded that Brack's fainting was connected to deep, unconscious anxieties rooted in his childhood experiences. The diagnosis involved basic immaturity, long-standing insecurity, and faulty identification with father. The incident of nearly being shot out of the sky was perceived as rather trivial, except as it precipitated anxiety in an already insecure and immature person. In contrast, Mischel (1968) offers a social behavior analysis of the case that emphasizes the severe emotional reaction that was conditioned to altitude cues specific to 10,000 feet. According to Mischel, it is a sufficient explanation of the fainting to recognize that the occurrence of any cues specific to the near-fatal incident would be sufficient to reelicit the emotional debilitation associated with that trauma.

It is my impression that virtually all fulfillment and consistency theorists would tend to agree with Mischel in his interpretation of the case of Brack. This underscores even more that Mischel's main dispute regarding motivation is with the Freudians, who persist in postulating basically unconscious conflicts and purposes underlying behavior. But if what I am saying is so, it would aid clarity for Mischel to acknowledge that there are indeed other personalistic approaches to the motivation construct much more compatible with his own.

The final social learning theorist we will consider is Rotter (1954), who takes as his task an understanding of the probability that a particular act will occur. He calls this probability the *behavior potential.* You will recall that in moderate behaviorism, the probability of a response is given by the strength of the habit or S-R bond. The more times in the past that the response has followed a particular stimulus cue and been stamped in by a reinforcement, the greater the likelihood that the cue will elicit the response in the future. Radical behaviorism offers a similar formulation, except that the terminology of habit is not used and it is explicitly recognized that intermittent reinforcement may produce a higher response probability than invariant reinforcement. The differences between these formulations and that of Rotter pinpoints what is new about social learning theory. For Rotter (1954), *behavior potential is a function both of the expectancy that reinforcement will follow the behavior, and the perceived value of the expected reinforcement.* First, the emphasis on expectancy and perceived value shows the strong cognitive commitment that Rotter has made. Expectancies and perceived values are internal mental events, and are given the role of jointly determining whether or not action will take place. Secondly, Rotter is dealing with a subjective rather than objective basis for predicting behavior. One person's expectancy that reinforcement will follow a response may be different than another person's expectancy. Similarly, there may well be individual differences in the perceived value of any particular reinforcement. Consequently, what is being said is that if you wish to understand why humans behave or fail to, you must refer to their own individualized view of the world. Indeed, Rotter has a name for this, the *psychological situation*. This is clearly intended to be the person's general construction of the value and likelihood of the stimuli making up his environment.

True to his social learning assumptions, Rotter does not regard individual differences in reinforcement expectancy and value to stem merely from instincts or underlying motives. Rather, such differences strongly reflect differences in previous experience. Having assumed this, Rotter could take a reasonably conservative stance that would hue as close as possible to an objective position. He could say that the value one places on a reinforcement reflects what its actual utility has been in one's past. Thus, sports cars would have more reinforcement value for someone who has won the company of attractive girls by owning them than for someone whose female associates regard fancy cars as ostentatious. Further, he could say that the expectancy of a reinforcement mirrors its actual frequency of occurrence in a person's past. Such an approach would certainly generate an ability to understand individual differences, for it could be safely assumed that the chances are great for objective differences among people in their past experiences.

Certainly, Rotter recognizes these actuarial bases for differences in reinforcement value and expectancy in the present. But he goes even further than this. In a leap into subjectivism from which there is no return, he (Rotter, Chance, & Phares, 1972) asserts that "People's probability statements, and other behaviors relating to the probability of occurrence of an event, often differ systematically from their actuarial experience with the event in the past." A variety of factors are regarded to influence one's probability estimates away from objective occurrence. Among these factors are the way in which a situation is categorized, various patterning and sequential considerations, the uniqueness of events, the degree of generalization that occurs, and how the person perceives causality. These factors are not meant to be derived from the person's reinforcement history in any precise way. Rather, they are best understood as cognitive commitments or decisions that interact with the objective frequency and utility of reinforcements to produce each person's particular reinforcement expectancies and values, or his psychological situation. It is this psychological situation that determines the relative likelihood of various actions he might take in the future.

In his reference to factors influencing cognition and perception away from actuarial experience, Rotter shows the influence of his longtime colleague, George A. Kelly (see Chapter 4, especially). Interestingly enough, Mischel studied for his Ph.D. with both Rotter and Kelly. It should be clear by now why I think that the cognitive emphasis of these social learning theorists and Bandura is so extreme as to place them outside behaviorism. To try somehow to subsume not only the notion of observational learning but also of subjective perceptions as determinants of reinforcement value and expectancy under behaviorism would literally destroy its original intent. When social learning theorists assert that they remain behaviorists nonetheless, it seems to me that what they really mean is that they still wish to be regarded as serious scientists. They are still concerned with the prediction and control of behavior, and they fervently believe that the cognitive concepts they employ are measurable and manipulatable experimentally. Most personologists would agree with them in this. But that does not make them behaviorists.

If you are wondering whether the conclusion that social learning theory is beyond the limits of behaviorism really applies to Bandura, set your mind at rest. In his recent presidential address before the American Psychological Association, Bandura (1974) goes as far as Rotter. Bandura first reasserts the preeminence of cognition by indicating that, in his judgment, research has shown that there is no operant conditioning at all without awareness on the part of the subject of the contingencies existing between responses and reinforcements, and consent to being manipulated by the experimenter in this fashion! Secondly, he regards self-regulation of one's own behavior through manipulation of the environment as the hallmark of human functioning. According to him, the human progresses toward maturity by gaining greater and greater control over his behavior through a combination of internal or self-reward, and actual shaping of the external environment so as to be more self-rewarding. Moreover, the procedure whereby certain events become more or less rewarding than other events is for Bandura an essentially internal one. Not only is it internal but also subjective in the sense that there may not be complete correspondence between reinforcement value and reinforcement histories.

His third point that is of importance here is an amplification of the previously-mentioned assumption that the person largely learns through observation of the reinforcement consequences of action, without having to perform any act or experience any reinforcement himself. Bandura does not intend that this imitative learning imply a slavish following of the literal behaviors that have been observed. If this were so, nothing new would ever happen. In attempting to explain how new behaviors could occur through imitative learning, Bandura considers how it is possible to learn by merely observing at all. The key is the human capacity to represent observed behaviors symbolically, not just literally. In other words, the person can generalize from what he sees to categories of behavior. Says Bandura (1974):

> From observing others, one forms an idea of how certain behavior is
> performed, and on later occasions the coded information serves as a

guide for action. . . . Some of the limitations commonly ascribed to behavior theory are based on the mistaken belief that modeling can produce at best mimicry of specific acts. This view is disputed by growing evidence that abstract modeling is a highly effective means of inducing rule-governed cognitive behavior.

Going further, he gives clear recognition to the fact that in the process of abstracting from specific acts observed, the person utilizes internal "judgmental orientations, conceptual schemes, linguistic styles, information-processing strategies, as well as other forms of cognitive functioning." It goes without saying, at this point, that Bandura can only mean, when he calls himself a behaviorist, that he is still a rigorous scientist.

THE IMPACT OF SOCIAL LEARNING RESEARCH

To some psychologists, the cognitive, internal, subjective emphasis of social learning theory will indeed brand it as no longer fully scientific. But Bandura, Mischel, Rotter and others who share their beliefs consider themselves quite interested in and capable of articulating, measuring, manipulating, and predicting the cognitive variables and learning processes they have assumed. Although in some purist sense, a behaviorist might argue that there is no way of measuring a thought or an idea because it is internal and intangible (remember that to a philosopher it would be spirit not material), social learning theorists insist that adequate measurement is possible through oral and written verbal report. This is the same assumption all personologists make. Were it not for the subject's verbalizations, be they spontaneous or responses to interview questions or paper-and-pencil tests, little by way of empirical study of personality would be possible. Thus, it would be hard for personologists to fault social learning theorists in their contention that they are serious scientists.

Moreover, if impact is any gauge of research soundness, the work of social learning theorists has certainly had that. It is not irrelevant that Bandura was President of the American Psychological Association in 1974. He and his colleagues have provided a body of research, an example of which was mentioned before, showing that observational learning takes place in humans, is more rapid than standard conditioning, and can lead to generalization beyond what is literally observed. The content of the studies has often been aggressive behavior (e.g., Bandura & Walters, 1963). By choosing in this fashion, Bandura and his associates have brought their work close to present concerns in their society. Their conclusion is clear: by merely observing on TV or in the movie theaters aggressive behavior that is rewarded or at least not punished, a person can learn that it pays to be aggressive! And this will happen even if the film contains only cartoon characters. Findings such as these raise an insistent question for a society beset by a steadily increasing rate of violence. When and under what circumstances is censorship of public communications appropriate? You may be appalled by the merest posing of the question of censorship. But let me remind you that Plato in *The Republic* puts into Socrates's mouth the defense of censorship, in order to preserve the ideal state and foster sound character in its members. And, after all, the work of Bandura and his associates does not lead to the conclusion that all portrayal of violence breeds violence in the observer. When what is observed is aggression leading to punishment, then aggressive behavior is learned but performance of it is not likely.

Another important research theme that Bandura shares with Mischel concerns self-control, a matter that is one of the major differences between social learning theory and ordinary behaviorism. A general procedure has been devised for studying the person's criteria for self-reward. The usual subjects are school children, who are asked to work on a performance task that seems to require skill. In actuality, their scores on the task are predetermined by the experimenter so that they have the experience of varying degrees of success or failure. They also have available to them a large supply of rewards (e.g., candy, cake, toys), and they are usually left alone, though secretly observed, during testing. But before testing, the procedure calls for the children to observe an adult performing the same or a similar task, and rewarding himself according to a high or low criterion of success. Often the adult model also verbalizes rationales that are consistent with his self-reward decisions.

Using such a procedure, Bandura and Kupers (1964) demonstrated that patterns of self-reward are acquired through imitating models. Children who observed an adult model rewarding and praising himself after low scores on the performance test tended to do the same when they were subsequently tested. Children who observed self-reward and praise only after high scores followed that example. These findings are shown in Figure 12–1. It is important to note that the children were alone when tested, and hence should not have experienced any direct social pressure influencing self-reward. That they did not deviate from the self-reward pattern they had previously observed is quite consistent with social learning theory.

There are several additional studies consistent with this one. In these studies as a whole, there has been a range of performance tasks, criteria of performance, and model characteristics. The consistency of the finding that self-reward patterns are strongly influenced by observed behavior in models can therefore be considered to have some generality.

A particularly interesting direction in self-control research involves the decision for immediate or delayed gratification. It can certainly be argued that adequate adjustment to our society requires the ability to delay rewards. If, as social learning theorists contend, the person is at

FIGURE 12–1

Self-reinforcement at each performance level by control children and those exposed to adults modeling high and low standards for self-reward

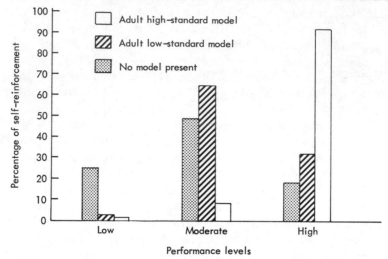

Source: Adapted from A. Bandura and C. J. Kupers, "Transmission of patterns of self-reinforcement through modeling." *J. abn. soc. Psychol.*, 1964.

least partially able to manipulate reinforcement contingencies in the environment rather than passively succumb to them as they exist, he must be able to delay reinforcement to some later time even though it is within his power to have it immediately. In research on this matter, subjects usually must choose among actual rewards that differ in time at which they occur and in value. Typically, the choice of immediate reinforcement brings a smaller reward whereas delaying reinforcement qualifies one for a larger reward. Again, children are the common subjects. And again, subjects observe an adult model making similar choices to those they will subsequently be asked to make.

In such a study, Bandura and Mischel (1965) preselected children such that their sample included subjects who characteristically sought immediate though small rewards and children who sought delayed and larger rewards. There were some of these children in each of the treatment groups of the experiment. In one treatment group, children observed an adult model who exhibited delay-of-reward choices that were counter to their own self-reward pattern. For example, if the child was initially high in delay of gratification, the adult model chose immediate rewards. And children who preferred immediate gratification during the pretest period observed a model who chose the delayed, larger rewards. Models always also gave verbal rationales for their choices. In another treatment group, subjects were again exposed to information about a model performing counter to their pretest pattern. But rather than viewing an actual model, they received the model's choices in written form. In a control group, children had no exposure or information about models.

The children's own choices to have immediate or delayed gratification were tested immediately after they had observed the model. Figure 12–2 shows clearly that the subject's choices were strongly influenced in the direction of the choices made by the model they had observed. The effects of the treatment persisted in a different social setting one month later. And the effect occurred even with written responses rather than a "live" model. These findings are impressive, especially when you keep in mind that observing the model actually reversed a predilection the child brought to the experimental situation!

A fair amount of work has been done attempting to pinpoint the mental state of subjects who are able to delay gratification. The subject must have the expectation or "trust" that the delayed reward will indeed be granted (e.g., Mischel, 1966). Also, in order to choose the delayed reward, the subject must be able to spend the time period preceding the reward either not thinking about anything in particular (Mischel & Ebbesen, 1970), or distracting himself with other pleasant thoughts (Mischel, Ebbesen, & Raskoff, 1971). Despite the many intriguing findings in this and other research themes involving initiative learning, an important question remains unanswered. To what extent is the learn-

FIGURE 12–2

Mean percentage of immediate-reward responses by high-delay children on each of three test periods for each of three experimental conditions

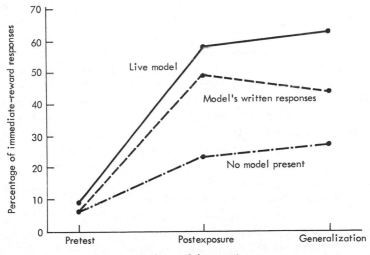

Source: Adapted from A. Bandura and W. Mischel, "Modification of self-imposed delay of reward through exposure to live and symbolic models." *J. pers. soc. Psychol.*, 1965.

ing and performance of adults influenced by observing models? After all, research to this point has almost invariably utilized children as subjects and adults as models. But adult subjects might be less impressionable in observing other adults or children as models.

The concern with the mental state of subjects who delay gratification forms a natural transition to research more squarely involving personality. This research treats the preference for *delayed versus immediate gratification* as a concrete peripheral characteristic. Mischel (1958) measured this in a simple fashion. After subjects had filled out a questionnaire, he displayed a large and a small piece of candy and indicated that he wished to give a piece to each of them, but that he did not have enough of the larger ones just then to go around. The subjects were given their choice of the smaller piece immediately, or the larger one a week later when another shipment arrived. Since this early study, the simple measure of immediacy or delay of gratification has been extended to include more choice situations. The resulting test seems to have adequate internal consistency and stability (e.g., Mischel, 1961).

Considerable research has been done correlating the measure of delayed versus immediate gratification with other behaviors. Persons who prefer delayed rewards are high in achievement orientation, social responsibility, resistance to temptation, older, live in a home where there is a father present, are future oriented, and plan carefully for distant goals (see Mischel, 1966; Klineberg, 1968). Socioculturally, preference for delayed gratification tends to be found most in the middle and upper classes, and in industrialized societies (e.g., Mischel, 1958). There is clearly empirical overlap between delay versus immediate gratification and McClelland's need for achievement (see Chapters 8 and 10). At some time the extent of this overlap will have to be determined. For the present, however, we can accept delay versus immediacy of gratification as a concrete peripheral characteristic with sufficient empirical support to be taken seriously.

Turning to Rotter's research, we find that the most influential theme in it has already been mentioned in Chapter 10 under existential psychology. The theme I am referring to is *internal versus external locus of control.* In this, Rotter is concerned with the generalized and pervasive expectancy in people that they have control over and responsibility for what happens to them as opposed to feeling manipulated and controlled by external factors. Strictly speaking, this concrete peripheral characteristic derives from the least explicit part of Rotter's theorizing. Generalized expectancies such as that concerning locus of control are not as concrete as the expectancies and values attributed to reinforcements. Rather, generalized expectancies are what forms the psychological situation, according to Rotter.

By now, considerable research has been done correlating various questionnaire measures of locus of control with other variables. But there is no point in repeating what has already been covered in Chapter 10. Suffice it to say that persons with internal locus of control emerge, at a personal level, as more individualistic, assertive, interested in gaining knowledge, and willing to rely upon their skill in risky situations than are persons believing they are externally controlled. At the societal level, persons with internal locus of control are more concerned with social problems and more activistic in attempting to solve these problems than are externally-oriented persons. It should also be kept in mind that Rotter and his associates have done experimental studies in this area that bolster the claim that internal versus external locus of control has a causal influence on behavior.

Recent evidence (e.g., Lao, 1970) has begun to suggest that the internal versus external locus of control construct is not as unitary as initially thought. Persons who regard themselves as able to influence their own lives and those of their friends do not necessarily believe that they can influence events in the broader society, and vice versa. Paralleling this empirical complication is the theoretical likelihood of overlap between locus of control and McClelland's need for achievement. And, as you know from Chapter 10, the overlap between locus of control and the emphasis in existential psychology upon the individualist's self-definition and world view is so great that Rotter's research is as relevant to that body of theory as to his own. Despite all these complications, the reaction of personologists to locus of control research has been enthusiastic. It seems to be an intuitively and rationally compelling concrete peripheral characteristic.

PERSONAL VERSUS SITUATIONAL DETERMINATION OF BEHAVIOR

For all of Mischel's emphasis upon self-control and a cognitively-based ability to delay gratification, he has somewhat reluctantly played a major role in the recent controversy over whether it is personal dispositions or situational forces that determine behavior. The controversy seems to have begun with Mischel's (1968) attempt to demonstrate that there is scant empirical support for the view that traits and underlying motivational states control behavior. In this argument, he was criticizing the view that traits and underlying motives have a pervasive, even ubiquitous influence upon behavior to the exclusion of situational forces. In the context of such a view, the modest reliability and validity correlations associated with nearly all measures of concrete peripheral characteristics is a damaging empirical fact. If a person's score on the measure of a trait or motive varies over time, and if its relationship to behavior is small, then how can traits and motives be conceived as important in the determination of action? Moreover, Mischel amassed evidence that situational factors seem to have a much larger role in controlling action.

As I have indicated earlier, this seemingly damning criticism must be examined more closely. For one thing, it takes as its starting point a version of trait theory that many personologists would recognize as sloppy. There is ample precedent among personality theorists (e.g., Allport, McClelland, Murray, Fiske, & Maddi) for a conceptualization of concrete peripheral characteristics as potentialities that await situational cues for arousal. Only when these potentialities are aroused should one expect them to influence action. This more rigorous usage than Mischel considered is not only rationally more satisfying, but would also lead to the empirical prediction of only moderate rather than large relationship between measures of concrete peripheral characteristics and other variables. Something very similar is true of the best examples of theorizing about underlying motivational states. As Mischel would clearly have to shoot down the best usage in order to demonstrate the inherent superiority of the view that it is the situation alone which controls behavior, what appeared at first to be a damning criticism ends being considerably blunted. As I indicated earlier, his criticism seems most cogent in the case of such views as psychoanalysis, which emphasize the constant effect upon action of underlying unconscious motivations. Such views do indeed explain even opposite behaviors as expressive of the same motivation. But Mischel has much less quarrel with fulfillment and consistency positions.

Mischel's critique ignited heated controversy that raged for several years and now shows signs of having abated. Defending the personological view, Alker (1972) argued that Mischel, in his zealous situationism, had overlooked several available studies crucial for the issue of whether the person or the situation determines action. These studies are crucial because they permit evaluation of the contribution to behavior of not only traits and situations but the interaction between them as well. In perhaps the best known of these studies, Endler, Hunt and Rosenstein (1962) constructed an *S-R Inventory* of anxiousness, consisting of 11 anxiety provoking situations and 14 modes of response indicating anxiety. Subjects indicated the intensity of each of their modes of response in each situation. Through their analysis of the data Endler et al., initially concluded that the situation was more predictive of behavior than the mode of response. But in a later reanalysis of the data, Endler and Hunt (1966) revised their conclusion to the position that the interaction between mode of response and situation was by far the best predictor of behavior. This finding was confirmed for the *S-R Inventory* in several subsequent studies (e.g., Endler & Hunt, 1969; Endler, 1973).

But the *S-R Inventory* is, after all, a questionnaire, which means that subjects were merely describing how they would respond in various situations without actually being in them. Moos (1968, 1969, 1970) improved upon this by putting subjects in a range of situations and observing their reactions in addition to obtaining their self-descriptions. His results also showed that the interaction between the person and the situation is a far better predictor of behavior than either the person or the situation alone.

Although Alker's citation of such studies seemed persuasive, the situationist argument was raised again by Bem (1972). He identified certain weak spots in Alker's position and insisted that the situationists should be given a chance since personology had assertedly failed. Although Mischel expressed discomfort with this extreme, the argument raged on for a time. It has now subsided in the face of strong agreement on an interactionist position. Many now believe that the controversy was a pseudo-issue in the first place.

In what seems to be a definitive settlement of the disagreements, Bowers (1973) amassed no less than 11 studies of the sort mentioned above demonstrating that behavior is largely a function of the interaction between personality and situation. Bowers also demonstrated the rational implausibility of asserting that either personality or situation is the whole explanation of behavior. A broader perspective on the controversy and its end has been provided by Ekehammar (1974), who reminds us of the various personologists and other psychologists who, years ago and now, have called for an interactionist approach. Recently, Mischel (1973) himself has endorsed interactionism. And no less a figure than Cronbach (1974) has reminded us that he years ago (Cronbach, 1957) called for the same thing.

Just what is the nature of the interactionist solution? It rejects the idea of traits as determiners of literal response repetition across situations regardless of their characteristics and demands. It also rejects the idea that the person is without structure and shifts behavior passively from one situation to the next. Rather, it focuses upon the way the person construes the situation and the effects of this construed or subjective environment on his behavior. It is assumed that there will be individual differences in construing the environment, and also individual differences in response to what has been construed. There is sufficient enthusiasm for this new accord that the difficulties it creates for empirical study do not seem to be a deterrent at this time.

The interactionist position is, of course, very similar to the emphases of several personologists, including Lewin, Angyal, Sullivan, Murray, Allport, McClelland, and the existentialists. True, some personologists put more emphasis upon personality and less upon situation than is consistent with the interactionist stance (e.g., Freud, Jung), essentially regarding reality as an internal mental state. But they are in the minority, however influential they may have been in the past.

I do not mean to suggest that there has been no value in the person-situation controversy. It has alerted psychologists to the need for an articulate theory of situations. A start on this has been made (see Ekehammar, 1974) which distinguishes (a) a priori definition of physical and social stimuli, (2) need concepts, (3) single reactions elicited by situations, and (4) perceptions of situations. The controversy has also pinpointed the need for personality theory to have a cognitive emphasis in order that we be able to explain how the person construes the environment. Although this cognitive emphasis is clearly consistent with the social learning approach and many personality theories, it is oddly out of place as moderate behaviorism, with its emphasis on mindless habits and automatic responses.

Although the controversy is largely over and the accord is fairly general, there is still a splinter position of situationism that lingers. Fiske (1974) is troubled not only by the low reliability of most personality trait measures but also by the many and diverse disagreements in the theorizing of personologists. Adopting the behaviorists' pessimism about theorizing, Fiske asserts that personologists can never reach agreement or measure reliably as long as they are focusing upon personality constructs because they probably do not really exist empirically. Disregarding the recently offered methodological and theoretical criticism of extreme situationism (and extreme personalism) cogently presented by Bowers (1973) and Ekehammar (1974), Fiske advocates that personologists abandon theorizing and devote themselves instead to the observational study of small, and therefore objective, actions and their controlling stimuli. He cites the work of Duncan (1972) as a model for personological research. In this study, Duncan has observed persons interacting together and has abstracted from those data the nonverbal cues or rules whereby signals are given that someone is starting or ending speech. The study does not consider individual differences.

But if the interactionist accord mentioned earlier is correct, then there really is no virtue to assuming an objective environment that affects all persons similarly. Duncan's work is as interpretive as anyone's. That he has thus far deemphasized individual differences in construing situations and responding to what has been construed emerges as a matter of choice on his part (researchers show individual differences in construing too) rather than what the data yield up inexorably. It would undoubtedly be possible to scrutinize the relationship between Duncan's data and findings to discover, in his choice to observe just certain cues for initiating and ending speech, his own subjective construction of the environment. It would also be possible to discern individual differences among subjects in perception and action. Similarly, Fiske's proposed direction for personology expresses a behavioristic preference on his part rather than a necessary conclusion for anyone else. Indeed, one might as easily be moved to excitement by the disagreements among personality theorists because they provide the occasion for comparative analytic research. Once the disagreements are taken seriously enough to be organized into precise issues, empirical and rational effort can well be expended in resolving them.

PERSONALITY IMPLICATIONS OF SOCIAL LEARNING THEORY

Social learning theorists clearly intend to have an impact on personality theory in addition to their emphasis on learning. In their statements, they recognize full well that the aim of personality theory is to specify those characteristics and tendencies of persons that are one factor in determining behavior. They also recognize that individual differences in perception, cognition, emotionality, and action form the main subject matter of personology. And they have indeed offered some theoretical statements that go in the direction of a viewpoint on personality. These statements are not sufficiently extensive and developed to constitute a full personality theory, but they do make a recognizable start.

Core considerations

It is at the level of core assumptions that the personality implications of social learning theory are least clear. Certainly, the statements they make about learned dispositions, which qualify as peripheral considerations, suggest underlying assumptions about core considerations. But discerning these core considerations is not particularly easy. Mischel (1973b) is clearest in the recognition that core assumptions are necessary in personology. He suggests that *all persons have an inherent tendency to construe the events of their experience, and thereby give them meaning.* As a core tendency, this bears resemblance to that of Kelly (see Chapter 4), though with less emphasis upon prediction and control of events. Indeed, much of what Mischel has to say about personality shows the unmistakable stamp of Kelly. But a word of caution is necessary. Mischel's main interest is in emphasizing individual differences in the ability to construe one's world. As these differences among persons are conceived of as inherent rather than learned, it is possible to regard them as aspects of a core statement. But it is quite rare for core statements to refer to individual differences. In any event, Mischel nominates the kinds of cognitive capabilities and skills that appear on intelligence tests (e.g., memory, perception of similarities, discernment of differences, ability to abstract) as what he means. He suggests that much of what others have referred to as ego strength, maturity, and competence is really a reflection of inherent differences in the cognitive abilities whereby meaning is attributed to events.

There is little else in social learning theory concerning core considerations. Little or no direction is provided whereby one can understand why persons construe in one direction or another. Rotter (1964, p. 58) makes passing reference to "unlearned or biologically based satisfactions of the organism," but says no more than that. The rest of the personality emphasis in social learning theory is at the peripheral level. That is, I suppose, only understandable in a position that derived from behaviorism and its preoccupation with the learning process.

Development

Whatever notion there is of personality development in social learning theory is simple enough. A person endowed with a particular level of cognitive capabilities encounters the social world, which is constituted of models to observe and persons who will apply positive and negative reinforcements to him. The greater the person's cognitive capabilities, the more active he will be in both construing the events and people of his world, in accepting or resisting the reinforcements applied to him, and in engaging in the self-control that mitigates the effects of those reinforcements.

As you know, the major form of learning is observational. Although models are important in this, that does not mean a necessarily slavish repetition of just what is observed. Presumably, the more cognitive capabilities a person has, the more he will generalize and transform what he observes into something more unique to him. Although there are no notions of developmental periods or stages in social learning theory, Bandura (1974) has indicated that the process of maturing involves progressively greater freedom from reinforcements imposed by others all the while there is progressively greater self-control of reinforcements.

Peripheral considerations

Most of what social learning theory has to say about personality involves learned orientations. There is general agreement that concrete peripheral characteristics develop out of the interaction between the person and his environment. But there is disagreement between Rotter and Mischel on how to conceptualize these learned characteristics.

According to Rotter (1964, pp. 58–60), development results in *motives* or *needs,* which vary from very specific to very general. He considers a need to have three essential components. The first component is the set of behaviors, all directed toward the same goal, that together define the expression of the need. The second need component is expectancies that certain behaviors will lead to satisfactions or goals that are valued. And the third component of the need is its value, or degree to which a person prefers the goal state associated with a need to some other goal state. You will recognize the three components as the behavior potential, reinforcement expectancy, and reinforcement value we considered earlier in this chapter.

To get a more complete sense of Rotter's approach, let us consider six very broad needs he offers as examples. They are listed in Table 12–1. According to Rotter, the needs for *recognition-status, dominance, independence, protection-dependency, love and affection,* and *physical comfort* are very common among people, though they are learned. He believes that each of the six broad needs would have to be broken down

TABLE 12–1

List of needs for Rotter

1. *Recognition-status:* The need to excel, to be considered competent, good or better than others in school, occupation, profession, athletics, social position, physical appeal, or play; that is, the need to obtain high position in a socially valued competitive scale.
2. *Dominance:* The need to control the actions of other people, including family and friends; to be in a position of power, to have others follow one's own ideas and desires.
3. *Independence:* The need to make one's own decisions, to rely on oneself, to develop the skill necessary to obtain satisfaction and reach goals without the help of others.
4. *Protection-dependency:* The need to have another person or persons prevent frustration, provide protection and security, and help obtain other desired goals.
5. *Love and affection:* The need for acceptance and liking by other people, to have their warm regard, interest, concern, and devotion.
6. *Physical comfort:* The need for physical satisfactions that have become associated with security and a state of well-being, the avoidance of pain, and the desire for bodily pleasures.

into subneeds in order to approach the level of specificity necessary to predict behavior. For example, the need for recognition-status could be regarded as including needs for certain social, occupational and intellectual activities.

Mischel's (1973b) approach is really quite different from that of Rotter. Any conceptualization that resembles the traditional approach concerning traits and needs is considered unwise by Mischel. He is quite unwilling to consider content definitions of person variables. Instead, he offers cognitive and response styles and strategies as concrete peripheral characteristics. One set of these is *encoding strategies,* which are very similar to Kelly's personal constructs in emphasis. According to Mischel, people do not passively absorb external stimulation. Rather, they reflect upon and transform stimulation, rendering it thereby more personally meaningful. These processes of transformation constitute how the information is coded, which in turn determines how it can be used then and in the future. Another set of concrete peripheral characteristics offered by Mischel is *expectancies concerning behavior-outcome and stimulus-outcome.* Behavior-outcome expectancies concern the perceived consequences of action, whereas stimulus-outcome expectancies concern perceptions as to how components of the stimulus surround relate to each other (the S-S laws mentioned previously). Behavior-outcome and stimulus-outcome expectancies give the person a sense that the environment is familiar and predictable. Also at the peripheral level are what Mischel calls *subjective stimulus values.* This concept is very similar to Rotter's reinforcement value, and is intended to refer to the varying degrees to which events are satisfying or dissatisfying for persons. The final set of concrete peripheral characteristics are *self-regulatory systems and plans.* Essentially these are contingency rules that guide the person's behavior in the absence of, or even despite, immediate external situational pressures and rewards. Such rules indicate to the person his own sense of the kinds of behavior appropriate under particular conditions, the performance levels he will require of himself, and the consequences of reaching or falling short of these standards.

As you can see from the discussion of self-regulatory systems, the five sets of concrete peripheral characteristics are conceived of as interacting complexly in the determination of behavior. In order to know what the person will do, you must know how he has coded information (what his personal constructs are), what relationships among stimuli and consequences of his actions he expects, what value he places on various outcomes of his actions, and his plans for regulating his own behavior. As if this were not complicated enough, Mischel insists that it is foolhardy to try to specify the common or typical content of these characteristics. He feels that they will reflect in each person some combination of his actual reinforcement history, his observational learning, and the fruits of internal cognitive competencies and transformations.

Echoing Allport's morphogenic approach (see Chapter 7), Mischel contends that each person is indeed unique, in the sense that the specific content of his personality cannot be determined in advance of studying him, and that his present concrete peripheral characteristics cannot accurately be discerned from a simple analysis of his past. Part of Mischel's objection to traditional trait and motive terms is, as Allport also contended, that they are too general to permit precise understanding or prediction of individual behavior. But in championing the morphogenic view, Allport gave us very little conceptual apparatus with which to know even how to scrutinize individuals in order to determine their peripheral personalities. Fortunately, Mischel gives us much more guidance by offering as concrete peripheral characteristics the five sets of cognitive styles and strategies.

As you might imagine, Mischel does not provide anything remotely approaching a typology. He does not regard such general categories to have any empirical value. Perhaps Rotter (1964) is less extreme, offering the notion of *generalized expectancies*. These are more or less conglomerates of need potentials, reinforcement expectancies, and reinforcement values, and together define the psychological situation as the person construes it. Internal versus external locus of control, as mentioned before, is an example of a generalized expectancy. But it is difficult to pursue this lead further, as Rotter has not been sufficiently explicit concerning the relationship of generalized expectancies to other peripheral aspects of personality.

CONCLUDING REMARKS

Although the social learning approach was born in the attempt to understand human learning, and has been critical of certain aspects of personology, it does have the beginnings of a theory of personality. It is too early in this development for extensive criticism to be a constructive enterprise. But in order to fulfill an important mission of this book, we should spend a bit of time considering what model of personality theorizing the social learning position seems to be developing toward.

It seems apparent that there is little in the approach suggestive of the conflict model. Indeed, social learning theorists are ardent critics of the psychoanalytic approach to theorizing and psychotherapy. It is possible, however, that the consistency model best illuminates the social learning approach. After all, Mischel's approximation to a core tendency nominates cognitive capabilities not at all unlike Kelly's approach. The expectations and plans formed by the person do not follow any content lines that are necessary in the sense of reflecting some inner nature. And the feedback obtained through interaction with the environment is regarded as important in changing one's expectations. Rotter's emphasis upon needs is not inconsistent with this classification, because they are conceptualized as learned, not inherent.

But one point provokes me to at least mention the fulfillment model as possibly relevant. Social learning theorists emphasize a very active use of cognitive processes. The person does not just sit back passively and receive information and meaning from outside. Rather, he actively develops encoding strategies, expectancies, reinforcement values, and plans. In this, he exercises considerable self-control. This suggests the existence of an implicit assumption, perhaps of the sort made by eixstential psychology, to the effect that the core tendency is to search for authenticity or meaning. Actually, Mischel (1973a) mentions existential psychology as a compatible approach to his own. Bandura's (1974) discussion of freedom is similarly suggestive. He regards it as important to conceptualize the human being's struggle to escape externally-imposed reinforcement and emerge into autonomous self-control. When there is conflict between what the person wants and what others want, the person is in difficulty, according to Bandura. But this conflict is not inherent, and can be surmounted through the person's gaining control of the reinforcement contingencies at play in his life.

It is probably best to regard the personality theorizing in the social learning approach as currently expressive of the consistency model. But I suspect that the theorizing is moving steadily toward the fulfillment model. The direction is away from Kelly and toward existential psychology.

Chapter 13 FORMAL AND SUBSTANTIVE CHARACTERISTICS OF THE GOOD THEORY OF PERSONALITY

In the preceding chapters, I have compared and contrasted theories, posed issues, and conducted rational and empirical analyses. My overall aim has been to identify the most promising bases for conceptualizing personality. In pursuit of this aim, I have made statements concerning the value of certain models for personality theorizing. Hopefully, these statements will serve as a guide to the development of theories of personality that are more sophisticated and effective than those considered in this book. What remains to be done in this concluding chapter is to set forth ality theorizing. This amounts to considering the formal and substantive characteristics that the good theory of personality will have. What I say here will not always agree with current orthodoxy. If I do not convince you entirely, perhaps you will at least be provoked to think again about the nature of the task of theorizing about personality.

FORMAL CHARACTERISTICS

In this section, I will consider the form that a good theory of personality should have, delaying discussion of content until later. There will be two aspects for discussion. One refers to the parts that properly comprise a personality theory, and the other refers to the overall criteria of formal adequacy that it should fulfill.

The parts of a personality theory

It will come as no surprise to you that I believe the good theory of personality will include both core and peripheral levels. The first of these levels will include both one or more core tendencies and the set of core characteristics implied in the core tendencies. Everything pertaining to the core of personality will be common to all persons. Emphasized here will be inherent attributes of the person, whether he be viewed individually or as part of a social aggregate. The attributes will tend to be inherent in the sense that they are not learned so much as being part of the nature of the organism. Although core characteristics may be physiological in nature, it is not at all necessary that they be so. They will only be so when the theorist assumes that the only commonalities in people are at the biological level. It would be just as possible, however, to consider ideals to be inherent attributes of the person, as do perfection theorists. From the formal point of view, it is only necessary that core level statements refer to that which is inherent, and common to all persons. What content is desirable in such statements is a matter to be evaluated later.

At the peripheral level of theorizing, emphasis is put on the easily discernible regularities in functioning that distinguish one person from another. Theorizing at this level should include a minimum of two kinds of concept. One I have called the concrete peripheral characteristic. It refers to those entities in people that cannot sensibly be subdivided further, and concerning which people show differences in intensity and content. From the formal point of view, the concrete peripheral characteristic is the smallest, most homogeneous unit of personality. It should be quantitative in nature, so that people can be said to have more or less of it than each other. It is also necessary that more than one concrete peripheral characteristic be assumed, if the peripheral theorizing is to have any success at celebrating the differences between people. The other kind of concept necessary to good peripheral level theorizing is what I have called the type. It has the function of indicating how the concrete peripheral characteristics get organized into broader units, more nearly approximating the styles of living that people show. Here too, the theorist must include a minimum of two types, if his peripheral theorizing is to permit understanding of differences among people. We have every reason to expect of the theorist a typology, or exhaustive listing of the types of peripheral personality he considers to be important, each type with its array of concrete peripheral characteristics. With such a typology in hand, we are sure of what the theorist considers to be an adequate description of the different ways it is possible for people to be.

Also necessary are developmental statements that express the nature of the interaction between the core tendencies and characteristics, on the one hand, and the external environment, on the other. Generally, it will be assumed that the core tendencies and characteristics are at such a high level of generality as to permit expression in a wide range of concrete forms. The actual forms of expression that become fixed are shaped by the external environment, in the form of parents, culture, social and economic conditions, and so forth. So, the personality theorist will disclose his position on the relationship between core and peripheral considerations through his assumptions concerning development.

Finally, the good theory of personality will include a data language, or set of conventions for observation having the function of indicating what it is important to explain. Application of a data language yields a group of behavioral variables arrived at through minimal interpretation of observations, certainly less interpretation than is involved in concrete peripheral characteristics. Because it involves minimal interpretation, a behavioral variable is usually considered descriptive rather than explanatory.

Thus far, I have been rather abstract about the parts of a personality theory, asserting their necessity rather than attempting to convince you of it. In the paragraphs that follow I shall try to be more concrete about why each of these parts is valuable, and just what explanatory capability would be lost without each of them.

Let us start with that which is to be explained. The whole point of theory is to provide understanding of something heretofore not understood. It is very clear, once you state the function of theory this way, that there must be some well-developed sense of what is to be explained. The data or phenomena that are perplexing must be clear enough in the mind of the theorist that he can direct his theoretical efforts in a problem-oriented way. This means that the good theory of personality must include a clear statement of the data it is attempting to explain. In other areas of theorizing, this point is so obvious it does not need to be articulated. But in the personality area, one tends to find an emphasis upon developing a theory with the data it is to explain left open for future discovery. This is perhaps understandable, in that the personality field is so broad that one is at a loss to be very specific about the data to be considered. Everything rushes to mind whenever one asks oneself about just what are the behavioral observations that need understanding in personality terms.

But the difficulty of specifying data does nothing to diminish the necessity of doing it. Indeed, perhaps the opposite is true. In any event, theorizing about the nature of personality without keeping in mind just what you want to understand about human behavior is like building a boat in the absence of knowledge of what water is like. The organization of the things people do, feel, and think into specifiable, communicable, tangible behavioral variables requires a data language. Personologists have failed sadly in developing or adopting a data language, however basic to theorizing such a step is. Rather than criticize further, let me simply conclude that a good theory of personality will specify a language for the description of human functioning in the terms indicating what the theory needs to explain. Whether the language has been invented by the theorist, or adopted by him from more widespread usage is unimportant, as long as it is clear what needs to be explained.

There is some guidance to be found in formulating the behavioral variables from numerous discussions in this book. An appropriate data language for the personologist will be heavily psychological, rather than biological or sociological in nature. In other words, the data language will describe complete thoughts, feelings, and actions as they occur in individual human beings. Especially important will be thoughts, feelings, and actions that are recurrent. Although personology does not yet have a consistently developed data language, it is clear that whatever rudimentary descriptions of data are currently attempted go in the direction just outlined. So in saying that a good theory of personality ought to specify a data language that is psychological in nature, I am at least not doing violence to the apparent intent of personologists.

As you know, the first level of explanation of the behavioral variables is the concrete peripheral characteristic. This characteristic is a postulated entity in the person that renders some number of behavioral variables understandable by indicating their similarity or functional equivalence. For example, the behavioral variables of competitiveness with work associates, moderate risk taking in situations where successful outcome can be influenced by skill, and greater involvement in complex than simple tasks, might all be explained as expressions of a particular concrete peripheral characteristic, the *need for achievement*. Invoking the need for achievement would not be merely to describe the behavioral variables. Rather, it would be to interpret, or explain them. Some personologists who strongly emphasize core level theorizing would dispute that what I am calling concrete peripheral characteristics have explanatory value, considering them no more than descriptive generalizations of behavioral variables. In order to convince yourself that concrete peripheral characteristics are more than data descriptions, consider in the example above how easy it would be to devise some other characteristic instead of the need for achievement to explain the observations. Ready alternatives would be *insecurity* and *dominance*. Considering the observations expressive of need for achievement rather than of these alternatives indicates that what has been done is an interpretation or explanation rather than a description.

Some of the personologists who raise the criticism that concrete peripheral characteristics are descriptive rather than explanatory may in reality have another criticism in mind that is more valid. It is the criticism that the postulated concrete peripheral characteristic, as presented above, has no logical existence apart from the behaviors it is supposed to explain, and hence, its adequacy as an explanation cannot be determined. Suppose, as in the example given before, that the presence or absence of the need for achievement could only be decided upon by inference from the presence or absence of the behaviors concerning risk taking, and so forth. If this were so, the need for achievement characteristic would have no existence apart from the data it is used to explain. Another personologist could easily invoke an alternative characteristic, like dominance, with as much convincingness. It would not be possible to determine which explanation was the best. The criticism being made here is not that the need for achievement would have no explanatory value, but rather that the explanation offered would be of an inconclusive sort.

Fortunately, there is a simple way around this criticism. It involves offering an operational definition for each concrete peripheral characteristic. An operational definition tells you how to measure the characteristic in terms that are different from the data it is meant to explain. In our example, once an operational definition of need for achievement is offered, it becomes possible to conduct an empirical test of the adequacy of explaining those particular behaviors with that particular characteristic. One would measure the strength of need for achievement in fantasy, let us say, and then determine the relationship between achievement fantasy and the relevant behavioral variables. It is in order to render the explanatory power of concrete peripheral characteristics more compelling that I conclude that the good theory of personality will include operational definitions of its concrete peripheral characteristics.

Continuing the discussion of the explanatory value of peripheral theorizing, it is time to consider the type concept and the associated typology I advocated previously. I have nothing very different to say here than I have already said about concrete peripheral characteristics. The explanatory value of types is at a more general level of behavior, but is similar in other respects. The behavior explained by a type is a composite of the behaviors explained by each of the concrete peripheral characteristics it subsumes. The typology explains differences between people that are grosser and in commonsense terms more obvious than those explained by single concrete peripheral characteristics. Perhaps I should mention that types need not include operational definitions, for they do no more than subsume a specified set of concrete peripheral characteristics, each member of which set already is operationally defined. The general style and directionality of individual lives is best understood in terms of the type concept and the associated typology. This is true even though it is possible to pinpoint a more restricted, less-sweeping directionality at the level of concrete peripheral characteristics, as do Murray and McClelland with their motive concepts.

We have reached a natural transition to the discussion of the explanatory value of core level theorizing. Core level theorizing explains the attributes and directions found in all persons by virtue of their common human nature. It is a necessary kind of theorizing insofar as one thinks in terms of mankind as a whole, and of contrasting it with other forms of life. In addition, the core tendency has the vital function of explicating the overall directionality of life. The concrete directions identified at the peripheral level must be derived from the overall directionality, and are not themselves understandable without it. The core tendency and characteristics are a level of theorizing farther removed from the behavioral observations that prompt peripheral level theorizing. As such, the core of personality is only indirectly explanatory of behavior, though its relationship to the periphery. There is no point, therefore, in attempting operational definition of core tendencies and characteristics. Empirical validity of core level theorizing is not to be assessed directly. Rather, in the process of testing peripheral theorizing empirically, one can determine the adequacy of core theorizing as well by weight of evidence. In theory that is only indirectly related to data, weight of evidence is the most sensible empirical standard.

But the weight of evidence cannot be brought to bear on core level theorizing, unless it is carefully articulated with peripheral level theorizing. This means that developmental statements relating core and periphery through the mediation of experience in the world are essential to a good theory of personality. As core theorizing refers to data only indirectly, its explanatory value may be questioned. Indeed, some personologists who prefer to stay very close to data in their attempts to understand, would consider core level theorizing not only dispensable but wasteful of time and effort. But anyone who feels it valuable to consider persons to share some inherent nature and direction would find it hard to agree. And anyone who considers it important, in an explanation of human behavior, to understand how there is an initial impetus to behave before any learning has taken place, could never agree. Core level theorizing explicates the prime mover of behavior, and clarifies the restrictions made on what is subsequently learned by the common characteristics of human nature. Any theory of personality making a claim to comprehensiveness must explain these matters, and therefore requires a core statement.

In summary, each of the parts of a theory of personality has a definite and important function. Without articulating with a data language, a theory cannot specify what it intends to explain. A theory in such a position is less an explanatory device than a world view, or a religion, or a myth. Concrete peripheral characteristics are necessary if one takes at all seriously that there are many obvious, though concrete and small differences among people. Without a typology, a theory is mute concerning larger patterns of difference among people. If a theory does not include a statement of core tendencies and associated core characteristics, it is not possible to consider persons to share some attributes by virtue of their common species, nor is it possible to consider how any functioning occurs in the absence of considerable learning. And the explication, through statements about development, of the process whereby core considerations come to be expressed in particular peripheral personalities, is essential if the core statements are ever to be even indirectly accessible to an empirical test of adequacy.

Obviously, complete theories of personality do not spring full blown from the mind of the theorist. One part or another may well be developed before the rest. The theorist may want to, and should, express his views even before he can make as comprehensive a statement as would be ideal. Nonetheless, the ideal defines what the theorist should be trying to accomplish. Failure to include any part of a personality theory leads to a particular, recognizable kind of drawback. Comprehensive understanding of personality requires all the parts.

Overall criteria of formal adequacy

Even assuming that the good theory of personality will have all the parts discussed above, there are still some overall principles of theorizing that are generally considered of importance. These frequently mentioned principles are that a theory should be *important, operational, parsimonious, stimulating, usable,* and *empirically valid.* It is generally believed that a theory is adequate only if it can fulfill these formal criteria. I agree with some of the criteria more than others, and will therefore discuss each of them separately. Much of what I am about to say has been implicit, or even mentioned before. But it is high time now to be explicit.

A theory should be important. Although it is not infrequent for psychologists to evaluate theories on the basis of their triviality or importance, this is a very difficult kind of evaluation to justify. Mandler and Kessen (1959, pp. 253–54) make this point forcefully:

> Were there at hand a rigorous criterion for triviality, the psychological community could agree with confidence on the study of genuinely important issues, the ones that "really matter." Unfortunately no such criterion of exclusion can be stated. The polemic use of terms such as "inconsequential," "limited," "far from reality," and so on, when applied to theories of behavior, misses the fact that science has no dead-end markets. We can look back into the past and see with relatively high acuity the junctures at which a line of theory went awry, but no satisfactory method can be proposed for making a similar judgment about contemporary systems of explanation. A responsible scientist may choose to work on whatever problems interest him but he is fooling himself if he claims to *know* that he is on a more direct route to some future truth than his colleagues. Franklin and Faraday were both asked "What good is it?" by curious and puzzled friends who were watching the demonstration of a new device. Franklin's famous reply "What good is a new-born child?" was a pointed recognition of our ignorance of future utilities, but Faraday expressed more accurately the disdain of the pure scientist for questions of applicability when he responded to Gladstone, "Why, sir, there is every probability that you will soon be able to tax it." . . . Much the same answers can be made to attacks against psychological theories on grounds of triviality; their ultimate contribution to knowledge is determined by so many unknown considerations that it seems wisest to recognize that attacks of this order cannot be justified by reference to an unambiguous criterion.

As a spirited argument for theoretical freedom, this statement is very effective, and yet, we must consider just how far we would endorse it. Consider, in this regard, an equally spirited indictment of a theory made by Bruner on the grounds of triviality. The theory criticized is Spence's version of general behavior theory, which holds that the hallmark of human and animal learning is the associative bonding of stimuli and responses that have been experienced as contiguous in time. This theory has been formulated mainly on the basis of experiments performed on rats that involved learning a particular route through a maze. Railing out against this concretistic theory of learning, Bruner (1957a, p. 156) says:

> Let me illustrate one source of my discouragement in attempting to evaluate this truly distinguished book. It is estimated that there are 10^{75} possible sentences in the English language 50 words in length, and that in the course of a year we hear perhaps 10^6 sentences altogether. If one learned the sentences we uttered by a process that is Markovian [associationistic] in nature, eliminating alternatives according to the gradual build-up of excitatory strength, our lives would be far too short to master even the simple prattle of a child. And there is little doubt, moreover, that we would be able to indicate which sentences among the 10^{75} constructed by an algorithm were proper sentences and which not, even though we had never encountered them. It is obvious that "verbal responses" are not what is "learned" but, rather, rules and principles of structuring that make it possible for us to *generate* sentences. The answer to such a point as this is by now familiar: You cannot criticize a thing for what it does not attempt to account for. But the ultimate end of such a defense is that the critic is then forced to celebrate behavior theory of this type as the applied psychology of CS-US linkages, T mazes, and straight runways.

Elsewhere in his review, Bruner (1957a, p. 156) says in the same vein:

> Donald Hebb recently remarked that if one made a set of micro photographs of Cambridge, inch by inch, very likely one would fail to discover the Charles River.

In pointing out that Spence's theory will either have to answer his criticism or be celebrated as the applied psychology of mazes, Bruner is raising the question of triviality. He does not really dispute the fact that humans can learn in an associationistic fashion. What he disputes is that such learning is to be considered characteristic of how the human operates. He feels that it obviously cannot be, from his example concerning language learning. One does not need to do empirical research to recognize that Spence has trivialized the human being by failing to attribute to him the principle learning he obviously shows. It will not help Spence to say, with Mandler and Kessen, that one could hardly have known in advance of theorizing that people are predominantly principle rather than association learners. It will not help because

Bruner, in his very example, which is rational rather than empirical, is saying that he and lots of other psychologists would have known in advance. This is why he is so disappointed in the book.

What brought about the trivialization of learning theory constituted by Spence's approach? Surely it was not a necessary concomitant of adopting a laboratory paradigm for the investigation of learning. Indeed, the value of laboratory paradigms can be great, if they truly represent simpler, more controllable forms of the naturalistic phenomenon under consideration. Through systematically varying one variable at a time, while holding the others constant, a phenomenon like learning can be analyzed more effectively in the laboratory than in a natural setting. But in order for the promise of the laboratory to be realized, the paradigm chosen must be representative of, or at least homologous with, the phenomenon as it occurs in a naturalistic setting. If humans learn primarily principles rather than associations, then the T-maze is not a suitable paradigm because it is too simple to lend itself to principle learning. Further, if rats are primarily association rather than principle learners, no matter how carefully they are studied, application of what is concluded to human beings is likely to be an oversimplification. Whenever theorizing about some phenomenon is not directed toward understanding it as it naturally occurs, being directed instead at some laboratory paradigm supposedly similar but in reality not representative of it, the theorizing runs a great risk of being trivial. The difficulty with Spence's approach is not that it relied on a laboratory paradigm, but that there was insufficient grappling with the question of the suitability of the paradigm as a basis for generalizing to human learning as it occurs outside the laboratory.

In theorizing, one can minimize the risk of being trivial by deciding what should constitute the major phenomena to be explained on the basis of primary reliance upon naturalistic observation. If truly representative laboratory paradigms are available, then observations from them can also be relied upon. But the theorist need not be especially alarmed if he finds his position unable to account for laboratory observations whose relationship to natural occurrences is unclear (e.g., hypnotic behavior, because hypnosis does not occur naturally). Reliance upon naturalistic observation in theorizing is especially important for the personologist, whose aim of understanding the whole human being can be so easily trivialized by oversimplification. After formulating the rudiments of his theory through reliance upon naturalistic observation, he can, of course, design laboratory experiments to his heart's delight in order to determine whether his theorizing is really sound. If he starts with naturalistic observation, he is unlikely to be working on a trivial problem, and also unlikely to design laboratory experiments that are such oversimplifications as to be no longer representative of the phenomenon under consideration.

Actually, most personality theorists would agree with much of what I have said. They certainly rely upon naturalistic observation, as can be seen from the case histories and even appeals to common experience that are often made the bases for theorizing. The more formal and systematic ratings of subject's behavior in various tasks, so effectively employed by such personologists as Murray (1938) and Cattell (1946) are still close enough to everyday functioning to be considered naturalistic. Also close to naturalistic observation are those personality tests that are least structured (e.g., Thematic Apperception Test) in that they permit the person to disclose himself in his own way. Rarely do personologists rely heavily upon laboratory forms of phenomena as a guide in theorizing.

But the danger with some personologists is that they use the psychotherapeutic interaction with some of the same alacrity that Spence exhibits with the T-maze. After all, the psychotherapeutic situation is a highly specialized one, created to permit treatment to occur. It is not a natural, but rather an invented situation. To my mind, it is only partially representative of naturally occurring interactions. When a personologist devises a personality theory on the basis of psychotherapy observations alone, he is running a large risk of being trivial in the depth and breadth of his understanding of life. Perhaps you will recall that in Chapter 7, I suggested that the reason Rogers offered only two personality types— thereby simplifying life—is that his is a theory developed almost exclusively on the basis of observation of the behavior of patients. A theory of psychotherapy is one thing, and a theory of personality is another.

*A **theory should be operational**.*   Simply put, the doctrine of operationism indicates that the meaning of a concept is determined by the measurement operations associated with it. This has been a very useful notion to the scientist, because it forces him to be really precise about what he means, lest someone else measure it in a manner at variance with the meaning he intended for it, and because it alerts him to the implications of various measurement operations for influencing what one means. But some overzealous psychologists have interpreted the doctrine of operationism in ways that do not seem advantageous at all to me.

One disadvantageous version of operationism is that concepts mean whatever we want them to mean, nothing more and nothing less. This seems a misuse of operationism, which was never meant to be a substitute for theorizing. When we use our measurement operations to define the concept, rather than first defining the concept and then choosing the measurement operations most relevant for it, we assume that the concept is nothing more than an arbitrary symbol. This assumption is virtually always violated in psychology, which uses as concepts not mathematical symbols so much as words. Words acquire fairly consistent meanings as conventions of usage for them develop. And these conventions are not merely semantic; distinctions between words generally coincide with perceived differences between events in experience. Denying this "real" meaning of a concept (see Mandler & Kessen, 1959, pp. 93–101) and defining it merely in terms of a set of measurement operations (e.g., intelligence is the score on the Stanford-Binet Test) would lead us into even more blind alleys than it does were it not for the fact that we rarely in reality give up the real meaning completely. It usually hovers on the fringe of consciousness, all the while it is disavowed, and exercises an intuitive influence on our investigations. This intuitive influence is what probably keeps us from making too many mistakes, all the while we are foolishly saying that we know nothing of the meaning of our concepts except the steps we took in measuring them. We do not land in blind alleys unequivocally enough to force a reconsideration of the madness of capitulating as theorists to measurement operations arbitrarily chosen. After all, there is an infinite number of measurement operations, and if we have no theory to guide us in choosing among them, the choice is arbitrarily made. Our undetected intuition leads to just enough reward to perpetuate our insane belief in the value of remaking concepts in the image of our measurement operations!

Clearly, then, I believe that concept definition is a matter of theory, and that only when definition has already been achieved does it make sense to select measurement operations. The measurement operations selected may well add a shade of meaning of their own, and hence, a reconsideration of the meaning of the concept after measurement operations have been selected is in order. But the contribution of measurement operations to the meaning of a concept is secondary to the contribution made by the theorist using all the intuition and reason available to him. In the good theory of personality, therefore, the cart will not lead the horse, the measurement operations for concepts will follow from their theoretical definitions, rather than themselves constituting the definitions.

The other disadvantageous version of the doctrine of operationism is simply that all concepts, regardless of their logical function, must be operationized in order for their inclusion in a theory to be justifiable. You already know that I disagree with this from my indicating that only concrete peripheral characteristics need have operational definitions. I see little reason why a concept should have an operational definition if its primary function is not to explain data directly, but rather to indicate the relationship and organization between concepts. To require that only operationalized concepts be included in theories might have the unfortunate effect of decreasing emphasis on core statements. In the good theory of personality, only concrete peripheral characteristics will be equipped with operational definitions.

Most personality theorists are lax in providing operationalizations of their concrete peripheral characteristics. It is not likely, therefore, that they will fall prey to the two versions of operationism I have called disadvantageous. These versions are common in other fields of psychology, however, and perhaps what I have said can aid the personality theorist in defending himself against critics. Hopefully, I have also been convincing concerning the need for operational definitions of concrete peripheral characteristics. In providing such definitions, the theorist has much to gain and nothing to lose.

A *theory should be parsimonious.* For a long time in psychology, it has been orthodox to believe that parsimony is a standard of adequacy in theorizing. What parsimony means is that, given a set group of phenomena to be explained, the explanation is best, among those available, which makes the fewest assumptions. Assumptions, for present purposes, are roughly equivalent to concepts and the interrelationships among them. The aim of parsimony is simplicity in theorizing. Sensible and sound though it may seem, the principle of parsimony may be virtually impossible to apply in psychology. In order to apply it, one would have to specify the domain of behavioral variables to be explained, and the assumptions of all theories claiming to explain these variables. Specification of theoretical assumptions is difficult because psychological theory is generally so incomplete and implicitly formulated (Mandler & Kessen, 1959). Especially personality theories are more implicitly formulated than is consistent with an application of the principle of parsimony. Specification of the domain of behavioral variables cannot meaningfully be done because even similar personality theories show little agreement in the data they attempt to explain. As you know, some theories do not even specify the data to which they pertain. And even if there were both more specification of relevant data, and agreement or overlap among the specifications, at current rates of information increase in psychology, the data personality theorists would want to explain would hardly remain constant long enough to permit any meaningful assessment of parsimony. These conditions render the principle of parsimony virtually useless as a basis for evaluating alternative theories. After all, can anyone remember a personality theory being definitely found unparsimonious not only by its opponents, but by its adherents and disinterested persons as well? What this means is that the principle of parsimony has not been useful as a guide to theoretical fruitfulness in the personality area.

Indeed, even if parsimony were capable of assessment in the personality area, I am not so sure I would want to put much stock in it. Let us say that you could, at some point in time, specify some domain of data that theorists agreed was what they wanted to explain. Let us also say that you could make all the assumptions of the various theories explicit. Further, let us suppose that one theory emerged as explaining the facts with the fewest assumptions. Would you be willing, on the basis of this possibly transitory victory, to discard the unparsimonious theories? I would not be willing, because the victory tells us little about the capability of the parsimonious theory to continue providing good explanations of whatever additional data are uncovered in the future. Indeed, it is distinctly possible that a theory which looks parsimonious in explaining today's facts may actually be such an oversimplification in terms of explaining all human functioning as to be wholly inadequate to cope with tomorrow's facts without major overhaul. Recognizing this, it does not seem important in theorizing to strive for simplicity for its own sake. Better to use all your intuition, reason, and empirical knowledge in striving for a theory that is as comprehensive concerning human functioning as you can make it. Happily, personality theorists seem to have done this, being rather indifferent to the parsimony of their formulations.

A theory should be precise. A criterion of such obvious importance as to require little elaboration here is that a theory should be as clear and precise as possible. In defining concepts and relating them to each other and to data, the theorist should avoid being implicit and using figurative, metaphorical, or analogical language. The trouble with implicit formulations is that they are not recognized and therefore exert an ambiguous, frequently inconsistent influence on the use of a theory. Figurative, metaphorical, and analogical formulations also create ambiguity and inconsistency. To make such statements as that "the superego *does battle* with the id" or that "the ego is the *executive organ attempting to strike a compromise* between the id and superego" is inconsistent with clarity and precision. As I pointed out in Chapter 5, such statements cannot literally be true, for doing battle and striking compromises are attributes of whole organisms, whereas id, ego, and superego are only intended to be parts of organisms. To theorize in this loose fashion is to court misunderstanding.

At the earliest, most intuitive phase of theory formulation, metaphorical usage and some general implicitness is probably inevitable and perhaps even a stimulant to imaginativeness. But the theorist should nonetheless strive toward the goal of precision and clarity in his formulations. All too often in personology, theories remain characterized by implicitness and metaphorical usage long beyond the time of their inception. Actually, were theories of personality more precise, my task of analysis in this book would have been much simpler and my conclusions less equivocal.

There is a fairly simple way to determine whether a theory is sufficiently precise. Try to use it for what it was intended. Try to apply it to observations of people so as to understand them better. Or try to generate predictions concerning the behavior of particular kinds of people whom you have not yet observed. Try to decide how, in the theory's terms, these predictions should be tested. When you encounter difficulty in using the theory, it will be for one of two reasons: the theory is incomplete (recall the parts of a personality theory previously listed as necessary), or it is imprecise. If all the necessary parts are present in some form, then imprecision is the flaw. Often, a careful scrutiny of the theory will even disclose where the imprecision lies. Remember that a precise theory can be used readily even by some one who has no special faith in it. Indeed, theories that can only be applied by people who believe in their truth usually have some failing in precision, which can sometimes be overcome by zealous utilization of intuition. But it would be better to use the zeal to decrease the implicitness and metaphorical qualities of the theory, so that it can communicate to all would-be users.

A theory should be empirically valid. In discussing precision, operationism, parsimony, and triviality, I have been considering rational rather than empirical standards of adequacy. Demonstrating the rational adequacy of a theory is the first step, following which assessment of empirical validity becomes relevant. The crucial evidence about empirical validity involves systematic empirical tests of the predictions made by a theory. Explanations generated for data already known before the explanation was formulated are interesting and useful, but do not directly clarify the matter of empirical validity. Such explanations are called *post hoc*, to indicate that they do not involve putting yourself out on the limb of *predicting* the kind of data you will find before you have looked. In determining empirical validity, the empirical test of such predictions is much more important than the fineness of post hoc explanation. Given that theories of personality are very complex and inevitably somewhat elastic in construction, then it is just too possible that post hoc explanations sound as good as they do because of some degree of unintentional twisting and stretching of the theory in order to square with what you already know the data to be. No such theoretical body English can operate in predictions, the data relevant to which are not yet available. To test a prediction, one must determine whether the relevant data, obtained under strict scientific standards, are indeed as expected. If the predictions of a theory are disconfirmed often enough, then the theory is thrown into serious doubt, regardless of its rational adequacy and the apparent adequacy of its post hoc explanations.

The assessment of empirical validity, though a basic method of evaluation, is premature until the theory is sufficiently well developed so that the kinds of data that are actually relevant, and the precise manner in which the theory addresses itself to these, can be unequivocally discerned. The rational standards already discussed, in that they are marks of sufficient development, are prior concerns to that of empirical validity. Before rational adequacy has been attained, empirical observations are probably more effectively used for theory construction and refinement rather than test.

A theory should be stimulating. It is often said that a theory justifies its existence if it provokes others to thought and investigation. A personologist might find a theory congenial and be motivated to enhance and support it; he might simply associate freely to it and be caught up in the novel ideas thus generated; he might reach against it and be driven to demonstrate its inadequacies. It does not make much difference which of these courses is taken as long as careful thought and research are undertaken that might not otherwise have occurred. Clearly, a theory need not meet any other criterion of adequacy, rational or empirical, to be considered worthwhile by the stimulation standard. And certainly, I would agree that a theory that stimulates is a good thing.

But legitimate and important as stimulation value is, a theory will not make a lasting, specific contribution to understanding in a scientific discipline like personology unless it achieves rational adequacy and empirical validity. It is fruitless, however, to be condemnatory because personology has not gone far in producing such theories. The standards discussed here simply define a goal to be worked toward. But personologists should not permit themselves to avoid the tedious and painful work of rendering their theories more rationally and empirically adequate by satisfying themselves with the thought that they have been stimulating.

SUBSTANTIVE CHARACTERISTICS

It is the content, or substantive characteristics of a theory that determine the predictions it will make. If the predictions are supported by empirical research it will be because the substantive characteristics of the theory were wisely chosen. Therefore, in attempting to develop better theories of personality it would be sensible to take into account the substantive conclusions we have reached in analyzing the various positions included in this book. For vividness, I have organized substantive considerations into broad, somewhat interpretative units, with the most important statements indicated by italicizing.

One of the most salient substantive conclusions coming out of Chapter 5 is that *defensiveness is a common, though not ubiquitous occurrence in living.* There are likely to be differences between people in the degree of their defensiveness, and in the areas of living in which defensiveness occurs. The evidence suggests two general techniques of defense; *to repress,* by failing to remember or perceive, and *to be hypersensitive,* by remembering or perceiving only some especially problematic things. The stimuli shown to elicit defensiveness have been of an anxiety provoking, or socially taboo nature. All of these findings incline me to the belief that *defensiveness occurs in the attempt to avoid anxiety which arises out of some conflict pitting man and society against each other.* But such conflict is not an inevitable outcome of interaction between individuals and groups, for defensiveness is not ubiquitous.

Consistent with the view that the conflict involves person and society are the conclusions from Chapter 10 to the effect that two common characteristics concerning which people show differences in intensity are *conscience* (a set of values bearing on the regulation of personal motivation) and *commitment to or endorsement of existing social institutions and role structures.* Apparently, some people are more accepting of the importance of society and its restrictions than are others. The complimentary findings from Chapter 10 are that people differ in the degree to which they are *stable, predictable, and dependable,* which characteristics probably refer to the conformance of behavior to social responsibilities. At a more abstract level, Chapter 10 also testifies to the existence in people of *personal goals* (motives) as well as *social goals* (schemata). It is important to recognize that personal goals can have a wide range of content.

Let us conclude that there can, but need not, be anxiety-inducing conflict between personal and social goals. Let us also conclude that this anxiety is often reduced by defensiveness aimed at convincing oneself and others of the social purity of one's intent. We are left with the insistent question of whether defensiveness is a good thing. The evidence summarized in the next two paragraphs suggests that, whatever the possible short-term gains, defensiveness is disadvantageous to the individual and, in a general sense, even to the vigorous development of his society. Clearly, defensiveness implies conformity to what people around you do and believe. Evidence that people differ in the strength of such conforming tendencies when interacting with others is suggested in Chapter 10. Common bipolar characteristics emerging from factor analytic research are *gregariousness-aloofness, cooperativeness-competitiveness,* and *dominance-dependence.* In addition, the existence of *needs for power, achievement, and affiliation* are well documented.

Knowing that it is possible to be conforming or individualistic, we can then ask what are the implications of these ways of being? From Chapter 5, we learned that *people who transcend the roles and institutions of society, and are individualistic rather than conforming in their interpersonal behavior, are more likely to be creative in their work.* Chapter 10 contributes evidence that *people who conform by answering questions about themselves in a socially desirable fashion show less initiative and self-confidence, and can be more easily influenced by others.* In contrast, *people who accept themselves and their individuality are involved in a broader range of activities, have a more positive impact on other people and are especially able to accept them.* A number of studies suggest that *people who do not see themselves as masters of their own fate are less likely to show initiative and proaction in the service of not only their own goals, but social problems as well.* These kinds of findings suggest that the transcendent person is not only more capable of fulfilling his own personal goals, but is also more socially useful than is the conforming person. Supporting this conclusion is the evidence that a personal goal, *the need for achievement, is an important factor in the socially crucial matter of economic development.*

There is another group of findings prompting the substantive conclusion that activation and its adjustment are important attributes of the person. From the factor analytic studies reviewed in Chapter 10, we find that an important characteristic in which people show differences is *general energy or activation.* Chapter 4 made clear that *people decrease tension in only some of their functioning, and actually increase tension in the rest.* You will recall that tension and activation are virtually interchangeable terms. Another aspect of the picture is the evidence in Chapter 5 that *people seek moderate degrees of variety, while avoiding large degrees of it.* Additional evidence is provided in Chapter 10 to indicate that *there are individual differences in the strength of the motivation to seek or avoid variety.* It is not hard to believe that the seeking and avoiding of variety is in the service of increasing or decreasing activation, respectively. Other behaviors of possible relevance for increasing or decreasing activation that are shown in Chapter 10 to be differentially represented in people are *stability-impulsivity,* and *rigidity-flexibility.*

Also apparent from Chapter 5 is the fact that people differ in the degree to which their personalities show *differentiation, or complexity. Differentiation, moreover, increases from birth at least until some time in early adulthood.* Further, *integrative processes may well increase as the years pass.* Differentiation and integration are the two aspects of psychological growth, and hence these findings are important for that concept. Chapter 5 provides general evidence for *the occurrence of significant change in personality over the life-span.*

The aims of comparative analytic research

The substantive considerations mentioned above are provocative as a basis for improved personality theorizing. But there remains some uncertainty about what is crucial substantively because true comparative analytic research is still rare in personology. One way that research qualifies as comparative analysis is if it aims to resolve an issue or issues separating two or more theories or models (Chapter 5 gives examples of such issues). Another kind of comparative analytic research aims to determine the relative ability of one or more theories or models to account for the dimensions of individual differences that are observed (Chapter 10 is relevant). The methodology employed may vary widely, from experimental to correlational analysis, from naturalistic observation to structured tests, from longitudinal to cross-sectional approaches. As long as the methodology is appropriate to the problem, the main thing which qualifies a study as comparative analysis is an explicit emphasis on assessing the relative merits of differing theories. A concerted effort at such research on the part of many researchers would at the same time lead to a giant step forward in knowledge and give personology the boost it currently needs.

Ideally, comparative analysis deals with models or families of theories because in that manner one gets the greatest return for effort. But such a grand approach is not always feasible or practical. Comparative analysis can also deal fruitfully with mini-issues concerning two individual theories rather than broader models. It seems likely that most comparative analytic research that gets done in the near future will be of this sort.

Perhaps an example or two of what might be done will be helpful. One might address the issue concerning whether defensiveness is facilitatory or inhibiting of sound functioning (e.g., Rogers would regard it as inhibiting and Freud as facilitatory). Adopting an experimental approach, one might use the same threatening treatment on several experimental groups to arouse defensiveness, and have each of the groups then perform some relevant task. The threatening treatment would have to be theoretically appropriate to the arousal of defensiveness in both theories (e.g., constituting the criticism of conditional positive regard and a psychosexual insult). The tasks performed by each group together would have to constitute a broad and reasonably representative cross-section of life's activities (e.g., problem-solving performance, creative endeavor, interpersonal functioning). It would also be useful to have a built-in manner (e.g., post-test interviews) of determining whether (and in which subjects) defensiveness actually occurred. Control groups for each experimental group would perform the same tasks without prior defensiveness arousal. The aim of the study would be to chart the actual effect of defensiveness on the various tasks. The results would either show a general inhibition (favoring Rogers) or facilitation (favoring Freud) of performance, or some more complex pattern of inhibition on some tasks and facilitation on others. The latter result would also be quite valuable in that it would constitute a basis for modification of both theories or for new theorizing.

Another example would use correlational methodology in comparing the existential and Freudian views of guilt. As the actual experience of guilt is similar (e.g., self-criticism, feelings of unworthiness, pessimism, depression, lack of energy, self-destructiveness) in the conceptualizations of both theories, a common measure of this state (probably questionnaire or interview) could be applied to a group of subjects. The subjects would also complete tests (probably other questionnaires or interviews) indexing the explanations of guilt that prevail in the two theories (the chronic tendency to choose the past or status quo rather than the future or change, for existential psychology; an unresolved love for the opposite-sexed parent and hatred for the same-sexed parent and the representation of this in contemporary life, for Freud). Then by correlating the measure of guilt with the measures of ontological choice and psychosexual conflict, one could determine whether guilt is best explained by Freud or existential psychology. Once again, even complex patterns of results (e.g., some subjects appearing more "Freudian" and others more "existential") would be useful in theory modification or new theorizing.

The psychology of possibility

One of the most constant and unique features of personality theory is the identification of ideal life-styles and developmental directions. As you know (see Chapter 1), this willingness to make value judgements about the good life is basic to statements and techniques in the area of psychotherapy, with its aim of changing destructive behavior to something better. Personologists are often criticized by their colleagues for making such value judgements, which are often seen as unscientific and appropriate, if at all, only in those nonempirical disciplines, philosophy and theology.

But it seems to me that the personologist has a definite contribution to make to science through his concern with ideal functioning. Whereas most of empirical psychology is preoccupied with what is actual, with preponderance or majority, generalizing from this to the way things must inevitably be, the personologist has the capability, because of his theoretical concerns, to explicate bases for human improvement. He carries the seeds of a psychology of possibility.

All he need do is study persons approximating his ideal in a rigorous empirical fashion. By definition, few persons achieve ideal functioning. But some approximate it and by searching them out, a large enough sample for rigorous study can be accumulated. Then these supposedly ideal persons can be compared on many theoretically-relevant dimensions of living with a group of supposedly less ideal persons. Empirical information as to how the ideal persons live and how they got to be that way can then be translated into prescriptions for personal development, parental actions, and psychotherapy, so that those of us who wish to follow suit will have some guidance. Indeed, one might even have a comparative analysis of conceptualizations of the ideal life. There is nothing at all unscientific about this. Quite the contrary. And there is much for the human species to learn and become.

CONCLUDING NOTE

As you already know, I believe that the substantive considerations just summarized indicate the fruitfulness for theorizing about personality of some combination of the fulfillment model and the actualization version of the consistency model. But it is certainly possible that someone could order the important substantive considerations in even more powerful fashion by developing some other kind of personality theory. I will be satisfied if reading this book has rendered the task of personality theorizing more understandable, tangible, important, and engaging for you. As I mentioned in the Preface, this book carries within it the seeds of its own demise. In one sense, the demise will have taken place when a comparative analytic orientation takes such root as to lead to theories of personality more precise and powerful than any mentioned here. At that point, there will be little need for a book of this sort. But the demise could also take the form of the promulgation of a more trenchant comparative analysis than I have been able to manage. Certainly, within the framework of comparative analysis, mine cannot be assumed the only or even best specific approach. If this book spurs others to better comparative analyses, then it will truly, but fortunately, have ended its usefulness.

REFERENCES

ABELSON, R., ARONSON, E. MCGUIRE, W., NEWCOMB, T., ROSENBERG, M. & TANNENBAUM, P. (Eds.). *Theories of cognitive consistency: A sourcebook.* Chicago: Rand McNally, 1969.

ABRAHAM, K. The first pregenital stage of the libido. In K. ABRAHAM, *Selected papers.* London: Institute of psychoanalysis and Hogarth Press, 1927. (a)

ABRAHAM, K. The influence of oral erotism on character formation. In K. ABRAHAM, *Selected papers.* London: Institute for psychoanalysis and Hogarth Press, 1927. (b)

ABRAHAM, K. Contributions to the theory of the anal character. In K. ABRAHAM, *Selected papers.* London: Institute for psychoanalysis and Hogarth Press, 1927. (c)

ABRAHAM, K. Character formation on the genital level of libido development. In K. ABRAHAM, *Selected papers.* London: Institute for psychoanalysis and Hogarth Press, 1927. (d)

ABRAMOWITZ, S. Internal-external control and sociopolitical activism: A test of the dimensionality of Rotter's internal-external scale. *J. consult. clin. Psychol.,* 1973, 40, 196–201.

ADAMS, H. E. & VIDULICH, R. N. Dogmatism and belief congruence in paired-associate learning. *Psychol. Rep.,* 1962, 10, 90–94.

ADAMS, J. S. Reduction of cognitive dissonance by seeking consonant information. *J. abnorm. soc. Psychol.,* 1961, 62, 74–78.

ADAMS-WEBBER, J. R. An analysis of the discriminant validity of several repertory grid indices. *Brit. J. Psychol.,* 1970, 60, 1, 83–90.

ADELSON, J., & REDMOND, J. Personality differences in the capacity for verbal recall. *J. abnorm. soc. Psychol.,* 1958, 57, 244–248.

ADLER, A. *Study of organ inferiority and its psychical compensation.* New York: Nervous and Mental Diseases Publishing Co., 1917.

ADLER, A. *The practice and theory of individual psychology.* New York: Harcourt, Brace & World, 1927.

ADLER, A. Individual psychology. In C. MURCHINSON (Ed.), *Psychologies of 1930*. Worcester, Mass.: Clark University Press, 1930.

ADLER, A. *What life should mean to you*. Boston: Little, Brown, 1931.

ADLER, A. *Social interest*. New York: Putnam, 1939.

ADLER, A. *The individual psychology of Alfred Adler*. New York: Basic Books, 1956.

ADLER, A. *Problems of neurosis*. New York: Harper Torchbooks, 1964.

ADORNO, T. W., FRENKEL-BRUNSWIK, E., LEVINSON, D. J., & SANFORD, R. N. *The authoritarian personality*. New York: Harper, 1950.

ADRIAN, E. D. The physiological basis of perception. In E. D. ADRIAN et al. (Eds.), *Brain mechanisms and consciousness*. Oxford: Blackwell, 1954.

AHLER, H. A. Cognitive controls and the Hoan-Kroeker model of ego functioning. *J. abnorm. soc. Psychol.*, 1967, 72, 434–440.

AKERET, R. U. Interrelationships among various dimensions of the self-concept. *J. counsel. Psychol.*, 1959, 6, 199–201.

ALEGRE, C. & MURRAY, E. Locus of control, behavioral intention, and verbal conditioning. *J. Pers.*, 1974, 42, 668–681.

ALKER, H. A. Is personality situationally specific of intrapsychically consistent? *J. Pers.*, 1972, 40, 1–16.

ALLPORT, F. H., *Theories of perception and the concept of structure*. New York; Wiley, 1955.

ALLPORT, G. W. *Personality: A psychological interpretation*. New York: Holt, 1937.

ALLPORT, G. W. *The use of personal documents in psychological research*. New York: Social Science Research Council, 1942.

ALLPORT, G. W. *Becoming: Basic considerations for a psychology of personality*. New Haven, Conn.: Yale University Press, 1955.

ALLPORT, G. W. *Pattern and growth in personality*. New York: Holt, Rinehart, & Winston, 1961.

ALLPORT, G. W. The general and the unique in psychological science. *J. Pers.*, 1962, 30, 405–422.

ALLPORT, G. W. & CANTRIL, H. Judging personality from voice. *J. soc. Psychol.*, 1934, 5, 37–55.

ALLPORT, G. W. & ODBERT, H. S. Trait names: A psychological study. *Psychol. Monogr.*, 1936, 47, No. 211, 1–171.

ALLPORT, G. W. & VERNON, P. E. *Studies in expressive movement*. New York: Macmillan, 1933.

ALLPORT, G. W. & VERNON, P. E. & LINDZEY, G. A. *A study of values*. (2d ed.) Boston: Houghton Mifflin, 1951.

ALTROCCHI, J., PARSONS, O. A., & DICKOFF, HILDA. Changes in self-ideal discrepancy in repressors and sensitizers. *J. abn. soc. Psychol.*, 1060, 61, 67–72.

ALTUS, W. D. Birth order and its sequelae. *Science*, 1966, 151, 44–49.

ANASTASI, A. *Psychological testing*. (2d ed.) New York: Macmillan, 1961.

ANDERSON, J. E. Prediction of adjustment over time. In I. ISCOE & H. A. STEVENSON (Eds.), *Personality development in children*. Austin, Tex.: University of Texas Press, 1960.

ANGYAL, A. *Foundations for a science of personality*. New York: Commonwealth Fund. 1941.

ANGYAL, A. A theoretical model for personality studies. *J. Pers.*, 1951, 20, 131–142.

ANGYAL, A. *Neurosis and treatment: A holistic theory*. New York: Wiley, 1965.

ANSBACHER, H. L. Life style: A historical and systematic review. *J. indiv. Psychol.*, 1967, 23, 191–231.

ANSBACHER, H. L. & ANSBACHER, R. *The individual psychology of Alfred Adler*. New York: Basic Books, 1956.

ARONSON, E. The effect of effort on the attractiveness of rewarded and unrewarded stimuli. *J. abnorm. soc. Psychol.*, 1961, 63, 375–380.

ARONSON, E. & MILLS, J. The effect of severity of initiation on liking for a group. *J. abnorm. soc. Psychol.*, 1959, 59, 177–181.

ARONSON, M. L. A study of the Freudian theory of paranoia by means of the Blacky Pictures. *J. proj-tech.*, 1953, 17, 3–19.

ATKINSON, J. W. Studies in projective measurement of achievement motivation. Unpublished manuscript, Ann Arbor, Mich.: University of Michigan, 1950.

ATKINSON, J. W. Motivational determinants of risk-taking behavior. *Psychol. Rev.*, 1957, 64, 359–372.

ATKINSON, J. W. (Ed.). *Motives in fantasy, action, and society*. Princeton, N.J.: Van Nostrand, 1958.

ATKINSON, J. W. Personality dynamics. In P. R. FARNSWORTH and Q. McNEMAR (Eds.), *Annual review of psychology*. Palo Alto, Calif.: Banta, 1960.

ATKINSON, J. W., HEYNS, R. W. & VEROFF, J. The effect of experimental arousal of the affiliation motive on thematic apperception. *J. abnorm. soc. Psychol.*, 1954, 49, 405–410.

ATKINSON, J. W. & WALKER, E. L. The affiliation motive and perceptual sensitivity to facts. In J. W. ATKINSON (Ed.), *Motives in fantasy, action, and society*. Princeton, N.J.: Van Nostrand, 1958.

AXTELL, B. & COLE, C. W. Repression-Sensitization response mode and verbal avoidance. *J. pers. soc. Psychol.*, 1971, 18, 133–137.

AYLLON, T. & AZRIN, N. *The token economy*. New York: Appleton-Century-Crofts, 1968.

BAKAN, D. *The duality of human existence*. Chicago: Rand McNally, 1966.

BAKAN, D. *Disease, pain, and sacrifice*. Chicago: University of Chicago Press, 1968.

BAKAN, D. *Slaughter of the innocents*. San Francisco: Jossey-Bass, 1971.

BAKER, S. R. A study of the relationship of dogmatism to the retention of psychological concepts: A research note. *Journal of Human Relations*, 1964, 12, 311–313.

BANDURA, A. Vicarious processes: A case of no-trial learning. In L. BERKOWITZ (Ed.), *Advances in experimental social psychology.* Vol. II. New York: Academic Press, 1965.

BANDURA, A. Behavioral modifications through modeling procedures. In L. KRASNER & I. P. ULLMAN (Eds.), *Research in behavior modification.* New York: Holt, Rinehart, & Winston, 1966.

BANDURA, A. *Principles of behavior modification.* New York: Holt, Rinehart, & Winston, 1969.

BANDURA, A. Behavior theory and the models of man. *Amer. Psychologist,* 1974, 29, 859–869.

BANDURA, A. & KUPERS, C. J. Transmission of patterns of self-reinforcement through modeling. *J. abn. soc. Psychol.,* 1964, 69, 1–9.

BANDURA, A. & MISCHEL, W. Modification of self-imposed delay of reward through exposure to live and symbolic models. *J. pers. soc. Psychol.,* 1965, 2, 698–705.

BANDURA, A. & WALTERS, R. H. *Social learning and personality development.* New York: Holt, Rinehart, & Winston, 1963.

BARKER, R., DEMBO, T., & LEWIN, K. Frustration and regression: An experiment with young children. *Univer. Iowa Stud. Child Welf.,* 1941, 18, No. 1, 1–314.

BARRON, F. *Creativity and psychological health.* Princeton, N.J.: Van Nostrand, 1963.

BATTLE, E. & ROTTER, J. B. Children's feelings of personal control as related to social class and ethnic group. *J. Pers.,* 1963, 31, 482–490.

BEM, D. J. Constructing cross-situational consistencies in behavior: Some thoughts on Alker's critique of Mischel. *J. Pers.,* 1972, 40, 17–26.

BENSON, J. K. Alienation and academic achievement: An empirical study of the reactions of college students to academic success and failure. Unpublished doctoral dissertation, University of Texas, 1966.

BERGER, E. M. The relation between expressed acceptance of self and expressed acceptance of others. *J. abnorm. soc. Psychol.,* 1953, 47, 778–782.

BERGER, E. M. Relationships among acceptance of self, acceptance of others and MMPI scores. *J. counsel. Psychol.,* 1955, 2, 279–284.

BERGER, L. & EVERSTINE, L. Test-retest reliability of the Blacky Pictures Test. *J. proj. Tech.,* 1962, 26, 225–226.

BERGONIS, B. W., LLOYD, J. & JOHANSSON, S. Individual differences among repressors and sensitizers in conceptual skills. *Soc. beh. Pers.,* 1973, 1, 144–152.

BERKOWITZ, L. *Aggression: A social psychological analysis.* New York: McGraw-Hill, 1962.

BERLEW, D. E. The achievement motive and the growth of Greek civilization. Unpublished bachelor's thesis. Middletown, Conn., Wesleyan University, 1956.

BERLYNE, D. E. The arousal and satiation of perceptual curiosity in the rat. *J. comp. physiol. Psychol.,* 1955, 48, 238–246.

BERLYNE, D. E. Uncertainty and conflict: A point of contact between information-theory and behavior-theory concepts. *Psychol. Rev.*, 1957, 64, 329–339.

BERLYNE, D. E. *Conflict, arousal, and curiosity.* New York: McGraw-Hill, 1960.

BERLYNE, D. E. Emotional aspects of learning. *Annu. Rev. Psychol.*, 1964, 15, 115–142.

BERLYNE, D. E. Arousal and reinforcement. *Nebraska Symposium on Motivation*, 1967, 1–110.

BERLYNE, D. E. Behavior theory as personality theory. In E. F. BORGATTO & W. W. LAMBERT (Eds.), *Handbook of personality theory and research.* Chicago: Rand McNally, 1968.

BERLYNE, D. E., BORSA, D. M., HAMACHER, J. H., & KOENIG, I. D. V. Paired-associate learning and the timing of arousal. *J. exp. Psychol.*, 1966, 72, 1–6.

BERNARDIN, A. C. & JESSOR, R. A construct validation of the Edwards Personal Preference Schedule with respect to dependency. *J. consult. Psychol.*, 1957, 21, 63–67.

BERRY, J. C., & MARTIN, B. GSR reactivity as a function of anxiety, instructions, and sex. *J. abnorm. soc. Psychol.*, 1957, 54, 9–12.

BIALER, I. Conceptualization of success and failure in mentally retarded and normal children. *J. Pers.*, 1961, 29, 303–320.

BIELER, S. H. Some correlates of the Jungian typology: Personal style variables. Master's thesis, Durham, N.C., Duke University, 1966.

BIERI, J. Complexity-simplicity as a personality variable in cognitive and preferential behavior. In D. W. FISKE & S. R. MADDI, *Functions of varied experience.* Homewood, Ill.: Dorsey, 1961.

BINDRA, D., PATERSON, A. L., & STRZELECKI, JOANNA. On the relation between anxiety and conditioning. *Canad. J. Psychol.*, 1955, 9, 1–6.

BINSWANGER, L. The existential analysis school of thought. In R. MAY, E. ANGEL, & H. F. ELLENBERGER (Eds.), *Existence: A new dimension in psychiatry and psychology.* New York: Basic Books, 1958.

BINSWANGER, L. *Being-in-the-world: Selected papers of Ludwig Binswanger.* New York: Basic Books, 1963.

BLOCK, J. Some differences between the concepts of social desirability and adjustments. *J. consult. Psychol.*, 1962, 26, 527–530.

BLOCK, J. *Lives through time.* Berkeley, Calif.: Bancroft, 1971.

BLUM, G. S. A study of the psychoanalytic theory of psychosexual development. *Genet. Psychol. Monogr.*, 1949, 39, 3–99.

BLUM, G. S. Perceptual defense revisited. *J. abnorm. soc. Psychol.*, 1955, 51, 24–29.

BLUM, G. S., & HUNT, H. F. The validity of the Blacky Pictures. *Psychol. Bull.*, 1952, 49, 238–250.

BLUM, G. S. & KAUFMAN, J. B. Two patterns of personality dynamics in male ulcer patients, as suggested by responses to the Blacky Pictures. *J. clin. Psychol.*, 1952, 8, 273–278.

BONEAU, C. A. Paradigm Regained? Cognitive behaviorism restated. *Amer. Psychologist*, 1974, 29, 297–309.

BOOTZIN, R. R. & NATSOULAS, T. Evidence for perceptual defense uncontaminated by response bias. *J. pers. soc. Psychol.*, 1965, 1, 461–468.

BOSS, M. *Psychoanalysis and Daseinanalysis*. New York: Basic Books, 1963.

BOSSARD, J. H. S. & BOLL, E. S. Personality roles in the large family. *Child Develpm.*, 1955, 26, 71–78.

BOWERS, K. S. Situationism in psychology: An analysis and a critique. *Psychol. Rev.*, 1973, 80, 307–336.

BRADBURN, N. M. & BERLEW, D. E. Need for achievement and English industrial growth. *Econ. Developm. cult. change*, 1961, 10, 8–20.

BRADLEY, R. W. Birth order and school-related behavior: A heuristic review. *Psychol. Bull.*, 1968, 70, 45–51.

BRAUN, J. & ASTA, P. Intercorrelations between the Personal Orientation Inventory and the Gordon Personal Inventory scores. *Psychol. Rep.*, 1968, 23, 1197–1198.

BREHM, J. W. Comment on "Counter-norm attitudes induced by consonant versus dissonant conditions of role-playing." *J. exp. Res. Personality*, 1965, 1, 61–64.

BREHM, J. W. & COHEN, A. R. Re-evaluation of choice alternatives as function of their number and qualitative similarity. *J. abnorm. soc. Psychol.*, 1959, 58, 373–378.

BREHM, J. W. & COHEN, A. R. Explorations in cognitive dissonance. New York: Wiley, 1962.

BREUER, J. & FREUD, S. Studies in hysteria. *Nerv. ment. Dis. Monogr.*, 1936, No. 61.

BRISSETTE, G. G. The significance of life goals in aging adjustment: A pilot study. *Calif. ment. Hlth. Res. Monogr.*, 1967, 9, 88.

BRONSON, G. W. Identity diffusion in late adolescents. *J. abnorm. soc. Psychol.*, 1959, 59, 414–417.

BROPHY, A. L. Self, role, and satisfaction. *Genet. Psychol. Monogr.*, 1959, 59, 236–308.

BROWN, D. & MARKS, P. A. Bakan's bi-polar constructs: Agency and communion. *Psychol. Rec.*, 1969, 19, 465–478.

BROWN, J. S. & FARBER, I. E. Emotions conceptualized as intervening variables with suggestions toward a theory of frustration. *Psychol. Bull.*, 1951, 38, 465–495.

BROWN, N. O. *Life against death*. Middletown, Conn.: Wesleyan University Press, 1959.

BROWN, N. O. Apocalypse. Phi Beta Kappa address. *Harper's*, 1961, 222, 46–49.

BRUNER, J. S. You are your constructs. *Contemp. Psychol.*, 1956, 1, 355–358.

BRUNER, J. S. Mechanism riding high. *Contemp. Psychol.*, 1957, 2, 155–157. (a)

BRUNER, J. S. Neural mechanisms in perception. *Psychol. Rev.*, 1957, 64, 340–358. (b)

BRUNER, J. S. *On knowing: Essays for the left hand.* Cambridge, Mass.: Harvard University Press, 1962. (a)

BRUNER, J. S. The creative surprise. In H. E. GRUBER, G. TERRELL & M. WERTHEIMER (Eds.), *Contemporary approaches to creative thinking.* New York: Atherton, 1962. (b)

BRUNER, J. S. & POSTMAN, L. Emotional selectivity in perception and reaction. *J. Pers.*, 1947, 16, 69–77. (a)

BRUNER, J. S. & POSTMAN, L. Tension and tension-release as organizing factors in perception. *J. Pers.*, 1947, 15, 300–308. (b)

BUGENTAL, J. F. T. *The search for authenticity.* New York: Holt, Rinehart, & Winston, 1965.

BUTLER, J. M. & HAIGH, G. V. Changes in the relation between self-concepts and ideal-concepts consequent upon client-centered counseling. In C. R. ROGERS & R. F. DYMOND (Eds.), *Psychotherapy and personality change.* Chicago: University of Chicago Press, 1954.

BUTLER, J. M. & RICE, L. Adience, self-actualization, and drive theory. In J. M. WEPMAN & R. W. HEINE (Eds.), *Concepts of personality.* Chicago: Aldine, 1963.

BUTLER, R. A. & ALEXANDER, H. M. Daily patterns of visual exploratory behavior in the monkey. *J. comp. physiol. Psychol.*, 1955, 48, 247–249.

BUTTERFIELD, E. C. Locus of control, test anxiety, reactions to frustration, and achievement attitudes. *J. Pers.*, 1964, 32, 298–311.

BYRNE, D. Anxiety and the experimental arousal of affiliation need. *J. abnorm. soc. Psychol.*, 1961, 63, 660–662. (a)

BRYNE, D. The Repression-Sensitization Scale: Rationale, reliability, and validity. *J. Pers.*, 1961, 29, 344–349. (b)

BRYNE, D. Repression-sensitization as a dimension of personality. In B. A. MAHER (Ed.), *Progress in experimental personality research.* New York: Academic Press, 1964.

BYRNE, D., BARRY, J. & NELSON, D. Relation of the revised Repression-Sensitization Scale to measures of self-description. *Psychol. Rep.*, 1963, 13, 323–334.

BYRNE, D., STEINBERG, M., & SCHWARTZ, M. S. Relationship between repression-sensitization and physical illness. *J. abn. soc. Psychol.*, 1968, 73, 154–155.

CALDER, B. J. & STAW, B. M. Interaction of Intrinsic and extrinsic motivation: Some methodological notes. *J. pers. soc. Psychol.*, 1975, 31, 76–80. (a)

CALDER, B. J. & STAW, B. M. Self-perception of intrinsic and extrinsic motivation. *J. pers. soc. Psychol.*, 1975, 31, 599–605. (b)

CAMPBELL, A. A. A study of the personality adjustments of only and intermediate children. *J. genet. Psychol.*, 1933, 43, 197–206.

CAMPBELL, A., CONVERSE, P. E., MILLER, W. E., & STOKES, D. E. *The American voter.* New York: Wiley, 1960.

CAMPBELL, D. T. & FISKE, D. W. Convergent and discriminant validation by the multitrait-multimethod matrix. *Psychol. Bull.*, 1959, 56, 81–105.

CAMUS, A. *The myth of Sisyphus and other essays* (tr. J. O'BRIEN). New York: Knopf, 1955.

CANNON, W. B. *Bodily changes in pain, hunger, fear, and rage.* New York: Appleton, 1929.

CARLSON, R. Sex differences in ego functioning: Exploratory studies of agency and communion. *J. consult. clin. Psychol.*, 1971, 37, 267–277. (a)

CARLSON, R. Where is the person in personality research? *Psychol. Bull.*, 1971, 75, 203–219. (b)

CARLSON, R. & LEVY, N. Studies of Jungian typology: 1. Memory, social perception, and social action. *J. Pers.*, 1973, 41, 559–576.

CARRIGAN, P. Extraversion-introversion as a dimension of personality: A reappraisal. *Psychol. Bull.*, 1960, 57, 329–360.

CATTELL, R. B. *Description and measurement of personality.* New York: World Book, 1946.

CATTELL, R. B. *Personality: A systematic, theoretical, and factual study.* New York: McGraw-Hill, 1950.

CATTELL, R. B. *Personality and motivation structure and measurement.* New York: World Book, 1957.

CATTELL, R. B. and DELHEES, K. Seven missing normal personality factors in the questionnaire primaries. *Multivariate Beh. Res.*, 1973, 8, 173–194.

CATTELL, R. B. & GIBBONS, B. D. Personality factor structure of the combined Guilford and Cattell personality questionnaire. *J. Pers. soc. Psychol.*, 1968, 9, 107–120.

CATTELL, R. B. & STICE, G. F. *Sixteen Personality Factor Questionnaire.* (Rev. ed.) Champaign, Ill.: Inst. Pers. Abil. Test., 1957.

CENTERS, R. The anal character and social severity in attitudes. *J. proj. Tech. & Personality Assess.*, 1969, 33, 501–506.

CHABOT, J. A. Repression-Sensitization: A critique of some neglected variables in the literature. *Psychol. Bull.*, 1973, 80, 122–129.

CHAPANIS, N. P. & CHAPANIS, A. Cognitive dissonance: Five years later. *Psychol. Bull.*, 1964, 61, 1–22.

CHAREN, S. Reliability of the Blacky Test. *J. consult. Psychol.*, 1956, 20, 16.

CHERULNIK, P. D. & CITRIN, M. M. Individual difference in psychological reactance: The interaction between locus of control and mode of elimination of freedom. *J. pers. soc. Psychol.*, 1974, 29, 398–404.

CHODORKOFF, B. Adjustment and the discrepancy between perceived and ideal self. *J. clin. Psychol.*, 1954, 10, 266–268. (a)

CHODORKOFF, B. Self-perception, perceptual defense, and adjustment. *J. abnorm. soc. Psychol.*, 1954, 49, 508–512. (b)

CLARK, C. *The conditions of economic progress.* (3d ed.) London: Macmillan, 1957.

CLARK, S. L. Authoritarian attitudes and field dependence. *Psychol. Rep.*, 1968, 22, 309–310.

CLARK, W. C. & HUNT, H. F. Pain. In J. A. POWNEY & R. C. DARLING (Eds.), *Physiological basis of rehabilitation medicine.* Philadelphia: Saunders, 1971.

COAN, B. W. Measurable components of openness to experience. *J. consult. clin. Psychol.,* 1972, 39, 346.

COHEN, A. R., BREHM, J. W., & FLEMING, W. H. Attitude change and justification for compliance. *J. abnorm. soc. Psychol.,* 1958, 56, 276–278.

COLEMAN, J. S., CAMPBELL, E. Q., HOBSON, C. J., McPARTLAND, J., MOOD, A. M., WEINFELD, F. D., & YORK, R. L. *Equality of educational opportunity.* Washington, D.C.: U.S. Office of Education (Superintendent of Documents, Catalog No. FS 5.238.38001), 1966.

COLLINS, B. E. Four components of the Rotter Internal-External Scale: Belief in a difficult world, a just world, a predictable world, and a politically responsive world. *J. pers. soc. Psychol.,* 1974, 29, 381–391.

COMREY, A. L. & DUFFY, K. E. Cattell and Eysenck factor scores related Comrey personality factors. *Multivariate Behav. Res.,* 1968, 3, 349–392.

CONANT, J. B. *On understanding science.* New Haven, Conn.: Yale University Press, 1947.

CONNERS, C. K. Birth order and needs for affiliation. *J. Pers.,* 1963, 31, 408–416.

CONSTANTINOPLE, A. An Eriksonian measure of personality development in college students. *Developmental Psychol.,* 1969, 1, 357–372.

COOK, P. Authoritarian or acquiescent: Some behavioral differences. *Amer. Psychologist,* 1958, 13, 338.

COOPER, J. & GOETHALS, G. R. Unforeseen events and the elimination of cognitive dissonance. *J. pers. soc. Psychol.,* 1974, 29, 441–445.

COOPER, J. & SCALISE, C. J. Dissonance produced by deviations from life styles: The interaction of Jungian typology and conformity. *J. pers. soc. Psychol.,* 1974, 29, 556–571.

COOPERMAN, M. & CHILD, I. L. Esthetic preference and active style. *Proc. of the 77th Annual Convention of the APA,* 1969, 4, 471–472.

CORTES, J. B. The achievement motive in the Spanish economy between the 13th and 18th centuries. *Econ. Develpm. cult. change,* 1960, 9, 144–163.

COSTA, P. T., JR. Multivariate analysis of the Maddi model of forms of need for variety. Unpublished Ph.D. dissertation, Chicago, University of Chicago, 1970.

COSTIN, F. Dogmatism and learning: A follow-up of contradictory findings. *J. educ. Res.,* 1965, 59, 186–188.

COSTIN, F. Dogmatism and the retention of psychological misconceptions. *Educ. psychol. Measmt.,* 1968, 28, 529–534.

COURTS, F. A. Relations between muscular tension and performance. *Psychol. Bull.,* 1942, 39, 347–367.

COWEN, E. L., & BEIER, E. G. Threat expectancy, word frequencies, and perceptual prerecognition hypotheses. *J. abnorm. soc. Psychol.,* 1954, 14, 469–477.

COWEN, E. L., HEILIZER, F., AXELROD, H. S., & SHELDON, A. The correlates of manifest anxiety in perceptual reactivity, rigidity, and self-conflict. *J. consult. Psychol.*, 1957, 21, 405–411.

CRANDALL, V. C., KATKOVSKY, W., & CRANDALL, V. J. Children's beliefs in their own control of reinforcement in intellectual-academic achievement situations. *Child Develpm.*, 1965, 36, 91–109.

CROMWELL, R., ROSENTHAL, D., SHAKOW, D., & KAHN, T. Reaction time, locus of control, choice behavior and descriptions of parental behavior in schizophrenic and normal subjects. *J. Pers.*, 1961, 29, 363–380.

CRONBACH, L. J. The two disciplines of scientific psychology. *Amer. Psychologist*, 1957, 12, 671–684.

CRONBACH, L. J. Beyond the two disciplines of scientific psychology. *Amer. Psychologist*, 1975, 30, 116–127.

CRONBACH, L. J. & MEEHL, P. E. Construct validity in psychological tests. *Psychol. Bull.*, 1955, 52, 281–302.

CROOKES, T. G. & PEARSON, P. R. The relationship between EPI scores and 16 PF second order factors in a clinical group. *Br. J. soc. & clin. Psychol.*, 1970, 9, 189–190.

CROSS, P. G., CATTELL, R. B., & BUTCHER, H. J. The personality pattern of creative artists. *Br. J. educ. Psychol.*, 1967, 37, 292–299.

CROSSON, S. & SCHWENDIMAN, G. Self-actualization as a predictor of conformity behavior. Unpublished manuscript. Marshall University, 1972.

CROWNE, D. P. & LIVERANT, S. Conformity under varying conditions of personal commitment. *J. abnorm. soc. Psychol.*, 1963, 66, 547–555.

CROWNE, D. P. & MARLOWE, D. A new scale of social desirability independent of psychopathology. *J. consult. Psychol.*, 1960, 24, 349–354.

CRUMBAUGH, J. C. & MAHOLICK, L. T. An experimental study in existentialism: The psychometric approach to Frankl's concept of noogenic neurosis. *J. clin. Psychol.*, 1964, 20, 200–207.

CRUMBAUGH, J. C. Cross-validation of the Purpose in Life Test based on Frankl's concepts. *J. indiv. Psychol.*, 1968, 24, 74–81.

DAMM, V. J. Overall measures of self actualization derived from the Personal Orientation Inventory. *Educ. psychol. Measmt.*, 1969, 29, 977–981.

DANDES, H. M. Psychological health and teaching effectiveness. *Journal of Teaching Education*, 1966, 17, 301–306.

DANSKIN, D. G. An introduction to KSU students. Unpublished report, Kansas State University, Student Counseling Center, September, 1964. Cited by J. B. WARREN, Birth order and social behavior. *Psychol. Bull.*, 1966, 65, 38–49.

DAVIS, A. & DOLLARD, J. *Children of bondage.* Washington, D.C.: Amer. Council on Education, 1940.

DE CHARMS, R. C. Affiliation motivation and productivity in small groups. *J. abnorm. soc. Psychol.*, 1957, 55, 222–226.

DE CHARMS, R. C., MORRISON, H. W., REITMAN, W., & McCLELLAND, D. C. Behavioral correlates of directly and indirectly measured achievement motivation. In D. C. McClelland (Ed.), *Studies in motivation.* New York: Appleton-Century-Crofts, 1955.

de Grace, G. R. The compatibility of anxiety and actualization. *J. clin. Psychol.,* 1974, 130, 566–568.

Dember, W. N. Response by the rat to environmental change. *J. comp. physiol. Psychol.,* 1956, 49, 93–95.

Dember, W. N. Alternation behavior. In D. W. Fiske & S. R. Maddi (Eds.), *Functions of varied experience.* Homewood, Ill.: Dorsey, 1961.

Dember, W. N. Birth order and need affiliation. *J. abnorm. soc. Psychol.,* 1964, 68, 555–557.

Dember, W. N. Motivation and the cognitive revolution. *Amer. Psychologist,* 1974, 29, 161–168.

Dennis, W. Spontaneous alternation in rats as an indicator of persistence of stimulus effects. *J. comp. Psychol.,* 1939, 28, 305–312.

Dimond, R. E. & Munz, D. C. Ordinal position of birth and self-disclosure in high school students. *Psychol. Rep.,* 1967, 21, 829–833.

Dittes, J. E. Birth order and vulnerability to differences in acceptance. *Amer. Psychologist,* 1961, 16, 358.

Dollard, J. & Miller, N. E. *Personality and psychotherapy: An analysis in terms of learning, thinking, and culture.* New York: McGraw-Hill, 1950.

Donley, R. E. & Winter, D. G. Measuring the motives of public officials at a distance: An exploratory study of American presidents. *Behavl. Sci.,* 1965, 3, 227–236.

Dorfman, D. D. Esthetic preference as a function of pattern information. *Psychon. Sci.,* 1965, 3, 85–86.

Dreikurs, R. Individual psychology: The Adlerian point of view. In J. M. Wepman & R. W. Heine (Eds.), *Concepts of personality.* Chicago: Aldine, 1963.

Duffy, E. *Activation and behavior.* New York: Wiley, 1963.

Duffy, K. E., Jamison, K., & Comrey, A. L. Assessment of a proposed expansion of the Comrey Personality Factor System. *Multivariate Behav. Res.,* 1969, 4, 295–307.

Dulany, D. E., Jr. The place of hypotheses and intentions: An analysis of verbal control in verbal conditioning. In C. W. Eriksen (Ed.), *Behavior and awareness.* Durham, N.C.: Duke University Press, 1962.

Dulany, D. E., Jr. Awareness, rules, and propositional control: A confrontation with S–R behavior theory. In T. R. Dixon and D. L. Horton (Eds.), *Verbal behavior and general behavior theory.* Englewood Cliffs, N.J.: Prentice-Hall, 1968.

Duncan, S. D., Jr. Some signals and rules for taking speaking turns in conversations. *J. pers. soc. Psychol.,* 1972, 23, 283–292.

Ebersole, P. Effects and classifications of peak experiences. *Psychol. Reports,* 1973, 40, 22–28.

Edwards, A. L. *Edwards Personal Preference Schedule.* New York: Psychol. Corp., 1963.

EDWARDS, A. L. *The social desirability variable in personality assessment and research.* New York: Dryden, 1957.

EHRLICH, D., GUTTMAN, I., SCHONBACH, P., & MILLS, J. Postdecision exposure to relevant information. *J. abnorm. soc. Psychol.*, 1957, 54, 98–102.

EHRLICH, H. J. Dogmatism and intellectual change. Unpublished master's thesis, Columbus, Ohio: Ohio State University, 1955.

EHRLICH, H. J. Dogmatism and learning. *J. abnorm. soc. Psychol.*, 1961, 62, 148–149. (a)

EHRLICH, H. J. Dogmatism and learning: A five-year follow-up. *Psychol. Rep.*, 1961, 9, 283–286. (b)

EHRLICH, H. J. & LEE, D. Dogmatism, learning and resistance to change: A review and a new paradigm. *Psychol. Bull.*, 1969, 71, 249–260.

EISENBERGER, R. Explanation of rewards that do not reduce tissue needs. *Psychol. Bull.*, 1972, 77, 319–339.

EISENBERGER, R., MYERS, A. K., SANDERS, R. & SHANAB, M. Stimulus control of spontaneous alternation in the rat. *J. comp. physiol. Psychol.*, 1970, 70, 136–140.

EISENMAN, R. & SCHUSSEL, N. R. Creativity, birth order and preference for symmetry. *J. consult. & clin. Psychol.*, 1970, 34, 275–280.

EKEHAMMAR, B. Interactionism in personality from a historical perspective. *Psychol. Bull.*, 1974, 81, 1026–1048.

ELDER, G. H., JR. Family structure: The effects of size of family, sex composition and ordinal position on academic motivation and achievement. In B. A. MAHER (Ed.), *Progress in experimental personality research.* New York: Academic Press, 1965.

ELLIOT, L. L. Effects of item construction and respondent aptitude on response acquiescence. *Educ. psychol. Measmt.*, 1961, 21, 405–415.

ELMS, A. C. Role playing, incentive, and dissonance. *Psychol. Bull.*, 1967, 68, 132–148.

ELMS, A. C. & JANIS, I. L. Counter-norm attitudes induced by consonant versus dissonant conditions of role-playing. *J. exp. Res. Personality*, 1965, 1, 50–60.

EMERSON, R. W. *The selected writings of Ralph Waldo Emerson.* (Ed. by B. ATKINSON). New York: Modern Library, 1940.

ENDLER, N. S. The person versus the situation—A pseudo issue? A response to Alker. *J. Pers.*, 1973, 41, 287–303.

ENDLER, N. S. and HUNT, J. McV. Sources of behavioral variance as measured by the S–R Inventory of Anxiousness. *Psychol. Bull.*, 1966, 65, 338–346.

ENDLER, N. S. and HUNT, J. McV. Generalizability of contributions from sources of variance in the S–R inventories of anxiousness. *J. Pers.*, 1969, 37, 1–24.

ENDLER, N. S., HUNT, J. McV., and ROSENSTEIN, A. J. An S–R Inventory of anxiousness. *Psychol. Monogr.*, 1962, 76, Whole No. 536.

ERIKSEN, C. W. Perceptual defense as a function of unacceptable needs. *J. abnorm. soc. Psychol.*, 1951, 46, 557–564. (a)

ERIKSEN, C. W. Some implications for TAT interpretation arising from need and perception experiments. *J. Pers.*, 1951, 19, 283–288. (b)

ERIKSEN, C. D. Defense against ego-threat in memory and perception. *J. abnorm. soc. Psychol.*, 1952, 47, 430–435.

ERIKSEN, C. W. Psychological defenses and ego strength in the recall of completed and incompleted tasks. *J. abnorm. soc. Psychol.*, 1954, 49, 45–50.

ERIKSEN, C. W. Perception and personality. In J. M. WEPMAN & R. W. HEINE (Eds.), *Concepts of personality*. Chicago: Aldine, 1963.

ERIKSEN, C. W. & BROWN, C. T. An experimental and theoretical analysis of perceptual defense. *J. abnorm. soc. Psychol.*, 1956, 52, 224–230.

ERIKSEN, C. W. & DAVIDS, A. The meaning and clinical validity of the Taylor Manifest Anxiety Scale in the hysteria psychasthenia scales from the MMPI. *J. abnorm. soc. Psychol.*, 1955, 50, 135–137.

ERIKSON, E. H. *Childhood and society*. New York: Norton, 1950.

ERIKSON, E. H. The problem of ego identity. *J. Amer. Psycholanal Ass.*, 1956, 4, 56–121.

ESTES, S. G. Judging personality from expressive behavior. *J. abnorm. soc. Psychol.*, 1938, 33, 217–236.

EYSENCK, H. J. *Dimensions of personality*. London: Routledge & Kegan Paul, 1947.

EYSENCK, H. J. *The dynamics of anxiety and hysteria: An experimental application of modern learning theory to psychiatry*. London: Routledge & Kegan Paul, 1957.

EYSENCK, H. J. & RACHMAN, S. *The causes and cures of neuroses*. San Diego: Knapp, 1965.

FARBER, I. E. Response fixation under anxiety and non-anxiety conditions. *J. exp. Psychol.*, 1948, 38, 111–131.

FARBER, I. E. & SPENCE, K. W. Complex learning and conditioning as a function of anxiety. *J. exp. Psychol.*, 1953, 45, 120–125.

FARBER, I. E., & SPENCE, K. W. Effects of anxiety, stress, and task variables on reaction time. *J. Pers.*, 1956, 25, 1–18.

FEATHER, N. T. Some personality correlates of external control. *Aust. J. Psychol.*, 1967, 19, 253–260.

FELDINGER, I. & MADDI, S. R. The motivational status of measures of the need for variety. Unpublished manuscript, Chicago, 1968.

FENICHEL, O. *The psychoanalytic theory of neurosis*. New York: Norton, 1945.

FESTINGER, L. *A Theory of cognitive dissonance*. Stanford: Stanford University Press, 1957.

FESTINGER, L. The motivating effect of cognitive dissonance. In G. LINDZEY (Ed.), *Assessment of human motives*. New York: Holt, Rinehart & Winston, 1958.

FESTINGER, L. & CARLSMITH, J. M. Cognitive consequences of forced compliance. *J. abnorm. soc. Psychol.*, 1959, 58, 203–210.

FINE, B. J. Conclusion-drawing, communication, credibility, and anxiety as factors in opinion change. *J. abnorm. soc. Psychol.*, 1957, 54, 369–374.

FINK, D. R., JR. Negative evidence concerning the generality of rigidity. *J. abnorm. soc. Psychol.*, 1958, 57, 252–254.

FISHER, G. Performance of psychopathic felons on a measure of self-actualization. *Educ. psychol. Measmt.*, 1968, 28, 561–563.

FISHER, G. & SILVERSTEIN, A. B. Simulation of poor adjustment on a measure of self-actualization. *J. clin. Psychol.*, 1969, 25, 198–199.

FISKE, D. W. Effects of monotonous and restricted stimulation. In D. W. FISKE & S. R. MADDI (Eds.), *Functions of varied experience.* Homewood, Ill.: Dorsey, 1961.

FISKE, D. W. Problems in measuring personality. In J. M. WEPMAN & R. W. HEINE (Eds.), *Concepts of personality.* Chicago: Aldine, 1963.

FISKE, D. W. The limits for the conventional science of personality. *J. Pers.*, 1974, 42, 1–11.

FISKE, D. W. & MADDI, S. R. (Eds.), *Functions of varied experience.* Homewood, Ill.: Dorsey, 1961.

FOULDS, M. L. Self-actualization and the communication of facilitative conditions during counseling. *J. counsel. Psychol.*, 1969, 16, 132–136.

FOULDS, M. L. and WAREHIME, R. G. Effects of a "fake good" response set on a measure of self-actualization. *J. counsel. Psychol.*, 1971, 18, 279–280.

FOX, J., KNAPP, R. & MICHAEL, W. Assessment of self-actualization of psychiatric patients: Validity of the Personal Orientation Inventory. *Educ. psychol. Measmt.*, 1968, 28, 565–569.

FRANKEL, M. Personality as a response: Behaviorism. In S. R. MADDI (Ed.), *Perspectives on personality.* Boston: Little, Brown, 1971.

FRANKL, V. *The doctor and the soul.* New York: Knopf, 1960.

FREEDMAN, M. B. & BEREITER, C. A longitudinal study of personality development in college alumnae. *Merrill-Palmer Quart.*, 1963, 9, 295–302.

FREEMAN, G. L. The facilitative and inhibitive effects of muscular tension upon performance. *Amer. J. Psychol.*, 1933, 45, 17–52.

FREEMAN, G. L. The optimal muscular tension for various performances. *Amer. J. Psychol.*, 1938, 51, 146–150.

FREEMAN, G. L. The relationship between performance level and bodily activity level. *J. exp. Psychol.*, 1940, 26, 602–608.

FRENCH, E. G. Some characteristics of achievement motivation. *J. exp. Psychol.*, 1955, 50, 232–236.

FRENCH, E. G. Motivation as a variable in work partner selection. *J. abnorm. soc. Psychol.*, 1956, 53, 96–99.

FREUD, A. *The ego and the mechanisms of defense.* New York: Int. Univer. Press, 1946.

FREUD, S. Quelques considérations pour une étude comparative des paralysies motrices organiques et hystériques. *Arch. de Neurologie*, 1893, 26, 29–43.

FREUD, S. *Beyond the pleasure principle.* London: International Psychoanalytic Press, 1922. (a)

FREUD, S. Character and anal erotism. In S. FREUD, *Collected papers.* London: Institute for Psychoanalysis and Hogarth Press, 1925. Vol. 2. (a)

FREUD, S. Instincts and their vicissitudes. In S. FREUD, *Collected papers*. London: Institute for Psychoanalysis and Hogarth Press, 1925. Vol. 4. (b)

FREUD, S. On the transformation of instincts with especial reference to anal erotism. In S. FREUD, *Collected papers*. London: Institute for Psychoanalysis and Hogarth Press, 1925. Vol. 2. (c)

FREUD, S. *Reflections*. (tr. A. A. Brill & A. B. Kuttner). New York: Moffat Yard, 1922. (b)

FREUD, S. Some character types met with in psychoanalysis work. In S. FREUD, *Collected papers*. London: Institute for Psychoanalysis and Hogarth Press, 1925. Vol. 4. (d)

FREUD, S. The infantile genital organization of the libido. In S. FREUD, *Collected papers*. London: Institute for Psychoanalysis and Hogarth Press, 1925. Vol. 2. (e)

FREUD, S. *The ego and the id*. London: Institute for Psychoanalysis and Hogarth Press, 1927.

FREUD, S. *Civilization and its discontents*. New York: Norton, 1930.

FREUD, S. *New introductory lectures to psychoanalysis* (tr. W. J. H. SPROTT). New York: Norton, 1933.

FREUD, S. *The problem of anxiety*. New York: Norton, 1936.

FREUD, S. Three contributions to the theory of sex. In *The basic writings of Sigmund Freud*. New York: Modern Library, 1938.

FREUD, S. *Totem and taboo*. New York: Norton, 1952.

FREUD, S. The history of the psychoanalytic movement. In J. STRACHEY (Ed.), *The standard edition of the complete psychological works*. London: Hogarth Press, 1957. Vol. 14.

FREUD, S. *The psychopathology of everyday life*. (Standard ed.) London: Hogarth Press, 1960. Vol. 6.

FRICK, J. W., GUILFORD, J. P., CHRISTENSEN, P. R., & MERRIFIELD, P. R. A factor-analytic study of flexibility of thinking. *Educ. psychol. Measmt.*, 1959, 19, 469–496.

FROMM, E. *Escape from freedom*. New York: Rinehart, 1941.

FROMM, E. Man for himself. New York: Holt, Rinehart, & Winston, 1947.

FROMM, E. *The sane society*. New York: Rinehart, 1955.

FROMM, E. *The art of loving*. New York: Harper, 1956.

FROMM, E. & MACCOBY, M. *Social character in a Mexican village*. Englewood Cliffs, N.J.: Prentice-Hall, 1970.

FUERST, K. & ZUBEK, J. P. Effects of sensory and perceptual deprivation on a battery of open-ended cognitive tasks. *Can. J. Psychol.*, 1968, 22, 122–130.

GALAMBOS, R. Suppression of auditory nerve activity by stimulation of efferent fibers to cochlea. *J. Neurophysiol.*, 1956, 19, 424–431.

GALAMBOS, R., SHEATZ, G., & VERNIER, V. G. Electro-physiological correlates of a conditioned response in cats. *Science*, 1956, 123, 376–377.

GARLINGTON, W. K. & SHIMOTA, H. The change seeker index: A measure of the need for variable stimulus input. *Psychol. Rep.*, 1964, 14, 191–924.

GELFAND, D. M. The influence of self-esteem on rate of verbal conditioning and social matching behavior. *J. abnorm. soc. Psychol.*, 1962, 65, 259–265.

GENDLIN, E. T. Experiential explication and truth. *J. Existent.*, 1965–66, 6, 131–146.

GENDLIN, E. T. & TOMLINSON, T. M. The process conception and its measurement. In C. R. ROGERS, E. T. GENDLIN, D. J. KIESLER, & C. B. TRUAX (Eds.). *The therapeutic relationship and its impact: A study of psychotherapy with schizophrenics.* Madison, Wis.: University of Wisconsin Press, 1967.

GERARD, H. B. & RABBIE, J. M. Fear and social comparison. *J. abnorm. soc. Psychol.*, 1961, 62, 586–592.

GLESER, G. C. & IHILEVICH, D. An objective instrument for measuring defense mechanisms. *J. consult. clin. Psychol.*, 1969, 33, 51–60.

GLESER, G. C. & SACKS, M. Ego defenses and reaction to stress: A validation study of the Defense Mechanisms Inventory. *J. consult. clin. Psychol.*, 1973, 40, 181–187.

GLOVER, E. Notes on oral character formation. *Int. J. Psychoanal.*, 1925, 6, 131–154.

GLOVER, E. Einige probleme der psychoanalytischen Characterologie. *Internationale Zeitschrift für Psychoanalyse*, 1926, 12, 326–333.

GLOVER, E. The etiology of alcoholism. *Proc. Royal Soc. Med.*, 1928, 21, 1351–1356.

GOLDFRIED, M. R. & D'ZURILLA, T. J. A behavioral-analytic model for assessing competence. In C. D. SPIELBERGER (Ed.), *Current topics in clinical and community psychology.* New York: Academic Press, 1969, pp. 151–196.

GOLDIAMOND, I. Moral behavior: A functional analysis. *Psychology Today*, 1968, P–31, 31–34, 70.

GOLDIAMOND, I. & DYRUD, J. Some applications and implications of behavioral analysis for psychotherapy. In *Research in psychotherapy.* Washington, D.C.: American Psychological Association, 1967. Vol. 3.

GOLDMAN, F. Breastfeeding and character-formation. *J. Pers.*, 1948, 17, 83–103.

GOLDMAN, F. The problem of "orality" and of its origin in early childhood. *J. ment. Sci.*, 1951, 97, 765–782.

GOLDSTEIN, K. *The organism.* Boston: Beacon Press, 1963.

GOOD, L. R. & GOOD, K. An objective measure of the motive to avoid appearing incompetent. *Psychol. Reports*, 1973, 32, 1075–1078.

GORE, P. M. & ROTTER, J. B. A personality correlate of social action *J. Pers.*, 1963, 31, 58–64.

GORNEY, J. E. & TOBIN, S. S. Experiencing and age: Patterns of reminiscence among the elderly. Reported at the 8th International Congress of Gerontology, Washington, D.C., 1969.

GRAFF, R. & BRADSHAW, H. Relationship of a measure of self-actualization to dormitory assistant effectiveness. *J. counsel. Psychol.*, 1970, 17, 502–505.

GRAHAM, W. K. & BALLOUN, J. An empirical test of Maslow's need hierarchy theory. *J. hum. Psychol.*, 1973, 13, 97–108.

GRANICK, S. & SCHEFLEN, N. A. Approaches to reliability of projective tests with special reference to the Blacky Pictures Test. *J. consult. Psychol.*, 1958, 22, 137–141.

GRANIT, R. *Receptors and sensory perception.* New Haven, Conn.: Yale University Press, 1955.

GRANT, C. H. Age differences in self-concept from early adulthood through old age. *Proc. of the 77th Annual Convention of the APA*, 1969, 4, 717–718.

GRAVES, T. D. Time perspective and the deferred gratification pattern in a tri-ethnic community. *Research Report No. 5*, Tri-Ethnic Research Project. Boulder, Colo.: University of Colorado, Institute of Behavioral Science, 1961.

GRAY, J. J. Effect of productivity on primary process thinking and creativity. *Proc. of the 77th Annual Convention of the APA*, 1969, 4, 157–158.

GREEVER, K. B., TSENG, M. S., & FRIEDLAND, B. U. Development of the Social Interest Index. *J. consult. clin. Psychol.*, 1973, 41, 454–458.

GRIFFIN, G. A. & HARLOW, H. F. Effects of three months of total social deprivation on social adjustment and learning in the rhesus monkey. *Child Develpm.*, 1966, 37, 533–547.

GRINKER, R. R. & SPIEGEL, J. P. *Men Under Stress.* Philadelphia: Blakiston, 1945.

GROESBECK, B. L. Toward description of personality in terms of configurations of motives. In J. W. ATKINSON (Ed.), *Motives in fantasy, action, and society.* Princeton, N.J.: Van Nostrand, 1958.

GROSSACK, M., ARMSTRONG, T. & LUSSIEU, G. Correlates of self-actualization. *J. Hum. Psychol.*, 1966, 37.

GUERTIN, W. H. Factor analysing two sorts of Kelly's personal construct productions. *J. pers. Assmt.*, 1973, 37, 69–71.

GUILFORD, J. P. *Personality.* New York: McGraw-Hill, 1959.

GUILFORD, J. P. *The Nature of human intelligence.* New York: McGraw-Hill, 1967.

GUILFORD, J. P. & ZIMMERMAN, W. S. *The Guilford-Zimmerman Temperament Survey.* Beverly Hills, Calif.: Sheridan Supply Co., 1949.

GUILFORD, J. P. & ZIMMERMAN, W. S. Fourteen dimensions of temperament. *Psychol. Monogr.*, 1956, 70, No. 10.

GUINAN, J. & FOULDS, M. Marathon group: Facilitator of personal growth? *J. counsel. Psychol.*, 1970, 17, 145–149.

GURIN, P., LAO, R. C., & BEATTIE, M. Internal-external control in the motivational dynamics of Negro youth. *J. soc. Issues*, 1969, 25, 29–53.

HAAN, N. & DEY, D. A longitudinal study of change and sameness in personality development: Adolescence to later adulthood. *Intnl. J. Aging Hum. Develpmt.*, 1974, 5, 11–39.

HABER, R. N. & ALBERT, R. The role of situation and picture cues in projective measurement of the achievement motive. In J. W. ATKINSON (Ed.), *Motives in fantasy, action, and society.* Princeton, N.J.: Van Nostrand, 1958.

HALL, C. S. & LINDZEY, G. *Theories of personality.* New York: Wiley, 1970.

HALL, C. S. & VAN DE CASTLE, R. L. An empirical investigation of the castration complex in dreams. *J. Pers.,* 1965, 33, 20–29.

HALL, E. Ordinal position and success in engagement and marriage. *J. indiv. Psychol.,* 1965, 21, 154–158.

HALL, E. & BARGER, B. Background data and expected activities of entering lower division students. *Mental Health Project Bulletin No. 7,* May 1964, Gainesville, Fla.: University of Florida. Cited by J. B. WARREN, Birth order and social behavior, *Psychol. Bull.,* 1966, 65, 38–39.

HALL, W. B. & MACKINNON, D. W. Personality inventory correlates of creativity among architects. *J. appl. Psychol.,* 1969, 53, 322–326.

HARLOW, H. F. Learning and satiation of response in intrinsically motivated complex puzzle performance by monkeys. *J. comp. physiol. Psychol.,* 1950, 43. 289–294.

HARLOW, H. F. Mice, monkeys, men, and motives. *Psychol. Rev.,* 1953, 60, 23–32.

HARLOW, H. F., HARLOW, M. K., DODSWORTH, R. O., & ARLING, G. L. Maternal behavior of rhesus monkeys deprived of mothering and peer associations in infancy. *Proc. Amer. Philos. Soc.,* 1966, 110, 58–66.

HARLOW, H. F., HARLOW, M. K. & MEYER, D. R. Learning motivated by a manipulation drive. *J. exp. Psychol.,* 1950, 40, 228–234.

HARRISON, A. A. Response competition and attitude change as a function of repeated stimulus exposure. Unpublished doctoral dissertation, Ann Arbor, Mich.: University of Michigan, 1967.

HARRISON, N. W. & MCLAUGHLIN, R. J. Self-rating validation of the Eysenck Personality Inventory. *Br. J. soc. & clin. Psychol.,* 1969, 8, 55–58.

HARTMANN, H., KRIS, E., & LOEWENSTEIN, R. M. Comments on the formation of psychic structure. In A. FREUD *et al.* (Eds.), *The psychoanalytic study of the child.* New York: International Universities Press, 1947.

HARVEY, J. H. & BARNES, R. Perceived choice as a function of internal-external locus of control. *J. Pers.,* 1974, 42, 437–452.

HAVENER, P. H. & IZARD, C. E. Unrealistic self-enhancement in paranoid schizophrenics. *J. consult. Psychol.,* 1962, 26, 65–68.

HEBB, D. O. Drives and the C.N.S. (conceptual nervous system). *Psychol. Rev.,* 1955, 62, 243–254.

HELSON, R. The heroic, the comic, and the tender: Patterns of literary fantasy and their authors. *J. Pers.,* 1973, 41, 163–184. (a)

HELSON, R. Heroic and tender modes in women authors of fantasy. *J. Pers.,* 1973, 41, 493–512. (b)

HELSON, R. & CRUTCHFIELD, R. S. Creative types in mathematics. *J. Pers.,* 1970, 38, 177–197.

HENDRICK, I. The discussion of the "instinct to master." *Psychoanal. Quart.,* 1943, 12, 561–565.

HERNANDEZ-POEN, R., SCHERRER, H., & JOUVET, M. Modification of electric activity in the cochlear nucleus during "attention" in unanesthetized cats. *Science,* 1956, 123, 331–332.

HEYNS, R. W., VEROFF, J., & ATKINSON, J. W. In J. W. ATKINSON (Ed.), *Motives in fantasy, action, and society.* Princeton, N.J.: Van Nostrand, 1958.

HILGARD, E. R. *Theories of learning.* (2d ed.) New York: Appleton-Century-Crofts, 1956.

HINDE, R. A. & STEVENSON-HINDE, J. (Eds.), *Constraints on learning.* New York: Academic Press, 1973.

HOERMANN, H. & TODT, E. Lärm und Lernen. *Z. exp. angew. Psychol.,* 1960, 7, 422–426.

HOLLANDER, E. P. & WILLIS, R. H. Some current issues in the psychology of conformity and nonconformity. *Psychol. Bull.,* 1967, 68, 62–76.

HOLMES, D. S. Dimensions of projection. *Psychol. Bull.,* 1968, 69, 248–268.

HOUSTON, B. K. & HOLMES, D. S. Effect of avoidant thinking and reappraisal for coping with threat involving temporal uncertainty. *J. pers. soc. Psychol.,* 1974, 30, 382–388.

HOWES, D. & SOLOMON, R. L., A note on McGinnies' emotionality and perceptual defense. *Psychol. Rev.,* 1950, 57, 229–234.

HOWES, D. & SOLOMON, R. L. Visual duration threshold as a function of word probability. *J. exp. Psychol.,* 1951, 41, 401–410.

HULL, C. L. *Principles of behavior.* New York: Appleton-Century-Crofts, 1943.

HULL, C. L. The place of innate individual and species differences in a natural science theory of behavior. *Psychol. Rev.,* 1945, 52, 55–60.

HUNT, H. F. Problems in the interpretation of "experimental neurosis." *Psychol. Rep.,* 1964, 15, 27–35.

HUNT, H. F. Behavior therapy for adults. In ARIETI, S. (Ed.), *American handbook of Psychiatry.* New York: Basic Books, in press.

HUNT, H. F. & DYRUD, J. E. Commentary: Perspective in behavior therapy. *Research in psychotherapy,* 1968, 3, 140–152.

HUNTLEY, C. W. Judgments of self based upon records of expressive behavior. *J. abnorm. soc. Psychol.,* 1940, 35, 398–427.

HYMAN, H. H. & SHEATSLEY, P. B. "The authoritarian personality"—A methodological critique. In R. CHRISTIE & M. JAHODA (Eds.), *Studies in the scope and method of "the authoritarian personality."* New York: Free Press, 1954.

ILARDI, R. & MAY, W. A reliability study of Shostrom's Personal Orientation Inventory. *J. Hum. Psychol.,* 1968, 8, 68–72.

ISAACSON, G. S. & LANDFIELD, A. W. Meaningfulness of personal vs. common constructs. *J. indiv. Psychol.,* 1965, 21, 160–166.

JACKSON, D. N. & MESSICK, S. Content and style in personality assessment. *Psychol. Bull.,* 1958, 55, 243–252.

JACKSON, P. W. & MESSICK, S. The person, the product, and the response: Conceptual problems in the assessment of creativity. *J. Pers.,* 1965, 33, 309–329.

JACOB, P. E. *Changing values in college.* New York: Harper, 1957.

JACOBY, J. Open-mindedness and creativity. *Psychol. Rep.,* 1967, 20, 822–823.

JAMES, W. Internal versus external control of reinforcements as a basic variable in learning theory. Unpublished doctoral dissertation, Columbus, Ohio, Ohio State University, 1957.

JAMES, W. & ROTTER, J. B. Partial and 100% reinforcement under chance and skill conditions. *J. exp. Psychol.*, 1958, 55, 397–403.

JANIS, I. L. Anxiety indices related to susceptibility to persuasion. *J. abnorm. soc. Psychol.*, 1955, 51, 663–667.

JANIS, I. L. & GILMORE, J. B. The influence of incentive conditions on the success of role playing in modifying attitudes. *J. pers. soc. Psychol.*, 1965, 1, 17–27.

JASPER, H. H. Reticular-cortical systems and theories of the integrative action of the brain. In H. F. HARLOW & C. N. WOOLSEY (Eds.), *Biological and biochemical bases of behavior.* Madison, Wis.: University of Wisconsin Press, 1958.

JENKINS, H. M. Effects of the stimulus-reinforcer relation on selected and unselected responses. In R. A. HINDE & J. STEVENSON-HINDE (Eds.), *Constraints on learning.* New York: Academic Press, 1973.

JONES, E. *The life and work of Sigmund Freud.* New York: Basic Books, 1955.

JONES, H. E. Consistency and change in early maturity. *Vit. Hum.*, 1960, 3, 17–31.

JUNG, C. G. *Modern man in search of a soul.* New York: Harcourt, Brace, & World, 1933. (a)

JUNG, C. G. *Psychological types.* New York: Harcourt, Brace, & World, 1933. (b)

JUNG, C. G. The psychology of the unconscious. In H. READ, M. FORDHAM, & G. ADLER (Eds.), *Collected works.* Princeton, N.J.: Princeton University Press, 1953. Vol. 7. (a)

JUNG, C. G. The relations between the ego and the unconscious. In H. READ, M. FORDHAM, & G. ADLER (Eds.), *Collected works.* Princeton, N.J.: Princeton University Press, 1953. (b)

JUNG, C. G. Concerning the archetypes, with special reference to the anima concept. In H. READ, M. FORDHAM, & G. ADLER (Eds.), *Collected works.* Princeton, N.J.: Princeton University Press, 1959. (a)

JUNG, C. G. The archetypes and the collective unconscious. In H. READ, M. FORDHAM & G. ADLER (Eds.), *Collected works.* Princeton, N.J.: Princeton University Press, 1959. Vol. 9. (b)

JUNG, C. G. On psychic energy. In H. READ, M. FORDHAM, & G. ADLER (Eds.), *Collected works.* Princeton, N.J.: Princeton University Press, 1960. Vol. 8. (a)

JUNG, C. G. Synchronicity: An acausal connecting principle. In H. READ, M. FORDHAM, & G. ADLER (Eds.), *Collected works.* Princeton, N.J.: Princeton University Press, 1960. Vol. 8. (b)

JUNG, C. G. The stages of life. In H. READ, M. FORDHAM, & G. ADLER (Eds.), *Collected works.* Princeton, N.J.: Princeton University Press, 1960. Vol. 8. (c)

JUNG, C. G. The theory of psychoanalysis. In H. READ, M. FORDHAM, & G. ADLER (Eds.), *Collected works.* Princeton, N.J.: Princeton University Press, 1961. Vol. 4.

KAGAN, J. Motives and development. *J. pers. soc. Psychol.*, 1972, 22, 51–66.

KAGAN, J. & MOSS, H. A. *Birth to maturity: A study in psychological development.* New York: Wiley, 1962.

KAMIN, L. J., & CLARK, J. W. The Taylor scale and reaction time. *J. abnorm. soc. Psychol.*, 1957, 54, 262–263.

KATKIN, E. S. The Marlowe-Crowne social desirability scale: Independent of psychopathology? *Psychol. Rep.*, 1964, 15, 703–706.

KATZ, D., SARNOFF, I., & McCLINTOCK, C. Ego defense and attitude change. *Hum. Relat.*, 1956, 9, 27–45.

KATZ, I. The socialization of academic motivation in minority group children. In D. LEVINE (Ed.), *Nebraska symposium on motivation.* Lincoln, Neb.: University of Nebraska Press, 1967.

KEEN, E. *Three faces of being: Toward an existential clinical psychology.* New York: Appleton-Century-Crofts, 1970.

KELLY, E. L. Consistency of the adult personality. *Amer. Psychologist*, 1955, 10, 659–681.

KELLY, G. A. *The psychology of personal constructs.* New York: Norton, 1955. Vol. 1.

KELLY, G. A. Europe's matrix of decision. In M. R. JONES (Ed.), *Nebraska symposium on motivation.* Lincoln, Neb.: University of Nebraska Press, 1962.

KENISTON, K. *The uncommitted: Alienated youth in American society.* New York: Harcourt, Brace, & World, 1966.

KIERKEGAARD, S. *The sickness unto death.* New York: Doubleday, 1954.

KLAVETTER, R. & MOGAR, R. Stability and internal consistency of a measure of self actualization. *Psychol. Rep.*, 1967, 21, 422–424.

KLECK, R. E. & WHEATON, J. Dogmatism and responses to opinion-consistent and opinion-inconsistent information. *J. pers. soc. Psychol.*, 1967, 5, 249–252.

KLEIN, E. B. & GOULD, J. Alienation and identification in college women. *J. Pers.*, 1969, 37, 468–480.

KLEIN, M. H., MATHIEU, P. L., GENDLIN, E. T., & KIESLER, D. J. *The Experiencing Scale: A research and training manual.* Madison, Wis.: Wisconsin Psychiatric Institute, 1969. Vol. 1.

KLEINSMITH, L. J. & KAPLAN, S. Paired-associate learning as a function of arousal and interpolated interval. *J. exp. Psychol.*, 1963, 65, 190–193.

KLEINSMITH, L. J. & KAPLAN, S. Interaction of arousal and recall interval in nonsense syllable paired-associate learning. *J. exp. Psychol.*, 1964, 67, 124–246.

KLEITMAN, N. *Sleep and wakefulness.* Chicago: University of Chicago Press, 1939.

KLEITMAN, N. & RAMSAROOP, A. Periodicity in body temperature and heart rate. *Endocrinology*, 1948, 43, 1–20.

KLINE, P. Obsessional traits, obsessional symptoms and anal erotism. *Br. J. med. Psychol.*, 1968, 41, 299–305.

KLINEBERG, S. L. Future time perspective and the preference for delayed reward. *J. pers. soc. Psychol.*, 1968, 8, 253–257.

KLINGER, E. Fantasy need achievement as a motivational construct. *Psychol. Bull.*, 1966, 66, 291–308.

KNAPP, R. Relationship of a measure of self actualization to neuroticism and extraversion. *J. consult. Psychol.*, 1965, 29, 168–172.

KOENIG, F. Definitions of self and ordinal position of birth. *J. soc. Psychol.*, 1969, 78, 287–288.

KOESTLER, A. *The lotus and the robot*. London: Hutchinson, 1960.

KÖHLER, W. *The mentality of apes* (tr. E. WINTER). New York: Harcourt, Brace, 1925.

KONRAD, K. W. & BAGSHAW, M. Effect of novel stimuli on cats reared in a restricted environment. *J. comp. physiol. Psychol.*, 1970, 70, 157–164.

KOUTRELAKOS, J. Authoritarian person's perception of his relationship with his father. *Perceptual mot. Skills*, 1968, 26, 967–973.

KRAMER, E. The Eysenck Personality Inventory and self-ratings of extraversion. *J. proj. Tech. pers. Assess.*, 1969, 33, 59–62.

KRAZNER, L. & ULLMANN, L. P. (Eds.). *Research in behavior modification*. New York: Holt, Rinehart, & Winston, 1965.

KRIS, E. *Psychoanalytic explorations in art*. New York: International Universities Press, 1952.

KUHLEN, R. G. Age differences in personality during adult years. *Psychol. Bull.*, 1945, 42, 333–358.

LACEY, J. I. Individual differences in somatic response patterns. *J. comp. physiol. Psychol.*, 1950, 43, 338–350.

LAUTERBACH, C. G. The Taylor A scale and clinical measures of anxiety. *J. consult. Psychol.*, 1958, 22, 314.

LAZARUS, R. S., ERIKSEN, C. W., & FONDA, C. P. Personality dynamics in auditory perceptual recognition, *J. Pers.*, 1951, 19, 471–482.

LEFCOURT, H. M. Risk-taking in Negro and white adults. *J. Personality & Soc. Psychol.*, 1965, 2, 765–770.

LEFCOURT, H. M. & LADWIG, G. W. The effect of reference group upon Negroes' task persistence in a biracial competitive game. *J. pers. soc. Psychol.*, 1965, 1, 668–671.

LEFCOURT, H. M. & LADWIG, G. W. Alienation in Negro and white reformatory inmates. *J. soc. Psychol.*, 1966, 68, 153–157.

LEHR, U. & RUDINGER, G. Consistency and change of social participation in old age. *Hum. Develpm.*, 1969, 12, 255–267.

LEITH, G. The relationships between intelligence, personality, and creativity under two conditions of stress. *Brit. J. Educat. Psychol.*, 1972, 42, 240–247.

LEMANN, G. F. J. Group characteristics as revealed in sociometric patterns and personality ratings. *Sociometry,* 1952, 15, 7–90.

LEMAY, M. & DAMM, V. The Personal Orientation Inventory as a measure of self actualization of underachievers. *Measurement and Evaluation in Guidance,* 1968, 110–114.

LESSAC, M. S., & SOLOMON, R. L. Effects of early isolation on later adaptive behavior of beagles: A methodological demonstration. *Develop. Psychol.,* 1969, 1, 14–25.

LEVINE, R. *Dreams and deeds: Achievement motivation in Nigeria.* Chicago: University of Chicago Press, 1966.

LIEM, G. R. Performance and satisfaction as affected by personal control over salient decisions. *J. pers. soc. Psychol.,* 1973, 31, 232–240.

LINDZEY, G., HEINEMAN, P. S. Thematic Apperception Test: A note on reliability and situational validity. *J. proj. Tech.,* 1955, 19, 36–42.

LINTON, R. *The cultural background of personality.* New York: Appleton-Century, 1945.

LIVERANT, S. & SCODEL, A. Internal and external control as determinants of decision-making under conditions of risk. *Psychol. Rep.,* 1960, 7, 59–67.

LONGSTRETH, L. E. Birth order and avoidance of dangerous activities. *Develop. Psychol.,* 1970, 2, 154.

LOWELL, E. L. A methodological study of projectively measured achievement motivation. Unpublished master's thesis. Middletown, Conn., Wesleyan University, 1950.

LUNDIN, R. W. *Personality: A behavioral analysis* (2nd Ed.) New York: Macmillan, 1974.

MACKINNON, D. W. Personality and the realization of creative potential. *Amer. Psychologist,* 1965, 20, 273–281.

MACKINNON, D. W. & DUKES, W. Repression. In L. POSTMAN (Ed.), *Psychology in the making.* New York: Knopf, 1962.

MADDI, S. R. Exploratory behavior and variation-seeking in man. In D. W. FISKE & S. R. MADDI (Eds.), *Functions of varied experience.* Homewood, Ill.: Dorsey, 1961. (a)

MADDI, S. R. Unexpectedness, affective tone, and behavior. In D. W. FISKE & S. R. MADDI (Eds.), *Functions of varied experience.* Homewood, Ill.: Dorsey, 1961. (b)

MADDI, S. R. Affective tone during environmental regularity and change. *J. abnorm. soc. Psychol.,* 1961, 62, 338–345. (c)

MADDI, S. R. Humanistic psychology: Allport and Murray. In J. M. WEPMAN & R. W. HEINE (Eds.), *Concepts of personality.* Chicago: Aldine, 1963.

MADDI, S. R. Motivational aspects of creativity. *J. Pers.,* 1965, 33, 330–347.

MADDI, S. R. The existential neurosis. *J. abnorm. Psychol.,* 1967, 72, 311–325.

MADDI, S. R. The seeking and avoiding of variety. Unpublished manuscript. Chicago, 1968. (a)

MADDI, S. R. Meaning, novelty, and affect: Comments on Zajonc's paper. *J. pers. soc. Psychol.,* Monogr. Suppl., 1968, 9, No. 2, 28–30. (b)

MADDI, S. R. The search for meaning. In M. PAGE (Ed.), *Nebraska symposium on motivation*. Lincoln, Neb.: University of Nebraska Press, 1970.

MADDI, S. R. Novelty, meaning, and intrinsic motivation. In H. I. DAY, D. E. BERLYNE & D. E. HUNT (Eds.), *Intrinsic motivation: A new direction in motivation*. Toronto: Holt, Rinehart, & Winston, 1971.

MADDI, S. R. The Alienation Test: A measure of the tendency toward existential sickness. Unpublished manuscript, Chicago, 1975.

MADDI, S. R. & ANDREWS, S. The need for variety in fantasy and self-description. *J. Pers.*, 1966, 34, 610–625.

MADDI, S. R. & BERNE, N. Novelty of productions and desire for novelty as active and passive forms of the need for variety. *J. Pers.*, 1964, 32, 270–277.

MADDI, S. R., CHARLENS, A. M., MADDI, D., & SMITH, A. Effects of monotony and novelty on imaginative productions. *J. Pers.*, 1962, 30, 513–527.

MADDI, S. R. & COSTA, P. T., JR. *Humanism in personology: Allport, Maslow, Murray*. Chicago: Aldine-Atherton, 1972.

MADDI, S. R. & PROPST, B. Activation theory and personality. In S. R. MADDI (Ed.), *Perspectives on personality: A comparative approach*. Boston: Little, Brown, 1971.

MADDI, S. R., PROPST, B., & FELDINGER, I. Three expressions of the need for variety. *J. Pers.*, 1965, 33, 82–98.

MAHONEY, J. & HARTNETT, J. Self-actualization and self-ideal discrepancy. *J. Psychol.*, 1973, 85, 37–42.

MANDLER, G. & KESSEN, W. *The language of psychology*. New York: Wiley, 1959.

MARCIA, J. E. Development and validation of ego-identity status. *J. pers. soc. Psychol.*, 1966, 3, 551–558.

MARSHALL, I. N. Extraversion and libido in Jung and Cattell. *J. analyt. Psychol.*, 1967, 12, 115–136.

MASLING, J., WEISS, L., & ROTHSCHILD, B. Relationships of oral imagery to yielding behavior and birth order. *J. consult. & clin. Psychol.*, 1968, 32, 89–91.

MASLOW, A. H. Deficiency motivation and growth motivation. In M. R. JONES (Ed.), *Nebraska symposium on motivation*. Lincoln, Neb.: University of Nebraska Press, 1955.

MASLOW, A. H. Some basic propositions of a growth and self-actualization psychology. In *Perceiving, behaving, becoming: A new focus for education*. Washington, D.C.: Yearbook of the Association for Supervision and Curriculum Development, 1962.

MASLOW, A. H. A theory of metamotivation: The biological rooting of the value-life. *J. hum. Psychol.*, 1967, 7, 93–127.

MASLOW, A. H. A theory of metamotivation: The biological rooting of the value-life. *Humanities*, 1969, 4, 301–343.

MASSERMAN, J. H. *Behavior and neurosis: An experimental psychoanalytic approach to psychobiological principles.* Chicago: University of Chicago Press, 1943.

MATARAZZO, J. D. & SASLOW, G. Psychological and related characteristics of smokers and nonsmokers. *Psychol. Bull.,* 1960, 57, 493–513.

MAY, R. Contributions of existential psychotherapy. In R. MAY, E. ANGEL, & H. F. ELLENBERGER (Eds.), *Existence: A new dimension in psychiatry and psychology.* New York: Basic Books, 1958.

MCCARROLL, J. E., MITCHELL, K. M., CARPENTER, R. J., & ANDERSON, J. P. Analysis of three stimulation-seeking scales. *Psychol. Rep.,* 1967, 21, 853–856.

MCCLAIN, E. Further validation of the Personal Orientation Inventory: Assessment of the self actualization of school counselors. *J. consult. & clin. Psychol.,* 1970, 35, 21–22.

MCCLEARY, R. A. & LAZARUS, R. S. Autonomic discrimination without awareness, *J. Pers.,* 1949, 18, 171–179.

MCCLELLAND, D. C. *Personality.* New York: Dryden, 1951.

MCCLELLAND, D. C. Risk taking in children with high and low need for achievement. In J. W. ATKINSON (Ed.), *Motives in fantasy, action, and society.* Princeton, N.J.: Van Nostrand, 1958.

MCCLELLAND, D. C. *The achieving society.* Princeton, N.J.: Van Nostrand, 1961.

MCCLELLAND, D. C. Assessing human motivation. New York: General Learning Press, 1971. No. 402IV00. (a)

MCCLELLAND, D. C. Motivational trends in society. New York: General Learning Press, 1971. No. 4020V00. (b)

MCCLELLAND, D. C., ATKINSON, J. W., & CLARK, R. A. The projective expression of needs: III. The effect of ego-involvement success and failure on perception. *J. Psychol.,* 1949, 27, 311–330.

MCCLELLAND, D. C., ATKINSON, J. W., CLARK, R. A., & LOWELL, E. L. *The achievement motive.* New York: Appleton-Century-Crofts, 1953.

MCCLELLAND, D. C., DAVIS, W. N., KALIN, R., & WANNER, II. E. *Alcohol and human motivation.* New York: Free Press, 1971.

MCCLELLAND, D. C., STURR, J. F., KNAPP, R. H., & WENDT, H. W. Obligations to self and to society in the United States and Germany. *J. abnorm. soc. Psychol.,* 1958, 56, 245–255.

MCGINNIES, E. Emotionality and perceptual defense. *Psychol. Rev.,* 1949, 56, 244–251.

MCQUAID, J. A note on trends in answers to Cattell personality questionnaire by Scottish subjects. *Br. J. Psychol.,* 1967, 58, 455–458.

MEDIN, D. L. Role of reinforcement in discrimination learning set in monkeys. *Psychol. Bull.,* 1972, 77, 305–318.

MEDINNUS, G. R. & CURTIS, F. J. The relation between maternal self-acceptance and child acceptance. *J. counsel. Psychol.,* 1963, 27, 542–544.

MEDNICK, M. T. Mediated generalization and the incubation effect as a function of manifest anxiety. *J. abnorm. soc. Psychol.,* 1957, 55, 315–321.

MEGARGEE, E. I. & PARKER, G. V. An exploration of the equivalence of Murrayan needs as assessed by the Adjective Check List, the TAT and Edwards Personal Preference Schedule. *J. clin. Psychol.*, 1968, 24, 47–51.

MEHLMAN, J. The "floating signifier": From Levi-Strauss to Lacan. *Yale French Studies*, 1972, 48, 10–37.

MEHRABIAN, A. & KSIONZKY, S. Models for affiliative and conformity behavior. *Psychol. Bull.*, 1970, 74, 110–126.

MEHRABIAN, A. & RUSSELL, J. A. A measure of arousal seeking tendency. *Environmt. Beh.*, 1973, 5, 315–333.

MELENDY, M. R. *Maiden, wife, and mother: How to attain health, beauty, happiness.* Chicago: Amer. Literary and Musical Assn., 1901.

MELZACK, R. & WALL, P. D. Gate control theory of pain. In A. SOULAIRAC, J. CAHN & J. CHARPENTIER (Eds.), *Pain.* New York: Academic Press, 1968.

MERBAUM, M. The simulation of normal MMPI profiles by repressors and sensitizers. *J. consult. clin. Psychol.*, 1972, 39, 171.

MIKOL, B. The enjoyment of new musical systems. In M. ROKEACH, *The open and closed mind.* New York: Basic Books, 1960.

MILLER, N. E. Liberalization of Basic S-R concepts: Extension to conflict behavior, motivation, and social learning. In S. KOCH (Ed.), *Psychology: A study of science.* New York: McGraw-Hill, 1959. Vol. 2.

MILLER, N. E. & DOLLARD, J. C. *Social learning and imitation.* New Haven, Conn.: Yale University Press, 1941.

MISCHEL, W. Preference for delayed reinforcement: An experimental study of a cultural observation. *J. abn. soc. Psychol.*, 1958, 56, 57–61.

MISCHEL, W. Delay of gratification, need for achievement, and acquiescence in another culture. *J. abn. soc. Psychol.*, 1961, 62, 543–552.

MISCHEL, W. Theory and research on the antecedents of self-imposed delay of reward. In B. A. Maher (Ed.), *Progress in experimental personality research.* Vol. 3. New York: Academic Press, 1966.

MISCHEL, W. *Personality and assessment.* New York: Wiley, 1968.

MISCHEL, W. *Introduction to personality.* New York: Holt, Rinehart, & Winston, 1971.

MISCHEL, W. On the empirical dilemmas of psychodynamic approaches. *J. abn. Psychol.*, 1973, 82, 335–344. (a)

MISCHEL, W. Toward a cognitive social learning reconceptualization of personality. *Psychol. Rev.*, 1973, 80, 252–283. (b)

MISCHEL, W. & EBBESEN, E. Attention in delay of gratification. *J. pers. soc. Psychol.*, 1970, 16, 329–337.

MOOS, R. H. Situational analysis of a therapeutic community milieu. *J. abn. Psychol.*, 1968, 73, 49–61.

MOOS, R. H. Sources of variance in responses to questionnaires and in behavior. *J. abn. Psychol.*, 1969, 74, 405–412.

MOOS, R. H. Differential effects of psychiatric ward settings on patient change. *J. ner. ment. Disease*, 1970, 5, 316–321.

MORGAN, C. D. & MURRAY, H. A. A method for investigating fantasies: The Thematic Apperception Test. *Arch. Neurol. Psychiat.*, 1935, 34, 289–306.

MOSAK, H. H. Life style. In *Techniques for behavior change: Applications of Adlerian theory.* Springfield, Ill.: Charles C Thomas, 1971.

MOWRER, O. H. An experimental analogue of "regression" with incidental observations on "reaction formation." *J. abnorm. soc. Psychol.*, 1940, 35, 56–87.

MOWRER, O. H. *Learning theory and personality dynamics.* New York: Ronald Press, 1950.

MUNROE, R. *Schools of psychoanalytic thought.* New York: Holt, 1955.

MUNSINGER, H. & KESSEN, W. Uncertainty, structure and preference. *Psychol. Monogr.*, 1964, 78, No. 9.

MURRAY, H. A. *Explorations in personality: A clinical and experimental study of fifty men of college age.* New York: Oxford, 1938.

MURRAY, H. A. *Thematic Apperception Test.* Cambridge, Mass.: Harvard University Press, 1943.

MURRAY, H. A. Toward a classification of interaction. In T. PARSONS & E. A. SHILS (Eds.), *Toward a general theory of action.* Cambridge, Mass.: Harvard University Press, 1954.

MURRAY, H. A. Preparations for the scaffold of a comprehensive system. In S. KOCH (Ed.), *Psychology: A study of a science.* New York: McGraw-Hill, 1959. Vol. 3.

MURRAY, H. A. & KLUCKHOHN, C. Outline of a conception of personality. In C. KLUCKHOHN, H. A. MURRAY, & D. M. SCHNEIDER (Eds.), *Personality in nature, society, and culture.* (2d ed.) New York: Knopf, 1956.

MURSTEIN, B. I. The projection of hostility on the Rorschach and as a result of ego-threat. *J. proj. Tech.*, 1956, 20, 418–428.

MURSTEIN, B. I. The relation of the Famous Sayings Test to self- and ideal-self-adjustment. *J. consult. Psychol.*, 1961, 25, 368.

MYERS, I. B. *Manual (1962), the Myers-Briggs type indicator.* Princeton, N.J.: Educational Testing Service, 1962.

NALVEN, F. B. Some perceptual decision-making correlates of repressive and intellectualizing defenses. *J. clin. Psychol.*, 1967, 23, 446–448.

NATSOULAS, T. Converging operations for perceptual defense. *Psychol. Bull.*, 1965, 64, 393–401.

NEUGARTEN, B. L. A developmental view of adult personality. In J. E. BIRREN (Ed.), *Relations of development and aging.* Springfield, Ill.: Charles C Thomas, 1964.

NEUMAN, G. G. & SALVATORE, J. C. The Blacky Test and psychoanalytic theory: A factor-analytic approach to validity. *J. proj. Tech.*, 1958, 22, 427–431.

NICHOLSON, W. M. The influence of anxiety upon learning. *J. Pers.*, 1958, 26, 303–319.

NUNNALLY, J. Visual attention to novel pictures. In H. I. DAY, D. E. BERLYNE, & D. S. HUNT (Eds.), *Intrinsic motivation: A new direction in education.* Toronto: Holt, Rinehart, & Winston, 1971.

O'CONNELL, W. E. The adaptive function of wit and humor. *J. abnorm. soc. Psychol.*, 1960, 61, 263–270.

ODELL, M. Personality correlates of independence and conformity. Unpublished master's thesis, Columbus, Ohio: Ohio State University, 1959.

O'LEARY, J. T. & COBEN, L. A. The reticular core—1957. *Physiol. Rev.*, 1958, 38, 243–276.

ORLOFSKY, J. L., MARCIA, J. E., & LESSER, I. M. Ego identity status and the intimacy versus isolation crisis in young adulthood. *J. pers. soc. Psychol.*, 1973, 27, 211–219.

OSGOOD, C. Studies on the generality of affect meaning systems. *Amer. Psychologist*, 1962, 17, 10–28.

PAGANO, D. Effects of task familiarity on stress responses of repressors and sensitizers. *J. consult. clin. Psychol.*, 1973, 40, 22–28.

PAGE, H. A. & MARKOWITZ, G. The relationship of defensiveness to rating scale bias. *J. Psychol.*, 1955, 40, 431–435.

PAVLOV, I. P. *Conditioned reflexes.* Oxford: Oxford University Press, 1927.

PEABOBY, D. Authoritarianism scales and response bias. *Psychol. Bull.*, 1966, 65, 11–23.

PEARSON, P. H. Openness to experience as related to organismic valuing. *J. Pers.*, 1969, 37, 481–496.

PEARSON, P. H. Relationships between global and specified measures of novelty seeking. *J. consult. & clin. Psychol.*, 1970, 34, 199–204.

PEARSON, P. H. Conceptualizing and measuring openness to experience in the context of psychotherapy. In D. A. WEXLER and LAURA N. RICE (Eds.), *Innovations in client-centered therapy.* New York: Wiley, 1974.

PECK, R. F. & HAVIGHURST, R. J. *The psychology of character development.* New York: Wiley, 1960.

PETERS, R. S. *The concept of motivation.* New York: Humanities Press, 1958.

PETERSEN, R. C. & HERGENHAHN, B. R. Test of cognitive dissonance theory in an elementary school setting. *Psychol. Rep.*, 1968, 22, 199–202.

PETTIT, T. F. Anality and time. *J. consult. & clin. Psychol.*, 1969, 33, 170–174.

PHARES, E. J. Expectancy changes in skill and chance situations. *J. abnorm. soc. Psychol.*, 1957, 54, 339–342.

PHARES, E. J. Perceptual threshold decrements as a function of skill and chance expectancies. *J. Psychol.*, 1962, 53, 399–407.

PHILLIPS, W. S. & GREENE, J. E. A preliminary study of the relationship of age, hobbies, and civil status to neuroticism among women teachers. *J. educ. Psychol.*, 1939, 30, 440–444.

PIERCE, J. V. *The educational motivation of superior students who do not achieve in high school.* Washington, D.C.: U.S. Department of Health, Education, and Welfare, Office of Education, 1959.

PISHKIN, V. & THORNE, F. C. A factorial study of existential state reactions. *J. clin. Psychol.*, 1973, 29, 392–402.

PLATT, J. J. & EISENMAN, R. Internal-external control of reinforcement, time perspective, adjustment, and anxiety. *J. genet. Psychol.*, 1968, 79, 121–128.

POE, C. A. Convergent and discriminant validation of measures of personal needs. *J. educ. Measmt.*, 1969, 6, 103–107.

POSTMAN, L., BRUNER, J. S., & McGINNIES, E. Personal value as selective factors in perception. *J. abnorm. soc. Psychol.*, 1948, 43, 142–154.

POWELL, F. A. Open- and closed-mindedness and the ability to differentiate source and message. *J. abnorm. soc. Psychol.*, 1962, 65, 61–64.

PYRON, B. & KAFER, J. Recall of nonsense and attitudinal rigidity. *J. pers. soc. Psychol.*, 1967, 5, 463–466.

RADLOFF, R. Opinion evaluation and affiliation. *J. abnorm. soc. Psychol.*, 1961, 62, 578–585.

RADO, S. Obsessive behavior. In S. ARIETI (Ed.), *American handbook of psychiatry*. New York: Basic Books, 1959. Vol. 1.

RANK, O. *The trauma of birth*. New York: Harcourt, Brace, 1929.

RANK, O. *Will therapy and truth and reality*. New York: Knopf, 1945.

RAPAPORT, D. The theory of ego autonomy: A generalization. *Bull. of Menninger Clinic*, 1958, 22, 13–25.

RAPHELSON, A. C. The relationships among imaginative, direct verbal, and physiological measures of anxiety in an achievement situation. *J. abnorm. soc. Psychol.*, 1957, 54, 13–18.

RAVEN, B. H. & FISHBEIN, M. Acceptance of punishment and change in belief. *J. abnorm. soc. Psychol.*, 1961, 63, 411–416.

RAZIK, T. A. *Bibliography of creativity studies and related areas*. Buffalo, N.Y.: State University of New York at Buffalo, 1965.

REICH, W. Character formation and the phobias of childhood. *Int. J. Psychoanal.*, 1931, 12, 219–230.

REICH, W. *Charakteranalyse*. Berlin: Selbstverlag des Verfassers, 1933.

REIMANIS, G. Childhood experience memories and anomie in adults and college students. *J. indiv. Psychol.*, 1966, 22, 56–64.

REIMANIS, G. Psychosocial development, anomie, and mood. *J. pers. soc. Psychol.*, 1974, 29, 355–357.

RESTLE, F., ANDREWS, M., & ROKEACH, M. Differences between open- and closed-minded subjects on learning-set and oddity problems. *J. abnorm. soc. Psychol.*, 1964, 68, 648–654.

RHINE, R. J. Some problems in dissonance theory research on information selectivity. *Psychol. Bull.*, 1967, 68, 21–28.

RICE, L. N. & WAGSTAFF, A. K. Client voice quality and expressive style as indexes of productive psychotherapy. *J. consult. Psychol.*, 1967, 31, 557–563.

RIESEN, A. H. Stimulation as a requirement for growth and function in behavioral development. In D. W. FISKE & S. R. MADDI (Eds.), *Functions of varied experience*. Homewood, Ill.: Dorsey, 1961.

ROBINSON, S. A. The development of a female form of the Blacky Pictures. *J. proj. Tech. pers. Assess.*, 1968, 32, 74–80.

ROBINSON, S. A. & HENDRIX, V. L. The Blacky Test and psychoanalytic theory: Another factor-analytic approach to validity. *J. proj. Tech. pers. Assess.*, 1966, 30, 597–603.

ROGERS, C. R. A theory of therapy, personality, and interpersonal relationships, as developed in the client-centered framework. In S. KOCH (Ed.), *Psychology: A study of a science.* New York: McGraw-Hill, 1959. Vol. 3.

ROGERS, C. R. *On becoming a person.* Boston: Houghton Mifflin, 1961.

ROGERS, C. R. Actualizing tendency in relation to "motives" and to consciousness. In M. R. JONES (Ed.), *Nebraska symposium on motivation.* Lincoln, Neb.: University of Nebraska Press, 1963.

ROHRER, J. H. & EDMONSON, M. S. (Eds.), *The eighth generation.* New York: Harper, 1960.

ROKEACH, M. Studies in beauty: II. Some determiners of the perception of beauty in women. *J. soc. Psychol.*, 1945, 22, 155–169.

ROKEACH, M. *The open and closed mind.* New York: Basic Books, 1960.

ROKEACH, M., SWANSON, T. S., & DENNY, M. R. The role of past experience: A comparison between chess players and non-chess players. In M. ROKEACH, *The open and closed mind.* New York: Basic Books, 1960.

ROSEN, B. C. Family structure and achievement motivation. *Amer. Sociological Review*, 1961, 26, 574–585.

ROSENBAUM, M. E., HORNE, W. C., & CHALMERS, D. K. Level of self-esteem and the learning of imitation and non-imitation. *J. Pers.*, 1962, 30, 147–156.

ROSENBERG, L. A. Idealization of self and social adjustment. *J. consult. Psychol.*, 1962, 26, 487.

ROSENBERG, M. J. When dissonance fails: On eliminating evaluation apprehension from attitude measurement. *J. pers. soc. Psychol.*, 1965, 1, 28–42.

ROSENMAN, S. Changes in the representations of self, others and interrelationship in therapy. *J. counsel. Psychol.*, 1955, 2, 271–277.

ROSENOW, C. & WHYTE, A. H. The ordinal position of problem children. *Amer. J. Orthopsychiat.*, 1931, 1, 430–444.

ROSENZWEIG, S. The recall of finished and unfinished tasks as affected by the purpose with which they were performed. *Psychol. Bull.*, 1933, 30, 698.

ROSENZWEIG, S. An experimental study of "repression" with special reference to need-persistive and ego-defensive reactions to frustrations. *J. exp. Psychol.*, 1943, 32, 64–74.

ROSENZWEIG, S. & MASON, G. An experimental study of memory in relation to the theory of repression. *Br. J. Psychol.*, 1934, 24, 247–265.

ROTTER, J. B. *Clinical psychology.* (2nd Ed.) Englewood Cliffs, N.J.: Prentice-Hall, 1964.

ROTTER, J. B. Generalized expectancies for internal versus external control of reinforcement. *Psychol. Monogr.*, 1966, 80 (1, Whole No. 609).

ROTTER, J. B., CHANCE, J. E., & PHARES, E. J. (Eds.), *Applications of a social learning theory of personality.* New York: Holt, Rinehart, & Winston, 1972.

ROTTER, J. B., SEEMAN, M., & LIVERANT, S. Internal versus external control of reinforcements: A major variable in behavior theory. In N. F. WASHBURNE (Ed.), *Decisions, values, and groups.* London: Pergamon Press, 1962, Vol. 2, 473–516.

SALAS, R. G. Some characteristics of the Eysenck Personality Inventory (EPI) found under Australian conditions. *Australian Military Forces Research Report,* 1967, 6, 11 pp.

SAMPSON, E. E. Birth order, need achievement, and conformity. *J. abnorm. soc. Psychol.,* 1962, 64, 155–159.

SAMPSON, E. E. The study of ordinal position: Antecedents and outcomes. In B. A. MAHER (Ed.), *Progress in experimental personality research.* New York: Academic Press, 1965.

SAMUELS, I. Reticular mechanisms and behavior. *Psychol. Bull.,* 1959, 56, 1–25.

SANFORD, N. (Ed.). *The American college.* New York: Wiley, 1962.

SARASON, I. G. The effect of anxiety and two kinds of failure on serial learning. *J. Pers.,* 1957, 25, 383–392. (a)

SARASON, I. G. Effect of anxiety and two kinds of motivating instructions on verbal learning. *J. abnorm. soc. Psychol.,* 1957, 54, 166–171. (b)

SARNOFF, I. Identification with the aggressor: Some personality correlates of anti-Semitism among Jews. *J. Pers.,* 1951, 20, 199–218.

SARNOFF, I. Reaction formation and cynicism. *J. Pers.,* 1960, 28, 129–143.

SARNOFF, I. *Personality: Dynamics and development.* New York: Wiley, 1962.

SARNOFF, I. & CORWIN, S. M. Castration anxiety and the fear of death. *J. Pers.,* 1959, 27, 374–385.

SARNOFF, I. & KATZ, D. The motivational bases of attitude change. *J. abnorm. soc. Psychol.,* 1954, 49, 115–124.

SARTRE, J. P. *Being and nothingness.* New York: Philosophical Library, 1956.

SCHACHTEL, E. G. On alienated concepts of identity. *Amer. J. Psychoanal.,* 1961, 21, 120–131.

SCHACHTER, S. *The psychology of affiliation: Experimental studies of the sources of gregariousness.* Stanford, Calif.: Stanford University Press, 1959.

SCHACHTER, S. Birth order, eminence, and higher education. *Amer. Sociological Review,* 1963, 28, 757–767.

SCHACHTER, S. Birth order and sociometric choice. *J. abnorm. soc. Psychol.,* 1964, 68, 453–456.

SCHAEFER, C. E. The self-concept of creative adolescents. *J. Psychol.,* 1969, 72, 233–242.

SCHAEFFER, D. L. Addenda to an annotated bibliography of the Blacky Test (1949–1967). *J. proj. Tech. pers. Assess.,* 1968, 32, 55–555.

SCHILL, R. Repression-sensitization differences in free-associative sex responses to double-entendre words. *J. clin. Psychol.,* 1969, 25, 368–369.

SCHOENPFLUG, W. Retention and Aktivation bei zusatzlicher Beanspruchung durch koperliche Tatigkeit. *Z. exp. angew. Psychol.,* 1964, 11, 130–154.

SCHOENPFLUG, W. & SCHAEFER, M. Retention and Aktivation bei akustischer Zusatzreizung. *Z. exp. angew. Psychol.,* 1962, 9, 452–464.

SCHOOLER, C. Birth order and schizophrenia. *Archs. gen. Psychiat.,* 1961, 4, 91–97.

SCHOOLER, C. Birth order and hospitalization for schizophrenia. *J. abnorm. soc. Psychol.*, 1964, 69, 574–579.

SCHUBERT, D. S. P. Impulsivity and other personality characteristics of cigarette smokers. *Amer. Psychologist*, 1959, 14, 354–355. (a)

SCHUBERT, D. S. P. Personality implications of cigarette smoking among college students. *J. consult. Psychol.*, 1958, 23, 376. (b)

SCHULBERG, H. Authoritarianism, tendency to agree, and interpersonal perception. *J. abnorm. soc. Psychol.*, 1961, 63, 101–108.

SCHULTZ, D. P. Spontaneous alternation behavior in humans: Implications for psychological research. *Psychol. Bull.*, 1964, 62, 394–400.

SCHWARTZ, B. J. The measurement of castration anxiety over loss of love. *J. Pers.*, 1955, 24, 204–219.

SCHWARTZ, B. J. An empirical test of two Freudian hypotheses concerning castration anxiety. *J. Pers.*, 1956, 24, 318–327.

SCHWARTZ, M. & GAINES, L. Self-actualization and the human tendency for varied experience. *J. pers. Assmt.*, 1974, 38, 423–427.

SEARS, R. R. Experimental studies of projection: I. Attribution of traits. *J. soc. Psychol.*, 1936, 7, 151–163.

SEARS, R. R. *Survey of objective studies of psychoanalytic concepts.* New York: Social Science Research Council, 1943.

SEARS, R. R. Experimental analysis of psychoanalytic phenomena. In J. McV. HUNT (Ed.), *Personality and the behavior disorders.* New York: Ronald Press, 1944, Vol. 1.

SEARS, R. R. Personality. In C. P. STONE & D. W. TAYLOR (Eds.), *Annual review of psychology.* Stanford, Calif.: Annual Reviews, Inc., 1950.

SECHREST, L. The psychology of personal constructs: George Kelly. In J. M. WEPMAN & R. W. HEINE (Eds.), *Concepts of personality.* Chicago: Aldine, 1963.

SECHREST, L. Personal constructs and personal characteristics. *J. indiv. Psychol.*, 1968, 24, 162–166.

SEEMAN, M. Alienation and social learning in a reformatory. *American Journal of Sociology*, 1963, 69, 270–284.

SEEMAN, M. & EVANS, J. Alienation and learning in a hospital setting. *American Sociological Review*, 1962, 27, 772–782.

SELLS, S. B. & ROFF, M. Peer acceptance-rejection and birth order. *Amer. Psychologist*, 1963, 18, 355.

SHAPIRO, K. J. & ALEXANDER, I. E. Extraversion-introversion, affiliation, and anxiety. *J. Pers.*, 1969, 37, 387–406.

SHARPE, D. & VINEY, L. Weltanschaung and the Purpose in Life Test. *J. clin. Psychol.*, 1973, 29, 489–491.

SHEERER, E. Analysis of the relationship between acceptance of and respect for self and acceptance of and respect for others. *J. consult. Psychol.*, 1949, 13, 169–175.

SHEFFIELD, F. D. & ROBY, T. B. Reward value of a non-nutrient sweet taste. *J. comp. physiol. Psychol.*, 1950, 43, 471–481.

SHLIEN, J. M. The self-concept in relation to behavior: Theoretical and empirical research. *Relig. Educ.*, 1962. Research Supplement.

SHLIEN, J. M. Phenomenology and personality. In J. M. WEPMAN & R. W. HEINE (Eds.), *Concepts of personality.* Chicago: Aldine, 1963.

SHOSTROM, E. An inventory for the measurement of self actualization. *Educ. psychol. Measmt.*, 1965, 24, 207–218.

SHOSTROM, E. *Manual for the Personal Orientation Inventory (POI): An inventory for the measurement of self actualization.* San Diego: Educational and Industrial Testing Service, 1966.

SHOSTROM, E. & KNAPP, R. The relationship of a measure of self actualization (POI) to a measure of pathology (MMPI) and to therapeutic growth. *Amer. J. Psychother.*, 1966, 20, 193–202.

SIDIS, B. An experimental study of sleep. *J. abnorm. Psychol.*, 1908, 3, 1–32, 63–96, 170–207.

SIEGAL, S. Certain determinants and correlates of authoritarianism. *Genetic psychol. Monogr.*, 1954, 49, 187–229.

SIEGELMAN, M. "Origins" of extraversion-introversion. *J. Psychol.*, 1968, 69, 85–91.

SILVERMAN, I. Defense of dissonance theory: Reply to Chapanis & Chapanis *Psychol. Bull.*, 1964, 62, 205–209.

SIMMEL, G. *The sociology of Georg Simmel.* Glencoe, Ill.: Free Press, 1950.

SKINNER, B. F. *The behavior of organisms: An experimental analysis.* New York: Appleton-Century-Crofts, 1938.

SKINNER, B. F. Are theories of learning necessary? *Psychol. Rev.*, 1950, 57, 193–216.

SKINNER, B. F. *Science and human behavior.* New York: Macmillan, 1953.

SKINNER, B. F. *Verbal behavior.* New York: Appleton-Century-Crofts, 1957.

SKINNER, B. F. *Cumulative Record.* New York: Appleton-Century-Crofts, 1961.

SKINNER, B. F. *Beyond freedom and dignity.* New York: Knopf, 1971.

SKINNER, N. F., HOWARTH, E. & BROWNE, J. A. Note on the role of neuroticism and extraversion in the "nice personality" stereotype. *Psychol. Rep.*, 1970, 26, 445–446.

SLETTOO, R. F. Sibling position and juvenile delinquency. *American Journal of Sociology*, 1934, 39, 657–669.

SMART, R. G. Alcoholism, birth order, and family size. *J. abnorm. soc. Psychol.*, 1963, 66, 17–23.

SMITH, M. B. Explorations in competence: A study of Peace Corps teachers in Ghana. *Amer. Psychologist*, 1966, 21, 555–566.

SMITH, M. B. Competence and socialization. In J. A. CLAUSEN (Ed.), *Socialization and society.* Boston: Little, Brown, 1968.

SOLOMON, R. L. & HOWES, D. Word frequency, personal values, and visual duration thresholds. *Psychol. Rev.*, 1951, 58, 256–270.

SONTAG, S. Against interpretation. New York: Noonday, 1961.

Spence, K. W. The postulates and methods of "behaviorism." *Psychol. Rev.,* 1948, 55, 67–78.

Spence, K. W. & Spence, Janet T. Sex and anxiety differences in eyelid conditioning. *Psychol. Bull.,* 1966, 65, 137–142.

Spielberger, C. D. Role of awareness in verbal conditioning. In C. W. Eriksen (Ed.), *Behavior and awareness.* Durham, N.C.: Duke University Press, 1962.

Spranger, E. Types of men (tr. by W. Pigors). Halle, Germany: Niemeyer, 1928.

Staffieri, J. R. Birth order and creativity. *J. clin. Psychol.,* 1970, 26, 65–66.

Stein, M. I. Creativity. In E. F. Borgatta & W. W. Lambert (Eds.), *Handbook of personality theory and research.* Chicago: Rand McNally, 1968.

Stephenson, W. The significance of Q-technique for the study of personality. In M. L. Reymert (Ed.), *Feelings and emotions: The Mooseheart symposium.* New York: McGraw-Hill, 1950.

Stephenson, W. *The study of behavior: Q-technique and its methodology.* Chicago: University of Chicago Press, 1953.

Stern, G. G. *Preliminary record: Activities index-College Characteristics Index.* Syracuse, N.Y.: Syracuse University Psychol. Res. Center, 1958.

Stevenson, I. Is the human personality more plastic in infancy and childhood? *Amer. J. Psychiat.,* 1957, 14, 152–161.

Stewart, R. A. C. Academic performance and components of self actualization. *Percept. mot. Skills,* 1968, 26, 918.

Stock, D. An investigation into the interrelations between self-concept and feelings directed toward persons and groups. *J. consult. Psychol.,* 1949, 13, 176–180.

Stotland, E. & Cottrell, N. B. Self-esteem, group interaction, and group influence on performance. *J. Pers.,* 1961, 29, 273–284.

Strickland, B. R. The prediction of social action from a dimension of internal-external control. *J. soc. Psychol.,* 1965, 66, 353–358.

Strong, E. K., Jr. Vocational interests of men and women. Stanford, Calif.: Stanford University Press, 1943.

Suinn, R. M. The relationship between self-acceptance and acceptance of others: A learning theory analysis. *J. abnorm. soc. Psychol.,* 1961, 63, 37–42.

Swanson, G. E. Some effects of member object-relationships on small groups. *Hum. Relat.,* 1951, 4, 355–380.

Symonds, P. M. *From adolescent to adult.* New York: Columbia University Press, 1961.

Taft, R. The validity of the Barron ego-strength scale and the Welsh anxiety index. *J. consult. Psychol.,* 1957, 21, 247–249.

Taft, R. Extraversion, neuroticism and expressive behavior: An application of Wallach's moderator effect to handwriting analysis. *J. Pers.,* 1967, 35, 570–584.

TAULBEE, E. S. & STENMARK, D. E. The Blacky Pictures Test: A comprehensive annotated and indexed bibliography (1949–1967). *J. proj. Tech. pers. Assess.*, 1968, 32, 102–137.

TAYLOR, C. W. *Creativity: Progress and potential.* New York: McGraw-Hill, 1963.

TAYLOR, J. A. A personality scale of manifest anxiety. *J. abnorm. soc. Psychol.*, 1953, 48, 285–290.

TAYLOR, J. A. The effects of anxiety level and psychological stress on verbal learning. *J. abnorm. soc. Psychol.*, 1958, 57, 55–60.

TAYLOR, J. A. & SPENCE, K. W. The relationship of anxiety level to performance in serial learning. *J. exp. Psychol.*, 1952, 44, 61–64.

TERMAN, L. M. & MILES, G. C. *Sex and personality.* New York: McGraw-Hill, 1936.

TERMAN, L. M. & ODEN, M. H. *The gifted group at mid-life.* Palo Alto, Calif.: Stanford University Press, 1959.

THAYER, R. E. Measurement of activation through self-report. *Psychol. Rep.*, 1967, 20, 663–678.

THOMPSON, W. R. & SCHAEFER, T. Early environmental stimulation. In D. W. FISKE & S. R. MADDI (Eds.), *Functions of varied experience.* Homewood, Ill.: Dorsey, 1961.

THORNDIKE, E. L. & LORGE, I. *The teacher's word book of 30,000 words.* New York: Teachers College, Columbia University, 1944.

THORNE, F. C. The Existential Study: A measure of existential status. *J. clin. Psychol.*, 1973, 29, 387–392.

THORNE, R. C. & PISHKIN, V. The Existential Study. *J. clin. Psychol.*, 1973, 29, 389–410.

TILLICH, P. *The courage to be.* New Haven, Conn.: Yale University Press, 1952.

TITTLER, B. A behavioral approach to the measurement of openness to experience. *J. pers. Assmt.*, 1974, 38, 335–340.

TODER, N. L. & MARCIA, J. E. Ego identity status and response to conformity pressure in college women. *J. pers. soc. Psychol.*, 1973, 26, 287–294.

TRAPP, E. P. & KAUSLER, P. H. Test anxiety level and goal-setting behavior. *J. consult. Psychol.*, 1958, 22, 31–34.

TRIBICH, D. & MESSER, S. Psychoanalytic character type and status of authority as determiners of suggestibility. *J. consult. clin. Psychol.*, 1974, 42, 842–848.

TUDDENHAM, R. D. Constancy of personality ratings over two decades. *Genet. Psychol. Monogr.*, 1959, 60, 3–29.

TURNER, R. H. & VANDERLIPPE, R. H. Self-ideal congruence as an index of adjustment. *J. abnorm. soc. Psychol.*, 1958, 57, 202–206.

ULEMAN, J. S. A new TAT measure of the need for power. Unpublished doctoral dissertation, Harvard University, 1965.

ULRICH, R. E. & AZRIN, N. H. Reflective fighting in response to aversive stimulation. *J. exp. anal. Behav.*, 1962, 5, 511–520.

ULRICH, R. E., DULANEY, S., KUCERA, T., & COLASACCO, A. Side effects of aversive control. In R. M. GILBERT & J. D. KEEHN (Eds.), *Schedule effects.* Toronto: University of Toronto Press, 1972.

VEROFF, J. A. A scoring manual for the power motive. In J. W. ATKINSON (Ed.), *Motives in fantasy, action, and society.* Princeton, N.J.: Van Nostrand, 1958.

VERPLANCK, W. S. Burryhus F. Skinner. In W. K. ESTES, S. KOCH, K. MACCORQUODALE, P. E. MEEHL, C. G. MUELLER, W. N. SCHOENFELD, & W. S. VERPLANCK (Eds.), *Modern learning theory.* New York: Appleton-Century-Crofts, 1954.

VIDULICH, R. N. & KAIMAN, I. P. The effects of the information source status and dogmatism upon conformity behavior. *J. abnorm. soc. Psychol.*, 1961, 63, 639–642.

VITZ, P. C. Affect as a function of stimulus variation. *J. exp. Psychol.*, 1966, 68, 176–183.

VROOM, V. H. Projection, negation, and self-concept. *Hum. Relat.*, 1959, 12, 235–244.

WALKER, E. L. & TARTE, R. D. Memory storage as a function of arousal and time with homogeneous and heterogeneous lists. *J. verbal Learn. & verbal Behav.*, 1963, 2, 113–119.

WALLACH, M. A. & GAHM, R. C. Personality functions of graphic construction and expansiveness. *J. Pers.*, 1960, 28, 73–88.

WAREHIME, R. G. & FOULDS, M. L. Social desirability response sets and a measure of self-actualization. *J. hum. Psychol.*, 1973, 13, 89–95.

WAREHIME, R. G., ROUTH, D. K., & FOULDS, M. L. Knowledge about self-actualization and the presentation of self as self-actualized. *J. pers. soc. Psychol.*, 1974, 30, 155–162.

WARREN, J. R. Birth order and social behavior. *Psychol. Bull.*, 1966, 65, 38–49.

WATERMAN, C. K., BUEBEL, M. E., & WATERMAN, A. S. Relationship between resolution of the identity crisis and outcomes of previous psychosocial crises. *Proc. of the Annual Convention of the APA*, 1970, 5, 467–468.

WATERS, L. K. Stability of Edwards PPS need scale scores and profiles over a seven-week period. *USNAMI Report*, 1967, 1019, 6 pp.

WATSON, J. B. *Behaviorism.* New York: Norton, 1924.

WATSON, J. B. *Psychology from the standpoint of a behaviorist.* (3d ed.) Philadelphia: Lippincott, 1929.

WATTS, A. W. *The way of Zen.* New York: Pantheon, 1957.

WEBER, M. *The Protestant ethic and the spirit of capitalism* (tr. by T. PARSONS). New York: Scribner, 1930.

WEIGEL, R. G. & FRAZIER, J. E. The effects of "feeling" and "behavior" instructions on responses to the Edwards Personal Preference Schedule. *J. educ. Measmt.*, 1968, 5, 337–338.

WELKER, W. I. Escape, exploratory, and food seeking responses of rats in a novel situation. *J. comp. physiol. Psychol.*, 1959, 52, 96–111.

WELLS, W. & GOLDSTEIN, R. Sears' study of projection: Replications and critique. *J. soc. Psychol.*, 1964, 64, 169–179.

WESSMAN, A. E. & RICKS, D. F. *Mood and personality.* New York: Holt, Rinehart & Winston, 1966.

WEXLER, D. Self actualization and cognitive processes. *J. consult. clin. Psychol.*, 1974, 42, 47–53.

WHERRY, R. J. & WATERS, L. K. Motivational constructs: A factorial analysis of feelings. *Educ. psychol. Measmt.*, 1968, 28, 1035–1046.

WHITE, R. W. Motivation reconsidered: The concept of competence. *Psychol. Rev.*, 1959, 66, 297–333.

WHITE, R. W. Competence and the psychosexual stages of development. In M. R. JONES (Ed.), *Nebraska symposium on motivation.* Lincoln, Neb.: University of Nebraska Press, 1960.

WHITE, R. W. Competence and the psychosexual stages of development. In D. W. FISKE & S. R. MADDI (Eds.), *Functions of varied experience.* Homewood, Ill.: Dorsey, 1961.

WHITE, R. W. Ego and reality in psychoanalytic theory. *Psychol. Issues*, 1963, 3, 1–210.

WINTER, D. G. The need for power in college men. In D. C. McCLELLAND, W. N. DAVIS, R. KALIN, & H. E. WANNER (Eds.), *Alcohol and human motivation.* New York: Free Press, 1971.

WINTER, D. G. *The power motive.* New York: Free Press, 1973.

WITKIN, H. A., DYK, R. B., FATERSON, H. F., GOODENOUGH, D. R., & KARP, S. A. *Psychological differentiation.* New York: Wiley, 1962.

WITKIN, H. A., LEWIS, H. B., HERTZMAN, M., MACHOVER, K., MEISSNER, P. B., & WAPNER, S. *Personality through perception.* New York: Harper, 1954.

WOLFF, P. H. Observations on newborn infants. *Psychosom. Med.*, 1959, 21, 110–118.

WOLPE, J. *Psychotherapy by reciprocal inhibition.* Stanford: Stanford University Press, 1958.

WOLPE, J. *The practice of behavior therapy.* New York: Pergamon, 1969.

WORTHEN, R. & O'CONNELL, W. E. Social interest and humor. *Int. J. soc. Psychiatry*, 1969, 15, 179–188.

WRIGHT, B. P. Selfishness, guilt feelings, and social distance. Unpublished doctoral dissertation, State University of Iowa, Iowa City, 1940.

WRIGHTSMAN, L. S., JR. Effects of waiting with others on changes in level of felt anxiety. *J. abnorm. soc. Psychol.*, 1960, 61, 216–222.

YARROW, L. J. Maternal deprivation: Toward an empirical and conceptual reevaluation. *Psychol. Bull.*, 1961, 58, 459–490.

YERKES, R. M. & DODSON, J. D. The relation of strength of stimulus to rapidity of habit formation. *J. comp. neurol. Psychol.*, 1908, 18, 459–482.

YUFIT, R. I. Variations of intimacy and isolation. *J. proj. pers. Assess.*, 1969, 33, 49–58.

ZACCARIA, J. S. & WEIR, W. R. A comparison of alcoholics and selected samples of non-alcoholics in terms of a positive concept of mental health. *J. soc. Psychol.*, 1967, 71, 151–157.

ZAGONA, S. V. & ZURCHER, L. Participation, interaction, and role behavior in groups selected from the extremes of the open-closed cognitive continuum. *J. Psychol.*, 1964, 58, 225–264.

ZAGONA, S. V. & ZURCHER, L. A. The relationship of verbal ability and other cognitive variables to the open-closed cognitive dimension. *J. Psychol.*, 1965, 60, 213–219.

ZAJONC, R. B. Attitudinal effects of mere exposure. *J. pers. soc. Psychol.*, *Monogr. Suppl.*, 1968, 9, No. 2.

ZEIGARNIK, B. Über das Behalten von erledigten und unerledigten Handlungen. *Psychol. Forsch.*, 1927, 9, 1–85.

ZUCKER, R. A., MANOSEVITZ, M., & LANGON, R. I. Birth order, anxiety, and affiliation during a crisis. *J. pers. soc. Psychol.*, 1968, 8, 354–359.

ZUCKERMAN, M., KOLIN, E. A., PRICE, L., & ZOOB, I. Development of a sensation-seeking scale. *J. consult. Psychol.*, 1964, 28, 477–482.

ZUCKERMAN, M., PERSKY, H., MILLER, L., & LEVIN, B. Contrasting effects of understimulation (sensory deprivation) and overstimulation (high stimulus variety). *Proceedings of the 77th Annual Convention of the APA*, 1969, 4, 319–320.

APPENDIX OF THEORETICAL SUMMARIES

FREUD'S THEORY

˙Core of personality

CORE TENDENCY: *To maximize instinctual gratification, while minimizing punishment and guilt* (called the reality principle). This is a compromise necessitated by the inevitable conflict between the individual (whose instincts are selfish) and society (which aims at the common good). The reality principle involves *secondary* process thinking, which is characterized by formulating and testing strategies for maximizing instinctual gratification while minimizing punishment and guilt.

CORE CHARACTERISTICS:

Id: Consists of the *instincts,* which are the original contents of mind. All instincts have their *source* in the biological (metabolic) requirements of the organism, and derive their *energy* from this source. The *aim* of all instincts is tension reduction (or satisfaction), which is achieved by obtaining objects appropriate to the source and aim. Instincts function according to the *pleasure principle,* or tendency to maximize instinctual gratification without regard for external reality. The pleasure principle involves *primary process* thinking, in which imagined objects give hallucinatory (and therefore only partial) satisfaction and tension reduction. All men possess life, death, and sexual instincts with the last being by far the most important.

Ego: With experience, a portion of the person's mind becomes differentiated for the purpose of facilitating reality principle functioning, through secondary process thinking. The major function of the ego is defensive, in that it permits only the forms and portions of instincts unlikely to engender punishment and guilt to remain in consciousness. The reality principle is largely engineered by the defensive process, which is itself unconscious.

649

Superego: Is a portion of the mind, differentiated from the ego, which contains the traditional *values* and *taboos* of society as interpreted to the child by his parents. It is the superego that makes *guilt* possible, which is the internal version of *punishment*. The values and taboos set restrictions on the forms of instinctual gratification that can be sought. When some instinctual impulse threatens to produce punishment or guilt, *anxiety* occurs as a warning. Some form of *defensiveness* occurs in order to avoid the anxiety by removing the instinctual impulse from consciousness. As conflict between id and either society or superego is inevitable, all behavior is defensive.

Development

PSYCHOSEXUAL STAGES:
>   *Oral* (first year of life), in which the erogenous zone is the mouth, and the primary activities are *receiving* (oral incorporative) and *taking* (oral aggressive). Feeding is the important area of conflict.
>   *Anal* (second year of life), in which the erogenous zone is the anus, and the primary activities are *giving* (anal expulsive) and *withholding* (anal retentive). Bowel training is the important area of conflict.
>   *Phallic* (third through fifth year of life), in which the erogenous zone is the genitals, and the primary activities involve *heterosexualizing interaction*. This is the time of the Oedipus conflict, when the child vies with the same-sexed parent for the affection of the opposite-sexed parent. Especially important for the boy is *castration anxiety*, and for the girl is *penis envy*.
>   *Latency* (sixth year through puberty), in which the sexual instinct is dormant, and the child is learning skills not directly related to sexuality.
>   *Genital* (puberty to death), characterized by mature sexuality that combines all that is learned in the pregenital stages and relies primarily upon *intercourse* and *orgasm*. The person reaching genitality is fully able to *love* and *work*.

FIXATION: When the inevitable conflict encountered at each psychosexual stage is minimal in intensity, the stage is successfully traversed. But when the parents intensify the conflict, by *depriving* or *indulging* the child unduly or inconsistently, growth is arrested through the occurrence of massive defensiveness aimed at avoiding anxiety through avoiding conflict. This arresting of growth is called *fixation*, and it signifies that the activities of the psychosexual stage involved will remain especially important to the person, even after he has achieved puberty.

Periphery of personality

CHARACTER TYPES COMPRISED OF TRAITS: The types are expressive, in adulthood, of the activities and conflicts of the various psychosexual stages of development, and *defenses* common to those stages.
>   *The Oral Character* has, as its major defenses, *projection* (attributing to others an objectionable trait that you really possess), *denial* (failing to

perceive some threatening object or event in the external world), and *introjection* (incorporating another person in order to avoid threat posed by him or one's own instincts), and some of its typical traits are *optimism-pessimism, gullibility-suspiciousness, manipulativeness-passivity,* and· *admiration-envy.*

The *Anal Character* has, as its major defenses, *intellectualization* (substituting a fictitious, socially acceptable reason for the genuine, instinctual reason behind one's wishes and actions), *reaction formation,* (substituting for one's true wishes, the directly opposite wishes), *isolation* (severing the connecting links normally present between the cognitive and emotional components of wishes, so that something of their true nature can remain conscious without a concomitant sense of threat), and *undoing* (certain thoughts and actions are engaged in so as to cancel out, or atone for, threatening thoughts or actions that have previously occurred), and some of its typical traits are *stinginess-overgenerosity, stubbornness-acquiescence, orderliness-messiness,* and *precision-vagueness.*

The *Phallic Character* has, as its major defense, *repression* (the active debarring from consciousness of instinctual wishes and actions of a threatening nature), and some of its typical traits are *vanity-self-hatred, pride-humility, blind courage-timidity, stylishness-plainness,* and *chastity-promiscuity.*

The *Genital Character* has, as its major defense, *sublimation* (changing the object of the sexual instinct so that it is more socially acceptable than the original, but in no other way blocking the instinct), and its traits indicate full socialization, adjustment and potency.

MURRAY'S THEORY

Core of personality

CORE TENDENCY: Similar to Freud. The possibility is raised that not all functioning is determined by the attempt to avoid conflict between individual and society.

CORE CHARACTERISTICS:

Id: Similar to Freud, but with addition that not all of the instincts are selfish and socially deleterious in nature.

Ego: Similar to Freud, but with considerable elaboration of nondefensive processes whereby the socially acceptable instincts can be vigorously expressed. These nondefensive ego processes include such cognitive and actional procedures as *rational thought* and *accurate perception.*

Superego: Similar to Freud, but with proviso that the values and taboos it contains are not fixed in childhood. Following childhood, one's peers and even the literature one reads can influence the superego.

Development

PSYCHOSEXUAL STAGES: Similar to Freud, but with the addition of two more stages, as follows:

Claustral (intrauterine period of life), in which there is no clearly definable erogenous zone, but there is passive dependency on mother.

Eurethral (between oral and anal stages), in which the urinary apparatus is the erogenous zone, and the primary activities involve urinary display.

FIXATION: Similar to Freud.

Periphery of personality

COMPLEXES: Similar to Freud's character types, with addition of two types corresponding to the two psychosexual stages that have been added.

Claustral Complex: The major defense is *denial,* and the traits are expressive of *passivity* and *withdrawal.*

Eurethral Complex: Major defenses resemble the anal character type, and traits stress *competitiveness* or *acquiescence.*

NEEDS: A major contribution of uncertain relation to the rest of the theory is the concept of need, which is defined as an entity that organizes perception, apperception, intellection, conation, and action in such a way as to transform in a certain direction an existing, unsatisfying situation. A list of 40 needs (e.g., achievement, power, affiliation, nurturance) is offered, along with several overlapping classifications of their functions and attributes. Needs are triggered by *press,* or environmental forces, real or perceived, that have arousing properties. Associated with the need concept, is the *need-integrate,* or set of stable values and action patterns that are learned as a function of need-expression.

ERIKSON'S THEORY

Core of personality

CORE TENDENCY: Similar to Freud. But there is definite emphasis upon some proportion of functioning that is not determined by the attempt to avoid conflict between individual and society.

CORE CHARACTERISTICS:

Id: Similar to Freud.

Ego: Similar to Freud, but with considerable elaboration of ego processes (such as rational thought and realistic perception) that are unrelated to the conflict between id and society. Ego is believed to be partially innate, and to have something like its own instincts.

Superego: Similar to Freud.

Development

PSYCHOSEXUAL STAGES: Similar to Freud, but with biological sexuality de-emphasized in favor of the psychosocial features of conflict between child and parents. Sees development as a process extending throughout life, which is divided into either periods or stages.

FIXATION: Similar to Freud.

Trust *v. Mistrust* (similar to Freud's oral stage), in which the amount of conflict determines whether the positive is learned.

Autonomy *v. Shame and Doubt* (similar to Freud's anal stage), in which the amount of conflict determines whether the positive or negative pole is learned.

Initiative and Responsibility *v. Guilty Functioning* (similar to Freud's phallic stage), in which the amount of conflict determines whether the positive or negative pole is learned.

Industry *v. Inferiority* (similar to Freud's latency stage), in which the amount of conflict determines whether the positive or negative pole is learned.

Identity *v. Role Diffusion* (puberty to the end of adolescence), in which conflict is produced by the socially imposed task of becoming an independent and effective adult, and the difficulty for the adolescent of performing this task. Again, the amount of conflict determines whether the positive or negative pole is learned.

Intimacy *v. Isolation* (young adulthood period), in which conflict is produced by the socially imposed task of developing close and comprehensive relationships, and the difficulty of so doing. Amount of conflict determines whether the positive or negative pole is learned.

Generativity *v. Stagnation* (middle adulthood), in which conflict is produced by socially imposed task of foregoing one's own immediate concerns in favor of fostering children and others, and the difficulty in doing this. Amount of conflict determines whether the positive or negative pole is learned.

Ego Integrity *v. Despair* (middle adulthood through death), in which conflict is produced by the decrease in important social and biological roles as old age approaches, and the difficulty in accepting this. Amount of conflict determines whether the positive or negative pole is learned.

Periphery of personality

Erikson is not explicit, but presumably assumes *character types* comprised of combinations of the sets of *traits* related to the eight stages of development. As development continues throughout life, one must know not only a person's history of fixation but also his general age, in order to express his personality. For example, a person in late adulthood who had not experienced fixations would show ego integrity, generativity, intimacy, identity, industry, initiative, autonomy, and trust, whereas a person also without fixations but only in young adulthood would probably not yet show generativity and ego integrity. Whenever a fixation occurs, it is likely to jeopardize sound development in subsequent stages as well. Thus, if a young adult shows isolation, rather than intimacy, it is likely that he will also show at least one negative quality relevant to earlier stages.

RANK'S THEORY

Core of personality

CORE TENDENCY: To minimize the fear of life while at the same time minimizing the fear of death. As these two fears are inherent, and opposed, conflict is inevitable, and compromise must be sought.

CORE CHARACTERISTICS: Fear of life, where life refers to the inevitable process of separation and individualization, starting with being born, and continuing through being weaned, locomoting independently, leaving the home for school, etc. *Fear of death,* where death refers to the inherent tendency toward union, fusion, and dependency. The *will,* or organized sense of who and what you are that in its most vigorous form if not defensive, functions to establish a basis for minimizing both the life and death fears.

Development

COUNTERWILL AND WILL: Soon after birth, the child begins to differentiate between himself and others, and develops a rudimentary form of the will. This rudimentary form is the *counterwill,* and involves the child's learning that he can say no to the pressures of adults and his own impulses. If this negativistic counterwill shatters union between child and parents, the result will be *guilt* (a specialized expression of fear of life). But if union between child and parent is not shattered, counterwill matures into will. No precise developmental stages are specified.

Periphery of personality

PERSONALITY TYPES COMPRISED OF TRAITS:

The *Artist* expresses ideal development, in which the fears of life and death are effectively minimized and will is strong. Characterized by high degree of *differentiation* and *integration* of thoughts, feelings, and actions; *intimacy* without slavish loyalties or concern for propriety; products are *unusual* but also *useful.*

The *Neurotic Man* expresses the tendency toward separation but has denied the tendency toward union, and shows counterwill more than will. He has committed himself to the pain of separation from the herd, but has not, like the artist, also won through to constructive interactions with the world. He is *hostile, negativistic, arrogant, isolationistic, critical of others, guilty,* etc. When developing counterwill, he was made to feel wrong and unworthy.

The *Average Man* expresses the tendency toward union but has denied the tendency toward separation. Out of fear of life, he never entertains the possibility of his own individuality. He is *conforming, dependable, superficial, suggestible,* and *dissatisfied.* The developmental handicap is an overwhelming negative response of parents to first expressions of counterwill.

ANGYAL'S THEORY

Core of personality

CORE TENDENCY: *The attempt to maximize both the expression of autonomy and the expression of surrender.* Autonomy and surrender are inherent and opposing tendencies, so conflict is inevitable and compromise must be sought.

CORE CHARACTERISTICS: *Autonomy* refers to the separation from others and the physical environment, with emphasis on independence and aloofness. *Surrender* refers to functioning leading to merger or union with other people, ideas, or the inanimate environment, with emphasis on dependency. Expressing both characteristics leads to simultaneous differentiation and integration. Relevant to Angyal's theorizing about the interaction between the person and his environment is the concept of *biosphere*, which encompasses individuals and their world. The personality is one component of the biosphere. The *symbolic self* is the sum total of the person's self-conceptions, but little specification of its content is available.

Development

No specific position is taken.

Periphery of personality

Although the distinction is made between periphery and core, little specification of periphery is available. Of possible relevance is the notion of *dimensions* (which may be somewhat like traits). A *vertical dimension* refers at one pole to concrete, overt behavior, and at the other to deep, underlying forces. A *progressive dimension* comprises a series of surface actions, which are organized in such fashion as to bring the person nearer to a goal. A *transverse dimension* involves the coordination of discrete acts into a larger, better integrated, and more effective behavior unit (such as the type, perhaps).

BAKAN'S THEORY

Core of personality

CORE TENDENCY: *The attempt to maximize the expression of both agency and communion.* Agency and communion are inherent, opposed tendencies, so conflict is inevitable and compromise must be sought.

CORE CHARACTERISTICS: *Agency* refers to the separation from others and the physical environment, with emphasis upon manipulativeness. *Communion* refers to merging with or joining other people, ideas, or the inanimate environment, with emphasis upon unity.

Development

No specific position taken.

Periphery of personality

No formal position taken, although implicit emphasis is put upon the importance of living according to the compromise involving expression of both agency and communion. The result is simultaneous differentiation and integration. When agency is expressed, with communion denied, the end result is psychological or physical illness.

JUNG'S THEORY

Core of personality

CORE TENDENCY: The tendency toward attainment of selfhood. Selfhood represents a balance between the opposing forces of personality, and includes both conscious and unconscious material. Energy concepts instrumental in achieving selfhood are the *principle of equivalence* (if the value of any aspect of personality increases or decreases, this shift will be compensated for by an opposite shift in another aspect), and the *principle of entropy* (the distribution of energy in the personality seeks an equilibrium or balance). Of uncertain relationship to the rest is the *transcendent function,* the aim of which is to integrate personality elements into an overall whole.

CORE CHARACTERISTICS: The *ego* (or conscious, individualistic mind), which is in conflict with the *personal unconscious* (formed of socially unacceptable mental content that was once conscious but has been forced out of awareness by defenses), and the *collective unconscious* (a communal, species memory, never achieving consciousness, representing the accumulated experiences of mankind and possibly even subhuman life). The collective unconscious is comprised of archetypes, or essences (universal forms) that predispose toward characteristically human thoughts and feelings. Although these thoughts and feelings can become conscious, the underlying archetypes cannot. Major archetypes are the *shadow* (the animalistic possibilities of man), the *anima* (the feminine possibility in men), the *animus* (the masculine possibility in women), the *persona* (the conventional mask adopted by persons in the face of social pressures), and the *self* (a conglomerate of all the opposing forces in a person).

Development

There is little emphasis on stages, though a distinction is made between early life and later adulthood. In early life, sexuality and the individualistic concerns of the ego are dominant. In later adulthood, there is a shift to spirituality and the universal emphases of the collective unconscious.

Concepts employed in understanding development are *causality* (influence on behavior of the past) v. *teleology* (influence on behavior of the anticipated future), *progression* (forward thrust) v. *regression* (shrinking to a safe past), and *sublimation* (energy transformed from primitive to cultural and spiritual concerns) v. *repression* (defensive blocking of consciousness and energy.

Periphery of personality

PERSONALITY TYPES COMPRISED OF FUNCTIONS AND MODES:
The *introversive-rational* type is oriented toward the inner world of experience (introversion) and emphasizes either the thinking or feeling modes of function (both are considered rational in that they involve evaluation of experience). Subtypes are introversive-thinking, and introversive-feeling.

The *extroversive-rational* type is oriented toward the outer world of experience (extroversion) and emphasizes either thinking or feeling, leading to subtypes as above.

The *introversive-irrational* type is oriented toward the inner world of experience (introversion) and emphasizes either the sensing or intuiting modes of function (both are considered irrational in that they passively record but do not evaluate experience). Subtypes are introversive-sensing and introversive-intuiting.

The *extroversive-irrational* type is oriented toward the outer world of experience (extroversion) and emphasizes either sensing or intuiting, leading to subtypes as above.

The ideal peripheral personality is *selfhood*, which involves a kind of transcendence of the other personality types such that introversion-extroversion and rational-irrational modes are balanced. Selfhood can be approached, but never completely attained.

ROGER'S THEORY

Core of personality

CORE TENDENCY: The tendency to actualize one's inherent potentialities. This tendency serves to maintain and enhance living not only for the individual but for his species as well. As there is nothing in inherent potentialities unacceptable to society, conflict is not inevitable. The actualizing tendency, as stated above, is common to all living things. In humans, the tendency takes the additional form of *the attempt to* actualize the self (discussed below).

CORE CHARACTERISTICS: Important in the *self-actualization tendency* are the *need for positive regard*, the *need for positive self-regard,* and the *self*. Both needs are offshoots of the self-actualizing tendency. The need for positive regard (from other people) renders the person influenceable by social approval and disapproval. The self (concept) refers to the person's conscious sense of who and what he is. The need for positive self-regard refers to the satisfaction involved in finding your experience of yourself consistent with your self-concept.

Development

No development stages are specified. In general, the important consideration is whether the person receives *unconditional positive regard* (basic, complete acceptance, and respect) or *conditional positive regard* (acceptance of some and rejection of other behaviors) from the significant others. If unconditional positive regard is received, then the self-concept reflects all that there is in the inherent potentialities (the self is considered *congruent* with the potentialities). But if the person encounters conditional positive regard, he will develop *conditions of worth* (evaluative notions concerning which of his behaviors are worthy and which unworthy). The self-concept will have been socially determined, and therefore is *incongruent* with the inherent potentialities. In order that this incongruence not become conscious, and hence the source of *anxiety* (concerning unworthiness, *defenses* are instituted. Defensive functioning involves either *repression* or *distortion*.

Periphery of personality

PERSONALITY TYPES COMPRISED OF TRAITS:
The *Fully Functioning Person* (or ideal person) has received unconditional positive regard. Hence, he has no conditions of worth, no defensiveness, and congruence between self and potentialities. He is characterized by *openness to experience* (emotional depth and reflectiveness), *existential living* (flexibility, adaptability, spontaneity, and inductive thinking), *organismic trusting* (intuitive living, self-reliance, confidence), *experiential freedom* (subjective sense of free will), and *creativity* (penchant for producing new and effective ideas and things).
The *Maladjusted Person,* has received conditional positive regard. Therefore he has *conditions of worth, incongruence* between self and potentialities, *defensiveness.* Also, he *lives according to a preconceived plan* rather than existentially, *disregards his organism* rather than trusting it, feels *manipulated* rather than free, and is *common and conforming* rather than creative.
For all his emphasis upon individuality, Rogers specifies only these two personality types. Subclassifications within each broad category might be possible if the contents of inherent potentialities were stated.

MASLOW'S THEORY

Core of personality

CORE TENDENCIES: The push toward actualization of inherent potentialities and *the push to satisfy needs ensuring physical and psychological survival.* The actualizing tendency leads to the enhancement of life (and is called *growth motivation*), whereas the survival tendency merely ensures the maintenance of life (and is called *deprivation motivation*). Although these tendencies are hierarchically organized, such that the survival tendency must be satisfied before the actualization tendency can be strongly expressed, they are not really in conflict with each other.

CORE CHARACTERISTICS: Associated with the survival tendency are *physiological needs* (food, water, etc.), *safety needs* (avoidance of pain), *needs for belongingness and love* (intimacy, gregariousness, identification), and *esteem needs* (the approval of self and others). Each of these needs becomes important only when those preceding it on the list are satisfied. When all the needs associated with survival are satisfied, those associated with actualization become salient. They are the *need for self-actualization* (emphasis upon special capabilities of people), and the *need for cognitive understanding* (emphasis upon information and stimulation hunger).

Development

Not much specification, though what there is agrees with Rogers. If the survival tendency is not blocked by other people, then the actualization tendency will be vigorously expressed. Blockage leads to defense.

Periphery of personality

PERSONALITY TYPE COMPRISED OF TRAITS AND VALUES: The *Self-Actualized Person* (has had satisfaction of the survival tendency) is characterized by *realistic orientation; acceptance* of self, others, and natural world; *spontaneity; task-orientation* (rather than self-preoccupation); *sense of privacy; independence;* vivid *appreciativeness; spirituality* that is not necessarily religious in a formal sense; sense of *identity with mankind;* feelings of *intimacy* with a few loved ones; democratic values; recognition of the *difference between means and ends; humor* that is philosophical rather than hostile; *creativeness;* and *nonconformism.*

ADLER'S THEORY

Core of personality

CORE TENDENCY: *To strive toward superiority or perfection.* This tendency applies not only to functioning as an individual, but as a member of society as well. Hence, there is no necessary conflict between the person and his society. An earlier form of the core tendency, *will to power,* had more competitive implications.

CORE CHARACTERISTICS: The bases of the perfection tendency are *organ inferiorities* (actual physical weaknesses and incapacities), *feelings of inferiority* (psychic states of inferiority regardless of physical condition), and *compensation* (the attempt to overcome real or imagined inferiorities). The direction of the compensations can be seen by the nature of the inferiorities, but also by the ideals of perfect living (which are called *fictional finalisms*). There is also the somewhat mysterious notion of *creative self,* which essentially expresses the person's capability of exercising free will to transcend the forces acting upon him.

Development

No stages are postulated. Instead, there is emphasis upon *family constellation* and *family atmosphere. Family constellation* refers to the sociological facts of the family as they effect each member. Included are such matters as ordinal position of the child, and presence or absence of the father. Family atmosphere refers more to the quality of emotional relationship among family members. Family constellation effects development by giving the child a particular set of problems (e.g., only child, or oldest child) with which to cope. Family atmosphere influences whether the child is active or passive, constructive or destructive in striving toward perfection. Cooperative atmospheres of mutual trust and respect encourage constructiveness, whereas the opposite atmosphere encourages destructiveness. Family emphasis upon personal initiative encourages activeness, whereas the opposite atmosphere encourages passiveness.

Periphery of personality

STYLES OF LIFE COMPRISED OF FICTIONAL FINALISMS AND TRAITS:
The *Active-Constructive Style* includes the fictional finalism of *service,* and the set of traits than can be summarized as *ambitiousness* or orientation toward success. This style may be the Adlerian ideal.
The *Passive-Constructive Style* includes the fictional finalism of *attention-getting,* and the set of traits summarized as *charm* or receiving special attention for what one is rather than for what one does. This style is also considered desirable.
The *Active-Destructive Style* includes the fictional finalisms of abrogation of *power,* achievement of *revenge,* and the bid to be *left alone.* The traits include *being a nuisance, rebelliousness, viciousness,* and *degeneration.*
The *Passive-Destructive Style* includes the fictional finalisms already mentioned for the Active-Destructive Style, but differs in including the traits of *laziness, stubbornness, passive aggression,* and *despair.*

WHITE'S THEORY

Core of personality

CORE TENDENCY: Discussed as *the attempt to produce effects through one's actions* (*effectance motivation*), and as the *attempt to achieve compe-*

tence in one's functioning (competence motivation). Probably effectance motivation occurs first, and becomes, with maturation, competence motivation.

CORE CHARACTERISTICS: Associated with effectance motivation is the requirement of the nervous system for *information* or stimulation. Associated with competence motivation is *actual competence* and *sense of competence,* though it is not yet clear what role in personality these characteristics play.

Development

Not specified, though White adopts some of the most psychosocial (least biological) features of Erikson's views on the eight stages of man.

Periphery of personality

Not specified extensively, though Erikson's emphases on trust v. mistrust, etc., are partially endorsed.

ALLPORT'S THEORY

Core of personality

CORE TENDENCIES: To function in a manner expressive of the self or proprium (called propriate functioning), and *to satisfy biological survival needs (called opportunistic functioning).* The self is phenomenologically defined, and functioning in terms of it is considered more important, human, and extraordinary than it is to function in terms of survival needs. There is little real conflict between the two tendencies. The survival tendency must be satisfied first, but once it is, the attempt to express the self becomes paramount.

CORE CHARACTERISTICS: Opportunistic functioning involves biological characteristics as *needs for food, water, air,* etc. Propriate functioning includes *sense of body, self-identity, self-esteem, self-extension, rational coping, self-image, and propriate striving.* Propriate functioning is *proactive* (influences the world), whereas opportunistic functioning is *reactive* (is influenced by the world).

Development

No specific stages are postulated. It is assumed that the organism is opportunistic at birth, and that it requires nurturance and affection. If the biological needs are satisfied easily, then propriate functioning develops vigorously. The first signs of a sense of body begin to develop by the end of the first year. The second and third years see the beginnings of self-identity and then self-image, and from 6 to 12, the rational coping qualities of the proprium become apparent. In adolescence, propriate striving is in increasing evidence. Although the various propriate functions begin their development at different times, they all act inter-dependently by the time adulthood is reached. All this presupposes nurturance and support of the child early in life. If this does not occur, then propriate development will not be vigorous, and opportunistic functioning will continue to be important in adulthood. The process of shifting from opportunistic to propriate functioning involves the principle of *functional autonomy,* which indicates that a behavior pattern originally instrumental to satisfaction of a biological need can persist as a fully independent aspect of living even after the biological need is no longer an important force.

Periphery of personality

No typology is offered. The major concrete peripheral characteristic is the PERSONAL DISPOSITION, which is a generalized neuro-psychic structure (peculiar to the individual), with the capacity to render many stimuli functionally equivalent, and to initiate and guide consistent (equivalent) forms of adaptive and stylistic behavior. Personal dispositions can be primarily *dynamic* (motivational) or *expressive* (stylistic). Personal dispositions are virtually unique to particular individuals, being expressive of individuality. In studying personal dispositions, Allport advocates the *morphogenic* (idiographic) approach, in which laws applying to individuals rather than groups are sought. Of secondary importance is the concept of *common trait,* an abstraction that describes the average rather than individual case. To study common traits, one adopts a *nomothetic* approach, the aim of which is laws arrived at by generalizing across people.

With the strong emphasis upon individuality, it is not surprising that little specification of content for personal dispositions is offered. The closest Allport comes to content specification is in his criteria of maturity, which are enduring *extensions of the self,* techniques for *warm relating to others* (such as tolerance), stable *emotional security* or self-acceptance, habits of *realistic perception, skills* and *problem-centered-ness,* established *self-objectification* in the form of *insight* and *humor,* and a *unifying philosophy of life* including particular *value orientations,* differentiated *religious sentiment,* and a generic, *personalized conscience.* These criteria of maturity seem to be the results, in stable aspects of behavior, of expressing the propriate functions.

FROMM'S THEORY

Core of personality

CORE TENDENCY: The attempt to express one's human nature. Man's human nature is radically different from his animal nature. Yet, the two are not really in conflict, first, because man's animal nature is the least important thing about him, and the second, because his animal nature is usually satisfied in a continuing way.

CORE CHARACTERISTICS: The content of human nature is expressed as the *needs for relatedness* (to be in contact with people and physical nature), *transcendence* (to be separate from other people and things), *rootedness* (to have a sense of belongingness), *identity* (to know who and what one is), and *frame of reference* (to have a stable way of perceiving and comprehending the world).

Development

There are three types of relationship between parents and child: *symbiotic relatedness*, in which the people are related, but never attain independence; *withdrawal-destructiveness*, in which there is a negative relatedness or distance and indifference; and *love*, in which there is mutual respect, support, and appreciation. Development is more a function of the type of relationship between child and parents, than of stages.

Periphery of personality

ORIENTATIONS (OR TYPES) COMPRISED OF TRAITS:
The *Receptive Orientation* or type stems from the masochistic patterns of behavior learned by the child who is the passive party in a symbiotic relationship with his parents. In this orientation, the person feels the source of all good to be outside himself, and expects to receive things passively. Typical traits show *passivity, lack of character, submissiveness,* and *cowardliness.*

The *Exploitative Orientation* stems from the sadistic behavior patterns learned by the child who is the dominant party in a symbiotic relationship with the parents. In this orientation, the person believes the source of all good to be outside himself, but does not expect to receive it so much as take it forcibly. Typical traits show *aggression, egocentrism, conceit, arrogance,* and *seductiveness.*

The *Hoarding Orientation* stems from the behavior pattern of destructiveness learned by the child who is reacting to parental withdrawal in the withdrawal-destructiveness type of relationship. In this orientation, there is little faith in anything new to be obtained from the outside world; security is based on hoarding and saving what one already has. Typical traits are *stinginess, unimaginativeness, suspiciousness, stubbornness, and possessiveness.*

The *Marketing Orientation* stems from the behavior pattern of withdrawal learned by the child who is reacting to parental destructiveness in the withdrawal-destructiveness type of relationship. In this orientation, one experiences oneself as a commodity obeying the laws of supply and demand, and has the values of the marketplace. Typical traits are *opportunism, inconsistency, aimlessness, lack of principle, relativism, wastefulness.*

The *Productive Orientation* stems from the behavior patterns learned through a love relationship with the parents. In this orientation, the person values himself and others for what they are, and experiences security and inner peace. Typical traits reflect the potentially useful aspects of the other orientations (e.g., *modesty, adaptability, trust, activeness, pride, confidence, practicality, patience, loyalty, flexibility, openmindedness, experimenting spirit.* Clearly, the productive orientation is Fromm's ideal.

EXISTENTIAL PSYCHOLOGY

Core of personality

CORE TENDENCY:

To Achieve Authentic Being: Being signifies the special quality of human mentality (aptly called *intentionality*), that makes of life a series of decisions, each involving an alternative precipitating the person into an unknown future, and an alternative pushing him back into a routine, predictable past. Choosing the unknown future brings *ontological anxiety*, whereas choosing the safe status quo brings *ontological guilt* (sense of missed opportunity). Authenticity involves accepting this painful state of affairs, and finding the *courage* (through a sense of human dignity) to persist in the face of ontological anxiety and choose the future, thereby minimizing ontological guilt.

CORE CHARACTERISTICS: Being-in-the-world emphasizes the unity of person and environment, since, in this heavily phenomenological position, both are personally or subjectively defined. Being-in-the-world has three components: *Umwelt* (the construed biological and physical world), *Mitwelt* (the construed social world), and *Eigenwelt* (the internal dialogue of relationship to oneself). It is assumed that behind these three components stand man's inherent biological, social, and psychological (symbolization, imagination, and judgment) needs.

Development

No specific position taken beyond the statement that parental and school conditions stimulating psychological (symbolization, imagination, and judgment) expression, in the context of acceptance of biological and social sides of life, is ideal. Nonideal development fails to accept or punishes psychological (and perhaps also biological and social) expression.

Periphery of personality

PERSONALITY TYPES EMPHASIZING SELF-DEFINITION AND WORLD VIEW:

The *individualist*, or ideal person, defines himself as someone with a mental life through which he can understand and influence his social and biological experiences. In his world view, he sees society as the creation of men and properly in their service. His functioning has unity, and shows originality and change. His biological and social experiencing shows subtlety, taste, intimacy, and love. Although he experiences doubt (ontological anxiety) as a natural concommitant of being his own measure of meaning, he does not let this emotion undermine his decision-making process. This personality type is the outcome of ideal development and expresses man's inherent biological, social, and psychological needs fully.

The *conformist* defines himself as nothing more than a player of social roles and an embodiment of biological needs. In effect, he inhibits expression of symbolization, imagination, and judgment, which has the effect of rendering his functioning fragmentary and stereotyped. His biological experiencing is isolated and gross, his social experiencing is contractual rather than intimate, and he feels worthless and insecure. In his world view, he stresses materialism and pragmatism. This type is the outcome of nonideal development, and represents a predisposition to existential sickness, which predisposition becomes an actuality when environmental stresses occur that are sufficient to disconfirm the self-definition and world view inherent in conformism.

KELLY'S THEORY

Core of personality

CORE TENDENCY: The attempt to predict and control the events one experiences. The model adopted for understanding man is that of the scientist, construing events and subjecting the constructs thus developed to test, retaining those that are confirmed and rejecting or changing those that are disconfirmed.

CORE CHARACTERISTICS: Constructs are abstractions or generalizations from concrete experience, and all have the form of a dichotomy with the two poles having opposite meaning (e.g., good-bad). Constructs are organized into *construction systems* on the basis of two hierarchical principles: A construct may be superordinate to another because each pole of the subordinate construct forms a part of the context for the two poles of the superordinate; An entire construct may fit in one pole of another construct, without relevance to the remaining pole.

In anticipating events, one selects the constructs that seem relevant, and then chooses which of the poles of the relevant constructs he will apply. Choosing the pole of the construct is called the *elaborate choice,* and it reflects deciding upon the alternative through which one anticipates the greater possibility for extension and definition of one's construction system.

Although constructs that are disconfirmed by actual events are changed or discarded, Kelly is not explicit about the procedure of testing constructs. But he does indicate something of the emotional conditions surrounding construct disconfirmation and change. *Anxiety* is the awareness that the events with which one is confronted lie outside the predictive capabilities of one's construction system. *Hostility* is the continued effort to extort validational evidence in favor of a social prediction that has already been recognized as a failure. *Guilt* is the awareness of dislodgement of the self from one's core role structure.

Development

There is no consideration of development, aside from the statements concerning the construing of events, and the changing of disconfirmed constructs. The nature of significant relationships in childhood and adulthood is not considered of importance.

Periphery of personality

There is no specification of typical constructs or organization of constructs into personal styles. Some differentiations concerning constructs are offered, however, that could be of use in understanding individual differences. Constructs differ in their degree of *permeability* (hitherto unencountered events can be subsumed within a construct if it is permeable) and *preemptiveness* (a preemptive construct renders the events it subsumes unavailable for subsumption within other constructs). In addition, constructs can be *preverbal* (having no consistent word symbols to represent them), *comprehensive* (subsuming a wide variety of events), *incidental* (subsuming a narrow variety of events), *superordinate* (including other constructs as one of their elements), *subordinate* (being included as an element of other constructs), and *loose* (leading to varying predictions while still maintaining their identity).

McCLELLAND'S THEORY

Core of personality

CORE TENDENCY: To minimize large discrepancies between expectation and occurrence, while maximizing small discrepancies between expectation and occurrence. People are perceived as craving small degrees of unpredictability, in order to offset boredom, and avoiding large degrees of unpredictability, in order to avoid threat.

CORE CHARACTERISTICS: Expectancies are cognitive units, referring to what you believe will be the content and timing of events in the future. *Positive* (pleasurable) and *negative* (displeasurable) *affect* (emotion), are inherent reactions to small and large discrepancies between expectation and occurrence, respectively. Also on an inherent basis, positive affect leads to *approach* whereas negative affect leads to *avoidance.*

Development

There is little emphasis upon stages. More simply, the developmental position is that if the parents arrange to make most of the child's experiences, in a particular area of endeavor, small rather than large discrepancies, then the child will learn stable patterns of approach behavior for that area. If large discrepancies predominate, what will be learned are stable patterns of avoidance behavior. If there is little discrepancy at all, the child will be indifferent to the area.

Periphery of personality

For concrete peripheral characteristics, MOTIVES, TRAITS, and SCHEMATA are offered. The *motive* is a strong effective association characterized by an anticipatory goal reaction and based on past association of certain cues with positive or negative affect. There are *approach motives,* in which the person tries to act in such fashion that his anticipation will indeed become a reality, and *avoidance motives,* in which the person works to keep his anticipation from becoming a reality. Approach motives are the stable behavior patterns learned on the basis of a predominance of small discrepancies between expectation and occurrence. Avoidance motives are the result of large discrepancies between expectation and occurrence. McClelland adopts Murray's needs (e.g., achievement, affiliation, power), postulating an approach and an avoidance version of each one.

The *trait* is a learned tendency in a person to react as he has reacted more or less successfully in the past in similar situations when similarly motivated. The trait is much like the habit, and is not considered motivational because it leads to repetitive rather than goal-directed behavior. It is not clear how the trait is developed, and it almost certainly does not express the core tendency mentioned above. No list of traits is offered.

The *schema* is a unit of cognition or mentation, which symbolizes past experience. Three major classes of schemata are *ideas, values,* and *social roles.* For content, McClelland suggests that ideas and values importantly concern *economic, aesthetic, social, political, religious,* and purely *theoretical* realms. Social roles can be understood as involving *age, sex, family position, occupation,* and *association group membership.* The manner in which schemata are developed is not clearly specified, although they are considered cultural knowledge communicated socially. They also do not seem expressive of the core tendency mentioned above.

No personality types are postulated.

FISKE'S AND MADDI'S THEORY

Core of personality

CORE TENDENCY: The attempt to maintain the level of activation to which one is accustomed (that is characteristic of one). At any given moment, activation may be higher or lower than that which is customary, leading to an avoidance of or search for additional activation.

CORE CHARACTERISTICS: Activation refers on the psychological side to excitement or tension, and on the physiological side to the state of

excitation in a postulated brain center. *Customary* or *characteristic activation* refers to the typical levels of activation experienced by a person over the course of many days. The level of activation at any time is determined by the *impact of stimulation,* by which is meant the degree of *intensity, meaningfulness,* and *variety* of stimulation emanating from *internal* and *external sources.*
When the actual level of activation has fallen below that which is customary, *impact-increasing behavior* occurs. When the actual level of activation is above what is customary, *impact-decreasing behavior occurs.*

Development

No specific developmental statements are made. But it is assumed that early experience contributes to the development of a customary level of activation. People will differ in the amount of activation they require, depending upon their customary level of activation. High-activation requirements will lead to development of *needs* for stimulus *intensity, meaningfulness,* or *variety.* Low-activation requirements will lead to *fears* of stimulus *intensity, meaningfulness,* or *variety.* Further, it is assumed that some people learn to *anticipate* activation requirements well (through an activeness trait), whereas others are frequently in the position of having to *correct* (through a *passiveness trait*) for discrepancies between actual and customary activation levels. The former people show simultaneously increasing differentiation and integration of thoughts, feelings and actions (future impact is increased by differentiation and decreased by integration). Also, it is assumed that some people learn to rely upon external sources of stimulation, whereas other people rely upon internal sources.

Periphery of personality

PERSONALITY TYPES COMPRISED OF MOTIVES AND TRAITS:
The *High-Activation Person* with *active* and *external* traits will be a "go-getter," seeking out challenges to meet in the physical and social environment. He will be energetic and voracious in his appetites. If he also has a high *need for meaningfulness,* he will be a pursuer of causes and problems. But if he has a high *need for intensity,* he may pursue action and tumult per se. And if he has a high *need for variety,* he will show curiosity, adventurousness, and impulsiveness.
The *High-Activation Person* with *active* and *internal* traits will pursue impact through thinking, daydreaming, responding to challenges posed by limitations of mind and body, without much regard for the tangible affairs of the external world. He will be subtle and complex. With a *high need for meaningfulness,* he will lead the life of the mind. With a high *need for intensity,* he will pursue sensations and emotions. With a high *need for variety,* he will strive for originality in some creative endeavor.
The *Low-Activation Person* with *active* and *external traits* will be the eternal conservationist, bent on heading off social and physical disorganization and conflict through negotiation and control. He will tend

to be a conformist, and show simplicity in his tastes. If he also has a high *fear of meaningfulness*, he will try to oversimplify problems and avoid ambiguity. With a high *fear of intensity*, he will exert a dampening effect on vigorous, disorganized external events. If he has a high *fear of variety*, he will seek to force routine on the environment, preferring the familiar to the new.

The *Low-Activation Person* with *active* and *internal* traits will be conservative with his own organism by advocating the golden mean, being careful to avoid excesses and indulgences of any kind. He will be simple, uncomplex, devoid of inconsistencies. With a high *fear of meaningfulness*, he will show absence of detailed or diverse thoughts and daydreams. With a high *fear of intensity*, he will have an especially ascetic emphasis about him. With a high *fear of variety*, he will force himself to function consistently and stably, in a manner devoid of flamboyance.

For all of the personality types mentioned above, there are counterparts in which the passive rather than the active trait occurs. All these passive personality types will seem similar to those with the active trait in stated aims, values, and interests. But, on finer analysis, those with the passive trait emerge as somewhat unable to practice what they preach. If they have high-activation requirements, they will be consumers rather than producers of impact. They will frequently be in the uncomfortable position of having to correct for activation levels that have become too low. If they are low in activation requirements, they will not actively and effectively manipulate the world or themselves to keep impact low. Rather they will just try to renounce stimulation, ending frequently in the uncomfortable position of having to correct for activation levels that have become too high.

MODERATE BEHAVIORISM

Core of personality

CORE TENDENCY:
  To Reduce Tension or General Drive: Tension is defined as the somatic effect of drives.

CORE CHARACTERISTICS: The *primary drives* (e.g., hunger, thirst, sex, pain avoidance, curiosity), which are biological in nature, and the satisfaction of which is consistent with physical survival. *General drive* is the tension from all drives at any given time. Also relevant are the *primary reinforcements*, which are the rewards and punishments corresponding to the primary drives (e.g., food, water, sexual experience, cessation of pain, information). The social learning variant is now emphasizing memory and choice, as human capabilities.

Development

No stages are specified. Development amounts to learning, which is defined as an increase in the probability of a response in the presence of a particular stimulus. This increase in probability occurs when the response is followed by a reinforcement. In effect, tension reduction can be brought about by performance of the response. *Resistence to extinction,* a major measure of the strength of what is learned, refers to the number of times a learned response will occur when it has ceased to lead to reinforcement. The social learning variant emphasizes imitation learning, in which learning takes place through observation and without a response being necessary. Whether what is learned will be acted upon depends upon the reward or punishment the model received.

Periphery of personality

For concrete peripheral characteristics, there are *habits, secondary drives,* and *secondary reinforcements.* A habit is a stable stimulus-response bond having been established by the regular occurrence of reinforcement. Through *stimulus generalization,* a learned response can occur in the presence of stimuli similar to (but not identical with) the original stimulus. Through *response generalization,* responses similar to (but not identical with) the original learned response can occur in the presence of the original stimulus. A *secondary drive* (e.g., anxiety) occurs when the stimulus conditions which have regularly been associated with primary drive arousal take on arousing properties themselves. A *secondary reinforcement* occurs when the stimulus conditions which have regularly been associated with primary reinforcement take on reinforcing properties. Although both secondary drives and reinforcements are learned, they can also mediate further learning.

RADICAL BEHAVIORISM

Core of personality

CORE TENDENCY: None· specified.
CORE CHARACTERISTICS: None specified.

Development

Operant conditioning refers to the process of bringing a voluntary ("spontaneously occurring") response under stimulus control. Learning has taken place when a particular stimulus serves as a cue (*discriminative stimulus*) for the operant response. This learning is brought about by following the operant response with a *positive* or *negative reinforcement.* A reinforcement is defined as anything which can increase or decrease the rate of occurrence of an operant response.

Respondent conditioning refers to the occurrence of responses in the presence of stimuli, but where the response is a "natural" sequel to the stimulus (e.g., an eyeblink response to the stimulus of a puff of air in the eye).

Schedules of reinforcement of different kinds have different effects on the rate of acquisition and extinction of a learned response. *Partial reinforcement* (where reinforcements occur intermittently) produce learned responses with greater resistance to extinction than *continuous reinforcement*.

Periphery of personality

No position taken. But statements about a response's *resistance to extinction,* and about *stimulus* and *response generalization* have some relevance (see Moderate Behaviorism).

SOCIAL LEARNING THEORY

Core of personality

CORE TENDENCY: Expressions of inherent individual differences in cognitive capabilities (e.g., memory, differentiation, generalization). This approach is rare in considered certain cognitive differences among persons to be unlearned and of importance for personality. These inherent differences underlie differences in amount and content of meaning.

Development

Observational learning is emphasized. Learning does not require the occurrence of either responses or reinforcements on the part of the learner. It is enough to observe a model responding. In such observation, the person associates stimuli with each other (S-S laws). Whether the model observed receives positive or negative reinforcement for his responses will determine if and when the learner will perform what he has learned.

Operant conditioning is also considered to occur, but is given little importance at the human level. The person matures by gaining greater and greater autonomy from reinforcements applied by others, and increasing in the ability to apply reinforcements to himself through a process of self-control that changes his environment.

Periphery of personality

For concrete peripheral characteristics, there are *needs,* comprised of *behavior potentials, reinforcement expectancies,* and *reinforcement values.* Reinforcement value refers to how satisfying the goal of the need is to the person. Reinforcement expectancy refers to how likely he thinks the attainment of the goal is. Behavior potential summarizes the implications of the other two components for actual performance, and also specifies the set of actions that such performance would entail. Examples of broad sets of needs common in people are *recognition-*

status, dominance, independence, protection-dependency, love and affection, and *physical comfort.*

Other concrete peripheral characteristics offered are more strategies and styles and less content considerations. These include *encoding strategies, behavior and stimulus outcome expectancies, stimulus values,* and *self-regulatory systems and plans.* Behavior and stimulus outcome expectancies and stimulus values are similar to the reinforcement expectancies and reinforcement values already mentioned. Encoding strategies emphasize the manner in which persons transform and lend meaning to information, and the resulting personal constructs. Self-regulatory systems and plans involve settled procedures for controlling oneself and regulating one's environment, and as such, constitute combinations of the other strategies and styles.

Strictly speaking, no types are specified. But one theme in social learning theory does refer to broader concrete peripheral characteristics such as *generalized expectancies.* An example is the person's view as to whether he is controlled externally, or controls himself.

GLOSSARY OF TERMS

ACTIVATION-DEACTIVATION ADJECTIVE CHECK LIST: A checklist devised by Thayer, to measure customary level of activation according to Fiske and Maddi. (See Chapter 10.)

ACTIVITIES INDEX: A questionnaire of 300 items, devised by William Stern, which yields scores on some of Murray's needs. (See Chapter 10.)

ADAPTATION: Usually refers to adjusting to social and physical pressures, rather than avoiding or changing them. (See Chapter 5, and *transcendence.*)

ADLER'S POSITION: See Appendix.

ALIENATION TEST: A 60-item questionnaire, devised by Maddi, which measures powerlessness, adventurousness, nihilism, and vegetativeness in the person's relationship to work, persons, social institutions, family, and self. (See Chapter 10.)

ALLPORT'S POSITION: See Appendix.

ANGYAL'S POSITION: See Appendix.

BAKAN'S POSITION: See Appendix.

BENEVOLENT ECLECTICISM: An attitude toward inquiry in which all points of view are accepted as plausible, and there is little effort to pinpoint and evaluate differences among the views. (See Chapter 1, *partisan zealotry,* and *comparative analysis.*)

BLACKY TEST: A set of pictures, devised by Gerald S. Blum, which depict a young dog in various situations, mainly with his parents, having special significance in psychoanalytic theory. The subject is to compose stories about the pictures, thereby projecting his personality for the tester to observe. (See Chapters 5 and 10.)

BRIGGS-MYERS TYPE INDICATOR: A questionnaire, devised by Myers, to measure introversion-extroversion, and the thinking, feeling, sensing, and intuiting modes of Jung. (See Chapter 10.)

673

CALIFORNIA PERSONALITY INVENTORY (CPI): A questionnaire yielding scores on many concrete peripheral characteristics covering mentally healthy functioning. (See Chapter 5.)

COMPARATIVE ANALYSIS: An attitude toward inquiry in which similarities and differences are sought among the various viewpoints on a subject matter, with the aim of posing issues to be resolved by thought and research. (See Chapter 1, *benevolent eclecticism* and *partisan zealotry*.)

COMPREHENSIVE UNDERSTANDING: When empirical, rational, and intuitive knowledge match. (See Chapter 1, and the kinds of knowledge mentioned.)

CONCRETE PERIPHERAL CHARACTERISTIC: The smallest, most homogeneous learned aspect of personality that a theorist believes can properly be conceptualized. It exerts an influence on thoughts, feelings, and/or actions such that they show continuity in time and over stimulus situations. (See Chapters 1, 6, through 10, and 12, and *periphery of personality*.)

CONFLICT MODEL: A form of personality theorizing which postulates that the person is continuously in the grips of the clash between two great, opposing forces. Life is necessarily a compromise, which at best involves a balance of the two forces, and at worst involves a foredoomed attempt to deny the existence of one of them. In the *psychosocial version*, the source of one great force is in the individual and the other in society. In the *intrapsychic version*, both great forces arise from within the person. (See Chapters 2 through 10, *fulfillment model*, *consistency model*, and *personality theory*.)

CONSISTENCY MODEL: A form of personality theorizing in which there is little emphasis upon great forces, be they single or dual, in conflict or not. Rather, there is emphasis on the formative influence of feedback from the external world. Life is to be understood as the extended attempt to maintain consistency. But consistencies and inconsistencies can have any content, themselves having been determined by prior experience. In the *cognitive dissonance version*, the relevant aspects of the person in which there may or may not be consistency are cognitive in nature. In the *activation version*, it is the degree to which bodily tension is consistent or inconsistent with what is customary that is important. (See Chapters 2 through 10, *conflict model*, *fulfillment model*, and *personality theory*.)

CORE CHARACTERISTICS: An unlearned, inherent structural entity of personality shared by all human beings. (See Chapters 1 through 5, 12, and *core of personality*.)

CORE OF PERSONALITY: The unlearned, inherent aspects of human nature we all share. Included are one (or two) core tendencies, which give the overall directionality or purpose of human life, and the core characteristics, or structural entities, implied by the tendency. (See Chapters 1 through 5, Chapter 12, and *personality theory*.)

CORE TENDENCY: The unlearned, inherent, overall direction or purpose of life shared by all human beings. (See Chapters 1 through 5, 12, and *core of personality*.)

CORRELATIONAL RESEARCH: Relatively naturalistic research in which information about the intensity of two or more (usually more) aspects of behavior are obtained from all subjects, the intent being to determine how the aspects are related. If many aspects of behavior are included, factor analysis is a frequent technique used on the data in order to determine how the aspects cluster. Correlational research is especially relevant to identifying concrete peripheral characteristics and types. (See Chapters 5, 10, and 12, and *concrete peripheral characteristics, types,* and *experimental research.*)

CREATIVITY: In a person, the predisposition to produce ideas and things that are new and have value. In an idea or thing, the quality of novelty and value. (See Chapter 5.)

CRITERION ANALYSIS: A special case of factor-analytic method, which is deductive (hypothesis-testing) rather than inductive (exploratory). (See Chapter 10 and *factor analysis.*)

DATA LANGUAGE: The designation of the thoughts, feelings, and actions (personality data) that are to be used in personology. No such language has yet been adopted. (See Chapter 10.)

DEFENSE MECHANISM INVENTORY: Devised by Gleser and Ihilevich, this test requires subjects to respond to stories, and yields scores on five sets of defenses (turning against object, projection, principalization, turning against self, and reversal). (See Chapter 10.)

DEFENSIVENESS: The tendency to distort reality in order that what one is conscious of conforms to what is socially acceptable. Theorists differ in their reliance upon this concept, in what they think is defended against, and in the elaborateness and precision with which they conceptualize the techniques of defense. But all agree that the technique of defense must itself be unconscious. (See Chapters 2 through 10.)

DEVELOPMENT: The interaction between expressions of the personality core and social and physical influences in the external world which culminates in the particular life-style or type of personality that is learned. (See Chapters 1 through 12, and *core of personality, periphery of personality,* and *personality theory.*)

DOGMATISM SCALE: A questionnaire, devised by Rokeach, to measure inflexibility in thinking. (See Chapter 10.)

DRIVE: Often used synonymously with need, motive, or motivation. But connotes something more biological and mechanical, less self-conscious and intellective than the term motive. (See Chapter 9, *motive, motivation,* and *need.*)

EDWARDS PERSONAL PREFERENCE SCHEDULE: A preference test, devised by Edwards, which uses the forced-choice format to obtain scores on several of Murray's needs. (See Chapter 10.)

EGO PSYCHOLOGY: See Appendix.

EMPIRICAL KNOWLEDGE: Hypotheses, derived carefully from theories, that have been confirmed in rigorous, systematic, and relevant research studies. This knowledge is public, precise, and systematic. (See Chapter 1, *rational knowledge* and *intuitive knowledge.*)

ERIKSON'S POSITION: See Appendix.

EXISTENTIAL PSYCHOLOGY: See Appendix.

EXISTENTIAL STUDY: A questionnaire devised by Thorne to measure several dimensions of general relevance to the existential position, including self-status, self-actualization, existential morale, existential vacuum, humanistic identification, and existence and destiny. (See Chapter 10.)

EXPERIENCE INVENTORY: A factor-analytically developed questionnaire, devised by Coan, to measure various aspects of openness to experience, such as aesthetic sensitivity, openness to hypothetical ideas, constructive utilization of fantasy, unconventional ideas of reality, and unusual perceptions and associations. (See Chapter 10.)

EXPERIMENTAL RESEARCH: Research in which subjects in an experimental group are treated in a particular manner in order to determine what the effect of the treatment will be. Subjects not receiving the treatment are used as a control group, to ensure that the effect observed in the experimental group really did not result from the treatment. Experiments are best employed in the testing of hypotheses. (See Chapters 5, 10, and 12, and *correlational research.*)

EXPLORATORY BEHAVIOR: Behavior bringing the subject into contact with previously unfamiliar aspects of the environment. A special case of this is *spontaneous alternation,* in which an organism having chosen one portion of the environment (usually a maze) on the first trial will choose the other on the next trial. (See Chapter 5.)

FANTASY TEST: Often called a projective test, this unstructured technique for obtaining scores on some variable or variables is often used in personality research. The subject is presented with ambiguous stimuli (usually pictures) and given the task of rendering them less ambiguous (by identifying them or using them in a story). The test should be shown to have adequate interscorer agreement, reliability, and validity. Such a test can be regarded as a form of performance test of indirect sort. (See Chapters 5 and 10, *unstructured test, personality research, questionnaire, performance test, reliability,* and *validity*).

FASCISM (F) SCALE: A questionnaire, devised by Adorno and colleagues, to measure fascistic attitudes and values. (See Chapter 10.)

FEAR OF APPEARING INCOMPETENT SCALE: A 36 item questionnaire, devised by Good and Good, to measure White's emphasis on sense of incompetence. (See Chapter 10).

FIELD DEPENDENCE-INDEPENDENCE: Individual differences, studied by Witkin and his associates, in the degree to which the person is able to utilize gravitational rather than visual cues to orient his body or other objects in space. The term *psychological differentiation* tends to be substituted when emphasizing the related phenomenon of discerning a simple figure embedded in a complex one. Typical tests are the *Body Adjustment Test* and the *Embedded-Figures Test.* (See Chapter 5.)

FISKE'S AND MADDI'S POSITION: See Appendix.

FORCED-CHOICE FORMAT: A variant on the questionnaire, in which each item is presented as a pair with each other item, and the subject's task is to choose which of each pair he prefers or considers right. The items can be ranked on the basis of number of choices. This test is regarded as less vulnerable to response sets than the ordinary questionnaire. But the test should be shown to have reliability and validity. (See Chapters 5 and 10, *questionnaire, personality research, reliability,* and *validity.*)

FORMAL CRITERIA OF THEORETICAL ADEQUACY: Theories have been evaluated with regard to their importance, operationalization, parsimony, precision, stimulating nature, and empirical validity. (See Chapter 12, *operational definition, parsimony, precision of theory,* and *importance of theory.*)

FREUD'S POSITION: See Appendix.

FROMM'S POSITION: See Appendix.

FULFILLMENT MODEL: A form of personality theorizing which postulates that the person embodies one great force. Life, at best, involves a progressively greater expression of this force, and at worst, involves inhibition of it. Conflict between individual and society is possible (indeed, causes inhibition), but not necessary, as in the conflict model. In the *actualization version,* the great force is in the form of a genetic blueprint of the person's special capabilities. In the *perfection version,* the great force constitutes ideals of what is fine, excellent, and meaningful. (See Chapters 2 through 10, *conflict model, consistency model,* and *personality theory.*)

GALVANIC SKIN RESPONSE (GSR): A procedure for measuring increases in sweating (considered emotional arousal) by the ease with which a mild electric current passes over the skin. Sweating increases skin conductivity. (See Chapters 5, 10, and 11.)

GATING: The phenomenon promulgated by Jerome S. Bruner, in which some central nervous system process "tunes" peripheral sense organs as to what stimulation they shall receive and reject. This could be a physiological substratum of defensiveness. (See Chapter 5 and *defensiveness.*)

GUILFORD-ZIMMERMAN TEMPERMENT SURVEY: A questionnaire, devised by the persons in the title, which yields 10 personality factors from a large pool of items. (See Chapter 10.)

HABIT: See *Trait.*

IDIOGRAPHIC (OR MORPHOGENIC) LAW: A law which concerns the functioning of particular individuals rather than the average case. The term is emphasized by Allport. (See Chapter 9 and *individuality.*)

IMPORTANCE OF A THEORY: There is disagreement as to whether the importance of a theory can be determined except after the fact. One viewpoint is that in order to ensure its importance, a theory should take as its subject matter (data to be explained) that which can be observed naturalistically, rather than behavior produced in the laboratory by experimental manipulation (and hence contrived). (See Chapter 11.)

INDIVIDUAL COMMONALITIES: Similarities on one or more dimensions or variables among any group of persons. Of special interests to personology are those commonalities that seem to reflect the inherent nature of man rather than the regularizing effect (or demand characteristics) of stimulus or social pressures. (See Chapter 1 and *individual differences.*)

INDIVIDUAL DIFFERENCES: Differences on one or more dimensions or variables among any group of persons. Of special relevance for personology are differences that occur under what appear to be the same stimulus situations, and differences that persist over time and situations. (See Chapter 1 and *individual commonalities.*)

INDIVIDUALITY: The uniqueness of persons, usually considered to reside in the total pattern of their personality, rather than one aspect of it. This is an extreme case of individual differences, especially emphasized by some theorists such as Allport, Kelly, Rogers, Maslow, ego psychology, and existential psychology. (See Chapter 1, the theorists mentioned, and *individual differences.*)

INTERNAL-EXTERNAL LOCUS OF CONTROL (I-E Scale): A questionnaire refined by James, which measures whether the subject believes he is in control of his own fate, or is externally controlled. (See Chapter 10.)

INTER-SCORER RELIABILITY: The degree to which two scorers analyzing the same ambiguous data agree as to what is there. (See Chapter 10.)

INTERVIEW: A procedure, which can be relatively structured or unstructured, whereby information about the subject is obtained through a face-to-face, question-and-answer session. This technique has greater flexibility than the questionnaire, and is therefore useful when the investigator is exploring. Also, the option of patterning one's questions on the subject's responses to prior questions makes this technique sometimes more desirable than even performance and fantasy tests, which are more restrictive. (See Chapters 5 and 10, *structured test, unstructured test, questionnaire, performance test,* and *fantasy test.*)

INTUITIVE KNOWLEDGE: The relatively inarticulate, private, emotional, though vivid, immediate, and compelling sense of the meaning of things. (See Chapter 1, *empirical knowledge,* and *rational knowledge.*)

INVENTORY OF PSYCHOSOCIAL DEVELOPMENT: A questionnaire, developed by Constantinople, to measure the salience of Erikson's stages of development. (See Chapter 10.)

JUNG'S POSITION: See Appendix.

KELLY'S POSITION: See Appendix.

LATENT LEARNING: The phenomenon whereby a subect seems to learn a maze (or other task) even when he receives no reinforcement for so doing. (See Chapter 5.)

LIFE-STYLE: See *Type.*

MANIFEST ANXIETY SCALE (MAS): A questionnaire, devised by Janet Taylor and Spence, to measure general drive, in the framework of moderate behaviorism. (See Chapter 11.)

MARLOWE-CROWNE SOCIAL DESIRABILITY SCALE (M-C SDS): A questionnaire, devised by the authors mentioned, to measure the tendency to respond in socially desirable fashion. (See Chapter 10.)

MASLOW'S POSITION: See Appendix.

MAUDSLEY PERSONALITY INVENTORY (MPI): A questionnaire, devised by Hans Eysenck, to measure neuroticism, and introversion-extroversion. (See Chapter 10.)

MAZE: Usually in the form of a T, the maze has been a ubiquitous apparatus for studying learning in rats. In more complex, paper and pencil or stylus form, mazes have also been used on human subjects. (See Chapter 5.)

McCLELLAND'S POSITION: See Appendix.

MINNESOTA MULTIPHASIC PERSONALITY INVENTORY (MMPI): A questionnaire comprised of many items to be answered "true" or "false" which provides many scores concerning psychopathological trends in personality. The scales from which the scores derive have adequate reliability and have been validated by determining that they predict the psychopathological entities assumed. (See Chapters 5 and 10.)

MODELING BEHAVIOR: Imitative or observational learning, in which it is assumed that what is learned is linkage between stimuli, rather than between stimuli and responses. Learning takes place without necessity of responses or reinforcements. (See Chapter 12.)

MODERATE BEHAVIORISM: See Appendix.

MOTIVATION: The pressure or energy to produce activity and the goal or direction to guide the activity. Some core tendencies are considered motivational, even though they are probably too abstract to achieve mental representation as goals. Some theorists reserve the concept of motivation for concrete peripheral characteristics. (See Chapters 1 through 12.)

MOTIVE: Usually refers to a kind of concrete peripheral characteristic having motivational properties in that it produces directional behavior aimed at reaching a goal. (See Chapters 6 through 10, *motivation,* and *concrete peripheral characteristic.*)

MURRAY'S POSITION: See Appendix.

NEED: Often used synonymously with drive, motive, or motivation. Usage varies widely by theorist. (See Chapter 9, *motive, motivation,* and *drive.*)

NOMOTHETIC LAW: A law which concerns the functioning of the average case, rather than any particular individual. The term is emphasized by Allport. (See Chapter 9.)

OPERATIONAL DEFINITION: A precise, literal statement of what operations to perform in order to measure concepts and variables. In personology, such definitions are especially important for identifying concrete peripheral characteristics. (See Chapters 10 and 12, and *concrete peripheral characteristic.*)

PARSIMONY: It is usually assumed that, other things being equal, the best of several explanations of a phenomenon is the one that makes the fewest assumptions. This criterion is difficult to apply to personality theory and may stifle imagination. (See Chapter 11.)

PARTISAN ZEALOTRY: An attitude toward inquiry in which the viewpoint one already believes is regarded as true, and championed energetically, regardless of plausible arguments and disagreements to the contrary. (See Chapter 1, *benevolent eclecticism,* and *comparative analysis.*)

PERCEPTUAL DEFENSE: The phenomenon whereby subjects require longer tachistoscopic exposures of threatening than nonthreatening stimuli in order to recognize them. (See Chapter 5, *tachistoscope,* and *perceptual vigilance.*)

PERCEPTUAL VIGILANCE: The phenomenon whereby subjects require shorter tachistoscoptic exposure times to recognize threatening as opposed to nonthreatening stimuli. (See Chapter 5, *tachistoscope,* and *perceptual defense.*)

PERFORMANCE TEST: A standardized technique, usually structured, for obtaining scores on some variable or variables which is sometimes used in personality research. The subject reveals himself by his effectiveness at and manner of performing the task, rather than in describing himself directly. The test should be shown to have reliability and validity. (See Chapters 5 and 10, *structured test, personality research, questionnaire, reliability,* and *validity.*)

PERIPHERY OF PERSONALITY: The learned, relatively concrete aspects of personality that develop out of the interaction of the personality core and the external, mainly social, world. Included in periphery statements are the types of personality (or life-styles) it is possible to develop and the concrete peripheral characteristics (motives, traits, schemata) that comprise the types. (See Chapters 1, 6 through 10, 12, and *personality theory.*)

PERSONALITY: A stable set of characteristics and tendencies that determine those commonalities and differences in the psychological behavior (thoughts, feelings, and actions) of people that have continuity in time and that may or may not be easily understood in terms of the social and biological pressures of the immediate situation alone. (See Chapter 1 and *personology.*)

PERSONALITY CHANGE: Theorists differ in views as to the degree of personality change which occurs as a function of aging. For some, little real change takes place after childhood, whereas others see change as continual throughout life. Most believe that even radical change can take place through psychotherapy. (See Chapter 5.)

PERSONALITY DATA: Thoughts, feelings, and actions that show continuity in time and over various stimulus situations. (See Chapter 1 and *personology.*)

PERSONALITY RESEARCH: This may be primarily to test hypotheses (deductive method) or to explore in order to generate hypotheses (inductive method). Naturalistic observation and correlational data analyses seem well suited to exploratory research, whereas experimental designs seem well suited to hypothesis testing. Research is particularly relevant to personality when, whether exploratory or hypothesis testing, it concerns thoughts, feelings and actions having continuity in time and over situations. Usually, this will involve stable individual differences. Often, personality research also concerns large amounts of each person's behavior, rather than only one or two elements. (See Chapters 1, 5, 10, 12, and *personality theory, personality data, correlational research,* and *experimental research.*)

PERSONALITY THEORY: A set of interconnected and logically consistent assumptions, having the aim of explaining personality data (thoughts, feelings, and actions having continuity in time and over situations). The parts of a personality theory are the core statement (concerning the inherent nature that is unlearned and common to all), the periphery statement (concerning the life-styles that are learned and differentiate persons), and the developmental statement (which explicates how expressions of the core lead, through interaction with the external, mainly social, environment, to the periphery). (See Chapters 1, 5, 9, 12, and *personality data, core of personality, periphery of personality,* and *development.*)

PERSONAL ORIENTATION INVENTORY (POI): A questionnaire devised by Shostrom, to measure various characteristics of actualization fulfillment theory, e.g., Rogers and Maslow. (See Chapter 10.)

PERSONOLOGIST: Someone who practices personology. (See Chapter 1 and *personology.*)

PERSONOLOGY: A field of psychology concerned with the study of entire persons. The data for the field are thoughts, feelings, and actions that characterize a person over time and situations, and the explanations employed concern personality (a set of concepts that are within the skin, rather than in the surround, and may or may not have biological substrata). In addition to this theorizing function, personology includes the conducting of research (to test the theorizing), and the practical application of knowledge in the form of assessment (the systematic identification of a person's personality), and psychotherapy (the systematic attempt to change personality to greater approximate some theoretical ideal). (See Chapter 1, *personality, personality theory, personality research, personality data, personality assessment,* and *psychotherapy.*)

PRECISION OF THEORY: A useful goal in theorizing is precision. Effort should be made to avoid inconsistencies, loose ends, and metaphorical language. (See Chapter 11.)

PSYCHOLOGICAL GROWTH: Progressively greater differentiation and integration of experience, especially emphasized by Allport, Adler, Maslow, Fiske, Maddi, and existential psychology. (See Chapters 2 through 8.)

QUESTIONNAIRE: Sometimes called an inventory, this structured technique for obtaining quantitative scores on some variable or variables is often used in personality research. The subject is presented with questions to be responded to ("true" or "false," "like" or "dislike," multiple choice). The test should be shown to have adequate reliability and validity. Such a test involves self-description of a relatively direct sort, and hence is vulnerable to distortions produced by the sets to respond in socially desirable and acquiescent fashions. (See Chapters 5 and 10, *structured test, personality research, reliability,* and *validity.*)

RADICAL BEHAVIORISM: See Appendix.

RANK'S POSITION: See Appendix.

RATIONAL KNOWLEDGE: Conclusions that are deduced from a set of assumptions by the careful, reflective use of logic, rather than arrived at by systematic observation. (See Chapter 1, *empirical knowledge,* and *intuitive knowledge.*)

RELIABILITY: The degree to which a test or scale yields scores on individuals that agree from one time to another. This is sometimes called *stability,* to contrast it with internal consistency. *Internal consistency,* which refers to the degree to which items on a test or scale are all measuring the same thing, is also an aspect of reliability. (See Chapters 5, 10, and 12.)

REPRESSION-SENSITIZATION SCALE: A questionnaire, devised by Byrne, to measure the defensiveness dimension concerning too little and too much sensitivity to stimuli. (See Chapter 10.)

RESPONSE SET: It has been discovered that, particularly when taking questionnaires, subjects respond in set ways bearing little relationship to the content of the questions. Major response sets are to be socially desirable, and to be acquiescent. (See Chapter 10.)

ROGERS' POSITION: See Appendix.

ROLE CONSTRUCTS REPERTORY TEST (REP): A categorizing performance test, devised by Kelly, which measures the subject's personal constructs and their organization into a construct system. (See Chapter 10.)

RORSCHACH TEST: A series of inkblots, devised by Herman Rorschach, which the subject is asked to identify. In indicating what the blots resemble, he discloses his personality. (See Chapter 5.)

SCHEMA: Usually refers to a kind of concrete peripheral characteristic that is mainly cognitive in nature and expressive of cultural or social influences. Examples are values and social roles. (See Chapters 6 through 10, 12, and *concrete peripheral characteristic.*)

SELF CONTROL: An emphasis in social learning theory (see Chapter 12) and a bit in behaviorism (see Chapter 11) on the person gaining control over the reinforcements influencing his behavior. This is considered a sign of maturity.

SELF-IDEAL Q SORT: A test, employing a procedure for sorting statements into groups (devised by Stevenson), that has been used to measure the discrepancy between self-concept and self-ideal, in a Rogerian framework. Butler and Haigh devised this particular Q sort. (See Chapter 10.)

SENSORY DEPRIVATION: An experimental procedure whereby the amount of stimulation from external (and sometimes internal sources as well) is markedly decreased. Sleep and disorder of thought frequently ensue. (See Chapter 5.)

SENTENCE-COMPLETION TEST: A semi-unstructured test in which the subject is provided with a series of sentence beginnings which he is to finish in some way. The test should be shown to have adequate inter-scorer agreement, reliability, and validity. (See Chapters 5 and 10, *personality research, unstructured test, interscorer agreement, reliability,* and *validity.*)

SIXTEEN PERSONALITY FACTOR QUESTIONNAIRE: A questionnaire, devised by Raymond Cattell, yielding scores on 16 first-order and 8 second-order factors. The factors result from numerous factor analyses of the items, and the test offers a comprehensive description of personality. (See Chapters 5 and 10.)

SOCIAL INTEREST INDEX: Devised by Greever, Tseng, and Friedland, this questionnaire measures Adler's emphasis upon constructive interest in other persons and society. (See Chapter 10.)

SOCIAL LEARNING THEORY: An offshoot of moderate behaviorism which stresses the importance of imitative or observational learning. Children especially are frequent learners by observing a model, with subsequent performance of what they learned dependent upon anticipated reinforcement contingencies. In its emphasis upon cognition, and de-emphasis of reinforcement as necessary for learning to take place, this position, as developed by Bandura, Walters, and Mischel, deviates significantly from moderate behaviorism. (See Chapter 12.)

S-R INVENTORY: Devised by Endler, Hunt and Rosenstein, this questionnaire measures various types of anxiety response over a range of situations. (See Chapter 10.)

STAGES OF DEVELOPMENT: Some theorists demarcate stages during which particular core functions mature and social experiences of a particular sort can have special impact on personality. (See Chapters 2 through 10 and *development.*)

STRONG VOCATIONAL INTEREST BLANK: A questionnaire, devised by Strong, often used to assess vocational interests. (See Chapter 5.)

STRUCTURED TEST: Often called objective, this type of test presents the subject with a structured, organized, specific situation to which to respond. Usually, structured tests are questionnaires, but they can also be performance tasks. Some techniques, like the interview, can be either rather structured or unstructured. Structured tests have greater reliability than unstructured tests, and are regarded by some theorists to be of special value in assessing socially directed personality characteristics. (See Chapters 5 and 10, *unstructured test, performance test, questionnaire, interview, reliability,* and *validity.*)

SUBCEPTION: The phenomenon in which the subject responds physiologically (e.g., by sweating) even when stimuli are presented tachistoscopically at exposure times too brief for conscious recognition. (See Chapter 5, *perceptual defense,* and *tachistoscope.*)

SURVEY OF PROBLEMATIC SITUATIONS: A questionnaire, developed by Goldfried and D'Zurilla, to measure White's emphasis on actual competence. See Chapter 10.)

SYSTEMATIC DESENSITIZATION: Wolpe's psychotherapy, in which the person is encouraged to relax while thinking of threatening material, in hopes that it will become less threatening. (See Chapter 11.)

TACHISTOSCOPE: A device for presenting visual stimuli for controllable and very brief lengths of time. It has been used extensively in personality research to study how and whether there are differences between subjects and between types of stimuli in recognition time. (See Chapter 5, *perceptual defense,* and *perceptual vigilance.*)

TENSION REDUCTION OR INCREASE: Tension (sometimes called arousal or activation) is usually regarded as a state of bodily discomfort or pent-up energy. Many theorists believe tension reduction to be pleasurable and the major aim of life. Other theorists define aims otherwise and believe that tension increases will be tolerated (even enjoyed) in order to achieve the aims. (See Chapter 5.)

THEMATIC APPERCEPTION TEST: A set of pictures, devised by Henry A. Murray, showing persons alone or in various relationships with each other. The subject, in composing stories for the pictures, projects his personality for the tester to observe. (See Chapters 5 and 10.)

TRAIT: Usually refers to kinds of concrete peripheral characteristics producing habitual, routinized, unreflective behaviors having little or no apparent motivational significance. (See Chapters 6 through 10, 12, and *concrete peripheral characteristic.*)

TRANSCENDENCE: Usually refers to transforming or surmounting social and physical pressures, rather than adjusting or acquiescing to them. (See Chapter 5 and *adaptation.*)

TYPE: A learned life-style comprised of concrete peripheral characteristics (motives, traits, schema) exerting an influence on thoughts, feelings, and actions. (See Chapters 1, 6 through 10, 12, and *periphery of personality.*)

TYPOLOGY: A classification of types that is part of a statement of the periphery of personality. (See *type* and *periphery of personality.*)

UNSTRUCTURED TEST: Often called projective, this type of test presents the subject with an unstructured, ambiguous situation to which to respond. Usually, unstructured tests engage the fantasy of the subject, but they can also involve other aspects of performance. Some techniques, like the interview, can be either rather structured or unstructured. Although unstructured tests have lower reliability than structured tests, many theorists regard the former as more appropriate than the latter for assessing underlying defenses, conflicts, and unconscious material that may not be readily apparent in overt behavior. (See Chapters 5 and 10, *structured test, personality research, performance test, interview, fantasy test, reliability,* and *validity.*)

VALIDITY: The degree to which a test or scale predicts the naturally occurring behavior it was intended to forecast. In personality research, construct validity is most relevant. Here, there is no one naturally occurring behavior important in the validation of a scale, but rather several, each linked to the scale (perhaps indirectly) by theory. The process of validating the scale is the same as validating the constructs underlying it. (See Chapters 10 and 12.)

WHITE'S POSITION: See Appendix.

WORD ASSOCIATION TEST: A procedure for studying personality, devised by Jung, in which a series of words is presented to the subject one at a time and he associates a word to each of them as quickly as he can. (See Chapter 10.)

INDEX

This book has been set in 10 and 9 point Caledonia, leaded 2 points. Chapter numbers are 16 point Helvetica Medium and chapter titles are 16 point Helvetica. The size of the type page is 27 × 46½ picas.